NEW OXFORD HISTORY OF MUSIC
VOLUME X

THE VOLUMES OF THE
NEW OXFORD HISTORY OF MUSIC

SKRYABIN'S *PROMETHEUS*, 1911 (*see p. 35*)

The front cover of the score designed by the theosophist poet Jean Delville. It is orange, the colour of fire, and shows a huge flaming sun with an androgynous face (symbolizing the union of male and female) enclosed in a 'world-lyre' and surrounded by magical and cosmic symbols—stars, comets, and spiralling clouds. The piercing eyes 'express *the will*', according to Skryabin, and the face is surrounded by primeval chaos 'from which the world-will calls everything to life', first to material life, after which matter is dissolved into spirit and in an orgiastic dance united with God.

THE MODERN AGE

AGE

1890–1960

EDITED BY

MARTIN COOPER

LONDON
OXFORD UNIVERSITY PRESS
NEW YORK TORONTO
1974

Oxford University Press, Ely House, London W.1

GLASGOW NEW YORK TORONTO MELBOURNE WELLINGTON
CAPE TOWN SALISBURY IBADAN NAIROBI LUSAKA ADDIS ABABA
BOMBAY CALCUTTA MADRAS KARACHI LAHORE DACCA
KUALA LUMPUR SINGAPORE HONG KONG TOKYO

ISBN 0 19 316310 1

© *Oxford University Press 1974*

PRINTED IN GREAT BRITAIN BY
EBENEZER BAYLIS AND SON LTD
THE TRINITY PRESS, WORCESTER, AND LONDON

GENERAL INTRODUCTION

THE *New Oxford History of Music* is not a revision of the older *Oxford History of Music*, first published in six volumes under the general editorship of Sir Henry Hadow between 1901 and 1905. It has been planned as an entirely new survey of music from the earliest times down to comparatively recent years, including not only the achievements of the Western world but also the contributions made by eastern civilizations and primitive societies. The examination of this immense field is the work of a large number of contributors, English and foreign. The attempt has been made to achieve uniformity without any loss of individuality. If this attempt has been successful, the result is due largely to the patience and co-operation shown by the contributors themselves. Overlapping has to some extent been avoided by the use of frequent cross-references; but we have not thought it proper to prevent different authors from expressing different views about the same subject, where it could legitimately be regarded as falling into more than one category.

The scope of the work is sufficiently indicated by the titles of the several volumes. Our object throughout has been to present music, not as an isolated phenomenon or the work of outstanding composers, but as an art developing in constant association with every form of human culture and activity. The biographies of individuals are therefore merely incidental to the main plan of the history, and those who want detailed information of this kind must seek it elsewhere. No hard and fast system of division into chapters has been attempted. The treatment is sometimes by forms, sometimes by periods, sometimes also by countries, according to the importance which one element or another may assume. The division into volumes has to some extent been determined by practical considerations; but pains have been taken to ensure that the breaks occur at points which are logically and historically justifiable. The result may be that the work of a single composer who lived to a ripe age is divided between two volumes. The later operas of Monteverdi, for example, belong to the history of Venetian opera and hence find their natural place in volume v, not with the discussion of his earlier operas to be found in volume iv. On the other hand, we have not insisted on a rigid chronological division where the result would be illogical or confusing. If a subject finds its natural conclusion some ten years after the date assigned for the end of a period, it is obviously preferable to complete it within the limits of one volume rather than to allow it to overflow into a second. An exception to the general scheme of continuous chronology is to be found in volumes v and vi, which deal with different aspects of the same period and so are complementary to each other.

The history as a whole is intended to be useful to the professed student of music, for whom the documentation of sources and the bibliographies are particularly designed. But the growing interest in the music of all periods shown by music-lovers in general has encouraged us to bear their interests also in mind. It is inevitable that a work of this kind should employ a large number of technical terms and deal with highly specialized matters. We have, however, tried to ensure that the technical terms are intelligible to the ordinary reader and that what is specialized is not necessarily wrapped in obscurity. Finally, since music must be heard to be fully appreciated, we have given references throughout to the records issued by His Master's Voice (R.C.A. Victor) under the general title *The History of Music in Sound*. These records are collected in a series of albums which correspond to the volumes of the present work, and have been designed to be used with it.

J. A. WESTRUP
GERALD ABRAHAM
ANSELM HUGHES
EGON WELLESZ
MARTIN COOPER

CONTENTS

ILLUSTRATIONS

ACKNOWLEDGEMENTS

Copyright music examples in this volume are quoted by kind permission of the following:

Associated Music Publishers Inc.: Elliott Carter, String Quartet (1951); Henry Cowell, Tiger.

Boosey & Hawkes Music Publishers Ltd: Béla Bartók, Concerto for Orchestra, Microcosmos, Rhapsody for Piano, String Quartet No. 6, Sonata for Solo Violin; Benjamin Britten, Holy Sonnets, Midsummer Night's Dream, Peter Grimes, Serenade Op. 31, Sinfonia da Requiem, Winter Words; Aaron Copland, Appalachian Spring, Piano Fantasy; Frederick Delius, A Village Romeo and Juliet, In a Summer Garden; Leoš Janáček, Diary of One Who Vanished; Dmitry Kabalevsky, Violin Concerto; Vadim Salmanov, The Twelve; Dmitry Shostakovich, 2nd Piano Concerto; Richard Strauss, Der Rosenkavalier, Elektra, Salome, Waldseligkeit; Igor Stravinsky, Movements, The Rake's Progress, Rite of Spring, Symphony of Psalms, Three Songs from Shakespeare, Threni.

Bote & Bock Verlag: Francesco Malipiero, Torneo Notturno.

Breitkopf & Härtel (London) Ltd, on behalf of Breitkopf & Härtel, Wiesbaden: Ferruccio Busoni, Toccata and Fugue in C Major, Arlecchino.

Chappell & Co Ltd: Arnold Bax, Symphonies Nos. 2 & 3; George Gershwin, Rhapsody in Blue; Roy Harris, Third Symphony; William Schuman, Symphony No. IV; Arnold Schoenberg, Violin Concerto.

J. & W. Chester Ltd: Manuel de Falla, Harpsichord Concerto; Arthur Honegger, Le Roi David; Francesco Malipiero, Rispetti e Strambotti; Arnold Schoenberg, Serenade; Igor Stravinsky, L'Histoire du Soldat, Les Noces.

J. Curwen & Sons Ltd: Ralph Vaughan Williams, Pastoral Symphony.

Durand & Cie, Paris: Vincent D'Indy, Fervaal, L'Étranger, Symphony No. 2; Paul Dukas, Ariane et Barbe-bleu, Piano Sonata (1901), Le Péri; Darius Milhaud, Catalogue des fleurs; Olivier Messiaen, Visions de l'Amen; Maurice Ravel, Gaspard de la Nuit, L'Heure espagnole; Florent Schmitt, La Tragédie de Salome.

Editions J. Hamelle, Paris: Gabriel Fauré, Green Op. 58.

Editions A. Leduc, Paris: Alfred Bruneau, Messidor.

Edition Peters: Richard Strauss, Ein Heldenleben.

Editions Salabert: Arthur Honegger, Quartet No. 3; Albert Roussel, Piano Suite; Erik Satie, Le Fils des étoiles, Sonneries de la Rose Croix.

Editio Musica Budapest: Béla Bartók, In Full Flower, Op. 10 No. 1.

Faber Music Limited on behalf of J. Curwen & Sons Ltd: Gustav Holst, Savitri.

Franco Colombo Inc., New York: Edgard Varèse, Hyperprism.

Heugel & Cie, Paris: Pierre Boulez, Piano Sonata No. 2; Darius Milhaud, Symphony No. 2.

Alfred Lengnick & Co Ltd: Edmund Rubbra, Symphony No. 5.

F. E. C. Leuckart Musikverlag: Richard Strauss, A Hero's Life.

Marks Music Corporation, New York: Roger Sessions, Quintet for Strings (1958).

xiv   ACKNOWLEDGEMENTS

Mercury Music Corporation: Charles Ives, Anti-Abolitionist Riots, The Housatonic at Stockbridge, Three Places in New England, Variations on 'America' (1891); Leon Kirchner, String Quartet (1949).

Merrymount Music Inc.: Wallingford Riegger, Music for Brass Choir Op. 45.

Virgil Thomson and Mercury Music Corporation: Virgil Thomson, Four Saints in Three Acts.

Messrs. Novello & Co Ltd: Edward Elgar, Symphony No. 2.

Oxford University Press: Constant Lambert, Summer's Last Will and Testament; Alan Rawsthorne, Piano Concerto No. 1, The Sprat, Symphonic Studies; William Walton, Symphony No. 1; Ralph Vaughan Williams, Symphonies Nos. 4 and 5.

G. Ricordi & Co: Alfredo Catalani, La Wally; Pietro Mascagni, Iris; Italo Montemezzi, L'Amore dei tre Re; Ildebrando Pizzetti, Debora e Jaele, Messa di Requiem; Giacomo Puccini, La Bohème, Tosca.

Schlesinger: Alban Berg, Piano Sonata Op. 1.

Mrs. Gertrude Schoenberg: Arnold Schoenberg, Die Jacobsleiter.

Schott & Co: Boris Blacher, Orchester-Ornament; Karl-Birger Blomdahl, Aniara; Luigi Dallapiccola, Canti di Liberazione; Wolfgang Fortner, Movement for Orchestra; Peter Racine Fricker, Elegy, Symphony No. 2; Karl Amadeus Hartmann, Concerto for Viola; Hans Werner Henze, Drei Dithyramben, Piano Variations, Symphony No. 2; Paul Hindemith, Das Marienleben, Das Unaufhörliche No. 4, Kammermusik Op. 24 No. 1, Ludus Tonalis, Mathis der Maler, Philharmonia Concerto; Luigi Nono, Canto Sospeso, Diario polacca, Incontri; Igor Stravinsky, Concerto for two pianos, Symphony in C; Michael Tippett, String Quartet No. 2.

Schott & Co on behalf of B. Schotts Söhne: Igor Stravinsky, Firebird, Scherzo Fantastique.

Schott & Co on behalf of Max Eschig, Paris: Darius Milhaud, La Création du monde; Maurice Ravel, Alborado del Gracioso; Francis Poulenc, Le Bestiaire; Erik Satie, La Mort de Socrate.

Stainer & Bell Ltd: Holst, Hymn of Jesus.

Sonzogno, Milan: Umberto Giordano, Andrea Chénier.

Universal Edition (London) Ltd: Béla Bartók, Dance Suite (1923) Finale; Luciano Berio, Circles; Pierre Boulez, Improvisation sur Mallarmé, Le Marteau sans maître, Structures; Olivier Messiaen, Oiseaux Exotiques; Darius Milhaud, Christophe Colomb; Bo Nilsson, Zwanzig Gruppen; Nikos Skalkottas, 4th Piano Suite; Karlheinz Stockhausen, Gruppen, Kontrapunkte, Klavierstück 1.

Universal Edition (Alfred A. Kalmus Ltd) Ltd: Alban Berg, Lulu, Lyric Suite, Violin Concerto; Alois Hába, String Quartet Op. 12; Leoš Janáček, Cunning Little Vixen, Glagolithic Mass, Jenůfa; Arnold Schoenberg, Erwartung, Fünf Orchesterstücke No. 2, Kammersymphonie, Op. 11 No. 1, Op. 11 No. 3, Pierrot Lunaire, Pelleas & Melisande, Piano Pieces Op. 33 No. 1, Quartet in A, Sechs Lieder Op. 8 No. 1, String Quartet No. 1, Variations for Orchestra; Franz Schreker, Der Ferne Klang; Karol Szymanowski, King Roger; Anton Webern, Cantata No. 1, Drei Gesänge Op. 23, Drei Lieder Op. 18 No. 1, Das Augenlicht, Orchesterstück Op. 6 No. 2, Passacaglia, Piano Variations Op. 27, Zwei Lieder Op. 19 No. 1, Symphony Op. 21.

Universal Edition (London) Ltd on behalf of Boosey & Hawkes Inc., copyright for the USA: Béla Bartók, Bluebeard's Castle, String Quartet No. 4, Violin Sonata No. 1.

Wilhelm Hansen, Musik-Forlag, Copenhagen: Carl Nielsen, Maskarade.

INTRODUCTION TO VOLUME X

THE precise dating of any historical period can never be more than a convention or a convenience, and in the case of this last volume of the *New Oxford History of Music* the decision has been complicated by a further question implicit in the nature of history. If we are to date any historical period from the first emergence rather than the full development of its most characteristic features, it seemed reasonable to choose 1890 as one term of the modern period. The *terminus ad quem* was more difficult to determine. At what remove of time does it become possible to see events, personalities, and individual works in that perspective which we call historical rather than as isolated points in our own experience, or markings on a map of whose exact orientation we are still uncertain? Those who interpret the concept of history rigorously argue that it is still too early to obtain a balanced and objective view of any musical events that have taken place in the last quarter of a century; and voices were in fact raised in support of making 1950 the end-date of the present volume. This would have been both safe and convenient, since it would have avoided the necessity of controversial selections among the phenomena of contemporary music and made it possible for this last volume to maintain the same strictly objective character as the other nine. Against this it was very strongly felt that the tempo of change in the third quarter of the twentieth century has been such that a gap of some quarter of a century between the latest events considered in the *New Oxford History of Music* and the appearance of the last volume would appear unreal and pedantic. Writers dealing with the most recent musical phenomena have naturally been obliged to content themselves with chronicling facts rather than interpreting or evaluating; and even the interval between the writing and the publication of these latest chapters has in some cases been long enough to alter the perspective. This is the price that must be paid for continuing the narrative up to the comparatively recent past, a tribute to Time whose payment has fallen particularly heavily on Peter Evans and Richard Franko Goldman.

If the time-span of the present volume is open to question, the sub-division of the seventy years under consideration may well seem even more arbitrary. It was determined by two main considerations: the emergence of an unmistakably new conception of music after the First World War, and the very different rate at which this new conception became general among composers in different countries. The head-waters of the New Music were in Central Europe, that is to say within a

quadrilateral bounded by Berlin, Paris, Milan, and Budapest; so that it
seemed logical to regard the development of music in those countries as
a European mainstream. On the periphery of this central area neither
Scandinavia nor Iberia seemed to warrant separate treatment; but
musical developments in the Soviet Union, the United States, and
Great Britain have been rich enough in themselves, and different
enough from each other and from those in countries of the European
mainland, to demand individual handling.

The movement in musical thought and practice since 1890 has been
so fast and so complex, and the movements themselves so multifarious,
that it is possible to make only the broadest generalizations about the
period as a whole. Until the last ten years of the period under review, it
might have been possible to describe the transformation which began
to show in music after 1890 and became complete before 1920 as the
superseding of the idea of music as a language by the idea of music as
an architecture. In panserialism, however, architecture was itself superseded by a concept nearer to that of engineering, which has in its turn
been superseded by random, indeterminate, and aleatory principles
which suggest, however misleadingly, a more than cursory glance in the
direction of the higher mathematics. Even the autonomy of music, once
regarded as possibly the most hard-won of all the principles underlying
the New Music, has been surrendered; and the baroque rhetoric of
the composer's statements accompanying Olivier Messiaen's *Et vitam
venturi saeculi* or Karlheinz Stockhausen's *Setzt die Segel zur Sonne*
far outshine the vague cosmic pretensions of Skryabin's *Prometheus* or
Ives's *Universal Symphony*, which seemed so ludicrous to the generation
that came to maturity in the heyday of neo-classicism and
Gebrauchsmusik.

If it was possible to trace a definite pattern in the distribution and
progress of the New Music between the wars, patterns since 1950 have
changed so quickly into each other that the effect is kaleidoscopic. The
war of 1939–45 obliterated the neat geographical demarcations which
allotted spheres of interest—Central Europe to Bartók and Schoenberg,
the rest of Germany and Northern Europe to Hindemith, Paris, and the
Latin world to Stravinsky—by sending each of these composers to the
U.S.A. When the war ended the music of Stravinsky, Hindemith, and
Bartók was comparatively well known to musicians outside Germany,
and isolated examples of their works were winning acceptance with the
public; but 'serial' music was still a closed book to all but a tiny
minority. When the National Socialist ban on the music of Schoenberg
and his followers was raised by the defeat of Hitler, serialism became
almost overnight equivalent to a certificate of opposition to National

Socialist ideology, and serial music was suddenly in demand in Germany on a large scale. But frequent performance revealed in Schoenberg's own music a deeply romantic, as well as a drily didactic vein and in Berg's a strong post-romantic impulse alien to the mood of the younger generation of composers, who turned their attention to the third, most radical, and least publicized member of the Second Viennese School, Anton von Webern. The discovery of Webern's music was the most important of the discoveries made by composers during the 1950s; and when Stravinsky himself admitted, on his own terms and very much in his own manner, conversion to serialism, it looked for a moment as though a firm new general pattern might be about to declare itself. Instead of this, panserialism produced a predictable reaction, complicated by the new presence of electronic music and by the first stirring of what has proved to be a strong, though by definition unorganized anti-intellectual movement, or 'servile revolt', directed against the élitism inherent in all mandarin art and indeed in all art that makes intellectual demands.

If composers since 1920 have often seemed confused by the shifting interests and attitudes of the pioneers, this whole period has been marked by a refusal on the part of the public, at first resolute and all but absolute and still only cautiously yielding, to interest itself in the New Music. This refusal has been the more marked in that the huge expansion and technical improvement in the recording and broadcasting of music during the second half of our period has multiplied the demand for music to an enormous extent. Up to 1950 the New Music was accepted by the public in direct proportion to the number of its links with the old. The stumbling-blocks were two: constructivism (music as architecture) and atonality. That is to say, the huge majority of music-lovers everywhere still regarded music as a language for communication and was not prepared to accept any idiom that could not be related, clearly even if remotely, to the diatonic or modal systems. This double barrier explains why Stravinsky, Hindemith, and Bartók achieved partial and cautious acceptance before Berg: Berg before Schoenberg: and Schoenberg before Webern.

This reluctance on the part of the public to accept the New Music, in conjunction with the new demand, accounts for the extraordinary spate of revivals or discoveries which have been a major feature of the last half century in every country except the U.S.S.R., where both composer and consumer have been guided by authority along lines determined by national and ideological exclusiveness. Elsewhere the eclipse of Wagner, whose music embodies late nineteenth-century romantic ideals, was followed by revivals and reinterpretations of the

2

operas of Mozart, Verdi, Handel, and more recently Bellini and Donizetti. The rediscovery of Vivaldi stimulated a new interest in baroque music generally, and Monteverdi's music has been more performed in the last twenty years than in the three centuries which have elapsed since his death. Medieval music, though still a minority interest, has made considerable progress with the general public and exercised a clear influence on young composers. A corollary of these revivals has been the rediscovery of unfamiliar or forgotten timbres, most notably that of the countertenor voice, the recorder, lute, viol family, and chamber organ. Still more remarkable has been the growing popularity of Oriental, especially Indian, music whose influence on composers (Messiaen and Boulez) began earlier. Even the over-exploited nineteenth century has yielded some unexpected novelties, and the few devoted and indefatigable champions who sponsored the apparently lost causes of Berlioz and Mahler have been rewarded in England by an overwhelming public response comparable to that which during the 1930s met Olin Downes's campaign for Sibelius in the U.S.A. and Sir Thomas Beecham's for Delius in Great Britain.

This picture of a sharply divided musical world, in which a small *avant-garde* pioneers almost out of sight of the main body of performers and listeners, who concern themselves with musical archaeology and indiscriminate truffle-hunting, is something entirely new. It suggests a parallel with Alexandrine historicizing and eclecticism, and an apparent falling-off in creative vitality. It should not, however, be forgotten that an indeterminable, but certainly large proportion of the creative power hitherto employed in the arts now finds an outlet in science, and that the triumphs of the human spirit in the twentieth century are likely to be found by future generations in its scientific rather than its artistic achievements. In the New Music itself the rejection of a heteronomous, quasi-literary art in favour of autonomy and constructivism represented a clear rapprochement with the scientific ideal, and one which has become increasingly close. Meanwhile the gap between composer and public closes very slowly. Peter Evans writes of 'the entirely new powers of discrimination' and 'new aural training' demanded by the latest music; and although Richard Franko Goldman considers that public hostility may be a valuable 'teething-ring' for young composers, he also emphasizes the significant loss of 'an audience that demands and rejects', while Professor Evans speaks of works being 'performed because no one is sure that they should not be'.

The danger of a 'composer's music' developing in a vacuum (or a studio), which at one time seemed very real, has been countered by the appearance of the 'servile revolt' against intellectual effort as a form of élitism, and by the willingness of a number of composers to abandon the idea of music as a discipline and to regard it as a labile, polymorphous activity comprising social protest and black humour, emotional 'togetherness', spiritual aspiration, and deliberate triviality in proportions chosen by the individual listener, who may well find himself also a part-time performer. This new form of 'concert', in which the composer provides hardly more than a ground-plan and music is chiefly important as a background or atmosphere, certainly owes something not only to oriental music and theatre, but also to oriental religion. It is perhaps as much a non-liturgy as an anti-concert.

Of all men the historian should be the least tempted to prophecy; and since the disappearance of the old norms by which music was formerly judged has not yet been followed by the appearance of new, there is no historical precedent to tempt the drawing of a parallel. At present there is no sign of any diminishing interest in the music of the European past, and interest in non-European music is on the increase. The future of the anti-intellectual movement, which I have called 'the servile revolt', is closely bound up with the future development of today's younger generation who are its chief supporters.

Perhaps the greatest threat to music as an art comes from its increased availability, a slowly growing inclination to regard as a kind of piped Muzak first the small change of the minor baroque composers, then the *Tafelmusik*, the divertimenti, cassations and dance suites of the masters, and so by an easy, insensible transition the symphonies of Haydn, Mozart, and perhaps Beethoven. The accepted institution of music as a background to other activities, and even to no activity at all, plainly dulls the listening faculty itself, eventually blurring the line that divides passive hearing from active listening. The distinction between noise and music, already much less clear than formerly, may easily become as indeterminate as that which divides writing from literature, often a matter of opinion and nomenclature rather than exact definition. Certainly the future of the public concert on its present scale is uncertain; and although music-theatre is very much alive, it seems improbable that there will be any but sporadic additions to the repertory of works suitable for performance in opera-houses as we know them today. European music, which once expressed man's idea of what he *should* be, his aspirations, now reflects what in his own eye he *is*; and it seems likely that this will continue to be true of music in the immediate future.

I

THE APOGEE AND DECLINE OF ROMANTICISM:
1890–1914

By GERALD ABRAHAM

INTRODUCTION

THE last decade of the nineteenth century and the first of the twentieth witnessed the final, though not the finest, efflorescence of all those musical conceptions, phenomena, and tendencies that can be subsumed in the general idea of romanticism: music as a record of the most subtle and intimate personal emotions and impressions, music as a rhetorical language addressed to large audiences (and, as in the cases of Tchaikovsky's last works and of Mahler's in general, the two were by no means mutually exclusive), music fertilized more richly than ever before by literature and painting, with the vast expansion of tonality, the complication of chromatic harmony and texture in general, and the richness and rarefaction of orchestration that were developed by the striving for wider and more refined expressive power. No doubt European music would have reached this condition of highly charged romanticism even if Wagner had never existed, but in fact Wagner had so completely summed up the various tendencies of musical romanticism and carried them to fresh heights—particularly in *Tristan, Götter-dämmerung* and *Parsifal*—that it is easy and not altogether erroneous to regard as Wagnerian everything that is romantic in the music of the period. The lay public of the time certainly did, thanks to his non-musical cultural prestige as well as to the fashionableness of his music. The romantic artist saw himself as an interpreter of the transcendental, and consequently felt himself to be above and apart from the common man; the musician was the ideal romantic artist and Wagner the ideal romantic musician. Much that was not Wagnerian was tinged with Wagner and those who resisted Wagner or reacted against him did so very consciously. Even the fresh wind which had begun to blow from Russia was contaminated by Wagnerian scents in the 1890s.

In the years immediately after Wagner's death his ideas were commonly misunderstood—for instance, any operatic theme associated with a character was regarded as a leitmotive—and the influence of his idiom and technique was very superficial. As Romain Rolland put it, 'les musiciens français traduisaient dans le style de Wagner des pensées de Gounod ou de Massenet'.[1] But as performances of *Tristan* and the *Ring* outside Bayreuth became more common, filling out the imperfect impressions gained from scores and concert excerpts—*Parsifal* was legally restricted to Bayreuth until 1913 though illegal performances were given earlier, notably in America—the influence deepened. Such typical works as Strauss's *Guntram* (comp. 1893), d'Indy's *Fervaal* (1895), Schoenberg's *Verklärte Nacht* (1899), Chausson's *Le Roi Arthus* (1899), and Elgar's *Dream of Gerontius* (1900), are saturated with it. Even composers who fought against it, as Debussy fought against 'le fantôme du vieux Klingsor',[2] partially succumbed. The Wagnerian empire, the supreme embodiment of musical romanticism, was at its heyday; like all empires, artistic and political, it bore within it the seeds of decay. Signs of reaction had already begun to appear and their development will be described in the following chapter. The present one is limited to a rapid survey of the European situation and a discussion of late romanticism and its decline.

CENTRAL EUROPE

Central Europe—Germany and Austria together with the non-German countries ruled by the Habsburgs—had been the heart-land of romanticism; consequently it was there that the crisis of romanticism was most severely felt. Perhaps the most obvious symptom of crisis was the exaggeration of antithetic moods: the brashness and exuberant virility which it is tempting to relate to the aggressive confidence of Wilhelmine Germany, and the autumnal melancholy of a culture that was drifting away from its foundations of religious faith and finding nothing to replace them. The first is most apparent in the work of Richard Strauss (1864–1949) but appears also in Gustav Mahler (1860–1911)—for instance in the finale of his First Symphony (completed 1888)—and in much of the music of their lesser German contemporaries. The second is much more characteristic of Mahler but also appears in many pages of even the young Strauss of the 1890s and dominates the last works of Brahms (d. 1897): the Clarinet Quintet, the piano pieces Op. 116–19, and the chorale preludes. (Although Brahms resisted the techniques of late romanticism, he was very sensitive to its spirit.) One finds both in the third leading representative of the Strauss-Mahler generation, Hugo Wolf (1860–1903), whose achievement seems so much less than theirs

[1] *Musiciens d'aujourd'hui* (Paris, 3rd edition, 1908), p. 243.
[2] Letter to Chausson, 2 October 1893, 'Correspondance inédite de Claude Debussy et Ernest Chausson', *Revue musicale*, vii (1925–6), p. 120.

only because it was mainly confined to the miniature form of the *Lied*[1]
and terminated untimely by his mental collapse.

Beside Brahms, other older figures still played an important part in
the musical scene: his friend, the more eclectic and progressive Dvořák
(d. 1904), the Wagner-worshipping Bruckner (d. 1896) whose symphonies are very much less influenced by Wagner than they appeared to
his contemporaries who knew them only in versions doctored by well-
meaning admirers, and such representatives of genuine conservatism as
Josef Rheinberger (d. 1901) and Max Bruch (who lived on till 1920).
For some time these, even Brahms, seemed to have no artistic progeny
of any importance; even the other progressive composers of the
Strauss-Mahler-Wolf generation (Emil Nikolaus von Reznicek, Eugen
d'Albert, Georg Schumann, Max von Schillings) were very secondary
musicians, distributaries rather than tributaries of the Wagnerian
mainstream. Only Hans Pfitzner (1869–1949), a Wagnerian but a very
conservative Wagnerian who in later years became a pugnacious
defender of conservatism, and his older contemporary Engelbert
Humperdinck (1854–1921) stand out of the ruck—the latter mainly on
the strength of a single work, *Hänsel und Gretel*. Most of them were
first and foremost opera-composers and their work is dealt with elsewhere in this volume.[2]

In the climate of the period it was natural that every progressive
musician should think first of writing for the stage and that even his
instrumental compositions should be saturated with extra-musical ideas.
Absolute music and its ideal medium, chamber music, were abandoned
to the conservatives. In the orchestral field the dominant figure was
Richard Strauss, who had built his reputation on programmatic works—
Aus Italien, Macbeth, Don Juan, Tod und Verklärung—and extended it
during the 1890s with four more tone-poems: *Till Eulenspiegels lustige
Streiche* (1895) and *Also sprach Zarathustra* (1896), *Don Quixote* (1897),
and *Ein Heldenleben* (1898).[3] With these scores, works of extraordinary
inventive exuberance and virtuosity of scoring, he established himself
as the outstanding German composer of the end of the century. The
thematic orchestral polyphony of the mature Wagner style is not only
employed with complete, confident mastery but with heightened
brilliance and with a lightness and vivacity rare in Wagner and the
Wagnerians. The range and sweep of a melody such as the opening of
Ein Heldenleben, which does not really draw breath until the seventeenth

---

[1] Wolf's songs and instrumental compositions, which date mainly from the pre-1890
period, are discussed in Vol. IX.

[2] See chap. 3.

[3] Strauss's symphonic poems, as such, are discussed in Vol. IX.

bar, would be as difficult to match in earlier music as would the incessant battering rhythm of the 'battle' section, where rhythm for its own sake anticipates the admittedly more subtle rhythmic triumphs of a decade or so later. If the structures of *Zarathustra* and *Heldenleben* are too sectional to be satisfactory, they are more daring than those of any earlier symphonic poems, and the conceptions of programmatic variations in *Don Quixote* and condensed symphony in the later *Symphonia domestica* (1903) were equally striking. And music was no longer only a language of emotion; it was now, more than with any earlier composer, a language not capable of describing concrete objects but offering acceptable symbols for them. Only in his normal harmony did Strauss usually fail to overtrump his contemporaries or even his immediate predecessors: when he did so, as at the end of *Zarathustra* and in some passages of *Elektra*, it was for a special effect of shock:

Ex. 1

ELEKTRA, Act I

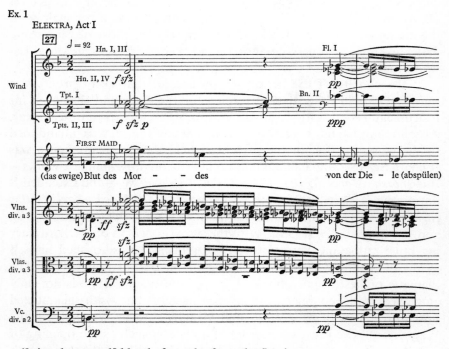

([wipe the eternal] blood of murder from the floor)

A typically rich-sounding passage, such as that at figure 24 in *Ein Heldenleben,* consists of four melodic strands:

Ex. 2

embroidered on a solid and, for the period, unadventurous harmonic
background:

Ex. 3

filled in by clarinet tremolos, horn chords, and the tremolo of divided
violas, with harp or trombones at points of emphasis. The points where
the part-writing sometimes momentarily breaks out of the harmonic
frame, as at the starred B in bar 3 of Ex. 2, pass unnoticed because of the
difference of timbre.

During the period of *Till*, *Zarathustra*, and *Heldenleben*, Mahler produced three symphonies, no. 2 in C minor (1894), no. 3 in D minor
(1896) and no. 4 in G (1900), equally involved with extra-musical
conceptions but in a very different way. Strauss was an extrovert,
technically self-confident, and fascinated by the musical depiction of
characters and events; he was a born dramatist and as his powers
matured he passed in *Don Quixote* from brilliant and sympathetic
external characterization to something more profound, that inner sympathy with another character which is the mark and indispensable
property of a true dramatic composer. Conversely, when he attempted
avowed autobiography in *Ein Heldenleben* and the *Symphonia domestica*,
he dramatized himself—and his wife—without revealing his inner

self; these works are over-concerned with external circumstances. Although his first essays in opera, *Guntram* (1893) and *Feuersnot* (1901), had not been particularly successful, he must now have recognized that the dramatic and descriptive powers of purely instrumental music could be carried no further and, with the single exception of the superficial and pictorial *Alpensymphonie* (1915), he abandoned it for his true *métier*, musical drama. On the other hand Mahler, despite his life-long occupation with the conducting of opera, culminating in his directorship of the Vienna Court Opera from 1897 to 1907, never wrote an opera at all—other than a youthful *Ernst von Schwaben*, which he destroyed.[1] His most dramatic work is the cantata *Das Klagende Lied*, which dates substantially from 1880.[2] A profound and complicated introvert, he composed hardly anything that was not autobiographical. With all his experience as a conductor, he lacked self-confidence as an orchestral composer, as is manifest from his innumerable revisions and other changes of mind and by the nervous meticulousness of his detailed instructions for performance.

Mahler's symphonies are no more absolute music than Strauss's tone-poems but they are at the same time both more and less explicit. Whereas with Strauss the external world nearly always plays a vivid part in his conception, with Mahler it exists only as indeterminate 'nature', symbolized by bird-song and cowbells and posthorn calls, as a setting for the poet's subjective brooding. For his First Symphony, a purely orchestral composition, Mahler had written, and then suppressed, a literary programme;[3] in the three symphonies of the 1890s he found it necessary, as Beethoven had done in the Ninth, to call in a poet's words. As he wrote to Arthur Seidl in 1897[4] 'When I conceive a great musical creation, I always come to the point where I must draw on the "word" as bearer of my musical idea.' We have it on his own authority[5] that the first movement of the Second Symphony is a funeral ceremony for the hero of the First—who is perhaps his own youth; that the second movement, innocent as Schubert or Dvořák, is a happy recollection of a sunny day in this hero's life; that the third represents a return to the senseless and repellent hurly-burly of everyday life (it is based on his song-setting of 'Des Antonius von Padua Fischpredigt' from *Des Knaben Wunderhorn*, just as the First Symphony is partly based on themes from his *Lieder eines fahrenden Gesellen*); and that the finale is an answer to 'the great question "*Why have you lived*? Why have you

---

[1] Gustav Mahler, *Briefe, 1879–1911* (Berlin, Vienna and Leipzig, 1925), p. 8, n. 1.
[2] See Donald Mitchell, *Gustav Mahler: The Early Years* (London, 1958), pp. 152–3.
[3] Printed in full in Paul Stefan, *Gustav Mahler* (Neue, vermehrte und veränderte Ausgabe; Munich, 1920), p. 113.
[4] *Briefe*, p. 228.   [5] Ibid., pp. 188–9.

suffered? Is that all merely a huge and frightful joke?" '. The answer is a grandiose choral setting of a slight adaptation of Klopstock's Resurrection ode, 'Auferstehen, ja auferstehen', which Mahler had just heard sung at Hans von Bülow's funeral, to which the transition from the bitter humour of the third movement is made through another *Wunderhorn* poem, 'Urlicht', sung by a solo voice, one of the most Brucknerian things Mahler ever wrote. He had already, with this distension of both the form and media of the symphony—the Third is scored for an enormous orchestra—reached the point when he could say, 'Symphony means to me the building up of a world with all the technical means available' ('Mir heisst Symphonie: mit allen Mitteln der vorhandenen Technik mir eine Welt aufbauen.') Mahler regarded his Third Symphony, to which the Fourth may be considered an epilogue, as 'a musical poem embracing all the stages of development step by step. It begins with inanimate nature and rises to the love of God.'[1] It was originally conceived with a title derived from Nietzsche, 'Meine fröhliche Wissenschaft'; later it became 'Pan', not only as the god's name but as the idea of 'allness'; then again it became 'A Summer Morning's Dream', the big initial movement in sonata-form being called 'Pan awakes; the summer marches in' and followed by shorter ones: 'What the flowers in the field tell me', 'What the animals in the wood tell me' (based on one of the earliest of his *Wunderhorn* songs, 'Ablösung im Sommer'), 'What Man tells me' (the midnight song from Nietzsche's *Zarathustra*, which Strauss was suggesting in his tone-poem almost at the same time, but composed by Mahler for alto solo), 'What the angels tell me' ('Es sungen drei Engel' from the *Wunderhorn*, set for alto and boys' choir), and 'What love tells me' (an Adagio for orchestra only). But these titles were suppressed before publication, leaving the naïve listener with an impression of a heterogeneous suite not even unified by a key-scheme, since the movements are respectively in D minor, A major, C minor, D major, F major, and A major. (Mahler once suggested that his unconventional key-schemes were motivated by the pursuit of innovation for its own sake; nevertheless they underlie all but two, nos. 6 and 8, of his later symphonies.) The exquisitely naïve finale of the Fourth Symphony, yet another *Wunderhorn* setting, was to have been the penultimate movement of the Third: 'What the child tells me', and the Symphony is, for Mahler, remarkably free from darker shades; only in the second movement does Death with his fiddle (a solo violin tuned up a tone) cast his shadow—and by no means over the whole of that.

These three symphonies, naïve in almost everything but their irony,

[1] Ibid. p. 161.

gangliated in structure, closely akin to song even when they do not actually break into it, are much more truly romantic both in musical substance and in their programmes than the symphonic poems of Strauss, where beside the genuine romanticism of such wonderful passages as the death of Don Quixote one finds much that is only superficial romantic gesture and the exaggeration of romantic language in conjunction with a realism (Quixote's bleating sheep, the battle-section in *Heldenleben*) that, as in opera of the period, is downright anti-romantic. And after the turn of the century, when Strauss soon withdrew from the symphonic field while his rival went on to produce first a trilogy of purely instrumental symphonies, no. 5 (1902), no. 6 (1904), and no. 7 (1905), then a gigantic totally choral symphony, no. 8 (1907), and yet another for orchestra alone, no. 9 (1909)—as well as the torso of a Tenth—Mahler's position as the leading Central European symphonist was uncontested. He had markedly developed. In the three symphonies of 1902–5, which are as definitely related to each other as the four *Wunderhorn* symphonies, he not only found it possible to dispense with 'the word'; they are—particularly nos. 6 and 7—much less disconcertingly naïve, more closely knit; the orchestral polyphony rivals Strauss's in its mastery while the massive effects (above all, in the finale of the Sixth and opening of the Seventh) recall the granite monumentality of Bruckner. Only the Adagietto of no. 5 seems to belong to the earlier group. But the music is no less romantic in essence—the funeral-march first movement of no. 5 with the Wagnerian cello cantilena of both this and the slow sections of the following Allegro, the autobiographical suggestions of no. 6 (which according to his widow[1] has elements of a *symphonia domestica*) with the hammer death-blows of its finale, the three 'inside' movements—the two pieces of 'night music' and the 'shadowlike' scherzo—no less subjective and secretly programmatic. The Eighth Symphony, monumental both in proportions and in the forces employed, also struck out in a new direction despite an obvious affinity with the finale of the earlier giant, no. 2; a symphony in two movements, one a setting of 'Veni creator spiritus', the second (embracing elements of Adagio, scherzo, and finale) of the closing scene of Goethe's *Faust*, employing eight vocal soloists, double chorus, and boys' choir, as well as an orchestra of unprecedented size, demanded and was given a more impressive power of coordination than the earlier, partly vocal symphonies. This was the last of the colossi of musical romanticism, a line stretching from the outdoor compositions

---

[1] Alma Maria Mahler, *Gustav Mahler: Erinnerungen und Briefe* (Amsterdam, 1940); English trans. by Basil Creighton (London, 1946); enlarged and revised edition (London, 1968), p. 70.

of the French Revolution through Berlioz, and Mahler followed it with two works which express with exceptional poignancy the autumnal mood and sunset colouring of musical romanticism itself: *Das Lied von der Erde* (1908), a song-cycle for alto, tenor, and orchestra that he himself styled a 'symphony', and the closely related but purely orchestral Ninth Symphony. In sharp contrast with the Eighth, these last scores are remarkable for the almost chamber-musiclike finesse of the orchestral writing, a finesse already adumbrated in the accompaniment of the cycle of *Kindertotenlieder* (Dirges for children) (1904) and the second *Nachtmusik* of the Seventh Symphony.

In this as in the influence of Bach, which is apparent in the fugal elements in the finale of his Fifth Symphony and the feats of invertible counterpoint in the Eighth, Mahler showed himself sensitive to the spirit of the decade, for of the Central European composers born in the seventies who came to the fore after the turn of the century, the two most important—Max Reger (1873–1916) and Arnold Schoenberg (1874–1951)—both were under the spell of Bach and both were attracted to chamber music. This was a generation of reconcilers; the days of partisanship were coming to an end; musicians could, and commonly did, admire both Wagner and Brahms. And often Dvořák as well: Schoenberg's early D major String Quartet (1897) shows particularly in its texture and in the opening subject of the finale that he too came under the influence of the Czech master. Schoenberg's leaning to Brahms was strengthened by his teacher (and later brother-in-law) Alexander von Zemlinsky (1872–1942), who was also drawn to chamber music though he became better known as a composer and conductor of opera. Franz Schreker (1878–1934) began as a Brahmsian and evolved into a full-blooded eclectic, though his really notable works, mainly operas, appeared only just before the First World War, while the more conservative Franz Schmidt (1874–1939) was even slower in finding a creative personality. The young Hungarian Brahmsian Ernö Dohnányi (1877–1960) and Dvořák's two most talented pupils, Vitězslav Novák (1870–1949) and Josef Suk (1874–1935), all developed into complete eclectics, sensitive to Strauss or Tchaikovsky, following the will-o'-the-wisps of impressionism or nationalism, and thus freely and often eloquently employing the *lingua franca* of late romanticism without extending it. The older and far more original Leoš Janáček (1854–1928) remained in obscurity throughout this period; even his most successful opera *Její pastorkyňa* (better known as *Jenůfa*), was performed only in the provincial city of Brünn (Brno) in 1904, and then forgotten until 1916, when it was followed by all his major works.[1]

[1] See pp. 179–82 and 301–4.

Some of the slightly younger men, Béla Bartók (1881–1945) and Zoltán Kodály (1882–1967) in Hungary, and Schoenberg's disciples Anton von Webern (1883–1945) and Alban Berg (1885–1935) in Austria, were much more significant figures, still romantics when they first appeared on the scene; Bartók's *Kossuth* Symphony (1903), for instance, was very closely modelled on *Ein Heldenleben* and the *Portraits, Elegies,* and *Dirges* (1907–10) were autobiographical in essence, even though the nature of his musical language was changing. These were the composers who, with Schoenberg and Reger, were to succeed Mahler when he died and Strauss when he began to repeat himself. It is symptomatic that, unlike most of the true romantics, none of them was in a hurry to write his first opera and that, when they did, both Bartók's *A kékszakállú herceg vára* (*Duke Bluebeard's Castle*) (1911) and Schoenberg's *Die glückliche Hand* (1913) were short and highly experimental works, reaching out in entirely new directions.[1] Berg and Kodály—ultimately more important as a teacher and stimulator in his native country than as a creator—were even later in entering this field, while Reger and Webern never entered it at all. On the other hand they all cultivated chamber music, both in the usual sense of instrumental ensemble music and in the wider one of intimate media generally, including solo piano music and the solo song with piano.

A great chapter in the history of chamber music closed in 1895 with Brahms's compositions for clarinet and other instruments and Dvořák's last quartets. Wolf might have opened a new one if he had remained sane, but Strauss, who turned away from chamber music and piano music after his youth, and Mahler, who was never interested in either, were too intoxicated with the possibilities of the post-Wagnerian orchestra to find modest, more or less monochrome media congenial. It is true that Strauss, unlike Mahler, continued to write songs with piano after his youth; indeed most of the songs by which he is best known—'Cäcilie', 'Heimliche Aufforderung', 'Morgen', 'Traum durch die Dämmerung'— date from the 1890s, while the songs of the new century, from Op. 48 onward, include such masterpieces as 'Blindenklage', Op. 56, no. 2.[2] That they should show the influence of Wolf in their often declamatory voice-parts and their rich, almost more important piano-parts was only to be expected. No important German song-composer of the period, neither Reger nor Schoenberg nor that gentler talent, Joseph Marx (1882–1964), a latter-day Robert Franz, completely escaped Wolf's influence. They might begin song-writing in emulation of Brahms or the earlier nineteenth-century masters of the *Lied*, but they inevitably

---

[1] See pp. 202–3 and 206.
[2] Recorded in *The History of Music in Sound*, x.

passed deeply through the experience of Wolf before they found their true selves, Strauss through the sheer exuberance of his creative personality, Reger in the series of *Schlichte Weisen* begun in 1904 by deliberate simplification. Reger's 'Maienblüten', Op. 66, no. 5, and the opening of his 'Morgen', Op. 66, no. 10 (1902), show his debt, even in maturity, to Wolf:

Ex. 4

(And tomorrow the sun will shine again, and on the way where I shall go.)

Reger's greater harmonic sophistication, compared with Strauss's in the latter's much better known composition of the same poem (1894), is again apparent in the settings of Richard Dehmel's 'Waldseligkeit' which both composers made in 1901:

Ex. 5 (i) STRAUSS (Op. 49, No. 1)

- - - men naht

die Nacht;

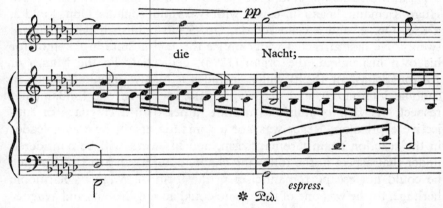

(ii) REGER (Op. 62, No. 2)

Äusserst zart, ausdrucksvoll *(doch nie schleppend)*

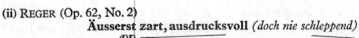

Der Wald be-ginnt zu rau - schen, den

assai delicato

sempre una corda

sempre con Pedale, ma assai delicato

(The wood begins to rustle, night draws near the trees;)

As an instrumental composer Reger, pupil of the musical polymath Hugo Riemann, began his career with two violin sonatas, Opp. 1 and 3, a trio, Op. 2, and a cello sonata, Op. 5, all published before he was twenty. He first attracted wider notice through a Suite in E minor for his own instrument, the organ (1895), dedicated 'To the Manes of Johann Sebastian Bach' which includes a highly ingenious fugue, a canonic intermezzo, and a baroque passacaglia. In one fundamental respect, his view of music as a craft rather than a language of subjective expression, Reger was not a romantic at all; he was a leader in the reaction against romanticism, and his work will be considered under that aspect in the following chapter. But as an artist of his time he could not escape romanticism in the form of Wagner's harmonic heritage, for he was one of those who could accept Brahms and Wagner —and also Strauss, whose orchestral technique was not without its effect on his own. His conception of Bach, common to his contemporaries, was a romantic conception and his own organ compositions on chorales, above all the three *Phantasien*, Op. 52 (1900), are highly romantic, not to say programmatic. The C major Violin Sonata (1903), the first movement of which spells out his enemies as 'sheep' and 'ape' (E♭ = S, C, B♮ = H, A, F, E and A, F, F, E), is as frankly autobiographical as *Ein Heldenleben*. Nor was the composer of such orchestral works as the G major Serenade (1906), which so impressed the young Prokofyev, the *Sinfonischer Prolog zu einer Tragödie* (1908) and the *Vier Tondichtungen nach Arnold Böcklin* (1913), a pure craftsman, certainly not a simple one. Even his chamber music, which is greater in bulk than his orchestral and organ music put together, is sometimes romantic in the broader sense; Guido Bagier[1] justly speaks of

[1] *Max Reger* (Stuttgart and Berlin, 1923), p. 256.

the C minor Piano Quintet, Op. 64 (1898) as 'a masterpiece of *Sturm und Drang*'. He goes on to describe it as 'an uncompleted symphony in the guise of chamber music'. Reger never did write a symphony; the Sinfonietta (1905), originally conceived as a serenade and scored for what at the beginning of the century was a 'small' orchestra, that is, one of classical size with the addition of a harp, was a failure and the *Sinfonischer Prolog*, the first movement of a projected symphony, was left on its own. As Bagier puts it,[1] 'each chamber-music work is a preliminary step toward this goal'. But chamber music was a much more congenial medium[2] and Reger's intensive cultivation of it accords with this basic preference for the forms of absolute music.

Yet the earliest major work of Schoenberg, a more fundamental romantic then Reger, was a bold essay in programmatic chamber music, a string sextet inspired by a poem of Richard Dehmel, *Verklärte Nacht* (1899). Schoenberg knew his Wagner really thoroughly at an early age, much earlier than Reger had done, and as his next compositions show he was also familiar with both Mahler and Strauss. The *Gurrelieder*, poems by Jens Peter Jacobsen[3] set for colossal vocal and instrumental forces, were composed by May 1901 though the instrumentation was not completed till ten years later; the work would hardly have been planned in that form without the Mahlerian precedents, although the Eighth Symphony was still to come. The symphonic poem, *Pelleas und Melisande* (1903), too, was clearly written in emulation of Strauss, who actually suggested the subject to him, though for operatic treatment: it portrays a series of episodes from Maeterlinck's play, with themes for Golaud, Mélisande, and Pelléas (the two latter combined at ⌐26⌐ against a picturesque background when Mélisande lets fall her hair from the tower-window); the dense orchestral polyphony, often bursting out of the harmonic framework, is very Straussian and the climax of the love-scene from ⌐39⌐ onward is closely related to the love-music of *Ein Heldenleben* (cf. Exs. 2–3). On the other hand, Mélisande's playing with the ring ⌐16⌐ is painted in a Mahlerian *Ländler*. The sequence of Schoenberg's early chamber compositions is equally significant in a different way. First after *Verklärte Nacht* came the String Quartet in D minor, Op. 7, which was published as 'No. 1' (1905), a thematically dense score in which, it has been claimed without too much exaggeration,[4] 'there is not an inside part or a figure that is not thematic', then the *Kammersymphonie*, Op. 9 (1906) for fifteen solo

---

[1] Ibid., p. 266.   [2] Witness the String Trio, op. 77b (1904), of which the slow movement is recorded in *The History of Music in Sound*, x.

[3] Translated from the Danish by R. F. Arnold.

[4] Egon Wellesz, *Arnold Schönberg* (Leipzig, 1921), p. 101; English translation by W. H. Kerridge (London, 1925 and 1971).

instruments, some of its material again oddly Straussian in outline—Strauss distorted by the whole-tone scale. In both of these, as indeed in *Verklärte Nacht* and *Pelleas und Melisande*, the elements of the four-movement sonata are compressed into a single, very long movement, scherzo and slow movement being inserted before and after the main development, and reprise understood in the freest sense. But whereas this was the complete antithesis of Mahler's practice of expansion, in the Second Quartet (F sharp minor, Op. 10) (1908)[1] Schoenberg, like Mahler, 'drew on the "word" as bearer of the musical idea'; in the third movement, *adagio con variazioni*, the soprano sings Stefan George's 'Litanei', in the finale the same poet's 'Entrückung' with its peculiarly apposite first line, 'Ich fühle Luft von anderen Planeten' ('I feel air from other planets'). And, as Dika Newlin has pointed out, 'the spirit of Mahler hovers even more persistently over the scherzo, with its bizarre quotation (in the trio section) of "Ach, du lieber Augustin".'[2] The dedication of the *Harmonielehre* (1911) speaks for itself; in later years too Schoenberg often 'expressed indebtedness to Mahler',[3] and during 1907-8 their personal relationship was at its closest. Yet there were profound differences, even greater differences than between Schoenberg and Reger, in whose music he also 'admired many things'.[4] Mahler's art was an end, Reger's seemingly a dead end, Schoenberg's at once an end and a beginning. The upward-leaping horn theme in perfect fourths at the beginning of the *Kammersymphonie* is, taken by itself, more anti-tonal than anything in Mahler or Reger, who took wild liberties with tonality but always left its pillars standing. And here, too, the Schoenberg passage stands between buttresses of F major and E major. But in the finale of the Second Quartet Schoenberg arrived at full atonality.

With the fanatical courage that was the predominant strain in his character, he did not shrink from the consequences and turn back. Atonal music presented many problems, of which the most difficult was that of structure in general and the construction of extended instrumental compositions in particular. Hence the works of the next few years which lean on drama—the monodrama *Erwartung* (1909) and the music-drama *Die glückliche Hand* (1913)—and those with poetic texts, the George song-cycle *Das Buch der hängenden Gärten* (1909), the Maeterlinck *Herzgewächse* (1911), the melodrama *Pierrot lunaire* (on Otto Erich Hartleben's translation of Albert Giraud's poems) (1912), and the four songs with orchestra, Op. 22 (1913-14)—are more assured

---

[1] First movement recorded in *The History of Music in Sound*, x.
[2] *Bruckner—Mahler—Schoenberg* (New York, 1947), p. 235.
[3] Ibid., pp. vii and 241-2.   [4] Ibid., p. 275.

than the purely instrumental pieces, the *Drei Klavierstücke*, Op. 11[1], and *Fünf Orchesterstücke*, Op. 16,[2] of 1909, epoch-making as they were, and the *Sechs kleine Klavierstücke*, Op. 19, of 1911. This group of compositions, in which both the romantic conception of music as a language of expression and the musical techniques of romanticism are carried to their ultimate extremity, was written under the sign of the *avant-garde* movement that was leaving its mark on all forms of European art at the time: expressionism, the antithesis of impressionism, the morbidly intense expressive content of concentrated particles of speech or line or sound, content with the minimum of matter and form. Representational painting was reduced to geometrical relationships such as the cube, dramatic characters to dreamlike abstractions from the subconscious like 'The Man', 'The Woman', and 'The Gentleman' in *Die glückliche Hand*.[3] In such music as Op. 11, no. 3, each thematic idea was self-sufficient, unrepeated, not balanced symmetrically by a following phrase; repetition was at all tolerable only in the form of constructive, developing variation. With tonality mortally strained by late-romantic techniques and undermined by those of impressionism,[4] chords had finally lost their functional significance. With the 'emancipation of dissonance',[5] which Schoenberg adumbrated in his *Harmonielehre*,[6] cadence no longer had meaning as a point of relaxed harmonic tension. Atonal music was, in fact, also athematic and, apart from the supports of text or drama, nearly amorphous.[7] The crucial element in *Pierrot lunaire* was not the *Sprechstimme* of the reciter, speaking at approximate musical pitches, which attracted so much attention at the time—it had already been used in the *Gurrelieder* and *Die glückliche Hand*—but the means by which Schoenberg attempted to counter amorphousness: the devices of canon and inversion which were to lead him to the note-row and twelve-note serialism. Yet the decadent, sado-masochistic subject of *Pierrot lunaire* is, as Stuckenschmidt has pointed out,[8] typical of late romanticism, with origins reaching back to *Parsifal* and coming to a climax in *Salome* and *Elektra*. Even at this point when Schoenberg's music had become totally un-Wagnerian and

---

[1] For an intensive study of Op. 11, and the works leading up to it, see Reinhold Brinkmann, *Arnold Schönberg: Drei Klavierstücke Op. 11* (Wiesbaden, 1969); on *Das Buch der hängenden Gärten,* see idem, 'Schönberg und George', *Archiv für Musikwissenschaft*, xxvi (1969), p. 1.

[2] There is a good study of Op. 16 in Anthony Payne, *Schoenberg* (London, 1968), pp. 20–8.

[3] On Schoenberg and expressionism, see Karl H. Wörner, *Neue Musik in der Entscheidung* (Mainz, 1954), pp. 58–9.

[4] See p. 90.   [5] Schoenberg, *Style and Idea* (New York, 1950), p. 104.

[6] Leipzig and Vienna, 1911, e.g. pp. 370, 433, and elsewhere.

[7] Cf. *infra*, pp. 140–1.

[8] Hans Heinz Stuckenschmidt, *Arnold Schönberg* (Zürich, 2nd ed. 1957). English translation by E. T. Roberts and Humphrey Searle (London, 1959), p. 65.

anti-romantic, the underlying ideas are often romantic and Wagnerian. *Erwartung* and *Die glückliche Hand* are conceived in the image of the *Gesamtkunstwerk*; one, at least, of the *Five Orchestral Pieces* had a poetic connotation—the changing chord-colours of no. 3 were 'comparable, as Schoenberg says, with the ever-changing colour-impression of the lightly agitated surface of a lake';[1] and the funeral bell tolls for Mahler in the little piano piece, Op. 19, no. 6.

Webern had written atonal, non-thematic miniatures, the *Fünf Sätze* for string quartet, Op. 5 (1909) and the *Sechs Stücke* for orchestra, Op. 6 (1910), before Schoenberg's Op. 19; but although expressionism may be considered the final convulsion of romanticism, and despite the *alla marcia funebre* of Op 6, no. 4, and the suppressed titles of his next orchestral work, the *Fünf Stücke*, Op. 10 (1911–13), Webern was not— after *Im Sommerwind* and the other juvenilia of 1904–5—a genuine romantic. His earliest acknowledged composition, the orchestral *Passacaglia* of 1908, already manifests a Regerian love of construction for its own sake. Its very large orchestra, like that of Op. 6, is characteristic of the period, just as the chamber orchestras of Op. 10 and the *Vier Lieder*, Op. 13 (1914–18), are characteristic of the reaction from it. Even the extreme condensation of expressionism lasted only until Schoenberg showed him a way of escape from it. But if Webern was never a romantic, his friend Berg was never—to the last—anything else. The majority of the still mostly unpublished early songs[2] and some of the published ones (such as the beautiful 'Traumgekrönt' of 1907) are in the true tradition of the romantic *Lied*; the expressionistic *Vier Lieder*, Op. 2 (1909–10)[3] mark the end of that tradition. Berg's early instrumental works follow closely the curve of development traced by the Schoenberg pieces on which they were to some extent modelled: the Piano Sonata, Op. 1 (1908) on the *Kammersymphonie*, the String Quartet, Op. 3 (1910) on Quartets nos. 1 and 2, and the *Vier Stücke* for clarinet and piano Op. 5 (1913) on the aphoristic piano pieces of Schoenberg's Op. 19, while the *Drei Stücke* for large orchestra, Op. 6 (1914) shows a curious affinity with Mahler.[4] But the romantic vein in Berg remained fairly constantly obvious in the music of his maturity,[5] and never more so than in the final Violin Concerto.

The early course of Bartók's evolution was not dissimilar. Turning from Schumann and Brahms to Wagner, he was overwhelmed in 1902

[1] Webern, 'Schönbergs Musik', in the symposium *Arnold Schönberg* (Munich, 1912), p. 44.
[2] Nicholas Chadwick, 'Berg's Unpublished Songs in the Österreichische National-bibliothek', *Music and Letters*, lii (1971), p. 123.
[3] Nos. 2 and 3 recorded in *The History of Music in Sound*, x.
[4] On this see particularly Hans F. Redlich, *Alban Berg—Versuch einer Würdigung* (Vienna, 1957), pp. 93ff., and its condensed English version (New York, 1957), pp. 65–72.
[5] See *infra*, pp. 362 ff.

by the discovery of Strauss, particularly of *Also sprach Zarathustra*[1] and *Ein Heldenleben*. What set Bartók apart from his Austrian contemporaries was his passionate nationalism, conventionally Hungarian in the Rhapsody for piano, Op. 1 (1904) and the first Suite for orchestra, Op. 3 (1905), but soon given a fresh direction by his discovery, in Kodály's footsteps, in 1905–6 of the authentic, un-gypsified folk-music of the Hungarian peasants. A belated acquaintance with Debussy's music in 1907[2] was the second most important factor in guiding him away from tonality and the Central European mainstream toward simpler, less dense textures and new melodic modes, and his *Bagatelles* for piano, Op. 6 (1908) constitute a miniature thesaurus of the new harmonic and tonal devices of the period: counterpoint of chord-blocks (no. 4), bitonality (no. 1), fourth chords (no. 11), a foreshadowing of 12-note composition (no. 3),[3] the non-functional side-slipping of dissonances.[4] Schoenberg quoted (inaccurately) from no. 10 to illustrate the last of these, side by side with excerpts from Webern and Schreker's *Der ferne Klang*, in his *Harmonielehre*.[5] Bartók got to know Schoenberg's music only in 1910; it affected both his harmony and the boldness of his line-drawing, and he wrote of it with warmth,[6] though even in 1937 he had still not heard *Pierrot lunaire*. Yet the last two of the *Bagatelles* are cryptically autobiographical quite in the Schumann manner, belonging to the group of works (including the First Violin Concerto and the *Két arckép* (Two Portraits), Op. 5) associated with the violinist Stefi Geyer; and in the piano *Elegies*, Op. 8b (1908–9) and the *Két kép* (Two pictures) for orchestra, Op. 10 (1910), Bartók reverted to romantic or impressionistic textures. It was only in 1911 with *Bluebeard's Castle* and the *Allegro barbaro* for piano that Bartók achieved a satisfactory and highly personal synthesis of these diverse elements.

FRANCE

Except in the earlier works of Berlioz and the mature ones of César Franck, romanticism had never penetrated French music very deeply. Fruitful contacts with literature and the pictorial are characteristic of romantic music, but they had been characteristic of French music long before the romantic movement. Chopin left his mark. Liszt influenced Saint-Saëns, the oldest French composer of any significance during the

[1] Bartók, 'Selbstbiographie', *Musikblätter des Anbruch*, iii (1921), p. 88.
[2] Ibid., p. 89.
[3] Oliver Neighbour, 'The Evolution of Twelve-Note Music', *Proceedings of the Royal Musical Association*, lxxxi (1954–5), p. 53.
[4] See, particularly, Edwin von der Nüll, *Béla Bartók* (Halle, 1930), pp. 3–14.
[5] p. 469.
[6] See his article, 'Arnold Schönbergs Musik in Ungarn', *Musikblätter des Anbruch*, ii (1920), p. 647.

1890s, and Franck and his followers, particularly in their use of theme-transformation in major instrumental works. French opera from Chabrier's *Gwendoline* onward abounds in leitmotives and other Wagnerian properties—even Massenet was not totally unaware of them —but d'Indy rightly held that the Wagnerism of *Gwendoline* is 'more apparent than real' and that Chausson's *Roi Arthus*, 'the most complete specimen of a work influenced by the Bayreuth master', is saved by 'the intervention of our French nature' from 'exaggerations which no German writer would have known how to resist',[1] a judgement which is equally true of his own *Fervaal*. The romanticism of French orchestral music is often only picturesque and superficial, as with Dukas's *L'Apprenti sorcier* (1897). It is not surprising that France began to reject romanticism before Germany, but it is typical of the period generally that two of the most effective agents of the rejection were composers who had fallen heavily under the spell of Wagner: Vincent d'Indy (1851-1931), by his foundation in 1896 of the Schola Cantorum which had as its main objects 'a return to the Gregorian tradition of performing plainsong' (i.e. the Solesmes tradition) and 'the rehabilitation of the music known as Palestrinian',[2] and Claude Debussy (1862-1918) by his rejection of functional harmony and his obedience to Verlaine's command[3] 'Prends l'éloquence et tords-lui son cou!'

Despite the antagonism of their ideals and temperaments, an antagonism which did not preclude a limited amount of mutual admiration and even influence,[4] d'Indy and Debussy had more in common than an early enchantment with Wagner—from which the older man finally escaped only much later, after the other's death. Both preferred to work with small units of sound rather than long-breathed melody; both had a distaste for clear, symmetrical rhythmic patterns, though d'Indy vigorously distorted them whereas Debussy gently dissolved them; both orchestrated generally with characteristically French restraint and clarity. But the differences went much deeper, as deep as the personal difference between devout, even bigoted Catholic and free-thinking, free-living faun. Debussy was the very ideal of the late-nineteenth-century artist, all sensuality and sensibility; d'Indy, like Reger, was essentially a cerebral craftsman. Paul Landormy quotes his 'peremptory affirmation' that 'une oeuvre d'art se *fait*'[5] and the analyses of his own compositions in his *Cours de composition musicale*[6] make amply clear

[1] *Richard Wagner et son influence sur l'art musical français* (Paris, 1930), pp. 69 and 75.

[2] Prospectus of *La Tribune de Saint-Gervais*, i (1895).

[3] In *Jadis et naguère* (Paris, 1884).

[4] See Léon Vallas, *Vincent d'Indy*, ii (Paris, 1950), pp. 195–6, 255, 319–21.

[5] *La Musique française de Franck à Debussy* (Paris, 1943), p. 77.

[6] Paris, three vols., i, 1903; ii, première partie (1909); ii, seconde partie (1933); iii (1950).

his concern with structural ingenuity for its own sake. Even his attitude to harmony was the complete antithesis of Debussy's; he wrote that 'chords as combinations of sounds appear only as the effect of a *halt* in the movement of the *melodic* parts . . . musically *chords* do not exist and harmony is not the *science of chords*. . . . The study of them for *their own sake* is an absolute aesthetic error.'[1] His approach to texture in his mature works was primarily contrapuntal, culminating in the polyphony of the Second Symphony (1903).[2]

The conflicts of the romantic crisis are much more strongly marked in d'Indy's orchestral music than in his operas, in which can be traced a gentle decline from the strongly Wagnerian *Fervaal*, through *L'Étranger*, to the unsuccessful *Légende de Saint Christophe* to which he devoted most of the years 1908–15.[3] His earlier instrumental music had been almost entirely programmatic;[4] after the death of his master Franck in 1890 there was a marked turn to absolute or relatively absolute music. In that very year he wrote his First String Quartet, and in the Second, in E major (1897), written in deliberate emulation of Franck, he carried the principle of essential thematic unity almost to its last extreme eight years before Schoenberg's Op. 7, all its themes being generated by the four-note motive which stands as its 'epigraph'.[5] The same thematic density and tightness of construction mark the Second Symphony and the Piano Sonata in E (1907).[6] Yet the spirit of romanticism was not completely extinct even in these. The programmatic *Istar* of 1896 had been cast in the form of fairly strict 'symphonic variations'; conversely the seemingly 'absolute' B flat Symphony is a struggle between two basic themes, symbols of darkness and light or evil and good, and the Piano Sonata, though profoundly different from the programmatic, Schumannesquely autobiographical piano compositions of the 1880s— the *Poème des montagnes* and the *Tableaux de voyage*—is not without remains of romantic rhetoric. Moreover the Symphony was followed in 1905 by the 'symphonic triptych' *Jour d'été à la montagne*: picturesque, romantic in essence and expression, even based on a detailed programme.[7] Like so many of d'Indy's mature compositions *Jour d'été* introduces folk-tunes, which he had collected from the late 1880s onward, and is crowned by a melody derived from plainsong, the two elements which—particularly plainsong—played in his work a role

---

[1] *Cours de composition*, i. p. 91. Schoenberg repeats this almost exactly in his *Harmonie-lehre*: in polyphony 'die Akkorde entstehen nur also *Zufälle der Stimmenführung* und sind, da die Verantwortung für das Zusammenklangliche vom Melodischen getragen wird, ohne Bedeutung für die Konstruktion' (p. 348). But he adds, 'That is naturally only half true. . . .'
[2] See Ex. 46 on pp. 108–9.
[3] On the operas, see *infra*, pp. 169–71 and *Cours*, iii, pp. 201 ff.
[4] See Vol. IX.   [5] Analysis in *Cours*, ii[2], pp. 267–70.
[6] Ibid., pp. 175 and 429.   [7] Ibid., pp. 327–30.

comparable with that of peasant-song in Bartók's in freeing it from Germanic ways of thought.

D'Indy was the most doctrinaire and the most influential of the Franckists, but his pre-eminence is partly due to the early silence of Duparc, who ceased to compose in 1885, the early death of Ernest Chausson (1855–1899), and the still more premature death of the brilliant young Belgian, Guillaume Lekeu (1870–1894). More individual than the other actual pupils of Franck, such as Guy Ropartz (1864–1955), were their allies: Albéric Magnard (1864–1914), Paul Dukas (1865–1935), and Albert Roussel (1869–1937). The operas of this group, above all Chausson's *Roi Arthus* and Dukas's *Ariane et Barbe-bleue* (1907), were more authentically Wagnerian than those of Massenet's so-called 'realist' pupils, Alfred Bruneau (1857–1934) and Gustave Charpentier (1860–1956),[1] but in *Ariane* the Wagnerism is strongly modified by Debussy's influence and both Dukas and Chausson were primarily instrumental composers; it is in their instrumental music that the crisis of romanticism is more perceptible, particularly in the way they treat their heritage from Franck. Duparc said that, 'Chausson comes more directly from Franck than any of us'[2] and his B flat Symphony (1890), his *Poème* for violin and orchestra (1896), and his chamber music are certainly Franckian in style though marked by a very individual vein of refined lyrical poetry. Magnard's symphonies, particularly No. 3 in B flat minor (1896), are subjectively, even rhetorically romantic, but reject his master d'Indy's cherished 'cyclic form'. The open fifths that begin the Third Symphony:

Ex. 6

----

[1] On French opera of this period, see *infra*, pp. 164 ff.
[2] Quoted by Landormy, op. cit., p. 89.

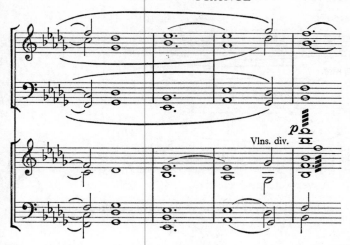

actually seem to stand between the openings of *La Damoiselle élue* and *Pelléas*. Dukas's *Ariane* also betrays an awareness of Debussy (see Ex. 7)

Ex. 7

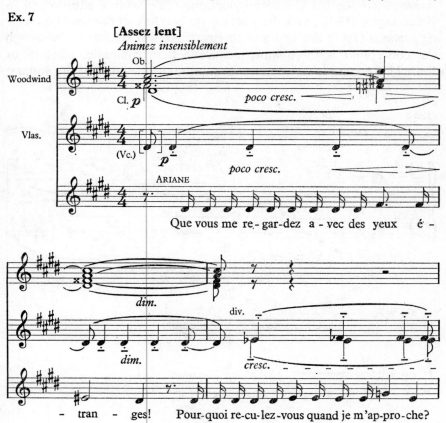

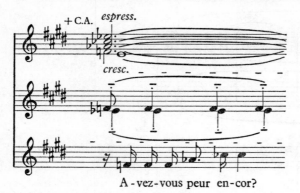

A - vez - vous peur en - cor?

(How strangely you look at me! . . . Why do you draw back when I approach? . . .
Are you still afraid?)

in its vocal writing, its harmony, and its texture and of Strauss in its full-
bodied orchestration. In sharp contrast to the earlier programmatic
Apprenti sorcier, his C major Symphony (1897), his Piano Sonata in
E flat minor (1901), and the *Variations, interlude et final sur un thème
de Rameau* (1903) are first and foremost musical structures. Although
the conception is often more academic than romantic, Lisztian or
Franckian romanticism comes to the surface in the finale of the Sonata:

Ex. 8

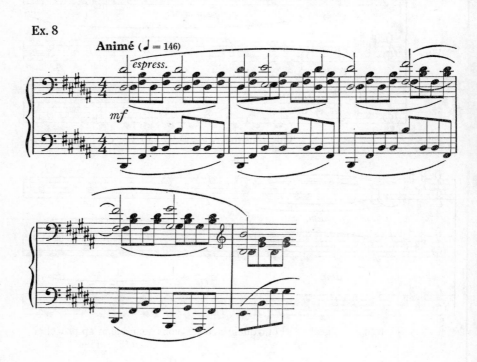

and there are picturesque suggestions in the slow movement of the Symphony (e.g. where flute and clarinet call *ppp, lointain*). On the contrary, Roussel's early work, with the exception of some d'Indyish chamber music—particularly the *Divertissement* for piano and wind quintet (1906) closely modelled on d'Indy's wind *Divertissement* of 1898[1]—is frankly picturesque romanticism. His so-called First Symphony, *Le Poème de la forêt*, is an impression of a specific place, like d'Indy's *Jour d'été*, and consists of four pieces written independently: *Forêt d'hiver* (1906), *Renouveau* (1905), *Soir d'été* (1904) and *Faunes et dryades* (1906). Stylistically it answers completely to his too modest description of all his music of the period 1898–1913: 'marked by the weak influence of Debussy but above all by the struggle with the technique learned from d'Indy'.[2] *Évocations* for soli and chorus (in the last movement) and orchestra (composed 1910–11) are avowedly impressions of travel in India; the ballet-pantomime *Le Festin de l'araignée* is naturally programmatic; and the opera-ballet *Padmâvatî*, mostly composed before the outbreak of the 1914–18 war though the scoring was not completed till after it, is in the same vein as *Évocations*. All three reveal an individuality that by no means rests on the Indian elements in two of them. Roussel would have been the last to deny their romanticism; for him even Debussy was 'a romantic in the best sense of the term'.[3] Yet he had already in 1906–8, in the *Divertissement* and parts of the D minor Violin Sonata, made essays in a much more spare and quasi-classical style and it was to this that he turned more and more, finally almost exclusively, in the post-war years. As for Dukas, after his ballet *La Péri* (1912) he remained almost completely silent.

Chausson has been described as 'un trait d'union non négligeable entre Franck et Debussy'.[4] Substitute 'd'Indy' for 'Franck' and the same could be said of Dukas and Roussel, but Chausson might be more truly described as a link between Franck and Fauré. Gabriel Fauré (1845–1924), an older man, was a pupil of Saint-Saëns more original than his master, more French than Franck. His music—mostly songs, piano music, and chamber music—is finely polished, classically restrained in expression yet saturated with a warm tender lyrical poetry which must be called romantic unless we are prepared to deny the epithet to Chopin as well, though Fauré has more often but less aptly been called the French Schumann. Fauré's earliest published works had been songs, and in the 1890s he reached his apogee as a song-writer with the

---

[1] See Basil Deane, *Albert Roussel* (London, 1961), pp. 102–4.
[2] Octave Séré, *Cinquante ans de musique française* (Paris, 1925) ii, p. 398.
[3] See Arthur Hoérée, *Albert Roussel* (Paris, 1938), p. 108.
[4] Hoérée, 'Chausson et la musique française', in *Ernest Chausson*, special number of *La Revue musicale* (December 1925), p. 193.

Mélodies, Op. 58 (1890), and the cycle *La Bonne Chanson* (1892); both consist entirely of Verlaine settings—indeed nearly all Fauré's Verlaine songs date from about this time, as do most of Debussy's.

Even before 1890 Fauré's role in the history of the French *mélodie*[1] was comparable with that of Wolf—perhaps one should say 'of Brahms and Wolf'—in the history of the *Lied*: the songs of Duparc, Chausson, and the young Debussy were all in some degree affected by him. The poetry of Verlaine and the other symbolists, which Debussy discovered earlier than Fauré, was the catalyst which precipitated some of his best work—and of Debussy's in this field. Fauré's earlier songs are marked by a lyrical expansiveness which is almost invariably saved from the commonplace or sentimental by some subtle touch of melody or harmony or both, as in the first eight bars of 'Les Présents'.[2] A suggestion of modalism is conveyed less often by actual flattening of a leading-note than tacitly by the omission of the seventh altogether, as at the end of the same song or at the end of 'Green', Op. 58, no. 3:

(And let me sleep awhile, since you are resting.)

[1] On Fauré's songs see particularly Vladimir Jankélévitch, *Gabriel Fauré: Ses mélodies— Son esthétique* (revised edition, Paris, 1951).

[2] Recorded in *The History of Music in Sound*, ix.

The parallel passage in Debussy's setting of two years earlier has a
romantic warmth that reminds one of Fauré at his less subtle.

Ex. 10

But when Debussy came to compose 'En sourdine' in 1892 he had
arrived at both a more personal piano style, as at the beginning of the

Ex. 11

(i)

song, and a much less melodic way of setting words which, even when he is closest to Fauré's general style, as at 'Laissons-nous persuader' (Ex. 11(ii)), is in marked contrast with Fauré's own setting in Op. 58, no. 2 (Ex. 11(i)).

(ii)

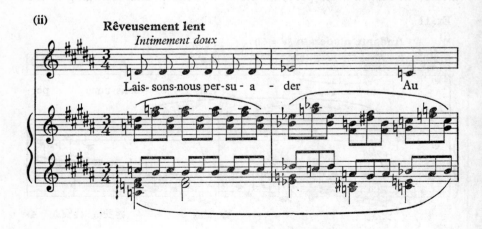

souf-fle ber-ceur et doux

(Let us be persuaded by the gentle lulling breeze.)

There is less lyrical expansiveness in the songs of *La bonne chanson* and an exquisite sensitivity to every detail of the text which makes this cycle an outstanding masterpiece. In the later song-cycles, from *La Chanson d'Ève* (1907–10) onward, this lyrical restraint is more and more noticeable; voice-part, harmony, general texture become ever simpler. The same increasing austerity is apparent in Fauré's later instrumental music. In his own way he too turned his back on romanticism.

Debussy had done so long before. Although 'old Klingsor's ghost' was still haunting him in 1893 he had already been touched by two influences which played some part in laying it: a Javanese *gamelan* and the music of the Russian nationalists, both heard at the Paris Exposition Universelle of 1889, although he had already encountered the Russians in 1881–2. He continued to employ some of the techniques and outward forms of romanticism—'cyclic' form in the String Quartet (1893) and leitmotives in *Pelléas*, programmatic or picturesque orchestral and piano music, even a suggestion of Franck's strident urgency in the 'Dialogue du vent et de la mer' of *La Mer* (1905)—long after his music had been drained of romantic emotion and romantic eloquence. This was only the Debussyan form of the dualism common to most of his musical contemporaries; in the *Douze Études* and *En blanc et noir* for piano (1915) and the three chamber sonatas (1915–17) he finally resolved it. The younger musicians who grew up under Fauré's wing, such as Charles Koechlin (1867–1951), Florent Schmitt (1870–1958), Roger-Ducasse (1873–1954) and Maurice Ravel (1875–1937) never formed a 'school' comparable with the d'Indy circle but all shared their master's romantic-classic dualism, with classical tendencies gradually gaining the upper hand; all came to a greater or less degree under the influence of Debussy. The most romantic of them was Schmitt whose large-scale Piano Quintet, the composition of which was spread over the years 1901–8, is held together by the cyclic principle and whose *Psaume XLVI* (1904) for soprano, chorus, organ and orchestra is 'monumental' in the sense of Strauss and Mahler. (Schmitt was, as Calvocoressi remarked,[1] 'more directly influenced by the German romantics than any other French composer of any standing'.) In the case of Ravel, by far the most important, one catches him in the very act of 'wringing the neck of eloquence' in his String Quartet (1903); while the picturesque-objective dualism of the piano works of 1905–8—the *Miroirs*, the Sonatina, and *Gaspard de la nuit* (which Ravel himself described as 'trois poèmes romantiques')[2]—is still manifest in the ballet *Daphnis et Chloé*, composed during the period 1906–11. The scales were tipped more and more in the direction of absolute music in the *Valses nobles et sentimentales* (1911), the *Trois Poèmes de Stéphane Mallarmé* (1913), the Piano Trio (1915), *Le Tombeau de Couperin* (1917), the Sonata for violin and cello (1922), and still later works.[3]

SPAIN AND ITALY

Apart from Italian opera, neither Italy nor Spain had contributed significantly to musical romanticism. Indeed Spain had contributed nothing but the violin compositions of Pablo Sarasate (1844–1908) and the folk melodies that were borrowed or imitated by various Frenchmen and Russians. Even her opera had not developed beyond the *zarzuela* and the *género chico* (the *petit genre*) exemplified by the *Verbena de la paloma* (1894) of Tomás Bretón (1850–1923) and the *Revoltosa* (1897) of Ruperto Chapí (1851–1909), until Felipe Pedrell (1841–1922) composed his ambitious but unsuccessful Catalan trilogy *Els Pireneus* (1891) which characteristically had to wait till 1902 for its first performance—in Italian. Pedrell gave a much greater impulse to Spanish musical nationalism by his writings and musicological publications, though the first volume of his *Cancionero musical popular español* appeared only in 1919, while Conrado del Campo (1876–1953) belatedly imported Central European romanticism in his symphonic poem *La divina comedia* (1904) and his *Bocetos fantásticos* for string quartet (1908). Thus romanticism reached Spain only as it was dying, and mainly from France and therefore heavily diluted. It was under the influence of contemporary French piano-writing that Pedrell's pupil, Isaac Albéniz (1860–1909), crowned an undistinguished creative career with his four sets of remarkable piano pieces *Iberia* (1906–09), and under that of Albéniz, modified by Domenico Scarlatti's, that Enrique Granados (1867–1916) wrote his *Goyescas* (1912–14). Granados lived in Paris

---

[1] *Musicians Gallery* (London, 1933), p. 56.
[2] 'Esquisse autobiographique', *Revue musicale*, xix (1938), p. 213.　　[3] See p. 235.

during the late 1880s and both Manuel de Falla (1876–1946) and Joaquín Turina (1882–1949) were there for six or seven years until the 1914 war drove them home again. Of these two, Turina always remained a romantic in essence but Falla, much the more gifted, evolved from a glorified *zarzuela, La Vida breve* (1905; prod. 1913 in French), through the romantic impressionism of the *Quatre pièces espagnoles* for piano (1908)[1] and the much less romantic impressionism of the orchestral *Noches en los jardines de España* (begun in 1909, completed in 1915), *El amor brujo* (1915), and *El sombrero de tres picos* (1917), to the classic austerity of the *Fantasia bética for piano* (1919) and the other post-1918 works.[2]

Whereas Wagner left Spanish music totally untouched, at least the superficial features of his technique—more or less continuous orchestral texture and what were supposed to be leitmotives—were appropriated by Giacomo Puccini (1858–1924) and the lesser composers of *verismo*, Ruggiero Leoncavallo (1858–1919), Pietro Mascagni (1863–1945), and Umberto Giordano (1867–1948) whose work is discussed in Chapter 3, while Italo Montemezzi (1875–1952) penetrated a little more deeply into Wagner's style in *L'amore dei tre re* (1913). Outside the theatre, the orchestral, chamber, and piano music of Giovanni Sgambati (1841–1914) and Giuseppe Martucci (1856–1909), disciples of Liszt and champions of Wagner, neither a very strong artistic personality, is very much poorer in genuine romantic sensibility than the scores of Puccini, while Leone Sinigaglia (1868–1944), a disciple of Dvořák, was important mainly as a collector and utilizer of Piedmontese folk-music and Antonio Scontrino (1850–1922) can hardly be considered a romantic at all.

The only outstanding instrumental composer of the Puccini generation, Ferruccio Busoni (1866–1924), elected as early as 1886 to leave his native land for Germany, Finland, Russia, and America before finally settling in Berlin in 1894. A great pianist and outstanding conductor, champion of every variety of contemporary music that needed a champion, Busoni seemed a reincarnation of Liszt, whose music he greatly admired. A true internationalist, he belonged to Italy no more than Liszt to Hungary and his own music has stronger affinities with Germany—he had some German blood—than with Italy. But the musical Germany that attracted him was not romantic Germany but the Germany of Bach (above all), Beethoven, and Brahms, and the Italian elements in his make-up which lighten the Violin Concerto (1897) and shine out in the *Lustspielouvertüre* (1897), the fourth movement of the Piano Concerto (1904), the suite inspired by Gozzi's *Turandot* (1904),

---

[1] No. 3, 'Montañesa' is recorded in *The History of Music in Sound*, x.
[2] On these, see *infra* pp. 200–1 and 315–17.

and the opera *Arlecchino* (1917) belong to the world of Verdi's *Falstaff* (1893) and have nothing of *morbidezza* in their melody. Busoni's music is by no means devoid of romantic traits, both technical (the Lisztian organization of the Violin Concerto; the colossal scale and choral finale of the Piano Concerto) and in spirit (the *Symphonisches Tongedicht* of 1893, the tragic third movement of the Piano Concerto). His first opera, *Die Brautwahl* (1912) was based on E. T. A. Hoffmann and his final masterpiece on the most characteristic of all romantic subjects, *Doktor Faust* (begun 1914; prod. 1925).[1] But the ideal which he constantly strove to realize was that which toward the end of his life he designated 'young classicism' (*junge Klassizität*) and defined as

the mastering, the sifting and turning to account of all the gains of previous experiments and their inclusion in strong and beautiful forms. This art will at first be old and new at the same time. The definite departure from what is thematic and the return to melody ... as the bearer of the idea and the begetter of harmony, in short the most highly developed (not the most complicated) polyphony. ... The renunciation of subjectivity ... and the re-conquest of serenity. ... Not profundity, and personal feeling and metaphysics, but music which is absolute, distilled, and never under the mask of figures and ideas borrowed from other spheres. Human feeling, but not human affairs ... not assigning to an art tasks which lie outside its nature. Description in music, for instance.[2]

He belongs therefore to another chapter as do for one reason or another the best of the younger composers of the *generazione dell' '80*.

RUSSIA AND POLAND

Wagner was relatively little known and less admired by Russian musicians until 1889, when Angelo Neumann's opera company brought the *Ring* to St. Petersburg and Moscow. The impact of mature Wagner impressed Rimsky-Korsakov and was perhaps responsible for his conversion from an occasional to an almost exclusive opera-composer; yet, beyond an enrichment of his already extremely colourful orchestral palette and a more systematic use of leitmotives, it had no marked influence on his style. With the very important exception of Tchaïkovsky, the romanticism of Russian composers had seldom taken the form of expression of exclusively personal emotion. Modelled on Berlioz, Liszt, and Glinka's *Ruslan* (and thus on Weber at second hand instead of Wagner at first), it adopted the forms and picturesque gestures of romanticism and entered into the romantic cult of past ages and the magical and exotic, but seldom with deep personal emotional involve-

---

[1] See *infra*, pp. 194–5.

[2] Open letter to Paul Bekker, *Frankfurter Zeitung*, 7 February 1920. Reprinted in *Von der Einheit der Musik* (Berlin, 1922) p. 276–9; trs. Rosamond Ley, *The Essence of Music* (London, 1957), pp. 20–2.

ment. It was Tchaïkovsky who was the supreme Russian romanticist and, after his death in 1893, while much in his style and technique passed into common usage, only three or four composers of any significance followed him in his employment of music as an emotional language: Sergey Rakhmaninov (1873–1943) most closely, Sergey Taneyev (1856–1915) and Nikolay Metner (1880–1951) whose romanticism was of the restrained nature of Brahms's, and Aleksandr Skryabin (1872–1915) who must be counted among those who attempted to push the aesthetic of the *Gesamtkunstwerk* to its farthest consequence. The surviving members of the former Mighty Handful continued and extended its tradition of colourful, Russian-flavoured music. Rimsky-Korsakov (d. 1908) in a series of operas three of which, *Kashchey bessmertny* (Kashchey the Immortal) (1902), *Kitezh* (1905; prod. 1907), and *Zolotoy Petushok* (The Golden Cockerel) (1907: prod. 1909), manifest a further deepening of his veins of mysticism and satire and a further development of his pungent but highly artificial harmonic vocabulary,[1] Balakirev (d. 1910) creating new works in his old vein. (Cui (d. 1918), the third survivor, had always lived mainly on glory reflected from his colleagues.) Their numerous pupils, Anatoly Lyadov (1855–1914), Sergey Lyapunov (1859–1924), Aleksandr Glazunov (1865–1936), and others less talented, produced syntheses of the idiom inherited from the Handful with a highly polished, euphonious style in which technical fluency often outran the flow of creative ideas. All were overshadowed by Rimsky-Korsakov's last notable pupil, Igor Stravinsky (1881–1971), who in three full-length ballets, *Zhar-ptitsa* (The Firebird) (1910), *Petrushka* (1911), and *Vesna svyashchennaya* (The Rite of Spring) (1913), enriched and extended the old 'nationalist' idiom with harmonic and rhythmic conceptions drawn partly from late Rimsky-Korsakov and Skryabin, partly from the West, and more and more from his own fertile inventiveness, but also drained away from it the last hint of the romantic.

The concentration on craftsmanship in the music of the nationalist epigones and the emotions and philosophical ideas underlying the equally highly polished music of Rakhmaninov and Skryabin are both attributable in part to the intellectual climate of Russia at this period. The optimistic positivism of the third quarter of the nineteenth century, when artistic truth mattered much more than beauty, had long since lost its force. Under an increasingly reactionary political regime only the revolutionary extremists preserved the energy that comes from despair; and in the general atmosphere of futility which Chekhov derided, the creative artist tended to take refuge in a sterile cult of

[1] See below pp. 174–7.

'Parnassianism', of 'pure' beauty, in symbolism and mysticism. Musically this took the form of the 'mièvre lyrisme' of Tchaïkovsky's imitators, which Stravinsky derided.[1] Rakhmaninov's pessimism is much less
anguished and personal than Tchaïkovsky's or Mahler's, and often
shows itself in flaccidity of invention rather than positive expression.
His most successful essay in actual programme-music, the tone-poem
inspired by Böcklin's painting *Die Toteninsel* (1908), is typical of the
polished superficiality of his elegiac art. Fine craftsmanship is also a
distinctive quality of Skryabin's music, but almost from the first, in
the piano Preludes, Opp. 11, 13, 15, 16 and 17 (mostly 1894–5), it
was informed by a poetry more individual than Rakhmaninov's and
expressing a much wider range of moods. Quickly absorbing and out-
growing the influence of Chopin and Schumann, he developed from an
exquisite piano-miniaturist into a musical mystic,[2] increasingly obsessed
with a pathological belief in his own Messiahship. His early piano
sonatas, nos. 1–3 (1893–8), are normal late-romantic compositions, but
from 1900 onward he became more and more deeply drawn into a
mystical philosophy of art and his First Symphony, completed in 1900,
ends with a setting for mezzo-soprano, tenor, and chorus of a poem of
his own in which art is nearly equated with religion. Whether he had
first-hand knowledge of Mahler's first three symphonies is uncertain
though he must have known of them by hearsay. In any case, he
followed neither Mahler nor earlier composers of partly choral symphonies, for in effect his vocal finale is an epilogue in E major, partly
based on one of the themes of the purely orchestral first movement, a
lento also in E major:

Ex. 12

[1] *Poétique musicale* (Cambridge, Mass., 1942), p. 65.
[2] Martin Cooper, 'Aleksandr Skryabin and the Russian Renaissance', *Studi musicali*, i
(1972), p. 327, shows the relationship of his ideas to those of the Russian thinkers and poets
of the day.

These two slow movements in E major frame a conventional four-movement symphony in E minor. The catastrophic failure of the experiment was caused by Skryabin's inability to devise anything better than a square-cut diatonic fugue, of a type more often written by students than by full-fledged composers, for the chorus. After the purely orchestral Second Symphony (1901), showing the influence of Liszt and Wagner (and perhaps also of Nietzschean philosophy, which obsessed him for a time) but also drawing nearer in style to his own far more individual piano music, he began to dream of 'a fusion of all the arts, but not a theatrical one like Wagner's'. 'Art', he said, 'must unite with philosophy and religion in an indivisible whole to form a new gospel, which will replace the old Gospel we have outlived. I cherish the dream of creating such a "mystery". For it, it would be necessary to build a special temple—perhaps here, perhaps far away in India. But mankind is not yet ready for it'.[1] Skryabin's Third Symphony, *Le divin poème* (1904)—preceded by the harmonically advanced Fourth Sonata (1903) —is in three movements, 'Struggles', 'Delights', 'Divine Play', and, according to the programme written by his mistress, Tatyana Schlözer,

represents the evolution of the human spirit which, torn from an entire past of beliefs and mysteries which it surmounts and overturns, passes through Pantheism and attains to a joyous and intoxicated affirmation of its liberty and its unity with the universe (the divine 'Ego').

The one-movement *Poem ekstaza* (Poem of Ecstasy) (1907), for very large orchestra with, for instance, quadruple woodwind, eight horns, and organ, and the Fifth Piano Sonata (1908) which quickly followed it,[2] elaborate similar ideas with a further intensification of post-Wagnerian harmony. In his next and last orchestral work, *Prometheus* (1910), 'for full orchestra and piano, with organ, [wordless] chorus, and *clavier à lumières*', Skryabin carried his harmonic language a stage further still to the very brink of atonality;[3] this was a preliminary study for the long contemplated but never written 'mystery', a 'liturgical act' combining dancing, music, poetry, colours, and scents, which would induce 'a supreme, final ecstasy' in which 'the physical plane of our consciousness would disappear and a world cataclysm would begin'.[4] The part for the *clavier à lumières* is in normal musical notation, but

---

[1] Yuly D. Engel, 'A. N. Skryabin. Biografichesky ocherk', *Muzïkalny Sovremennik* (1916), no. 4–5, p. 56.

[2] Skryabin published the verbal poem, the first part of which (lines 1–224) provided the programme of the orchestral poem, at Geneva in 1906; lines 227–35 were printed as an epigraph to the Fifth Sonata. The whole poem (original text and German translation by Ernst Moritz Arndt) is printed as an appendix to Clemens-Christoph Johannes von Gleich, *Die sinfonischen Werke von Alexander Skrjabin* (Bilthoven, 1963), p. 113.

[3] See *infra* pp. 136–7, and the Frontispiece of this volume.   [4] Engel, op. cit., p. 89.

Skryabin intended that the pressure of each key should produce not a musical sound but an intense light, coloured in accordance with his associations of sound and colour (e.g. C = red, C sharp–D flat = violet, D = yellow, and so on), and flooding the concert-hall; mere projection of colours on a screen was a compromise which he rejected as 'trivial'.[1] The Sonatas No. 6–10 (1912–13) and the other post-Promethean piano-compositions probably—Opp. 71–4 (1914) certainly —originated as music for the 'mystery'. Thus Skryabin's *Gesamtkunstwerk* was never realized and his nearest approach to it, *Prometheus,* fell short of Schoenberg's *Die glückliche Hand*, even—most ironically— of the ballets of the outstanding anti-Wagnerian, Stravinsky.

The *mélomimiques* of Vladimir Rebikov (1866–1920), short dramatic studies of psychological situations for one or two characters, with piano accompaniment, and his 'musico-psychographic dramas', attracted a good deal of attention during the early part of the century; but like his harmonic experiments with chords of superimposed perfect fourths, they were foredoomed to failure by the weakness of his musical invention. Nevertheless they were known to Janáček and may have suggested the form of his *Zápisník zmizelého* (Diary of one who vanished).[2]

Although traces of Skryabin's stylistic influence are perceptible in *The Firebird* and the early works of Myaskovsky and other Soviet composers of the early post-Revolution period, even in the young Prokofyev, only one important non-Russian composer was deeply affected by him, the Pole Karol Szymanowski (1882–1937),[3] who towered above the other members of the 'Mlada Polska' (Young Poland) group, Mieczysław Karłowicz (1876–1909), Grzegorz Fitelberg (1879–1953), Ludomir Różycki (1884–1953), and others. The common aim of these 'young Poles' was a renaissance of Polish music to be effected by the reconciliation of the national idiom with more or less contemporary forms and harmony; all were influenced by Strauss. But Szymanowski, after a First Symphony (1907) in which the shadow of Reger also appears, a symphonic colossus typical of the period, went on to write a Second (1909) and a partly vocal Third (1915–16) in which Skryabin and French music played a liberating role. The influence of Skryabin's style is still more marked in Szymanowski's *Métopes* (1915) and *Masques* (1917) for piano and his *Mythes* (1915) for violin and piano, while the blending of the mystic, the erotic, and the

---

[1] Leonid Sabaneyev, *Vospominaniya o Skryabine* (Moscow, 1925), p. 61.
[2] See *infra*, pp. 307–8.
[3] See particularly Józef Chomiński, 'Szymanowski i Skryabin' in Igor Belza (ed.), *Russko-polskie muzïkalnïe svyazi* (Moscow, 1963), p. 375.

orgiastic in his later opera *Król Roger* (King Roger) (1926) also smacks strongly of Skryabin.[1]

SCANDINAVIA

Those countries which may, more conveniently than accurately, be called Nordic and Anglo-Saxon, were most strongly influenced by Germanic techniques and idioms, less by French, and hardly at all by Slavonic even after Dvořák and Tchaïkovsky had become familiar and even popular. But there was an affinity with the Slavonic lands in that clinging to national idioms which has always been associated with musical romanticism although the impersonality of such idioms is in direct conflict with the subjectivity that is the essence of romanticism. The Norwegian Christian Sinding (1865–1941) and the Swede Wilhelm Stenhammar (1871–1927) are typical of the German-orientated composers of the period who yet managed to infuse national qualities—and in Stenhammar's case an element of neoclassicism—into their later works. But it was the older Grieg (1843–1907) who still dominated the Scandinavian scene, ever a thoroughbred romantic but in some respects a new Grieg as in the *Haugtussa Sang-Cyclus* (1898) and the piano arrangements of *Norske Folkeviser*, Op. 66 (1896) and *Slåtter* (1902), the harmony of which last is influenced by a folk instrument, the *hardingfele* or 'Hardanger fiddle'.[2]

Grieg was hardly ever completely successful when he attempted large-scale composition; even the so-called *Symphonic Dances* on Norwegian folk-tunes (1898) are essentially compilations of miniatures. But the two Scandinavians who came to the fore during his later years, the Finn Jean Sibelius (1865–1957) and the Dane Carl Nielsen (1865–1931), were both masters of the larger forms, particularly of the symphony. Both were markedly individual talents and, although it is not difficult to detect the influence of Bruckner's *ostinati* on Sibelius or to trace this or that melodic turn in his earlier works to Borodin or Tchaïkovsky, his mature idiom is strikingly unlike that of any of his predecessors or contemporaries. It is always clearly diatonic, as is Nielsen's. Although Sibelius anticipated Mahler in employing the chorus in a very large-scale symphonic work (*Kullervo*, 'symphonic poem for soloists, chorus and orchestra', 1892),[3] he was the antipode of Mahler, reacting in his symphonies—even in the First (1899)—against all those procedures in the nineteenth-century symphony which Mahler

---

[1] On Szymanowski's later works, see *infra*, pp. 311–15.

[2] See John Horton, 'Grieg's "Slaatter" for Pianoforte', *Music and Letters*, xxvi (1945), p. 229.

[3] See Robert Layton, *Sibelius* (London, 1965), pp. 107–14.

developed further. Structures are tightened; transitions are from the first most skilfully made; and the thematic work is severely dialectical so that, while theme-transformation goes on continually, a totally organic web of sound is woven without need of such mechanical devices as the motto-theme to give it a sense of unity. In the Fourth Symphony (1911), which the composer himself described as 'a protest against the compositions of today',[1] compression is carried so far that the first subject consists of only 25 *adagio* bars, the second of only 8; but this compression and the chamber-like treatment of the orchestra, if a 'protest' against elephantiasis, was very much in line with the other tendencies of that date which have already been remarked on. Compression led to actual fusion of the movements in the Seventh Symphony (1924). Although Sibelius's earlier symphonies are romantic in tone, they are not programmatic and he protested vigorously against attempts to interpret them so.[2] The strong romantic element in his make-up was, as it were, siphoned off in a series of tone-poems from *En Saga* (original version, 1892; revised 1901) to *Tapiola* (1926) and other works. On the other hand Nielsen, after a First Symphony (1892) chiefly remarkable for its unconventional treatment of tonality, went on to write a completely programmatic Second, *De fire Temperamenter* (The Four Temperaments) (1902),[3] and others with suggestive titles: no. 3 *Sinfonia espansiva* (1911), no. 4 *Det Uudslukkelige* (The Unquenchable) (1916), no. 6 *Sinfonia semplice* (1925). His justification for such titles was that 'while a short hint or title can illuminate the music in many ways . . . the programme or title may indicate a mood or emotion but not an idea or concrete action'.[4]

BRITAIN AND THE UNITED STATES

Music in the English-speaking countries remained until the end of the nineteenth century, and after, under influences that were not only German but rather conservatively German. It was Brahms rather than Wagner who attracted Alexander Mackenzie (1847–1935)—whose best work, like Sullivan's, was all done before 1890—Hubert Parry (1848–1918) and Charles Stanford (1852–1924). The American talents of Edward MacDowell (1861–1908) and Horatio Parker (1863–1919) were initially fostered by Raff and Rheinberger. But the strongest and most

---

[1] Harold E. Johnson, *Sibelius* (London, 1960), p. 126.
[2] See, for instance, Karl Ekman, *Jean Sibelius* (Helsinki, 1935; English translation by Edward Birse, London, 1936), pp. 191–2 (English edition).
[3] For Nielsen's own explanation see Robert Simpson, *Carl Nielsen, Symphonist* (London, 1952), pp. 42–3.
[4] Nielsen, *Levende Musik* (Copenhagen, 1925), p. 41.

individual Anglo-Saxon of their period, Edward Elgar (1857–1934), after a long slow development in the debilitating climate of the English provinces, discovered for himself the real fountainheads of later romanticism, Schumann, Liszt and Wagner, and applied their techniques of harmony, orchestration, and leitmotive first in the dead forms of the Victorian cantata and the dying one of the oratorio, most successfully in *The Dream of Gerontius* (1900), and then in a series of intensely personal orchestral works—the *Enigma* Variations (1899), two symphonies (1908 and 1910), the symphonic study *Falstaff* (1913), the concertos for violin and for cello (1910 and 1919)—which constitute the high-water mark of English musical romanticism. Elgar really stands alone; the work of the only comparable figure, Frederick Delius (1862–1934), English merely by the accident of birth, has nothing in common with any English tradition and little with the mainstream of Continental romanticism. Delius was an isolated cosmopolitan like Busoni, poetically far more and technically far less gifted. (A comparable, though less individual, character was his almost exact contemporary, the Alsatian-born Charles Martin Loeffler (1861–1935), an American from 1881 onward.) He stands nearest to his colleagues not in his musical style but in his sources. Like Schoenberg he was attracted by the poetry of Jens Peter Jacobsen (the opera *Fennimore and Gerda* (1910), the *Arabesk* for baritone, chorus and orchestra (1911), and a number of songs); like Strauss and Mahler, he came under the spell of Nietzsche's *Zarathustra* (*A Mass of Life*, 1905); like his younger English contemporaries, he set Walt Whitman (*Sea Drift*, 1903) and based compositions on folk-melodies: *Appalachia* (1902), *Brigg Fair* (1907), and *On hearing the first cuckoo in spring* (1912). But his borrowed folk-melodies were American Negro and Norwegian as well as English and he used them merely as catalysts for his ultra-romantic nostalgia, embedding them in his personal dialect of Griegian harmony, whereas the best of his younger English contemporaries sought in English folk-melody for the basis of a musical style that should be independent of the German tradition.

These were Ralph Vaughan Williams (1872–1958) and Gustav Holst (1874–1934),[1] both pupils of Stanford who had himself written a symphony and orchestral rhapsodies on Irish tunes. But Stanford treated folk-music as 'material' for traditional composition, while for his pupils it was the principal—though not the sole—instrument of emancipation from the heritage of both Brahms and Wagner, from the forms and idioms of the European mainstream altogether. Although

---

[1] See pp. 507–19.

there are plentiful traces of romanticism in their extra-musical thinking, their suppression of subjective emotion and rhetoric was almost as complete as their rejection of chromaticism and rich, complicated textures. In Holst's directness of expression and fresh approach to the essentials of music, and in his vein of transcendentalism, it is possible to find hidden affinities with his American contemporary, the Horatio Parker pupil, Charles Ives (1874-1935);[1] but Holst was never as radical as Ives and he achieved general recognition with the performance of *The Planets* in 1918; Ives had to wait considerably longer. The more conservative Vaughan Williams made his mark more quickly; before the choral *Sea Symphony* (1910), his name was already well known to his fellow-countrymen.

THE MUSICAL LANGUAGE OF LATE ROMANTICISM

It is significant that Vaughan Williams, Holst, and Ives rejected not only the idioms of their European contemporaries but their sophisticated techniques. To say what they wanted to say, more idiosyncratic homespun techniques were not so much adequate as necessary. But Holst's ostinati and static basses, Vaughan Williams's fumbling with the methods he had learned from Parry and Stanford, Ives's 'collisions of musical events', seem embarrassingly naïve beside the harmonic and orchestral refinements of the Continental composers of the period. Even the Europeans who were turning back to sound-for-sound's-sake and away from the concept of music as a quasi-language were still often employing the techniques which the late romantics had evolved in their striving to catch and communicate the subtlest nuances of complicated, even perverse, emotion and mystical or ironic ideas. The erotic oriental mysticism of Szymanowski struggles in the song 'Smutna wiosna', Op. 24, no. 6 (1911) to express simultaneously the sense of spring returning and sorrow for a dead love through typical romantic harmony and a plethora of meticulous markings. 'Where art thou?' his lover cries (Ex. 13). Three years earlier Holst had set the same words, in nearly the same sense, in his oriental-mystical chamber-opera *Sāvitri*, with the utmost austerity (Ex. 14). And although Holst's voice-part outlines an F minor triad, the typical ostinato bass shows that he has really parted company with tonality, while the Szymanowski song is in D major despite the constant sound of minor sorrow in the harmony and despite the fact that only one phrase in the voice-part—the last—is in D major and floats down to a piano cadence which perfectly illustrates the final stage of functional harmony in dissolution (Ex. 15).

[1] See pp. 574-83.

Ex. 13

Ex. 14

Ex. 15

(loveliest flower of spring!)

This process of dissolution had certainly been protracted. It had already reached an advanced stage in the opening of Act III of *Parsifal* which was written in 1879, but its progress must be measured not so much by its intensity in certain passages as by the extent of its cancer-like spread through entire movements and works. It was essentially a harmonic process and fundamentally affected melody only in so far as melody is the surface of harmony; much seemingly chromatic melody, even in *Tristan*, is no more than a rippling of the surface with chromatic appoggiaturas and passing-notes. But basically diatonic melody, even purely diatonic melody, with its tonal associations and implications was still an important feature of the late romantic sound-language and few composers discarded it entirely. Strauss, Elgar, Dukas, Rakhmaninov were but a few of those who often employed clear diatonic harmony and melody; these provide the language for

Ex. 16

Delius (*Songs of Sunset*, 1907), Elgar (end of the Second Symphony, 1910), and Mahler ('Abschied' of *Das Lied von der Erde*, 1908) to sing their saddest farewells. Diatonic melody was often treated as the core of otherwise deliquescent or tonally uncertain or obscure harmony, or deliberately contrasted with tonally disturbed passages, as in *Parsifal*, *Ein Heldenleben*, *The Golden Cockerel*, to suggest antitheses of good and evil or real and unreal. Even the purely diatonic could be subjected to strange juxtapositions and dislocations like the flattening of the second and third degrees of the scale in the seventh bar of *Ein Heldenleben* and the expanded 'Neapolitan' interpolation of bars 11–12, which is logical and almost orthodox by comparison with the Introduction to *Rosenkavalier* where E major is dazzlingly expanded by purely diatonic means (Ex. 16).

There is a close technical parallel to the 'Neapolitan interpolation' of *Heldenleben* near the beginning of the Andante of Mahler's Sixth Symphony:

Ex. 17

though this seems to be motivated by some extra-musical purpose, Strauss's by sheer musical exuberance. Even while Mahler was working on the Sixth Symphony in 1904, Schoenberg was opening the first of his *Sechs Lieder*, Op. 8, with a succession of common chords equally disruptive of the tonic key, E major:

Ex. 18

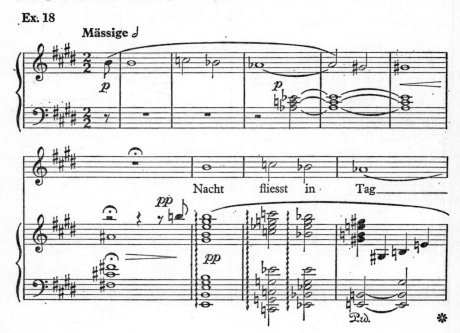

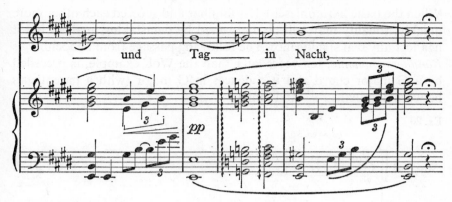

und Tag___ in Nacht,___

(Night flows into day, day into night,)

Thus, even in diatonic contexts, functional key-relationship remained no more than an outworn convention which, as we have seen,[1] Mahler had already discarded in his Third Symphony; the E major coda to the very G major Fourth Symphony, a master-stroke of imagination, is motivated by no law of tonal gravity but by its contrast of key-colour. Or rather it is used as a means of suggesting the unearthly radiance of angelic music, just as the tonal aberrations of the *Rosenkavalier* Introduction convey the orgiastic turbulence of Oktavian and the Marschallin. Such passages can often be justified by extra-musical considerations; indeed they usually originate in them; but by this time they had become part of the normal language of music.

If rapid harmonic change could weaken key-sense even in essentially diatonic music, it could destroy it completely when the harmony is chromatic. A mere veil of chromatic appoggiaturas and passing-notes can totally disguise the most familiar of chords, as Wolf showed in the opening of the twenty-seventh song of the *Italienisches Liederbuch*, 'Schon streckt' ich aus' (1896), where he broods on a single chord of the diminished seventh for the best part of two bars before revealing at the very end of the second bar that the key is A flat:

Ex. 19

Sehr langsam ($\quad$ = 42)

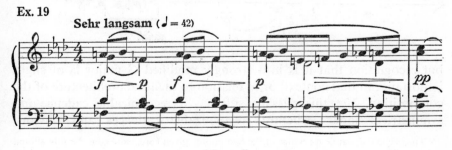

[1] See p. 7.

When the basic harmonies are less familiar and succeed each other more quickly, tonality may still be discovered by painstaking analysis but it has lost any real significance. The following passage from Schoenberg's *Kammersymphonie*, ten years later than the Wolf example, is preceded by a G major chord and it cadences in G major (with a parenthesis between dominant—x—and tonic):[1]

Ex. 20

but recognition that it is in a strongly modified G major is of slight importance in that context, or in relation to the total architecture of the composition. Yet this passage still has a recognizable cadence and symmetrical inner structure; recognizable cadences and obvious

---

[1] The original dynamic markings of the Symphony, given here, were considerably altered in later editions.

periodicity became ever less frequent in the language of late romanticism, giving way to a species of opaque musical 'prose'. At the other extreme, Strauss, Mahler, and Reger—to say nothing of such conservatives as Pfitzner—sometimes revert to a provocatively naïve, symmetrical and diatonic type of melody.

The old drives and tensions of harmony and key having, by over stretching, been weakened almost to non-existence, the energy of music was mainly concentrated in line: melody, motive, or more often something less easily definable. 'Prose' lines of great flexibility, angularity, and sensitiveness are brought into relationship through, or sometimes against, somewhat lymphatic harmony of various kinds: chromatically modified diatonic, experimental (for instance, based on superimposed fourths instead of thirds) or purely empirical. In the first decade of the century one can still often detect a family likeness among the melodic lines of very different composers, traceable to their common filiation from Wagner—which is naturally most obvious in the passages from d'Indy and Mahler, the earliest of the seven quotations grouped in Ex. 21.

Ex. 21
(i) D'INDY (1895)

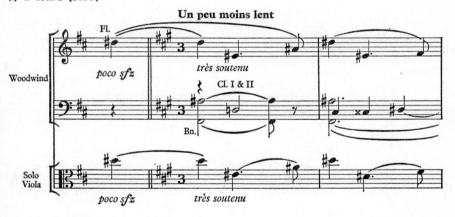

(ii) MAHLER (1900)

(iii) Bartók (1903)

(iv) SCHOENBERG **(1906)**

(v) Skryabin (1907)

(vi) WEBERN (1908)

(vii) STRAUSS (1909)

Und rühr Dich nicht!   Wenn er   mich dort

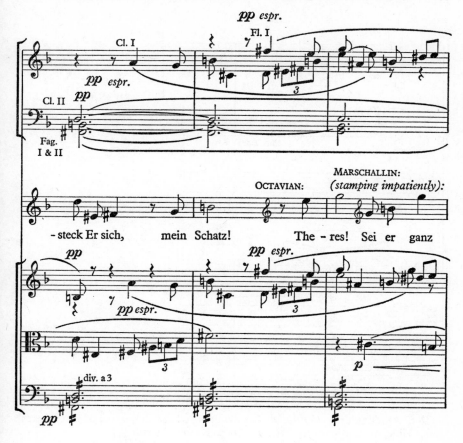

(*Oct.:* And don't move! If he catches me there, what will become of you, Theres?
Mar.: Hide, my darling! *Oct.:* Theres! *Mar.:* Keep quite still!)

These passages are characteristic of the musical language of what may reasonably be called the main stream of late romanticism, 'language' not merely in the sense of 'technical idiom' but in the sense of conveying— essentially in the initial dropping interval with its suggestion of a caress—a definite emotional significance. In all but two of them, the composers tell us we are correct in understanding his music as an expression of love or tenderness: (i) is from the Prologue to *Fervaal*, where the wounded hero first turns his eyes to the princess Guilhen; in (ii), from the first movement of Mahler's Fourth Symphony, the Wagnerian melodic language is clear beyond doubt; (iii) opens the section in the *Kossuth* Symphony headed 'What sorrow weighs on your spirit, dear husband?'; (iv) is from the first section of the *Kammersymphonie*; in (v) from the *Poem of Ecstasy* the theme has just been played by a solo violin, with the marking *dolce espress. carezzando*; in (vi), the thirteenth variation of Webern's Passacaglia, the markings also speak for themselves, as does the anxiety of the lovers in (vii) from the opening scene of *Rosenkavalier*. In each case the sharply defined initial motive generates, or dissolves into, a more or less indeterminate non-motivic continuation. A more motivic continuation of the same basic idea occurs in the second movement of Roussel's D minor Violin Sonata, Op. 11 (1907–8) which comes particularly close in some of its later appearances, such as Ex. 22, to the Skryabin version.

THE TEXTURES OF LATE ROMANTICISM

These passages also repay study from the point of view of texture: the harmonic bases, the warp and woof of the music, and the instrumental colouring of the strands. Although selected in the first place solely on the basis of similar emotion expressed melodically, they have a number of common characteristics beneath their very obvious differences.

The harmonic pace is moderate and equable, usually changing with the bar. And the basic chords, considered simply as agglomerations of sounds, are generally unremarkable; even Bartók's 'Hungarian' melodic line is borne on very ordinary harmonies before it collapses in the Wagnerian cadence at the end of bar 4. But these basic chords are thickly overlaid with passing-notes, appoggiaturas, and less easily explicable 'foreign' notes, and they are more easily related to each other as a simple concatenation than functionally and with reference to a firm tonal centre. 'Key' is obvious enough from point to point but is seldom orientated to a more distant horizon-mark. Only d'Indy's F sharp minor and Mahler's G major have any real meaning; Strauss's B minor and the D major to which it leads are only passing incidents, as

Ex. 22

the one-flat key-signature suggests—yet that one-flat signature is really valid only for two passages, each of a dozen bars or so, separated by nearly three hundred bars of non-F major. Webern's 8-bar variation is a miniature version of the same thing; it begins and ends with tonic chords, buttressed by augmented triads which function as substitute dominant sevenths (F natural replacing E-G), but the intervening harmonies can be related to D major only by ingenious sophistry. In itself the chord of superimposed fourths in bar 5, F-B-E flat-A flat, is an instrument of tonal dislocation, as are the augmented fourths/ diminished fifths of Skryabin's bass. Compared with these passages of Webern and Skryabin, that from *Rosenkavalier* is strikingly conservative, but it should be remembered that *Rosenkavalier* in general is harmonically more conservative than its predecessor, *Elektra*; Strauss was an older man, and *Rosenkavalier* marked the beginning of his creative climacteric.

Despite this contrast of harmonic vocabulary and of Strauss's *al fresco* writing, such as opera demands, with the jewellers' work of

Mahler, Skryabin, and Webern, the basic texture is the same in all four—and in the other examples: through or over the harmonic background are drawn one or two horizontal strands which may or may not be related to each other. But, except in the Schoenberg passage, these lines do not interact on each other and propel the music forward, any more than the harmonic successions give a sense of progression toward a goal. The vitality of the music lies in the nervous energy of the individual lines themselves; it is thus easily exhausted and climaxes tend to be achieved artificially, not to say mechanically, by '*Tristan-Steigerungen*' and mere volume of sound and elaboration of texture.

The finest craftsmanship of the late romantics was expended on the dovetailing and instrumental colouring of the horizontal lines, whether of primary or secondary importance—*Hauptstimmen* or *Nebenstimmen*, as Schoenberg was to distinguish them some time after the *Kammersymphonie*. Indeed dovetailing and colour-shading are often part of the same process, as may be heard at its most subtle in Skryabin's woodwind writing in Ex. 21 (v) or in Elgar's shattering tutti in Ex. 27 (on pp. 76–7). The amount of line-drawing entrusted primarily to the wind, whether or not supported by strings, is very characteristic of the period. And not only woodwind or horns: eighteen bars after (v) Skryabin gives his principal melodic line to two trumpets in unison, *f ma dolce* (and the secondary line to solo horn and cellos). Egon Wellesz has traced this way of employing the trumpet melodically, in the later Strauss, early Berg, and elsewhere, not only 'at moments of heightened brilliance, power and solemnity', from the example of Mahler.[1] He goes on perceptively:

This is connected with the endeavour to heighten the intensity of the sound without drawing on the full orchestra, with the need to give the melodic line the highest degree of emotion without interfering with the clarity of the line-drawing. In this tendency ultimately one can see a romantic element, that of over-playing one's hand (*Überpointierung*). The romantic musician— as one may already observe in Liszt—is not content to state objectively the values latent in the musical substance but, through the instrumentation, adds to it from his own subjective—one might almost say *literary*—feeling a wish-idea more complete, richer, more fulfilled than the apparent sound. With Mahler this conflict between *will to represent* and *what is represented*, typical of all romantic creativity, is partially resolved by his ability to extend the limits of invention through the colour of the orchestra.

And he illustrates this with a passage from the first movement of Mahler's Fifth Symphony:

[1] *Die neue Instrumentation* (Berlin, 1928), i, pp. 106–7.

Ex. 23

Plötzlich schneller. Leidenschaftlich. Wild

the *al fresco* scoring of which is as far removed as possible from Skryabin's exaggerated finesse. But Mahler and Strauss, indeed Sibelius and Elgar and the more conservative composers of the period generally, thought directly in terms of the orchestra, while their slightly younger contemporaries were not only affected by Debussy's *pointillisme*— Skryabin had a score of *La Mer* at his elbow, as well as *Ein Heldenleben*, when he was orchestrating *Prometheus*[1]—but tended to translate pianistic textures. The instrumental refinements of Ex. 21 (v) reflect the exquisite refinements of the composer's piano-playing. The lay-out of Webern's variation reminds one of some late Brahms piano-piece, and that of the Schoenberg passage, Ex. 21 (iv) corresponds to a great deal of nineteenth-century piano-music: a vital top and bottom, with a filling-in of conventional figuration.

Nevertheless, although orchestral writing did not always originate in purely orchestral thinking, this was perhaps the last great age of orchestral composition, distinguished by the hectic colouring of decadence. The orchestra—often a giant orchestra, even for tiny pieces such as Webern's Op. 6—was the favourite medium of the later romantics, including such doubtful romantics as Ravel. It was the medium through which they—and their half-brothers the impressionists —depicted with the utmost possible realism the adventures of Don

---

[1] Sabaneyev, *Vospominaniya*, p. 54.

Quixote and Falstaff, painted seascapes and erotic fantasies, expressed immortal longings, and exposed the tragic secrets of their tormented souls. It dominated their operas[1] and influenced even their chamber-music and piano-music. Their characteristic chamber works are those which seem to aspire to the condition of orchestral music: Reger's C minor Piano Quintet, Florent Schmitt's Quintet, *Verklärte Nacht* which Schoenberg himself afterwards arranged for string orchestra, just as he made two quite different full-orchestral versions (*c.* 1914 and 1935) of the first *Kammersymphonie*. The string quartet, in spite of its adaptability to almost every change of stylistic fashion, denied them not only wide range of colour but full, saturated sound. Most of them ignored it and, after the César Franck (1889), the Debussy (1893) written to some extent under its influence, and Dvořák's last two masterpieces, the form was almost totally neglected by significant composers until Bartók and the Schoenberg group turned to it—and, as Schoenberg himself admitted,[2] his First Quartet (1905) was written in too 'thick' a style, from which he found his way back to a true chamber-music texture only gradually. (Webern made a string orchestral version of his own *Fünf Sätze* for string quartet (1909).) Even the exceptions, of which the most notable is Ravel's, have many passages that strain toward the orchestral.

The attitude to solo piano music was also symptomatic. No other composer was as wholesale as Ravel in the later orchestration of his own piano pieces, but there was a widespread tendency, stemming more from Liszt than from Brahms, toward quasi-orchestral effects. Sometimes this amounts to little more than a full romantic sound; sometimes it shows in dense and complicated textures which, like those of their orchestral counterparts, are not always necessitated by dense and complicated thought, but which, when examined in detail, often reveal more subtlety and acute sensibility than the listening ear can readily take in. This tendency toward very full, quasi-orchestral piano-writing is the highest common factor of otherwise totally different styles[3] (Ex. 24) and is fatally deleterious when reflected in organ-music.

It appears also in the overloaded piano-parts of songs, though in this field the quasi-orchestral was now often replaced by the really orchestral. Wolf orchestrated the accompaniments of three of his *Mörike-Lieder* in 1889, at least fifteen songs the following year, and others later. At about the same time Rimsky-Korsakov began to orchestrate songs originally composed with piano; Grieg followed suit in 1894; and in 1897 Strauss

[1] See Chap. 3. [2] Newlin, op. cit., pp. 215–16.
[3] Cf. also Exs. 28 and 29 on pp. 82–4.

Ex. 24

(i) SKRYABIN: Satanic Poem, Op. 36 (1903)

Allegro ($\downarrow$. = 92--108)

(ii) SCHOENBERG: Op. 11, no. 3 (1909)

(iii) GRANADOS, 'Coloquio en la reja' *(Goyescas)* (1911)

Andantino allegretto

orchestrated 'Cäcilie' and 'Morgen' and composed the *Vier Gesänge*, Op. 33, the first of his 'songs with orchestra', the genre with which he took so touching a farewell to life in the *Vier letzte Lieder* half a century later. But it was Mahler who won recognition as the supreme master of the *Orchesterlied* with his *Lieder eines fahrenden Gesellen* (with piano, 1884; orchestrated in the early 1890s)[1], *Lieder aus 'Des Knaben Wunderhorn'* (1888–99), *Kindertotenlieder* (1904), *Fünf Lieder nach Rückert* (1904), and above all *Das Lied von der Erde* (1908) in which the song-cycle with orchestra is expanded to symphonic proportions and actually styled 'symphony'. In the same year as the *Kindertotenlieder* and *Rückert-Lieder* Schoenberg wrote his *Sechs Orchester-Lieder*, Op. 8 (including two *Wunderhorn* settings, one of which, 'Sehnsucht', sounds oddly like distorted Mahler). It is significant that Ravel, despite his mania for orchestration, never scored any of his songs; that Debussy did so only once (a late version, in 1907, of a very early song); and that, whereas Alban Berg wrote his *Altenberg-Lieder* (1912) for voice and large orchestra, his friend Webern abandoned piano-accompaniment only in favour of small chamber ensembles. The *Orchesterlied* had a romantic ancestry in Berlioz and it was essentially a late romantic phenomenon.

PROBLEMS OF STRUCTURE

The opulence of sound which is the most characteristic symptom of romantic texture in its last phase was paralleled by cultivation of grandiose structure, and the organization of compositions on a vast scale presented problems even more difficult than usual to a generation that was in the process of devaluing by inflation the tonal and harmonic currency it had inherited. Coherence of detail was carried further than ever before, but it was a coherence which generally lacked that vitalizing quality which may be grotesquely compared with the muscular activity of the gut: the tiny thrusts and pulls of appoggiaturas and inter-dominant chords, the magnetism of local tonics and vestigial cadences. The outward appearances of all these remained but they had lost their tension-relaxation effect through over-use and through the general raising of the norm of dissonance. The *effect* of dissonance could be achieved only by further intensification of dissonance or by 'illogical' progressions, in which it appeared that any chord might follow any other and which consequently disrupted inner cohesion. Infrastructure still depended either on the weakened remains of the familiar small-scale symmetry of lyrical phrases, which in Skryabin's totally thematic miniatures sound mechanical, or on asymmetrical 'prose',

---

[1] Cf. Donald Mitchell, introduction to Alma Mahler, op. cit., pp. xviii-xxi.

which in Webern's non-thematic miniatures sounds incoherent. And these were the two master-miniaturists of late romanticism.

All the same, miniature forms can exist as aurally comprehensible forms without key. The weakening of key-sense was much more serious in its effect on large-scale forms. Indeed very large forms in themselves weaken key-sense so far as the listener is concerned, even if he possesses absolute pitch. But a key-plan remained important, or at least useful, to composers in laying out music on a vast scale, even if the central key no longer exercised any gravitational pull and no normal listener could recognize that the composition ended in the key with which it had begun. Few listeners notice that Debussy's *Nocturnes* begin in B minor and end in B major, that the *Symphonia Domestica* is 'in' F major and the *Poem of Ecstasy* 'in' C major; that *Salome* begins in C sharp minor and would have ended in C sharp major if Herod had not commanded Salome's execution eleven bars before the end. Key-organization of this kind is so unreal as to deprive the so-called 'progressive tonality' of Mahler and Nielsen[1] of all meaning or impact; but it was a practical convenience in architectural planning rather than conformity to an obsolescent convention. So, when all but the last vestiges of key had disappeared, a composer would bring back his second subject at a different pitch in the recapitulation (as Berg does in his Piano Sonata, Op. 1):

Ex. 25

from that in the exposition:

Ex. 26

---

[1] See pp. 7 and 38.

though neither stands in any realistic functional relationship to the nominal tonic key of the movement (B minor).

When key had become nothing more than a point of reference on a blue-print, the only structural element apparent to the listener was theme, and musical architecture became more and more a matter of the treatment of thematic material, even of texture. The quasi-spatial conception of musical form began to decay, not as the immediate consequence of the decay of tonal feeling but as a later consequence. In the end form might almost be defined as no more than 'essential relationships of material'. Distinctions of nomenclature, as between 'symphony' and 'symphonic poem', often became as meaningless as key-names: the *Symphonia Domestica*, though it includes slow movement and scherzo, is indistinguishable from a *Tondichtung*. The real difference was now not so much between symphony and symphonic poem as between one kind of symphony and another. The very term 'symphony' had long before the twentieth century become as loose a term as 'novel', which can include *A la recherche du temps perdu* as well as *Madame Bovary*; and the basic distinction has little to do with general lay-out. A symphony might be as taut and compressed as Schoenberg's *Kammersymphonie* or as loose and sprawling as one of Mahler's symphonic 'worlds'—or as superficially conventional as one of Elgar's. The fundamental distinction between one kind of symphony and another lay in the presence, and degree of presence, of a quasi-dialectic element—the processes by which musical ideas generate each other, not by obviously mechanical transformation, but by seemingly organic growth of tissue. These were the processes, sometimes comparable with those of the logical syllogism, sometimes in the nature of what Schoenberg called 'developing variation' (*entwickelnde Variation*),[1] which had constituted the main tissue of instrumental musical thinking since the Viennese classics; its presence in nineteenth-century music had been considered a strength, its absence a weakness. In the decade before 1914 it suffered its final crisis.

In the hands of the out-and-out romantics musical consequence and contrast became less important than emotional, or otherwise extra-musical, consequence and contrast. In the vast area of a Mahler symphony all kinds of disparate and disconnected material could be employed to record and communicate successive states of mind. At the other extreme, composers as different as Schoenberg and Sibelius (whom Schoenberg recognized as having 'the breath of a symphonist')[2] by tightening thematic procedures as the one did in his Third and Fourth Symphonies (1907 and 1911) and the String Quartet (*Voces intimae*)

[1] *Style and Idea*, p. 185.   [2] Ibid., p. 195.

(1909) and the other in the *Kammersymphonie* (1906) and the first two numbered string quartets (1905 and 1908), were either consciously or unconsciously gradually sacrificing emotional meaning and consequence to musical constructivism. At the same time, by packing more and more intense significance into confined musical space, they brought instrumental coherence to the edge of a precipice from which Sibelius turned back in his Fifth Symphony but from which Schoenberg boldly leapt in the *Klavierstücke*, Op. 11, no. 3 (1909). In these pieces, as Webern wrote,[1] 'Once stated, the theme expresses everything that it has to say; it must be followed by something new.'

The dilemma posed by intense concentration of expression may be illustrated by a passage from an extremely different, intensely romantic, work completed eighteen months later: Elgar's Second Symphony. Here into two bars of the Larghetto (Ex. 27), sketched seven years earlier under the immediate impact of great sorrow, Elgar compressed an overwhelming expression of naked and quivering grief. Everything is said, musically, in two bars; but Elgar, an expansive and improvisatory genius rather than a great musical architect or thinker, can only repeat them with different scoring and then let them run down in a feeble continuation. The whole passage remains an incident in the movement, though an incident repeated later with heightened hysteria but no intensification of musical expressiveness. As a large-scale instrumental composer, in his symphonies and concertos, Elgar represents the typical conservative late-romantic compromise, submitting autobiographical expression to the discipline of at least the appearance of more or less traditional form and integrating improvisation by the Franckist devices of theme-transformation, sometimes very subtly, sometimes with mere mechanical ingenuity, as in the transformation of the Allegro molto semiquavers of the scherzo of the First Symphony into the main theme of the Adagio.

Elgar's conservatism is equally apparent in his oratorios, which were 'modern' only in relation to the form itself. Neither his creative gifts nor his technical innovations could save oratorio from the death that overtakes all outmoded art-forms, as he recognized by abandoning the third part of the trilogy begun with *The Apostles* (1903) and *The Kingdom* (1906). The only comparable works of any importance in this period were two nearly contemporary 'monumental' compositions for vast forces: Delius's *Mass of Life* (1905)—the much shorter *Sea-Drift* would have been described as a *Ballade* half a century earlier—and Schoenberg's *Gurrelieder* (composed, though not orchestrated, in 1900) where even the triple male chorus is not heard until Part III and the

---

[1] 'Schönbergs Musik' in *Arnold Schönberg* (symposium), (Munich, 1912), p. 41.

Ex. 27

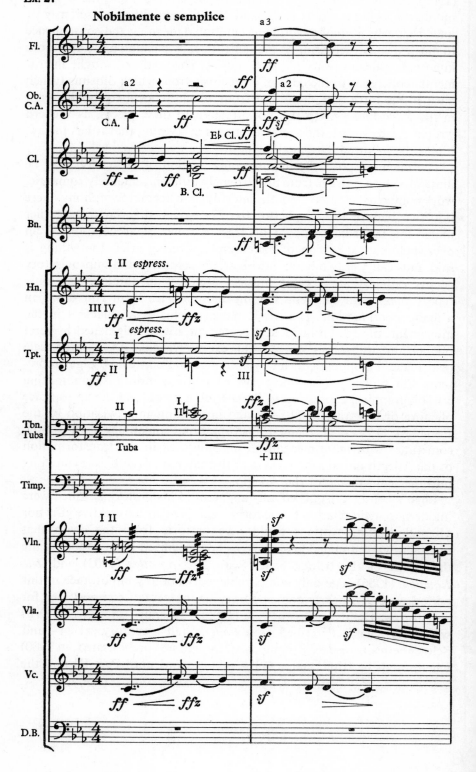

full chorus only at the very end of the work. (The two works have a certain stylistic affinity; not only the orchestral introduction and final chorus of the *Gurrelieder* but such passages as Tove's 'O, wenn des Mondes Strahlen leise gleiten' could easily belong to *A Mass of Life*.) The relative unimportance of the chorus in the *Gurrelieder* is characteristic of the period; large-scale works involving chorus, with or without vocal soloists, tend to be fundamentally orchestral. The chorus is incorporated into symphonic or quasi-symphonic frameworks, as in Sibelius's *Kullervo* and Mahler's Second, Third and Eighth Symphonies; or, as in the *Gurrelieder*—following the precedent of Liszt's *Faust* Symphony rather than Beethoven's Ninth—composers bring in the chorus to clinch the finale: Skryabin's First Symphony (1900), Delius's *Appalachia* (1902), Busoni's Piano Concerto (1904), the last section of Roussel's *Evocations* (1911). It was perhaps the example of Mahler's Eighth (1907) which suggested the employment of voices throughout symphonies organized in the conventional four movements: Vaughan Williams's *Sea Symphony* (1910) and Rakhmaninov's *Kolokola* (The Bells) (1913). Even more symptomatic was the more and more frequent use, after Debussy's *Sirènes* (1899), of a wordless chorus simply as a part of the orchestra either for the sake of its sound-colour—as in Ravel's *Daphnis* and Delius's *Song of the High Hills* (both 1911) and the end of Holst's *Planets* (1917)—or merely to add to the volume of sound, as seems to be the case in Skryabin's *Prometheus* (1910).

END OF AN EPOCH

The period that began with *Falstaff* and *Hänsel und Gretel*, the *New World* Symphony and the *Pathétique*, Brahms's Clarinet Quintet and the Spanish and Italian *Liederbücher* of Hugo Wolf, and ended with *Rosenkavalier* and *Petrushka*, *Prometheus* and *Das Lied von der Erde*, the period which includes practically all the best work of Strauss, Mahler, Reger, Elgar, Delius, Puccini, Rakhmaninov, Skryabin, Debussy, Busoni, appears heterogeneous enough when one examines it in detail—still more heterogeneous if one draws in other names and works—yet, seen in historical perspective, shows an over-riding aesthetic unity. It was an over-ripe art that, so far as it has been examined in this chapter, owed almost everything to the past. Its sumptuous operas and sumptuous orchestral scores were composed for a public that was wealthy enough to support large orchestras and great opera-houses, and that was also musically intelligent enough to appreciate superb singing not only of opera but of polished *Lied* and *mélodie* and to enjoy the refinements of instrumental chamber-music. It was possible for the composer of the period to use music as a language because he could count on his hearers' understanding the language evolved particularly during the previous century, with all its sound-symbols and associations and conventions; he could also count on their making some effort to follow him so long as he could be seen to be logically extending and enriching that language. Conversely the real innovator knew that he must be prepared to face not merely misunderstanding, but the accusation that his music was nonsense.

Yet, for all its close correspondence to the relatively stable and prosperous European civilization that nourished it, its decline cannot be attributed to the war which dealt that civilization such a staggering blow. The social and economic conditions would never again be so favourable to music of that kind, but the symptoms of decay and exhaustion were already apparent years before 1914. Sumptuousness of sonority, hypertrophic harmony, emotional intensity, music-as-a-language could be carried no farther. The future of music lay in other directions, which other composers—indeed sometimes the late romantics themselves—had long been pointing to and exploring.

II

THE REACTION AGAINST ROMANTICISM:
1890–1914

By GERALD ABRAHAM

INTRODUCTION

THE forces which revitalized music during the rich and colourful decadence of romanticism were in appearance and in origins totally opposed to each other. One was conservative, the other radical. One had always held out against romanticism, though romantic composers such as Schumann had sometimes been fascinated by it and given it play in their music; the other came into existence actually as a form of romanticism. One was concerned with musical pattern and structure for its own sake, the other with sonority for its own sake, but even this was not really a common factor. However, the rejection of music as a rhetorical or autobiographical language ultimately brought them together; and the musician who wished to be a pure craftsman, applying seemingly outworn techniques of composition to the treatment of 'purely' musical ideas, found that the musician exploring new sonorous effects could provide him with new materials for the exercise of his craft. The aesthetic of the nineteenth-century conservatives was that expounded by Eduard Hanslick in *Vom Musikalisch-Schönen*:[1] 'a complete musical idea . . . is an end in itself and by no means medium or material for the representation of feelings and thoughts' and composition is not 'the translation of an imagined material (*eines gedachten Stoffs*) into sounds; the sounds themselves are the untranslatable primitive language (*Ursprache*)'.[2]

THE IMPACT OF BACH

The conservatives were saved from technical stagnation less by the borrowing of devices associated with romanticism (such as theme-transformation) for purely musical ends than by the revival of baroque methods, largely as a result of the cult of Bach. But the impact of Bach, as he changed from a rediscovered historical figure to a living influence, was ambiguous. When Schumann composed Bachian fugues in his

---

[1] Leipzig, 1854; sixth, enlarged and improved edition, 1881.
[2] Sixth edition, pp. 65 and 194.

Opp. 60 and 72, he was temporarily denying his essential romanticism, and the fugal ideas he acquired in these technical exercises enriched the musical vocabulary of his later years[1] more than they affected his technique. Many composers who were not 'absolute' musicians or conservatives in any sense learned technical lessons from Bach and even the idea of fugue could be used as a symbol—of *science*—in Strauss's *Zarathustra*. Indeed Bach himself was claimed as a romantic by the Alsatian Wagner-disciple Albert Schweitzer in his *J. S. Bach, le musicien-poète*,[2] which, as Charles Marie Widor put it in his preface, revealed the chorale-preludes as not merely 'modèles de contrepoint pur' but a 'suite de poèmes d'une éloquence, d'une intensité d'émotion sans pareilles'. In fact Schweitzer mistook the baroque symbols of *Affekte* for quasi-Wagnerian 'motifs de la démarche, de la quiétude, de la douleur . . . de la lassitude, de la terreur'. But it was Bach's demonstration that 'contrepoint pur' could be living musical tissue, neither empty sound-patterns nor precise 'langage musical', which did so much to revitalize absolute music at this period.

It was not from Bach but from Wagner, the Wagner of *Meistersinger* and *Götterdämmerung*, that Strauss and Mahler and the other late romantic masters learned their kind of polyphony: the polyphony of thematic lines, or thematic and subordinate lines, controlled by harmonic progressions. But there is a world of difference between the counterpoint which consists of the combination of themes all based on the same chord and the 'contrepoint pur' which, equally secure in its harmonic basis, propels itself by the thrusts and stresses of suspension and friction and resolution, between free polyphony employed to romantic ends and disciplined polyphonic thinking for its own sake. The practice of fugue or quasi-fugal writing not only lowers the romantic temperature—as Mahler demonstrates in the finale of his Fifth Symphony (1902)—but provides a firm bone-structure in place of flaccid tissue, just as the passacaglia technique provides an element of formal discipline. Nor was this merely a matter of structure, important only to the composer himself; he wished the listener to listen to the details of the music instead of allowing himself to be immersed in washes of rich, emotional sound.

BUSONI AND REGER

The two masters of the generation after Brahms mostly deeply

[1] Wolfgang Boetticher, *Robert Schumann: Einführung in Persönlichkeit und Werk* (Berlin, 1941), p. 572.

[2] Leipzig, 1905; later vastly expanded in a German version (Leipzig, 1908) which was in turn revised and expanded for the English translation made by Ernest Newman (London, 1911).

impressed by Bach were Ferruccio Busoni (1866–1924) and Max Reger (1873–1916), the first a Germanized Italian, the second the most Teutonic of Germans. Neither was by any means free from romantic strains.[1] Busoni was a passionate admirer of Liszt; Reger's harmony is often hypertrophied to the last degree. Indeed their Janus-faces have given them an historical importance beyond that of their original creative powers. They met in 1895, became close friends and 'exchanged their compositions and piano-arrangements of Bach organ-works',[2] but to what extent there was any real mutual influence, it is difficult to determine. Both adopted the contemporary attitude to Bach, as a master who must be rescued from the dry-as-dust academics and presented to the public in contemporary terms with all the resources of contemporary instruments, an attitude which led to such inflated transcriptions as the conclusion of Busoni's piano version of Bach's organ Toccata in C major (BWV 564):

Ex. 28

---

[1] See *supra*, pp. 14–15 and 32.
[2] Fritz Stein, *Max Reger* (Potsdam, 1939), p. 20.

They naturally carried this monumental style of piano-writing over into original compositions in which they paid homage to Bach: Busoni's *Fantasia contrappuntistica* (1910) and Reger's *Variationen und Fuge über ein Thema von J. S. Bach*, Op. 81 (1904). Near the end of the latter, a double *Monumentalfuge*,[1] Reger presents both first (right hand) and second (left hand) subjects not simply combined but with typically thick harmonies:

[1] An apt term coined by Emanuel Gatscher, *Die Fugentechnik Max Regers in ihrer Entwicklung* (Stuttgart, 1925).

Ex. 29

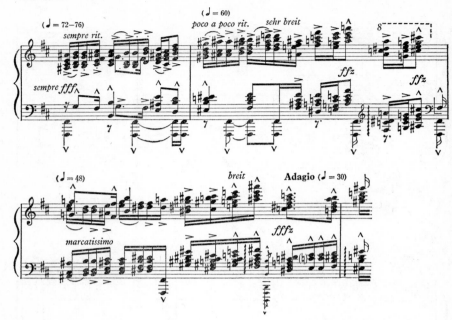

But an excerpt from the exposition will show Reger's genuine, if always rather harmony-bound, linear feeling:

Ex. 30

espress.

a severe style which is maintained until the third section of the fugue and which represents the Reger who influenced his younger contemporaries, including Schoenberg. ('Schoenberg had always been interested in the music of Reger and had admired many things in it';[1] when Schoenberg wrote of 'the great masters of our time' he habitually included Reger among their number.) Reger's sets of variations—Op. 81, the Beethoven Variations, Op. 86 (1904), the Telemann Variations, Op. 134 (1914) for piano, the Hiller and Mozart sets for orchestra, Op. 100 (1907) and Op. 132 (1914)—all end with fugues, as do a number of his other works, and nearly all, like Op. 81, with fugues whose dynamic plan reflects his own way of playing Bach. He would begin a fugue almost inaudibly and end with a triple forte; his own fugue in the Bach Variations begins *pp (una corda)* and ends *ffff*, and those of the Beethoven, Hiller and Mozart sets, after a *mf* or *sfz* call to attention, begin *pp* and proceed to a massive, heavily reined-in conclusion. There are highly romantic changes of tempo, and almost every entry of the subject is *marcato* in accordance with the common way of playing Bach at that period.

Not all Reger's very numerous fugues lean so heavily toward the romantic, though even the less *monumental* often preserve the basic conception of an overall crescendo. Near the very end of his life in the *Preludes and Fugues*, Op. 131a, for solo violin and *Drei Duos (Kanons und Fugen im alten Stil)* Op. 131b, for two violins (1914), he did achieve mastery of pure and classical line-drawing. Yet the lasting significance of Reger's copious fugue-writing lay not in his romanticizing of the fugue—he had begun, in the organ pieces of Op. 7 (1892) by imitating Bach without harmonic inflation—but in the fugal discipline he imposed on romantic music. Here the intellect reasserted its power to think *in* music rather than *about* music; and his later works in general, notably the Telemann Variations and the Clarinet Quintet (1916), recapture genuine classical feeling as well as classical techniques. This was no

---

[1] Dika Newlin, *Bruckner—Mahler—Schoenberg* (New York, 1947), p. 275.

more than a personal achievement, however. It was reached too late to affect Reger's contemporaries, among whom classical feeling—balance and textural clarity, emotional restraint, and the other qualities commonly subsumed under the idea of the classical—was cherished by composers, particularly Ravel and his compatriots, who were little concerned with the techniques of polyphonic discipline and harshly intellectual harmonic schemes, and in any case knew nothing or little of Reger. (When Honegger went to Paris in 1911, 'féru de Richard Strauss et de Max Reger', he found the latter completely unknown there.)[1] On the other hand, those who were so concerned showed little sense of classical ideals, despite their increasing preoccupation with music and its technical devices for their own sake.

NON-FUNCTIONAL HARMONY

The cultivation of composition-techniques for their own sake was fecundated only by contact with the cultivation of sonorities for their own sake, which originated not in any conception of absolute music but in typically romantic attempts to extend the expressive and suggestive or descriptive language of music. A characteristic example is the added note: two notes, a minor or major second apart, are sounded together instead of only one of them, as at the end of the voice-part of Wagner's song 'Im Treibhaus' (In the hothouse) (1858). The piano suggests the 'heavy drops' by minor seconds, D–E flat, which can be explained in terms of tonal harmony in conjunction with the G–B flat of the left hand but which the listener irresistibly hears as irrational sounds, a blurred *Naturlaut* as Mahler might have called it:

Ex. 31

(On the green edge of the leaves.)

---

[1] *Je suis compositeur* (Paris, 1951, p. 128; English translation by Wilson O. Clough, London, 1966).

And Wagner proceeds to resolve the E flat on to E natural, producing a normal added-sixth chord. Similarly, ten years later, in the ninth of his *Romanzen aus Tiecks 'Magelone'*, 'Ruhe, Süssliebchen', Brahms evoked the magic indistinctness of woods at night by a soft syncopated major second, persisting for five slow bars, but immediately explained by its context as part of a dominant seventh and soon given an orthodox resolution. By an extraordinary coincidence Borodin had already, in 1867, also composed a song about a fairy-tale princess sleeping at night, surrounded by forest, 'Spyashchaya knyazhna' (The sleeping princess). His song also is in A flat and it also begins with the same syncopated *pp* major second, D flat–E flat, casting the same drowsy spell; but the major second is not part of dominant seventh harmony and instead of being resolved it moves to another major second:

Ex. 32

(In the dense forest sleeps,)

Syncopated major seconds, constituting a single 'line' of the piano part, continue uninterruptedly for fourteen bars and are only briefly and unconventionally resolved; major or minor seconds continue to play an extremely important part throughout the song. This is something fundamentally different from Brahms; it is often possible to analyse

Borodin's individual chords in terms of conventional harmony and the first sixteen bars are in the purest A flat, except for a couple of flattened leading notes; but it is impossible to hear the chords in that way. The harmony is not functional harmony. Every chord is blurred by the added note in the highest part; the two G flats neutralize the faintest suggestion of a dominant pull. It is sound without conventional musical sense, sound relying on its purely sensuous impact to produce a quasi-mesmeric effect; the seconds ask not to be resolved but to be savoured.

In the setting of the next stanza, which tells how the noisy rout of witches and wood-demons flies over the princess without wakening her, Borodin even more thoroughly destroys the functional property of harmony by a powerful whole-tone scale descending through two octaves:

Ex. 33

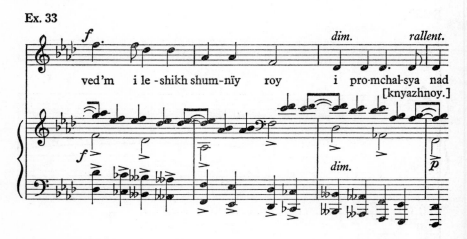

although the firmly outlined subdominant chord prevents any feeling of atonality and only the first four notes of the scale (and their repetition) are harmonized in the whole-tone mode. Here again the intention is suggestive: from Glinka's *Ruslan* onward, the descending whole-tone scale has in Russian music been associated with evil magic, harshness, and cruelty. But even without whole-tone harmonies, like those in the first bar of Ex. 33 or the music of the avenging statue in Dargomïzhsky's *Stone Guest*,[1] it destroys the functional sense of harmony, which depends ultimately on gravitation toward points defined by the semitones in the scale and by the rise or fall of the perfect fourth or fifth in the bass.

Throughout the second half of the nineteenth century functional harmony was being weakened, through its melodic surface, by modal

[1] See Vol. IX.

influences from folk-song, as in Russia, and plainsong as in France, to say nothing of pentatonic influences from the music of the Far East, such as that which impressed Claude Debussy (1862–1918) at the Paris Exposition Universelle in 1889. Fauré's flattening or evasion of the seventh degree of the scale, very characteristic of his style, has been mentioned in the previous chapter.[1] Chabrier has flattened sevenths; and Debussy in his early songs thought nothing of preceding a final tonic chord by a chord with no dominant function. In 'Beau soir' (1878), in E major, the penultimate chord is a G major triad; indeed the whole song is marked by juxtapositions of unrelated diatonic chords. 'Mandoline' (1882) is still bolder. The suggestion of strumming on the open strings of the instrument, G D A, is unmistakably dominant, but the C major triad has hardly been heard when at bar 8 the composer breaks into a succession of unrelated triads and inversions:

Ex. 34

(Exchange idle chat under the whispering boughs.)

[1] p. 26 and Ex. 9.

This is followed by another kind of unconventional succession, held together by the common notes, A G, but giving the ear the impression of consonances enriched by added notes. Near the end of the song the tonic chord alternates constantly with a 4/3 chord the dominant force of which is eliminated by the flattening of the B; in the last seven bars the two superimposed fifths of the opening become three—C G D A—of which the A is finally silent and the D moves to E. Every one of these procedures is in total opposition to the doctrine d'Indy was to enunciate later: that 'chords as combinations of sounds appear only as the effect of a *halt* in the movement of the *melodic* parts . . . musically *chords* do not exist . . .';[1] Debussy's chords exist purely as combinations of sounds for their sonorous effect, and are related to their neighbours often as much by contrast as by connection. The constitution, colour and lay-out of the chord are more important than its context; concord or theoretical discord, it is treated as a single unit to be manipulated as earlier composers had used consecutive thirds or sixths.[2] (It should be added that Debussy employed major seconds, possibly suggested by Borodin's, as early as 'Le Jet d'eau' (1889) and 'Les Angélus' (1891)—as indeed d'Indy did later, with no obvious poetic justification, in the prologue to *Fervaal*: Guilhen's 'Au nom du soleil, roi du monde'.) The fabric of classical harmony was thus being gently eroded on the diatonic side at the same time that it was disintegrating under the more violent strains of constantly intensified chromaticism. And it was the gentler process that was the more revolutionary, for while it originated as a symptom of romanticism it was by its very nature a denial of romanticism.

THE EVOLUTION OF DEBUSSY'S STYLE

It is natural to attribute Debussy's exploitation of sonority for its own sake to the influence of current aesthetic ideas. No musician has been more sensitive to his cultural ambience;[3] and Rimbaud's 'Alchimie du verbe' (1873)—'J'inventai la couleur des voyelles!—A noir, E blanc, I rouge, O bleu, U vert.—Je réglai la forme et le mouvement de chaque consonne, et, avec des rythmes instinctifs, je me flattai d'inventer un verbe poétique accessible un jour ou l'autre à tous les sens. Je réservais la traduction'—had opened the door to the Symbolists and their poetry of subtly suggestive non-sense, a play of sounds and images and

---

[1] See p. 21.

[2] On Debussy's non-functional harmony, see Ilse Storb, *Untersuchungen zur Auflösung der funktionaler Harmonik in den Klavierwerken von Claude Debussy* (Cologne Diss., 1967).

[3] On the relationship of Debussy to the artistic and literary tendencies and theories of his day, see Andreas Liess, *Claude Debussy: das Werk im Zeitbild* (two vols., Strasbourg, 1936) and Edward Lockspeiser, *Debussy: his Life and Mind* (two vols., London, 1962 and 1965).

rhythms that should act on the reader as music acts on the listener. Similarly Debussy rejected those musical procedures in which the intelligence intervenes at the expense of simple perception:

One combines, constructs, imagines themes intended to express ideas; one develops them, modifies them in conjunction with other themes which represent other ideas; *one makes metaphysics but one doesn't make music.* Music should be registered by the listener's ear without his having to discover abstract ideas in the maze of a complicated development.[1]

In 1909 Monet was to acknowledge an affinity between Debussy's aesthetic and his own when he spoke to Roger Marx of his 'harmonies and concords of colours which are sufficient in themselves and which succeed in touching us, as a musical phrase or chord touches us ... without the aid of a more precise or clearly enunciated idea'.[2]

All the same, it is possible to exaggerate Debussy's impressionability to cultural fashions. The pentatonic flute theme which opens his orchestral *Printemps* (1887):

Ex. 35

was written two years before he heard the *gamelan* at the International Exhibition, and it is very likely that he was introduced to pentatonic and other unusual scales by his theory teacher at the Paris Conservatoire, Albert Lavignac, who also introduced him to Wagner.[3]

Debussy's continued employment of Wagnerian and Franckian techniques, in music very different in substance and ethos from theirs, has been mentioned in the previous chapter.[4] Such dual nature was not uncommon in the music of that period; but whereas with most composers it consisted of real symbiosis, with Debussy such devices as theme-transformation were only the least disagreeable means of saving his music from deliquescence. Not only is his harmony in quite early compositions 'weightless', without sense of tonal gravity, but even his

[1] Léon Vallas, *Les Idées de Claude Debussy, musicien français* (Paris, 1927), p. 30.

[2] Roger Marx, '*Les Nymphéas* de M. Claude Monet', *Gazette des Beaux-Arts*, i (1909), p. 523; quoted in George H. Hamilton, *Painting and Sculpture in Europe: 1880–1940* (London, 1967), p. 19.

[3] An impressive catalogue of pentatonic motives and segments in Debussy's music has been compiled by Constantin Brailou, 'Pentatony in Debussy's Music' in *Studia Memoriae Belae Bartók Sacra* (3rd ed., London, 1959), p. 377. But the first and earliest example, from the song 'Fleur des blés' (1877), is only part of a phrase which is not completely pentatonic.

[4] See p. 29.

melody floats, as Ex. 35 does, and tends to return to the same note, beautiful but lymphatic and listless, outlining shapes in which—as in the filigree detail of background texture—it is impossible to deny a close affinity with what was, a little later, to become known as *art nouveau*.[1] When he wished to construct an extended piece of absolute music in the String Quartet (1893) he was obliged not only to employ the romantic technique of theme-transformation but to lean heavily on an actual model: Grieg's Quartet in the same key.[2] He goes through many of the motions appropriate to a large-scale work of this kind: sequence, pseudo-imitation (particularly in the finale, the most clumsily made movement of the four), the return of themes in different keys. But the motions are meaningless and distract one from that exquisite mosaic of motives constantly shown in fresh harmonic lights and from fresh tonal angles, which constitutes the real essence of the music. Key-organization is of even less importance than in the work Mahler was composing at the same time, his Second Symphony.

In the compositions of the period between the String Quartet and the completion of the score of *Pelléas et Mélisande* in 1902—the *Prélude à l'après-midi d'un faune* (1892–4) and *Nocturnes* (1897–1901) for orchestra, the *Proses lyriques* (1893) and *Chansons de Bilitis* (1897) for voice and piano, 'Jardins sous la pluie' (1894) (the other two *Estampes* seemingly came eight or nine years later) and *Pour le piano* (1894–1902) —he completed the establishment of an extraordinarily personal style and harmonic vocabulary which he was more or less content to work and re-work and refine during the following decade, until it was nearly exhausted. In *L'après-midi* there are still traces of Balakirev or Rimsky-Korsakov (the flute triplet-figure three bars before fig. 3) and Massenet (the section in D flat), but after that the various influences that contributed to the formation of his idiom were fully absorbed. Some of these have been greatly exaggerated. The unorthodoxy of Mussorgsky's empirical harmony, for instance, is quite different in nature from Debussy's, even if it was known to him earlier than *c*. 1896; and it would be difficult indeed to isolate any element in Debussy's music which he could have picked up only from Erik Satie (1866–1925)[3] and not from the common stock. In 1897 he orchestrated two of Satie's three *Gymnopédies*[4] (1888) for piano but they made no impression on his own work except perhaps in the unimportant 'Danse profane' for

[1] On Debussy and *art nouveau*, see Lockspeiser, op. cit., i, pp. 116 ff. and *infra*, pp. 166 ff.

[2] See Gerald Abraham, *Grieg: a Symposium* (London, 1948), p. 8.

[3] On the early personal relationship between Debussy and Satie, see Lockspeiser, op. cit., i, pp. 145–9; on his early knowledge of Russian music, ibid, pp. 47–52, and André Schaeffner, 'Debussy et ses rapports avec la musique russe', in *Musique russe* (ed. Pierre Souvtchinsky) (Paris, 1953), i.

[4] The Greek γυμνοπαιδία was a festival marked by the dancing of naked youths.

harp and strings (1904); it was Maurice Ravel (1875–1937) who came near to plagiarizing them in 'Les entretiens de la Belle et de la Bête' in *Ma mère l'Oye* (1908). As for Satie's three *Sarabandes* (1887), it is impossible to see any connection between them and the Sarabande of *Pour le piano* beyond one insignificant motive and the fact that both revive an old dance-form. (The revival of old dance-forms was in any case fashionable in France at the time, witness Chabrier's *Bourrée fantasque* (1891), Chausson's *Quelques danses* (including sarabande, pavane and forlane) (1896), and Ravel's *Menuet antique* (1895) and *Pavane pour une Infante défunte* (1899).) Chabrier had introduced series of unresolved ninth chords in several passages of *Le roi malgré lui* (1887). (To fill out an impression of French harmony at this period it should be remembered that such relatively conservative composers as Saint-Saëns and Bruneau wrote passages melodically and harmonically in the whole-tone mode, in the Scherzo, Op. 87, for two pianos (1890), and *Le Rêve* (1891) respectively.) Satie's *Gnossiennes* (1890), his three preludes for Sar Péladan's *Le Fils des étoiles* (1891), his *Sonneries de la Rose+Croix* (1892) and *Prélude de la Porte Héroïque du Ciel* (1894), all for piano, did open up new ground—unbarred and rhythmless successions of unrelated chords—but Debussy did not follow him on to it. Admittedly the chords themselves are sometimes interestingly experimental, as is the case with the piled up fourths at the beginning of the first *Fils des étoiles* prelude (i); but although the passage of common chords that opens the *Sonneries* (ii) may have sprung from mystical emotion, it could hardly communicate it:

Ex. 36

En blanc et immobile

8

Highly romantic conceptions are reduced to nullity by extremely anti-romantic musical devices. Romantic symptoms—pictorial and literary affinities—are neutralized by non-expressive music in Debussy also; but Debussy's music, while it does not seek to express directly the emotion aroused by contemplation of an object, is nevertheless a vivid reaction to the object in terms of purely sensuous sound, which evokes an imprecise but delightful response akin to that produced by Rimbaud's verbal alchemy or Monet's visual harmonies.

The apparent paucity of Debussy's output during this period is easily accounted for by his preoccupation with *Pelléas*, which is discussed in the next chapter, and with other projects which never came to fruition. Few as they are, these compositions reveal significant tendencies. Following the String Quartet, Debussy experimented further with 'absolute' music in the Sarabande and two later pieces of *Pour le piano*: the side-slipping of triads, sometimes augmented (whole-tone) triads, and complete whole-tone passages in the Prelude, side-slipping of chords of the seventh and added-note chords in the Sarabande, pentatonic patterns in the Toccata (to which 'Jardins sous la pluie' is a faintly pictorial counterpart). Despite the non-functional nature of the harmony, the pieces are given very clear definition by the nature of the piano writing, by diatonic sequences, and by the recurrence of patterns and sections. In the *Proses lyriques* and *Chansons de Bilitis*, settings of prose–poems by Debussy himself and Pierre Louÿs respectively, Debussy moved even further from lyrical song than in the Verlaine sets of 1891 and 1892 (the *Trois mélodies* and the first set of *Fêtes galantes*); the piano is often the more important partner and the voice only comments, though the *Bilitis* songs approach the exquisite subtlety of the near-parlando style of *Pelléas*. The sense of the texts and the use of all-pervading patterns in the piano-part, in the traditional manner, brush aside that problem of form which Debussy still handled clumsily and somewhat perfunctorily in his instrumental music. It was in the orchestral *Nocturnes* that Debussy first perfected his instrumental technique, not in the tarantella-like 'Fêtes' with its echoes of Balakirev's *Tamara* nor even in the drifting, changing cloud-shapes of 'Nuages', but in 'Sirènes' which is a pure sound-mosaic of fragmented, subtly coloured chords and tiny motives, moniliform and athematic except that some minute pattern may appear briefly as an ostinato and reappear lightly transformed and in ever-changing harmonic and orchestral lights:

Ex. 37

'Sirènes' begins with a 'dominant' chord in B major and ends with a B major triad, and here and there the ear catches other familiar harmonies; but they bring no sense of tonal unity or contrast, of modulation, or of tension and relaxation. The distinction of consonance and dissonance had been obliterated long before this in Debussy; each chord has its isolated value as sound-effect only.

These techniques were exploited exhaustively in some of the works of the next decade, *La Mer* (1903–5) and the *Images* for orchestra (1906–12) and the two sets of *Images* (1905 and 1907) and two books of *Préludes* (1910 and 1910–13) for piano. The sustaining of low bass-notes on the piano necessitates suspension of the damper action and further enriches and blurs the sonorous effect. Equally idiosyncratic is the treatment of the orchestra, in which doubling between groups is extremely rare: a figure is usually limited to woodwind or horns or strings only, and set against an equally complex pattern in another instrumental colour. When doubling between groups does occur, it is employed to produce effects of great subtlety, as in the section 'Les Parfums de la nuit' in 'Ibéria' (1908), the second orchestral *Image* (p. 69), where a 'distant' melody (*lointain et expressif*) is played by a solo violin, muted, and a solo bassoon in its 'pinched' highest register; or a little later in the same score (p. 72) where a melody characteristically thickened out in 6/4 chords is played by two flutes, two piccolos, three trumpets (two of them muted), two solo violins, and two solo cellos, the main strand being delicately outlined:

Ex. 38

An equally subtle blend of sonorities, this time accompanimental as background to a horn solo—the same melody which is soon to be heard in quicker tempo, *lointain et expressif*—occurs a little earlier:

Ex. 39

In all these compositions, orchestral or pianistic, which may justly be described as impressionistic or (better) *pointilliste*, the basic methods are the same: whether modal or pentatonic or whole-tone, the melodic fragments are often thickened out into parallel seconds, simple or augmented triads or higher-powered chords with or without added notes, to form variegated patterns. The fabric is held together not by thematic logic or rhetoric, though sometimes by relationships between the various tesserae, but by pedals or ostinato figures. Rhythmic patterns are also used for the same purpose, though rhythmic impulse— sometimes vigorous enough, as in the first and third section of 'Ibéria' or 'Golliwogg's cake walk' from *Children's Corner* for piano (1906–8), or even quasi-mechanical as in 'Mouvement' from the first set of piano *Images*—is frequently feeble to the point of near-extinction. (On the other hand, Debussy's micro-rhythms can be exquisitely subtle.) Sometimes whole sound-complexes are the binding agents as in 'Voiles' from the first book of *Préludes*:

Ex. 40

which becomes

or the right-hand figure of the section *Un peu animé et plus clair* of 'Cloches à travers les feuilles' from the second set of *Images*.[1]

Yet side by side with his purely impressionistic compositions Debussy never ceased to write others, almost equally non-tonal but hovering on

[1] 'Cloches', a compendium of Debussyan technique, is recorded in *The History of Music in Sound*, x.

the edge of the diatonic and employing simpler harmonies and textures and more sober colouring: the settings of Charles d'Orléans for voice and piano (nos. 1 and 3 of the *Trois chansons de France*, 1904) and unaccompanied chorus (*Trois chansons de Charles d'Orléans*, 1908) and Villon (*Trois ballades*, 1910),[1] the music for d'Annunzio's *Le Martyre de saint Sébastien* (1911), the *Trois Poèmes de Stéphane Mallarmé* for voice and piano (1913), and the *Douze Études* for piano (1915). All these in their different ways—renunciation of 'jewellers' work', absence of extra-musical suggestion, simple modality of melody and harmony, economy of texture—suggest, particularly when all these qualities show themselves at the same time, an ever-increasing preoccupation with the values we describe as 'classical'. It was a tendency that reached its apogee in Debussy's last works, the three *Sonates* of 1915–17, for cello and piano, for flute, viola and harp, and for piano and violin. It is difficult to imagine music more severely classical than the opening of the last Sonata:

Ex. 41

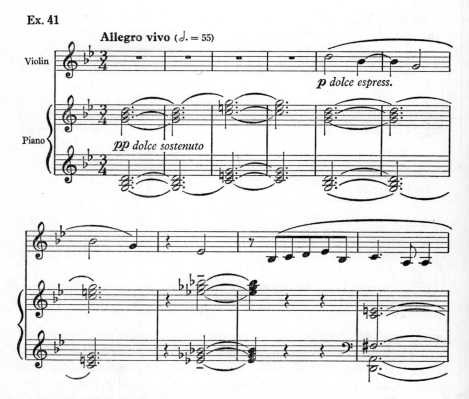

[1] The second, 'Ballade que feit Villon à la requeste de sa mère pour prier Nostre Dame' is recorded in *The History of Music in Sound*, x.

DEBUSSY AND RAVEL

Although Debussy's development after *Pelléas* was little affected by the music of other composers—in 1913 he told Calvocoressi he was rather out of touch with contemporary music 'because he wished to concentrate and had made it a rule to hear as little music as possible'[1]—there was one young contemporary who undoubtedly came under his influence and to whom, it seems possible, he was to a slight extent indebted. In March 1898 he heard a performance of Ravel's *Les Sites auriculaires* for two pianos (1895–6) and was so impressed by the first of them, the 'Habanera' afterwards orchestrated as the third movement of the *Rapsodie espagnole* (1907), that he asked the younger composer to lend him the score. This led ultimately to charges of plagiarism in his own 'Soirée dans Grenade' (1903), second of the *Estampes* for piano, where the resemblance is certainly very striking, and his *Lindaraja* for two pianos (1901), where it is limited to the dance-rhythm and a single bar of melody common to other habaneras; indeed Ravel's was itself heavily indebted to Chabrier's piano-piece of 1885, or, rather, the later version in D flat. Similar claims have been made for the influence of Ravel's *Jeux d'eau* (1901) on Debussy's piano-style; they are counterbalanced by the fact that *Jeux d'eau* is itself marked by Debussyan procedures.[2] And Ravel admired the Sarabande from *Pour le piano* enough to orchestrate it in 1903, conversely arranged *L'Après-midi* for two pianos, and admitted in 1928 that in his *Shéhérazade* songs of 1903, 'l'influence, au moins spirituelle, de Debussy est assez visible'.[3] The fact is that under the influences of Saint-Saëns, Fauré, and Chabrier French piano-composers had for some time been exploring the resources of the instrument; even minor figures such as Déodat de Séverac (1873–1921) in his suites *Le Chant de la terre* (1901) and *En Languedoc* (1904) made highly individual harmonic experiments before succumbing to Debussy's influence in the *Baigneuses au soleil* (1908), so it is hardly surprising that the two leading figures found each other mutually stimulating. But even in this field of piano music, where in his five *Miroirs* (1905) and the three pieces of *Gaspard de la nuit* (1908) Ravel comes nearest to Debussy—and the *Sonatine* (1905) may perhaps be regarded as a counterpart of *Pour le piano*—the differences are very obvious. Harmonic vocabulary and pianistic figuration are similar yet

---

[1] M. D. Calvocoressi, *Musicians Gallery* (London, 1933), p. 122.

[2] On Debussy's piano-style, see Frank Dawes, *Debussy: Piano Music* (London, 1969) and Robert Schmitz, *The Piano Works of Claude Debussy* (New York, 1950); on Ravel's, Kurt Akeret, *Studien zum Klavierwerk von Maurice Ravel* (Zürich, 1941), and Henri Gil-Marchex, 'La technique de piano', *Revue musicale* (special Ravel number), vi (1925), no. 6, p. 38.

[3] 'Esquisse autobiographique', *Revue musicale*, xix (1938), p. 212. On the musical and personal relationships of Debussy and Ravel, see Lockspeiser, op. cit., ii, pp. 33–44, and Martin Cooper, *French Music* (London, 1951), pp. 134–40.

different; Ravel's piano-writing is virtuosic in the sense of Liszt and Balakirev (who meant quite as much to him as to Debussy), it is rhythmically incisive as Debussy's seldom is, its shapes are generally clear rather than blurred and they succeed each other with that logical connection which Debussy minimized or spurned. For all the modernity of his musical language—the pentatonic and modal elements, the complication of individual chords, the parallel seconds and sevenths, and so on—tonal feeling is nearer the surface of Ravel's music than of Debussy's. Even the added seconds which blunt the edge of Debussy's sound seem to sharpen the edge of Ravel's, as in these passages from 'Scarbo', the third piece of *Gaspard de la nuit*:

Ex. 42
(i)

Again unlike Debussy, Ravel cared more for instrumental line than for instrumental colour. His orchestration—and he delighted in orchestrating even his own piano-music—is totally different. The lines are not often variegated in themselves as in the romantic line derived from Wagner's orchestra, which may pass from horns and lower strings to upper woodwind (Ex. 27) or begin on flutes, be doubled by clarinet for half a bar and then (while flutes pursue a different line) by violas, ending on violas alone—all within four bars (Ex. 21 (v)). Ravel makes no effort to avoid doubling and when he contrasts groups of instrumental colour he does so not to obtain subtle, iridescent effects but for the sake of brilliant transparency in the Russian tradition. Thus, when he scored the following passage from the 'Alborada del gracioso', the fourth of the *Miroirs*:

Ex. 43

he gave the melody to piccolo, oboes, cor anglais, bassoons, half the first violins, half the seconds, half the violas, and half the cellos (in their highest register) in octaves, and the 'inside pedal' A—always a favourite device of Ravel's from the 'Habanera' onward—to the remaining strings (in octaves), double basses, double bassoon, and tuba; the rich harmony is left to flutes, clarinets, harps, and brass, and the second chord of each bar (which is just off the second beat) is piquantly emphasized, again in the manner of Rimsky-Korsakov, by triangle, tambourine, side-drum, and cymbals. Similarly the harmony of the opening of the *Valses nobles et sentimentales* for piano (1911) sounds much clearer in the orchestral version. When Ravel wishes to create a wash of imprecise sound as in the 'Lever du jour' of the ballet *Daphnis et Chloé* (1909–12), it is paradoxically done with extreme precision and serves as a background against which firm, clear lines are drawn in contrasted instrumental colours.

When one turns from the two great sets of piano pieces and the song-cycle *Histoires naturelles* (1906), the most Debussyish of all Ravel's mature works, the completely different basis of his aesthetic becomes even more apparent. 'Mon Quatuor en fa' (1902–1903), he told Roland-Manuel, 'répond à une volonté de construction musicale ... qui apparait beaucoup plus nette que dans mes précédentes compositions'.[1] It was to appear again in the *Sonatine* for piano and the *Introduction et Allegro* for harp with flute, clarinet, and string quartet (1906). The wish to make a 'musical structure', *tout simple*, seldom visited Debussy even in the non-impressionistic works of his maturity; it possessed him only at the very end of his life in the three *Sonates*. But, looking back at the frankly impressionistic *Jeux d'eau* after seventeen years, Ravel thought it worthwhile to point out not only that it was 'the starting-point of all the pianistic novelties' of his music but that it is 'based on two themes in the manner of the first movement of a sonata, though not however subjected to the classic key-scheme'. The classical ground-plan of sonata-form, rudimentary in *Jeux d'eau*, is more obvious in the String Quartet and *Sonatine* but they are equally emancipated from the classical key-scheme. It is true the first subject of the first movement of the *Sonatine* would be in F sharp minor if its Es were not all natural, and the key suggested (but always evaded) by the second-subject material is the orthodox relative major; moreover the second subject is recapitulated in an identical evasion of F sharp—which actually identifies itself only in the final bar of the movement. But these ghosts of keys no more exercise pulls of tonal gravity than the themes in which they are embodied act and react on each other. The String Quartet had evidenced more thematic logic and is held together as a whole by familiar cyclic methods; both slow movement and finale refer back to the first. But the sonata-form of the first movement is even less orthodox than that of the *Sonatine*; the second subject is not in a contrasting key and is recapitulated in the same key; the tonal changes in the recapitulation, which is otherwise nearly literal, occur within the subjects and in the transition-passages—which thus become merely reliefs from tonal monotony. But survival of the mere shell of sonata-form, void of everything that had given it life and purpose, is a common phenomenon of the period.[2] Without the gravitational pulls of tonality, neither the loosely flowing diatonic or modal lines of a Ravel nor the tightly woven chromatic fabrics of the Central Europeans could use sonata-form in any significant way.

Although Ravel dispensed with the dynamism of key, his formal

[1] 'Esquisse autobiographique', p. 212.
[2] Cf. the remarks on Alban Berg's Piano Sonata on p. 73.

structure is perfectly lucid in ways that place him apart from Debussy and at the opposite pole from the Central Europeans, not so much because his melodic lines and harmony are free from hyper-chromaticism, his textures from over-density and his rhythms from flaccidity, but mainly because of its clear articulation by cadences. His cadences are not corner-stones and key-stones of tonality; nothing gravitates toward them; but their frank definition of periods is in striking contrast with the practices of impressionism, where they were of no importance, and of late romanticism, where every effort was made to nullify or conceal them. A 'musical structure', as Ravel conceived it, neither an expression of emotion nor a play of exquisite sonorities, was a work of high artifice and he saw no reason to conceal the fact. Thus in every way he found himself congenially assuming eighteenth-century attitudes toward music, just as when, in realizing 'the Greece of his dreams' in *Daphnis*, he found that his 'vast musical fresco' readily harmonized with 'that which had been imagined and depicted by the French artists of the end of the eighteenth century'.[1] Ravel was only in a few of his works and in a limited sense an 'impressionist', but he adapted some of Debussy's techniques, particularly his harmonic language, to a quite different end, a renaissance of classicism, just as others borrowed them to enrich the palette of exhausted romanticism: for example, the slow strange chords evoking the atmosphere of Herod's palace at the beginning of Florent Schmitt's *mimodrame*, *La Tragédie de Salomé* (1907; symphonic version, quoted here, 1911), (Ex. 44), or Dukas's Debussyan orchestration in *La Péri* (1912), (Ex. 45).

In considering Debussy in the context of history, it is always necessary to distinguish between 'impressionism' in the narrowest sense, which was—at any rate for the time being—a dead end, and his conscious 'emancipation of dissonance'[2] twenty years or more before Schoenberg used the phrase in his *Harmonielehre*. Admittedly, the dissonances Debussy set free were a great deal less fierce than Schoenberg's.

THE WIDER INFLUENCE OF DEBUSSY

Considerable as Debussy's reputation had been before the performance of *Pelléas* (30 April 1902, the first major landmark in the history of twentieth-century music), it was much greater afterwards. During the next decade Debussy and Strauss were almost universally regarded as the two outstanding figures, the leaders of strongly opposed tendencies, in contemporary music. Debussy and Strauss, be it noted, not Ravel and Mahler. In France Debussy's influence was naturally very great;

[1] 'Esquisse', p. 213.
[2] See Lockspeiser, op. cit., i, pp. 204–8.

Ex. 44

Ex. 45.

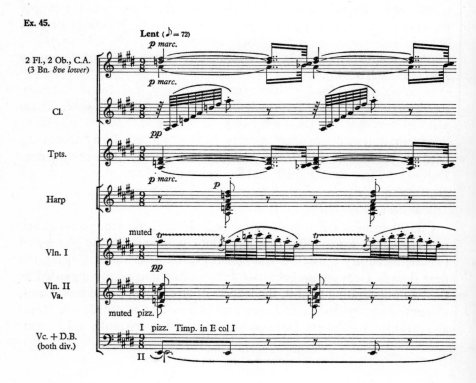

composers of widely different character submitted to his influence in
one way or another, and only those of an older generation—Saint-
Saëns, Fauré, d'Indy—were immune to it; and in d'Indy's case the
immunity was not total.[1] As Léon Vallas put it, 'Personne vers 1902–
1905 ne pouvait se défendre complètement de la contagion musicale de
Pelléas et Mélisande'.[2] That d'Indy should have been even slightly
infected is the more remarkable in that his variety of classicism, which
he imparted to Dukas, was more rigorous than that of Saint-Saëns;
Ravel could in later years recognize an affinity with Saint-Saëns but the
elegance of their classicism was quite foreign to d'Indy; the polyphony
of d'Indy's Second Symphony (1903) is often as harsh and angular as
Reger's:

Ex. 46

---

[1] See p. 20, n. 4.
[2] *Vincent d'Indy*, ii (Paris, 1950), p. 255.

and the fugal middle section of the third movement of Dukas's Piano Sonata (1901):

Ex. 47

doucement marqué

comes from the same school. If composers such as these could not resist the infection (cf. also Exs. 44 and 45, the trio of the scherzo of d'Indy's Violin Sonata (1904) and his *Jour d'été à la montagne* (1905)), it is not surprising that such natural eclectics as Albert Roussel and Charles Koechlin succumbed heavily before finding their own artistic personalities.

Roussel's acknowledgement of 'the weak influence of Debussy' has already been quoted.[1] It is naturally most obvious in such early works as the first set of *Quatre poèmes* (by Henri de Régnier), Op. 3 (1903), the *Rustiques* for piano, Op. 5, and First Symphony (*Le Poème de la forêt*), Op. 7 (both 1904–6), and persists until the orchestral triptych of Indian impressions *Évocations*, Op. 15 (1910–11), but even in the earliest of these works a distinctive personality begins to show itself; the language of Debussy is used in a different sense. And actually at the same time Roussel was writing things like the *Divertissement*, Op. 6, for flute, oboe, clarinet, bassoon, horn and piano (1906) (i), and certain parts of the D minor Violin Sonata, Op. 11 (1908) (ii), which are as neo-classical as Ravel without being particularly Ravelian:

[1] See p. 25.

Ex. 48

Nor, despite their structural leaning on d'Indy, are the *Divertissement* and Sonata d'Indyesque. Like Debussy and Ravel, Roussel delighted not only in the sound of added-note seconds but in the pentatonic mode (from the 'Ode à un jeune gentilhomme' (1907), second of the *Deux poèmes chinois*, onward); exotic scales and the harmonies based on them then played a more and more important part in Roussel's music.[1] And, like Florent Schmitt, Koechlin, and others, he employs 'scholastic' chords of the ninth, not obtained by added notes as Debussy's usually are, with a freedom of non-resolution and chromatic alteration like that with which rather earlier composers had treated chords of the seventh. The dissonances set free by Debussy were used in music very unlike his, for example the bourrée of Roussel's Suite for piano, Op. 14 (1910):

[1] See Arthur Hoérée, 'La Technique', *Revue musicale* (special Roussel number) x (1929), no. 6, p. 84; this article, of which Roussel himself approved, is reprinted in condensed form in Hoérée, *Albert Roussel* (Paris, 1938), p. 87.

Ex. 49

Unlike Roussel's eclecticism, Koechlin's was never focused by a strong creative personality. During his long life (1867–1951) he composed in every style of the day—at least in every French style and in some not particularly French—very often with individual touches. One hears this at once in his Op. 1, the first set of *Rondels* for voice and piano (1890–94), where the delicious setting of Théodore de Banville's 'Le Thé' could not quite have been written by Fauré. The opening of the prelude to Part I of his *L'Abbaye* (*suite religieuse pour choeurs, orchestre et orgue*), Op. 16:[1]

Ex. 50

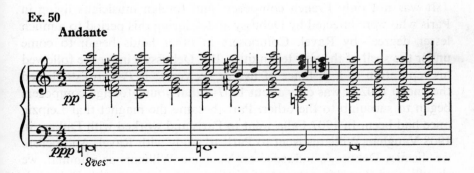

[1] Quoted from the composer's piano reduction, the only published form.

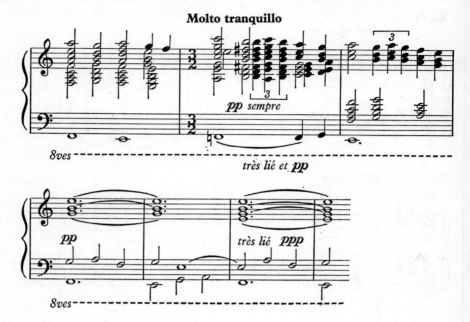

is remarkable in that it was composed during 1899–1901, long before 'La Cathédrale engloutie'. Debussyish harmony, Ravelian line-drawing, Satie's deliberate naïveté and eccentricity, experiments of every kind, often combining to produce music of undeniable beauty, converged most satisfactorily in such trifles as the two sets of *Esquisses* for piano, Op. 41, the more substantial *Paysages et Marines*, Op. 63 (1905–15), and the *Quatres Sonatines françaises* (Op. 60) for piano duet (1919). In so far as Koechlin was influential, which was really only in the post-war period, he certainly contributed to the current of French neo-classicism.

It was not only French composers and foreign musicians living in Paris who were infected by Debussy and—during this period to a much lesser degree—by Ravel. Composers in other lands began to come under the spell of the new techniques. But Debussy's influence followed his reputation at a distance of five or six years; if *Pelléas* established the one in 1902, it was only about 1907–8 that young foreign composers began to succumb to the other. Paris became the magnet that Leipzig once had been. In 1907 Falla went to Paris and worked with Dukas; in 1908 Vaughan Williams went to Paris to study with Ravel. And before we dismiss Debussy's influence on Vaughan Williams as minimal, we should note Bartók's account of his first acquaintance with Debussy's music:

When, urged by Kodály in 1907, I began to know and study Debussy's compositions, I was astonished to find that certain pentatonic motives corresponding to ones in our folk-song similarly play a great role in his melody.[1]

It was not the harmony that struck him first, though it did soon, not the piano-writing or the *pointilliste* technique which never made much impression on him. (Bartók's most Debussyish composition is the first of the *Két kép* (Two pictures) for orchestra, Op. 10, no. 1 (1910): cf. (Ex. 52 (iv).) As Edwin von der Nüll put it:[2]

He escaped from the atmosphere of neo-romanticism and subscribed to Debussyism. He did not, it is true, fall under the spell of Debussy's highly strung femininity . . . He took from the Frenchman what he could incorporate in his own self-willed, angular nature. He gladly accepted the enrichment of harmonic means but did not give up his sharply profiled melodic line; thus from the combination of these two forces arose far more radical forms than was ever the case with Debussy. Nor did he have at his disposal that narcotic twilight which made complicated chord-formations tolerable to the ear of 1908.

The same might be said of Schoenberg, though it is difficult to determine so precisely when and how Schoenberg became acquainted with Debussy's music; according to his own statement in the *Harmonielehre*,[3] it was 'three or four years' after 1902. However, the influence of Debussy's piano-writing is unmistakable in much of the piano-part of *Pierrot lunaire*—a work which, in turn, was to exercise through its *facture* a transitory impression on both Stravinsky ('Mazatsumi' from *Tri stikhotvoreniya iz yaponskoy liriki* (Japanese lyric poems)) and Ravel ('Placet futile' from *Trois Poèmes de Stéphane Mallarmé*) in 1913.

1908 was also the year of the earliest works in which the young Stravinsky reflected the influence of Debussy: the *Scherzo fantastique* and *Fireworks* for orchestra, followed by the First Act of his opera, *Solovey* (The Nightingale) in 1909. The Lento middle section of *Fireworks* also borrows from the opening of Dukas's *L'Apprenti sorcier*, and some of the 'unmistakable Debussy-like . . . harmonic combinations' that have been discovered in early Stravinsky[4] really derive from his teacher Rimsky-Korsakov. For more than sixty years Russian composers had shown a certain interest in artificial scales and the harmonies derived from them: not only the whole-tone scale[5] but the scale of

---

[1] 'Önéletrajz', *Magyar Irás* (1921); reprinted in Bartók, *Válogatott zenei irásai* (Budapest, 1948), p. 9. German version in *Musikblätter des Anbruch*, iii (1921), p. 89.
[2] *Béla Bartók: Ein Beitrag zur Morphologie der neuen Musik* (Halle, 1930), p. 2.
[3] p. 438.   [4] e.g. by Roman Vlad, *Stravinsky* (London, 1960), p. 6.
[5] See *supra*, p. 88.

alternate tones and semitones invented by Rimsky-Korsakov and first employed by him in his opera *Mlada* (1890), and not only the whole-tone mode with its augmented-triad harmonies, but ingeniously fabricated, non-functional chord-progressions founded on the whole-tone scale—as in the prologue to *Zolotoy Petushok* (The Golden Cockerel) (1907):

Ex. 51

where the alternation of 6/4 and 6/3 chords based on the descending scale admirably suggests the magical character of the Astrologer. It was from the same toy-box that Stravinsky took the harmonic ingenuities from which he fashioned the music of Kashchey and the Fire-Bird in *Zhar-Ptitsa* (The Fire-Bird) (1910)[1]. But great as was Stravinsky's debt to Rimsky-Korsakov and other innovators of the period, the greatest (as he acknowledged) was to Debussy: 'The musicians of my generation and I myself owe the most to Debussy.'[2]

The technical devices, especially the orchestral devices, of impressionism—the kaleidoscopic open-work of melodic scraps and spots of instrumental colour, the additional dimension given to pure line by doubling at conventional or unconventional intervals simultaneously (often amounting to side-slipping of chords), varied or unvaried repetition of motives or mere figures or rhythmic patterns instead of thematic development—all tending to the disintegration of the hitherto accepted norms of texture and consequence, were adopted or adapted by composers whose creative personalities differed markedly from each other's and from Debussy's, as may be seen in the six excerpts shown in Ex. 52. (The contemporary listener had no opportunity to hear the Webern piece until March 1913; he would doubtless have been incredulous of any prophecy that this would prove the most seminal of the six.) Not everything that seems 'impressionistic' in the music of the period stems from Debussy; the passage in Schoenberg's *Pelleas und Melisande* (1903), pp. 42–5, where Mélisande lets down her hair from the tower, probably owes more to passages in 'Am Strande von Sorrent' in Strauss's *Aus Italien* than to Debussy; but even composers whose appreciation of Debussy was severely limited were indebted to him technically. Such a one was Holst, who admired *L'Après-midi* and liked the *Nocturnes* 'but was never very happy about anything else' and 'hated' *Pelléas*,[3] yet 'Saturn' and 'Neptune' (composed 1914) in *The Planets* could hardly have been written without the pre-existence of Debussy's scores. It was another side of Debussy that appealed to Vaughan Williams, the diatonic or modal vein that runs from *La Damoiselle élue* (1888) to *Le Martyre de Saint Sébastien* (1911).

---

[1] See, for instance, André Schaeffner, *Strawinsky* (Paris, 1931), p. 21, and Edwin Evans, 'The Fire-Bird' and 'Petrushka' (London, 1933), p. 10.
[2] *Conversations with Igor Stravinsky* (London, 1959), p. 48.
[3] Imogen Holst, *Gustav Holst* (London, 1938), p. 147.

Ex. 52

(i) DELIUS: In a Summer Garden (1908)

Slower and more reposefully

(ii) STRAVINSKY: Scherzo fantastique (1908)

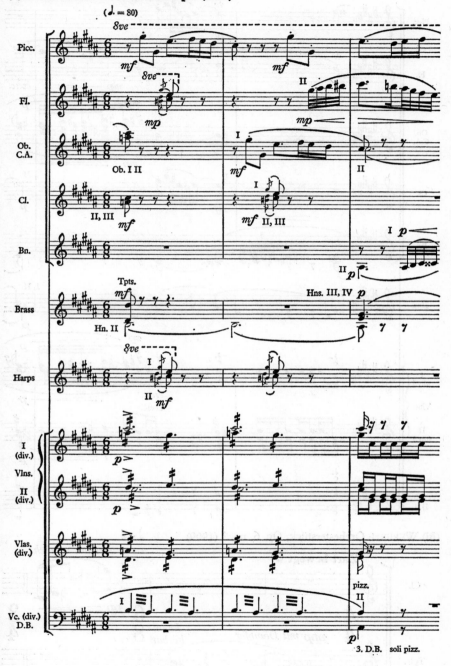

(iii) WEBERN: Orchesterstück, Op. 6, no. 3 (1909)

(iv) Bartók: In Full Flower, Op. 10, no. 1 (1910)

THE NEW HARMONY IN NEW CONTEXTS

The general techniques of impressionism lived on after the demise of the aesthetic that had given birth to them, and were employed mainly in attempts to rejuvenate romanticism (as in Skryabin's later style), but gradually exhausted themselves. With the new harmonic resources opened up by Debussy and his compatriots it was a different matter. Instead of being employed as elements in *pointillisme* or dissolved into 'romantic' figuration and texture, often softened by appoggiaturas and the like, they were commonly used—even by Debussy himself in such late works as the *Douze études* of 1915—as the material of 'pure music'.[1] Ironically, the added notes which Debussy had employed to blur the outlines of sound were now used to harden those outlines; the piled-up chords producing a sensuous haze of sonority into which he breathed the minimum of rhythmical life now gave dynamic weight and were pounded out in vigorous or subtle rhythms which often seemed the most, instead of the least, important element in the music, as in the 'Russian Dance' of *Petrushka* (1911) and the final dance of *The Rite of Spring* (1912). By 1908 piled-up chords were becoming common currency, but they were seldom introduced as starkly and uncompromisingly as by Bartók in his piano *Bagatelles*. Bartók was a pioneer of the new percussiveness on the very instrument Debussy had treated with such magical delicacy, but in any case the piano emphasized the 'block' character of chord agglomerations. The clarification of Ravel's harmony in the *Valses nobles*, when he orchestrated them, has already been pointed out[2] and in a piece written at almost exactly the same time as Bartók's *Bagatelles*, the second of the *Fünf Orchesterstücke*, Op. 16, Schoenberg gave a classic demonstration of prismatic scoring. The first sketch[3] shows the naked harmonic basis (i), though the instrumentation is already indicated, but the effect to the ear is very different (ii):

Ex. 53

(i)

---

[1] Debussy, letter to Stravinsky, 24 October 1915.   [2] See p. 103.
[3] Reproduced in Egon Wellesz, *Arnold Schoenberg* (Leipzig and Vienna, 1921), facing p. 122.

(ii) **Mässige Viertel**

The importance of fourths in the chord-structure, as in nos. 10 and 11 of the *Bagatelles*, was no novelty by this date although the treatment of them was. Chords of superimposed fourths had existed as early as Satie's *Fils des étoiles* (see Ex. 36 (i))—to say nothing of Beckmesser's lute—and had been an occasional component of the impressionist vocabulary (Debussy's *L'Isle joyeuse*, Ravel's 'Vallée des cloches' in *Miroirs*, and elsewhere). Schoenberg himself had introduced them in *Pelleas und Melisande* just before the appearance of the 'Pelléas' theme, where they sound less daring in their context and threaded through by the 'Mélisande' theme (Ex. 54) than when quoted in isolation, as they are in the *Harmonielehre*,[1] though he claims there that they occur 'quite isolated . . . as the expression of a mood, the strangeness of which obliged me against my will to find a new means of expression'. Furthermore, each is resolved; they are not 'emancipated' chords like Debussy's and Ravel's. But in 1905 both Mahler and Strauss (Ex. 55) employed quartal harmony and melodic lines derived from it in the Seventh Symphony (i) and *Salome* (ii) and (iii).

So the celebrated opening of Schoenberg's *Kammersymphonie* was in

[1] p. 450.

Ex. 54

Ex. 55

Ex. 56

itself only abreast of other German music of its date (1906); the fourth-chordal climax of the *Kammersymphonie* (Ex. 56), occurs later, at the end of the 'development'. Quartal music on this scale is the furthest possible reaction from hyper-chromaticism. What was new about the horn-theme was that it was 'pure music'. Whereas Mahler and Strauss and Schoenberg himself in *Pelleas* had turned to quartal music to express a strange mood, or tense excitement, or to symbolize the prophet's inflexibility or suggest the barbaric, it now existed for its own sake as it was to do in Berg's Piano Sonata, Bartók's Tenth and Eleventh *Bagatelles*, the end of his First String Quartet (1907) and very much of his Second (1915–17), and a great deal of other music of the next decade. In the 'Spring Divinations' of *The Rite of Spring* (1912) Stravinsky throws in Schoenberg's six-note quartal chord (Ex. 56) as the climax to an ostinato pattern just before fig. 18. A similar accumulation of perfect fifths occurs half a dozen bars earlier (see Ex. 57).

Like the whole-tone mode, quartal music generally remained an adjunct to more normal music. Except the egregious Rebikov,[1] who had certainly employed occasional fourth-chords in undistinguished piano-pieces of the late 1890s but whose monstrosities of quartal commonplace, the *Belïya pesni* (Chansons blanches), Op. 48, and *Dances*, Op. 51, for piano, date from *c.* 1913, the only composer to construct a system of fourth-chords was Skryabin. Unlike almost all his contemporaries, Skryabin did not confine himself mainly to the perfect or diatonic fourths derived from impressionism though he employed them in his early works in passing (cf. Ex. 12, bar 3); nor was his basic chord a purely intellectual conception.[2] When he began to compose his orchestral *Prometheus* in 1908, he consciously based it on what he called his 'synthetic harmony': the basic chord C, F sharp, B flat, E, A, D, an arrangement in fourths of the scale C, D, E, F sharp, A, B flat which corresponds to 8, 9, 10, 11, 13, 14 in the harmonic series —or, rather, to the approximation attainable on the piano keyboard— and also differs only in one note (A instead of G sharp) from the whole-tone scale. According to Leonid Sabaneyev, it was he who devised *ex post facto* the theory of overtone derivation, which was then appropriated by the composer 'almost as a dogma',[3] but Skryabin's

---

[1] See p. 36.

[2] For a survey of Skryabin's harmonic evolution see C. C. J. von Gleich, *Die sinfonischen Werke von Alexander Skrjabin* (Bilthoven, 1963), pp. 85–90. Paul Dickenmann, *Die Entwicklung der Harmonik bei A. Skrjabin* (Bern, 1935) deals only with his pre-Promethean harmony.

[3] Sabaneyev, *Vospominaniya o Skryabine* (Moscow, 1925), p. 227. Schoenberg likewise held that 'dissonances . . . are merely more remote consonances in the series of overtones' (*Structural Functions of Harmony* (London, 1954), p. 193).

Ex. 57

piano-playing fingers had already discovered the sound of the 'Promethean chord', no doubt empirically, in the course of natural evolution from the post-Chopinesque harmony of his early compositions. Two examples occur in the second and third bars of the Prelude, Op. 37, no. 3, written in 1903:

Ex. 58

The technique is, of course, fundamentally different from the block treatment of quartal harmony, though it is equally non-functional. When Rebikov hit on something surprisingly close to the 'Promethean chord' in 1907, in his 'musico-psychological tale' *Bezdna* (The Abyss, based on Leonid Andreyev's story), he could do nothing better than side-slip it to accompany the moment when the student 'gazes rapturously' at the schoolgirl:

Ex. 59

But Skryabin, having taken his basic harmony as a concord, treats it freely in any transposition, breaking it up into melodic fragments and figuration, and admitting 'foreign' notes as appoggiaturas or passing-notes. The chromatic parallel ninths which open the Étude, Op. 65, no. 1 (1911–12), are drawn across Promethean chords as a nineteenth-century composer would have drawn a simple chromatic scale across conventional harmonies. In *Prometheus* itself the complete six-note chord is used, but in Skryabin's post-Promethean compositions the last partial may be omitted, as in 'Étrangeté', Op. 63, no. 2 (1911–12),[1] while in the seventh Sonata, Op. 64 (1911–12) it is flattened.

The paradox of Skryabin, the arch-romantic with apocalyptic visions of an art, or at least an act, embracing all humanity, is that he should have invented a musical language of non-communication, a language the extra-musical sense of which only he could understand. Sabaneyev tells us[2] that Skryabin considered the passage in *Prometheus* quoted as Ex. 60 'the most tragic thing I have written in my whole life', but although Sabaneyev was closer to him than any other colleague he was quite unable to agree. Skryabin contributed as much to the final destruction of functional harmony as any of the Central Europeans, and the 'artificial' constructivism of his last works was not merely symptomatic of a tendency, like Rimsky-Korsakov's in the *Cockerel* and Stravinsky's in *The Fire-Bird*: it pointed a way—which no one exactly followed, though Schoenberg was soon to trace a parallel one—through the potential chaos of atonality. Both the Promethean chord and the twelve-note row provide synthetic nuclei for a composition and since the one can be 'verticalized' into chords and the other 'horizontalized' into melodic lines, they appear superficially to be opposite sides of the same coin. But the notes of the Promethean chord are not 'related to one another' in Schoenberg's sense, and the six-note scale deducible from the chord (without transposition) is apt to sound like a chromatically altered diatonic scale, though it lacks points of tonic, dominant and leading-note function. In his last compositions, the five Preludes, Op. 74, of 1914, Skryabin introduced such a profusion of 'foreign' chromatic notes that he reached a kind of twelve-note music, but it is certainly not the Schoenbergian kind.[3]

A rather younger Russian contemporary of Skryabin's, Nikolay Roslavets (1880–1944), did actually (for instance, in his *Deux Composi-tions pour piano* (1915)) go farther than Skryabin toward twelve-note music.[4] In an autobiographical article published in 1924,[5] Roslavets—while denying that his system of *sintetakkordï* of '6 to 8 or more notes' owed anything to post-Promethean Skryabin or to Schoenberg—admitted that 'Skryabin (in a musical-formal respect, but in no wise ideologically [Roslavets was an anti-romantic constructivist]) is of

---

[1] Recorded in *The History of Music in Sound*, x.   [2] Op. cit., p. 228.

[3] On the analogies and differences between Promethean and twelve-note structures, see Zofia Lissa, 'Geschichtliche Vorform der Zwölftontechnik', *Acta Musicologica*, vii (1935), p. 15. George Perle, *Serial Composition and Atonality* (Berkeley and Los Angeles, 1962), p. 41, considers Skryabin as a 'nondodecaphonic serialist'.

[4] See Detlef Gojowy, 'Nikolaj Andreevic Roslavec, ein früher Zwölftonkomponist', *Die Musikforschung*, xxii (1969), p. 22.

[5] 'Nik. A. Roslavets o sebe i svoem tvorchestve', *Sovremennaya muzïka*, no. 5 (November–December 1924), p. 132.

Ex. 60

course far nearer to me than Schoenberg, whose work, I confess, I have got to know only comparatively recently'.

SCHOENBERG

Compared with the brilliantly erratic side-track of Skryabin's Promethean experiment, Schoenberg's progress from romanticism, through expressionism and non-serial atonality,[1] seems a straightforward, even logical process of evolution. For it was he who gathered the harmonic fruits of impressionism—we must take note of his claim to have discovered them independently of Debussy[2]—and integrated their free dissonance with post-Wagnerian harmony and then with the polyphonic devices of 'absolute music'. In a lecture given in 1941[3] he described the position around 1908, and hence his own historical role, with great accuracy:

[Debussy's] harmonies, without constructive meaning, often served the coloristic purpose of expressing moods and pictures [which] . . . thus became constructive elements, incorporated in the musical functions; they produced a sort of emotional comprehensibility. In this way [as in post-Wagnerian harmony] tonality was already dethroned in practise, if not in theory. This alone would perhaps not have caused a radical change in compositional technique. However, such a change became necessary when there occurred simultaneously a development which ended in . . . the *emancipation of the dissonance*. . . . One no longer expected . . . resolutions of Strauss' discords; one was not disturbed by Debussy's non-functional harmonies, or by the harsh counterpoint of later composers. . . .
   A style based on this premise [emancipation of 'Wagner's, Strauss', Moussorgsky's, Debussy's, Mahler's, Puccini's, and Reger's more remote dissonances'] treats dissonances like consonances and renounces a tonal center. By avoiding the establishment of a key modulation is excluded. . . .

He then goes on to describe the problems raised by the first compositions in this style by himself and his pupils Webern and Berg. 'The foremost characteristics of these pieces *in statu nascendi* were their extreme expressiveness and their extraordinary brevity.' Hitherto, harmony 'had served as a means of distinguishing the features of the form'; transitional passages demanded different harmonic treatment from those leading to cadence-points; 'harmonic variation could be executed intelligently and logically only with due consideration of the fundamental meaning of the harmonies':

Fulfillment of all these functions . . . could scarcely be assured with chords whose constructive values had not as yet been explored. Hence, it seemed at first impossible to compose pieces of complicated organization or of great

---

[1] See chapter 1, pp. 15–17.   [2] *Harmonielehre*, pp. 435, 438, 450–1.
[3] Printed in *Style and Idea* (New York, 1950), particularly pp. 104–6.

length. A little later I discovered how to construct larger forms by following a text or a poem. . . .

But it was only 'after many unsuccessful attempts during a period of approximately twelve years' that Schoenberg 'laid the foundations for a new procedure in musical construction which seemed fitted to replace those structural differentiations provided formerly by tonal harmonies': the method of the twelve-note series.[1]

At first there was no question of 'absolute music'. Schoenberg re-emphasized the 'extreme expressiveness', the 'extreme emotionality', of his pre-serial atonal compositions—though they were no more successful than Skryabin's in communicating their message to a wider circle. And for the same reason: the message was in a language comprehensible to few but the composer himself. But the real problem, as Schoenberg makes abundantly clear, was not of expression but of construction, a purely musical problem, and the search for a solution forced Schoenberg to concentrate his thought on the structural devices of 'pure' music: canon and ostinato, inversion and variation. He had very early shown a predilection for canon: for instance in the first movement of the early String Quartet in D (1897) at the beginning of the development:

Ex. 61

_____
[1] See *infra*, pp. 341 ff.

and in the finale of the same work (bars 65 ff.) where the close canon between first violin and cello is much more 'classical' than the canon—also between solo violin and solo cello—in Tove's first song in the *Gurrelieder*. Now he began to construct with microscopic ingenuity, as in the first piece of Op. 11:

Ex. 62

In Op. 19, no. 2, an ingenious analyst[1] has discovered a foreshadowing of serial construction and at the same time (1911) Schoenberg felt the need to write a textbook that should 'thoroughly impart to a student the handicraft of our art, as a carpenter always can'.[2] The highest point of his own craftsmanship at this period was reached in the later numbers of *Pierrot lunaire* (1912), for instance, no. 17, 'Parodie', which begins with a canon by inversion between viola and clarinet, while the *Sprechstimme* follows the viola exactly at a bar's distance (Ex. 63).

At the repeat this theme becomes a normal canon between *Sprechstimme* and piccolo, to which is now added another canon by inversion between viola and clarinet; the 'accompanying' piano part is also freely varied. In the next number 'Der Mondfleck' similar ingenuities are compounded by retrograde movement. Not all the numbers of *Pierrot lunaire* are as intellectually constructed as this. No. 8, 'Nacht' is a passacaglia, as

[1] Rudolf Wille, 'Reihentechnik in Schönbergs opus 19, 2', *Die Musikforschung*, xix (1966), p. 42.
[2] *Harmonielehre*, p. 7.

Ex. 63

(Knitting-needles, polished and gleaming, in her grey hair,)

the composer points out. (The first of the *Orchestral Pieces*, Op. 16, is held together by a three-note ostinato figure in the bass.) But despite the ultra-romantic decadence of the Giraud-Hartleben poems, a decadence subtly suggested rather than expressed by much of the music of the 'three-times seven melodramas', 'Parodie' and 'Der Mondfleck' are essays in constructivism as 'purely' musical as the works of 1923, the *Klavierstücke*, Op. 23, and the Serenade, Op. 24, in which Schoenberg began to 'compose with twelve notes'. They are not neo-classical, any more than Reger's fugues are neo-classical—or the overture to *Ariadne auf Naxos* or *The Rite of Spring*. More deserving of that epithet are some of the French compositions of the War years: Fauré's song-cycle *Le Jardin clos*, Ravel's Trio, Debussy's piano *Études* and the *Sonates pour divers instruments*, of the first of which—for cello and piano—he himself claimed that the proportions and form were 'presque classique, dans le bon sens du mot'.[1] But all are symptoms of the same turning away from romanticism, the same preoccupation with the basic materials of music for their own sake, which were to characterize the mainstream of Western music from the 1920s for the next half-century.

[1] Quoted by Vallas, op. cit., p. 365.

III

STAGE WORKS: 1890–1918

By MARTIN COOPER

WHEN Wagner died in Venice on 13 February 1883, his music was still hotly discussed but the works had been very little staged outside Germany and Austria. Elsewhere *Tristan und Isolde* had been given only in London, *Die Meistersinger von Nürnberg* only in Riga, London, Copenhagen, and Holland; and complete performances of *Der Ring des Nibelungen* only in London, Brussels, and Amsterdam. Paris did not have a performance of *Lohengrin* until 1887, followed by *Die Walküre* in 1893 and the complete *Ring* cycle only in 1911. Bayreuth and Munich were places of pilgrimage for all Wagnerians, and the list of French composers who made this pilgrimage during the seventies and eighties includes all the most gifted and distinguished of the rising generation. Places of pilgrimage, however, cater by definition for the converted; and the large majority of opera-goers outside German-speaking countries, and a very high proportion of musicians everywhere, had had very little opportunity to judge Wagner's works except by isolated passages transferred from their context to the concert-hall. When these works began to be generally performed and became familiar, it took only a single generation to discover that, far from heralding the dawn of a new musical era, Wagner's music represented the all but final stage in a great musical epoch which had begun in the second half of the sixteenth century. Much, too, of what Wagner and his immediate disciples had believed to be of universal significance proved to be either personal in application, or relevant at most to German composers for the stage.

In spite of this, opera during the years between 1890 and 1918 was dominated by Wagner's shadow, and every composer for the stage was forced to adopt an attitude to Wagner's music and to Wagner's ideas of dramaturgy. It was possible to accept the one and reject the other, as happened in France, and outright rejection of both became increasingly common; but it was impossible to ignore the questions that Wagner had asked or the answers which his own works had provided.

CENTRAL EUROPE

Wagner's fundamental contention that symphonic and chamber music belonged to the past and that the future of music lay with the music-drama rested on twin generalizations, of his own personal gifts on the one hand and of German musical aptitudes and conditions on the other. His further identification of German music with himself was proved unjustified; but not until his influence had done much to weaken the strong national traditions which had hitherto divided the operatic world into largely self-subsistent compartments. It is not surprising that this influence was strongest in Germany and Austria, where Wagner's dramatic theories were linked to literary, intellectual, and even political movements, and *Musikdrama* appeared not only as the latest development in the history of opera, but also as the first fully mature embodiment of the form in wholly Germanic terms. Wagner's expansion and enrichment of the orchestra, and its greater part in defining as well as supporting the drama, were universally copied; but his conception of opera as symphony proved to have a limited personal validity and was ultimately rejected by even his most enthusiastic followers. The most gifted of these was Richard Strauss (1864–1949), whose first opera *Guntram* (1894) is a naïve continuation of the knightly world of *Lohengrin*, while in *Feuersnot* (1901) we have an example of that specifically German delight in an idealized version of the national past, mythical or historical, viewed in the same golden, transfiguring, and largely diatonic light that Wagner had created for *Die Meistersinger*, enhanced by a nostalgic counterpoint employed to heighten the illusion of the medieval past. Although *Tristan* continued to be the most musically influential of Wagner's works, it was *Parsifal* and *Meistersinger* that were most copied by opera-composers of this period.

The *Meistersinger* world, as we may for convenience call it, proved a particularly rich vein. It was exploited successfully by Engelbert Humperdinck (1854–1921), who had worked for a time at Bayreuth as Wagner's assistant, in two *Märchenoper*, or fairy-story operas, in which a Wagnerian harmonic and orchestral style is scaled down so that the disproportion between manner and matter is not offensive. *Hänsel und Gretel* (1893) belongs to a class not uncommon in the nineteenth century: a work of art conceived ostensibly for children but in fact reflecting an adult's sentimental idealization of childhood and very little appreciated by children themselves. It is musically inferior to *Königskinder* (Royal Children) (1910), where the medieval atmosphere is plainly modelled on that of *Die Meistersinger*, and there is even a boys' dance that suggests an obvious parallel with Wagner's apprentices.

A more important parallel is the personification of the power of music in the character of Der Spielmann, whose (offstage) violin solo in Act III provides the focal point of the drama, like Walther von Stolzing's Prize Song; and the children's music, which Humperdinck introduces in the same spirit as the opening chorale of *Die Meistersinger*, emphasizes the naïve, folk-like element in the work.

Ex. 64

(Dear Mr Player, all the children and I have begged and prayed for you)

The personification of music in a single character[1] and the sophisticated use of simple, popular material as a reassuring feature in intellectually demanding or emotionally threatening situations[2] are common features of opera in this period. Hugo Wolf (1860–1903) further exploited the 'golden' *Meistersinger* atmosphere in *Der Corregidor* (1896), formally weak but musically rewarding and containing a Beckmesser part in the amorous Alcalde. A different kind of Wagnerian affiliation appears in *Der arme Heinrich* (1895), the first opera of Hans Pfitzner (1869–1949). Here the music owes as much to Weber as to Wagner, but there is a clear echo of *Parsifal* in the harmonies associated with the relationship between Agnes and the wounded Heinrich. Pfitzner's *Märchenoper, Die Rose vom Liebesgarten* (1901) is an essay in that sophisticated simplicity more successfully exploited by Humperdinck, and it was admired and performed by Gustav Mahler, whose own music contains many of the same features that distinguish the operas written by members of the first generation after Wagner's death— idealization of an imaginary past (*Des Knaben Wunderhorn* songs) and

[1] Cf. Beppe in Mascagni's *L'Amico Fritz* (1891), Sadko in Rimsky-Korsakov's *Sadko* (1898), Floria Tosca in Puccini's *Tosca* (1900), the Jongleur in Massenet's *Jongleur de Notre Dame* (1902), the Dark Fiddler in Delius's *Romeo und Julia auf dem Dorfe* (1907), the Italian Singer in Strauss's *Der Rosenkavalier* (1911), and Palestrina in Pfitzner's *Palestrina* (1917).

[2] E.g. the shepherd boy at the opening of Puccini's *Tosca*, Act III; the child's piano practice in Leoncavallo's *Zaza*, Act II; the children's Christmas song in Massenet's *Werther*; and the fisher-girl's humming a folk-song at the opening of d'Indy's *L'Étranger*.

the innocence of folk- or child-elements contrasted with psychological complexity and suffering (Symphonies 3, 4 and 8). In the operas of Siegfried Wagner (1869–1930), Wagner's son and Humperdinck's pupil, humour is added to the symbolism of the *Märchenoper* (*Der Bärenhäuter*, 1899); and Austria produced a variety of popular post-Wagnerian crossings with folk-music in *Der Evangelimann* (1895) by Wilhelm Kienzl (1857–1941) and *Der Musikant* (1910) and *Das höllisch Gold* (1916) by Julius Bittner (1874–1939).

It was not only the example of Wagner's music, or his professed belief that myth and symbol were the proper concern of the music-drama, that turned the minds of many composers in this direction when searching for a libretto. The Symbolist movement in France, led by the poet Stéphane Mallarmé, had itself been influenced by Wagner's theories[1] and was in its turn to furnish composers with the new ideals of hermetic reserve and indirect allusiveness characteristic of a mandarin art. Symbolism appeared as a reaction against the realism, or naturalism, that marked the development of the French novel in the hands of Flaubert, Zola, and Maupassant; and realism and symbolism were the dominant elements in opera between 1890 and 1910, at first strongly contrasted but later amalgamating in many instances.

Both the mosaic-like structure of Wagner's musical idiom involving an intricate system of cross-references, and the richly poetic and evocative resources of the Wagnerian orchestra clearly corresponded more closely to the Symbolists' use of language in poetry than to the prose of the naturalist novelist. Wagner's own symbolic conception of opera was carried to its logical extreme in the two works that Strauss wrote after *Feuersnot*—*Salome* (1905) and *Elektra* (1909). In both of these the role of the orchestra is more important than in any of Wagner's works, and the structure and even the scale recall those of Strauss's tone-poems. Oscar Wilde wrote his *Salome*, on which Strauss based his opera, in French, and the central figure was inspired by Gustave Moreau's picture 'L'Apparition'; but Wilde's reference to 'refrains whose recurring motifs make the poem like a piece of music and bind it together as a ballad'[2] almost certainly betrays a superficial acquaintance with Wagnerian theory. His description of the work to Sarah Bernhardt as 'quelque chose de curieux et de sensuel'[3] suggests that, like Debussy, he was already interested in the so-called 'theatre of cruelty'; and the perverted eroticism of *Salome*, which gave the work a *succès de scandale*

---

[1] See Mallarmé, 'Richard Wagner, rêverie d'un poète français', *Revue wagnérienne*, no. 7 (August, 1885) p. 195. For a study of the impact of Wagner's ideas on French literature see Eliot Zuckerman, *The first 100 years of Wagner's 'Tristan'* (New York, 1964), pp. 83–122.

[2] Oscar Wilde, *De Profundis* (London, 1905), 26th ed., p. 66.

[3] Quoted in Norman Del Mar, *Richard Strauss* (London, 1962), i, p. 240.

PLATE I

STRAUSS'S *SALOME*, 1905 (*see p. 148*)

The dance of the seven veils in the original Dresden production

clearly foreseen by the composer, provided a piquant sauce welcome to jaded *fin de siècle* appetites. Although the crucial Dance of the Seven Veils[1] is as weak and commonplace as the dance section in Strauss's *Also sprach Zarathustra*, and Jochanaan's music has the flat, oleaginous quality of much painting of the Nazarene School, *Salome* is a brilliant tour de force unique in the history of opera. The characterization of every member of the Idumaean court is needle-sharp and concise, and Strauss applied all his phenomenal orchestral virtuosity and musical inventiveness to set his characters in high relief against the general background of sultry, acrid hysteria. Psychological motivation is supplied by the ingenious cross-references which form the web of the music, whose nervous plasticity follows every physical movement or gesture by corresponding rhythmic and melodic shapes as skilfully chosen as in the finest of the tone-poems. Ex. 65 (i) expresses Salome's violence and perversity, (ii) Jochanaan's prophetic conviction:

In *Elektra* Strauss collaborated for the first time with the Austrian poet Hugo von Hofmannsthal, whose libretto is deeply coloured by Nietzsche's insistence on the part played in Greek tragedy by the dark Dionysian world as a counterweight to the bright Apollonian air of Goethe's *griechische Heiterkeit*. The difference between Strauss's thematic vocabulary here and in *Salome* is immediately noticeable in the simple and majestic phrase associated throughout the work with the figure of Agamemnon, and providing the *Grundgestalt* for countless psychologically significant derivations and variations (Ex. 66 (i)). By the side of this diatonic fanfare the theme associated with Klytemnestra has the same penetrating and concentrated suggestion of perverse evil as is to be found in *Salome* (Ex. 66 (ii)):

---

[1] See pl. I.

Ex. 66

(i)

(ii)

There is a further parallel between the two operas in the figure of
Chrysothemis, Elektra's sister who stands, like Jochanaan in *Salome*,
outside the main preoccupations of the drama. But whereas Jochanaan's
austere and unbending ethical idealism prompted only second-hand
reminiscences in the composer, Strauss's natural sympathies were
stirred by the impassioned femininity and life-affirming instincts of
Chrysothemis, the broad lyrical sweep and diatonic strength of whose
music sets her in harsh contrast to the rest of the characters. It is
significant that in the scene with Orestes even the obsessed, half-crazed
Elektra catches some of this vital warmth:

Ex. 67

Au - gen mich sehn, Traum - bild,

mir ge - schenk-tes Traum - bild schö - -

pp

cresc.

- - - ner als al - le Träu - - me.

(O let me behold your eyes, vision that has been granted to me, lovelier than any dream)

It is in such ecstatic, long-breathed passages as these, often forming extended cadences on an enormous scale, that Strauss's debt to Wagner is most clear; and he was to write them to the end of his life, always for one, two, or even three soprano voices. Indeed a number of duets and a trio of this kind formed some of the climactic moments in his next opera, *Der Rosenkavalier* (1911).

The collaboration with Hofmannsthal had led Strauss into a world of literary sophistication that he would hardly have entered otherwise, and it is to Hofmannsthal's brilliant recreation of late eighteenth-century Viennese society that *Der Rosenkavalier* owed much of its success. This work is in essence a comedy, but so richly complicated by sentiment and spectacle that the comic element is largely overlaid. The Marschallin's levée in Act I and the presentation of the Silver Rose in Act II, on which the composer lavishes all his extraordinary gifts of harmonic and orchestral invention for their own sake rather than for specific dramatic effect, recall the great tableaux and divertissements of Meyerbeer's operas; and it is only in Act III that the comic element, represented by Baron Ochs, predominates unequivocally. In the Marschallin's music Strauss made himself the mouthpiece of that nostalgia that characterizes so much of the art of this period, in which Mahler's *Sehnsucht nach der Kindheit* was only exceeded by Rakhmaninov's more radical and unqualified nostalgia—the Buddhistic 'longing for non-existence' (*toska nebïtiya*) of Alexander Blok's poems. The Marschallin's nostalgia is ostensibly for her vanished youth, but her desire 'to put the clocks back in the night' is in fact a symbol of that deeper nostalgia for the past that had already played an important part in Hofmannsthal's early lyric poetry. As early as 1893 he wrote in the Prologue to Artur Schnitzler's *Anatol*:

> Hohe Götter, Taxushecken,
> Wappen nimmermehr vergoldet,
> Sphinxe, durch das Dickicht schimmernd,
> Knarrend öffnen sich die Tore.
> Mit verschlagenen Kaskaden
> und verschlafenen Tritonen,
> Rokoko verstaubt und lieblich,
> Seht . . . das Wien des Canaletto,
> Wien von siebzehn hundert sechzig.

In his case this was not simply a longing for a vanished innocence and simplicity, such as we find in Mahler's symphonies and Humperdinck's operas, nor even an idealization of the past in the manner of Wagner's *Meistersinger*. It was rather a delight in what he felt to be the richness, variety, and vitality of an older society, including its inhumanity and injustice. Baron Ochs represents that society's unregenerate face, the selfishness and ruthlessness of feudalism; and although Ochs is defeated, neither Hofmannsthal nor Strauss conceals his sympathy with the defeated. Beneath its smiling surface *Der Rosenkavalier* is in fact a 'reactionary' work of art which owes much of its popularity to that nostalgia for 'the good old days' that since 1900 has been a powerful, if not always acknowledged, emotional force in the bourgeoisie of Western Europe.

Again, as in *Salome* and *Elektra*, the fascination of Strauss's score lies in the skilful contrasting of the familiar and the novel, an abundant diatonic melodiousness (the Marschallin's soliloquy and the Italian Singer's aria in Act I, Sophie's music and Ochs's waltzes in Act II and the trio and final duet in Act III) and the more complex, chromatic style of the intervening passages in which these form points of rest, exactly like the closed forms of the old opera, which are in fact here resurrected. In Strauss's next collaboration with Hofmannsthal, *Ariadne auf Naxos* (1912), the disparate elements are presented with more sophistication, first by the scheme of presenting a play (or plays) within a play and then even more strikingly by giving a *commedia dell'arte* improvisation and an *opera seria* simultaneously. This device may perhaps be regarded as a type-figuring of the schizophrenia which marked much of the art of these years immediately before the First World War. Historically it is interesting that Strauss, who started his career in the theatre as an enthusiastic Wagnerian, should have returned in *Der Rosenkavalier* to the closed forms and even, in the Italian Singer's aria, to the *bel canto* of nineteenth-century Italian opera. In *Ariadne auf Naxos* his taste for the most mellifluous possible combinations (three soprano voices and harps in a D flat major trio) is even more marked; and in Zerbinetta's aria he resurrected coloratura as an expression of character. This had not been attempted in Western Europe since Delibes's *Lakmé* (1883), with the possible exception of Catalani's *La Wally* (1892), where La Wally's 'Canzon del Edelweiss' adds a fantastic, unreal note to a character in other ways fiercely realistic.

ITALY AND THE NEW REALISM

Although realism might appear to be of all aesthetic attitudes the one least compatible with so highly artificial an art-form as opera, it was in fact the influence of the French realist, or *naturaliste*, school of writers— and above all Emile Zola, whose often brutal novels of contemporary life began to appear in the seventies—that gave rise to the movement which carried opera equally far from the historical or exotic world popularized by Meyerbeer and his followers and the world of myth or legend which Wagner chose for his music dramas. Just as Zola himself had found inspiration for his new approach to the novel in Gustave Flaubert's *Madame Bovary* (1857), so opera-composers of the next generation found for the first time since Verdi's *La Traviata* (1853) something like a window on contemporary life in Bizet's *Carmen* (1875).[1] The extraordinary aristocratic finesse of Bizet's music and his instinctive distancing, or stylizing, of the popular, 'vulgar', element to a great extent masked the real originality of *Carmen*. Unfortunately very few of the composers who were tempted to follow his example possessed either his purely musical gifts or that instinct, which can only be called classical, for the effortless conversion of raw vulgarities into the material for a serious work of art.

Although in France there are realistic elements in Delibes's *Lakmé*, and a collaboration between Zola himself and Alfred Bruneau (1857–1934)[2] began in 1891, it was in Italy that realism in opera first developed as a distinct movement, under the name of *verismo*. The Sicilian village-drama of *Cavalleria rusticana* (1890) is innocent of any attempt at distancing, and the composer Pietro Mascagni (1863–1945), was content with the same naïve criteria of simple, sensuous, and passionate melody that would have been applied in real life by the characters of Giovanni Verga's story. *Cavalleria rusticana* may be regarded as an instinctive, unconscious Italian protest against the 'mandarin' music-drama, the infiltration of even the Italian operatic world by Wagnerian theories. *Pagliacci* (1892) is only slightly more sophisticated musically, and the sentimentality of popular melodrama is equally dominant in both works. The composer, Ruggiero Leoncavallo (1858–1919), had in fact personal experience of the life of a touring company, though on a different level from that shown in *Pagliacci* and nearer to the comparatively polite demi-monde which he used as the background for his *Zazà* (1900). In Mascagni's *Iris* (1898), realism is tempered not only by the exotic Japanese setting but by a strong note of poetic fantasy introduced by the librettist, Giovanni Illica. In the opening scene, for instance, a hidden chorus makes itself the mouthpiece of the rising sun with the words 'Son Io! son Io la Vita! son la Beltà, la Luce e il Calor!', and this reappears at the end of the work, when the heroine has jumped from a window into what proves to be the town's main drain, where she encounters the rag-pickers, symbols of social rejection whom we are to meet again in the masterpiece of French realistic opera, *Louise* (1900) by Gustave Charpentier (1860–1956). There is an interesting example of what was to become a common feature in *art nouveau*

---

[1] See Vol. IX.   [2] See below, p. 164.

music, not only opera: the wordless chorus singing *bocca chiusa*. The geisha chorus opens Act II of *Iris* thus:[1]

Ex. 68

Lentamento

a bocca chiusa, accompagnandosi al suono di samisen e tam-tam delle altre guechas

This interlarding of an often crudely realistic modern story with decorative, and fundamentally inorganic, symbolism became increasingly common and represents a bridge between veristic and mythological or fairytale opera.

Leoncavallo's *La Bohème* (1897), based on Henri Murger's *Vie de Bohème*, contained none of these unrealistic elements, but was unable to support the inevitable comparison with an opera with the same title produced a few months earlier by the composer who was to prove the only undoubted master among the Italian *veristi*, Giacomo Puccini (1858–1924). Puccini turned for his librettos to a very different class of French writer, and no vitalistic symbolism such as we find in Zola was to be found in Prévost, Murger, or Sardou. Apart from Verdi, the productions of whose last years towered above all other Italian music of the day, the strongest influence in Puccini's musical formation was Jules Massenet (1842–1912), whose *Manon* (1884) prompted Puccini's first mature work, *Manon Lescaut* (1893). To his librettist, Emilio Praga, he observed very truly that 'Massenet may feel his subject with the powder and the minuets. I shall feel it with a despairing passion'[2] and this *passione disperata* is the keynote of Puccini's music, a lyrical outpouring that puts into the shade the eighteenth-century French graces which had formed an important attraction in the older man's work. In two of the three operas which followed—*La Bohème* (1896), *Tosca* (1900),[3] and *Madama Butterfly* (1904)—Puccini turned again to

[1] Similar choruses are to be found in Puccini's *Madama Butterfly* and Rakhmaninov's *Francesca da Rimini*, in the Sirènes in the third of Debussy's *Nocturnes*, and in Delius *passim*.

[2] Quoted in Mosco Carner, *Puccini* (London, 1958), p. 57.   [3] See pl. II.

French sources; but in each case his librettists, Giacomo Giacosa and Luigi Illica, faithfully presented him with versions of Murger and Sardou that allowed full scope for the despair as well as the passion in the composer's personality. If this despairing quality in Puccini's lyricism had its immediate origin in his own personal psychology, it also corresponded to a more general mood in the public, a vague emotional unrest and presentiment of future disaster that found poignant expression in the almost funereal melodies, which have often escaped notice among Puccini's innumerable expressions of erotic passion. In Act II, scene 5, of *Tosca* the Andante sostenuto, with muted violins playing on the G string, could be the funeral march not simply of Scarpia but of a whole civilization, like the slow movement of Elgar's Second Symphony written ten years later.

Ex. 69

PLATE II

PUCCINI'S *TOSCA*, 1900 *(see p. 156)*

A poster advertising the first performance

The frailty of Puccini's heroines and the fated character of their loves had a sentimental and sensual appeal for his listeners similar to that which Verdi's *La Traviata* had enjoyed half a century earlier. Only this appeal was now greatly enhanced by the obscure, and often unacknowledged, sense of moral and social insecurity, of enjoying the last uncertain splendours of an age of European civilization that was unmistakeably coming to an end. In this sense Puccini's relationship to Verdi is exactly paralleled by Strauss's relationship to Wagner. In each case we can observe the characteristic marks of a decadence— the replacing of strength by violence, the exclusive concern with the subjective interests of the individual and the constant demand for emotional extremes, reflected in dynamic and other markings of expression formerly reserved for climactic moments.

The elements of melodrama and sadism in Puccini's works are not without parallel in nineteenth-century opera, including Wagner; but they had never been so nakedly exposed, even exploited. The description of Mimi's physical and emotional distress in Act III of *La Bohème* has a gloating quality, to which Puccini added a macabre note of banality by using a thinly disguised version of the fashionable 'hesitation' waltz (Ex. 70).

The lengthy and detailed exploitation of Cavaradossi's torturing in Act II of *Tosca*, and its close linking with Scarpia's physical desire for

Ex. 70

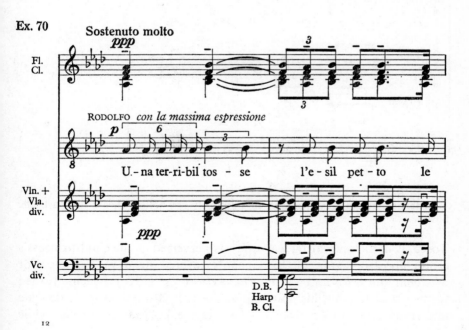

(A terrible cough racks her thin chest, already her hollow cheeks have a hectic flush)

Tosca, is in its less glaring way quite as perverted as the child-princess's erotic apostrophizing of Jochanaan's severed head in *Salome*. For *Madama Butterfly* and *La Fanciulla del West* (1910) Puccini turned to the novelette; but his handling of the orchestra, at its most delicate and transparent in *La Bohème*, grew increasingly adventurous, while his harmonic language was increasingly enriched by the absorption of the last of many French influences—the elements of Debussy's style to be found in whole-tone chords, sequences of block harmonies and atmospheric chains of fifths. The last and most powerful of his purely veristic operas, *Il Tabarro*, appeared in 1918 in the *Trittico*, with the convent opera *Suor Angelica* (women's voices only) and *Gianni Schicchi*, a Dante-based comedy the vicious bitterness of whose humour has not always been observed. In *Turandot*, which he left unfinished at his death in 1924, Puccini returned to a type of Italian grand opera which he had done more than any other single composer to supersede. The exotic magnificence of the spectacle is often matched by the music, especially in the central scene of the three riddles; and in Liù Puccini created the last of his fragile, fated heroines pitted against hopelessly unequal odds, here represented by the pathologically cold and revengeful Turandot, a sketch for whose portrait had already appeared in the Zia Principessa of *Suor Angelica*.

THE MUSICAL LANGUAGE OF VERISMO

Opera became an increasingly popular art during the nineteenth century in Italy, where Verdi's personal devotion to the cause of Italian liberation and unity even lent it on occasion a political colouring. Only a very small group of Italian musicians and intellectuals, of whom the most distinguished was Arrigo Boito, interested themselves in Wagner's music and theories. The chief foreign influences were Meyerbeer and Massenet, both of whom contributed to that progressive popularization of musical style and manner of presentation which followed naturally on the musical enfranchisement of a wider section of the public. In the operas which Verdi wrote for Paris, and later in *Aida*, the element of orchestral and scenic display, the ambitious use of the chorus in large quasi-symphonic tableaux, and a new dramatic style of vocal virtuosity reveal Meyerbeer's influence. Following Gounod, and in conscious reaction against Meyerbeer, Massenet developed a new, intimate type of opera in which scenic display is less important and the chief emphasis is on erotically poignant melody, short-breathed and presented with the greatest possible emotional impact. The touch of realism lent by comparative informality was considerably increased by the Italian *veristi*, whose melodies often show the unmistakably melodramatic character of Italian popular speech. Irregular phrase-lengths and frequent variations of metre are interspersed with dramatic pauses. Triplet figures lend an added urgency and, combined with stylized sobs, produce an almost physical effect on the unsophisticated listener, as in *Tosca*, Act III:

Ex. 71

(The hour is past and I am dying in despair! And never have I loved life so much)

Like Diderot and Greuze in the 1750s, the *veristi* chose conventionally heart-rending subjects, cultivating in their operas a similar
larmoyant emotionalism aimed at the unsophisticated. It was not only
erotic scenes that were presented in this perfervid way. In Act I of
Andrea Chénier (1896) by Umberto Giordano (1867–1948), the hero
Gérard indignantly commiserates with his old father who has worked
for sixty years in serf-like conditions for arrogant aristocratic masters.
The free declamation follows the more formal melody in the orchestra:

Ex. 72

la for - za dei tuo   ner   –   vi

(You have been a servant for sixty years, old man! and have given freely to your
impudent, arrogant masters your loyalty, the sweat of your brow, and the strength
of your muscles)

The doubling of the melodic line in the orchestra, the pauses, the
appoggiature or stylized sobs and the final unison are well calculated to
give the scene an intensity that will stir even the dullest listener. Harmonic effects were often calculated in the same way to stun the listener,
as in the opening chords of *Tosca*; while at the opposite extreme an
almost conversational lyrical style often takes on a caressing, childlike
character, as in Mascagni's *Iris* (Act II), (Ex. 73).

If block sequences proved the simplest and most effective weapon
in the emotional arsenal of the *veristi*, Puccini in particular makes use
of altered chords of all kinds in order to extract the last refinements of
poignancy from a motif often simple in itself, as in Act IV of *La Bohème*:

Ex. 73

Larghetto mosso – con molta semplicità

Vo - glio il giar-di-no   mi - o! io voglio il mio giar-di - no,___

(I want my garden with its surrounding hedge, and my white cottage)

where the dying Mimi is represented by a mortally sick version of her original motif:

Ex. 74

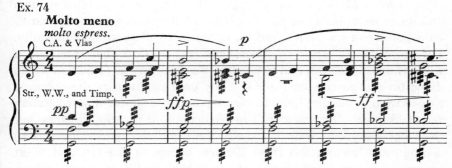

As early as 1892 Alfredo Catalani (1854–93) had used in *La Wally* more sophisticated and Wagnerian sequences in order to heighten the tension:

Ex. 75

(As adoration is known in heaven, so would I adore you)

But *verismo* in Italy was only rarely to follow this path, which was subsequently adopted by veristic composers in Germany and Austria.

As we have seen, French subjects were particularly favoured by the Italian *veristi*, and Prévost, Murger, and Sardou had furnished material for three of Puccini's most successful operas. He was to turn to France again for the first of the three operas in his *Trittico* (1918), and *Il Tabarro* may be counted as the last masterpiece of the movement which had spent its vital force by 1910. It was not only Puccini who had fallen under Massenet's spell. The whole Act III of Leoncavallo's *Zazà* (1900), which takes place in a Paris drawing-room, is redolent of Massenet, and Milio's elegiac reflections clearly echo des Grieux's dream in Act II of *Manon*.

FRANCE AND THE REACTION AGAINST REALISM

Meanwhile Massenet himself repaid the compliment implicit in such imitations when he wrote *La Navarraise* (1894), which might appear to be a parody of an Italian veristic opera in its violence and brutality. Far more characteristic of Massenet's real musical character, and a work of delicate charm and sensibility, was his *Werther* (1892), in which domestic and genre scenes are skilfully used to diversify the unhappy love-story in a manner quite foreign to the more simple-minded Italian *veristi*. Sophie's 'Le gai soleil', in particular, which distinguishes her from her sister Charlotte in exactly the same way as Strauss was to distinguish Chrysothemis from Elektra, is one of the last and finest examples of a characterization which goes back to the old *opéra comique*. (Soeur Constance in Poulenc's *Dialogues les Carmélites* (1957) is perhaps the latest avatar of this traditionally French type of character.) *Thaïs* (1894) is yet another working of the popular theme of the prostitute redeemed by love, and the ballet, in which a ballroom waltz is danced by La Perdition, even harks back to Meyerbeer's *Robert le Diable*. More in harmony with the new tastes that Massenet himself had done much to create was *Sapho* (1897), based on a story of contemporary life by Alphonse Daudet, while in *Grisélidis* (1901) and *Le Jongleur de Notre Dame* (1902) Massenet moved into the field of medieval legend without abandoning his own personal lyrical style.

If operatic realism was really foreign to Massenet, it was the whole inspiration of Alfred Bruneau (1857-1934), who chose Zola's stories for five operas written between 1891 and 1905. In *L'Attaque du moulin*, which is the most strictly realistic in character, Bruneau used one of the *Soirées de Médan* dealing with an incident in the Franco-Prussian war. *Messidor* (1897) and *L'Ouragan* (1901), on the other hand, contain strong veins of symbolism. In *Messidor* the contrast between the evil power of Gold and the beneficent Water dominates, while in *L'Ouragan* weather and scenery are used to symbolize the passions of the characters. Bruneau's music, though unmistakably French and considerably in-indebted to Massenet, also shows Wagnerian influence in the orchestra-tion. The third act of *Messidor* is an interesting example of the apparently incompatible elements that Bruneau combined in his operas. The first scene is entitled 'La Légende d'Or' and is a full-length ballet, full of symbolical figures including the Madonna and Child, set in a vast cathedral-like cave. On the other hand the second scene shows a newly installed machine for washing the gold brought down from the mountains by the river. As the curtain rises, the large wheel of the machine is shown in motion. Bruneau plainly turned to Wagner in his music for the opening of the scene, and the epic of man's mastering natural forces by mechanical power suggested to him a parallel with the primitive forces of the Valkyries:

Ex. 76

It is characteristic of French opera in general, and of Bruneau in particular, that the final scene of *Messidor* shows a return to the conventions of Latin rustic life. After the villain, Mathias, has admitted the murder of Véronique's husband and committed suicide by jumping from a rock, the smiling crops that have sprung up under the beneficent influence of the Water are solemnly blessed, in the traditional Latin liturgical formulae, by the village priest. This suggests a link with Gounod rather than with Massenet,

The same is true of the most remarkable of all French realistic operas, Charpentier's *Louise* (1900). Here the banal story of a Parisian working-girl's love-affair and her escape from parental authority is set against a romantic vision of the street and factory-life of Paris, envisaged as the Ville-Lumière and itself a product of that *art nouveau* that was subtly modifying the attitude of French artists to their materials. Charpentier's musical invention is undistinguished and his melodic ideas have a facile sentimental appeal (and even a preference for triplet-phrases, as in Louise's 'Depuis le jour') similar to that of the lesser Italian *veristi*. The very naïveté and plasticity of his style, however, the absence of all academic stiffness and the suggestion of mysterious vital forces present beneath the commonplace surface of everyday life were novel.

These features were to find expression of a very different kind in the *Pelléas et Mélisande* (1902) of Claude Debussy (1862–1918), where the reaction against realism appears at its most marked. Debussy had already shown in his cantata *La Damoiselle élue* (1888) his sympathy with the ideals of the English Pre-Raphaelites, which were at the root of *art nouveau*[1]—the freely flowing, plant-like arabesque, the sinuous and mysterious femininity whose misleadingly 'chaste' contours and anaemic complexion barely conceal a sophisticated sensuality, and the hushed palette and matt surfaces that give an equally misleading impression of monastic tranquillity. In Maeterlinck's poem Debussy found a perfect literary expression of these features, and in addition a scale of moral values dominated by compassion in the face of human suffering and the acknowledgement of the mystery of human existence, a rejection of the too easy optimism of scientific materialism and of Nietzsche's philosophy of power. In retreat from, yet still deeply marked by his early Wagnerian fervours, Debussy had come upon a score of Mussorgsky's *Boris Godunov* which had suggested to him rhythms, phrase-shapes, and harmonies useful in his search for a new dramatic language and a new musical prosody for the French language. A systematic use of the whole-tone scale and its resulting harmonies

[1] See below p. 183.

hitherto used only in isolated passages for dramatic or decorative purposes by Liszt and his Russian followers, enabled Debussy to avoid the emphatic statements and rhetorical cadences conventionally associated with the opera. The echo of ecclesiastical modes heard in the very opening bars seems to set the action of *Pelléas* outside chronological time and topographical space; and it is followed immediately by the pliable, floating motif that suggests the passive movement of weed in a gently flowing stream—an image of human powerlessness against the flow of events.

Ex. 77

Debussy's views on dramaturgy and the part to be played in the drama by the orchestra are reflected in a conversation, reported by Jean Cocteau, where Debussy quoted with approval the advice of Erik Satie. 'There is no need for the orchestra to grimace when a character comes on to the stage. Do the trees in the scenery grimace? What we have to do is to create a musical scenery, a musical atmosphere in which the characters of the drama move and talk.'[1]

In spite of many echoes of Wagner (particularly *Parsifal*) in Debussy's harmony, and frequent almost verbatim quotations of Mussorgsky's *Boris Godunov* (mostly Pimen's music)[2] Debussy's score is wholly original in conception and texture. The handling of the unaccented

---

[1] Quoted in Rollo Myers, *Erik Satie* (London, 1948), p. 32.
[2] For *Parsifal* see e.g. the Lent section in the orchestral interlude between Act II, scenes 1 and 2. For *Boris Godunov* see Act II, scene 2, the orchestral introduction to Act IV, and Act III, scene 2. Debussy's two-bar structures are also of Russian origin.

French language, to which the emphatic accentuation proper to both German and Italian is completely alien, is faithful throughout to the muted understatements and elusiveness of Maeterlinck's text. The breathless simplicity of the lovers' declaration is characteristic and unique in operatic literature. Having set the scene, the orchestra is suddenly silent:

Ex. 78

Je t'ai-me.   Je t'aime aus - si. Oh! qu'as tu dit, Mé-lis-an-de!

[Orchestra *tacet*]

je ne l'ai pres-que pas en -ten-du!___

(P: You don't know why I have to go away . . . you don't know that it is because . . . I love you. M: I love you too. P: Oh! what did you say, Mélisande? I could hardly hear!)

Although pastel colours and the pliable arabesques of *art nouveau* play a large part in the score, Golaud's explosions of anger are anything but muted and the scene (Act III, scene 4) in which he sets the child Yniold to spy on the lovers is in its way as terrible a depiction of ungovernable jealousy as anything in Verdi's *Otello*, and represents a heightened form of realism beside which the naïvetés of Italian *verismo* seem pale indeed.

With *Pelléas* opera moved for the first time unequivocally outside the conventions of the nineteenth-century opera-house. Debussy's new conception of opera clearly influenced Paul Dukas (1865–1935) in another setting of a Maeterlinck play, *Ariane et Barbe-Bleue* (1907), in which choral, descriptive, and even purely decorative scenes represent links with the past. Themes are treated symphonically and cyclically, and thematic material shaped into a grandiose coda. These musical procedures are largely hidden from the ordinary listener by Dukas's orchestration, which often has the amplitude and much of the brilliance of Strauss's. A less accomplished example of the style is to be found in *Macbeth* (1910), the single opera written by Ernest Bloch (1880–1959) where Lady Macbeth in the sleep-walking scene improbably echoes Mélisande (Ex. 79).

During the same years as the realistic operas of Bruneau and Charpentier and the innovatory *Pelléas* there appeared the last monuments of the Wagnerian enthusiasm which had made so deep a mark on French music in the eighties. Something has already been said of Vincent d'Indy's Parsifal-like *Fervaal* (1897) and Ernest Chausson's posthumously performed *Le Roi Arthus* (1903), which witnesses to that obsession with *Tristan* traceable as far back as Duparc's earlier songs ('Soupir', 1868). In the same year as *Le Roi Arthus*, Vincent d'Indy produced *L'Étranger*. This is a very free reworking by the composer of the Flying Dutchman story. The mysterious Stranger, whose success as a fisherman and evangelical behaviour cause havoc in a small French

Ex. 79

(Fie, my lord, fie! A soldier and afraid!)

fishing-village, seeks redemption from an unspecified guilt in the love of the symbolically-named Vita. She already has a pretender to her hand, a dashing excise-man very unlike Wagner's Erik. Torn between her feelings for the two men Vita, like Senta, sacrifices her life when she shares the Stranger's attempt to rescue a ship in distress. D'Indy makes effective use of folk-song choruses, and a traditional *opéra comique* style of characterization for Vita's mother; but the music of the Stranger and his scenes with Vita have a Wagnerian harmonic density and flavour. In bar 4 of the following passage from Act II the Franck fingerprint is unmistakable:

Ex. 80

(Forgive me the rash words that escaped me yesterday. Forgive me, tell me that you forgive me and that I can go away absolved)

It is interesting to find Debussy, in his article for *Gil Blas* on the first performance of *L'Étranger* (Brussels, Théâtre de la Monnaie) observing that 'this work is an admirable lesson for those who believe in the crude imported style which consists in crushing music under cartloads of realism.'[1]

André Messager (1853–1929), whom Debussy had chosen to conduct the first performance of *Pelléas*, showed an excellent craftsmanship and a delightful lyrical gift in a series of operettas which included *Madame Chrysanthème* (1893), *Les p'tites Michu* (1897), and *Véronique* (1898). The only other country in which light opera was treated with comparable skill was Austria, where Franz Léhar (1870–1948) produced in *Die lustige Witwe* (The Merry Widow) (1905) a work which has outlived all but a few of the serious post-Wagnerian or veristic operas of the day. Certainly the final numbers of Massenet's long portrait-gallery of women, which ended only with his death in 1912, contained

---

[1] Reprinted in *Monsieur Croche the Dilettante-Hater* (English ed., London, 1927).

nothing more distinguished than the slight *Thérèse* (1907); and the advent of Sergey Dyagilev's *Ballet russe* to Paris in 1909 had the effect of distracting the attention of the most gifted composers away from the lyrical drama. Apart from the musically interesting but dramatically weak *Pénélope* (1912) by Gabriel Fauré (1845–1924) the only opera of distinction produced in France between 1908 and 1918 was *L'Heure espagnole* (1911) by Maurice Ravel (1875–1934). In this, a deliberately frivolous subject, which might seem to belong to the operetta rather than to the opera, is handled with a care and skill that at first seem disproportionate. Ravel, however, was seeking for a solution of the problem facing all French composers of the day: that of avoiding the shadows of both Wagner and Debussy and presenting the public with a work that made full allowance for the well-developed French sense of the ridiculous yet still allowed a place for fine musical craftsmanship.

Ravel's characters are no more than exquisitely fashioned puppets, but they express their conventional sentiments in a perfectly calculated and highly polished language, in which Spanish rhythms and melodic phrases are presented with French gracefulness and a strong sense of parody. The plot has the symmetry of a *mouvement de ballet*, and Ravel and his librettist Franc-Nohain emphasize this fragile artificiality in the final quintet which, like the vaudeville in the old *opéra comique*, points the moral. Here Ravel harks back to the clowning of Offenbach's *Belle Hélène*, with his take-off of vocal *fioriture*.

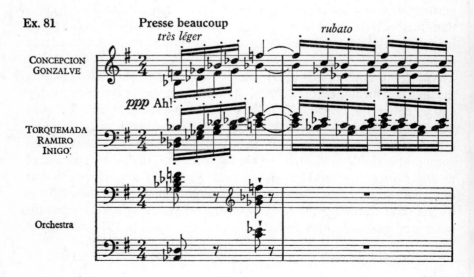

(Ah! The muleteer has his turn!)

Ravel did not write another opera until 1925, when he collaborated with Colette in a *fantaisie lyrique*, *L'Enfant et les sortilèges*, which is as much ballet as opera. Here the *divertissements* provided by animals and inanimate objects far outweigh the slender central theme in importance. This was in effect a return to the ideals of the French eighteenth century, which had already prompted the most important of the works which Ravel wrote for the *Ballets russes*. Before examining these ballets it will be as well to trace the history of opera in Russia itself during the last years before it was largely replaced by ballet.

RUSSIA AND THE SLAVONIC PERIPHERY

The year 1890 witnessed the production in St. Petersburg of two different flawed masterpieces, Tchaikovsky's *Pikovaya Dama* (The Queen of Spades) and Borodin's posthumous *Knyaz Igor* (Prince Igor).[1] Tchaikovsky was to write only one more opera before his death in 1893, the comparatively feeble fairytale *Iolanta* (1892), and it was fairytale operas that were to predominate among the dozen operas that Nikolay Rimsky-Korsakov (1844–1908) was to write during the last fifteen years of his life. Already in his *Snegurochka* (Snowmaiden) (1882) there had been a marked accentuation of the fantastic and spectacular elements at the expense of character-delineation and human interest in general; and this emphasis, all but complete in *Mlada* (1892), was very marked in *Noch pered Rozhdestvom* (Christmas Eve) (1895) and the brilliant *Sadko* (1898). The decorative scenes and *divertissements* showing the bustling commercial life of Novgorod and the submarine kingdom to which Sadko is carried off by the Sea King's daughter quite outweigh the rest of the work in musical interest. Rimsky-Korsakov's preoccupation with fantasy and spectacle, and the banality of the love-music in his operas, no doubt reflect a certain lack of humanity in his character; but this is counterbalanced by the skill and inventiveness displayed in his cold and glittering instrumental combinations, as in the scene in *Sadko* where the fish are turned into ingots of gold.

In *Mozart i Salieri*, which was produced in the same year as *Sadko* (1898), Rimsky-Korsakov imitated Dargomïzhsky[1] in setting a complete Pushkin text, but used a pastiche 'classical' style in every way different from his own and Dargomïzhsky's. Human interest is strong in *Tsarskaya Nevesta* (The Tsar's Bride) (1899) and *Servilia* (1902) but these are feeble works compared with the four fairy-stories or legends *Skazka o Tsare Saltane* (The Tale of Tsar Saltan) (1900) *Kashchey*

---

[1] See Vol. IX.

Bessmertny (Immortal Kashchey) (1902), *Skazanie o nevidimom grade Kitezhe i deve Fevronii* (The Legend of the Invisible City of Kitezh and the Maiden Fevronia) (1907) and *Zolotoy Petushok* (The Golden Cockerel) (1909).

The first two of these are fantasies, fairy-stories from the Russian past that provide the composer with scenes in which he can simply exploit to the full his colouristic imagination. In *Kitezh* and *The Golden Cockerel*, on the other hand, the fairy-story is used as a parable for the times, the deeply troubled years of the Russo-Japanese War and the 1905 revolution. *Kitezh* reflects the ferment in Russian religious and philosophical thought during these years, when Vladimir Solovyev was developing the final stages of his new ideas of Christian mysticism and Leo Tolstoy a new version of evangelical simplicity, while theosophical and anthroposophical speculations were under the influence of Rudolf Steiner. Although Rimsky-Korsakov himself was a typical nineteenth-century rationalist, he felt the aesthetic attraction of the legend, medieval and originally Platonic, of a Holy City conceived in terms of Orthodox liturgy and symbolism. His librettist, V. I. Belsky, based his text on a thirteenth-century legend and his language is deliberately archaic, influenced by that of Wagner's librettos. The composer drew not only on the traditional songs and chants which had provided much of the material of his earlier operas, but on Wagnerian models. For instance, the opening scene, which shows the maiden Fevronia alone in the depth of the forest in summer, recalls the Forest Murmurs of Wagner's *Siegfried*; and in Act IV there are clear reminiscences of the Flower Maidens in *Parsifal*. The figure of Grishka Kuterma, who betrays the city of Kitezh to the Tatars and is nevertheless forgiven and redeemed by Fevronia, is a cross between the holy simpleton of Russian tradition and the tortured psychological criminals of Dostoevsky. Throughout the opera the conflation of Orthodox ideals and imagery with the pantheistic nature-worship of the pre-Christian Slavs is reflected in the music, which alternates between a stiff, archaic and fundamentally modal idiom and Wagnerian colour and flexibility. There are passages in *Kitezh* where Rimsky-Korsakov denies himself his customary luxury of orchestration and adopts, in the interests of the drama, a much more austere manner that recalls Mussorgsky. In Act III, scene 2, where Grishka Kuterma's guilt is beginning to send him out of his mind, the insistent expanding figure representing the bells of Kitezh ringing in his head is heard echoing in the lowest reaches of the orchestra, a psychological transformation that is very telling.

Ex. 82

(No escape from hellish torments—no life for me on God's fair earth! I shall cast myself headlong into the depths)

Pushkin's *The Golden Cockerel*[1] is a fable which shows a stupid, ease-loving king deaf to warnings of imminent disaster and unwilling to keep his promises, engaged with a mysterious Eastern enemy with whose queen he falls in love. The parallel with the political situation in Russia at the time of the war with Japan was close enough for the censor to raise obstacles to the performance of the work; but this last of Rimsky-Korsakov's fourteen operas is the finest example of his powers both as dramatist and orchestrator. The clever musical contrasting of the solid King Dodon and his court with the mysterious trio of the Astrologer, the Golden Cockerel, and the Queen of Shemakha shows clearly his unusual ability to create atmosphere rather than human character by musical means. His use of coloratura, as in the shimmering roulades of the Queen of Shemakha, anticipates the Zerbinetta of Strauss's *Ariadne auf Naxos*.

[1] See pl. III.

PLATE III

RIMSKY-KORSAKOV'S *THE GOLDEN COCKEREL*, 1909 (*see p. 176*)

The stage set of Act Three of the original production designed by I. Bilibin

The Golden Cockerel was later performed in a ballet version by Dyagilev's *Ballet russe*, and in Rimsky-Korsakov's earlier *Kashchey the Immortal* (1902) the element of ballet was already strong. Everything in this 'autumn fairy-story', which is in fact another winter-spring myth like the earlier *Snegurochka*, is magic. The Stormwind suggests a dancer rather than a singer, and the Princess Kashcheevna is characterized as much by the orchestra and by her movements as by her actual singing. It was, in fact, with a ballet based on another version of the same story that Rimsky-Korsakov's most gifted pupil, Igor Stravinsky (1882–1971), was to make his name.

The principles of realism, which had found an early expression in parts of Mussorgsky's *Boris Godunov* and in Serov's *The Power of Evil* during the 1870s, hardly interested Russian composers of the nineties. Sergey Rakhmaninov (1873–1943) was influenced by Mascagni's example in his *Aleko* (1893); but he showed his real dramatic powers much later in the more ambitious setting of Pushkin's *Skupoy Ritsar* (The Miserly Knight), and an awareness of contemporary fashion in the *bouche fermée* choruses of the more feeble *Francesca da Rimini*, both of which appeared in 1906.

BOHEMIA

Russian music and literature played an increasingly important role in the artistic developments of Bohemia as dissatisfaction with Austrian rule and the centralizing policy of Vienna grew more acute. Dvořák had chosen a Russian subject for his *Dimitrij* as early as 1881, but the influence of Wagner is paramount in the most important of his later operas, *Čert a Káča* (The Devil and Kate, 1899) and *Rusalka* (1901), a fairy-story which had inspired Dargomïzhsky. Wagner and Smetana largely determine the style and character of *Šárka* (1897) one of the handful of stage-works by Zdeněk Fibich (1850–1900), which include an historically interesting trilogy in which the composer attempted to revive the *melodrama*. An earlier Bohemian composer, Jiří Benda (1722–95), had experimented with some success in setting a spoken text against orchestral accompaniment and comment;[1] but Fibich's musical language, in which the already old-fashioned language of Schumann is only superficially modernized by a Wagnerian leitmotive technique, was not strong enough to bear the weight of the drama in his trilogy of heroic Greek legends based on the character of Hippodamia—*Námluvy Pelopovy* (Pelops' Wooing) (1889), *Smír Tantalův* (Tantalus's Atonement (1890) and *Smrt Hippodamie* (Hippodamia's Death) (1891). The following excerpt from *Námluvy Pelopovy*, Act IV, scene 2, is typical:

[1] See Vol. VII, pp. 76–9.

Ex. 83

vzplál ohněm, proti němuž malý jest žár věčného tam slunce na nebi,

kdo v očích v tvoje patře ú - v srdci zápalil se blahostí, kdo nemoh' jinak, něz tě
směvem a milovat.

(*Pelops:* I mean to plumb the depths of this hideous treachery, leave nothing unexplored until I find the traitor. *Hippod:* You will not have far to seek. P: Then it is Myrtillos! H: Only his hand, not his the design. P: Then who guided that infamous hand? H: One, Pelops, who loved you from the moment you crossed our threshold, with a love more burning than the sun in the heavens. One who looked smiling into your eyes, one whose heart blazed in ecstasy and could not but love you.)

The only opera of outstanding quality and originality to appear in Bohemia (or rather Moravia) at this time passed unnoticed by the outside world, and had to wait twelve years for its first performance in Prague. This was *Její pastorkyňa* (Her Step-daughter) (1904) by Leoš Janáček (1854–1928). The story by Gabriela Preissová is one of peasant life, involving primitive passions as violent, in a setting as realistic, as those of Mascagni's *Cavalleria rusticana*. In fact this opera, which made its reputation in the outside world under the title of *Jenufa*, may be considered as the supreme masterpiece of *verismo* although the composer insisted on 'naturism', rather than naturalism, as his guiding principle. In this, as in his use of a prose libretto, he followed the example of Alfred Bruneau.

Janáček's musical style is naturalistic in the sense that his vocal line was modelled on the rhythms of Moravian peasant speech, just as Mussorgsky had shaped his phrases and rhythms on those of the Russian language. Unrealistic elements, however, appear in the many repetitions of words or single phrases, sometimes emphasizing a single idea but often modifying it slightly; and in Janáček's handling of the denouement where the characteristically veristic horror and despair are replaced by the catharsis brought about by the Kostelnička's confession of her crime. Janáček's use of cross-rhythms and repetition, for intensifying and slightly modifying a phrase, often has a quasi-hypnotic effect:

Ex. 84   Act I, scene 1

Mužs - ký ro - zum máš

(What joy that gives you, my girl, what joy! You taught even the servant-girl to
read! You have a man's intelligence)

Or a vocal line unaccompanied but echoed, or interrupted, by the
orchestra may be given the solemnity of a primitive spell:

Ex. 85   Act II, scene 1
          Meno mosso

KOSTELNIČKA

Už od té chví - le, co jsem tě do-ved-la

dom,   na - pad - lo mně z tvé - - - - ho

na-ří-ká-ní ne-ště-stí.   A když jsi se mi

po-tom   při-zna-la se svým   po-kles-kem—

my-sle-la jsem, že i mne to mu-sí   do hro-bu spro-vo-dit,

(From the day that I brought you home I noticed your grieving and your misery, and when you confessed your guilt I thought that it would be the end of me)

AFTER VERISMO: ART NOUVEAU AND THE CLASSICAL REACTION

Wagner's legacy, though most fruitfully invested by the composers of Central Europe, had certainly enriched opera in both France and Russia. Realism, too, though primarily an Italian movement in opera, proved a fertilizing agent well beyond the borders of Italy, first in France and then in Central Europe, where it was combined with Wagnerian elements in a number of works which caught the imagination of the day, though they proved to possess small lasting power. A third element which played an important part in modifying both neo-Wagnerian and realistic opera has already been mentioned on several occasions: the *art nouveau*, or *Jugendstil*, movement which originated in the visual arts. It was a minority movement, one of the many protests against the accepted presuppositions of artistic academies and so, in the last resort, against the industrial society of nineteenth-century Western Europe. The roots of the movement can be easily traced, through the Aesthetic Movement of the eighties in England, back to the Pre-Raphaelite painters of the fifties; and they in their turn were indebted to the German school of 'Nazarene' painters, who owed their origin to the secessionist Guild of St. Luke founded in Vienna in 1809 by Overbeck. The rejection of the Renaissance image of man and the return to an imagined Middle Ages was accompanied by a new cult of nature, a conscious turning away from the literal representation of human life at its fullest and most magnificent to a study of the forms and textures of inanimate nature. Man's place in the new art was humbler and more mysterious, no longer that of 'the lord of creation' but suggesting rather an order of being shared with plant and animal life and equally at the mercy of destructive forces. During the eighties this new attitude found expression in an enthusiasm for Japanese art, especially prints and pottery, and in the cultivation of the arabesque or stylized plant-forms of oriental art; and it soon spread to feminine fashions, which dictated clothes moulded naturally to the figure instead of the exaggerations and stylizations of the crinoline and the bustle. Floating veils and gauzes, clinging stuffs and floral designs such as those elaborated by William Morris replaced stiff brocades and velvets, and the bourgeois ideal of opulent display yielded to a subtler and more poetic conception of feminine beauty.

Art nouveau elements in the opera go back as far as Wagner's Rhine-maidens and Flowermaidens, and oriental and flower motifs often modify the realism of Italian opera in the 1890s (e.g. Puccini's *Madama Butterfly* and Mascagni's *Iris* and *L'Amico Fritz*). The sense of human fragility, the mysteriousness of existence and an overriding sense of pity, which characterize the writing of Maurice Maeterlinck, found musical expression in the operas based on his works, and supremely in Debussy's *Pelléas et Mélisande*. In Charpentier's *Louise* and in Dukas's treatment of Maeterlinck's *Ariane et Barbe-Bleue* there is more than an echo of the contemporary struggle to obtain for women a position in society if not equal to that of men at least superior to that of minors. Outside the Latin countries an amalgam of Wagnerian (or later Straussian) harmony and orchestration with typically veristic Italian melody is to be found in the operas of Eugen d'Albert (1864–

1932) and, in a more personal idiom, Frederick Delius (1862–1934) and Franz Schreker (1878–1934). D'Albert's *Tiefland* (1903) is a skilful and effective score almost equally indebted to Puccini and Wagner, and the story of violent passions in a Pyrenean village is comparable to that of Janáček's almost exactly contemporary *Její pastorkyňa* ('Jenufa'). *Art nouveau* elements are much stronger in Delius. His first opera, *Koanga* (1904), is set in Florida and the heavily chromatic post-Wagnerian style of the white planters' music is happily relieved by the slave choruses, whose old-fashioned 'nigger-minstrel' style suggests an acquaintance with the ballads of Alfred Scott-Gatty. *Romeo und Julia auf dem Dorfe* (A Village Romeo and Juliet) (1907), based on a story from Gottfried Keller's *Die Leute von Seldwyla*, presents a pair of child lovers defying the conventions of a small-minded, property-conscious society and ends in the *Liebestod* of a double suicide. The Black Fiddler is a personification of music as a sinister power, and Delius's melting chromatic harmonies spread a very characteristic *art nouveau* veil over melodic lines which are often of extreme simplicity.

Ex. 86

ei - le dir nach, dein ver - lass - en - er Gei - ger: Wir
I must limp af - ter thy fidd - ler for - sa - ken, but

sind ja doch Brü - der, du ruh - lo - ser Wind.
are we not com - rades, o Va - ga - bond wind!

In Schreker's *Der ferne Klang* (The Distant Sound) (1912) the heavy unisons and fortissimo sequences of unrelated triads recall *verismo*, the thick texture and opulent orchestration are borrowed from Strauss, and much of the harmony shows the superficial influence of Debussy. The realistic opening scenes of Act I gradually take on a symbolical, unreal character; and Act II takes place in the Casa delle Maschere, a fantastic brothel on an island in the Venetian lagoon, which is a thinly disguised modernization of Klingsor's garden in Act II of *Parsifal*. In this act the contrasting of gipsy music on the stage in close antiphony with the orchestra (a device not lost on Alban Berg, who made the piano-reduction of Schreker's score) alternates with passages of character-istically overblown late romantic harmony, like Grete's dream.

Ex. 87

Appassionato rubato, *sehr rhythmisch, scharf, doch die Viertel gleich lang.*
(The count, surprised and intrigued, sends the gipsies away.)

Traum.

cresc.   f

(For many years, it seems to me, I have been dreaming a wild dream.)

The heroine of *Der ferne Klang*, Grete, is a minor character in the long portrait-gallery of erotic pathology, which stretches from Verdi's Violetta to Alban Berg's Lulu, through Wagner's Kundry and Massenet's Manon and Thaïs, Strauss's Salome and Puccini's Turandot. The exploitation of sexual elements is an even stronger feature of Schreker's *Die Gezeichneten* (The Branded) (1918).

Art nouveau in its most innocent, even etiolated form strongly influenced two English operas of the period. The mystery of life and death and the all-prevailing power of conjugal love are presented in an Indian scriptural setting, and in a musical language of extreme chastity by Gustav Holst (1874–1934) in his chamber opera *Sāvitri* (1916), and a Celtic fairy twilight provided the background for *The Immortal Hour* (1914) by Rutland Boughton (1878–1960). The revived interest in Celtic mythology, and the example of Wagner, prompted three operas by Joseph Holbrooke (1878–1958), *The Children of Don* (1912), *Dylan, Son of the Wave* (1914), and *Bronwen* (1929). These stood out as novel compared with the well-made but musically characterless operas of Sir Charles Stanford (1852–1924), whose *Shamus O'Brien* (1896) put conventional Irish comedy on the operatic stage for the first time. *Art nouveau* elements appear in the wood-spirits of *Der Wald* (1902) by Ethel Smyth (1858–1944), whose *Strandrecht* (The Wreckers) (1906) would have insured her a future as an operatic composer in any country but England, where opera at this time was virtually confined to a summer season at Covent Garden closely linked with the social life of London and provided almost entirely by foreign artists. A later comedy, *The Boatswain's Mate* (1916), contains much shrewd characterization and clear references to the still continuing struggle for women's rights.

In Italy Gabriele d'Annunzio's highly coloured and scented, but sterile poetry had a powerful effect on all the arts, prolonging the 'decadence' of the nineties by at least two decades. As *verismo* lost its novelty, d'Annunzio's influence prompted a wave of spectacular neo-romanticism to be felt in *Francesca da Rimini* (1914) by Riccardo Zandonai (1883–1944), a work full of medieval pageantry including a stage orchestra of flute, piffero, clarinet in C, viola pomposa, and lute. This, like *Fedra* (1915), the first opera by Ildebrando Pizzetti (1880–1968), was based on a play by d'Annunzio, who also provided the subject of *La Nave* (1918) by Italo Montemezzi (1875–1952). Montemezzi's *L'Amore dei tre Re* (1913) is outstandingly the finest of these neo-romantic operas, a powerful story presented in a musical language quite free of the more facile theatrical exaggerations and stylistic coarseness of *verismo*, but still plainly indebted to *Tristan* in the love-music which forms the greater part of the work, one way and another.

Ex. 88

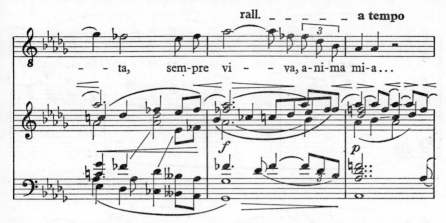

(I do not want to look at you before you speak, beloved, chosen one, ever-living, my soul . . .)

At least a decade before *verismo* had produced its last major flowering in Puccini's *Il Tabarro* (1918) or combined with the neo-romantic fashion in *I Gioelli della Madonna* (The Jewels of the Madonna) (1911) by Ermanno Wolf-Ferrari (1876–1948), this gifted half-German, half-Italian composer was anticipating what was to become the classical reaction in two operas based on Goldoni. Both *Die neugierigen Frauen* (The Inquisitive Women) (1903) and *Die vier Grobiane* (A School for Fathers) (1906) were given at Munich, where the Venetian-born composer had studied with Rheinberger, acquiring an excellent and robust musico-dramatic technique which he used to evoke the world of the Italian eighteenth century. Wolf-Ferrari's musical language is traditional, but his use of it is personal and his strong melodic gift often seems to lie midway between Mahler and Puccini, as in this song from Act I of *Die vier Grobiane*:

Ex. 89

(Be nice to me again, dear father, for after all I am your little daughter, and a good and obedient little girl. It's Carnival too—but of course I can be joyful and happy without a mask or a ball.)

The very topical *Susannens Geheimnis* (Susanna's Secret) (1909), where the plot turns on a husband's discovery that his wife smokes cigarettes, is a 'modern-style' comedy such as Strauss was later to write in his autobiographical *Intermezzo*.

Neither the mood of the times nor the musical language available favoured the writing of such broadly human comedies as *Die Meister-singer* or *Falstaff* during the first two decades of the twentieth century. The outstanding exceptions, *Der Rosenkavalier* and *L'Heure espagnole*, though musically far more ambitious than Wolf-Ferrari's charming and slender period pieces, do not stand comparison with Wagner or Verdi. *Maskarade* (1906) by the Danish composer Carl Nielsen, is a comedy based, like Wolf-Ferrari's Goldoni operas, on an eighteenth-century classic—Holberg's comedy of 1723—and alternating between a lively neo-classical style, partly pastiche and partly Regerish in character (overture, the *folie d'Espagne* and archaic dances in Act I, Hieronymus's C major aria in praise of 'the good old days', and the three-part madrigal in Act III) and memories of nineteenth-century models. These include *Die Meistersinger* (the character of Arv recalls David, and the Night-watchman in Act III is an obvious borrowing) and, at a deeper level, Berlioz. In an earlier opera, *Saul og David* (1902), the love-duet between David and Saul's daughter, Michal, already recalls the unique combina-tion of sensuality and chastity that distinguishes the love-music in Berlioz's *Roméo et Juliette* and *Les Troyens*; and the scene between Leander and Leonora in Act II of *Maskarade* confirms this impression:

Ex. 90

(*Leander:* No, let me drink from rosy beakers the happiness, the life which you have given me by that single word. *Leonore:* Yes, drink on!)

In the character of the valet Henrik, Nielsen created one of the great servant-roles of operatic literature, a worthy Danish successor to Mozart's Leporello.

A very different kind of wit from that of either Nielsen or Wolf-Ferrari marks the operas of another half-German, half-Italian composer, Ferruccio Busoni (1866–1924). His double nationality found a striking parallel in a double indebtedness to J. S. Bach and Liszt, who between them dominated his twin careers of composer-theorist and piano virtuoso. It is significant that, whereas Wolf-Ferrari turned for the subjects of his operas to Goldoni, Busoni's choice among Italian writers was the fantastic, even visionary Gozzi, for whose *Turandot* he wrote incidental music in 1911. From this he later constructed an opera of the same name, given in a double-bill with his *Arlecchino* in 1917. These and *Die Brautwahl* (1912) represent the first conscious intrusion into the operatic field of the neo-classical spirit—objective, quick-witted, dry, and contrived, in the sense of stylistically eclectic—which had already appeared in Busoni's own *Fantasia contrappuntistica* and even earlier in the works of his friend Max Reger.[1]

[1] See above pp. 82 ff.

Mascagni had already attempted, though unsuccessfully, to reclaim for the opera the figures of the Italian *commedia dell'arte* in his *Le Maschere* (The Masks) (1901). Busoni's *Arlecchino* is altogether different from the sentimental and decorative, Watteauesque use of the old comedy figures which became fashionable in French literature after the publication of Jules and Edmond de Goncourt's *L'Art du dix-huitième siècle* (1859–75) and developed into a mannerism among poets of the nineties who imitated Verlaine.[1] The masks in *Arlecchino* are used to lend greater objectivity and more general relevance to Busoni's very shrewd and individual comments on human existence. The musical style of *Arlecchino* is desperately taut and nervous, as full of allusions as Busoni's text, which shows an intimate knowledge of Dante and Goethe. Musical references include quotations or parodies of Don Giovanni's 'Finch' han del vino' and Beethoven's Fifth Symphony and the *Fidelio* march, with sidelong glances at Rossini and Wagner, and some eighteenth-century pastiche. Much of the music has a nervous, staccato glitter that looks forward to Stravinsky's *Rake's Progress*—the last of the neo-classical operas, as this is the first—but the sham funeral march in Act IV might be a parody of Mahler, and there are passages in which the telling awkwardness of the vocal line and the orchestral spacing recall those of Dargomïzhsky's *Stone Guest*, though the more probable and immediate source is Strauss's *Elektra*:

Ex. 91

[1] The composer's own curiously ambiguous attitude to his *Arlecchino*, and to opera in general, can be found in his essay *Entwurf einer neuer Aesthetik der Tonkunst* (1907), relevant passages of which appear in *The Essence of Music* (English translation, London, 1957), pp. 40, 60–70.

- dien-ten   in   eu -   -   - rer Be-hand-lung zu | stehn

(I know of cardinals who would deserve to be treated by you.)

The music of *Turandot* has little except some oriental pastiche in common with the opera that Puccini left unfinished at his death in 1924. The fantastic plays an even more important role here than in *Arlecchino*, and the eclectic, consciously fabricated nature of Busoni's music is emphasized when he introduces the old English tune of 'Greensleeves' at the opening of Act II. Intellectual contrivance, a vivid musical imagination, and vast musical and literary erudition are combined in *Dr. Faustus*, the opera which the composer left unfinished at his death in 1924.[1] Busoni's libretto shows a literary gift very similar, and not much inferior, to his musical powers. After the opening symphonia, which evokes the spring festival of Easter, two preludes show Faustus approached by three mysterious students from Cracow and then summoning Mephistopheles. As Faustus signs away his soul, Busoni's 'Credo' and 'Gloria' emphasize the world that he is deliberately rejecting; and the extended organ-solo in the following church scene, where Gretchen's brother is seen praying for vengeance, is used for the same effect, while the vivace Te Deum in 6/8 time in the second scene of the *Hauptspiel* becomes a song to wine and women. The first scene of the *Hauptspiel*, which shows Mephistopheles at the court of Parma, contains many characteristics of nineteenth-century grand opera—a polonaise, pages duelling to waltz-music, noble girls with wreaths, and scenes of magic in which Mephistopheles conjures up apparitions of Solomon and Balkis, Samson and Delilah, John the Baptist and Salome, before spiriting away the Duchess. In the following scene, Mephistopheles appears in a Wittenberg tavern among quarrelling students (*Te Deum* pitted against 'Ein' feste Burg' in the manner of Meyerbeer's *Huguenots*).

In the final scenes the appearance of the Nightwatchman and

---

[1] It was completed by his pupil Philipp Jarnach and performed in 1925.

Mephistopheles's *tempo di minuetto* serenade with pizzicato accompaniment inevitably call up the ghosts of Wagner and Berlioz. But the end of the opera is a monologue for Faustus, in which Busoni's own Faustian spirit of enquiry and 'young classicism' find worthy expression. Busoni's eclectic historicism with its many literary as well as musical overtones from the European past, seemed altogether too contrived and intellectual when *Dr. Faustus* first appeared. Fifty years later the perspective has changed as completely as in any conjuring-trick of Mephistopheles himself; and what seemed the freakish, if brilliant concoction of an intellectual visionary has found an honourable place in the mainstream of operatic history.

If there was something of the Abbé Vogler about Busoni, Hans Pfitzner's lonely championship of late romantic musical ideals and language in the revolutionary atmosphere of the 1914–18 war suggests rather a musical Don Quixote.[1] His *Palestrina* (1917) is the latest of the operas centred around a character in whom the power of music is personified, as earlier opera-composers had chosen Orpheus and Wagner Hans Sachs, although Hindemith was to choose artist-heroes for his *Cardillac* (1926) and *Mathis der Maler* (1938). Pfitzner's musical idiom is basically Wagnerian, though extended by harmonic freedoms that owe something to Strauss, perhaps more to Reger. The legend of Palestrina's composing the so-called 'Missa Papae Marcelli' in a single night gave Pfitzner, who wrote his own libretto, the opportunity for a powerfully conceived choral scene (Act I, scenes 4–6) in which composers of earlier ages urge him on and a chorus of angels echoes phrases of the Mass as he writes them. In Act II the scenes depicting the Council of Trent contain masterly vignettes of the leaders of the different national factions and their suites—the Bishop of Budoja characterized by brisk neo-classical music, for example, the Assyrian Patriarch using oriental melismata and the Master of Ceremonies, Ercole Severolus, depicted in austere brass unisons. In the final scene of the opera, where Palestrina is shown sitting peacefully at the organ while crowds outside hail him as 'rescuer of music', Pfitzner clearly reflected his idea of his own position as legitimate champion of musical traditions which he saw on all sides rejected. His loyalty to the past was to become increasingly intense, and blind, during the next thirty years, while the musical revolution was to establish its legitimacy often in the face of social ostracism and even, in some cases, political persecution. Nineteenth-century traditions, whether of Wagnerian music-drama or Italian *verismo*, could not resist the new forces which were transfiguring society as well as the arts. Puccini wrote the last Italian grand opera

[1] Pfitzner made a personal attack on Busoni in an essay of 1917, 'Futuristengefahr'.

with *Turandot* and died in 1924. Strauss, like Pfitzner, was less fortunate in living another quarter of a century and continuing to write, against the current of the times, complex and luxuriant fables like *Die Frau ohne Schatten* (The Woman without a Shadow) (1919), *Die aegyptische Helena* (1928) and *Die Liebe der Danae* (1940) or nostalgic comedies in the vein of *Der Rosenkavalier*, like *Arabella* (1933). Despite real individual merits these proved as ineffective against the tide of events as his own Marschallin's desire to put the clocks back in order to preserve her youth. The lyrical drama was far from dead, but its spirit had deserted the old forms and was searching for the new.

TOWARDS NEW SHORES

Although Strauss and Pfitzner eventually rejected Wagnerian music-drama in favour of a return to the traditional opera, we have seen that in Russia Rimsky-Korsakov's last operas suggest a quite different way out of a situation which most intelligent composers felt to be an impasse. Instead of insisting, like the Italian *veristi* and their followers in France and Central Europe, on ignoring the gulf between a highly artificial form and naturalistic subject-matter, Rimsky-Korsakov chose exclusively fantastic subjects; and Debussy, though avoiding all hint of fantasy and the supernatural, found in Maeterlinck's *Pelléas et Mélisande* a largely interior, only half articulate drama. These were in effect the two paths explored by the composers who came to maturity around 1910, and they led to two quite different solutions: on the one hand the ballet and on the other hand the symbolist or 'expressionist' drama with music, the one essentially an extrovert form and the other raising introversion to a principle.

BALLET

Although ballet had been cultivated in Russia on quite a different footing from any Western European country, with the possible exception of Denmark, at least since the days of Noverre, ballet music first became a serious art-form in France with Adolphe Adam and, far more importantly, Leo Delibes (1836-91). The first great ballet scores in Russia were Tchaikovsky's,[1] much indebted to Delibes in detail but incomparably richer and more varied musically. It was the musical standard set by Tchaikovsky in *Swan Lake*, *The Sleeping Beauty*, and *The Nutcracker* that made it possible for the young Igor Stravinsky (1882-1971) to consider ballet as a possible form, and the example of

[1] See Vol. IX.

his teacher, Rimsky-Korsakov, that showed him how the fundamentally
plastic language of ballet could be employed in a work which lay on the
borderline between this and opera. The first act of his opera *The
Nightingale* was written in 1908–9, before his three ballets *Zhar-ptitsa*
(The Fire-Bird) (1910), *Petrushka* (1911) and *Le Sacre du printemps*
(The Rite of Spring) (1913) were presented in Paris by Sergey Dyagilev's
Ballet Russe. In both *The Nightingale* and *The Fire-Bird* Stravinsky is
still very much indebted to Rimsky-Korsakov's 'magic' orchestration.
The intermezzo 'Courants d'air' is full of harp and horn glissandos,
glittering trills and tremolandos from the whole orchestra; and the
Nightingale's song recalls the coloratura of the Queen of Shemakha in
The Golden Cockerel:

In *The Fire-Bird* Stravinsky shows his acquaintance with contemporary
French music very clearly, and the earliest example of what was to
become his characteristic mature style, laconic in utterance, with
irregular ostinato rhythms, and analytical rather than synthetic orchestration is to be found in the 'Danse infernale';

Ex. 93

In *Petrushka*, a puppet fantasy played against the background of a Russian Shrovetide fair, the crude, incisive, spiky harmonies are either superimposed to form a giant accordion-like orchestral sound, still recognizably diatonic, or detached from this background with exaggerated emphasis and high relief that recall those of a Fauviste painting. The quotation of deliberately trival music—a French café song and a Tyrolese waltz by Lanner—and the embedding of this material in a score where echoes of Russian folk-music closely jostle fragments of a highly sophisticated *Konzertstück* for piano and orchestra, together form a clear portrait of Stravinsky's musical character, in which sharp intelligence, curious erudition and the gifts of a colourist and a miniaturist rather than those of a musical architect are directed by a forcible, even aggressive personality. This aggressive trait was to find formidable expression in *The Rite of Spring*, 'pictures of pagan Russia' presented with a neo-primitive savagery of rhythm and a frequent piling-up of disparate harmonic aggregates that seemed at first provocatively revolutionary. In fact, however, the substance of Stravinsky's harmony in *Le Sacre* is seldom bolder than that to be found in the last piano works of Aleksandr Skryabin,[1] and it was the vertiginous rhythmic vitality and the enormous percussive impact of the music that gave it a unique character. Where Stravinsky's harmonic daring differed from Skryabin's was in its application; and here *The Rite* shows clearly the influence of his French friends, Maurice Ravel (1875–1937) and Florent Schmitt (1870–1958). In *La Tragédie de Salomé* (1907–12) Schmitt wrote a 'Danse des éclairs' with a rhythm of $\dfrac{(3 + 1\frac{1}{2})}{4}$ and a 'Danse de l'effroi', which plainly anticipate *The Rite*. Already in *Petrushka*, and even in *Zhar-ptitsa*, Stravinsky had exploited with brilliant effect the clash of triads whose tonics lie an augmented fourth apart (C–F sharp)—a bitonal effect already used by Ravel for the cadenza of his *Jeux d'eau* (1902); in *The Rite* it is Stravinsky's methodical insistence, at the opening of the 'Cercles mystérieux des adolescentes', on a chord consisting of a dominant seventh on E flat and a chord of F flat (E) major, rather than the chord itself, that was novel. On the other hand the rhythmic pattern in the final 'Danse sacrale'—9/8–5/8–3/8–2/4–7/4–3/4–7/4–3/8–2/4 and so on—was a unique innovation in European music.[2] The leading French composers of the day were soon fired by the new possibilities suggested by Dyagilev's *Ballet russe*. Debussy's *Jeux* and Ravel's *Daphnis et Chloe*, both dating from 1912, represent the latest and highest achievements in that Impressionist writing for the orchestra which had been developing since Debussy's *Prélude à l'après-midi d'un faune* (1894). The pointillistic style already developed in painting by Georges Pierre Seurat, who died in 1891, was effectively imitated in *Jeux*, where Debussy breaks down his material to the smallest possible units, writing music that is not so much thematic as cellular. Ravel's score is perfectly judged and organized to the

[1] See chapter 2, pp. 133–7.
[2] Cf. Jean Cocteau, *Le Coq et l'Arlequin* (Paris, 1918), p. 64 '*Le Sacre* est encore une "oeuvre fauve"—une oeuvre fauve organisée'.

smallest detail, a monument of that refinement of taste and that poetic sensibility expressed in terms of colour and rhythm, which were to be superseded by the neo-primitive savagery of *The Rite* and the dry, objective prose style of the neo-classical reaction. An elegant, well-made ballet-score of the same period is Paul Dukas's *La Péri* (1912), in which Russian influence is again strong.

Quite different from this Franco-Russian ballet style which developed from the mutual exchanges of ideas between Rimsky-Korsakov and Stravinsky on the one hand and Debussy and Ravel on the other, was *Le Martyre de Saint Sébastien* (1911), incidental music written by Debussy for a mystery-play by Gabriele d'Annunzio. Here the most disparate and unexpected sources are drawn upon by the composer—Palestrina, the Wagner of *Parsifal*, and the Liszt of *Christus*—to form a modern version of that *fresque musicale* at which Gounod had aimed at the end of his life. D'Annunzio's hypertrophic and profoundly insensitive art was at the opposite pole to Debussy's; but *Le Martyre* lies on the same borderline between opera and ballet as the symbolist dramas of Bartók and Schoenberg. Much of the music is in a flat-toned fresco style that suggests the oratorio rather than the theatre (Ex. 94).

Debussy and Ravel both obliged Dyagilev by either supplying him with new ballet-scores or permitting the use of former works or arrangements of former works (*Prélude à l'après-midi d'un faune, Ma Mère l'oye, Valses nobles et sentimentales,* renamed *Adelaïde ou le langage des fleurs*). Manuel de Falla (1876–1946) was the most gifted of the composers, after Stravinsky, who owed their international reputation to music written for the Russian Ballet. In *El amor brujo* (Love the Sorcerer)

Ex. 94

PLATE IV

FALLA'S *THE THREE-CORNERED HAT*, 1919 (*see p. 201*)

The opening scene, showing the stage set by Picasso and the choreographer Massine in the part of the miller

(1915) and *El sombrero de tres picos* (The Three-cornered Hat) (1919)[1] he moved forward from the refined *zarzuela* style of his early *La vida breve* (1913) to a language in which Spanish dance-rhythms and melodies based on Spanish folk-song patterns are combined with a French elegance and polish, and the neo-classical element played a considerable part. In *El sombrero de tres picos*, where the influence of *Petrushka* is often felt, the use of a quasi-symphonic style gives the 'Dance of the Neighbours', which opens Part II, a size and a breadth quite new to music based on Spanish folk-songs and folk-dances.

In *El retablo de Maese Pedro* (Master Peter's Puppet Show) (1923) Falla wrote the finest and most intelligent of puppet-operas, reproducing with extraordinary skill the atmosphere of sixteenth-century Spain and drawing, like his master Felipe Pedrell (1841–1922), on contemporary material as his inspiration. *El Retablo* is as untranslatable as Dargo-mïzhsky's *Stone Guest*, but it is a small masterpiece. In Pedrell's own opera, *Els Pirineus* (The Pyrenees) (published 1894, performed 1902), archaic material is combined with music written in a style that owes something to Wagner yet remains fundamentally Latin in its graceful sentiment and physical verve. There was no flowering of opera, however, in Spain; Falla's dance-dramas remain the only serious Iberian contribution to the lyrical theatre in the first quarter of the twentieth century.

[1] See pl. IV.

SYMBOLIST DRAMA

Music formed an integral part of the Symbolist aesthetic, since it represented an ideal, abstract art to which all other arts are continually approximating. A Symbolist poem is essentially an act of contemplation, a magic evocation of the metaphysical reality behind appearances. Action belongs to the other, phenomenal world; and we have seen how Maeterlinck's dramas attracted both Debussy and Dukas by their interior nature, an intense life of the spirit that is hardly exteriorized in gesture or action. 'Vous avez brisé la glace avec des fers rougis' says Pelléas, after Mélisande's confession of love; and it is characteristic of symbolist drama in general that the surface of life is there shown as disturbed only when a character's emotional life has reached volcanic heat. In *A kékszakállú herceg vára* (Duke Bluebeard's Castle) (written in 1911, performed 1918) Béla Bartók (1881–1945) set an Hungarian adaptation by Béla Balázs of Maeterlinck's *Ariane et Barbe Bleue* in a style where the tonic accent of the Hungarian language combines with a *parlando rubato* to create vocal lines entirely new to European music. There is no action, only the change of mood induced in Judith by the successive opening of the seven doors in Bluebeard's castle. These are symbolized not only by the changing nature of the orchestral music (a 46-bar trill, recalling Strauss's *Salome*, for the torture-chamber: a horn theme against string tremolos for the flower-garden; an orchestral tutti, with organ and Debussy-like sequences of major triads for Bluebeard's wide domains) but also by the play of light and colour. This is an important element in the work, which moves out of darkness into light and back again into darkness. This association of colour with music, which had already interested Skryabin[1] and was to concern Schoenberg, is indicative of the synaesthesia which had been adumbrated by E. T. A. Hoffmann and Baudelaire and consciously aimed at by Wagner in his ideal of the *Gesamtkunstwerk*, against which Stravinsky and the whole neo-classical school were to protest. Although action is minimal, the psychological reflection of the music is clear: Bluebeard's happiness is contingent on those he loves, and he can possess them only in memory. Judith, by arousing these memories, automatically becomes one of them. Although there are momentary echoes of Debussy and Strauss (the D flat major 6/4 chord at Bluebeard's protestation of love after the opening of the sixth door) Bartók's language is already an individual blend of Hungarian and Western European elements, with chains of sevenths or minor seconds often built into powerful combinations.

[1] See above p. 36.

Ex. 95

(Tell me, Bluebeard, whom have you loved before me?)

Maeterlinck had attracted the attention of other writers and musicians quite outside the orbit of the French-speaking world, and Arnold Schoenberg (1874–1951) had written his symphonic poem *Pelleas und Melisande* (1902–3) 'after Maeterlinck', as well as setting *Herzgewächse* for soprano, celesta, harmonium, and harp (1911). More important in determining the character of Schoenberg's work for the theatre, however, were his experiences as a painter. These began in 1907, when he created portraits and masks which foreshadowed those of the artists who, five years later, were to form the Blaue Reiter group in Munich—Kandinsky, Klee, and Marc. Expression—'not the rendering of the visible, but the rendering visible'—was the object of this art; and Expressionism had from the outset something of the amorphous quality of the human psyche itself, lacking both the geometrical foundations of French Cubism and the intellectually defined aims of Italian Futurism. Schoenberg's monodrama *Erwartung* (Expectation) (composed in 1909, performed 1924) is a minutely detailed study of erotic tension and existential anxiety. Although the speech-like prosody is naturalistic, the exaggeration characteristic of all Expressionist art is to be found in the enormous melodic intervals, which give the vocal line the nature as well as the appearance of a fever chart.[1] Marie Pappenheim's text presents the monologue of a woman walking through a forest at night in search of her lover, whom she eventually finds dead. Every minute inflexion of her feelings is reflected in the myriad changes of instrumental colour, pitch, texture, and dynamics; and unacknowledged resentments and hostilities are exteriorized with the acuteness of the new psychological analysts. Schoenberg's language owes something still to the *Salome* and *Elektra* of Richard Strauss, but its nervous tension and fragmented texture are entirely novel, and the detailed, often delicate scoring for the large orchestra achieves a feverish delicacy.

Ex. 96

II. Szene (Very dark, wide path, tall, closely planted trees. She gropes her way forward)

[1] H. H. Stuckenschmidt, *Arnold Schoenberg* (Zürich, 1951: English translation, London, 1959), p. 54.

(Is that still the path? . . . Ah! here it is. What's that? Leave go of me! . . . hemmed in? . . . No—there was something creeping . . . and here too . . . who is that touching me? Go away—I must go on . . .)

In *Die glückliche Hand* (The Lucky Hand) (written in 1910–13, performed 1924) Schoenberg wrote an Expressionist drama in which the distinction between dream and reality is abolished. There is no logical sequence in the scenes between the Man, the Woman, and the Gentleman, only an often confused rhythmic polyphony and 'an insatiable piling up of harmonic complexes as an allegory of the many layers of the psychological subject.'[1] The writing for the chorus of six men and six women includes whispering and speaking as well as singing, and Schoenberg's insistence on the exact visual representation includes crescendos of colour, or shifting colour-schemes which reflect the emotions of the characters, as in the 25-bar sequence brown-dirty green-dark blue-grey which corresponds to a growing tension in the Man, and leads eventually to a bright-yellow climax.

These two works of Schoenberg's are the first examples in music of that exclusive concern with the suppressed elements in human existence that Adorno regards as necessarily characteristic of twentieth-century art.[2] 'In so far as art to-day has any real substance, it reflects without any concessions, and brings to the level of consciousness, what people would like to forget.' Radicalism such as this, pursued with such total and exclusive passion, posed the problem of musical theatre in terms which made any substantial continuity with the old opera out of the question. It was left to Schoenberg's pupil Alban Berg (1885–1935) to find a compromise.[3]

Outside Central Europe composers were not attracted by Symbolist

[1] Theodor W. Adorno, *Philosophie der neuen Musik* (Tübingen, 1949), p. 20.
[2] Ibid., p. 8.   [3] See below pp. 363 ff.

drama and knew little or nothing of Expressionism in these years. Rebikov's 'musico-psychological drama' *Alpha i Omega* (1911), which purports to show the beginning and the end of the human race in terms of diabolical seduction, is no more than a curiosity rendered musically tedious by an all too thorough and unimaginative use of whole-tone harmony. Stravinsky, on the other hand, was to experiment during the war years, when the resources of Dyagilev's ballet were no longer available, with chamber-music entertainments such as *Renard* (composed in 1916–17, performed 1922) and *L'Histoire du soldat* (1918). But both these must be considered as substitutes for opera rather than extensions of operatic form, and their examination belongs to the next chapter.[1]

[1] See pp. 211–15.

IV

MUSIC IN THE MAINLAND OF EUROPE: 1918–1939

By MOSCO CARNER

GENERAL CHARACTERISTICS

HERACLITUS'S 'All is flux, nothing is stationary' is true of all epochs that have witnessed a radical moral, political, intellectual, and artistic transvaluation; but it would appear to apply with particular force to the arts in the years between 1918 and 1939. Centripetal and centrifugal forces were pulling in opposite directions, school stood against school each proclaiming a different aesthetic creed, and the air was full of slogans and counter-slogans. It was as though a new *Sturm und Drang* had seized the European mind. In music, rumblings of the coming storm had been heard during the decade or so before the First World War. Both Debussy's impressionism and Schoenberg's expressionism sprang from a new 'feeling' about music and both represented far-reaching and successful attempts to free musical thinking from the fetters of tradition and to advance into new territory. Yet it was not until the beginning of the 1920s that the full strength of these powerful forces was felt—in Central Europe, where revolutionary political and social changes followed in the wake of a lost war and strongly influenced the arts, particularly in Germany, but also among young artists in France and Italy, who were profoundly affected by the new ideas that had sprung up during and shortly after the war. The general feeling was that one epoch had come to an end and another was born which held the promise of a regeneration, if not indeed a rebirth, of the human spirit, bringing with it a liberation from the obsolescent traditions and conventions of the romantic past. The millennium, so it seemed, was round the corner. If this optimism proved unjustified in the light of subsequent developments in the political and social life of most European nations, it nevertheless had the effect of creating in the arts a new outlook, a spectacular change of orientation among artists.

In music this transformation manifested itself in two aspects. On the one hand, open war was declared on the lingering romanticism and all it implied—pronounced subjectivism, unhindered projection of the artist's private ego into his work, the tendency to make music a means to an end by using it as a vehicle for emotional expression and psychological exploration or rendering it a reflecting mirror of literary and programmatic ideas. The most violent attacks were reserved for the Wagnerian music-drama and its progeny as the chief culprit in having led music away from its true self by the emphasis on emotional, psychological, philosophical, and mythological elements, by the sensuality and opulence of its tone colours and by the huge array of instrumental forces. More positively artists sought to write music that avoided at all costs the subjective, expressive factor and that aimed instead at a detached, objective attitude such, it was assumed, as had been cultivated in the Baroque period. Composers turned to a new consideration of the musical material as such, exploring its immanent laws of texture and structure and treating it in an analogous manner to the architect's handling of bricks and stone. 'Construction' became the alpha and omega of this New Music. The work of building in sounds and achieving a clear order and organization assumed the significance which the former emotional 'content' had possessed. Technical craftsmanship was placed on a higher plane than inspiration, the sheer *métier* was often exalted over imagination. This attitude scarcely affected the aesthetic merits of the works of such masters as Stravinsky, Bartók, or Schoenberg, but with less creative artists it led to a species of dry, cerebral academicism. Form, design, and texture were reduced to essentials and this explains the characteristic predilection for chamber music and chamber orchestras, in which each part of the fabric was set out with succinctness and clarity and was of individual musical account. This was the antithesis of the large forms and dense overloaded texture shown in late-romantic music, particularly the opera and the symphonic poem. In search of this ideal of pure construction a return was made to the style of Baroque polyphony, yet with a marked difference of emphasis; for the vast extension and final attenuation of tonality and the emancipation of the dissonance to an equal status with the consonance had led to the gradual destruction of functional harmony, and thus the new contrapuntal style developed largely non-harmonic, linear patterns, in which vertical configurations became the accidental result of horizontal part-writing. In the same way the Baroque forms of suite, concerto, and cantata were revived, as ideal moulds into which to pour a purely musical content, whereas the dramatic form of the sonata was correspondingly neglected. Expression became an incidental by-product of construction and even where it was intentional, as in operas and cantatas, it was expression not of subjective ego-bound feeling, but of an impersonal, more universal order. The object was to concentrate attention not on the individual's personal feelings, but on types of sentiment which possessed general validity. Whether it was the neo-classicism of Stravinsky, the New Objectivity of Hindemith, or the mixture of experiment with the urge to 'épater le bourgeois' of the young French artists known as 'Les Six'—all shared in common the negation of subjectivism and the concentration on an objective interplay of the constituents of the musical material. The sole exceptions in this general trend towards emotional detachment were Schoenberg, Berg, and, chiefly during his pre-dodecaphonic period, Webern. These composers adhered essentially to the aesthetic tenets of romanticism, pressing construction into the almost exclusive service of espressivo; and thus they represented, in a sense, the 'reaction'. Yet, on the other hand, Schoenberg's establishment of the serial method constituted an entirely novel and revolutionary approach to the technique of composition and resulted in the creation of what may be termed a true *ars nova*.

In short, the years between the German Wars formed a period of intense search for means whereby to transform radically the face of music and lend it a new physiognomy—a process that is parallel to the beginning of the seventeenth century when the old polyphony gave way to homophonic thinking and a whole new musical outlook was born. The strong impulse to find fresh solutions for old problems led to a rage of experiment, some of it issuing in merely ephemeral results but leading in other cases to enduring achievements which may be ranked with the great masterpieces of past ages.

STRAVINSKY AFTER THE *RITE*

One of the foremost exponents of the movement to break with the heritage of romanticism and evolve a new aesthetic outlook was Igor Stravinsky[1] (1882–1971). After the monster score of *The Rite of Spring* (1913) in which primitive 'barbaric' expression is combined with the highest degree of technical sophistication, especially in rhythm and instrumentation, Stravinsky realized that an extension of the boundaries of music in this direction was not possible and he changed his course, making simplicity and economy of means his guiding principle. Characteristic of this new development were already three pre-war compositions —the vocal *Three Japanese Lyrics* and *Pribautki* (written between 1912 and 1914) and the Three Pieces for String Quartet (1914),[2] intimate small-scale works of which the first two are scored for a chamber orchestra. This treatment was probably suggested by the peculiar instrumentation of Schoenberg's *Pierrot Lunaire* which Stravinsky heard in Berlin in

---

[1] For Stravinsky's earlier music see Chapter II.
[2] No. 1 is recorded in *The History of Music in Sound*, x.

1912, but it largely corresponded with the new aim he was setting himself in his artistic aspirations. The great restriction of forces available, particularly in the *Ballets Russes*, during the war years between 1914 and 1918, also played a purely practical part in determining Stravinsky's change of front.

This departure from his previous style reached its first culmination in a series of three chamber works for the stage—*Renard* (1917), *L'Histoire du soldat* (1918) and *Les Noces* (1917, orch. 1923)—in which Stravinsky evolved novel musico-dramatic forms and a new type of orchestration. Though they were written at the period when the composer had severed his connexion with his native country and was living in Switzerland, they still belong in style to his 'Russian' period and their texts all derive from Russian sources—in the case of *Renard* and *L'Histoire* from folk-tales and in *Les Noces* from records of ancient Russian folk customs and wedding rites. Stravinsky, who began as a nationalist, inherited his love of Russian folk-material from his teacher Rimsky-Korsakov, but the younger composer treated it in a strikingly different manner from his master. In *Renard* and *L'Histoire* he does not anchor the story in a definite time or place, but sets it in the timelessness and unreality of a fairy-tale; and as early as *Petrushka* (1911), instead of individual living characters he presents puppet-like figures governed by rudimentary primitive instincts. This mechanical, automaton-like element appears to correspond with a trait in Stravinsky's artistic make-up and finds its musical expression in the stereotyped, continuous repetition of short melodic-rhythmic patterns whose machine-like regularity is, however, broken up by the conflict between metre and rhythm, resulting in the displacement of the strong beats in the bar and in an ideal, if not actual, negation of the bar-line division of the phrases (see Ex. 97). In setting the texts of these three works Stravinsky was, of course, attracted by the story, by its poetic images and metaphors; but what exercised on him an equal, if not indeed stronger, fascination was the sequence of words and syllables—in short, the purely phonetic element which 'produces an effect on one's sensibility very closely akin to that of music'.[1]

Renard is a 'Burlesque in Song and Dance', one of whose novel features is the division of the cast into singers and actors, with the former (two tenors and two basses) placed in the orchestra. This procedure was adopted in order to ensure, on the one hand, the greatest possible concentration on the music and, on the other, the greatest liberty in the representation of the stage action; and it sprang from Stravinsky's dissatisfaction with the absence of close union between

[1] Igor Stravinsky, *Chroniques de ma vie* (Paris, 1935; English translation 1936, p. 91.)

music and action observed in the production of his opera *Rossignol* (The Nightingale) (1914). The plot of *Renard* unfolds in two dramatic episodes of which the second, with the exception of the ending, is a literal repetition of the first. The Fox lures the Cock from his perch and seizes him but, owing to the intervention of the Cat and the Goat, has to release him. The play starts again, but this time ends with the killing of the Fox by the Cat, followed by a jubilant dance, and the burlesque closes with the mummers' ancient request to the public:

> 'Et si l'histoir' vous a plu,
> Payez-moi c'qui m'est dû!'

The style of the work is Russian in the sense that it is marked by the repetition of short melodic phrases. But a typically Stravinskyian quality is noticeable in their outline, which is clear-cut and sharp-edged as though etched with a stylus, a feature that remains characteristic of all his later periods. Some of the melodies possess the flavour of Russian folk-song, as the introductory March which is partly Dorian, partly Phrygian, or the duet between the Cat and the Goat, sung to the accompaniment of a gusli.[1] The instrumental ensemble consists of flute, cor anglais, E flat clarinet, two horns, trumpet, string quintet, percussion, and cimbalom. This last instrument, for which the composer developed a strong liking, is largely used to accompany the Cock, playing sustained pedals and marking the rhythmic accents, and generally serves the purpose of holding the harmonic textures together. The sound produced by this unusual combination of instruments, particularly by the cimbalom, the various percussion instruments and the strings plucked and martellato, is dry, sharp, and very resonant.

Renard is a genuine burlesque with a strong element of caricature, as when, for instance, the Fox, disguised as a monk, sings to the Cock with an expression of mock-piety,[2] or when the Cock replies in an arrogant, complacent vein.[3] Stravinsky exacts from the four singers a large measure of vocal virtuosity and special effects, their music frequently imitating in a stylized fashion the noises of the farmyard. There is, however, no attempt at a fusion of the diverse musical, poetic, and dramatic elements, which are complementary rather than blended together, and the work as a whole creates a static effect partly due to the symmetrical arrangement of the action but more especially to the automaton-like, circumscribed, and formalized nature of the music.

L'Histoire du soldat was conceived in peculiar circumstances. During the latter part of the war Stravinsky found himself cut off from Russia,

---

[1] At 62.   [2] At 11.   [3] At 13.

and after the Russian Revolution of 1917 he decided never to return and settled for the time being in Switzerland. This meant that he could expect no income from Russia and it occurred to him to improve his situation by writing a stage work that would require only two or three characters and a handful of instruments and that could be produced in a mobile theatre to be transported from place to place and staged in the smallest locality. The Swiss poet, C. F. Ramuz, who had provided the French version of *Renard*, suggested a mimed narration, a story to be read, acted, and danced. Stravinsky's choice fell on Afanasyev's collection of Russian tales, which contains a cycle of stories dealing with the adventures of a deserter and his compact with the devil.

L'Histoire has four characters: the Soldier and the Devil who have speaking parts, the Princess who is a dancer, and the Narrator who combines several functions: he recounts the tale, sometimes comments on the action as an outsider rather in the manner of a Greek chorus, and at other times participates in it, expressing the Soldier's thoughts and feelings and occasionally addressing him in direct speech. The orchestra consists of a violin and a double bass, a clarinet (on account of its possessing the widest compass among the woodwind) and bassoon, a cornet-à-pistons, trumpet and trombone, and finally a variety of eight percussion to be managed by a single player, the whole to be directed by a conductor.

Stravinsky was partly influenced in his choice of this combination by contemporary jazz, a selection of which had been brought to him from America in 1918 by the conductor, Ernest Ansermet. Jazz was bound to appeal to a musician with such interest in rhythmic-percussive experiments as Stravinsky, and indeed he included a tango and a ragtime among the Princess's dances and followed this up by his *Ragtime* for eleven instruments (1918) and the *Piano Rag-Music* (1919).

The instrumental ensemble is to be placed on the stage, for it was the composer's view that seeing the movements of the players facilitates the spectator's auditory perception. On another 'drum' at the opposite side of the stage sits the Narrator, before a little table 'with a pint of white wine', while the centre is occupied by the actors. For the thirteen musical numbers, to be played simultaneously with the action or interpolated in the narration, Stravinsky drew on a great variety of sources: Russian folk-song, American ragtime, Argentine tango, Viennese waltz, Swiss brass band, and Bach chorale.[1] Yet all these heterogeneous elements are fused together in the alembic of Stravinsky's imagination, resulting in a perfect homogeneity of style. The melodic and contra-

[1] The Royal March, recorded in *The History of Music in Sound*, x, is pseudo-Andalusian.

puntal lines are invented in terms of the particular nature of the
instruments producing textures of sharply defined sonorities, and the
fact that the part-writing is linear rather than harmonically determined
accounts for the astringently dissonant character of the music, as illustrated in the following example which also shows the pull of rhythmic
phrases against the underlying metre:

Ex. 97

Stravinsky, it should be observed, pretends to no sympathy, no compassion for the Soldier; he is not emotionally involved and illustrates
from outside, dispassionate and objective. This tallies with the view he
expounded in his autobiography[1] where he wrote that

music, by its very nature, is essentially powerless to *express* anything at all,
whether a feeling, an attitude of mind, a psychological mood, a phenomenon
of nature, etc. . . . *Expression* has never been an inherent property of music.
That is by no means the purpose of its existence. If, as is nearly always the
case, music appears simply to express something, this is only an illusion and
not a reality . . . The phenomenon of music is given to us with the sole
purpose of establishing an order in things, including particularly the coordination between *man* and *time*. To be put into practice, its indispensable
and single requirement is construction. Construction once completed, this
order has been attained, and there is nothing more to be said . . . One
could not better define the sensation produced by music than by saying that it

[1] *Chronicle of my Life*, p. 91.

is identical with that evoked by contemplation of the interplay of architectural forms.

Stravinsky's theoretical axiom, however, does not entirely square with his actual practice which fell somewhat short of his strict demands for non-expressive music and pure construction. Even in his neo-classical works emotive impulses press to the surface, especially in the stage

works where something of the characters' feelings and sentiments is projected into the music, and it was not until Stravinsky embraced serial technique that he came near his ideal of pure construction. Nevertheless, it was left to the dodecaphonic Webern and the succeeding generation of advanced composers to realize (if this is not a contradiction in terms) the Platonic idea of construction. *Les Noces*, which was completed before *L'Histoire du soldat* but not orchestrated until 1923, expresses, together with the joys and exultation of bride and bridegroom, the awe and trepidation felt by man at the renewal of life. Stravinsky adapted the text from Kireyevsky's collection of Russian folk poems which contains a number bearing on the subject of peasant wedding customs, but he used this material in a very free manner, paying little heed to ethnographical considerations and aiming to reproduce not the actual character of the wedding ritual, but its essential spirit and feeling. Though entitled 'Russian Choreographic Scenes', the work is more in the nature of a stage cantata, with four scenes which follow one another without a break and employ four soloists (soprano, mezzo soprano, tenor and bass), chorus, four pianos, and percussion. There is no real plot, the action unfolding in four static tableaux which describe the preparations and the actual wedding of the couple.

The work displays an extraordinary unity of conception and treatment. Virtually all the material is derived from a single cell—the interval of the fourth divided into a major second and minor third and vice versa, and there are also other permutations. This basic motive is heard at the very beginning:

Ex. 98

The motive is pentatonic, being modelled on Russian folk-song, but in its elaborations it frequently takes on a modal character, and the presence in it of the major second leads, harmonically, to bitonal chords at the distance of that interval. In addition to the themes derived from the germ cell, there are several other ideas which are first introduced as counterpoints and subsequently achieve independence. The entire melodic material is of Stravinsky's own invention, with the exception of three themes which are, however, so closely integrated with the composer's individual language that they all but lose their original identity. The setting of the Russian text is syllabic almost throughout and emphasizes the sonorous (phonetic) quality of the words. It must be admitted that this peculiar treatment, in combination with the melodic-rhythmic repetitions, results in a certain monotony which was probably intentional, but it is a monotony which has an extraordinary mesmeric effect comparable to that of primitive Asian and African music.

Stravinsky's neo-classical phase, which began after *Les Noces*, has sometimes been dismissed as 'time travelling', 'musical impersonation', 'music about music', or simply as a 'pastiche' of older styles. Yet Stravinsky's neo-classicism reflects quite as much his own sharply defined individuality as the acute historical sense which he developed in order to fuse the Russian elements in his musical personality with the wide range of Western musical thought of the last three centuries. To possess a sense of the past is to enrich the present; and by his references to the styles of former composers Stravinsky has reconstituted a picture of Western musical tradition seen through the prism of his own imagination. The original music, observed with the sensibility and taste of an artist of a later age, is so metamorphosed as to acquire an altogether new meaning or, to put it differently, the old material is so rethought and commented upon in the light of Stravinsky's own artistic experience that the result is a genuine individual creation. Closely linked with this neo-classicizing tendency was Stravinsky's preoccupation with the Nietzschean dialectic of Apollonian and Dionysian art. The Apollonian artist has for his supreme object the creation of order by means of self-restriction and self-imposed laws. The Dionysian artist, on the other hand, is ruled by irrational urges and a pronounced tendency towards the frenzied and chaotic. After *The Rite of Spring* Stravinsky gradually turned from Dionysian to Apollonian art, moving on to a more or less abstract plane, where the invention appears at times cold, cerebral, and even arid. Even in those of his works which are coloured by a certain expressive element—*Oedipus Rex*, the *Symphony of Psalms*, and *Perséphone*—the emotions are of a generic, universal order finding expression in highly stylized and formalized music from which all suggestions of an anecdotal, picturesque, psychological, or philosophical nature are absent.

STRAVINSKY'S NEO-CLASSICISM

Stravinsky's neo-classical period was initiated by the ballet *Pulcinella* (1920), after music by Pergolesi, but the process of remoulding and rethinking the old material is here seen still in its initial and tentative stage. Pergolesi's themes are taken over intact, and while Stravinsky adheres to their original melodic outlines it is chiefly in the inner harmony and the rhythm that he begins to press his own stamp on the music; the harmonic texture is stiffened and given more violent impact by astringent chords, the symmetry of the phrases is broken and their regular accent often displaced by syncopation. Where Stravinsky is entirely himself is in the orchestration, in which he adapts the eighteenth-century concertante manner to his own brilliant purposes. The subsequent *Symphonies of Wind Instruments* (1920) and the Octet (1923) both employ an instrumental combination which is the outward expression of the impersonal, objective nature of the music. The absence from both works of the strings is significant.

The Octet, scored for flute, clarinet, two bassoons, two trumpets, and a tenor and bass trombone, is modelled partly on the Venetian renaissance style (Gabrieli) and partly on Bach. It consists of three compact movements—a Sinfonia (overture), an Air with five variations, and a

Finale. If the *Symphonies of Wind Instruments* already contained many passages of non-harmonic, linear counterpoint—to be distinguished from the technique of short ostinatos and heterophony characteristic of Stravinsky's Russian period—the Octet shows the total application of this typically twentieth-century Western device.

Between the *Symphonies of Wind Instruments* and the Octet Stravinsky composed the one-act opera *Mavra* (1922) which is in a sense a throwback to his Russian style, yet at the same time is influenced by his neo-classicistic preoccupation. In it he adopts and adapts to his own manner of speech the language of Glinka, Dargomïzhsky, and Tchaikovsky and writes in the convention of Russo-Italian opera. The libretto is based on a rhymed story, *The Little House in Kolomna*, by Pushkin— Pushkin who in the composer's own words 'was the most perfect representation of that wonderful line which began with Peter the Great and which, by a fortunate alloy, has united the most characteristically Russian elements with the spiritual riches of the West . . . As for myself, I had always been aware that I had in me the germs of this same mentality only needing development, and I subsequently deliberately cultivated it'.[1] This precise statement helps to explain one of the guiding aims which Stravinsky pursued after his 'Russian' period, and *Mavra* is a characteristic example of this in its resuscitation of the shades of Glinka and Tchaikovsky, whose Europeanized nationalism the composer compares favourably with the 'doctrinaire aestheticism' of the pure Russian nationalists. The opera, dedicated to the memory of Pushkin, Glinka, and Tchaikovsky, conveys, despite its comic action, a feeling of nostalgia and even bitterness which no doubt reflects Stravinsky's mixed feelings about Russia, ancient as well as modern. In style the work is an *opera buffa* consisting of arias, duets, and ensembles, but it has no recitatives.

Stravinsky's strong attraction to the wind ensemble, demonstrated in the *Symphonies of Wind Instruments*, the Octet and *Mavra*, was followed by an equally keen interest in the piano as a solo instrument. True, during his previous years he had written some piano pieces, such as the *Five Easy Pieces* (1917) and *The Five Fingers* (1921), but these were intended for his children; at the opposite end stand the *Piano Rag-Music* and the Three Movements from *Petrushka* (1921) (written for Artur Rubinstein) which are virtuoso pieces. In his use of the piano as an orchestral instrument he strongly emphasized its percussive aspect (*Petrushka*) developing this to a *ne plus ultra* in the martellato style of the four pianos in *Les Noces*. In the works of his neo-classical period he still exploits the percussive quality, but he takes advantage also of the

[1] *Chronicle of my Life*, p. 159.

legato and cantabile potentialities of the keyboard. This preoccupation with the piano led first to the Concerto for piano, wind orchestra, double basses and timpani (1924), then the Piano Sonata (1924), the Serenade in A (1925) and, after a lapse of four years, the Capriccio for piano and orchestra (1929). The characteristic common to these four works is the propulsive 'motoric' and 'open' writing for the piano and, in the first three works, the influence of the Baroque harpsichord style, while the Capriccio emulated the brilliant virtuoso writing of Weber or Mendelssohn.

The Piano Concerto was the first work that suggested Stravinsky's 'return to Bach'. The first movement is in the style of a Bach toccata whose introductory Largo recalls in its measured dotted rhythm Lully and the seventeenth-century French overture. The middle movement, a Larghissimo, unfolds with a stately tread somewhat reminiscent of Vivaldi, while the middle section contains a cantabile of incantatory effect, the orchestral melody in 2/4 being accompanied in the treble of the piano and the double basses by an implied 3/8 rhythm. The finale combines the flavour of eighteenth-century music with fierce syncopations which recall remotely the 'barbaric' rhythms of *Petrushka* and *The Rite of Spring*, proving that, despite the adoption of the Apollonian principle, Stravinsky's old Dionysian urge could not be altogether suppressed. The Piano Sonata is noteworthy for the sparse, attenuated texture of the first and last movements, mostly in two parts, with the treble of the opening Allegro at times thickened out with euphonious thirds and sixths. Yet the music as a whole strikes the ear as cold and calculated, and almost the only relief is provided by the lyrical charm of the middle movement, an Adagietto that is reminiscent, in its rich ornamentation and the ostinato-like appoggiaturas of the middle section, of early Beethoven. Though Stravinsky studied Beethoven's piano sonatas before his own composition, the latter is entirely different in form and in development of thought. The title 'sonata' is intended in its pre-classical, Baroque, sense denoting music to be played as against 'cantata', i.e. music to be sung. The Serenade in A is a far more genial and immediately attractive work emulating the style of eighteenth-century 'night music' and consisting of four short, well-contrasted movements. It provides a characteristic example of his concept of 'polar' or extended tonality, the note A acting as the point of harmonic attraction in the completely free flow of keys, and at various times assuming the function of tonic, dominant or major and minor third.

Stravinsky's neo-classicism assumed a profounder, more spiritual aspect after his discovery of the world of Greek antiquity. 'Discovery' is perhaps not quite the appropriate term since two of his very early works, the song cycle *Faun and Shepherdess* (1906) and the wordless song *Pastoral* (1908), already proclaim a certain affinity with the spiritual landscape of the Hellenic world. But it was not until Stravinsky came to live in Paris and felt the influence of Cocteau, Gide, and other writers that classical antiquity with its idealistic yet essentially tragic view of life—man living in a realm of purity and serenity but pursued by a remorseless Fate—exercised a fascination on him, and gave rise to a series of important stage-works—the opera-oratorio *Oedipus Rex* (1927), the ballet *Apollo Musagetes* (1928), the melodrama *Perséphone* (1934), and the ballet *Orpheus* (1948).

The choice of the Sophoclean *Oedipus* as a subject for an opera-oratorio was determined by two facts. One was Stravinsky's desire to use a plot known to the generality of spectators, so that their undivided attention could be given to the musical treatment. The second and, perhaps, more important fact is to be found in an affinity between something in Stravinsky's own personality and the spirit of the Greek play, which shows man as the plaything of higher, supernatural forces, entangled in the meshes of a snare that gradually closes on him and eventually destroys him. This idea of a tragic destiny suspended like the sword of Damocles over the human being had in the past given rise to three of Stravinsky's works—*Petrushka*, *The Rite of Spring* and *L'Histoire du soldat*—but *Oedipus Rex* projects it in the most un-equivocal, direct terms yet with a striking economy of dramatic gestures. What there is of external action is chiefly confined to the latter part of the drama—the revelation of the Messenger and Shepherd, the suicide of Jocasta, and the self-mutilation of Oedipus. For the greater part Stravinsky concentrates on the inner, psychological, action—the fall of Oedipus from his height as the proud and self-confident King of Thebes into an abyss of misery and tragic guilt. Cocteau's libretto, which is masterly in the compression of the ancient tragedy and impressive in the simple dignity of the language, was translated into Latin (by Jean Daniélou) which was Stravinsky's idea. Reading Joergensen's book *St. Francis of Assisi* he discovered that the saint (whose native language was Italian) used French on all solemn occasions; and by analogy he decided to have a Latin text, which had the advantage of being 'a medium not dead but turned to stone and so monumentalized as to have become immune from all risk of vulgarization'.[1]

The static, hieratic, and impersonal character of the drama is already emphasized in the 'alienation' effect created by its method of produc-tion: the stage has no depth, the whole action taking place on one level suggesting a bas-relief. With the exception of Tiresias, the Shepherd, and

[1] *Chronicle of my Life*, p. 210.

the Messenger, the characters appear in built-up costumes and masks, moving only their heads and arms and producing the effect of living statues; their entries and exits are made through trap doors which are alternately veiled and unveiled by special curtains; the chorus sits on three tiers. To assist the spectators in recalling the detail of the plot, a Speaker in evening dress explains, in the vernacular, the action in an impersonal, detached way like a lecturer. In his musical design Stravinsky follows the scheme of eighteenth-century opera and oratorio: self-contained arias, duets, and choruses which have no thematic connection and are arranged like stark contiguous blocks of granite, the cumulative effect of which is one of awe-inspiring monumentality. The idiom is for the most part diatonic, another means by which the composer achieves directness, immediacy, and simplicity of expression. The pervasive rigidity of the rhythmic language corresponds with the ritualistic character of the tragedy, and it is only at the peripeteia—the highly dramatic scene between the Messenger and the Shepherd—that the cast-iron regularity of the metrical scheme is abandoned in favour of a more irregular treatment, with asymmetrical phrases reminiscent of the composer's 'Russian' style.

The musical material of *Oedipus Rex* is derived from widely differing sources—Handel and Bach, Verdi and the early nineteenth-century Italian opera, and Russian music. But these heterogeneous materials are moulded together into a new and entirely original synthesis in which not a single bar could have been written by any other composer but Stravinsky. Oedipus is the sole character who is shown in a consistent psychological development—from the first aria 'Liberi, vos liberabo', expressing his self-assurance and supreme pride in the stiffness of the vocal writing which is marked by a high tessitura and oriental melismas, to the final 'Natus sum quo nefastum est' where at last he recognizes the enormity of his guilt and reaches the point of utter humiliation. His thrice-repeated phrase rotating round the constituent notes of the B minor chord (accompanied by shuddering strings and woodwind) and his last 'Lux facta est' are characteristic examples of Stravinsky's use of the simplest harmonic formulae in the service of an intense dramatic expression. These and other instances in this work demonstrate the extent to which he revitalizes seemingly outworn harmonic devices and achieves a strikingly fresh effect by divesting them of their original tonal function and grafting them on the living tissues of his personal style.

If *Oedipus Rex* was an illustration of the tragic aspect of Greek mythology, the ballet *Apollo Musagetes*, written a year after, represents the opposite world—the world of Arcadian bliss, unruffled calm, and supreme serenity and beauty. It may be taken as an allegory on the theme of artistic creation: Apollo inspires the muses and leads them to a final apotheosis on Mount Parnassus. The composer intended the work as a *ballet blanc*, devoid of all psychological, narrative and expressive interest, with an abstract choreography based on the traditional classical forms of pas d'action, pas de deux, and variation and using simple scenery and monochrome antique costumes. Musically this finds its counterpart in a predominantly diatonic style from which all harmonic tension and conflict are banished, and the effect of extreme calm and purity is heightened by the use of a string orchestra to which the composer returned after twelve years of comparative neglect. In his *Chronicle of my Life*[1] he writes of the utter delight he experienced in employing the string medium whose original purpose, he says, was the cultivation of *canto*, and he wished to compose music in which 'everything evolved round the melodic principle' making 'the multi-sonorous euphony of the strings penetrate even the furthest fibre of the polyphonic web'.

Perséphone, for which André Gide supplied the text, bears the subtitle 'melodrama', a description not to be understood in the traditional sense of music accompanying a spoken text but as indicating a hybrid between opera and ballet, which combines music, singing, dancing, miming, and spoken recitative. The work is divided into three parts—*The Abduction of Perséphone, Persephone in the Underworld* and *The Rebirth of Persephone*. In the treatment of the text Stravinsky is seen to apply his by now customary method of repeating words and whole sentences in order to build up his musical phrases, a striking instance of which is the four-part chorus of Nymphs, Danaids, and Shades in the second part. Similarly, to suit his rhythmic patterns he broke up the words into syllables, to the discomfiture of Gide who, rightly, felt that this method did violence to his prosody. This aerated style of writing, which Stravinsky had already used in *Oedipus Rex*, lends the music an extraordinary limpidity and transparency and the idiom is in an even more pronounced diatonicism than in *Apollo Musagetes*, while the rhythms are remarkably fluent and subtle but frequently of a regular pattern, entire sections adhering to the identical metre. The melodic invention is distinguished by a natural, unforced flow and almost the whole of the work is marked by a remarkable tenderness of expression.

Stravinsky's love and admiration for Tchaikovsky, to which he first gave expression in the opera *Mavra*, prompted him six years later to a ballet *Le Baiser de la Fée* (The Fairy's Kiss) (1928), composed in commemoration of the thirty-fifth anniversary of the composer's death; the choreographic action is taken from Hans Andersen's *The Ice Maiden*.

[1] pp. 221-2.

While in *Mavra* it is only the style which is reminiscent of Tchaikovsky, the themes being Stravinsky's own, in the ballet the material is borrowed *in toto* from the older composer and treated in something like the manner of *Pulcinella* yet without the sense of parody and caricature characteristic of that earlier score. *The Fairy's Kiss* foreshadows another and far more successful work written by Stravinsky eight years later. This was *Jeu de cartes* (Card Game) (1936), a ballet in 'Three Deals', whose choreographic plot revolves round a game of poker, with the various characters represented by the chief cards. In the first two deals the Joker, because of his ability to become any desired card, stirs up all sorts of trouble, but in the last deal he is beaten by a Royal Flush of Hearts which puts an end to his malice and knavery. In a sense this ballet forms a counterpart to *L'Histoire du soldat* which is also concerned with the force of evil but closes with the triumph of the devil, while *Jeu de cartes* ends with his defeat. Each of the three 'deals', which follow without a break, is prefaced by the same 'processional' music, intended to suggest the shuffling of the card pack; each of the main movements, however, bears a distinct character of its own and although the musical ingredients derive from a great variety of sources—Haydn and Weber, Delibes and Tchaikovsky, Johann Strauss and Ravel—the result is unmistakably original.

THE 'SYMPHONY OF PSALMS' AND LATER WORKS

We must now retrace our steps to the year 1930 to examine the first major work in which Stravinsky gave eloquent expression to his deep-seated religious feelings. The *Symphony of Psalms* originated in a request by Sergey Kusevitsky to compose a work in celebration of the fiftieth anniversary of the foundation of the Boston Symphony Orchestra; but a profounder and more exalted impulse is revealed in the inscription 'composed to the Glory of God'. In his *Poetics of Music*[1] the composer ascribed to music the aim of promoting 'a communion with our fellow-men and with the Supreme Being' which gives a clear indication of the spiritual significance he perceived in music in general and in sacred music in particular.

In choosing three of the Psalms from the Vulgate (38: 13–14; 39: 2–4; 150) Stravinsky was concerned with man's relation to God in the spirit of the Old Testament which, in contrast to the Christian doctrine, knows of no redemption but only offers the consolation of hope and comfort in the struggle and sufferings of life on this earth, in response to man's humble prayer and obedience. It is to this conception, compounded of utter humility and severity, that the work gives unique expression,

[1] Harvard, 1947, p. 18.

avoiding all undue dramatization of the text, toning down the impulse of all subjective feeling, aspiring to a devout contemplation of divine mystery and thus raising its message to the plane of universality. The work is of an extraordinary compactness and terseness, lasting about twenty minutes; and although there is a marked contrast in the structure and texture of the three linked movements—'Prayer' (Prelude), 'Thanksgiving' (Double Fugue) and 'Hymn of Praise' (Symphonic Allegro)—it yet conveys the distinct feeling of a higher, spiritual, unity which is largely achieved by the application of Stravinsky's principle of similarity. What contributes to this impression is a motive of two interlinked minor thirds which in various permutations recurs in all three movements, yet does not possess the role of germ cell from which, as in *Les Noces*, all the essential material is evolved. In the opening movement this basic motif is to be found mainly as an accompanying figure, in the second movement it forms part of the subject of the instrumental fugue, with the second minor third now inverted to a major sixth, and in the finale it appears in the opening chorus 'Laudate Dominum':

Ex. 99

In the 'Prayer' the contrapuntal burden is carried by the orchestra while the choral writing is predominantly homophonic and is marked, first, by small intervals, as in the subdued 'Exaudi orationem meum, Domine', sung on the two adjacent notes E and F; but, as the prayer grows more fervent, the intervallic steps become wider. The 'Thanksgiving' is fugal, showing the composer at the height of his polyphonic ingenuity, especially in the manner in which he achieves a close yet entirely effortless interlocking of the instrumental and choral subjects. The most extensive piece is the 'Hymn of Praise' which is less concentrated in the structure than the two preceding movements but of a more varied texture. The gulf that separates Stravinsky from musicians of the past centuries is seen in the way in which he sets the opening line, 'Alleluia. Laudate Dominum' (Ex. 99(iii)). Where other composers would have burst forth in loud jubilations he preserves an attitude of utter calm and humility and even where the text invites a pictorial image, as in 'Laudate Eum in cymbalis', the music remains subdued and inward-glancing. This is not to say that the 'Hymn of Praise' is entirely devoid of a feeling of joyful exultation and ecstatic fervour, but its general tendency is towards the expression of tranquil, sublimated emotions, and, significantly, it closes with the same ethereal choral phrase with which it began.

After the *Symphony of Psalms* Stravinsky turned to a medium which, except for a passing excursion in *L'Histoire du soldat*, he had not attempted before—music for the solo violin. The immediate cause for this awakening of a new interest was his acquaintance in early 1931 with the violinist Samuel Dushkin, for whom he composed the Violin Concerto (1931) and the Duo Concertante for violin and piano (1932). This task afforded the composer the opportunity for a more serious study of the expressive and virtuosic possibilities of the violin, while Dushkin collaborated with him in the matter of technical details. The Concerto which, following established precedents, is in the 'violinistic' key of D, and shows in general character a certain affinity with the Capriccio for piano and orchestra. Of the four movements, the opening Toccata and the closing Capriccio are modelled on eighteenth-century patterns (Bach and Mozart) and represent *Spielmusik* in the true sense, displaying the composer's delight in the sheer manipulation of form, design, and texture for their own, purely musical sakes. In the Toccata soloist and orchestra have interchangeable material. By contrast, the Aria I and II are in an expressive lyrical vein, with much sustained cantabile writing, and in the Aria II the melodic line dissolves into rich yet most supple filigrees (runs and arpeggios). Roman Vlad[1] perceives in the two arias Stravinsky's wistful longing for the full expressiveness that music once possessed, an abandonment to a nostalgic 'recherche du temps perdu'. In the Duo Stravinsky explores the potentialities of the violin in conjunction with the piano. The work is a small-scale illustration of Stravinsky's attraction to the ancient Hellenic world, for in spirit and formal structure it is intended as a musical counterpart to the pastoral poetry and scholarly art of antiquity,

[1] *Stravinsky* (Turin, 1958; English translation 1960), pp. 115–16.

with its enforcement of strict rules and an iron discipline on lyrical composition. A common theme runs through all the five movements, lending them coherence and unity; it first occurs in the fifteenth bar of the opening Cantilena and is given its most articulate shape in the slow Eclogue II, the central piece of the work round which the other movements are symmetrically grouped. The tranquil, serene lyricism of this Eclogue is admirably matched by the bucolic charm of Eclogue I, which opens with a delightful bagpipe episode, the bass of the piano playing a patterned drone-like ostinato while the treble echoes in canon the chanter tune of the violin, the note A being sustained as an inner pedal. The brilliant Gigue is a perpetuo mobile and the final Dithyrambe is noteworthy for its gently undulating piano phrases in three and four parts and an expressive violin cantilena which reaches its climax in a passage of truly ecstatic fervour.

In the Concerto for Two Pianos (1935) Stravinsky displays the same delight in making music for its own sake, the same enjoyment in solving specific stylistic and technical problems as characterized the Violin Concerto and the Duo Concertante. It is on an imposing scale consisting of four movements, of which the first is remarkable for the trenchant force of its rhythmic invention and its extraordinary dynamic impulse. The Notturno excels in delicate lyrical writing, the ensuing Four Variations are a *locus classicus* of the composer's unremitting search for novel construction, and in the four-part fugue all existing contrapuntal devices are brought into vivid play. As in Mozart's Sonata for Two Pianos (K.448), which served Stravinsky as a point of departure, the two instruments share the same material, but the twentieth-century musician goes a step further in achieving a rare

Ex. 100

degree of taut, close-knit texture, frequently cutting up a thematic idea and dividing it between the two instruments, a style of writing that creates the impression of a contest between two wrestlers (Ex. 100).

A feature of the Four Variations is the absence of an explicitly stated theme, the first variation starting with a zigzagging motive of wide intervals which only gradually takes on a firmer outline until it achieves its fully developed shape as the vigorous subject of the final fugue. And for all the wide range of keys touched in the course of the music there is, nevertheless, a strong pull towards the note E as the tonal pole of the entire work, which opens and closes in a clear E major.

In the Dumbarton Oaks Concerto in E flat (1938), so called after the place in America where it was composed, Stravinsky aimed at a work which, on his own admission, follows the style of Bach's Brandenburg Concertos. Yet his indebtedness to Bach is largely confined to emulating the general shapes of themes and to the choice of a chamber orchestra of fifteen players. The strings and wind are treated in concertante style but, unlike his model, Stravinsky makes no attempt at writing a proper concertino.

In concluding this section we may attempt a brief definition of the general significance of Stravinsky's achievement during the period of the inter-war years. A number of points emerge. In the first place, Stravinsky was one of the first to exploit Debussy's rediscovery of the primary nature of music, i.e. the meaningful organization of sound, and liberate it from the extra-musical superstructure of psychological, philosophical, and metaphysical notions and ideas imposed on it by the romantics. He saw his role in terms of the medieval master-craftsman for whom his material was something to be worked upon according to its inherent properties—hence Stravinsky's concentration on texture, design, harmony, counterpoint, and instrumentation. In this he was guided by a most highly developed sense of order, discipline, and adjustment of means to ends—the principal characteristics of the Apollonian spirit at whose shrine Stravinsky worshipped after his Dionysian 'Russian' period. Few modern composers have displayed greater technical ingenuity, skill, and resourcefulness in handling and moulding the raw material of music. If, for a time, Stravinsky adopted an almost inhuman, coldly objective detachment from all emotion and feeling, this was only a passing phase. While it lasted Stravinsky showed a marked predilection for an orchestral style *sec*, trenchant and coruscating in which, significantly, wind instruments, piano, and percussion occupied the forefront while the expressive strings were relegated to the background. Later works such as *Oedipus Rex*, the *Symphony of Psalms*, and *Perséphone*, while ostensibly aiming at an 'alienation', in fact refute Stravinsky's theoretical axiom that music was incapable of expressing anything at all and that construction was both its meaning and scope.

Neo-classicism appears, in retrospect, to have sprung from a deep-rooted urge to fuse the East with the West by bringing Western styles and techniques to bear upon an intrinsically Eastern or Russian mode of thought. (Bartók pursued a similar aim after his discovery of Hungarian folk-song, see p. 275.) For example, the constant reiteration of short melodic-rhythmic fragments, though much attenuated in his neo-classical works, derives ultimately from Stravinsky's Russian heritage and was grafted on to devices common to European music of several centuries. As with Bartók, this process of assimilation resulted in compositions of a highly original order, which present a panoramic view of musical history reinterpreted and used as a potent fertilizer. Within the neo-classical framework Stravinsky developed an astonishing diversity of styles and manners of projection, due to his particular approach which considers each new work as a new adventure, a novel and isolated creation demanding a novel and appropriate mode of treatment. Stravinsky is the perfect stylist, in the sense that to each new work he brought a wholly apt and commensurate technical apparatus. In spite of the kaleidoscopic changes in his style, changes comparable to Picasso's zigzagging evolution, a basic unity can be discerned in Stravinsky's music of the inter-war years, the corollary of a fully integrated artistic personality which pervades and holds together the complex and variegated character of his utterance. Lastly, he stands almost unrivalled in the harnessing of a crystal-clear, penetrating, and highly analytical intellect strictly controlling the conscious part of his creative processes, to a rich, vivid, and most versatile imagination. A whole generation of younger composers benefited from his widening of the horizon, and this was particularly true of the French musicians of the 1920s whose country Stravinsky had adopted as his physical and spiritual home and where his personality and influence were, therefore, most strongly felt.

SERGEY PROKOFYEV

Born a decade later than Stravinsky and in many ways his opposite in musical character, Sergey Prokofyev was the *enfant terrible* of his generation at the St. Petersburg Conservatoire, where he studied composition with Lyadov and orchestration with Rimsky-Korsakov and became, under Anna Esipova's tuition, a brilliant pianist of a kind hitherto unknown, an athlete rather than a poet of the keyboard. An interest in neo-classicism was first prompted by the visit of Max Reger to St. Petersburg in 1906, when he conducted a programme of his own works including the Serenade in G major, Op. 95. Prokofyev's *Ten Pieces for Piano* (1908–13) reflect this interest, and so even more clearly does the eighteenth-century pastiche of his *Classical Symphony* (1916–1917). He also admired the orchestral music of Richard Strauss and Aleksandr Skryabin, making a piano transcription of the first movement of *Le Divin Poème*; and both admirations are reflected in his own First Piano Concerto (1912). The music of Debussy and the early work of Stravinsky had little attraction for the young Prokofyev, whose extraordinary musical fertility and rough, irreverent high spirits resembled those of the young Hindemith and made him all but totally unacceptable to the cultured and sophisticated members of the Dyagilev set. Even so Prokofyev's *Scythian Suite* (*Ala and Lolly*) (1914–15) was clearly prompted by the same contemporary movement of interest in the Russian past (*Skifstvo*) as Stravinsky's *Rite of Spring*, which it rivals in aggressive 'modernism' of harmony and rhythm. There was to be little in Prokofyev's music comparable with the French sophistication, and later the erudite historicism, which played civilizing, westernizing roles in Stravinsky's musical development.

The role of iconoclast and rebel was indeed an important part of the young Prokofyev's image of himself, and his reputation as composer and performer was predominantly one of ruthlessness and physical energy. Certainly the public found these qualities in the first three piano concertos and the *Toccata*, overshadowing the delicate and very personal *Sarcasms* and *Visions fugitives* and the almost Mussorgskian *Tales of the Old Grandmother*, all piano works written between 1912 and 1918. His first ballet *Shut* (The Buffoon, 1920), the cantata *Semero ikh* (Seven, they are seven, 1918) and two of his first three operas reveal how deeply Prokofyev was rooted in the literary and artistic world of pre-revolutionary Russia. The cantata is the setting of a hermetic text by Konstantin Balmont, while the libretto of *Lyubov k trem apelsinam* (Love for Three Oranges, 1921) is taken from the sardonic and fantastic Gozzi and that of *Ognenniy Angel* (The Flaming Angel, composed 1919–27 but first performed 1955) from the 'decadent' Symbolist poet Valery Bryusov. Only his *Igrok* (The Gambler, 1915–16) was based on a realistic story by Dostoevsky.

Prokofyev's musical language during the years which he spent outside Russia (1917–32), though even more strongly diatonic in basic character than Stravinsky's, was marked by jagged tonal shifts, which often replaced traditional modulation; wide-spaced and deliberately angular melodic patterns; aggressive harmonies formed by chromatic added notes often with distinct bitonal implications; and most notably by rhythms of whirlwind force and motoric regularity and persistence. The devil-may-care humour, mordant satire and sheer physical excitement of this music have much in common with those of the young Hindemith, and also of the younger generation of French composers (Milhaud, Poulenc) who were among his friends during the years he spent in Paris (1923–32). Much later in life he was to write 'The cardinal virtue (or sin, if you like) of my life has been the search for an original musical language, a musical language of my own. I detest imitation; I detest hackneyed methods. I always want to be myself.'[1] That the lyrical gift

[1] Quoted in I. V. Nestyev, *Prokofyev* (Moscow, 1957, Eng. trans. 1961, p. 466).

which he cultivated consciously after his return to Russia in 1932 was from the beginning part of his musical character is clear from the First Violin Concerto (1916–17) and the Third Piano Concerto (1917–21) among many other works. But it was obscured by the consciously harsh, 'constructivist' character of many of the works of Prokofyev's Parisian days—the Second Symphony and the ballet *Le Pas d'acier* (both 1925) and the Third Symphony (1929) in which the composer reworked themes from the hysterical *Flaming Angel*. Prokofyev was in touch with Russian musical life for almost ten years before he returned finally to live there. There were performances of his works in Russia as early as 1923 and he paid a visit there in 1927. As he became increasingly disillusioned with what seemed to him the artificial nature and narrowly restricted appeal of contemporary music in Western Europe, it was natural that he should become more aware of the ties that bound him to his native country and the possibilities that it promised him as a composer.[1]

THE OLDER GENERATION IN FRANCE

The musical scene in France between the two wars presented a confusing but extremely vivid picture. There was the old guard consisting of Fauré, Roussel, and Ravel, who were the last representatives of 'le troisième âge d'or' in French music and, with the exception of Fauré, belonged to the same generation as Debussy. In strong opposition 'Les Nouveaux Jeunes' were inspired by new ideals and, under the collective name of 'Les Six', at first rallied round the figure of the ageing Satie making him their involuntary *chef d'école*. Lastly, in the mid-1930s a new group, 'La Jeune France', in its turn reacted against the supposedly excessive cosmopolitanism of the previous generation and sought a regeneration of French music on national lines.

Gabriel Fauré (1845–1924) was seventy-three when the war ended, but in his few remaining years he composed six chamber works, chamber music having always been a particular interest, a few piano compositions, and three song cycles. An exclusive and reticent musician, Fauré had always been inclined to write for himself and a select circle of connoisseurs rather than for the large public, and during his last years he became even more discreet, subtle, and elliptical in his utterance. This latest development was partly due to his total deafness which may account for the fact—as it does in the case of Beethoven—that Fauré's last works reveal a marked attitude of self-communion and a tendency to explore to its furthest limits an esoteric and ascetic manner of expression. As his English biographer says,[2] in the chamber works 'the

[1] On his career in the Soviet Union, see Chapter VIII.
[2] Norman Suckling, *Fauré* (London, 1946), p. 118.

opening movements are vigorous without protestation, their finales without effervescence; and the intervening andantes in particular distil an atmosphere of peaceful intensity where every vibration is significant without being insistent, by means of a sensitiveness of the mind's ear'. Fauré's textures become extraordinarily sparse and transparent, the harmony achieves a new simplicity, and the thematic material shows a remarkable condensation. True, the long flowing melodic lines so characteristic of his previous style still occur here and there, as in the slow movements of the First Cello Sonata (1918) or the opening movement of the Second Cello Sonata (1921), but they are more often than not replaced by cellular melodic units, as in the second movement of the Piano Quintet (1921) and the String Quartet (1924), a transcendental work and, like his late songs, tenuous and elusive. In the works for piano, such as the *Fantaisie* (1919), the keyboard writing is so designed as to achieve a measure of coherence by means of such typically Fauréan devices as scale passages, crossing and recrossing of the melodic lines and harp-like arpeggios; but there are exceptions as seen in the antiphonal treatment of piano and strings in the Trio (1924) which for a composer approaching his eightieth year is remarkably fresh and vivid. In the two song cycles, *Mirages* (1919) and *L'Horizon chimérique* (1922), a setting of four poems by Jean de la Ville de Mirmont, Fauré captures the evocative power of the text and the significance of individual sentences with an unexampled artistry. These songs exhale an air of aristocratic refinement and discretion, a civilized tranquillity in which the underlying emotions are but vaguely sensed. Together with Roussel, Fauré was the last great traditionalist of French music, embodying the spirit of French culture in its purest form and combining it with a classical serenity of an almost Hellenic quality.

Albert Roussel (1869–1937), who was a pupil of Vincent d'Indy and for many years teacher at the Schola Cantorum, allied the serious outlook of his master and the technical solidity and discipline of that School to a sensibility that, though increasingly affected by the new post-war spirit, never lost its refined and poetic qualities. Roussel was a fastidious and highly self-critical artist who aimed 'to achieve music which is self-contained, music which is divorced from any illustrative and descriptive elements and is free from any localization in place . . . Far from wishing to write descriptive music, I constantly try to obliterate from my mind the memory of objects and forms capable of being translated into musical terms. I want my music to be nothing but music.'[1] Whether Roussel adopted this austere attitude under the influence of the neo-classical Stravinsky or followed his own inclination

[1] Quoted in Arthur Hoérée, *Albert Roussel* (Paris, 1937), p. 66.

the fact is that, with advancing maturity, he was more and more given to an abstract conception rare in a French musician, yet his individual style remained strongly marked and manifested itself, above all, in a highly developed rhythmic sense and a natural ability for polyphonic writing. The majority of his post-war works reveal a rough-hewn, granite-like quality which is in sharp contrast to the subtle and seductive textures of Debussy or the highly ornate patterns of Ravel; and they possess a directness of expression that makes its points without circumlocution. Roussel was an unsentimental, powerful figure in whom there was an element of the peasant and the long, piercing glance of the sailor.

His descriptive *Pour une Fête de printemps* (1920), with its romantic and impressionistic features, was the last work of Roussel's to look back to his previous style, and it is only the bitonal clash of the opening chord that gives an indication of the direction in which the composer was to progress. With the Second Symphony (1921) begins what has been termed his 'classical' period when he discarded earlier influences, chiefly Debussy's. This was followed by the Suite in F (1926) and the Concerto for Small Orchestra (1927), both of which are examples of Roussel's growing realization of his mature self which found complete and masterful expression in the Third Symphony (1930) and the Fourth Symphony (1934). The Third manipulates a basic five-note theme with an extraordinary resourcefulness, and the entire work is remarkable for its extreme formal compression, the taut, clear-cut texture and its tremendous rhythmic force—the embodiment, it would seem, of sheer energy. The Fourth Symphony is more detached in outlook and its salient stylistic features are to be seen in a sinewy counterpoint and bare astringent harmonies (tritone, major sevenths, and the chord of the eleventh) which are the result of the uncompromising part-writing. The robust vitality of the opening movement is offset by the poetic quality of the slow movement for which is reserved the main emotional climax of the work, while the finale brings the crowning affirmation of the music's predominant spirit.

If Roussel's later orchestral works are characteristic of the classical bent of his art, his stage works pursue a more varied stylistic course. *Padmâvatî*, an opera-ballet in two acts (1918), to a libretto by Louis Laloy, deals with a barbaric episode in Indian history of the thirteenth century and is based on Hindu scales employed both in the melody and harmony and organically integrated into Roussel's own individual style, which is expanded and enriched through his free conception of modality and a more varied and more supple application of rhythmic patterns. In the classical ballet, *La Naissance de la lyre* (1924), which has a scenario after Sophocles, the chief basis of the material is the ancient

Greek modes. A second ballet with a classical subject, *Bacchus et Ariane* (1930), is characterized by a vigorous rhythmic style and clear, sharply defined melodic lines, while the orchestration echoes at times the exquisite lights and shades of Debussy's impressionism. *Aeneas* (1935), the composer's third classical ballet, is exceptional in that it is more choral than orchestral music, and contains a percussion part for piano in which Roussel pays homage to Stravinsky. He always wanted to write an opera in a light and humorous vein which he achieved in the delightful though perhaps rather *risqué* comedy, *Le Testament de la Tante Caroline* (1933), which stands apart from the canon of his works.

Roussel showed no natural feeling for the piano. His Piano Concerto (1927) is an introspective and technically forbidding work in which the solo instrument largely explores the lower registers. The Cello Concerto (1936), his last orchestral composition, resembles a concerto grosso in that the orchestra is more individually treated than is usual in a concerto. Of Roussel's post-war chamber music, the String Quartet (1932) and String Trio (1937)[1] stand out for the combination of a taut logical thought with a fastidious taste and a highly refined sensibility.

Roussel's chief achievement lies in the solidity and distinction of his craftmanship with which he upheld the precepts of the Schola Cantorum; in his purely musical approach to matters of form, design, and texture, and in the way in which, emerging from the impressionism of his early and middle periods, he fashioned a powerful personal style that is deeply rooted in the time-honoured traditions of French culture and art. Like Fauré, he belonged to what has been aptly called 'the silver age of Latin civilization',[2] but being a younger man than Fauré, he survived into a time which saw the dissociation and even disruption of traditional values.

Maurice Ravel (1875-1937), the youngest member of the older generation, continued to enjoy the world-wide reputation which he had established for himself by his pre-war works,[3] but in his own country he was entirely out of favour with the young group of 'Les Six' who reproached his music for excessive refinement and ornateness, regarding him as an exponent of obsolete aesthetics. Ravel felt a strong resentment at losing his position among the leaders of musical fashion and strove hard towards a transformation and even rejuvenation of his style and technical methods. The results, however, were not altogether convincing. Ravel had done his best work before 1920 and, although his extraordinary refinement of taste, his perfect sense of form and his most

---

[1] From which the first movement is recorded in *The History of Music in Sound*, x.

[2] Martin Cooper, *French Music. From the death of Berlioz to the death of Fauré* (London, 1951), p. 214.   [3] See Chapter II, particularly pp. 101-5.

fastidious and brilliant workmanship were as much in evidence as of old, his creative energy now began to show tell-tale signs of impatience, strain, and fatigue. As one of his French biographers implies,[1] Ravel was touching the boundaries of his nature—boundaries around which the very perfection of his technique had created all but impassable barriers. This is already noticeable in the first of his post-war compositions, the choreographic poem *La Valse* (1920), an evocation of the atmosphere of a Second Empire ballroom in which an apotheosis of the Viennese waltz is linked with the suggestion of a fantastic whirl of destiny. Yet the febrile character of this *danse macabre* really sprang from Ravel's dissatisfaction with himself and the work is hardly more than a brilliant technical essay in veiled pastiche, of which he was a master unrivalled in skill and resourcefulness. In the Sonata for Violin and Cello (1922), which is a cyclic work, the music is reduced to essentials, the composer almost completely abandoning the fascination of harmony and concentrating on purely melodic writing, the effect of which is often harsh and angular. In the Sonata for Violin and Piano (1927) the two instruments share some of the material, but Ravel emphasizes their fundamental incompatibility by making them not co-operate, but contrast with each other. The second movement is a blues and shows the composer following the contemporary fashion for jazz. The popular *Bolero* (1928), originally conceived as a ballet for Ida Rubinstein, is a *tour de force* in the achievement of a long orchestral crescendo which becomes more highly coloured with each return of the two themes; there is no modulation and no development but a persistent reiteration of the same ideas. The Piano Concerto in G major and the Piano Concerto for the Left Hand (both 1931) show a distinct contrast in conception. The former is in the style of a magnified chamber concerto (Ravel originally intended to call it a *divertissement*) while the latter, almost in defiance of the limitation imposed on him by having to write a solo part for the left hand only (for the one-armed Viennese pianist, Paul Wittgenstein), is marked by a highly elaborate virtuoso element. In both works the influence of jazz is conspicuous, but through the light-hearted G major Concerto there also stalk the ghosts of Couperin, Scarlatti, Mozart, and Fauré. In the left-hand Concerto, which is a far more inspired and more forceful work, it is Liszt and the sombre Spain of Mérimée whose echoes are heard.

It was largely in the opera, *L'Enfant et les sortilèges* (1925), to Colette's fantastic and exquisite children's tale, that Ravel succeeded in recapturing something of his former self and rediscovered something of the enchanting world of his first opera *L'Heure espagnole*. In the

[1] Roland Manuel, *Maurice Ravel* (Paris, 1938; Eng. ed. London, 1947), p. 86.

music of the Princess there appears again that note of shy, tender, yet sophisticated lyricism by which the composer always attempted to conquer his innate reluctance to express natural, full-blooded sentiments; and each of the characters—animals and pieces of furniture—is succinctly and most aptly delineated: the sardonic humour of the Teapot in ironic jazz rhythms, the malevolence of the Little Old Man in short acidulated phrases and the mewing of the Two Cats and the croaking of the Frogs, in imitative music of the most brilliant invention. The vocal writing in this opera is of a remarkable flexibility and predominates over the orchestra which, for all its virtuosity, is chiefly characterized by light, aerated sonorities. Thematic development is all but abandoned and the continuity of the recitative is frequently broken up by arioso passages. Except for the music of the Princess, *L'Enfant* is perhaps Ravel's furthest attempt to rid himself of all subjective feeling and portray the world of things as they appear in objective reality.

ERIK SATIE AND 'LES SIX'

While Ravel tried to adapt himself to the spirit of the 1920s, no such adjustment was needed by Erik Satie (1866–1925), the only member of Debussy's generation who all his life had held high the flag of heterodoxy and rebellion. As a composer Satie was a minor figure, the intrinsic value of whose work is far outstripped by his significance as a prompter of tendencies which younger composers moulded into an artistic creed.[1] He was an eccentric, an intellectual clown, a deliberate hoaxer and mystifier—in short, an *enfant terrible* who under his clown's mask concealed, however, a certain child-like tenderness and gentle melancholy. Throughout his life he had a horror of the style of the Establishment, which was synonymous for him with stagnant and staid academic authority. Satie thus fitted ideally into those Parisian circles before and after the First World War in which 'l'esprit frondeur'—the Frenchman's instinctive resistance to all authority—was assiduously cultivated.

In 1915 Satie met the young Cocteau who combined in his person the roles of poet, dramatist, painter, and animator and leader of the literary *avant-garde*, and this encounter marked the beginning of Satie's belated fame. For Cocteau found in his music all those elements that corresponded with his own novel aesthetic ideals—simplicity, brevity, ironic humour, unromantic melancholy, and a complete absence of those 'half-lights, muslin, enervating charms and scents' with which he reproached the symbolists and impressionists. Cocteau decided to collaborate with Satie and the fruit of their united efforts was the ballet *Parade* (1916), for which the poet wrote the scenario and Picasso

[1] For Satie's earlier music see p. 93.

designed the sets. The scene is a booth at a fair before which perform a Chinese juggler, a couple of acrobats, a young American girl who is a parody of the type then made popular by transatlantic films, and three showmen or managers whose antics give a foretaste of what the public are to see inside. The audience and the majority of critics were shocked by what they supposed to be a manifestation of Cubism in the choreography and the music; yet in reality the latter is disconcertingly simple and naïve, consisting mostly of two-bar phrases which are monotonously repeated over and over again. The acrobats perform to circus music, the first manager is given a theme evocative of the bustle of a fairground, and jazz music accompanies the incredible feats executed by the American girl. The orchestra contains such 'instruments' as a typewriter, a revolver, a ship's siren, a Morse apparatus and the like, which were added by Satie partly to give the work an exaggerated realistic touch and partly to raise the hackles of the audience. Whatever the intrinsic value of Satie's music, *Parade* was certainly a landmark in the history of the modern theatre. The ballet *Mercure* (1924), subtitled 'Poses plastiques', for which Picasso again provided the décor, deals with an adventure of the Greek god and Satie's contribution represents only a subordinate part of the spectacle—the work was in fact called 'a painter's ballet'. The music is rather academic in treatment, though it recalls the atmosphere of the circus and the music-hall which was in deliberate contrast to the high degree of ingeniousness and sophistication shown by Picasso's scenic construction. The surrealistic ballet *Relâche* (1924), to a scenario by Francis Picabia, carries to what then seemed the limit, the spirit of aesthetic nihilism, the inconsequential and crazy plot being seemingly devoid of all intelligible meaning. For this Satie solemnly wrote a series of serious and dry dance movements which are, however, occasionally relieved by popular themes selected for their 'evocative' quality.

One of Satie's principal aims was to achieve authenticity and simplicity of expression and to cultivate 'dépouillement'—the stripping down of the music to bare essentials—and this led him in 1920 to compose his 'musique d'ameublement', 'furnishing music', which originated in a remark by Matisse that 'he visualized an art without distracting subject-matter and comparable to a good armchair'. The occasion was provided by an exhibition of paintings at which a play by Max Jacob was staged for which Satie wrote accompanying music. This consisted of well-known fragments from Thomas's *Mignon* and Saint-Saëns's *Danse macabre* juxtaposed with simple isolated themes of Satie's own invention, in stereotyped repetition and reminiscent of the patterns of a wallpaper or carpet. It was intended as mere background music and the

17

composer went around urging the visitors to talk and not to take any notice of what was being played. Satie applied the same kind of writing to the film music he wrote for the entr'acte in *Relâche*.

Satie always maintained that in the setting of a text music should never usurp to itself the dramatic and narrative elements but furnish only a suitably coloured background, and he provided the best illustration of this self-denying ordinance in the cantata *Socrate* (1919), a setting for four female voices and chamber orchestra of excerpts taken from Victor Cousin's French translation of passages from the Platonic dialogues. The voices progress in continuous chant-like lines, with a monotony that is intentional, while the instrumental parts proceed in often repeated figures (Ex. 101).

The quiet uneventful flow of this music is occasionally punctuated by the expression of muted emotion, particularly in the last part—'The Death of Socrates'. The work, which in Satie's words is 'an act of piety . . . a humble homage', is his masterpiece and the apotheosis of the style he had developed in reaction to the luscious harmonic language and the enervating melodic refinement of impressionism. It may be said to have paved the way for the neo-classicism of Stravin-

Ex. 101

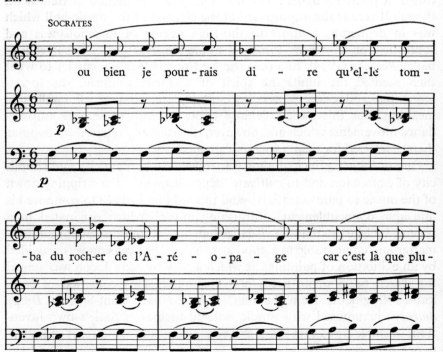

(Or I could also say that she fell from the rock of the Areopagus, for it is to that spot that some transfer the scene.)

sky and other composers in the following years. Although Satie belonged to no group, he had always manifested enthusiasm for what was novel and adventurous in the music of his time, and this explains why in the last four years of his life he became the champion of four composers who were brought to him by Milhaud and who became known as 'L'École d'Arcueil'—so called after the Parisian suburb where Satie lived. The most distinguished member of this group was Henri Sauguet (b. 1901) whose music showed the influence of Satie in its easy fluency and a certain wit. Spontaneous and unpretentious, it eschews profundity, seeking to please by its gracefulness and polished charm.

Far more important than 'L'École d'Arcueil' was the group of six young musicians who after the first performance of *Parade* had gathered around Satie as the embodiment of the new spirit, a spirit of invigoration and rejuvenation at which they all aimed in their different ways. In 1926 the critic Henri Collet dubbed them 'Les Six', an analogy to the Russian 'Five'. 'Les Six' consisted of Louis Durey (b. 1888) who had already left the group, Germaine Tailleferre (b. 1892), Darius Milhaud (b. 1892), Arthur Honegger (1892–1955), Francis Poulenc (1899–1963) and Georges Auric (b. 1899). If they formed a group at all, with common aims and aspirations, this was only true in the early 1920s, after which each composer developed in his own individual manner. Moreover much of the aesthetic doctrine considered as characteristic of 'Les Six' belonged more properly to Poulenc and Auric who, unlike the older members of the group, came to Satie without being bound by any previous loyalties. The literary mouthpiece of 'Les Six' was Cocteau who provided them with a brilliant manifesto, *Le Coq et l'Harlequin* (1918),[1] in which he proclaimed their artistic tenets and elevated the reluctant Satie to the position of a *chef d'école*. The Cock of the title represented the new progressive forces, while the Harlequin stood for everything that in Cocteau's view was

[1] English translation by Rollo Myers (London, 1921).

antiquated and reactionary in the arts. What united 'Les Six' for a brief space of time was their declared antagonism to romanticism and impressionism, their emphasis on simplicity, clarity and terseness of expression, and the avoidance of all pretentiousness and boredom in music. They aimed at a masculine art and, stimulated by the enthusiasms for Negro art among contemporary painters, they discovered in jazz what they perceived to be a potent antidote to the vague, static rhythms and the sophisticated harmonic refinement of impressionism. Poulenc and Auric in particular manifested a strong predilection for the music of the circus, of the fairground and the music-hall in which, according to Cocteau, they looked 'not for the charm of clowns and negroes but for a lesson in equilibrium. This school which teaches hard work, strength, the exact use of force and a functional elegance is a real *haute école*'. 'Les Six' deliberately cultivated the banal, the commonplace, and the brutal, yet at the same time they loved the prettiness of *musiquette*, writing pastiches in the style of eighteenth-century French ballet music and of French opera of the mid-nineteenth century, and frequently all these disparate elements were amusingly but incongruously brought together in one and the same work.

Durey and Tailleferre are the least significant members of the group. Durey, after initially embracing the new aesthetic tenets, soon dissociated himself from them and his later style showed an affinity with that of Debussy and Ravel. Tailleferre wrote for the most part small-scale, unpretentious, and rather short-winded works possessing, however, a typically Parisian chic and elegance. The two leading figures of 'Les Six' were Milhaud and Honegger. Milhaud, who was born at Aix-en-Provence, was, as he suggests in his autobiography,[1] conditioned by Latin-Mediterranean culture, and as a young man he displayed a strong aversion to German music, notably Wagner's. Latin clarity of form and Latin elegance and conciseness of melody combine in him with an inveterate love for harmonic and contrapuntal experiments, and he made polytonality, both in the harmonic sense and in the sense of several diatonic melodies being superimposed on one another, a characteristic feature of his style. Milhaud's approach to his material is purely musical, and one would be tempted to describe him as a 'natural', were it not that he possesses an extraordinarily sharp musical intelligence which permits him to essay an immense variety of genres with great self-confidence, though he lacks the self-criticism characteristic of less fertile composers. Writing with immense speed he has produced an *oeuvre* enormous in volume but very uneven in invention, although in technical craftsmanship he proves himself unfailingly resourceful

[1] Darius Milhaud, *Notes sans musique* (Paris, 1949; English translation, 1952, p. 21).

and accomplished. During the 1920s and early 1930s Milhaud was attracted by extraordinarily various ideas and trends which account for the curious zigzag course his style pursued—neo-classicism and South American music, jazz and African ballet, ritual cult and classical-drama.

From 1917 to 1919 Milhaud was attached to the French Embassy at Rio de Janeiro and this afforded him the opportunity to study Brazilian folk-music on the spot. The creative result of these studies is seen in the orchestral piece, *Le Bœuf sur le toit* (1920)—the title derives from a popular Brazilian song used in it—in which Milhaud transcribed tangos, maxixes, sambas and a Portuguese fado linking them with a theme of his own invention which recurs, rondo-like, a number of times. Cocteau later wrote for it a choreographic scenario that is enacted in an American bar during the Prohibition period. In the ballet *La Création du monde* (1923), with choreography based on African mythology about the creation of the world, the jazz element is pervasive:

Ex. 102

Milhaud, who wrote it after a visit to Harlem during his American tour in 1922, adopted for it the identical orchestra of seventeen instruments found in the Negro jazz bands of the time. *Cinq Symphonies* for small orchestra (1917–23), *Machines agricoles* (1919), and *Catalogue des fleurs* (1920) are conceived in a predominantly neo-classic style. The symphonies are marked by a rudimentary kind of counterpoint often approaching heterophony and by polytonal passages in several simultaneous keys as, for instance, in the third movement of Symphony No. 2:

Ex. 103

The harmonic idiom is rather acid but the melodic writing is frequently punctuated by simple folk-song-like themes of a Mediterranean character. *Machines agricoles* and *Catalogue des fleurs* are settings for voice and chamber orchestra of descriptions, respectively, of agricultural implements and flowers from a seedsman's catalogue, and they combine a pastoral vein with an impersonal objective expression. Milhaud intended them not as a joke but in the spirit of Virgil's *Georgics*; yet an element of incongruity cannot be denied to exist between the dry, factual nature of the text and the inventive musical treatment (Ex. 104).

One of Milhaud's finest works is the opera *Les Malheurs d'Orphée* (1925), a modern adaptation of the classical myth in which Orpheus is a healer in the Camargue and Eurydice a gypsy girl; the music has the luminosity as well as the intensity of the Provençal landscape and the economy of means employed is most remarkable. In *Le Pauvre Matelot* (1926), 'une complainte en trois actes', which is Milhaud's best-known opera, Cocteau, who was the librettist, derived the subject from an incident reported in a newspaper, and treated in a realistic, almost veristic manner. A sailor returning home incognito passes himself off to his wife as a rich friend of her husband and is murdered by her for his money. In strong contrast to the character of the action Cocteau's language imitates the detached and impersonal style of sailors' tales, and this is matched by Milhaud's setting which is completely stylized and objective and frequently creates an 'alienation' effect such as Stravinsky achieved by similar means in *L'Histoire du soldat* and *Oedipus Rex*. In the three miniature operas, *L'Enlèvement d'Europe, L'Abandon d'Ariane,* and *La Délivrance de Thésée* (1927), which together last about thirty minutes, Milhaud followed the vogue fashionable at that time in Germany for short one-act operas. The antique myths are treated in a half poetic, half ironic, and off-hand vein, with a modern tango in the second and jazz rhythms in the third opera. *Christophe Colomb* (1928), to a libretto by his friend Paul Claudel, is Milhaud's most ambitious and spiritually most profound stage-work of the inter-war period, in which he achieved a remarkable fusion of a medieval mystery play with a modern opera-oratorio, a fusion deserving the epithet 'unique'. The action concerns the life of Christopher Columbus as seen from the point of view of posterity; and to enhance and intensify the stage drama, a cinematographic film duplicates the stage scenes on a screen, presenting images which vary in their degree of verisimilitude to the action, ranging from a more or less accurate reproduction of the stage scenes to unreal, dream-like pictures which concentrate on the poetic essence of the subject. Accompanied by percussion, a Narrator, reading from an

Ex. 104

(Begonia Aurora, very double flower, apricot mixed with coral, very attractive
shades, unusual and interesting.)

old chronicle, explains and links the twenty-seven scenes in a strictly rhythmical recitation in which a speaking chorus frequently joins. There is a numerous cast of singers but, with the exception of Columbus and Isabella of Spain, these parts are all subsidiary and the singing chorus is given the most important musical sections. Milhaud set the text to grave, sombre, and exalted music, rather in the manner of a classical oratorio, and effectively contrasts lyrical and epic elements with the dramatic. The vocal style oscillates between recitative-like declamation and arioso, while the predominantly diatonic character of the instrumental themes is concealed behind a bitonal and polytonal treatment. Thus, in the nineteenth scene, 'Le Rédempteur', one orchestral part consists of no fewer than seven superimposed thirds, another part moves chromatically in block harmonies and a third part has a bell-like ostinato to play; the first chorus sings an independent part in octaves while the second chorus is given a five-part organum (Ex. 105).

Such tremendous complexities—and they are also to be found in many of his later works—are difficult to reconcile with Milhaud's declared aversion to German music. In fact *Christophe Colomb* and some of his subsequent operas such as *Maximilien* (1930) and *Medée* (1938) show an affinity with the ideals of the German expressionism rather than with Milhaud's own ideals of clarity, simplicity, and economy of means and attempt 'not to render the visible but to render visible' the individual's deep-seated irrational instincts and drives. Yet in his chamber music and song cycles with orchestra of the same period (String Quartets nos. 5–9, 1920–35; *Trois chansons de troubadour*, 1936; *Les quatre éléments* and *Trois élégies*, both 1938) Milhaud produced music which, despite harmonic astringencies and complicated polytonal passages, demonstrates that aspect of his artistic make-up which finds expression in a delicate and often alluring Latin lyricism.[1]

Arthur Honegger, the son of Swiss parents but born and brought up in France, shows in both his musical personality and in his aesthetic outlook a mixture of German and French traits. It is significant that he displayed no great sympathy for the anti-emotional, 'objective' tendencies of 'Les Six' to which he adhered only during the early 1920s, nor did he share the interest in the music of the fairground and music-hall so characteristic of Poulenc and Auric. Unlike the other members of this group, he favoured large-scale architectural designs and linear polyphony; and, so far as his stage works are concerned, he showed a strong predilection for grave, tragic subjects treating them in a statuesque monumental fashion, yet at the same time revealing a highly developed sense of dramatic gesture and theatrical effectiveness.

[1] As in the slow movement of no. 6, recorded in *The History of Music in Sound*, x.

Ex. 105

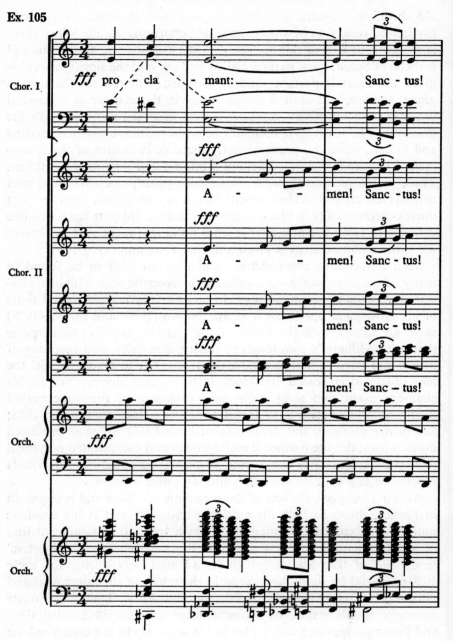

Honegger was comparatively slow in developing a personal style. In his early works (First String Quartet, 1917, and two Violin Sonatas, 1918 and 1919, respectively) he is seen to oscillate between homophonic writing and a complex contrapuntal manner, a dichotomy which was to persist though the demarcation between the two styles was to grow less clear-cut in his maturity. A more personal note is revealed in his *Pastoral d'été* for chamber orchestra (1920) which is unpretentious and direct in its appeal and thus embodies one of the chief tenets of 'Les Six'. It is based on two themes, one lyrical and the other bucolic, and displays a relatively simple texture in which a rhythmic ostinato serves to generate the atmosphere of a pastoral idyll. Another aspect of Honegger's musical character is shown in *Pacific 231* (1923) and *Rugby* (1928) both of which are symphonic movements with an illustrative tendency, though the composer disclaimed any descriptive intentions. *Pacific 231* resembles in its form a figured chorale and one of its salient features lies in the fact that, while the metronomical speed progressively diminishes, the metric units are filled with increasingly more notes. The piece translates the exciting visual impression created by a train engine of 300 tons hurtling down the track at 75 miles per hour and captures the sheer physical exhilaration aroused by this spectacle. Though Honegger was probably the first to have attempted it in music, this intoxication with speed and the impersonal beauty of mechanical objects had been extolled as early as 1911 by the Italian Futurists. In *Rugby*, sport and physical movement are made the subject for musical treatment though in this Honegger was anticipated by Martinů in his *Half Time* (1925). The work hardly varies in speed and uses a swinging theme as its main idea. Yet another and more intrinsic side of Honegger's personality is shown in the Symphony in Three Movements (1930)— music of great muscular strength, rhythmic vigour and lean texture. The String Quartets Nos. 2 and 3 (both 1936) display the same characteristics as the Symphony but combine with their close formal control and cogent thematic thinking a large measure of contrapuntal skill. Honegger prefers to set the various themes against one another (mostly in the recapitulation) rather than exploit any motivic kinship between them. In the finale of Quartet No. 3 he appears to flirt with dodecaphony, as illustrated in its opening:

Ex. 106

but he was too deeply anchored in tonality to go further in his experimentation with serialism, and the movement closes in an unambiguous
E major.

Honegger wrote numerous stage works in the majority of which he
aimed at combining an appeal to large unsophisticated audiences with
an interest for the educated music lover and professional musician. They
are large frescos of a static, monumental character, whose subjects are
drawn from the Bible, Greek tragedy and French medieval history.
The best known of these is *Le Roi David* (1921) which was originally
written as incidental music to a play by René Morax but later transformed into a Symphonic Psalm in three parts—in fact, a dramatic
oratorio in which a Narrator describes the intervening stage action.
Honegger had not yet quite found himself in this work and the stylistic
sources on which he draws are of the most heterogeneous kind:
Handelian counterpoint and folk-song-like melodies, exotic, oriental-
sounding music and Bachian chorale, simple diatonic harmonies and
polytonality. But whatever Honegger's borrowings, the whole is more
than its constituent parts and the composer succeeds in re-creating the
spirit and atmosphere of the Old Testament with an impressive vividness and directness of expression. The music alternates between harsh,
barbaric grandeur and lyrical simplicity best exemplified in the various
choral psalms and solo numbers. Thus, the 'Song of David the Shepherd'
employs a vocal melody of a simple diatonic character—combined,
however, with chromatic harmonies in the orchestra, while in the
'Lament of Gilboa' oriental arabesques and melismas are used for an
expressive purpose:

Ex. 107

The 'Invocation of the Witch of Endor' shows the composer as a master of suggestive instrumental evocation, while the 'Dance before the Ark' is a choral movement of tremendous vitality and primitive corybantic power. *Judith* (1925)[1] was also originally conceived as incidental music for a play by Morax, though subsequently Honegger turned it into a three-act opera. The subject, which is taken from the well-known biblical story of Judith and Holofernes, is set to music remarkable for its evocation of a stark primitive atmosphere, notably by means of highly dramatic choruses, and among the chief devices used for characterization of the protagonists are oriental melismas and psalmodic melodies with a marked modal tendency.

Compared with *Le Roi David*, the opera shows a far more homogeneous stylistic character. Honegger's most dramatic opera is unquestionably *Antigone* (1927) whose glowing intensity of expression stands at the opposite end to the hieratic grandeur of Stravinsky's *Oedipus Rex*. Cocteau's libretto, freely adapted from the tragedy of Sophocles, strictly observes the three Aristotelian unities and is most direct in its language. In character with this tragic subject the music is marked by violent dissonances and atonal-sounding polyphonic writing; the individual scenes are firmly held together by a close-knit symphonic structure. The treatment of the text avoids the traditional recitative which is replaced by a word-inspired melodic line such as the composer had already attempted in *Judith* and which is comparable to Janáček's realistic speech-song and Pizzetti's declamatory arioso. *Jeanne d'Arc au bûcher* (Joan of Arc at the stake) (1935) is a vast and spectacular stage oratorio in which Paul Claudel aimed at a synthesis of ancient mystery play, *chanson de geste* and modern drama. Honegger's music possesses the immediate graphic quality of a film but it more often accompanies than interprets the action.

Francis Poulenc and Georges Auric were the youngest members of the 'Les Six' and stood, as has been said, closest to the aesthetics of Satie which they even carried a step further. Both composers gained an early reputation as musical clowns who wrote with tongue in cheek. Both were soon dubbed 'les sportifs de la musique', owing to the robust-

[1] See pl. V(a).

PLATE V

HONEGGER'S *JUDITH*, 1925 (*see p. 250*)

A scene from the original production at the People's Theatre, Darmstadt

KŘENEK'S *JONNY SPIELT AUF*, 1927 (*see p. 340*)

The station scene from the original production at the Neues Theater, Leipzig

ness of the sentiments expressed and a sense of physical hustle and bustle which emanates from their compositions. Poulenc felt the pull of several influences—in the first place Satie's and in varying degrees those of Chabrier, Ravel, and Stravinsky. Yet, as he matured, his style developed an unmistakable personal cachet compounded of playfulness and gravity, of simplicity and sophistication, while some of his compositions exhale the flavour of 'la vieille France' lending them a certain nostalgic charm. In his music spontaneous melodic invention and a well-developed sense of pointed rhythmic structure are allied to a neat and deft craftsmanship. Poulenc's preference was for the smaller forms. He was eighteen when in the wake of Europe's 'discovery' of American jazz he wrote the *Rhapsodie nègre* (1917) and this was soon followed by the *Mouvements perpétuels* (1918), three pieces for piano which derive their title from the fact that each is based on a rhythmic ostinato figure which is almost incessantly repeated. They are simple two-part inventions of an unpretentious but vivid charm, with bitonality as a characteristic feature. An effective interpreter of his own piano music, Poulenc wrote a great number of pieces for the instrument among which the *Sept Nocturnes* (1935) must be reckoned as the most important; a tender and delicate melancholy (nos. 1 and 4) and calm serenity (no. 6) are matched by the expression of ironic humour (no. 2) and the exhilaration engendered by rapid physical movement (no. 5). Some of his vocal chamber music reveals perhaps best the two prominent aspects of Poulenc's artistic personality. In *Cocarde* (1919), to poems by Cocteau which are intended as parodies of the style of the French Symbolists, the music perfectly matches the spirit of the words in a humorously inconsequential manner, the scoring for violin, cornet, trombone, bass drum and triangle imitating the fortuitous ensembles found in Parisian music-halls and dance-halls. On the other hand, *Le Bestiaire* for voice, string quartet, flute, clarinet, and bassoon (1919), six settings of animal verses by Guillaume Apollinaire, is remarkable for the blend of gentle irony and prettiness and for the delicate and pointed texture in which each note seems to stand in its right place (Ex. 108).

The individual songs are of the utmost brevity, with 'La Sauterelle' extending to no more than four bars. In the ballet *Les Biches* (1923) Poulenc conjures up partly the *vieille France* of the eighteenth century (Rondeau and Adagietto), partly the spirit of the jazz age (Rag-Mazurka), while the exquisitely wrought *Concert champêtre* for harpsichord and orchestra (1928) echoes the world of Chambonnières and Couperin. Outstanding among Poulenc's religious works is the Mass for unaccompanied chorus (1937), which in its marked purity of

Ex. 108

vous et moi nous nous en al - lons

p très doux

com - me s'en vont les é - cre - visses:

(Uncertainty, O! my delight, you and I go away as crayfish do.)

style and serenity of spirit provides a demonstration of the fact that this composer was at times able to discard his tongue-in-cheek approach and probe into more profound emotions. The *Litanies à la Vierge Noire de Rocamadour* (1936), and *Quatre Motets pour un temps de pénitence* (1938–39) belong to this same serious and often impressive vein.

Like Poulenc, Auric showed a precocious talent, composing, it has been stated, more than 300 songs and piano pieces between the ages of twelve and sixteen. His early admiration of Ravel led him first to imitate the former's style but subsequently Auric came under the influence of Satie and, partly, Stravinsky when he adopted Satie's precept that the largest measure of audacity lies in simplicity. Thus, in the *Huit Poèmes* (1920), settings of wittily ironic verses by Cocteau, the voice part is formed by a straightforward diatonic melodic line, rather in the style of a French folk-song or popular tune, and is embedded in an equally simple but very pliant piano accompaniment that often serves to point the witticism of the text. But this phase of deliberate simplicity soon passed and Auric, developing a more personal note, harnessed a muscular rhythm and violent discordant harmonies to a plain melodic statement. For instance, in *Les Joues en feu* (1921), a setting of three poems by Raymond Radiguet, the voice part of the first song modulates no further than the subdominant but the piano indulges in the most dissonant clashes between E flat and B major while the third song is characterized by first successive and then simultaneous bitonality. Technically Auric avoids phrases of any length and elaboration and, like Poulenc, he juxtaposes sections of the most heterogeneous character in order to produce a violent shock of contrasts. Thus, in the ballet *Les Fâcheux* (1925), after Molière, a highly adorned dance marked 'très lente et expressive' is offset by a fast staccato movement suggesting sheer motor energy. Since the great success of René Clair's film, *A nous la liberté*, for which he wrote the music, Auric has been much in demand as a screen composer. In his general artistic make-up a sense of comedy, irony, and scepticism and a sharp intelligence are perhaps the most salient features.

'LA JEUNE FRANCE'

Since the time of the *querelle des bouffons* Parisian artists have shown a strong inclination to group themselves into separatist bodies, each representing a particular aesthetic creed and engaging in heated polemics with their antagonists. This phenomenon is the manifestation of a typically Gallic spirit of individuality and heterodoxy not encountered to the same extent in any other European country. We have seen how in the years shortly after the First World War the short-lived group of 'Les Six' was formed in reaction against impressionism, and sixteen years later, in 1936, four members of the rising young generation grouped themselves into 'La Jeune France' whose chief aim was to achieve yet another rejuvenation of French music by attempting to re-instate those deeper and more permanent values which they found lacking in the creations of their elders. At the same time they en-deavoured, like the young Italian composers of the 1920s, to revive a national spirit neglected by the older generation in favour of an excessive internationalism, and in general they were opposed both to revolution-ary tendencies and to faint-hearted academicism. All four members of 'La Jeune France' were born in the first decade of the twentieth century —André Jolivet (1905), Yves Baudrier (1906), Daniel Lesur (1908), and Olivier Messiaen (1908). The mature works of these composers do not fall into the purview of this chapter but their early style demands a brief consideration here.

From the first Jolivet and Messiaen were the outstanding members of the group, a fact amply confirmed by their later achievements. Jolivet, who was a pupil of Edgard Varèse, first adopted the 'hermetic' style of his teacher, with its constant search for extraordinary instrumental timbres and novel effects in the field of rhythm. During his early period Jolivet was much preoccupied with ideas about such primitive forms of religion as magic and the appropriation of cosmic forces, believing in vibrations from unseen psychical 'fluids' which he thought he could detect in all manifestations of life and even in inanimate objects. Already the titles of those works intended as an expression of these psychic phenomena are indicative of Jolivet's ideas and his concept of music as a 'cosmic' force endowed with magical properties[1]—the piano suite *Mana* (1935), *Incantation: Pour que l'image devienne symbole* for ondes martenot or flute (1937), the orchestral prelude *Cosmogonie* (1938), and *Cinq Danses rituelles* (1939). The declared purpose of this music was to cast a magic spell, and in pursuing this object Jolivet evolved a personal style of great harmonic freedom and marked by a wide range of novel rhythmic and dynamic effects, all with the aim of generating in the listener an appropriate state of mind. After the Second World War, however, Jolivet began to turn to music which is more closely concerned with man and his natural feelings.

Messiaen, who was a pupil of Paul Dukas and the organist Marcel Dupré, showed very early a strong leaning towards a particular form of Catholic mysticism, a subject which, according to his note for the first London performance (1938) of his *La Nativité du Seigneur*, 'is the best subject, for it encompasses all subjects. And the abundance of technical

---

[1] Cf. the case of Skryabin, p. 34.

means allows the heart to open up freely.' It was largely as a composer of organ music that Messiaen made his name in the 1930s, and particularly by *La Nativité du Seigneur* (1935), a series of nine meditations on Christian themes, and *Le Corps glorieux* (1939). These and some other works of that period form the transition to Messiaen's later style, in which plainsong, elements from Hindu music and a novel conception of rhythmic structure play an important part. Yet what remained constant in his music, whether vocal or instrumental, is the expression of intense emotional sincerity, religious ecstasy and mystical contemplation.

Composers who remained more or less independent of the aesthetic doctrines advanced by the group of 'Les Six' and 'La Jeune France' include Jacques Ibert (1890–1962), and Jean Françaix (b. 1912) whose prodigal fertility and extreme facility are matched by elegance and brilliance of workmanship rather than any profounder qualities.

ITALY: LA GENERAZIONE DELL'80

In Italy the roots from which the new post-war ideas were to spring were planted in the first decade of the present century and showed a pronouncedly national bias. Under the intellectual leadership of the musicologist Fausto Torrefranca, who published a fiercely polemical book on Puccini,[1] the young composers of that time—chief among them Ildebrando Pizzetti (1880–1968), Gian Francesco Malipiero (1882–1973), and Alfredo Casella (1883–1947) representing the generation after Puccini's—gathered together. The so-called *generazione dell'80* shared the conviction that native opera had run its course and become effete and that a *risorgimento*, a renascence of Italian music, could only be brought about by the assimilation of the spirit and style of the great instrumental masters of the past: Frescobaldi, Vivaldi, Corelli, Veracini, and others. The monopoly that opera occupied in the musical life of the nation was deeply resented, vocalism was condemned and finally the stage was reached when the young iconoclasts clamoured for a ban on all those composers who had exclusively devoted themselves to opera (Puccini, Mascagni, Leoncavallo). By diverting the creative energies from *melodramma* to instrumental music the *avant-garde* hoped to achieve that *ristabilimento dell' equilibrio* which it so much desired and which, indeed, was restored by the large amount of instrumental works composed in Italy during the inter-war period. But it is to be noted that this process had already been begun, though in isolation, in the 1880s by such composers as Martucci, Bossi, Sinigaglia, and Sgambati. These however, had carried out their reform largely by imitat-

---

[1] *Giacomo Puccini e l'opera internazionale* (Turin, 1912).

ing the German symphonists, whereas the new movement sought to achieve the same object by a return to the instrumental forms of seventeenth- and eighteenth-century Italian music. The new anti-operatic tendencies were both idealistic and nationalistic. Idealistic, because they set out to turn away from the bourgeois mentality of realist opera, with its lack of spirituality and high moral values; nationalistic, because they demanded an art exclusively nurtured in old Italian soil and freed from the influence of both later German romanti-cism and French impressionism. In a thoughtful book,[1] which includes a fairly balanced study of Puccini, Pizzetti reproached the entire impres-sionistic school for its over-refinement, its growing exclusion of the life of the emotions and 'its prodigious faculty of stifling the will to live'.[2] On the other hand, he accused Puccini and the rest of the Italian realists of having sinned in the opposite direction by their emotional excesses and their superabundance of crude vitality which, according to Pizzetti, defied full translation into satisfactory aesthetic expression.[3] Yet the extreme position taken up by these young firebrands was gradually relinquished with growing maturity when both Pizzetti and Malipiero devoted their attention to opera, although guided by aesthetic and stylistic principles totally different from those of *verismo* and realist opera in general.

While the hostility towards this kind of opera, particularly as represented by Puccini, was at its height, Puccini himself had been undergoing, from about 1912, a certain change of outlook and began to detach himself from the line he had pursued in *Tosca, Madama Butterfly*, and *La fanciulla del West*. The first milestone of this changed course was *Il trittico* (1918) of which only the first episode, *Il tabarro*, after a French play *La Houppelande*, contained a strong touch of *verismo* in its brutal ending. A *pièce noire*, this opera is a masterpiece of dramatic concentration and in its evocation of a most unusual atmosphere— the wretched life of bargees on the River Seine at the beginning of the present century, which forms the background to a triangular drama between husband, wife and lover. The second episode, *Suor Angelica*, shared with the first an uncommon subject and uncommon setting— the tragic frustration of maternal love and the suicide of a nun in an Italian convent at the end of the seventeenth century. The opera, in which all the characters are women, suffers from the quietism and passivity inseparable from the monastic atmosphere. The final miracle, too, remains only a stage spectacle, Puccini lacking the power to convey mystic ecstasy and the cathartic force of Divine Grace. But the music

---

[1] Ildebrando Pizzetti, *Musicisti contemporanei. Saggi critici* (Milan, 1914).
[2] Ibid., p. 130.   [3] Ibid., p. 51.

is of impeccable craftmanship and particularly successful in its portrayal of the cruel aunt and of the monastic milieu. The third panel of *Il trittico*, *Gianni Schicchi*, was Puccini's sole comic opera and shows a most remarkable extension of his creative range. The subject, which was drawn from a brief anecdote in Dante's *Inferno*, concerns the duping of scheming heirs by the impersonator of the dead testator and is turned into a riotous comedy of situation. The music, reviving the spirit of eighteenth-century *opera buffa*, is brilliantly witty and ironic; the only slight blemish in it is Lauretta's sentimental air 'O mio babbino caro'. Compared with Verdi's *Falstaff*, *Gianni Schicchi* shows a brand of humour which is bitter, mordant, even harshly cynical. *Turandot* (1924), after the play of the same name by Carlo Gozzi, is Puccini's greatest masterpiece. Its larger theme is the liberating and uniting power of true love which lends the work a universal significance absent from the rest of Puccini's operas. Moreover, with the exception of the final two scenes, left only in sketch by the composer and completed by Franco Alfano, the dramatic structure is masterly, and the music represents a synthesis and, with it, a consummation of the four separate aspects of Puccini's previous style: the lyric-sentimental (Liù), the heroic-grandiose (Turandot and Calaf), the comic-grotesque (Masks), and the exotic.

By the time *Turandot* was first produced (1926) both Pizzetti and Malipiero had launched into opera; but their stage conception, conditioned and guided by new operatic aesthetics, was entirely different from those of both Verdi and the bourgeois dramatists of *verismo*. The main point in Pizzetti's theory of reform was the argument that if opera is musical drama, then everything must be subordinate to the tying of the dramatic knot, to the surmounting of the emotional crisis and to the unfolding of the characters' psychology. In such a scheme lyricism must never be allowed to interrupt the flow of the inner action, no lyrical halts should interrupt the development of the drama. 'For five centuries,' Pizzetti wrote with dubious accuracy,[1] 'from the fourteenth to the nineteenth centuries, there was an uninterrupted tendency in opera to lyricism at all costs. . . . It is not the characters who have sung, or rather lived; the poets have spoken and the musicians have sung.' Unless lyricism arises directly out of the dramatic context it has no justification. In consequence of this theory Pizzetti developed a style of operatic writing in which declamation is the paramount feature, a kind of declamation encompassing both dramatic recitative and arioso and thus providing a solution of the antithesis between drama and lyricism. This heightened declamation, which combines drama and song in a higher unity, follows the inflexions of the Italian language so

---

[1] *Musica e dramma* (Rome, 1945), p. 41.

accurately that it renders the translation of the text into other languages, without distorting alteration of the vocal line, almost impossible, as for instance in this passage from *Debora e Jaele*:

Ex. 109

(And they shall slay the slayers, and prey on the predators, the vultures shall make of the towns and fortresses fields of ruins for the owls. And Sisera shall be given into the hands of my people.)

This unity of words and music—different from Wagner's *Wortvers-melodie* but similar to Debussy's word-inspired declamation—was in Pizzetti's case greatly aided by the fact that he was his own librettist, who created text and main musical themes and motives simultaneously. A further corollary of his theory is seen in the stripping from the text of all verbiage, and in the projecting of the action without superfluous episodes in which music could only play the part of an adjunct, whereas it should be the vital and direct translation of the inner drama. Although by these means Pizzetti succeeded in achieving a remarkable continuity and pliancy of musical structure and expression, it must still be admitted that his exclusive use of the declamatory principle often creates a distinct feeling of monotony.

Fedra (1912), to a libretto by d'Annunzio, was the first opera in which Pizzetti applied his theory, though as yet in a tentative manner; it was not until he wrote the trilogy *Debora e Jaele* (1921), *Lo straniero* (1925), and *Fra Gherardo* (1927), that he succeeded in putting it into full effect. Pizzetti, a deeply religious man, went to the Bible for the subject of the

first two operas, while for the later part of the trilogy he chose a historical subject drawn from a Parma chronicle of the thirteenth century,
though the ultimate tragedy of Fra Gherardo was wholly invented by the
composer. The underlying theme of the trilogy is redemption through
the power of self-sacrificing love and the devotion of human beings
surrounded by an uncompromising, hostile, and fiercely dogmatic
world. Though in theory Pizzetti abjured the inclusion of purely lyrical
episodes, in practice he did not altogether banish them: *Lo straniero*,
for example, is marked by more static, sustained, and lyrically expressive
sections, and *Fra Gherardo* contains even self-contained vocal music
of a strophic character. In all these three operas as also in *Orsèolo*
(1935) and *L'Oro* (1942), the chorus plays an extremely active role. With
the function of the chorus in Greek tragedy at the back of his mind,
Pizzetti treats it as a *dramatis persona* in its own right and with a
psychology of its own, assigning to it some of his most powerful music.

Hardly less important than the stage works which form the nucleus
of his output are Pizzetti's choral compositions. These represent a
synthesis of his own style with influences from Gregorian chant and
fifteenth- and sixteenth-century Italian vocal polyphony. Outstanding
here is the unaccompanied *Messa da Requiem* (1922), a markedly lyrical
work in the Dorian mode and representing a serene meditation on
the theme of death which eschews all dramatic accents. Even the 'Dies
Irae', the most extensive and most elaborate of the five movements, is
in a reticent, subdued vein:

Ex. 110

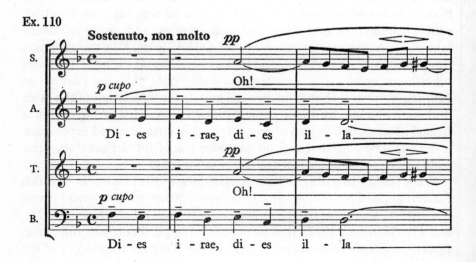

The magnificent 'Sanctus' is for three choruses, one of which is for
women's voices and the other two for male voices, which alternate
between antiphony and singing in concert. Most of Pizzetti's instrumental works are implicitly programmatic and conform to his aesthetic
tenet that music must stand in close relation to life and nature. On this
theory there is no room for 'pure' or 'objective' music, music that is not
evocative of nature or expressive of human emotions; and a whole
series of Pizzetti's instrumental compositions provides testimony to this
view. Thus, the *Concerto dell'estate* for orchestra (1928) consists of three
movements, 'Mattutino', 'Notturno', and 'Gagliarda e finale', which
are expressive, respectively, of the pristine freshness of a summer
morning, of the many voices with which nocturnal nature speaks to

man, and of the joys and the zest for life summer inspires in human beings. In the *Rondo veneziano* (1929) the ritornello symbolizes the pride and splendour of ancient Venice while the three episodes depict scenes from Venetian life. Characteristic of these and other works, such as the *Canti della stagione alta* for piano and orchestra (1930), is the essentially vocal nature of the themes though their elaboration conforms to symphonic principles.

Malipiero, as uneven and over-prolific in his production as Milhaud, is nevertheless the most eminent among the *generazione dell'80*. Profoundly steeped in the music of the Italian Baroque,[1] he derived from it the austerity and nobility of his general artistic aspirations. To baroque music he also owes something of his well-developed sense of melody, while his studies of Gregorian chant bore fruit in the modality and free structure of his melodic idiom. In his early work Malipiero was subject to influences from German and, notably, French music (Debussy); and although the latter influence diminished, his harmonic style retained parallel shifts of triads, fauxburdons, and chords of superimposed fourths and fifths. French impressionism is partly responsible, too, for his marked inclination to evoke characteristic states of mind and emotional attitudes aroused by the contemplation of nature, people and places and by a nostalgic longing for the past. Thus, in *Pause del silenzio* (1917) he describes in seven 'symphonic expressions' the different moods he experienced during the war when the tension and turmoil of external life made it very difficult to achieve peace of mind and spiritual serenity. In this work he applied for the first time the principle of thematic non-development, themes being stated and repeated in slight harmonic and rhythmic alterations, after which they make room for fresh ideas. Each of the seven sections has its own theme but, with no development, the texture is fragmentary and kaleidoscopic, though an element of unity is provided by the opening horn fanfare which recurs like a ritornello after each section. This method of construction, for which a hint is to be found in the instrumental works of the ancient Italian masters and also in Debussy, may be compared to the psychological process of 'association by contrast'. The application of this method is seen at its clearest in Malipiero's first three string quartets—*Rispetti e strambotti* (1920), *Stornelli e ballate* (1923) and *Cantari alla madrigalesca* (1931). The titles of the first two works are derived from old Italian verse-forms consisting of a series of short poems of different content and mood to which unity is given by the verbal style. The music displays

---

[1] Malipiero edited a complete edition of Monteverdi's works and collaborated in the collected edition of Vivaldi's music.

an analogous structure in that there are twenty sections in the first quartet and fourteen in the second, all of the most diverse character— grave and comic, tender and ironical, fantastic and bucolic. In both works a unifying element is generated by a kind of ritornello, which in the first quartet takes the form of a succession of quadruple and double stops on the open strings (first violin and viola) evoking the characteristic sound made by the tuning of strings.

Ex. 111

Malipiero arrived comparatively late at pure symphonic composition in his *Prima sinfonia, in quattro tempi come le quattro stagioni* (1933) and *Seconda sinfonia (Elegiaca)* (1936) to which he later added seven more symphonies. The First Symphony was largely inspired by a nostalgia for Venice's great past and partly by *Stagione*, poems by X. Lamberti, and is modelled on the Italian *sinfonia* of the seventeenth and eighteenth centuries, with a characteristic concertante treatment of woodwind and horns, while the structure shows a return to the traditional symphonic technique abjured by Malipiero in his previous period. In the Second Symphony this feature is even more pronounced, and the work demonstrates his art of achieving a close fusion between musical thought and emotional expression.

In his operas Malipiero evolved a style diametrically opposed to that of Pizzetti. While Pizzetti aimed at dramatic development, continuity and flexibility by means of a half-declamatory, half-arioso recitative, Malipiero's operatic aesthetics exclude all dramatic dialectics: action and characters are not developed but are static like a bas-relief; there is no before and no after. The recitative is abandoned as a naturalistic device and as an obstacle to lyricism; in other words, lyrical *melos* is the prime feature of Malipiero's operas. Despite the great variety of his output, the stage works represent his most characteristic and, undoubtedly, his most significant creations. It is in them that his northern romanticism, his love of the fantastic, of the supernatural and of nocturnal mystery, finds its most eloquent expression. This trait showed from his earliest years and persisted through the radical changes which Malipiero's artistic outlook underwent, changes which must be interpreted as a rebellion against nineteenth-century music, notably German symphonism and Italian *melodramma*. His operatic ethos is at once idealistic, romantic, and poetic—'the classical ideal of an unquiet romantic spirit', as one of the composer's Italian biographers defined it[1]—and this is already seen in Malipiero's choice of subjects from ancient Italian poetry, Goldoni, Euripides, Shakespeare, E. T. A. Hoffmann, and Pirandello.

Most typical of Malipiero's novel conception of opera are *L'Orfeide* (1922) and *Torneo notturno* (1929). The first work is a trilogy of which the central piece, *Sette canzoni*, written in 1919, is perhaps the most noteworthy. The text of these 'seven dramatic expressions' is drawn from verses by Lorenzo de' Medici, Poliziano, and Jacopone da Todi, to which Malipiero invented a series of short incidents (some inspired by personal experiences) which form independent tableaux or 'panels' and follow one another in quick succession like a cinematographic sequence, with exposition of the action and peripeteia unfolding in a few pages. The seven episodes are realistic in essential character but tinged with fantastic, dream-like colours, alternating between the tragic, the macabre, and the comic-grotesque. Unity is achieved by the character of the music which is almost exclusively lyrical and more or less independent of the external stage action, but penetrates to the heart of the poetic and psychological character of each episode. Malipiero made a significant comment on this when he said that for him 'the dramatic is what *one sees* while the music expresses that which one *does not see*'. The musical centre and core of each episode is formed by a *canzone* which is a simple straightforward song in the ancient Italian manner, recalling the airs of native peasants and fishermen.

The first part of the trilogy, *La morte delle maschere*, though written three years after *Sette canzoni*, is intended as a kind of prelude and is in the style of the old *opera buffa*. The action is an allegory, implying caricature and ultimate condemnation, of conventional attitudes towards art, which are personified in seven figures from the *commedia dell'arte* who, in a symbolical act at the end, are shut away in a huge wardrobe. Then Orpheus appears embodying the idea of pure idealistic art and introducing the characters who are to play in *Sette canzoni*. The musical delineation of the Masks and of Orpheus is

---

[1] Guido M. Gatti, in the symposium *L'Opera di Gian Francesco Malipiero* (Treviso, 1952), p. IX.

sharply contrasted in style and expression. The third and last part of the trilogy, *Orfeo, ovvero l'ottava canzone*, is intended as a satire on the indifference, incomprehension, or sterile enthusiasm which were shown by the large public towards *Sette canzoni*. The opera presents a play within a play, spectators on the stage watching the performance of a puppet-show, with the Emperor Nero as an insane and ludicrous hero. At the end Orpheus appears singing an impassioned air about his hapless fate which touches the Queen's heart, while the rest of the spectators are fast asleep from boredom. The music is a most skilful parody of the style of Italian grand opera and of Puccinian lyricism.

Torneo notturno shows the same dramatic and musical pattern as *Sette canzoni*. As in the earlier work, the text is drawn from ancient Italian poetry to which Malipiero invented incidents that are arranged into seven night scenes, but the characters are far more static and puppet-like than in the earlier opera. They symbolize elemental human passions in conflict with one another, and the incidents unfold in the unreal, fantastic sphere of some timeless myth or legend. In the two main characters, the Disperato and the Spensierato, who appear in all seven episodes, the composer portrays two fundamental and diametrically opposed attitudes to life—despair and hedonism; the final murder of the Spensierato by the Disperato is a symbolic act implying the victory of the life-destroying over the life-asserting forces. The ultimate scene shows a funeral procession in a shadowy distance suggesting that the Disperato still continues his hopeless search for happiness. Like *Sette canzoni, Torneo notturno* points to a profound pessimism—life seen as a vale of tears and as the mirror of death. As in the earlier work, a pronounced lyricism serves to create unity and coherence, while a musical link between the individual episodes is provided by the recurrence of the Spensierato's *Canzone del tempo*, which, according to the composer, represents the dramatic centre:

Ex. 112

Andante

Chi ha tem - po e tem-po as - pet - ta, il tem - po per - de il tem - po fug - ge

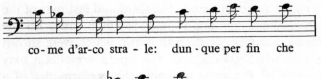

co-me d'ar-co stra - le: dun - que per fin   che

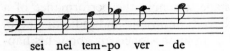

sei nel tem-po ver - de

(He who has time and awaits time, wastes time and time flies like an arrow from a bow: thus even while you are in your youth . . .)

Although Malipiero's style in this opera is eclectic in the sense that it draws on diverse sources—Gregorian chant, the ancient arioso, old dance forms (*ballate*), Debussyan harmony and Stravinskyan rhythm—these heterogeneous elements coalesce into an organic whole which shows a distinct individual physiognomy.

In *Tre commedie goldoniane* (1922), whose spiritual origin is to be traced back to his nostalgia for the ancient splendour of his native Venice, Malipiero aims at an illustration of the characteristic atmosphere of Venetian life in the past: the streets and piazzette, in *Bottega de caffé*; domestic life with its petty intrigues and complications, in *Sior Todoro Brontolon*; and the hustle and bustle in the port and the lagoons, in *Le baruffe chiozzotte*. The subjects are taken from three of Goldoni's plays but Malipiero greatly simplified the dramatic intrigues, reduced the number of characters to a minimum and, in the last opera, combined incidents from several other Goldonian comedies. The three works revive the spirit of the eighteenth-century comic opera on the basis of a more or less symphonic treatment of the orchestra, and whereas the recitative is all but completely banished from *L'Orfeide*, in *Tre commedie* it plays a more conspicuous role, while the number of lyrical arias is restricted. In *Le baruffe chiozzotte* there is also a song sung in Venetian dialect and the imitation of the cries of Venetian street-vendors. Another notable opera is *La favola del figlio cambiato* (1933) for which Pirandello provided the libretto. The ancient fairy-tale of the changeling is so altered as to make the child of a poor mother, a young boy sane and ambitious, become the son of the King while the King's true son is a poor demented creature. The story is to be interpreted as an allegory demonstrating that absolute truth is unascertainable and that what people believe passes as truth. The most impressive part of the drama is the second act which plays in a port tavern, with harlots, sailors, and street urchins as a vivid and colourful background to the action. The musical treatment is on the whole less happy than in

Malipiero's earlier operas, but there is sharp delineation of the chief characters and some remarkable vocal effects, such as an ostinato chorus of sailors and guttersnipes in Act II and internal voices singing on one note in Act III.

Casella's works before the first German War displayed a wide range of the most disparate influences—from Mahler and Richard Strauss to Debussy, Ravel, and the 'Russian' Stravinsky; and though he later settled to a more personal style he remained a more eclectic composer than Pizzetti or Malipiero. His essential strength lay in a neat and very resourceful craftmanship applied either to straightforward pastiche (*Scarlattiana*, 1926; *Paganiniana*, 1942) or to the resuscitation of older music on the basis of modern technical devices. The neo-classicism of the inter-war period found in Casella's cool and speculative mind a responsive echo (*Concerto for strings*, 1927; *Concerto for Orchestra*, 1937; *Sinfonia*, 1940)—all the more so since he was an assiduous student of the music of the ancient Italian masters. Apart from his work as a composer, Casella was very active in the propagation of music by contemporary foreign composers and combined in his person the roles of conductor, pianist, writer and lecturer.

With his orchestral compositions Casella was instrumental in establishing a school of Italian symphonic music. The theatre also held a great attraction for him and he wrote a number of works all marked by a shrewd instinct for theatrical effectiveness. His ballet *La Giara* (1924), to his own scenario, based on a novel by Pirandello, aims at a synthesis of ancient *opera buffa* and rustic comedy and deftly employs some Sicilian folk tunes. His most ambitious stage-work is the three-act opera, *La donna serpente* (1932), after Carlo Gozzi's dramatic fable of the same name, and this represents a summary of Casella's mature stylistic development. True, elements from Baroque opera, comic opera of the eighteenth century (especially Pergolesi's), Spontini and neo-classicism are juxtaposed, but they are most skilfully used to interpret and accompany the dramatic action. The work is set in a legendary and spectacular Orient and combines the atmosphere of a fairytale with the simple human emotions displayed by the characters of the King and the fairy Miranda. The orchestral score presents an almost uninterrupted succession of vivid, brilliant, and rhythmically inventive ideas though Casella's imagination remains fundamentally cold and dry. In the same year in which he completed *La donna serpente*, Casella wrote the one-act chamber opera, *La favola d'Orfeo* (1932), to a text by Poliziano which follows with slight deviations the antique myth. The bulk of the work consists of laments, sung by Aristeus and Orpheus, which lean towards the manner of Caccini and

Monteverdi. An epic and objective character predominates, the exception being the ferocious and rhythmically agitated dance of the Bacchantes with which the opera closes.

OTTORINO RESPIGHI, GIORGIO GHEDINI, MARIO CASTELNUOVO-TEDESCO

Of the composers who belonged to the generation of Pizzetti, Malipiero, and Casella and who contributed their share to the national renascence of Italian music but show a less sharply defined musical profile, three are noteworthy—Ottorino Respighi (1879–1936), Giorgio Federico Ghedini (1892–1965), and Mario Castelnuovo-Tedesco (1895–1968). Respighi's musical pedigree can be traced to Rimsky-Korsakov (whose pupil he was at St. Petersburg), Strauss, Debussy, and, after the war, Stravinsky; at the same time he was much attracted to ancient Italian music and Gregorian chant. Italian critics divide Respighi's mature period into a 'Roman' and a 'Gregorian' phase, though the two overlapped in reality. The first phase, lasting roughly from 1916 to 1926, is characterized by sumptuousness and a highly coloured sensuality of expression which make Respighi the musical counterpart of d'Annunzio. Into those years fall the symphonic poems *Fontane di Roma* (1916), *Pini di Roma* (1924), and the *Trittico botticelliano* (1927), which represent a combination of mood-pictures, nature impressions, and descriptive music. In these works the passages of more intrinsic value occur in those parts that are in a muted poetic vein and tinged with a slight melancholy, such as in 'Fontana di Villa Medici' and 'Pini presso una catacomba', and 'L'Adorazione dei Magi' of the *Trittico*. The *Concerto gregoriano* for violin (1922) and the *Concerto in modo misolidico* for piano (1924) anticipate Respighi's later concentration on Gregorian chant and modality. Of his eight operas, at least three claim attention. *Belfagor* (1922), to a diverting libretto after the play of E. L. Morselli, displays great vivacity and a marked sense of comedy, with vocal writing that owes something to Puccini and an orchestral brilliance that echoes Richard Strauss. The one-act *Maria egiziaca—trittico per concerto* (1931), which belongs to Respighi's 'Gregorian' phase, has no proper action but represents *tableaux vivants* showing incidents from the conversion of St. Mary of Egypt. The music is in a predominantly static, lyrical vein and distinguished by a rare transparence of orchestral colours. The scene of the sombre and starkly dramatic *La Fiamma* (1933), after *The Witch* by G. Wiers-Jenssen, is laid in Ravenna in the seventh century and makes use of both Gregorian and Byzantine liturgical chant, notably in the choral sections of the first act and in the music of the Exarch Basilio and of Eudoxia. In *Lucrezia* (1935), which was his last opera, the composer reverts to the dramatic recitative of the oldest Italian opera, reducing the role of the orchestra to a minimum and entrusting the narration of the plot to a singer who is placed in the orchestra pit.

Ghedini's chief distinction lies in a finely controlled sense of form and texture and in his extremely solid workmanship best seen in the deft manipulation of a close-knit polyphony. These qualities tend, however, to outweigh his imaginative power which is rather academic and drily abstract. Ghedini has devoted himself to opera, chamber music, and choral and orchestral works of which the Symphony (1938) and *Archittetture* for orchestra (1940) are characteristic examples of his general style during the inter-war years.

Castelnuovo-Tedesco, a pupil of Pizzetti, began to develop a more personal style during the First World War. His song cycles, *Stelle cadenti* and *Coplas* (both 1915), are marked by extreme melodic fluency and refinement of the technical means of expression, against which must be set a lack of emotional depth and intellectual vigour. In his vocal compositions Castelnuovo-Tedesco is not merely content to throw into relief the imagery of the text but attempts to reproduce its poetic essence by the creation of a distinct musical atmosphere. He has set all the songs from the Shakespeare plays in the original English (1926), a notable undertaking for a foreign composer and all the more remarkable as his treatment of the prosody is impeccable. Of the three operas which he wrote during the inter-war period, *La Mandragola* (1926), after Machiavelli's comedy, is perhaps the most successful, and by employment of actual folk-songs skilfully re-creates the atmosphere of Renaissance Florence. The Overtures to seven Shakespeare plays (1931–42) are noteworthy examples of Castelnuovo-Tedesco's orchestral style while the *Concerto italiano* for violin (1924) is a work of great euphony in which the earlier arioso is applied to modern instrumental music; but it suffers from a certain tonal monotony, all three movements being cast in a modal G minor. Castelnuovo-Tedesco's awareness of his Jewish origin can be traced in the Second Violin Concerto (subtitled *The Prophets*) (1938), which combines the concerto form with elements from the symphonic poem, the three movements characterizing Isaiah, Jeremiah, and Elijah. In the Guitar Concerto (1939), written for Andrés Segovia, the temptation to imitate a Spanish manner is successfully avoided and much play is made of the contrast between the fragile and subtle sonority of the solo instrument and the more compact sounds of the orchestra which is, appropriately, of a modest size

LUIGI DALLAPICCOLA AND GOFFREDO PETRASSI

The next generation of Italian composers, who came to full maturity in the post-war years, did not ignore the stylistic and spiritual premises of old Italian music on which their predecessors had built, but they proved equally receptive to many ideas and ideals common among their contemporaries outside Italy. Two musicians stand out here—Luigi Dallapiccola (b.1904) and Goffredo Petrassi (b.1904). Dallapiccola, who shows the most sharply defined artistic profile among the composers of this later generation, began with the exploration of sixteenth-century polyphony whose technique and spirit he assimilated in a highly individual manner. Characteristic of this phase of his development are the three sets, *Cori di Michelangelo Buonarotti il Giovane* (1933–36), of which the first set is for unaccompanied mixed chorus while the two remaining sets are, respectively, for a female chorus and seventeen instruments and mixed chorus with large orchestra. In the choral writing Italian vocalism is paramount, though allied to a strongly marked rhythmic feeling and to a texture which displays the signs of a mind steeped in counterpoint:

Ex. 113

(And we say that he who takes her away shall see her become, in two days, a hellish devil.)

The more or less straightforward polyphony of the first set (see Ex. 113) is offset by the complex vocal and instrumental density of the later sets. In the mid-1930s Dallapiccola came into contact with the music of the Viennese dodecaphonic school and this was of decisive importance for his subsequent development, though in adopting the twelve-note method he did not go against his native temperament, which is out of sympathy with decadent romanticism and leans towards a Mediterranean brand of neo-classicism, such as was advocated by Busoni. An instructive instance of this are the three *Canti di prigonia* (1938–41), written for mixed chorus, two pianos, and percussion—a combination evidently suggested by Stravinsky's *Les Noces*—in which Dallapiccola handles the serial technique with considerable freedom, combining it with pure diatonic writing. Despite their ancient texts (Mary Queen of Scots, Boethius, and Girolamo Savonarola), these choral songs are a testimony to the composer's profound social conscience and that compassionate response to the sufferings of political victims in totalitarian countries—a compassion to which his second opera, *Il prigioniero*, written after the war, gives even more eloquent expression. As a composer for the stage Dallapiccola displays a remarkable dramatic instinct, especially in suggesting states of nightmare and anxiety which he achieves partly by the characteristic nature of his thematic material, partly by vocal and orchestral devices. This is already seen in his first opera, *Volo di notte* (1939), after Antoine de Saint-Exupéry's novel. This is the story of a South American airline company, prepared to sacrifice the life of a pilot in order to inaugurate night flights, thus hoping to serve the advancement of modern technology. The action is symbolic of the relation between man and machine, the machine taking full possession of the human mind. Like *Canti di prigionia*, the opera is written in a free serial style mixing tonality with atonality. Thus, it opens in B major and ends in E major but a very large part of the work resorts to dodecaphony, the music being based on the following note-row:

Ex. 114

Like Berg in *Wozzeck* and *Lulu*, Dallapiccola harnesses the individual scenes to 'closed' musical forms such as 'Tempo di blues', 'Pezzo ritmico', Chorale and Variations. Pure singing is interspersed with the Schoenbergian *Sprechstimme* to which Dallapiccola, following Berg, adds a rhythmic declamation half-way between speech and singing.

Petrassi's development was chiefly determined by his early friendship with Casella, who not only influenced him directly but guided his artistic outlook towards contemporary movements outside Italy. Hindemith and Stravinsky are the two composers who, apart from Casella, have contributed most to the formation of Petrassi's style—the first with his contrapuntal complexity and 'motoric' rhythm and the second, more generally, with his non-emotional, objective approach to musical composition. The first work demonstrating Petrassi's essential manner was the early Partita for orchestra (1932) which showed a remarkable technical maturity, especially in the assurance of the instrumental treatment, firmness of structure and unity of expression. The thematic material is sharply defined and this, combined with rhythmic vigour, lends the music a sinewy, athletic quality. While here Petrassi still leans on the form of Baroque dances ('Gagliarda', 'Ciaconna', 'Giga'), in the Concerto for Orchestra (1934) he penetrates into the intrinsic spirit of Baroque music, which is that of an antithesis. Apart from the broad contrast between the individual sections, the concerto principle is carried further in that the thematic ideas are allotted to different instrumental groups, and thus stand out with great clarity of outline while, as a corollary, the scoring avoids the blending of colours. As in the Partita, the tonal style is that of Hindemith's 'diatonicized' chromaticism. The Piano Concerto (1939), however, shows simplification of both tonality and texture, particularly in the expressive second movement—an air with variations in B flat major. For a number of years, beginning with 1934, Petrassi concentrated his chief energies on choral composition, such as the *Ninth Psalm* (1936), the *Magnificat* (1940) and the inspired *Cori di Morti* (1941) which is a dramatic madrigal set to a text by Leopardi. The first two works are expressive of a deeply religious vein and distantly echo the style of Italian vocal polyphony of the sixteenth century, with which Petrassi had come into direct contact as a young Roman choirboy.

BÉLA BARTÓK

As we have seen, Stravinsky began his career as a nationalist and after the First World War shed the national traits in order to evolve a style on Western lines. But there were contemporary composers in Eastern Europe and in Spain who cultivated and sustained a latter-day nationalism half a century after the first outbreak of national consciousness in music in Russia, Czechoslovakia, and Scandinavia. The case of these twentieth-century nationalists was put in a nutshell by Manuel de Falla who in speaking of Debussy said that 'folkmusic is most satisfactorily treated by the cultivated musician, not by using authentic tunes but by "feeling" them, by realizing the foundations on which they rest and conveying the essence of them in music which is all his own.'[1] Bartók, Kodály, Janáček, Szymanowski, Falla, and others have all done this in a deliberate manner; theirs is a nationalism which is more a matter of essential thought and general aesthetic attitude than a manifestation of concrete, tangible features though all have occasionally drawn on native folk material.

Of these composers Béla Bartók[2] (1881–1945) is the personality who combined nationalism and a highly original personal style in the most remarkable manner. It is true that Bartók's early training was Western, and throughout his career he availed himself of Western forms and techniques, especially sonata and variation form, and linear counterpoint; but the substance of his creative achievement is to be found in the close amalgamation of Hungarian elements with his own way of musical thinking. His researches into Hungarian folk-song, begun with his friend Kodály in 1905, revealed to him rich untapped sources which increasingly fertilized his own style and taught him a number of fundamental differences from Western art music. In his *Selbst-Biographie*,[3] Bartók has enumerated some of these differences:

The study of this peasant music was for me of decisive importance, for the reason that it revealed to me the possibility of a total emancipation from the hegemony of the major-minor system. For the largest and, indeed, the more valuable part of this treasure-house of melodies lies in the old church modes, in ancient Greek and certain still more primitive scales (notably the pentatonic), and also shows the most varied and free rhythms and time-changes in both *rubato* and *tempo giusto* performance. This was evidence that the old scales, which are no longer in use in out art-music, have by no means lost their vitality. Their application also makes novel harmonic combinations possible. This treatment of the diatonic scale also led to a liberation from the petrified (*erstarrt*) major-minor scale and, as an ultimate result, to a completely free handling of each single note of our chromatic twelve-note system.

To this must be added the characteristic syncopation (quaver-dotted crotchet and semiquaver-dotted quaver, comparable to the 'Scottish snap') which is so prevalent in Bartók's and Kodály's rhythmic style and derives from the peculiarity of the Hungarian language, in which the

---

[1] J. B. Trend, *Manuel de Falla and Spanish Music* (London, 1925), p. 55. In the Debussy number of the *Revue musicale* (December 1920) p. 209, Falla wrote: 'Mais tandis que le compositeur espagnol [Felipe Pedrell] fait emploi, dans une grande partie de sa musique, du document populaire authentique, on dirait que le maître français s'en est écarté pour créer une musique à lui, ne portant de celle qui l'a inspiré que l'essence des éléments fondamentaux.'

[2] For Bartók's early works see Chapters I–III.

[3] *Musikblätter des Anbruchs*, iii (1921), p. 89.

tonic accent falls invariably on the first syllable of the word. On the other hand, Bartók's technique of repeating short melodic-rhythmic units with the effect of creating a 'strange feverish excitement' may have originated in his studies of Arab music (see pp. 281–2); it forms one of the primitive traits of his style comparable to Stravinsky's melodic structure in his 'Russian' period.

Bartók began with simple transcriptions of authentic Hungarian, Rumanian, and Slovakian folk-songs and went on to use these tunes as 'material'—varying, breaking them up, and developing them according to Western technique. He finally arrived at the invention of themes bearing the melodic and rhythmic characteristics of genuine folk-songs; in other words, he wrote what have been called 'imaginary folk-songs'. To put it differently, in this last stage the folk element entered the very fibre of Bartók's own creative thought and was sublimated into a very personal utterance. In order to appreciate fully this fusing of East and West in his music, it will be necessary to look more closely at this process of gradual amalgamation.

Up to 1905, the year in which he started to collect and to research into Hungarian folklore, his nationalism expressed itself in the use of what was then considered to be authentic folk music but was in reality greatly distorted, westernized music. Such were the tunes employed by Liszt in his Hungarian Rhapsodies and Brahms in his Hungarian Dances. These tunes had been adapted to the major-minor system and, since they were mostly played by gypsy bands, they were decked out with rich embellishments, trills, and grace-notes and often made to conform to the so-called 'gypsy scale', 'natural' minor but with the fourth and seventh degrees raised. Bartók himself used such a melody, complete with ornaments and augmented intervals, in his Rhapsody for piano of 1904:

Ex. 115

With the discovery of Hungarian peasant music, which up to 1905 had been entirely unknown to professional musicians, a new chapter opened in Bartók's creative career. He profoundly appreciated these long-forgotten melodies: 'In their small proportions [the Hungarian folk-songs] are as perfect as the large-scale masterpieces of musical art. They are, indeed, classical models of the way in which a musical idea—in all its freshness and shapeliness—can be expressed in the most concise form and with the most modest means: in short, in the most perfect way possible.'[1] As established by Bartók, there are two fundamental types of Hungarian folk-song: the first, the more ancient type, which was on the point of dying out by the time he and Kodály began their studies, shows different features in different regions, though certain traits are common to all. By contrast, the more 'modern' type, flourishing in the nineteenth century, was identical in all regions of the country. What are the characteristics of the old songs? First, they are isometric, i.e. each line of the verse consists of the same number of syllables and, since most of the settings are syllabic, of the same number of notes. Secondly, they all show a quaternary structure, one section to one line of the quatrain; in other words, a chain-like arrangement patterned ABCD, ABBC, ABAB, or AABC in which A never occurs in the last section. Thirdly, the majority are pentatonic, others again are modal. Fourthly, they invariably show a downward tendency and never start with an anacrusis, in conformity with the first-syllable accentuation of Hungarian words. Here are two examples to show a pentatonic and a modal tune, respectively:[2]

Ex. 116

(i) **Parlando**

(ii)

---

[1] *Das ungarishe Volkslied* (Berlin and Leipzig, 1925), p. 4; English translation, London, 1931.

[2] Ibid., Exs. 15 and 45.

As to the general character of folk-song, Bartók distinguishes two major kinds. The first is a slow song in *parlando-rubato*, free in rhythm and of an improvisatory nature:[1]

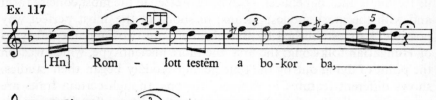

Ex. 117

[Hn] Rom - lott testëm a bo-kor - ba,_____

Piros vérem hull - a hó - ba;

(I lie wounded in the thicket,
My red blood trickles on the snow.)

Of Bartók's own music it is particularly the quartets where we find movements in the style of these slow improvisatory songs, e.g. the third movement of Quartet No. 4 (Ex. 133) and the 'night music' of the Andante of Quartet No. 5. Occasionally these slow songs repeat (like the related Rumanian *doină*, see below) the same note, as illustrated by the Andante of Quartet No. 5, the Più adagio section of the Second movement of the Piano Concerto No. 3, and the opening of the Adagio in the *Music for strings, percussion, and celesta.*

The second type of authentic Hungarian peasant music is represented by *tempo giusto* songs in strict time and dance rhythm:[2]

Ex. 118

which like the previous example shows the characteristic Hungarian 'snap'. There are instances in which Bartók uses *tempo giusto* and *rubato* in alternation, notably in works of his early period, an instructive example of which is the Introduction to the finale of his Quartet No. 1 of 1908.

As to the more 'modern' folk-song, Bartók sees its main difference from the authentic type in that the first section of its quaternary struc-

---

[1] Ibid., Ex. 21.   [2] Ibid., Ex. 61.

ture is always repeated in the last section (AAAA, AABA, ABBA, or ABCA), and the song employs modality more frequently than the old kind:[1]

Ex. 119

Otherwise, the 'modern' type is identical with the authentic, having absorbed most of its features.

Bartók also refers to a third type, the 'mixed' folk-song which possesses certain traits of the authentic song, such as the quaternary structure, but reveals the influence of the West in its major-minor tonality:[2]

Ex. 120

This 'mixed' type, commonly described in the nineteenth century as *airs favoris*, was especially popular with the upper classes of Hungarian society—it is the kind used by Liszt and Brahms—and Bartók himself occasionally resorts to it, as in the *Improvisations* for piano (1920)[3] and even as late as 1944, in the fourth movement of the Concerto for Orchestra:

Ex. 121

[1] Ibid., Ex. 105.   [2] Ibid., Ex. 271.
[3] Nos. 3, 4, 5, and 6 are recorded in *The History of Music in Sound*, x.

Inevitably, Hungarian folk music engaged Bartók's main interest. But he also made valuable studies of the musical folklore of Rumania, Slovakia, and the Arabs round Biskra, and occupied himself with the folk-songs of Bulgaria, Yugoslavia, the Ukraine, and Turkey. In Rumania he found four different kinds: the *colindă* or Christmas song, the dirge, instrumental dance music, and music not associated with any particular occasions. To this last variety belongs the *doină* or *horă lungă* preponderant in the regions of Maramures and Ugocsa, which is, perhaps, together with the dance music, the most important product of Rumanian folk music. Like the slow Hungarian song, the *doină* is in *parlando-rubato* style, free in rhythm and improvisatory but, in addition, marked by chant-like, incantatory passages on the same note[1] and the fairly frequent use of the downward third:[2]

Ex. 122

(Hey, my sweetheart, when I talked to you you were afraid I might bewitch you.)

How Bartók uses the *doină* in a stylized, highly individual form may be seen, for instance, from the first movement of his Violin Sonata No. 2 and, particularly, the Trio in the Marcia of the Quartet No. 6, in which the falling third is very prominent:

[1] These are sometimes also found in the Rumanian dirge.
[2] Bartók, *Die Volksmusik der Rumänen von Maramures* (Munich, 1923), Ex. 23.

Ex. 123

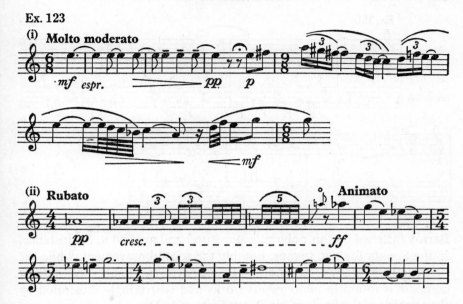

In his *tempo giusto* movements Bartók resorts very frequently to the characteristic dactylic-trochaic pattern of the Rumanian folk dance.[1]

Ex. 124

while his other favourite rhythmic pattern originates in Slovakian music:

Ex. 125

In the summer of 1913 Bartók made a journey to the region of Biskra, in Algeria, to study Arab music which he found to be very limited in compass, mostly moving between two or three neighbouring notes and constantly repeating tiny melodic fragments. This primitive structure, however, is strongly counterbalanced by the complex polyrhythmic character of Arab music as seen, for instance, in a woman-*kneja* or nuptial song:[2]

[1] Ibid., Ex. 166.

[2] Bartók, *Die Volksmusik der Araber von Biskra und Umgebung* (Leipzig, 1920), Ex. 26.

Ex. 126

Bartók fastened on this polyrhythmic aspect and applied it, for instance, in the Sonata for two pianos, notably the second movement, while the perpetual reiteration of short melodic-rhythmic figures of narrow compass is found in many of his works and is strikingly illustrated by the opening of the finale of his Dance Suite of 1923:

Ex. 127

Bartók's researches into the folk music of the Ukraine, Yugoslavia, Bulgaria, and Turkey were not carried far enough to allow him to arrive at any definite conclusions. What he wrote, for instance, on the irregular 'Bulgarian rhythm' has now been shown to be true also of the music of the Greeks, Turks, Armenians, Berbers and Hindus.[1] Here is an example of a Bulgarian folk-song in an 'irrational' rhythm:[2]

[1] John W. Downey, *La Musique populaire dans l'œuvre de Béla Bartók* (Paris, 1964), p. 151.
[2] Quoted p. 154, from Vasil Stoin, *Narodni pesni ot Timok do Vit* (Sofia, 1928).

Ex. 128

Bartók introduces such rhythmic patterns into the *Six Pieces in Bulgarian Rhythm* in Vol. VI of his *Microcosmos*, in the Scherzo and Trio of his Quartet No. 5 $\frac{(4+2+3}{8}$ and $\frac{3+2+2+3)}{8}$ and the finale of *Contrasts* $\frac{(8+5)}{8}$.

As regards Serbo-Croat folk-song, Bartók began to study it systematically only in 1941–2, when he examined various collections by other investigators. There he found one type, particularly widespread in Dalmatia, which is in two parts, the second voice holding a pedal or moving, heterophonically, in seconds and sevenths with the first voice. The following example opens with two *sopile*, double-reed wind instruments, which are always used in pairs:[1]

Ex. 129

2 Sopile

etc.   Voices

Bartók had used seconds and sevenths to thicken out a line and thus lend it greater pungency long before these studies, in fact as early as 1907, in his *14 Bagatelles* for piano. But his late occupation with Serbo-Croat folk music bore fresh fruit in the two-part writing in major sevenths and minor seconds in the *Giuoco delle coppie* of his Concerto for Orchestra.

[1] Quoted in Bartók and A. Lord, *Serbo-Croatian Folk Songs* (New York, 1951), p. 63.

Another fingerprint of Bartók's harmonic style also had its origin in folk music. In the folk-songs of the Balkan peninsula there is no clear major and minor third but a 'neutral' interval higher or lower in pitch than the Western interval. This is the natural corollary of the absence of a definite feeling for a major or minor key. Bartók absorbed this feature into his own music in two ways. He either combines the major and minor third in a single chord as, for instance, in No. 143 of his *Microcosmos* and the finale of his Quartet No. 5 (Ex. 130, i and ii); or he extends this 'neutralization' by casting one part into major and the other into minor, thus arriving at a simple bitonality, as in No. 59 of *Microcosmos* (Ex. 130, iii):

Ex. 130

To sum up, Bartók's amalgamation of East European folk-song with his own style was a gradual process, beginning with simple transcriptions and arrangements in which a peasant tune is taken

either unchanged or only slightly modified, a piano accompaniment
and, perhaps, a few bars of introduction and postlude added. Bartók
himself compared this to Bach's treatment of the Protestant chorales
some of which were originally popular songs.[1] In a later stage he
took the native tune as 'material' to be altered, developed, and
elaborated; and the final phase was the invention of 'imaginary'
folk tunes, i.e. melodies springing from the composer's mind and
bearing characteristics of both his own individual style and that of
authentic folk-song fused into an organic, indivisible unity. Pointers in
this direction can be clearly discerned in his Quartet No. 2 and the ballet
The Miraculous Mandarin (1919); but it was not until the First and
Second Violin Sonatas (1921 and 1922 respectively) that Bartók's
advance towards a realization of his new ideal became manifest. The
more obvious Hungarianisms are confined to the last movements which
are in the nature of primitive folk dances, while in the remaining movements he applies a novel expressionistic manner. The First Sonata is
larger in scope than the Second, and has an opening movement bursting
with a passionate and sweeping melodic line in the violin and with
savagely percussive chords in the piano. The obscuring of the underlying
tonality—an infinitely extended C sharp minor—is almost complete and,
availing himself of the advanced harmonic devices of contemporary
Western music, Bartók acquired a tonal sense very different from
that shown in his previous compositions. The individual notes of some
themes imply a kind of 'diatonicized' chromaticism which in appearance
is almost identical with serial writing and greatly differs from the
intense, Wagnerian chromaticism encountered in such an early work
as the first movement of the First String Quartet (1908). The Second
Sonata is more concentrated and more economical, consisting of
two parts only, which stand to each other in something like the relation
of *lassú* and *friss* of the *verbunkos* style—popular Hungarian music
of the eighteenth and early nineteenth centuries which was played at
army recruiting (German, *Werbung*). The first part is in *tempo rubato*,
slow and recitative-like, while the second is in fact *tempo giusto* and
shows a rondo-like arrangement of varied dance sections. The two
parts have the main thematic material in common; but in contrast to
the practice of the classical and romantic duo sonatas, the violin (which
is leading) and the piano of Bartók's two sonatas are allotted for the
most part separate material, which emphasizes the individual character
of the two instruments. Instead of interweaving them Bartók makes
them complementary to each other, which has the effect of apparent
contrast but ideal unity of thought. Both works show classical sonata

---

[1] *The Influence of Peasant Music on Modern Music* (New York, 1959), p. 71.

form, but Bartók varies the expository thematic material in the recapitulation almost beyond recognition and thus achieves a psychological rather than actual reprise.

In the Dance Suite (1923), which consists of five dances with a ritornello and a finale, Bartók reverts to the half authentic, half imaginary type of Hungarian folk-music, but the following Piano Sonata (1926), the suite *Out of Doors* for piano (1926), and the First Piano Concerto (1926) show a modification of the style initiated in the violin sonatas. The predominant feature of the Piano Sonata is its extreme percussiveness, with explosive chord-clusters compounded of seconds, fourths, sevenths, and ninths, and the structure built up by the ostinato-like repetition of short melodic phrases of a limited compass, whose connexion with Hungarian folk-music is so attenuated as to be almost non-existent. The dynamic thrust and power of the music leaves no room for lyricism and even the meditative slow movement avoids all sustained melody; in spirit the work is akin to the *Allegro barbaro* of fifteen years earlier, but the writing is far more concentrated and uncompromising. Although *Out of Doors* shows the same application of percussive and repetitive devices as the Piano Sonata, it is a more ingratiating composition and programmatic in character. The five pieces of which it consists are mood-pictures of which the fourth, 'Night Music', is the first fully developed example of Bartók's extraordinary sensitiveness to the sounds of a nocturnal world, with the chirpings, twitterings, and calls of night animals and insects reproduced in an impressionistic manner that owes almost nothing to Debussy but represents the composer's individual contribution to evocative music. The First Piano Concerto continues in the percussive martellato style of the Piano Sonata, but the sounds produced are less harsh and spiky than in the former work. This is due partly to the chordal texture being largely colouristic, and partly to the fact that a great deal of writing is dissolved into contrapuntal lines, whose clashes refuse to be interpreted in a vertical sense and pass very quickly. The individual strands of the polyphonic fabric are drawn succinctly and stand out with great clarity, features which may be traced back to Bartók's intense study of Bach and to his editing of Baroque music (Couperin, Frescobaldi, Scarlatti, and other composers). The influence of the Baroque concerto can be seen in the relation between the piano and the orchestra in which there is no clear-cut division and, though there are passages (as in the Baroque concerto) where the piano becomes a true solo instrument, especially in the slow movement, the general effect remains one of a competition between equals, the piano playing the role of a *primus inter pares*. As in the Piano Sonata, the material is fragmentary, with a predominance of scale motives that are very much alike, and the feeling for a definite tonality is very vague: to say that the Concerto is 'in' E minor is merely to indicate a general tendency of the music towards a tonal pole.

During this period, initiated by the two violin sonatas and lasting till about 1930, Bartók advanced to the utmost limits of his intellectual exploration, cultivating an expressionistic, abstract, and esoteric style of utterance. He appears during these years to be almost exclusively concerned with the projection of an inner world in which the dividing line between the conscious (rational) and the instinctive (irrational) is virtually non-existent. This is perhaps best seen in the Third String Quartet (1927) which in style represents a *ne plus ultra* in concentration and subtilization of thought. Like the Beethoven of the late quartets and piano sonatas, Bartók in this work seems to be communing with himself rather than attempting communication with the outside world. This is the main reason why this string quartet is the least accessible of his six, making extraordinary demands on the listener's perceptive powers; yet it is no less a masterpiece than the subsequent quartets, differing from them only in the inaccessibility of its aesthetic and technical premises. The six quartets occupy a central position in Bartók's creative career and may be likened to a diary to which the artist confided his most intimate intellectual and emotional experiences and adventures. Each of the six quartets stands at the culmination of a different phase of Barótk's artistic growth, summing up the essential problems, tendencies, and aspirations characteristic of each stylistic stage. Just as Beethoven's seventeen quartets represent the apogee of the classical form, so does the series of six Bartók quartets mark the consummation of the modern genre. For profundity of thought, imaginative power, structural logic, diversity of formal and textural features, and enlargement of the technical scope, they stand unrivalled. This quality of uniqueness is further enhanced by the following consideration: one of the mainsprings of Bartók's art was the attempt to achieve a perfect synthesis between East and West, and in his quartets this synthesis may be said to have been most nearly achieved. We can realize the full measure of this imaginative feat if we bear in mind that this fusion between two different musical cultures was brought about in a medium which has come to be regarded as the purest and most subtle manifestation of Western musical thinking. To have harnessed the instinctive primitive forces residing in Hungarian music to the most intellectual of Western musical forms—therein lies the historic significance of Bartók's quartets. This fusion, however, was achieved at a price. The criticism that must be levelled against Bartók's quartet style, as it may be also advanced against Beethoven's from the Razumovsky quartets onwards, is that it frequently bursts the framework of the medium. In Beethoven's case this was due to a powerful symphonic urge, while with Bartók it is the dynamic percussiveness of his harmonic and rhythmic language that contradicts the intimacy and 'inwardness' associated with the quartet medium.

The Third String Quartet is the shortest and, in expression, most intense of the six, consisting of one continuous movement of a highly unusual formal design. It is divided into four sections which follow one another in the simple pattern slow-fast-slow-fast and these are thematically closely related in a manner best illustrated by two interlocking arches:

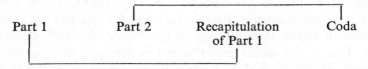

Part 1 furnishes a striking example of Bartók's technique of developing virtually an entire movement from a single germ-cell—here a pentatonic figure consisting of a rising fourth and descending minor third. As the last section of the ternary Part 1 proves, this basic idea derives from a broad sustained theme of Hungarian flavour which was probably Bartók's initial idea, but, instead of stating it at the beginning, he seizes on its most characteristic motive and evolves from it the major part of the movement before revealing the source from which it sprang. The immense regenerative force inherent in this germ-cell may be seen from the following examples:

Ex. 131

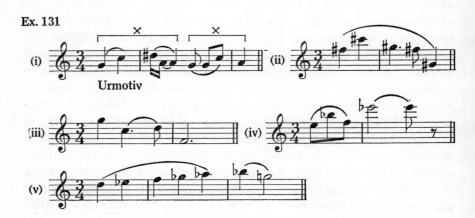

The recapitulation of Part 1 condenses the expository material to such an extent that a few bars have to do duty for a dozen bars or so of the exposition (the recapitulation is seventy bars long, as against 122 bars of Part 1). Part 2 clearly springs from native dances, with the main theme harmonized in 'primitive' parallel triads, and the music is driven along by an elemental rhythm in which percussive chords and syncopations predominate. Its form is that of a sonata-cum-variations. The treatment of the main subject proceeds by imitation and stretto; and while the melodic structure undergoes comparatively minor alterations, there are frequent changes of the metric units (2/4, 3/4, 3/8, 5/8, and 6/8). The second subject provides the material for the 'development' which takes the form of a series of variations culminating in a characteristic Bartókian fugue—a fast scurrying piece in *leggiero* style and with subdued dynamics. (Unlike the fugues of Beethoven's last works, Bartók's do not serve a dramatic purpose nor are they intended as an intellectual catharsis; they are motoric in character and serve to intensify the rhythmic drive of the movement in which they occur.) The coda is a much transformed reprise of Part 2, changing from Allegro to Allegro molto, with the contrapuntal texture becoming denser still (canons and inversions in stretto), until towards the end the music takes on a savagely aggressive character through the use of percussive note-repetitions, incessant ostinatos, double-stops, *glissandi*, and rising and falling arpeggios. The work closes on a chord of three superimposed fifths based on the note C sharp—the 'tonic', which, except for the very beginning and a brief passage in Part 1, is never in evidence until the concluding bars.

If the Third String Quartet represents Bartók's farthest advance in the direction of intellectual severity, uncompromising harshness of emotional expression and formal experiment, the Fourth (1928) marks a certain retreat from this extreme position, though it still has some hard things to say. Not that Bartók's advanced style undergoes an intrinsic change. The writing remains predominantly linear, without regard for the violent dissonances produced in the vertical texture; and there is a predilection for scholastic 'automatic' devices (canon, imitation, stretto, inversion and retrograde motion) which at times creates the impression of excess, a feeling that Bartók is straining these devices and making too self-conscious a use of them. But he does handle them with a remarkable freedom and it is not often that he sacrifices the shapeliness and equipoise of his melodic lines to the demands of strict contrapuntal logic. Moreover, the gains acquired in the Third Quartet are now consolidated on a broader formal basis, and such sections as the wonderful elegy of the third movement and the delightful serenade of the fourth suggest that Bartók's personality was maturing and becoming accessible to gentler and more relaxed moods. But the quest for unity and for correspondences between the movements by novel means continues. In the Third Quartet Bartók interlocks what are in fact two different movements. In the Fourth Quartet he resorts to the so-called *Bogen* or arch form in that its five movements follow in the pattern A–B–C–B'–A' in which the two outer and the two inner movements, respectively, mirror one another while the central piece C stands by itself. In other words, the music progresses from A to C and then retraces its steps back via B' to A':

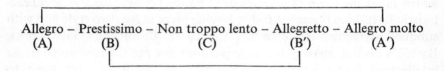

The links between the respective outer and inner movements are not simply confined to thematic correspondences but also embrace the general structure and the character of the music. The first and last movements derive their entire material from a germ-cell of six notes in the seventh bar of the opening Allegro:

Ex. 132

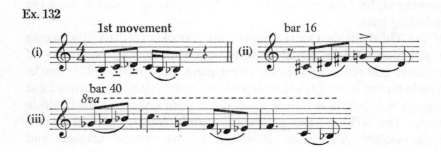

Ex. 132 (i) looks an unpromising enough motif but it is the measure of Bartók's art of organic thinking that from it he evolves a wealth of thematic ideas with which he builds up the constantly changing texture of the first and last movements. This he does by stretching and contracting the intervals, forming diatonic or chromatic versions of the same figure, subjecting it to fragmentation, inversion and retrograde motion, and rhythmic variation. It would be extremely hard to detect the inner connexion between the original idea and some of its metamorphoses, without hearing the intervening stages. As one of his recent biographers remarks,[1] it is because Bartók allows us to share his thought-processes rather than leaping from the basic motive to its furthest transformation that his music carries with it such utter conviction. The first movement is an abstract piece wholly concerned with problems of form, design, and texture; the finale, on the other hand, is a ferocious Hungarian dance which at times oversteps the proper string quartet medium by producing an almost orchestral sonority. The relationship between the second and the fourth movements is on several levels: both share the same thematic material, both are lightweight scherzos, and both are played in a special manner—the Prestissimo with muted strings and the Allegretto pizzicato. Yet there is a marked contrast of mood between these two movements: while the former is a kind of moto perpetuo to which the muted strings lend a strange shimmer (not unlike the effect produced by the Allegro misterioso of Berg's *Lyric Suite*), the latter has a delicate, guitar-like accompaniment in the manner of a serenade. It is in this fourth movement that Bartók first uses the 'snap' pizzicato in which the strings of the instrument are to be plucked with such a force that they rebound off the fingerboard with a percussive sound. The only point of

[1] Halsey Stevens, *The Life and Music of Béla Bartók* (New York, 1953), p. 188.

repose in this dynamic quartet is provided by the lyrical espressivo of the slow central movement, with its grave, wistful cello recitative of Hungarian character in the first section. Here Bartók recalls music peculiar to the tárogató, a woodwind instrument of ancient (Eastern) origin whose dark colour is akin to that of the *chalumeau* register of our clarinet:

Ex. 133

The middle section is an exquisite atmospheric study of the sounds of nocturnal nature. The Fifth String Quartet (1934) followed the fourth after an interval of six years, yet intrinsically they are sister works, though in the later composition the process of intellectual relaxation and lyrical expansion is carried a stage further. Significantly, it has two slow movements whereas the previous quartet had only one; and its melodic lines show a more clear-cut articulation and grow in amplitude almost in the manner of themes in the established sense, while the harmonic style is on the whole less astringent. Yet the formal organization is the same as in the Fourth Quartet—again an arch form, A–B–C–B'–A', in which C is now a scherzo flanked by two slow movements in which Bartók achieves a new height of evocative lyrical poetry. The correspondences between the opening movement and the finale comprise the sharing of the same thematic material, the casting of both movements in sonata form, and a clear definition of tonality (B flat). Both movements show an abundance of inversion, canons, stretti, and passages in invertible counterpoint—the recapitulation of the Allegro, for instance, reintroducing the expository material in its 'mirror' form. The finale is notable for the inclusion of a fugue which in its percussive note-reiteration on the two violins, *col legno*, and a drone-like ostinato on the cello, constitutes an illuminating example of Bartók's fusion of an Eastern and Western style. It also contains a strange episode, marked 'Allegretto con indifferenza', with a trivial tune in A major and harmonized in deliberately commonplace fashion with alternating tonic and dominant chords, the whole to be played 'meccanico'. The barrel-organ effect thus produced is like a grimace or mocking sneer, recalling Mahler's use of banal tunes to suggest the commonplace aspect of life. The second and the fourth movements— an Adagio and Andante—share the same ground plan (A–B–A plus coda) and the same material. Both open in an atmospheric manner, the fragmentary motives and trills of the Adagio corresponding to the repeated pizzicato notes, slurs and *gruppetti* of the Andante, and both movements contain a chorale, a feature almost invariably associated with Bartók's 'night music'. The central piece is an engaging scherzo in *alla bulgarese* rhythm for which Bartók showed a special predilection in his late period. The asymmetrical rhythmic pattern of the scherzo proper, $\frac{(4+2+3)}{8}$, grows more complex in the trio and a most noteworthy feature of the latter is a delicate arabesque formed by a ten-note ostinato which is repeated fifty-nine times, with an enchanting melody in the vein of Hungarian children's song set against it. With the Sixth String Quartet (1939), written five years after the Fifth, we reach the 'classical' stage of Bartók's development, which also includes such works as the *Music for Strings and Percussion*, the Sonata for Two Pianos and the Violin Concerto. This last period is characterized by a greater simplicity of form and technical devices, by the invention of themes of a broader, more sustained character, by a marked reduction of grating dissonances, by a greater transparency of texture and a sharper tonal perspective. These changes, which were first noticeable in the Fifth Quartet, reach their consummation in the Sixth. Thus it is significant that Bartók reverts to the classical scheme of four contrasting movements, that he anchors the work in a D major-minor tonality and that he employs a simpler, less intellectual device than the arch form in order to achieve formal unity between the movements. He resorts to a motto theme first announced at the very beginning by the viola which is a mournful melody of a marked drooping tendency, most beautifully shaped and balanced and (like the variation theme of the Violin Concerto) constituting an exquisite example of Bartók's skilful fusion of the melodic and rhythmic inflexions of a Hungarian melody with his own personal manner:

Ex. 134

Each of the first three movements is prefaced by this motto theme, but on each successive occasion it appears in a slightly different and texturally richer form, until in the finale it becomes the actual material of the movement, expanded and subjected to elaboration and at last revealing its full emotional significance. At the other extreme stands the gay, even exuberant opening movement. With the Marcia and Burletta, however, Bartók returns to the style of his expressionistic period; the march is harsh and aggressive and the Burletta's humour is grim and sardonic, with the first violin playing quarter-tones against the 'true' notes of the second violin and vice versa, thus creating a deliberate 'out of tune' effect. In the Burletta Bartók's 'barbaric' tendency is particularly emphasized in the fierce harmonic clashes, in glissandos and percussive chords to be played 'at the heel' of the bow. Indeed it is hard to resist the impression that the work possesses an extra-musical significance or an implicit programme.

The Second Piano Concerto (1931) is permeated by a feeling of extrovert exuberance comparatively rare with Bartók, its sinewy athletic strength proclaiming the composer at the height of his creative powers. Its tonic is an unambiguous G major and though the themes are still short and fragmentary, their outline is clear-cut and readily retained in the listener's mind. The formal structure is more articulate than in the First Concerto, the first movement being in sonata form, with the themes inverted in the recapitulation, while the finale consists essentially of the varied alternation of two ideas, recalling Haydn's favourite principle of construction. The slow movement combines an Adagio with a Scherzo in the form A–B–A, section A being an example of the composer's 'night music' style in which a string chorale, harmonized in five superimposed fifths, alternates with recitative-like passages of an improvisatory character on the piano. The work may be said to stand halfway between the Baroque type of the First Concerto and the classical layout of the Violin Concerto, with the solo part frequently rising from an obbligato to full individual status, though the allocation of separate material to the piano and the orchestra still points to the eighteenth-century model.

Bartók's interest in the rhythmic and colouristic possibilities of a percussion ensemble in combination with other instruments first showed itself in the two piano concertos; but it was not until the second half of the 1930s that he composed two works in which he explored to the full the potentialities of such a combination. Although the *Music for Strings, Percussion and Celesta* (1936) and the Sonata for Two Pianos and Percussion (1937) belong together as bold experiments with novel and fascinating sonorities, in the first work the percussion is intimately integrated with the rest of the orchestra, while in the second the percussive instruments are frequently treated in opposition to the two pianos. The *Music for Strings* is in effect a chamber symphony in four movements and is the more highly organized of the two works, demonstrating Bartók's ingenious use of Lisztian cyclic form and theme-transformation. The entire composition springs virtually from a single theme which in its narrow, mostly chromatic, intervals and its emotional expression is similar to the motto theme of the Sixth String Quartet. In the first movement it forms the subject of a five-part fugue and the successive entries of the fugal subject are on alternating rising and falling fifths from the initial A to the final E flat, the 'key' in which the climax is reached after being approached simultaneously from both the higher and the lower circle of fifths. The process is then reversed in a condensed form, with the fugal subject now turned upside down, and in the coda both its original and inverted versions appear in combination in the 'key' of A, the tonal pole of the movement. Dynamically, the movement represents a long crescendo-decrescendo, blazing into white heat at the climax and mirroring on a large scale the arch described by the fugal subject in four bars. There are no counter-subjects, no episodes, and no free contrapuntal lines—the whole fabric is woven into a single closely-knit organic structure. The remaining three movements, though introducing some fresh material, are essentially an exploration of the implications of the fugal subject in different directions.

The choice of a double string orchestra in combination with piano, harp, celesta and percussion instruments of definite and indefinite pitch provided Bartók with an immensely wide and varied range of timbres which he exploits with uncanny resourcefulness. The two string orchestras are used both in combination and antiphonally, with and without the percussion, which is employed to produce both traditional and novel sound effects. Just as the *Music for Strings* exploits both the expressive and percussive qualities of a chamber orchestra, so does the Sonata exploit these qualities within the more confined medium of two pianos and percussion. Bartók was himself a distinguished pianist and a wealth of characteristic piano devices are applied to the two instruments, which are treated on a completely equal footing. The percussion comprises three kettle-drums, a bass drum, two side drums, two cymbals, triangle, tam-tam, and, as the only melodic instrument, a xylophone, the whole to be handled by two players. In the opening movement the percussion is largely used for underlining and emphasizing the piano rhythm, while in the two remaining movements it acquires a solo role, the xylophone being entrusted with numerous passages of thematic importance. In 1940 Bartók transcribed the work as a Concerto for Two Pianos and Orchestra, and in this version the role of the percussion is less conspicuous, with a corresponding loss of the particular sonorous quality characteristic of the original version.

From the same year as the Sonata for Two Pianos and Percussion dates the completion of *Microcosmos* (1926-37) which consists of 153 piano pieces of varying length and of progressive technical difficulty. *Microcosmos* is in the first place a didactic work intended to develop a pianist's facility at specific stages of his technique, but it is also a compendium of the essential devices of modern music as seen in the light of Bartók's own style—chords of the fourth, major and minor seconds, cluster harmonies, modality, bitonality, whole-tone and other scales, contrapuntal techniques such as canon and inversion, and special rhythmic patterns such as syncopation and asymmetrical rhythms, of which the *Dances in Bulgarian Rhythm* are the finest examples.

The Violin Concerto (1938) illustrates the perfect equilibrium of all that is characteristic of Bartók's mature style. Thus, the Hungarian elements are subtilized to such an extent that they become intangible; they are like the scent that clings to a plant transplanted from an exotic soil. And while the music is immensely virile and shows that intellectual passion peculiar to Bartók, it is punctuated by a powerful expressive emotional note; this amalgamation of the dramatic with the lyrical is perhaps the most remarkable feature of the concerto. Bartók's mellowness is also evident in a number of technical features. Instead of short fragmentary ideas we now find song-like themes of a sustained character; the formal design is spacious, yet it creates the impression of the utmost concentration on account of the extraordinary vitality and cogency of the composer's musical thinking; there is a clear feeling of tonality (B minor), a less pronounced use of contrapuntal devices, and the soloist assumes a dominating role in a part marked by great virtuosity. The orchestral texture shows a noticeable increase in transparency, Bartók's former style of block instrumentation being replaced by a more individual treatment of single instruments with much subtle blending of colours, especially in the second movement. The work is conceived as a kind of variation; in addition to the second movement, which consists of theme and six variations, all the thematic material of the opening movement is repeated in varied guise in the finale, and this correspondence extends also to the architecture, the finale duplicating the formal design of the first movement (which is in sonata form) almost section by section.

In America Bartók wrote four major works—the Concerto for Orchestra (1943), the Sonata for Solo Violin (1944), the Third Piano Concerto (1945) and the Viola Concerto (1945), which remained unfinished. The Concerto for Orchestra was written for the Boston Symphony Orchestra which explains the extraordinary brilliance of the writing, single instruments and groups of homogeneous instruments (strings, woodwind, and brass) being treated in a virtuoso concertante style. The work is in fact a symphony or, better, a symphonic suite in five movements. Like the Violin Concerto, it represents a crystallization of all the features of Bartók's maturity—lucid textures in which contrapuntal devices are manipulated to vivid effect, trenchant rhythms and a strongly affirmed, though still widely extended, tonality. If anything, the Hungarian-inspired character of certain themes is more pronounced than in the previous work; the chain-like arrangement of the second and third movements also follows the pattern of multiple structure characteristic of old Hungarian folk-songs (p. 277). Thus, in the second movement, 'Giuoco delle coppie' (Play of the Couples), which takes the place of a symphonic scherzo, the chain structure is seen in the successive introduction two by two, each pair with its own theme, of bassoons in sixths, oboes in thirds, clarinets in sevenths, flutes in fifths, and muted trumpets in major seconds. The Sonata for Solo Violin stands apart from Bartók's 'American' work in that it reverts to the 'difficult' expressionistic style of the Third and Fourth String Quartets, at any rate so far as its first two movements are concerned. The work is severe both in emotional expression and in intellectual content, and to this severity must be added the deliberate angularity and austerity of the style. This is partly the corollary of this particular medium, which is restricted by the absence of a bass to provide tonal balance, the impossibility of sounding more than two notes together and the consequent necessity of breaking chords in triple and quadruple stops. The whole work represents a technical *tour de force* of extraordinary difficulty. Extremes of range are employed in all four movements and much use is made of simultaneous arco and pizzicato and of harmonics and glissando. The Fugue (second movement), whose subject, Ex. 135, with

Ex. 135

its narrow compass and chromatic steps, is most characteristic of Bartók, makes perhaps the greatest demands on the player though the first movement, in 'Tempo di ciaccona' but in sonata form, is scarcely less exacting. It is in the Melodia, whose long-spun chromatic line is subsequently subjected to variation treatment, and in the final Presto, a rondo with three episodes, that a more 'open' style of writing and a more relaxed mood are discernible. The influence of Bach's solo violin sonatas is felt not only in the technical treatment of the instrument but to some extent also in the neo-classical conception of the Tempo di ciaccona and the Fugue. Hungarian memories affect the melodic and rhythmic invention of the last two movements in a most subtle way.

The Third Piano Concerto was the last work Bartók was able virtually to complete before his death. It illustrates a further move towards structural and tonal simplification characteristic of Bartók's late style, the texture being light and the orchestration of great transparency, especially in the chorale and the 'night music' of the slow movement. The solo part is far less percussive and less exacting than in the first two piano concertos yet it is of sufficient brilliance to stamp the work as a true virtuoso concerto.

Looking back at Bartók's total achievement, one sees that several features stand out with great clarity. First, like Stravinsky but to a higher degree, he succeeded in an organic fusion of Western art-music with Eastern folk music, bringing all the technical resources of the West to bear upon native material. In his technique of composition Bartók was one of the most sophisticated Western composers, but his spiritual allegiance belonged to the 'primitive' East, whence he derived much of the freshness and seeming spontaneity of his melodic style and the immense vitality of his rhythmic invention. Secondly, while adhering to the traditional forms of sonata, rondo, and variation, he displayed supreme mastery in designing novel schemes and patterns best illustrated in his six string quartets, the Sonata for two pianos, the Music for strings, celesta and percussion, the Concerto for orchestra and the Sonata for solo violin. The same consummate command is shown in his management of the rhythmic and instrumental texture and his use of orchestral timbre, notably in the genre of his impressionist 'night music' which sprang from Debussy, but which Bartók developed into a highly original utterance. And thirdly, of the three musicians who dominated the musical scene during the first half of the twentieth century—Stravinsky, Schoenberg, and Bartók—it is the Hungarian master who, despite his immense intellectual control, remained nearest to the instinctual, the irrational in music and thus to the Dionysian spirit in art. He is the supreme example of the artist who, in the dialectic between emotional 'primitivism' and intellectual sophistication, never allowed the second ascendancy over the first.

ZOLTAN KODÁLY

Zoltan Kodály (1882–1967) was intimately associated with Bartók in his researches into Hungarian folk-music and also absorbed its characteristic melodic, rhythmic and tonal inflexions into his own idiom; but he shows a greater dependence in his melodic invention on folk material and is, altogether, a composer of less marked individuality than his compatriot. Less intellectual than Bartók, Kodály was a more direct and more sensuous musician whose early works show some allegiance to French impressionism. His strength lay in his lyricism, in a sustained, expressive line of melody; and it is, therefore, no accident that his best work is to be found in vocal music, particularly songs and choral compositions. In these he seems strongly influenced by Palestrina's ideal of transparent contrapuntal texture and clear part-writing. His outstanding choral work is the *Psalmus Hungaricus* for tenor solo, chorus and orchestra (1923), with a text based on Psalm 55, in which the sixteenth-century author identified his own sufferings and sorrows with those of King David and, indirectly, with those of the Hungarian people. The spirit of this archaic text is recaptured in lyrico-dramatic music of extraordinary power and vision, showing a tense melodic style, harmonic directness and great ingenuity in the choral writing. Rich in incidents and episodes, the work consists of a choral prelude and choral interludes which use identical pentatonic material modelled on the style of sixteenth-century Hungarian minstrel songs[1] and with the Hungarian fourth prominent in the cadences.

These interludes constitute the refrain for the various solo passages employing different themes, so that the form represents a freely treated rondo on a large scale; the vocal parts are reinforced but never overwhelmed by the orchestral accompaniment. By contrast, the *Te Deum* (1936), written in commemoration of the 250th anniversary of the relief of Buda from the Turkish occupation, is conceived in a triumphant vein and with a judicious balance between contrapuntal and more homophonic choral writing. And, while in the *Psalmus Hungaricus* the Hungarian element is conspicuous in the general melodic style, in the *Te Deum* it is largely confined to the subjects of the two fugues, and there are also references to plainsong melodies.

With *Háry János* (1926) and *Székelyfonó* (The Székely Spinning Room) (1932) Kodály made important contributions to national Hungarian opera. Both works employ native subjects, the first the legendary exploits of a kind of Hungarian Baron Munchausen and the second scenes from the life in a Transylvanian village. In contrast to Bartók, who adopted in his opera *Duke Bluebeard's Castle* the Wagnerian principle of musical continuity, Kodály adheres to the older 'number' design, with solos, duets, and choral ensembles separated by spoken dialogue, as in the *Singspiel* of *Háry János*, or orchestral bridge passages linking the various numbers, as in *The Spinning Room*. The music of the latter consists mainly of a succession of Transylvanian folk-tunes whose texts are so arranged as to imply an action, though the whole character of the work is rather that of a scenic cantata. Both operas are true folk-operas of a distinctly popular nature and with a strong Hungarian flavour, but in *Háry János* Kodály mixes the native element with ingredients from other sources: in the Hungarian scenes, a song from the Bukovina,

---

[1] See article 'Kodály' in *Grove's Dictionary of Music and Musicians* (5th ed. London, 1954), iv, p. 801.

verbunkos, and gypsy music; in the Austrian scenes, a Viennese carillon tune, an eighteenth-century minuet and Austrian marches. Kodály's orchestral music shows a highly developed sense of brilliant colouring, particularly in the concertante treatment of woodwind and the richly decorated style of the string writing. Characteristic examples of this are the *Dances of Marosszék* (1930) and *Dances of Galánta* (1933), the former based on Hungarian peasant tunes and the latter on *verbunkos* music. The *Variations on a Hungarian Folk-song* (1939) uses a pentatonic tune, 'The Peacock', which provides the theme for sixteen variations and a finale that combines a wide range of contrasting expression with orchestral virtuosity. The Concerto for Orchestra (1939) shows a contest between the different instrumental groups that emulates the style of the eighteenth-century concerto grosso.

LEOŠ JANÁČEK

Turning to Czechoslovakia, the outstanding figure after the death of Smetana and Dvořák was Leoš Janáček (1854–1928) who cultivated a nationalism more intrinsic, more 'intensive' than that of his two predecessors. Like Bartók and Kodály in Hungary, he modelled his style on the characteristics of native (chiefly Moravian) folk material, and showed a natural gift for inventing melodies in genuine folk style. In his vocal compositions he assimilated with immense skill the verbal rhythms and tonal inflexions of his native tongue, imitating Mussorgsky's similar musical treatment of Russian speech—as in this passage from *Příhody Lišky Bystroušky* (The experiences of the little vixen Sharp-Ears, generally known as *The Cunning Little Vixen*):

Ex. 136

(They accused each other of horrible things, indecent and immoral—that the old starling was a shameless philanderer who did unseemly things in the crown of the beech)

Janáček was the first Czech composer to emancipate himself from the prevailing Western influences and he gradually arrived at an entirely personal and, in some aspects, highly original style that opened up new musical territory. The characteristic features of Janáček's language are an aphoristic melodic utterance and a kaleidoscopic change of short themes and motives; a continual variation of the melodic and rhythmic material; an elliptical harmony in which linking modulatory chords are abolished; a fluid tonality which is largely modal and avoids tonic-dominant relationships and the leading-note; and a rhythmic idiom in which the employment of the smallest metric units (2/8, 3/8) is very prominent. Janáček, who belonged to the generation of Mahler, Strauss, and Debussy, matured very slowly and did not reach the height of his creative career until he was in his sixties. The peak of his later achievement is to be found in his five operas, each of which treats an unusual subject and provides testimony to the composer's interest in psychological conflicts.

The great success of his early opera *Jenůfa* (1903)[1] at the Prague production of 1916 appears to have released pent-up forces in Janáček and in the next twelve years he composed no less than five works for the stage. The first was *Výlety Páně Broučkovy* (The Excursions of Mr. Brouček) (1917), to a libretto by František Prochazka (after Svatopluk Čech), a good-humoured but sharply observed satire on the *petit bourgeois* mentality, with its narrow, smug, materialistic outlook, personified in the Prague landlord, Matěj Brouček. Apart from word-inspired motives in both parts, in the first (on the moon) it is the lyrical element that prevails, while the second part (in the fifteenth century) is characterized by a dramatic and ejaculatory style, and the thematic burden is carried by the orchestra, short and clear-cut phrases being repeated or varied on different degrees of the scale. Some phrases play the role of leitmotives and are transformed according to the external and psychological changes of the action; but Janáček employs them in such a free manner that they stand simultaneously for different characters and different situations. *Katya Kabanova* (1921), to Janáček's own libretto, derived from A. N. Ostrovsky's play *The Storm*, is the first of his two operas with Russian subjects. The story illustrates the conflict between the rights and the freedom of the individual, and the rigour of tradition in old Russia as seen in the despotism of family life, the servile status of married women and the iron grip of moral and social customs, Katya representing the urge of the individual to escape from the fetters of antiquated modes of life. In spite of the title of the opera, the ideological, if not actual, heroine is her mother-in-law Kabanicha, the

[1] See pp. 179–82.

embodiment of conservatism, and around her are grouped two contrasting pairs of lovers: Katya and Boris, Kudrjáš and Varvara. The psychological differences between these pairs are clearly reflected in the musical characterization, the ill-starred lovers being depicted in broad flowing themes with, frequently, wide intervals in the vocal parts while the bright, happy pair are portrayed in short, dance-like figures mostly in 2/4 and 3/8 metres of a distinctly Slavonic flavour. Janáček's mature genius is seen not only in his succinct delineation of these characters but in his rich invention and the absolute technical mastery of a work which, despite its predominantly objective treatment, soars at moments into tense dramatic life, as for instance in the last duet between Katya and Boris. The interplay of human drama with nature, which is a salient characteristic of this opera, affords the composer opportunities for atmospheric music, such as the magnificent storm of Act III or the wordless humming chorus of the last scene personifying the River Volga, which forms the background to the tragedy and is to be taken as the symbol of eternal unchangeable life.

Nature in both its human and animal manifestations is also the theme of *The Cunning Little Vixen* (1923) in which Janáček's pantheism and his idea of the essential unity of creation finds full expression. 'My themes,' he once wrote, 'grow out of the earth, out of animals, out of people.' The truth of this dictum is seen not only in the music which transmutes human-speech inflexions, the calls and cries of animals and nature sounds into imaginative utterances, but also in the action which unfolds at two levels—the actual and the symbolical. The opera represents a kind of modern fairy-tale for grown-ups and some scenes have the naïve air of a Christmas charade; but the Gamekeeper's apostrophe to Nature in the final scene is one of the finest lyrical passages in twentieth-century opera. *Věc Makropulos* (The Makropulos Affair) (1924), after Karel Čapek's comedy, is a strange mixture of everyday reality with fantasy. The fantastic element is represented by Elena Makropulos who, thanks to an elixir given her by her father, an alchemist at the Prague Court of Rudolf II of Habsburg, survives for three hundred years into modern times when we meet her as the opera singer, Emilia Marty. The opera suffers from too involved a libretto, with a complicated legacy-lawsuit in the centre and much dialectics arising from the heroine's long past, which impair the conciseness of the dramatic action. The music, however, shows an advance on the previous stage-works in the greater suppleness and plasticity of the orchestral comment accompanying the declamatory phrases of the singers, and, significantly, the traditional operatic cantilena is all but completely absent. All this heralds the style of Janáček's last opera,

Z mrtvého domu (From the House of the Dead) (1928), his most powerful realistic drama. The subject, adapted by the composer from Dostoevsky's autobiographical novel, has no coherent story but sets out to show various scenes from life in a Siberian prison, in all its terror, brutality, and desperation relieved only by occasional touches of humour and comedy. Instead of a real plot we are given three great narratives told by prisoners about the crimes that brought them to Siberia. Grouped around these three tales are two episodes—the arrival (first act) and the release (third act) of a political prisoner, and an interlude which takes the form of a pantomime *Don Juan*, performed by some prisoners for the amusement of the rest. The cast is, with one exception, all male. Most characteristic of the music are stark, bare motives of a violently dissonant nature produced by clashes of minor and major seconds, parallel shifts of chords and long metrical units (6/4, 9/4, and 4/2). The orchestral style is marked by sharply drawn instrumental lines and shows an unusual feature in that treble and bass instruments are set against each other at the extremes of their range, with no intermediate texture (anticipated in *The Makropulos Affair*), which serves to intensify the starkly dramatic character of this opera. The title-page bears the inscription: 'In every creature there is a spark of God'. The opera is a most eloquent summing-up of Janáček's deep-rooted belief in the essential goodness of man and an expression of his profound compassion for the sufferings of humanity.

A word or two must be said about the state of incompletion in which Janáček left *From the House of the Dead*. He had worked directly from Dostoevsky's Russian text and had prepared from it a synopsis of the action on four loose pages from which he wrote the libretto straight into the score—some lines in Russian, others in Czech, and yet others in Lachian dialect. After his death this had to be unified in Czech and adapted to the vocal line. Moreover, Janáček did not live to complete all the orchestration, often writing only the top line and bass which he intended to fill in later. This task was performed by two Brno musicians, the composer, Osvald Chlubna, and the conductor, Břetislav Bakala, both intimately acquainted with Janáček's late orchestral style; the latter conducted the first performance of the opera at Brno on 12 April 1930.

The majority of Janáček's choral music dates from his early, pre-war period, but he did not write his greatest work in that genre until 1926, two years before his death. This was the *Glagolská mše* (Glagolitic Mass) for soli, chorus, orchestra, and organ: that is, a Mass using, instead of the Latin text of the Ordinary, the equivalent text in Church Slavonic.[1] The

---

[1] In Croatia Glagolitic Masses have been written by such composers as Božidar Sirola (1889-1956), Albe Vidaković (1914-1964), Krsto Odak (1888–1965).

liturgical use of Old Slavonic had been banned by the Roman Church in
the eleventh century, although permitted again temporarily under
Charles IV (1316–78). In 1920 an edict was issued allowing the Slavonic
Mass to be celebrated in Bohemia on the Feasts of St. Cyril and St.
Methodius and other patron saints, and it was soon after this that
Janáček first contemplated a *Glagolitic Mass*. He took the text from the
church-music periodical *Cyril*, xlvi (1920) which reproduced it in a
linguistically inaccurate version. Moreover, he ignored the characteristic
semi-vowels and nasals of Church Slavonic and set the words according
to the accentuation of modern Czech. It consists of the traditional five
choral sections (the equivalent of *Kyrie*, *Gloria*, *Credo*, *Sanctus*, and
Agnus Dei) and of three instrumental numbers—an Introduction, an
organ solo after the 'Agneče Božij' (Agnus Dei), and a final Intrada.
Both the Introduction and the Intrada have a fanfare character, and
Janáček visualized the performance of his Mass in the open, with the
congregation returning to the church in solemn procession to the music
of the Intrada. The style of the work is boldly simple and at times
picturesquely dramatic—in a word, entirely original. The vocal melodies
frequently spring from the verbal rhythm and in the ejaculatory passages
for soloists and chorus the tessitura for the solo soprano and solo tenor
is often high, as for instance in the *Kyrie*:

Ex. 137

(Lord have mercy!)

The essential themes are entrusted to the orchestra on which the vocal superstructure rests, sometimes based on the instrumental material, at other times set against it chordally. As in Stravinsky's *Les Noces*, a few tiny motives pervade the *Mass* in various metamorphoses. As Hans Hollander has shown,[1] they are marked by some of the characteristics

[1] *Leoš Janáček* (London, 1963), pp. 99–100.

of Moravian folk-song. Moreover, Slavonic dance rhythms are as peculiar to the Credo and the Intrada as are incisive aphoristic themes to the remaining movements. The organ solo is an agitated piece in ostinato technique symbolizing the Last Judgement, while the ensuing Intrada is intended to conjure up the vision of the assembly of the Czech people before the throne of God. There is nothing comparable to the *Glagolitic Mass* in the whole of Western religious music and, though it must be accounted a Christian work, in its expression of primitive elemental joy and jubilation it sounds an unmistakably pantheistic note. Of Janáček's orchestral compositions written during his late period, the Rhapsody *Taras Bulba* (1918), inspired by Gogol's novel, and the ballad *Blanik* (1920) bear witness to his ardent Slav patriotism. More intrinsically characteristic of his late style, however, is the Sinfonietta (1926) which grew out of a fanfare for thirteen brass instruments intended for the Prague congress of the Sokols. Despite its title, the work is hardly symphonic in the established sense, themes being rarely developed but mostly repeated with slight variations, and no sooner is an idea introduced than it is discarded for another. The texture is mosaic-like and much use is made of pedals and ostinatos, as for instance in the fourth movement which is almost exclusively based on the incessant reiteration of a theme of folk-dance character. The progress of the five movements shows a suite-like order of sequence, and the form is rhapsodically loose, often creating the impression of an improvisation. There are no thematic connexions between the movements, but in order to provide an effective rounding-off Janáček repeats the opening fanfare in the finale. The orchestration is marked by novel and, in some instances, extraordinary sound-effects. The first movement, for example, is scored for eleven trumpets, two bass tubas, and drums, while elsewhere the composer aims at the transparent style of chamber music, with much concertante writing for woodwind and brass. The Sinfonietta is a typical illustration of Janáček's laconic and deliberately 'primitive' manner and is one of his few works which have no explicit or implicit programme.

Among Janáček's chamber works for vocal ensemble the *Zápisník zmizelého* (Diary of One Who Vanished) (1918) occupies a unique place. The anonymous verses, which were published in the Brno newspaper *Lidové noviny* in 1916, are in the vein of genuine folk-poetry telling of a young peasant, Jan, who yields to his love for the gypsy girl Zefka with whom he deserts his native village. The subject fascinated Janáček, partly because of its social implication—the lifting of the barriers that separate an inferior race (gypsies) from the rest of the community—and partly because its ardent passion and sensuality strongly echoed a relationship in his own private life. The verses, which are set for tenor, contralto, three women's voices, and piano, present sharp-edged dramatic vignettes in which the entire gamut of a young man's erotic sentiments are blended with nature moods and descriptive passages, for all of which Janáček found an immense variety of musical expressions. Yet the work, not unlike the *Glagolitic Mass*, is virtually monothematic, being based on a single brief idea, consisting of a rising or falling fourth and a major second, which undergoes permutations according to the dramatic and emotional progress of the text:

Ex. 138

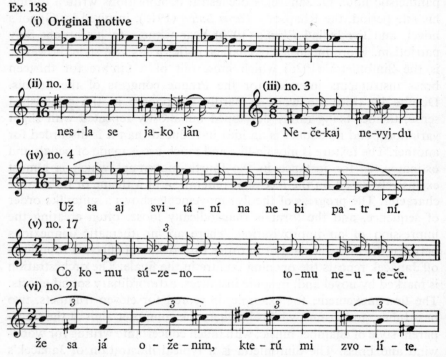

((ii) she carried herself like a hind; (iii) Don't wait, I'm not going out; (iv) Now already dawn appears in the sky; (v) If something is one's fate, there's no escape; (vi) that I marry her whom you chose for me.)

There are twenty-two songs,[1] the majority of which are for the tenor, mostly short in length and oscillating between a declamatory style and a more expressive arioso. Small metric units (2/8, 3/8, 4/16, 6/16) combine with short incisive figures to lend the vocal phrase a high degree of plasticity while the piano points and comments on the moods and incidents of the verses. Of Janáček's purely instrumental chamber music the First String Quartet (1923) (which owes its inspiration to Tolstoy's

[1] Nos. 15, 16, 17, and 18 are recorded in *The History of Music in Sound*, x.

The Kreutzer Sonata) is rhapsodic in form but creates a feeling of organic coherence largely due to the derivation of its main material from the opening dance theme and the use of a motto that itself presents a fore-shortening of the initial dance theme. The Second String Quartet (1928), written six months before his death, is, like Smetana's *From My Life* Quartet, of an autobiographical nature, its subtitle, *Intimate Letters,* referring to the composer's intimate friendship with Kamila Stösslová. Characteristic of the work are the abrupt changes of mood, from a tranquil and inward lyrical expression to dramatic outburst and im-passioned ecstasies. The writing, though not devoid of contrapuntal passages, tends towards a more homophonic treatment.

OTHER CZECH COMPOSERS

If Janáček's prime significance lay in a conscious and deliberate nationalism, the next generation of Czech composers stood in a less pronounced, looser relationship to native musical lore and took their chief bearings from movements in contemporary Western music. The most important figures here are Bohuslav Martinů (1890–1959) and Alois Hába (1893–1972). Martinů was a pupil of Roussel in Paris at a time (1923) when Milhaud, Honegger, and Poulenc were emerging as individual personalities. He soon came under their influence, notably Honegger's. Stravinsky's neo-classicism also exercised a considerable attraction on him. He was essentially a musical 'natural', writing with immense facility and great technical skill, but he did not avoid the com-monplace and the trivial, with the result that his output shows great unevenness. Martinů was a craftsman who did not aim at a settled style but was primarily concerned with the potentialities inherent in his musical material, notably structure, formal design and rhythmic move-ment. The majority of his Parisian works (before 1940, when he emi-grated to America) reveal an unemotional, objective attitude of mind from which vitality and a certain degree of originality are not absent. A composer of great versatility, Martinů devoted himself to the cultivation of all types of composition—opera, ballet, choral and orchestral works, chamber music, and music for violin and piano. He first made his name with an orchestral work, *Half-Time* (1925), an impression of a soccer game with which he anticipated Honegger's *Rugby* (1928); while noisy and even brutal in sound, it has an invigorating, sinewy rhythm. This was followed by *La Bagarre* (1927), commemorating the occasion of the landing of the American aviator Lindbergh at Le Bourget and is charged with the atmosphere of the movement of big crowds. In both these works the mere physical excitement created by a shifting mass of people was the primary incentive for the music. The Partita (1931) and the more ambitious Sinfonia Concertante (1932) show Martinů pursuing a neo-classical style into which he assimilated the melodic characteristics of Czech folk-song, which lend his works freshness and earthy vigour. Among his most successful compositions in the neo-classical vein are his Concerto Grosso (1938), a virile and dynamic piece in which the 'concertino' is the piano, and the Double Concerto for two string orchestras, piano, and timpani (1938) where the manipulation of the two groups of strings—now in opposition, now in concert and now alternating with each other—shows remarkable resourcefulness.

For Martinů opera does not present philosophical or psychological problems or a fragment of real life, but is a theatrical spectacle transformed by music into something *sui generis*, in all of which one strongly senses the potent influence of Stravinsky's operatic aesthetics. His most ambitious opera, illustrating Martinů's attitude in a startling manner, is *Juliette* (1937), to a libretto adapted from a play of the same name by Georges Neveux, the theme of which is the conflict between reality and the illusion of dreams. The work is in the nature of a lyrical poem that avoids all dramatic effect. The one-act radio opera, *Comedy on the Bridge* (1937), is written in an attractive light-hearted vein which combines a pastiche of eighteenth-century comic opera, notably Mozart's, with melodic-rhythmic elements from Czech folk-music. The transparent scoring guarantees the clear audibility of the singers' words.

Alois Hába, who was a pupil of Franz Schreker in Vienna and, later Berlin, was not a Czech nationalist in the proper sense, but belonged rather to the wider orbit formed by Central European music, and was in particular associated with an athematic style of writing and with microtonal experiments. Convinced that Western music must be liberated from the principle of thematic development, he developed a new manner in which he gradually rejected all traditional means of formal and melodic design and harmonic structure, such as sequence, repetition, recapitulation, and the polarity of harmonic zones. In his athematic works (string quartets and piano music) Hába aimed at a vigorous and continuous flow of free invention, though frequently at the expense of musical logic and structural coherence. As for his microtonality, his first ideas were suggested by his observations as a violinist, when he noticed the slight variations in pitch characteristic of the solo playing on stringed instruments. Moreover, his studies of Czech folk-song, notably of his native Moravia, made him aware of microtonal deviations in the singing of this music. These facts, combined with examples of oriental music and with the influence of certain of Busoni's aesthetic theories (which advocated the division of the semitone into third- and sixth-tones) induced Hába to experiment with the possibilities of

microtonality. As a result, some of his works are based on quarter-
tones, such as the opera *Matka* (The Mother) (1929), the String
Quartets, opp. 7, 12 (Ex. 139), and 14, and the various Fantasies for
piano, op. 25 to op. 31, for which the Czech piano firm of Förster constructed special instruments; other compositions use the sixth-tone, such

Ex. 139

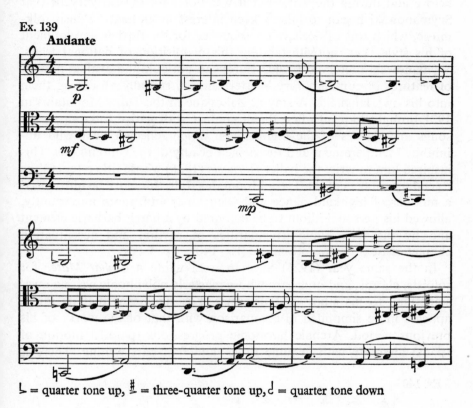

L = quarter tone up, ♯ = three-quarter tone up, ♩ = quarter tone down

as the opera *Přijd' království Tvé* (Thy kingdom come) (1942) and the
String Quartet, op. 15. Yet, interesting and ingenious as are Hába's
attempts to introduce novel notions of composition, neither his
athematic style nor his microtonal experimentation has proved a significant pathway to the future.

KAROL SZYMANOWSKI

Unlike Hungary and Czechoslovakia, Poland did not develop an
advanced national movement until after the First War. Its acknowledged leader was Karol Szymanowski (1883–1937), the most eminent
composer that Poland had produced since Chopin. Beginning his career

under the influence of Skryabin, he subsequently modelled his style on Reger and Richard Strauss, whose thematic complexity he took over until acquaintance with the music of Debussy and Ravel led to the emergence of a personal manner. A native Polish element is already manifest in the nostalgia and brooding melancholy of the works written before and during the war,[1] but it was not until the early 1920s that Szymanowski began to take a keen interest in authentic Polish folk-music, which was of decisive consequence for the further development of his style. Yet, notwithstanding this acquisition of national traits, Szymanowski preserved a wide European outlook and availed himself of features of contemporary Western music, skilfully absorbing them into his own language. A stay at Zakopane in the Tatra Mountains in 1921 brought him into first direct contact with native folk-music, the songs and dances of the highlanders, which reflected their wild uninhibited temperament and the rugged beauty of their mountains. This inspired him to write the ballet *Harnasie* (1926) whose title refers to the legendary robbers of the Tatra Mountains. Into this work he introduced a number of highland dance and song tunes and, more importantly, allowed his personal idiom to be coloured by a harsh barbaric element and by the remarkable irregularities of rhythm and accentuation characteristic of Tatra folk-music (Ex. 140).

In the same year (1926) Szymanowski wrote a *Stabat Mater* for soloists, chorus, and orchestra whose masterly polyphonic writing owes something to his study of Palestrina; it is significant that its idiom appears more simplified in comparison with that of the works of his previous period. Archaic harmonic progressions (parallel motion of triads) alternate with genuine three- and four-part writing. There is

Ex. 140

---

[1] See Chapter I, p. 36.

perhaps an excess of pure lyricism in the *Stabat Mater* but, with this
qualification, the work is an impressive example of the individual
projection of a profound religious emotion.

In *King Roger* (1924), a three-act opera to a libretto by Jaroslaw
Iwaszkiewicz, Szymanowski produced one of his most distinguished
works. The subject is the conflict between Christianity and Hellenic
paganism and the action takes place in twelfth-century Sicily centring
on King Roger (the historical Roger II lived in the eleventh century) and
a shepherd who casts a spell on Queen Roxane and in the last act reveals
himself as the god Dionysus, to whom Roger, in a symbolic act,
sacrifices his own soul. The opera contains overtones of Eastern
mysticism and philosophy which, combined with an erotic sensualism,
inspired the composer to some of his most characteristic and imaginative
music. The sensual element is associated with the shepherd and Roxane
and reaches its climax in the second act, in Roxane's melismatic song:

Ex. 141

and the orgiastic dance in 7/8 of the shepherd and his musicians. This
is contrasted with the hieratic Byzantine grandeur of other portions,
especially the music characterizing Roger and the court atmosphere.
The style of the work is intensely dramatic, often taking on a starkly
barbaric expression in which the role of the chorus is most important,
but there are other episodes in which an ecstatic lyricism prevails.
The organum-like progressions in much of the choral writing, thematic
complexity, bitonality, and a tense involuted chromaticism are as
typical of the music as are the chord-derived melodies of an impressionistic character.

The *Symphony concertante* for piano and orchestra (1936), frequently
referred to as the Fourth Symphony, shows a change of manner. Instead
of the romantic lyricism that informs Szymanowski's general style, most

of the music is brittle, dry, and brilliant, with the piano treated in a percussive manner which owes something to Stravinsky. But the second of the three movements, with its dreamy arabesque for the solo flute and an ornate, slightly overladen piano part, recalls the composer's earlier style. Of the two string quartets, the First Quartet (1917) is musically perhaps the more substantial, showing themes of great plasticity and a varied contrapuntal texture in the first two movements. The mood of the opening movement, which begins with an expressive Lento introduction, fluctuates between the exhilaration of the dance-like first subject and the melancholy lyricism of the second while the working-out section turns to a vein of grotesque mockery. The finale, a 'Scherzando alla burlesca', is an example of polytonal writing before Milhaud exploited this technique, the four parts being written in the respective keys of C, E flat, F sharp, and A major. The Second Quartet (1927) is of a more complex texture than the first, containing much linear counterpoint, with two fugato passages in the finale, but there are also passages of an impressionistic (chordal) character, and bitonality and polytonality play a conspicuous part.

MANUEL DE FALLA

Nationalism in Spain developed in a continuous line from Felipe Pedrell and Isaac Albéniz in the second half of the nineteenth century to Enrique Granados and Manuel de Falla (1876–1946) in the first half of the present century. It was Falla, the outstanding personality among those composers, who put Spain once again on the musical map of Europe, with works which are intrinsically as well as extrinsically Spanish and yet transcend the purely national element, by their combination of imaginative power and a clear-sighted, penetrating technical acumen. The basic feature of Falla's style is the brilliant application of an essentially impressionistic technique, which he learned before the war from Debussy, to the treatment of strongly nationalistic material, notably of his native Andalusia. Yet, like Janáček and the later Bartók, he scarcely ever introduced authentic folk themes into his music; it is rather that his essential thought is moulded by the spirit of Spanish folk-music and by some of its technical features. Apart from a handful of folk-song arrangements, *Siete canciones populares españolas* (1922), it was only on very rare occasions that Falla employed actual folk tunes: a few phrases associated with the Miller and his Wife in the ballet *El Sombrero de tres picos* (The Three-Cornered Hat) (1919), and two melodies in the puppet opera *El Retablo de Maese Pedro* (Master Peter's Puppet Show) (1923), based on an incident in Cervantes' *Don Quixote*—the Catalan dance when Don Quixote smashes the puppets to pieces, and the song of Melisendra in the tower, whose tune derives from an old Spanish ballad sung at the time of Cervantes. In this last work and in the Harpsichord Concerto (1926) Falla shed virtually all superficial nationalist traits, but conveyed its essence in music that bears his own entirely individual stamp. His chief means of expression are not so much harmony as melody and rhythm; short incisive phrases are presented in contrasting and unblended instrumental colours while the juxtaposition of accent and cross-accent results in conflicting rhythms of a fascinating effect (Ex. 142).

The guitar conditioned to a large extent Falla's harmonic idiom and his piano writing, as in the *Fantasía bética* (1919), and it is responsible for the internal pedals and the clear, percussive style of the Harpsichord Concerto. There is in this latter work something of Domenico Scarlatti's Italian clarity and coruscating brilliance, and it is significant

Ex. 142

that Falla made prolonged studies of Scarlatti's music before he composed the Concerto. During the last twenty years of his life Falla was occupied with a vast choral work, *Atlántida*, whose text deals with the story of the lost continent, Atlantis, sunk in the sea beyond the Western coast of Spain. This was performed at Milan in 1962 (completed by Ernesto Halffter) and proved to contain music of a high order of invention, though nothing that added to Falla's reputation.

ESPLÀ AND TURINA

Falla's relationship to Andalusian folk-music was paralleled by Oscar Esplà's (b. 1886) to the music of his native Alicante. Like Falla, Esplà made only rare use of authentic folk tunes—to the exceptions belongs his cantata, *La noche buena del diablo* (The Devil's Christmas Eve) (1931), based on traditional Spanish children's songs. A composer of a pronounced intellectual cast of mind—Esplà was originally an engineer who later turned to music, musicology and philosophy—he cultivated the symphonic form in the tone-poems *Don Quijote velando las armas* (Quixote keeping vigil by his arms) (1925) and *Fiesta* (1931). After his studies in Germany he adopted a scale of his own invention (C–D flat–E flat–E–F–G flat–A flat–B flat) on which he built a harmonic system that lent his music a regional, Spanish-Mediterranean flavour, without incorporating any genuine folk-song material, as for instance in the symphonic poem, *Ciclopes de Ifach* (1937), one of Esplà's most important works. Joaquin Turina (1882–1949) was largely inspired by Andalusian scenes (*Danzas fantásticas* for orchestra, 1920, and *Sinfonia sevillana*, 1921). A musician of limited range, endowed with a facile and rather superficial pen, Turina is best known outside his country for his many songs and piano pieces, notably the

Cuentos de España (Spanish Tales) (Set I, 1918; Set II, 1928) in which picturesqueness and charm are evenly balanced. With the exception of Esplà and Gerhard, the composers of Falla's generation, including Falla himself, considered Paris the Mecca of Music to which they made their pilgrimage after completing their studies in their native land.

LATER SPANISH COMPOSERS

Among the musicians of the next generation, Federico Mompou (b. 1893) and Roberto Gerhard (1896–1970) have attracted most attention. Mompou, born in Barcelona, is an exponent of Catalan nationalism, with an output largely confined to the miniature form of piano pieces and songs, the main characteristics of which are intimacy of feeling and refined, subtle workmanship (6 *Impresiones intimas*, 1914; *Cants magics*, 1919; *Quatre Mélodies*, 1926). Mompou has been called a *primitivista* on account of the marked simplicity of his technical style. Thematic development, foreign anyway to a miniaturist, and harmonic complexity he avoids in favour of a static lyricism of an evocative impressionist nature. Gerhard, who was of Swiss origin and after the end of the Spanish Civil War settled in England in 1939, was first a pupil of Pedrell, the founder of documentary Spanish nationalism, and then studied with Schoenberg in Berlin from 1923 to 1928, a fact that would partly account for Gerhard's remarkable technical *savoir faire*. Despite his adoption of the 12-note method his ties with his native Catalonia remained at first very close, as in the cantata, *L'alta naixença del Rei En Jaume* (The high birth of King James) (1931) and *Albada, interludi y dança* for orchestra (1936). In contrast to the predominantly contrapuntal character of dodecaphonic music, Gerhard initially stressed the vertical (harmonic) element, as in his Wind Quintet (1928) which adopts the same combination as Schoenberg's Op. 26, but with an instrumental timbre tinged with a Spanish (Catalan) flavour. Also in the music written after taking up residence in Britain, Gerhard continued to treat serialism in such a way as to allow a pronounced Spanish note to make itself felt as, for instance, in his ballet, *Alegr'as* (Festivals) (1942) and the opera, *The Duenna*, to a libretto after Sheridan (1948; rev. 1950). Gerhard was the first Spanish composer to harness thinking in 12-note terms to genuine Spanish feeling. Joaquin Rodrigo (b. 1902), who was blind from the age of three, is a prolific composer of minor stature who follows Falla yet cultivates a more advanced harmonic idiom. Outside Spain Rodrigo is perhaps best known by his *Concierto de Aranjuez* for guitar (1939). There remains a group of Spanish composers who, like *Les Six* in Paris, banded themselves together and under the intellectual leadership of the influential critic and writer, Adolfo Salazar (1890–

1958), formed what became known as *el grupo de los ocho* or *el grupo de Madrid* where this association was founded in the spring of 1930. They were: Ernesto Halffter (b. 1905), its most eminent member; his older brother, Rodolfo Halffter (b. 1900); Salvador Bacarisse (1898–1963); Juan José Mantecón (b. 1896); Fernando Remacha (b. 1898); Gustavo Pittaluga (b. 1906); and the woman composer, Rosa Maria Ascot (b. 1906). (Mantecón, the oldest member, was like Salazar in the first place a writer.) What united this group of eight post-Falla musicians was a bond of far stronger fibre than that which had originally brought the Parisian six together. This was the total rejection of all nationalism and impressionism. In a lecture given in Madrid on the aims of *el grupo de los ocho*, Pittaluga, the youngest of this group, took a completely negative view of Spanish musical folklore and stressed the necessity of composing 'authentic' music, i.e. music free from all ethnic roots and all association with literary, philosophical and metaphysical ideas. They set out to write works the sole criterion of which was their intrinsic musical and technical qualities. For the rest 'no romanticism, no chromaticism, no divagations—and no chord of the diminished seventh!'[1]

This advocacy of a kind of New Objectivity in Spanish music demonstrated the distance these younger composers had travelled from their nationalist predecessors (Pedrell, Falla, Esplà, and Turina), and had become receptive to the main trends in European music, notably to the neo-classicism of Stravinsky and Hindemith.

SWITZERLAND

Owing to íts peculiar geographical position, Switzerland has for many centuries been subject to the cultural influence from its great neighbours in the North-East, South, and West and it is therefore not surprising that its musical history should be closely bound up with that of Germany, France, and, to a lesser degree, Italy.

Of the German-Swiss composers born between 1880 and 1900, Othmar Schoeck (1886–1957) was the outstanding artistic personality and occupies an intermediate position between the late romanticism of Wolf and Reger (his master) and the modern world. It is as a song writer and musical dramatist that Schoeck made his most important contribution to Swiss music. His strong lyrical vein manifests itself in a prodigious number of songs in which the choice of poets, such as Goethe, Eichendorff, Uhland, Hebbel, Keller, and Lenau, proclaims his affinity with the great German song composers, notably Wolf. In his various operas (*Venus*, 1920; *Penthesilea*, 1925; *Vom Fischer un syner Fru* (The

[1] Quoted in Gilbert Chase, *The Music of Spain*, (New York, 1959). p. 203.

Fisherman and his wife), 1930; *Massimila Doni*, 1935, and *Das Schloss Dürande*, 1939), he achieved, through the exploitation of the considerable emotional tension inherent in his subjects, a rare combination of dramatic power with terse lyrical expression. If there is a common theme running through his operas it is that of man's better self in conflict with his evil, demoniac powers, and, owing to the particular psychological problems posed in his libretti, Schoeck's musical language in his operas appears to be more austere and more uncompromising than in his songs.

Schoeck was the acknowledged leader of the younger generation of German-Swiss composers which includes Albert Moeschinger (b. 1897), Conrad Beck (b. 1901) and Willy Burkhard (1900–55) whose oratorio, *Das Gesicht Jesajas* (The Vision of Isaiah) (1935) impresses by its direct forcefulness and the woodcut simplicity of its utterance. With these and other composers the influence of Busoni, who lived in Zürich from 1915 to 1920, as well as of Hindemith is noticeable, but their common denominator is their typically Swiss quality of ruggedness, severity, and economy of expression.

Of the musicians of French Switzerland, Frank Martin (b. 1890) presents the sharpest and most individual profile. Martin's early works show the strong influence of Franck and Fauré, and some leaning towards Ravel. During the inter-war years, however, he gradually developed an individual style and grappled with the technical problems raised by the New Music. A teacher for many years at the Jaques-Dalcroze Institute in Geneva, Martin was in close contact with eurhythmics which accounts for the fact that his chief interest was at first concentrated on rhythmic experiments, of which the *Trio sur des chants populaires irlandais* for violin, cello, and piano (1925) and the orchestral *Rhythmes* (1926) are notable examples. In 1930 Martin began to study Schoenberg's twelve-note technique, freely using this method with tonal implications while rejecting the aesthetic premises of the dodecaphonic school. In an article[1] he defined his attitude to Schoenberg's aesthetics by saying that 'every rule has for its sole aim the enrichment of style . . . the observation of rules is nothing but an elegance, a pleasure of the mind which is independent of any (aesthetic) value'. Characteristic of this stage in Martin's development are the Piano Concerto (1934), the Symphony (1937), and the first four Ballades for various solo instruments and orchestra (1938–40). The outstanding work of this period is the dramatic oratorio, *Le Vin herbé* (The magic potion) (1941), based on the *Roman de Tristan et Yseult* by Joseph Bédier, which made Martin's name known beyond the confines of Switzerland and in which he applied

---

[1] *Schweizerische Musikzeitung*, lxxxii (1942), no. 3.

the serial technique in conjunction with tonal and homophonic effects of a novel kind. The legendary atmosphere is recaptured by means of a chorus of twelve reciting voices, from which the two protagonists detach themselves as singing characters. The accompaniment consisting of a small orchestra of seven strings and piano shows a great variety in the thematic and rhythmic treatment. In two subsequent works—*Der Cornet* (1943), after Rilke, and the *Six Monologues* (1943) from Hofmannsthal's *Jedermann*—Martin achieves a still closer synthesis of serial technique with tonal writing in the service of an intense lyrical expression.

SCANDINAVIA AND HOLLAND

Music in Scandinavia and Holland during the inter-war years showed the same dichotomy as in other countries between conservative tendencies (which meant adherence, chiefly, to German romanticism) and a strong movement towards the assimilation of stylistic and technical features of contemporary music in Germany (Hindemith, Schoenberg) and France (Debussy, Ravel, and Stravinsky). Of the composers, who adopted technical devices and, to some extent, also the aesthetic creeds of the New Music, the Norwegian Fartein Valen (1887–1952) is noteworthy for his atonal style which he began to evolve in 1924 independently of Schoenberg's tone-rows. While occasionally employing a strict serial technique as, for instance, in the Piano Variations Op. 23 (1936), Valen most cultivated a texture characterized by combination of various independent lines in which the same note series occurs constantly; in some works an identical 'theme' pervades each of the parts.

The Dutchman Willem Pijper (1894–1947) was first influenced by Debussy but in his subsequent works he achieved a measure of individuality, making use of polytonality and polyrhythms and evolving a complex, elaborate style of writing which owes something to Schoenberg. In his later period, however, Pijper aimed at simplification and economy of means as in the Trio for flute, clarinet and bassoon (1927), the String Quartet no. 4 (1928) and the *Six Symphonic Epigrams* (1928). He also devoted himself to the study of Dutch folk-song, the chief creative fruits of which are two unaccompanied eight-part choruses, *Heer Halewijn* (1920) and *Heer Danielken* (1925). Henk Badings (b. 1907), a pupil of Pijper, is a prolific composer who has written orchestral works, concertos, and chamber music in which a neo-classicism, largely based on Bach's style, prevails and which combine experiments in form and tonality.

RICHARD STRAUSS'S LAST YEARS

The musical scene in Central Europe between the two wars presented a picture more complex and varied in its aesthetic and stylistic aspects than that of post-war France and Italy. Three main currents may be distinguished. There was the older generation, led by Richard Strauss and Hans Pfitzner, which in varying degrees continued the romanticism of the pre-war period. There was the *avant-garde* under the leadership of Hindemith, violently anti-romantic in its attitude, avoiding all subjectivity and cultivating 'New Objectivity' with a concentration on the technical and structural potentialities of the musical material *per se* and, so far as opera was concerned, seeking a close link with the political and social climate of its time. And there was, lastly, the Second Viennese School, essentially romantic in its aesthetic outlook and aims but working with Schoenberg's twelve-note system, a revolutionary method of composition that radically altered the face of music.

Richard Strauss (1864-1949)[1] had written his most significant works before the First World War. With the audacities of *Salome* and *Elektra* he had proved himself the most advanced German composer of his time, a position from which, partly under the influence of his librettist, Hugo von Hofmannsthal, he began to retreat in *Der Rosenkavalier* and *Ariadne auf Naxos*. In his subsequent operas he completely shut himself off from all contact with the modernism of the post-war period. At the same time an increasing falling-off became noticeable in his earlier vitality and invention, though his immense fertility and sovereign technical command continued undiminished to the end of his life. What also remained intact was Strauss's innate and restless intellectual curiosity and his ready response to the challenge of problems of style, form, and dramatic treatment. This explains the curious zigzag course of both his pre-war and post-war operas. *Die Frau ohne Schatten* (The Woman without a Shadow) (1919) is an oriental fairy-tale not wholly unlike Mozart's *Die Zauberflöte*, but Hofmannsthal's libretto is packed with a number of obscure symbolisms and allegories—the 'Shadow' of the title stands for female fertility —and the language, for all its poetic imagination, is involuted and full of esoteric semantic subtleties. Strauss treated this subject in the style of spectacular grand opera, with big ensembles and finales and with broad symphonic interludes, and the best part of the music lies in the refined, technically resourceful evocation of the magic element. Ever since *Der Rosenkavalier* Strauss had been exercised by the problem of word-setting in opera, and in *Intermezzo*, 'A Bourgeois Comedy with

---

[1] For Strauss's early and middle years see chapters I and III.

Symphonic Interludes' (1924), he found for it an original solution. The singing parts are largely treated in a light conversational manner imitating everyday speech and are accompanied by a remarkably transparent orchestra. It is only in the finales of the two acts that the vocal writing turns to sustained cantilena, with the lyrical element and also symphonic elaboration being mainly confined to the orchestral interludes. Despite the utterly banal nature of the libretto, which was Strauss's own, the work constitutes a brilliant experiment in the creation of a new type of German comic opera. In *Die aegyptische Helena* (1928) he returned to the mythological Baroque opera such as he had essayed in *Ariadne auf Naxos*, but with this difference that now both the protagonists are human characters. Hofmannsthal places in the centre of the action the matrimonial drama of Menelaus and Helen seen in the light of modern psychology; but he surrounds it with the trappings of the ancient myth, magic potions, supernatural figures, and the splendour and opulence of an imaginary Orient. Strauss responded to this strange concoction with music of the most luxuriant and richly proliferating character, in which a heroic hymn-like element predominates; but the score lacks truly significant utterances. In *Arabella* (1933), the libretto of which was the last Hofmannsthal wrote before his death in 1929, poet and composer endeavoured to repeat the style of *Der Rosenkavalier*. The story has much of the period charm and the poetic sentiment of the earlier work, Hofmannsthal returning in it to his favourite theme of youth's awakening to full awareness of itself through the experience of true love. Yet the psychological richness of *Der Rosenkavalier* is absent, and the work contains no dramatic character comparable to that of the Feldmarschallin. Arabella's suitor, a Slovene aristocrat, who is conceived as a kind of inverted Ochs von Lerchenau— young, noble, and generous—fails to inject into the plot the irresistible comic vein of Hofmannsthal's earlier character. The music is instinct with a rich lyricism, with a sensuous vocal melody of a melting, at times cloying, sweetness; and, since the action takes place in the Vienna of the 1860s, Strauss's waltzes are not felt to be incongruous with the period as they are with Maria Theresa's Vienna in *Der Rosenkavalier*. Yet, strangely enough, the composer here favoured the rustic, coarse-grained *Ländler* of Bavarian origin rather than his namesake Johann's elegant, town-bred waltzes. On the other hand, the orchestral texture of *Arabella*, if compared with that of *Der Rosenkavalier*, is more refined and more supple, frequently achieving the effect of chamber music, and the use of leitmotives is more subtle in the psychological delineation of the characters. The composer shows his age in the paucity of memorable melodic ideas, but the work has proved the most successful of his later operas. *Die schweigsame Frau* (The Silent Woman) (1935), to a libretto by Stefan Zweig who adapted it from Ben Jonson's *Epicoene*, represents Strauss's excursion into pure *opera buffa*, with vivacious ensembles and an immensely fluent parlando style which are testimony to his incomparable technical mastery. Themes from old English and Italian masters are most skilfully interwoven to suggest the atmosphere and time of the action.

The one-act *Der Friedenstag* (The Day of Peace) (1938) has a libretto by Joseph Gregor dealing with an episode at the end of the Thirty Years' War; but the subject takes on a universal human significance in the dramatic confrontation of the Commander, bound by his military duty to blow up the fortress rather than surrender it, with the population craving for peace. Less opera than dramatic oratorio, *Der Friedenstag* has big choral scenes at the beginning and end, and indeed concludes with a grandiose hymn for peace that owes something to the last-act finale of *Fidelio*. In *Daphne* (1938) and *Die Liebe der Danae* (1940), both to libretti by Gregor, Strauss returned for the last time to mythological Baroque opera of which he was particularly fond. The first, a one-act work, mingles tragedy with idyll, with the ancient myth interpreted in terms of modern psychology while the music, though devoid of potent melodic invention, is among Strauss's technical masterpieces—subtle, refined, rich in motivic work, and imbued with a feeling of Mediterranean serenity. *Die Liebe der Danae*, a 'Cheerful Mythology in Three Acts', based on an unfinished scenario by Hofmannsthal, telescopes the separate myths of Midas and Danae, the underlying theme being the victory of true love against which even a god is powerless. The musico-dramatic treatment of Jupiter is strongly reminiscent of that of Wotan in *Die Walküre*; and indeed the opera as a whole echoes the Wagner of the *Ring*, notably in its harmonic and orchestral idiom, though the vocal writing for Danae and Midas bears in its sustained cantabile Strauss's own individual signature.

Strauss's last opera, *Capriccio* (1941), is the culmination of the light-handed conversational manner which he cultivated in *Ariadne*, *Intermezzo*, and parts of *Arabella*. The subject, taken from a libretto by the Abbate Casti for Salieri's now forgotten opera, *Prima la musica e poi le parole*, was elaborated by the composer and the conductor Clemens Krauss into a play dealing with the problem of words and music in opera. The action, which takes place in a château near Paris about 1775, centres on a young countess who is to decide which of her two impetuous suitors—the poet Olivier and the musician Flamand—she is to marry. In the end she cannot decide for either, a symbolism implying the perfect equality of text and music. According to the dramatic exigencies, now the words, now the music must prevail and now again both will be poised in equilibrium. Strauss moves with the most natural ease between parlando, arioso, and more sustained lyrical styles, while the orchestral writing is in the sparse and supple style of chamber music.

Strauss was seventy-eight at the time of *Capriccio*, which he intended to be his last work. But his Indian summer continued and saw the composition of seven more works—the Second Horn Concerto (1942), the First and Second Sonatina for sixteen wind instruments (1943 and 1945, respectively), the *Metamorphosen* for twenty-three strings (1945), the Oboe Concerto (1946), the Duet Concertino for clarinet and bassoon (1947), and the *Vier letzte Lieder* (1948). Strauss jestingly referred to these works as 'wrist exercises' and 'snippets from my workshop'. With the exception of the *Metamorphosen*, they are all slight in musical substance and in a simple unassuming vein, written with the aim of keeping his hands busy and of delighting the senses. They are moulded, more or less closely, on classical (Mozartian) principles and thus Strauss's creative career came full circle: for a classical tendency, manifest in the young Strauss, showed itself again in the octogenarian, yet greatly enriched and mellowed by the artistic and human experiences of a life-time. The neo-classical tendency is displayed in a number of features: in the turn to pure instrumental music; in the avoidance of an emotionally charged expression and the emphasis on exquisitely refined and polished workmanship; in the symmetrical cut of thematic ideas (mostly in regular four and eight bars) and 'old-fashioned' cadences; in the marked preference for simple diatonic writing, and in the transparent scoring, whose sparseness and economy—already to be found in *Daphne* and *Capriccio*—is in strong contrast with the sumptuousness and lavishness of Strauss's symphonic poems and the majority of his operas. *Metamorphosen*, which is the most important of Strauss's late compositions, shows all these features at their most characteristic, to say nothing of a formidable skill displayed in the polyphonic interweaving of the parts. Written at the end of the last war and using as one of its four themes the first four bars of the Funeral March in Beethoven's *Eroica*, the work is a moving expression of the composer's sadness and grief at the catastrophe that had overtaken Germany and at the same time a nostalgic and melancholy reflection on his past life. Equally autobiographical is the cycle of the *Four Last Songs*, tinged as it is with a gentle melancholy. The soprano solo part is closely integrated with the orchestra, singer and instruments forming an organic whole and weaving a continuous finely drawn tapestry of sound from which the voice stands out merely by its different timbre. The cycle represents a miniature emotional drama, moving from the subdued animation of 'Im Frühling' to a complete withdrawal in the closing 'Im Abendrot'.

PFITZNER AND SCHREKER

In Hans Pfitzner (1869–1949) Strauss encountered his one serious rival to the claim of being the most representative German operatic composer of his time. Pfitzner's music is little known outside Central Europe, where he is generally considered as one of the great masters. Pfitzner described himself as 'the last Romantic' and advanced a theory that Germany's last great period in music was the Romantic era and that in the twentieth century the country had outlived its musical hegemony over the other nations. Not unexpectedly, this philosophy was accompanied by a declared enmity to all modern tendencies and trends, which Pfitzner expressed in two pamphlets—*Futuristengefahr* (1917) and *Die Neue Aesthetik der musikalischen Impotenz* (1919) which were both written in reply to Busoni's *Entwurf einer Neuen Aesthetik der Tonkunst* (1907). Pfitzner's music expresses a profound longing for the German past and is pervaded by a melancholy and a pessimism to be fairly expected of a composer so deeply steeped in Schopenhauer and Wagner. Characteristic of this attitude of mind are two works both of which look backward in their sentiment and style. In the 'romantic cantata', *Von deutscher Seele* (1921), to poems by Eichendorff, Pfitzner seeks to convey the mystical yearnings of the romantic artist for the ineffable and the transcendental. The opera *Palestrina* (1917), to his own libretto, presents a *Künstlerdrama* in which, freely adapting the life-story of the great sixteenth-century Italian church composer with whom he identifies himself, Pfitzner demonstrates the spiritual solitude and isolation of the artist amid the worldliness and the intrigues of his surroundings. The work is unquestionably Pfitzner's masterpiece and perhaps the only one by which posterity is likely to remember this conscious follower of Schumann and Wagner.[1]

The chief reputation of Franz Schreker (1878–1934), whose name was bracketed with those of Strauss and Schoenberg in the Germany of the 1920s, rests upon his operas of which the most important are *Der ferne Klang* (The Distant Sound) (1913),[2] *Die Gezeichneten* (The Branded) (1918) and *Der Schatzgräber* (The Treasure-Digger) (1920). They are eclectic in style, much indebted to Strauss (orchestral style), Puccini (melody), and Debussy (harmony), and, while dramatically and scenically effective, suffer from an obscure erotic symbolism based on ideas from Freud and Wedekind.

[1] See also p. 195.   [2] See pp. 185—7.

FERRUCCIO BUSONI[1]

One of the first champions of the New Music in Germany was Ferruccio Busoni (1866–1924), who sought to achieve an individual 'Young Classicism' by the fusion of Latin clarity of form with German technical solidity, a fusion in which form, content, and expression should be in equilibrium. The conflict between Italian and German in Busoni's heredity was reflected in his double life as performer and composer. He was one of the greatest piano virtuosi of his day, and a sense of kinship with Liszt found expression in studies, arrangements, and, perhaps most notably, in the *Chamber Fantasy on Bizet's Carmen*, the last of six piano 'sonatinas' written between 1910 and 1922. The fifth of these ('In signo Johannis Sebastiani Magni') reflects the other major influence in Busoni's own music, that of J. S. Bach, though the contrapuntal writing is unambitious compared with that of his *Fantasia Contrappuntistica* (four versions, the last for two pianos, 1922). This started as an attempt to solve the problem of the unfinished fugue in *Die Kunst der Fuge*, but proliferated to include a choral prelude and a quadruple fugue on the Bach fragment. Busoni's design leads gradually from the procedures of baroque counterpoint to the most daring polyphonic complexities, and the work represents a twentieth-century counterpart to *Die Kunst der Fuge*.

The same intellectual curiosity and intensity that prompted Busoni's writings are reflected in the second sonatina (1912), while the fourth ('In die Nativitatis Christi MCMXVII') shows a rare equilibrium between the classicizing formal tendencies and the deeply romantic kernel of Busoni's character as a creative artist. There are echoes here of Beethoven's last manner (especially of the *Diabelli Variations*), and the style is not unlike that of Fauré's last works in harmony and lay-out. The cerebral experimentation, which makes much of Busoni's music interesting rather than satisfying, is almost wholly absent.

PAUL HINDEMITH

Paul Hindemith (1895–1964) was outstanding in the generation of German composers which came to maturity during the late 1920s and whose works display the diverse facets of all that is implied in the term 'New Music'. If Hindemith became its acknowledged leader, this was for two main reasons: first, because the various modern tendencies in post-war German music crystallized in his personality with extraordinary clarity and force; and second because of his superior musical gifts, his tremendous fertility and vitality, his truly extraordinary technical resourcefulness and industry. Hindemith provides an illustra-

[1] On Busoni's operas, see pp. 192–5.

tion of that rare combination of a sheer *Musikant*—a musical 'natural'—
with a seemingly inexhaustible fund of creative energy and a technical
command that recalls the supreme craftsmanship of the great masters
of the seventeenth and eighteenth centuries. His own attitude towards
composition has indeed a great deal in common with the approach of
the pre-nineteenth-century composers. Like them, Hindemith regarded
himself as primarily a craftsman who pursues his métier with the utmost
of his skill and intelligence and with whom purely musical problems—
invention, form and design, balance and proportion, texture and instrumentation—take precedence over expressive qualities. The latter he
considered during his early period as merely incidental to his fundamental conception of the musical work as an edifice, a construction in
sound. In his younger years his artistic personality found its chief
expression in music characterized by a reckless iconoclastic spirit, an
irrepressible buoyancy and masculine vigour, a sense of irreverent fun
and a good-natured cynicism. At the time he was regarded as an *enfant
terrible*, thumbing his nose at established traditions and conventions and
disconcerting the public and the critics by his unpredictable antics.
With the beginning of the 1930s his more serious side came gradually to
the fore—a Hindemith high-minded and lofty in his attitude to art and
concerned with things of the mind, with general human problems and
with philosophical and metaphysical themes.

Hindemith started as a spiritual disciple of Brahms and even more
Reger, adopting the latter's use of Bachian counterpoint as a regenerative constructive means and soon a marked individuality begins to
show, as in the Second String Quartet, Op. 10 (1919), and the *Kammermusik*, Op. 24, no. 1 (1922), which display three salient features. First,
Hindemith is seen to establish an autonomous melodic principle: the
lines become energy-laden and take on a dynamic 'motoric' character
in which movement *per se* is the main concern:

Ex. 143

Secondly, functional harmony is in the process of being destroyed by an emphasis on seconds, fourths, and sevenths as constructive melodic and harmonic intervals which implied an equality between consonance and dissonance, though even in his extreme 'atonal' period Hindemith never accepted the complete 'emancipation of the dissonance' envisaged by Schoenberg. And thirdly, he now discarded Reger's harmonic counterpoint in favour of a bold linear style, in which the vertical factor was almost invariably the incidental result of the part-writing. At the same time jazz, which became known in Germany about 1920, begins to colour Hindemith's manner, as in the Piano Suite, Op. 26 (1922), and in the finale of the above-mentioned *Kammermusik* which is scored for a small orchestra, including nine percussion instruments. This was partly in imitation of a jazz band, partly to ensure the utmost clarity of the melodic and rhythmic patterns. The *Kammermusik* is the first instance of Hindemith's interest in orchestral chamber music, largely in reaction against the lavish orchestral style of the romantic period. The Third String Quartet, Op. 22 (1922), represents the summing-up of all the stylistic aims pursued by the young Hindemith, yet at the same time it is also a transitional work paving the way for the neo-classicism which finds its first clear expression in the song cycle *Das Marienleben*, Op. 27, for voice and piano (1923). This setting of poems by Rainer Maria Rilke consists of fifteen songs divided into four groups, each with a character of its own: idyllic and lyrical in the first group, dramatic in the second, growing in tension and emotive expression in the third, until the fourth group is marked by an almost abstract treatment of the text, the musical structure completely absorbing the *dramatis personae* and the action. In the majority of these songs the voice is handled in a rather unvocal, instrumental manner and often forms with the piano a two- or three-part polyphonic texture. The various forms employed are those of Baroque music: 'Die Darstellung Mariä im Tempel' (no. 2) for instance is a passacaglia, and 'Vom Tode Mariä II' (no. 14) is designed as a theme with five contrapuntal variations. The setting, in avoiding all descriptive and picturesque elements, expresses the poetic essence of the words in a more or less stylized and objective way. *Das Marienleben* is a significant landmark in Hindemith's technical development, and evidence of the importance he attached to it may be seen in the fact that in 1948 he subjected the music to a fairly extensive revision, smoothing down the harshness and angularity of the voice part and clarifying the harmonic and contrapuntal texture, but in the process sacrificing youthful boldness and spontaneity.[1]

[1] No. 12, 'Stillung Mariä mit dem Auferstandenen', the only song completely unchanged in the new version, is recorded in *The History of Music in Sound*, x. And see Ex. 189, pp. 407–8.

Hindemith's indebtedness to the spirit of Bach reached its highest point in the contrapuntal complexity and compactness of the Fourth String Quartet, Op. 22 (1924), with a fugue in the first movement and in the finale a passacaglia and fugato, which constitute a *ne plus ultra* in close polyphonic thinking. In subsequent works Hindemith began to free himself of this dense contrapuntal writing; texture becomes gradually looser, more clearly defined in the disposition of the parts, and a decorative element is seen to play an increasingly important role. In his orchestral style Hindemith more and more resorts to the concertante principle, with a resulting gain of clarity in the general texture; and, possibly influenced by Stravinsky, he tends to replace, within the single movement, construction-by-contrast with construction-by-similarity. Typical of this phase are the Piano Concerto, Op. 29 (1924), the Concerto for Orchestra, Op. 38 (1925) and the *Kammermusik*, Op. 36, nos. 3 and 4 (1925 and 1927 respectively) which are essentially concertos for violin and viola, the latter being a demonstration of Hindemith's concertante writing at its most felicitous.

His temporary interest in the 'Neue Sachlichheit' (New Objectivity) prompted Hindemith to devote himself to *Gebrauchsmusik*—'utility' or functional music conceived for special purposes such as the film, the radio and the school. His various *Kammermusiken* are in a sense also 'utilitarian' in that, like so much eighteenth-century music, they were written for special players or special occasions. Both he and Kurt Weill[1] composed works which are wholly subservient to those uses and also intended to bring music to the home and tempt the amateur to play it, thus trying to bridge the ever-widening chasm between the composer and the ordinary music lover or between 'the producer and the consumer of music', as Hindemith put it in the language of the economist. Works of this kind include the *Schulwerk für Instrumental-Zusammenspiel* (1927), the school opera, *Wir bauen eine Stadt* (We are building a town) (1930) and the *Sing-und-Spielmusik für Liebhaber und Musikfreunde* (1928-31). In a preface the composer points out that it is not written for the concert hall or the professional musician, but is intended to provide modern studies for those 'who wish, for their own pleasure, to sing and play or to perform before a small circle of people who share their taste'. Yet, after an initial vogue for this kind of music, which found its most concrete expression in the music festival held by and for young people at Plön in the summer of 1932, enthusiasm waned and the whole movement gradually petered out, though in retrospect it must be seen as a genuine attempt to win the interest of the ordinary music lover for contemporary music.

[1] On Weill, see *infra*, p. 339.

Although opera might seem alien, or, at any rate, not as congenial to Hindemith's cast of mind as 'absolute' instrumental music, his versatility, his strong creative energies, and his intellectual curiosity prompted him to a number of operatic works. He started with three one-act operas, all written in 1921: *Mörder, Hoffnung der Frauen* (Murderer, hope of women), to an expressionist libretto by the painter Oskar Kokoschka, the subject of which is symbol-laden to the point of unintelligibility; *Sancta Susanna*, whose libretto by August Stramm portrays female eroticism in conflict with the rigours of monastic life; and *Das Nusch-Nuschi*, a satirical play for Burmese marionettes by Franz Blei, treated by Hindemith in *buffo* style and with a great deal of musical parody. With the exception of the last work, there is a very noticeable incongruity between the involved and obscure libretto and the clear-cut, stylized nature of the musical setting.

His next opera, the three-act *Cardillac* (1926), to a libretto by Ferdinand Lion drawn from E. T. A. Hoffmann's story, *Das Fräulein von Scuderi*, demonstrates Hindemith's tendency towards objectivity and stylized treatment. All psychological and descriptive elements are avoided in favour of a strictly musical response to the drama, whose stage action frequently runs on a different plane from that of the music. Hindemith here aims at a return to the aesthetic of late baroque opera, the music having the first say and the individual scenes being not much more than a peg on which to hang such 'closed' autonomous musical forms as arias, duets, and ensembles. But it has to be admitted that the opera suffers from the immobility of these forms in relation to the dramatic happenings recalling the style of an oratorio, and from too rigid an application of polyphony that often creates the impression of being written for its own sake, as in the final chorus—a passacaglia of considerable length. Also Hindemith's portrayal of the chief *dramatis personae* as objective types is in conflict with the characters of the libretto, especially that of the title-hero—a Parisian goldsmith who, in his pathological mania to retrieve by murder the jewels purchased from him by his customers, is a truly romantic and very individual figure. Moreover, the differentiation in the musical delineation of the various characters is not carried far enough, though there is an attempt to depict Cardillac and his daughter in particular colours—the former by a tortuous, darkly scored theme and the latter by florid writing. In 1952 Hindemith subjected the opera to some dramatic revisions: a great deal of the text was entirely rewritten, the vocal lines were rendered more singable, parts of the score were amplified to match the alterations in the plot, and the orchestra was made to yield a richer and more varied quality of sound, in keeping with the composer's later style of instrumentation.[1] Yet, as in the case of *Das Marienleben*, much of the direct and uncompromising character of the original version was lost in this process of improving what Hindemith regarded as the indiscretions of his youth. The tragedy of *Cardillac* was followed by two comic operas both of which reflect the contemporary inclination to deal with topical subjects. The first of these was the one-act *Sketsch [sic] mit Musik, Hin und zurück* (There and Back) (1927), an example of the miniature type of opera then in vogue as a reaction against the ponderous seriousness and the huge dimensions of Wagnerian and Straussian music-drama. The action deals with a matrimonial tragedy in an amusingly flippant manner and reverses the plot halfway through, so that the opera ends as it began; the music moves from that point also partly in retrograde motion and makes use of elements from revue and cabaret. The three-act *Neues vom Tage* (News of the day) (1929), to a libretto by Marcellus Schiffer, who also wrote the book of the previous opera, deals with the sensationalism of modern newspapers which pry, recklessly and callously, into the private affairs of citizens. It is in the *buffa* style of *Hin und zurück*, but is more ambitiously conceived, with great choral scenes and orchestral interludes, and contains parodistic skits on the traditional romantic opera—a 'hate duet' instead of the customary 'love duet', and a 'divorce ensemble' instead of a 'wedding ensemble'. Altogether, it is a work that witnesses to Hindemith's high spirits and his good-natured irony, though it is a little weighed down by his obsessive urge for elaborate contrapuntal writing.

At the beginning of the 1930s, which also marks the beginning of his full maturity, Hindemith's style underwent a very noticeable change in the direction of greater relaxation and mellowness. Technically, this is seen in the abandonment of a massive, close-knit texture in favour of a

Ex. 144

---

[1] See H. L. Schilling, *Paul Hindemith's 'Cardillac'. Beiträge zu einem Vergleich der beiden Opernfassungen* (Würzburg, 1962).

lighter, more transparent treatment, in a greater differentiation being made, so far as polyphony is concerned, between main voices and subsidiary parts, and in a more clearly defined feeling for key, as in the Philharmonic Concerto of 1932 (Ex. 144).

Typical of this new phase is not only the Philharmonic Concerto, consisting of six variations on a markedly expressive theme, but the oratorio *Das Unaufhörliche* (The Incessant) for four soloists, mixed chorus, boys' chorus, and orchestra (1931), in which the expressive emotional element, that up to now had been allowed into his music through the back door, assumes an increasingly important role and lends Hindemith's neo-classicism a romantic overtone:

Ex. 145

(Night bears the end.)

The oratorio is a setting of a half-mystical, half-philosophical text by Gottfried Benn, which contrasts eternity with the transience of human life and the perpetuity of creation with the temporary aspirations and achievements of mankind. This monumental work is in three parts, of which the middle is chiefly allotted to the soloists and is flanked by two predominantly choral parts, where the great choruses in contrapuntal-imitatory style show Handel's influence while the melodic writing is coloured by Gregorian chant.

The work that best illustrates Hindemith's mature mode of expression, and that in its spirituality and musical vision must be accounted a masterpiece, is the opera *Mathis der Maler* (1934), to which he wrote his own libretto. Like *Die Meistersinger* and Pfitzner's *Palestrina*, this opera is an 'artist's drama' centring on the figure of Dürer's contemporary Mathis Grünewald, who is for the composer a symbol of the German artist of his own time. The story deals with significant events in the painter's life and is set against the background of the Peasant War in South Germany in the sixteenth century. The spiritual tensions and conflicts which torment Mathis's mind arise from his participation in the politics of his country and from his profound questioning of his artistic mission; and they take on a topical meaning when understood as a reflection of Hindemith's own problems as artist and man in Nazi Germany. The opera is a refutation of the totalitarian dogma that the artist must be a political animal, subservient to the State, and proclaims as its chief message that for an artist to serve any other master but himself is to forfeit his moral and intellectual integrity and to deny his true mission. More epic than dramatic in character, it approaches the style of a scenic oratorio, with big choral scenes in contrapuntal manner and with extensive slow-moving solo numbers, duets, and ensembles. Wagnerian leitmotive technique alternates with the formal devices of the older opera. Occasional use is made of

German folk-song such as the medieval tune 'Es sungen drei Engel'
(Ex. 146 (i)) in the Prelude, *Engelkonzert*, of Gregorian chant as at the
end of the seventh scene (ii) and of pentatonic melodies modelled on
Gregorian chant (iii):

Ex. 146

(Mighty Ruler, true God who controllest the changes of things.)

These lend the music an archaic flavour suited to the ambience of
this idealistic and noble work. The symphony *Mathis der Maler* (1934)
is based almost entirely on music from the opera.

Of Hindemith's three pre-war ballets, *Nobilissima Visione* (1938), to
a choreographic story by Leonid Massine, shows in eleven scenes the
life of St. Francis of Assisi. Lofty in conception, it is not primarily
ballet music in the Stravinsky sense, for the range and variety of pure
dance pattern is restricted. Other works of Hindemith's pre-war period
include *Der Schwanendreher* (1935), a kind of viola concerto whose
material is largely derived and elaborated from a German folk-song.
(Hindemith was for a number of years viola player in the Amar Quartet
and frequently appeared as soloist in his own works for that instrument,
as he did in *Der Schwanendreher*.) His three Piano Sonatas (all 1936)
and the Sonata for Piano Duet (1938) are splendid examples which
show the synthesis of an essentially neo-classical style with a romantically
expressive mode of utterance.

With a composer of Hindemith's temperament a profound interest in the theoretical aspect of his craft is not surprising. His was that rare combination of a creative and reproductive artist with a searching and lucid theoretical thinker. Evidence of this is provided by his textbook, *Unterweisung im Tonsatz*[1], which is an exposition of the theory and practice of his own methods, in which the organization of the entire melodic and harmonic material is based on a 'diatonization' of the twelve notes of the chromatic scale—the very opposite of Schoenberg's dodecaphonic system.

Like Schoenberg, Hindemith takes for his basis the twelve chromatic notes; but, unlike the Schoenbergian series, the twelve notes are strictly organized and stand in clearly defined relationships to both a central note, the tonic, and to one another. It is these relationships which determine the melodic and harmonic values of the twelve notes. Hindemith takes as his point of departure the harmonic or overtone series acclimatizing its 'impure' notes to the temperate scale, and derives from it two rows. In contrast to Schoenberg's complete equalization of the twelve chromatic notes, Row I shows a hierarchical order:

Ex. 147

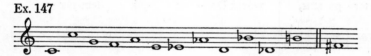

(Hindemith includes the octave as the note next in importance to the first note).

The nearer a note lies to C, the closer its relationship to it; the further away from it the weaker this relationship until in the twelfth note, B, it is at its weakest. The tritone F sharp is considered by Hindemith an outsider standing in a neutral relationship to the tonic C and playing an ambivalent role (see p. 337). In this he differs from the generally held modern view that the tritone is completely unrelated to C and therefore represents an extreme, or zero, in the scale of relationship.

The varying degrees of relationships to the central note, or tonic, constitute for Hindemith 'rule and measure for the linking of sounds, for the order of harmonic progressions and thus for the further course of the musical happenings'.[2] Row I is what has been called a 'functional mode',[3] i.e. it indicates the functional role of the twelve chromatic notes

---

[1] Mainz, 1937; translated as *The Craft of Musical Composition* (New York, 1942).
[2] Ibid., p. 74.
[3] This term was first used by Richard Hill, 'Schoenberg's Tone-Rows and the Tonal System of the Future', *Musical Quarterly*, xxii (1936), p. 14.

to a centre. There is, to repeat, a world of difference between this row and the Schoenbergian note-row. The latter is a melodic model or store of motives for practical use in a composition, whereas the Hindemithian series has no thematic significance whatsoever and is merely a graph showing functional relationships.

It gives only one set of tonal relationships, i.e. the degree of nearness to or distance from the tonic. Another row is needed to show the relationship *between* the twelve notes, namely their intervallic relationship which determines the harmonic value of an interval, according to its degree of consonance and dissonance. This purpose is served by Hindemith's Row II which he derived from the so-called combination tones:

Ex. 148

(The arrows indicate the respective roots of the intervals).

Hindemith takes full account of the modern conception of the relativity of consonance and dissonance by drawing no strict demarcation line between the two; there is merely a gradual transition from simple and perfect intervals (the first seven intervals of Row II) to less simple intervals of higher harmonic tension (the next four intervals) until extreme tension is reached in the major seventh. The tritone, on the other hand, which has no root, is a neutral interval whose harmonic value depends on the context in which it occurs.

On the basis of Row II Hindemith proceeds to build a system of chords comprising all possible combinations of intervals whose harmonic value is determined by what kind of simple and less simple intervals they contain. If chords of a higher harmonic tension move towards chords of lesser tension the result of such a progression is a *harmonischer Fall* or harmonic descent—in the opposite case, a *harmonischer Anstieg* or harmonic ascent. In other words, the harmonic tension decreases and increases in direct ratio to the progression from a *wertvoller*, or valuable, chord to a less valuable chord and vice versa. This crescendo and diminuendo in harmonic tension Hindemith calls *harmonisches Gefälle* or harmonic incline, and the planning of a gradual and balanced incline is, according to him, the purpose and test of a good chord progression, unless a sudden fall in harmonic tension is sought for some specific aesthetic effect. For instance, in the following progression of six chords, the harmonic tension is seen to increase slowly towards the fourth chord and then diminish towards the last:

Ex. 149

Thus, the harmonic *Gefälle* of this example is well-balanced. Hindemith argues that by assessing the harmonic values of chords with the help of Row II, composers are given a means whereby to organize and control in a deliberate manner the course of harmonic progressions and, indeed, the harmonic disposition of a whole piece.

A word must be said about Hindemith's theory of tonality in modern music. Since his system, based on the natural laws of musical acoustics, constitutes a 'diatonicized' chromaticism in which every one of the twelve notes is related to a central note—just as the seven diatonic notes of the major-minor system are related to a tonic—he maintains that it is possible to establish a tonality in every kind of music, including even twelve-note music, as he attempts to show in his analysis of a few bars from Schoenberg's Piano Piece, Op. 33a.[1] His procedure in finding the key of a given passage is, roughly, the following: he first looks for the roots of a given chord progression, then arranges these roots in a line, ascertains with the help of Row II the 'best' interval, and the root of this interval is the tonic of the passage in question: Thus, the line formed by the roots of Ex. 149 is:

Ex. 150

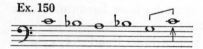

Its 'best' or simplest interval is the perfect fourth G—C whose root is C —hence C is the tonic of the above passage.

Whatever might be thought of the involved way in which Hindemith establishes the two fundamental rows on which his whole system rests, it must be said that *Unterweisung im Tonsatz* represents, even after the lapse of a whole generation, a very valuable contribution to compositional theory and a serious attempt to introduce tonal order and organization into the complex phenomena of music in the inter-war years.

KURT WEILL AND ERNST KŘENEK

The two most notable German contemporaries of Hindemith during

[1] *Unterweisung*, pp. 244–45.

the inter-war period were Kurt Weill (1900–50) and Ernst Křenek (b. 1900). Weill, a pupil of Busoni, began his career with works in which he pursued a boldly experimental, expressionistic and abstract line (Divertimento, 1923; String Quartet, 1923, and *Frauentanz* for soprano and five instruments, 1924). He subsequently turned to the stage as his main field of activity, adopting a more realistic and topical approach and creating a new type of German opera in which such heterogeneous elements as those from the old *Singspiel*, jazz, cabaret and *Überbrettl* (a German form of intimate revue) are moulded into an individual style. For this reason and also on account of the raciness of his melodic idiom and the pungency of his much simplified harmonic language, Weill's operas achieved at the time a wide popular success. Like the young Hindemith, Křenek, and other contemporary composers (Max Brand in *Maschinist Hopkins*, 1929), he cultivated *Zeitoper*, operas with a topical political and social subject in which bourgeois society was pilloried and made responsible for the social injustices of the class system, as in *Aufstieg und Fall der Stadt Mahagonny* (Rise and fall of the town of Mahagonny) (1927), *Die Dreigroschenoper* (Threepenny Opera) (1928), and *Die Bürgschaft* (The Security) (1932) in which a strong satirical vein is tempered by an intermittent serious attitude. He also followed the short-lived vogue for the *Lehrstück*, or educational music, in the school opera *Der Jasager* (The Yea-sayer) (1930). Significantly, five of Weill's stage works have libretti by the left-wing poet and playwright, Bert Brecht; and their collaboration produced, in *Die Dreigroschenoper*, their best-known and most successful work, the model for which was John Gay's *The Beggars' Opera*. This was a thinly veiled attack on the corruption of contemporary public characters and institutions, and similarly the German work represents a mordant satire on modern society and public institutions. It is not an opera in the traditional sense but a mixture of *Singspiel* and cabaret, consisting of set numbers (arias, duets, ensembles, and parodistic chorale) with interspersed spoken dialogue, the whole accompanied by a small orchestra. Weill replaces the popular melodies of the English original by jazz-like tunes of a most immediate appeal and of such simplicity that they can be sung by actors, not only by professional singers; his argument for using this device was that jazz represented the folk-music of modern times.

Whereas Weill's output was largely devoted to opera, Křenek displayed a Protean versatility; in fact, he may be said to be the German counterpart of Milhaud. The fact that Křenek's intellect has always been more potent than his creative instinct possibly explains the lack of a firm direction in his stylistic development. His zigzag course also reflects the spiritual insecurity and absence of a strong inner purpose characteristic of the German *Zeitgeist* in its extreme manifestations. Like Hindemith, Křenek allowed himself to be influenced by the various 'isms' of the 1920s, but, unlike Hindemith, he did not succeed in achieving a distinct personal mode of expression. He began as a radical and uncompromising experimentalist in an intransigent atonal style— three Symphonies (1921–22); four String Quartets (1921–24); the scenic cantata *Die Zwingburg* (The Citadel) (1922); the farcical detective thriller *Der Sprung über den Schatten* (The Leap over the Shadow) (1923), and the expressionist *Orpheus und Eurydike* (1923), the latter to a libretto by Kokoschka which treats the ancient myth in a modern psychological manner. Then Křenek executed a *volte face*, abandoning the experimental and abstract and turning to a frankly popular idiom. In *Jonny spielt auf* (Johnny strikes up) (1927) a Negro dance-band leader is the hero, and Křenek makes use of jazz and the spectacular devices of modern stage production, including the radio and a real locomotive.[1] After this he changed his course again, paying tribute to topical *Zeitoper* in the trilogy *Der Diktator* (1926), *Das geheime Königreich* (The Secret Kingdom) (1927), and *Schwergewicht oder die Ehre der Nation* (Dead Weight or the Honour of the Nation) (1927), all one-act operas. Then came a neo-romantic phase in which he drifted into a diatonic style best exemplified in the song cycle, *Reisebuch aus den österreichischen Alpen* (Travel Book from the Austrian Alps) (1929), which was largely modelled on Schubert's *Winterreise*; *Fiedellieder* (Fiddle Songs) (1930), and the tragedy *Das Leben des Orest* (The Life of Orestes) (1930), treated as an intensely passionate human drama in the manner of grand opera. Returning from his studies in Berlin with Franz Schreker to Vienna (1928) he came into close contact with the works of Schoenberg and his school, and after prolonged hesitation decided to embrace the twelve-note system with all its theoretical and practical implications.[2] From then onwards the majority of Křenek's compositions were written in serial style, such as the monumental *Karl V* (1933), which draws on elements from the historical drama, grand opera, dumb-show, and the film, and is comparable to Milhaud's *Christophe Colomb*.

THE SECOND VIENNESE SCHOOL—ARNOLD SCHOENBERG

In the flux of currents and cross-currents characterizing European music during most of the inter-war period, there was one firm rock formed by three composers who are collectively known as the Second Viennese School—Arnold Schoenberg (1874–1951) and his two disciples Alban Berg (1885–1935) and Anton Webern (1883–1945). This

[1] See pl. V (b).
[2] See his *Über neue Musik* (Vienna, 1937) and *Studies in Counterpoint* (New York, 1940).

was the only group of composers which showed a consistent development in a single direction, namely the exploitation of a new method of composition that represented a revolutionary departure from all other methods known in musical history. In its aesthetics, however, it adhered, with the exception of the later Webern, to the chief tenet of romanticism —music as the vehicle of subjective emotion—but music subjected to the immense pressure of largely unconscious irrational forces of the ego and thus becoming expressionist in character; in this sense the Second Viennese School may be said to represent a reaction against neo-classicism and the New Objectivity.

In earlier chapters of this volume it has been shown how Schoenberg, in developing and intensifying Wagner's chromaticism, arrived in the period 1908–1914 at a free chromatic or atonal style. His works written in this style—a fluid, amorphous, and invertebrate atonal mass— represent the liquidation of all previous means of formal and harmonic organization; and they were all very short works (Three Pieces for piano, Op. 11, Five Pieces for orchestra, Op. 16, Six Piano Pieces, Op. 19) for the relinquishing of all harmonic devices, used hitherto to create formal articulation in tonal music, precluded the employment of larger forms; while in those compositions which did show a measure of formal extension, it was the text that conditioned the form (*Das Buch der hängenden Gärten* (The Book of the Hanging Gardens), Op. 15, *Erwartung* (Expectation), Op. 17, *Die glückliche Hand* (The Lucky Hand), Op. 18, and *Pierrot lunaire*, Op. 21). In these 'free atonal' works Schoenberg had arrived at an end, he found himself in an impasse; and it was in consequence of this that he began experimenting with a novel principle of construction which, analogous to the formal organization of tonal music, would guarantee order and coherence and at the same time introduce a unifying principle into the melodic and harmonic material. These aims he achieved by the method of what he himself called 'composing with the twelve chromatic notes related only to one another' and which is generally known as the twelve-note or serial method, a method foreshadowed in some of Schoenberg's atonal works, such as *Pierrot lunaire* and the Orchestral Songs, Op. 22, where an attempt is made to tie together the structure by means of recurrent motives. Similarly, the last part of an abortive symphony (1915), which later became the oratorio *Die Jakobsleiter* (Jacob's Ladder), contained a scherzo with a dodecaphonic theme. In the oratorio it appears at the very opening— the first six notes in the form of a *basso ostinato*, the last six notes sustained in a chord above it:

Ex. 151

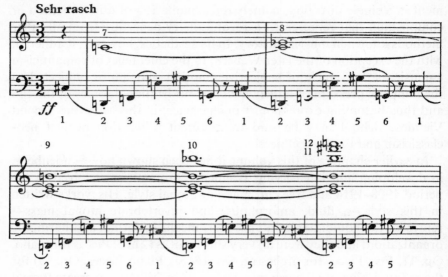

The fundamental idea behind this new mode of composition was to replace one structural force—tonality—by another force—thematic unity; or, seen from the point of view of Schoenburg's pre-dodecaphonic works, to substitute for unqualified free atonality organized atonality. This was to provide a firm basis for the achievement of a genuine atonal style, as in his previous compositions it was frequently hard to prevent tonal elements from intruding into the music and thus disrupting the carefully arranged atonal structure.

This search for the unification of the entire material of a composition by means of an inclusive system of note relationships had been in the air during the years shortly before the First World War. There were, for instance, Skryabin's attempts to base whole musical structures on what he termed 'synthetic chords'. The Austrian Josef Mathias Hauer (1883–1959) anticipated Schoenberg more directly and his theories had some influence on the latter's own thinking. As he admitted, 'Hauer's theories, even where I think them exaggerated, are profound and original, and his compositions, even where I regard them as examples rather than as compositions, reveal creative gifts'.[1] In 1908 Hauer began to write music based on a system which he later elaborated in several publications,[2] demonstrating that the chromatic scale can be arranged in 479,001,600

---

[1] *Harmonielehre* (third edition, Vienna, 1922), p. 488,

[2] *Vom Wesen des Musikalischen: Ein Lehrbuch der Zwölftonmusik* (Berlin, 1920), and *Zwölftontechnik: Die Lehre von den Tropen* (Vienna, 1926).

permutations; these are grouped into forty-four *Tropen* which are twelve-note patterns rather similar in character to Schoenberg's note-rows. Each of these *Tropen* can again be divided into two sections of six notes which stand in complementary intervallic relationship to one another; and, in addition, each *Trope* can be transposed to any other degree of the chromatic scale, with further internal regroupings of intervals which result in an astronomical number of permutations. As a composer Hauer was negligible, and in the event it was not his system but Schoenberg's that established itself and proved technically and aesthetically of far-reaching significance.

The dodecaphonic method was primarily a means of achieving order and coherence; but it also fulfilled two other purposes with which Schoenberg had been concerned almost from the beginning of his career. One was to develop a theme by continuous variation, a principle which he gradually evolved from hints found in Brahms as, for example, in the finale of the Quartet in A minor, Op. 52, no. 2:

Ex. 152

Such hints find in the twelve-note technique their consummation; for essentially a dodecaphonic composition represents a perpetual series of organically linked variations of a basic note-row and its derivations. The other purpose was to achieve complete thematic unity, that is, to evolve an entire work from a basic idea which is represented by the so-called note-row—a series formed by the twelve notes of the chromatic scale arranged in an individual order of sequence and invented by the composer. Yet so far as Schoenberg himself was concerned, the construction of a note-row was preceded by the invention of an idea which already possessed a thematic character; and it was from this idea that he worked back to the basic row—in other words, the creative act came first and then the play of the intellect on its product. The unity of the musical space is ensured by the use of the note-row in two dimensions, vertical and horizontal, which results in an intrinsic identity of the harmonic and melodic elements, in which the temporal-spatial elements are only two different aspects of the same musical idea. Each composition has to be based on a note-row, and to enlarge its scope three variants are to be added to the basic series: its inversion or mirror form, its cancrizans or retrograde form, and the inversion of the retrograde as, for instance, shown in Schoenberg's Suite, Op. 25:

Ex. 153

Moreover, the note-row and its derivations can be transposed to the other degrees of the chromatic scale, with the result that forty-eight possible versions of the basic idea are available to the composer—always supposing the truly musical 'identification' of note-series with their 'opposites', an intellectual rather than an aural process. These transpositions provide one of the principal means of achieving formal design, as moving from one transposition to another fulfils a similar function to that fulfilled by modulating from one key to another in tonal music.

The twelve-note row combines some of the functions of scale, key, and fundamental theme. Like a scale, it contains all the available notes of a given note system—in dodecaphonic music, the twelve notes of the chromatic scale are arranged not according to a gradually rising and falling pitch, but in an order of intervals freshly invented for each composition. Thus the row already possesses a *melodic* character but is not yet a melody or a theme because it is not yet rhythmically articulated.

Two rules in the early application of the note-row were that (*a*) the original order of its intervals must be maintained throughout a composition, and (*b*) no note must be repeated until the other eleven notes are sounded. After the row has been used up melodically or harmonically, or in both ways simultaneously, this procedure is repeated until the end of a piece. As the two chief purposes of the row are to ensure thematic unity and to replace the function of key in tonal music, it follows that it must be present in a composition at all times in either basic form (*Grundgestalt*) or its derivatives. As for the rule of the non-repetition of an individual note before the entire row is employed, this sprang from Schoenberg's anxiety during his early dodecaphonic period lest a repeated note might tend, by thus assuming undue importance, to destroy the equality of the twelve chromatic notes and suggest something similar to a tonal centre; for the same reason octave doublings of a note were forbidden. In the later stage of twelve-note theory these and other strict rules were relaxed—note-repetitions were permitted, dissonances were no longer employed indiscriminately but according to their varying degrees of harmonic tension,[1] and even consonances were readmitted. The note-row as such does not, of course, exclude tonal implications—it can be so designed as to include triads and other tonal formations, a procedure adopted in particular by Berg to mollify the extremely discordant character of pure twelve-note music, and by inventing rows with a tonal slant he may be said to have achieved a kind of symbiosis with tonal music. Methods of employing the note-row also include its sub-division into two or more segments, with groups of six, four, or three notes (see Exx. 151, 159, 162, 174, 177, and 179), without thereby affecting the all-pervasive thematic function of the *entire* row. For this reason the term 'functional mode' is an apt description of its true nature which bears a certain affinity to that of the *rāga* in Indian and the *maqām* in Arabic music.[2] Since the note-row is a horizontal structure, the music based on it is primarily contrapuntal in character and the ancient devices of inversion, reversion, imitation, and canon play a prominent part. Indeed it is in the use of polyphony and variation that a composer may show the extent of his inventive imagination and technical skill. On the other hand, it has to be admitted that the twelve-note method of composition represents an artificial, intellectually conceived system of tone relationships which, unlike the empirically derived theoretical basis of tonal music, was invented *ad hoc*. In this it resembles a language like Esperanto, without a natural history. The note-row and its manipulations, fascinating though they are to the intellect, have no basis in the observable natural phenomena of music; they are, as it were, test-tube creations, laboratory experiments, very close in character to the

---

[1] Křenek, in his *Studies of Counterpoint*, distinguishes between dissonances of a higher degree of tension or 'sharp' dissonances (minor second, major seventh), and dissonances of a lower degree of tension or 'mild' dissonances (major second, minor seventh).

[2] See Vol. I, pp. 195 and 421.

acrostic and other devices which have at different periods engaged the attention of poets. Yet what matters in the last analysis is not the nature of a system, but whether, by using that system, the composer is able to create works of an original and enduring quality, a question which has been answered in the affirmative by Schoenberg, Berg, Webern, Dallapiccola, and other musicians. Moreover, twelve-note music adheres to the same general aesthetic principles as govern the rest of Western music irrespective of style and technique—contrast and variety in unity, balance and proportion of the parts in relation to the whole, effective distribution of climax and anti-climax, and so on. These qualities make themselves felt without the listener being consciously aware of the particular technical means by which they are obtained. As Schoenberg once said, 'the twelve-note technique is a purely family affair'; and he insisted that in the term 'twelve-note composition' the accent was to be laid on the noun.

The great crisis in Schoenberg's creative career occurred during the years 1914–18 when as a composer he went underground, as it were, and experimented in a number of abortive works with the possibilities of a unifying principle based on the employment of the twelve notes of the chromatic scale. The first works which showed this principle in embryo were the Five Piano Pieces, Op. 23 and the Serenade, Op. 24, for seven instruments and solo voice (both 1923).[1] The fifth of the piano pieces, a waltz, and the fourth movement of the Serenade, which is an impassioned setting of Petrarch's Sonnet no. 217, are both based on twelve-note series; but the technique employed was, as Schoenberg himself admitted, comparatively rudimentary. Thus, in the vocal movement the baritone sings the identical series of twelve notes throughout, without any transpositions or derivatives:

[1]The first movement of the Serenade is recorded in *The History of Music in Sound*, X.

Ex. 154

(O could I ever recover from the revenge on her who destroys me with glance and speech alike, and then . . .)

The only structurally interesting feature lies in the successive distributions of the row: as every line of the poem is hendecasyllabic, the second line begins with the 12th note of the row, the third line with the 11th, the fourth line with the 10th and so on, the row gradually doubling back on itself until the thirteenth line is reached when the row begins again with its first note. The Waltz of Op. 23 is also based on a complete note-row while the other pieces show an approximation to it, in that each contains a recurring series of several notes—five for instance in the third movement:

Ex. 155

and twelve plus two in the variation movement of Op. 24. Both these works, which are in the composer's relaxed and light-hearted vein, are of a transitional character in their manipulation of the dodecaphonic method. By contrast, in the following Piano Suite, Op. 25 (1924) (though some movements were composed in 1921), and in the Wind Quintet, Op. 26 (1924), Schoenberg is seen to employ his new method with an inflexibility difficult to reconcile with a composer who, despite the marked intellectuality of his technique, always placed construction at the almost exclusive service of emotional expression. It was as though he wanted in these two works to prove to himself the practical validity of the twelve-note technique, its manifold structural and contrapuntal potentialities. Each of the two compositions is based in its entirety on a single row of a special form: that of the Piano Suite is arranged into three groups of four notes each, while in the row of the Wind Quintet the last six notes are an almost exact replica, transposed a fourth down, of the first six notes, a structure which corresponds to the divisions of a theme in tonal music into first (half) and second (full) close. In op. 26 Schoenberg returned to the classical four-movement scheme abandoned during his free atonal period, a return made possible through the achievement of large-scale structural organization by means of twelve-note technique. The Wind Quintet comprises an Allegro in free sonata form, a Scherzo, an Adagio in ternary form, and a Rondo, and is scored for flute, oboe, clarinet, bassoon, and horn which frequently produce an organ-like effect. It is Schoenberg's first large work in the new method and represents a compendium of all available contrapuntal devices, especially in the finale.

Schoenberg next applied his new-found technique to the choral medium, with special emphasis on the canonic aspect. The two works in question, both for mixed chorus, were Four Pieces, Op. 27, and *Three Satires*, Op. 28 (both 1925), in which, with the exception of the last two numbers of Op. 27, the settings are of his own texts. The *Satires* were occasioned by the attacks made on Schoenberg's new compositional principles in various quarters, and represent his declaration of war on all current 'isms' of the time—neo-classicism, folklorism, 'middle of the way' music and 'wrong note' tonal music. And to demonstrate that it may be as exacting to write good tonal music as dodecaphonic music he added three most complicated tonal canons which show the same contrapuntal boldness of writing as the serial pieces. The next three works were all instrumental. The Suite, op. 29, for seven instruments (1926), proves by its gay, unbuttoned mood, which reaches a point of sheer exuberance in the final gigue, that dodecaphonic music is not concerned exclusively with states of terror or anxiety, e.g. the second movement, *Tanzschritte* (dance steps) which is a witty caricature of jazz. As in the Serenade, the unusual combination is handled with superb mastery and insight into the peculiar character of the individual instruments, with the three strings (violin, viola, and cello), the three woodwind (two clarinets and bass clarinet) and the piano being treated both in opposition and in concert; the keyboard instrument is conceived partly as a concertante, partly as a very plastic accompaniment. Schoenberg's own strict rules are here relaxed—there are octave doublings, reiteration, and also omission of single notes of the basic row, and tonal formations such as major and minor thirds and sixths. The slow movement is a set of four well-contrasted variations on the song, 'Ännchen von Tharau', by Friedrich Silcher (1789–1860), which is perfectly integrated into the serial texture:

Ex. 156

Like the Wind Quintet, the Third String Quartet, Op. 30 (1927), is cast in a classical mould—a Moderato in free sonata form, an Adagio consisting of theme and variations, an Intermezzo in scherzo form, and a Rondo. Yet, compared with that earlier work, Schoenberg's formal handling here has acquired greater clarity of articulation, the themes have an increased plasticity, the contrapuntal lines are more fluid and the texture is more airy. And, as in the Suite, the twelve-note technique is treated with considerable freedom as, for instance, in the opening movement, where the initial five-note ostinato (G–E–D sharp–A–C) is not only continuous for twelve bars but pervades the entire movement in various permutations. With the Third String Quartet Schoenberg entered his 'classical' period. A year later came the Variations for Orchestra, Op. 31 (1928), which represents the crystallization of the dodecaphonic method in the exploitation of all the horizontal and vertical potentialities and is in a sense comparable to Bach's *Kunst der Fuge*. Although orchestral polyphony is carried to its utmost limits, yet, owing to the continuous changes in the distribution of the leading parts and the scoring, which frequently achieves the effect of infinitely varied chamber music, the general texture shows an extraordinary transparence, with a gossamer lightness in certain variations (nos. 2, 4, 6, 7, 9). Similarly, the colour scheme is marked by immense diversity—from the hazy, almost impressionist, introduction and the monochrome of the theme itself to the subtle woodwind hues of Variation 2, and from the fleeting colours of Variation 7 to the compact and massive sound of Variation 8. At no point is the orchestral palette used for the sake of extraneous effects but always in the service of the musical thought, of the individual structure and the general design. The introduction gradually reveals the contours of the basic theme and some of its transpositions and in its latter part quotes, in the solo trombone, the motive B flat–A–C–B natural. This in German spells BACH and is intended as a homage to the master of counterpoint. In fact, this introduction may be taken as a variation *before* the actual appearance of the variation theme. The latter shows quaternary form built up successively from the original row, its retrograde inversion (transposed), its retrograde and the inversion (transposed), and is a *locus classicus* to show how twelve-note music permits of the invention of a melody which is beautifully sustained, of the utmost purity of line and of a perfect equipoise in its rise and fall, to say nothing of its tender lyrical expression:

Ex. 157

Basic Row:

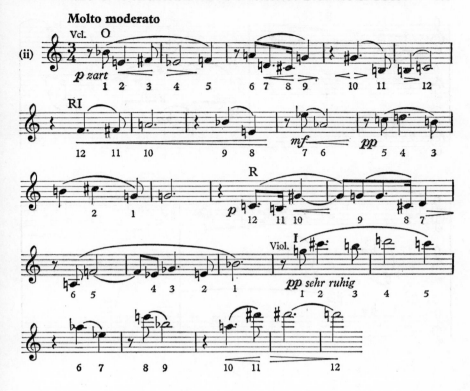

Of the numerous ingenuities which characterize the Variations, one deserves special mention. While the theme, in its initial statement, derives from the *successive* unfolding of the original row and its three derivatives, in the Adagio section, shortly before the close of the work, it appears *simultaneously* in all the four forms of the row:

Ex. 158

The Variations were Schoenberg's first full-scale orchestral work in serial technique, and the comic *Von Heute auf Morgen* (From Today till Tomorrow) (1929) was his first twelve-note opera. It reflects the vogue for opera with a topical subject, such as Hindemith's *Neues vom Tage* and Křenek's *Jonny spielt auf*; and the composer also wanted to prove that serial technique and a light-hearted vein of expression were not incompatible. The rather insipid libretto by Schoenberg's second wife Gertrud who concealed her identity behind the pseudonym 'Max Blonda', is a social satire illustrating the inconsistencies of modern matrimonial assumptions. There are five characters, one of whom, a child, is a speaking part. The opera is based on a single note-row that yields an infinite number of vocal themes of varying character—lyrical, arioso, and dramatic—which are handled with a considerable flexibility and lightness of touch, despite the fact that contrapuntal writing prevails. Thus, the quarrel duet between husband and wife is a canon, and to the final quartet the orchestra contributes two more parts so that the texture contains altogether six independent voices. Yet the instrumental style—the opera is scored for an orchestra of normal size but includes a large number of percussion instruments—is for the most part restrained and the audibility of the singers' words generally unimpaired. Apart from the Suite, Op. 29, the opera is the only work of Schoenberg's to make use of jazz elements.

The two Piano Pieces, Op. 33a and b (1929), show an advance on the style of Schoenberg's previous dodecaphonic piano music, in that they are more clear-cut in design and that his mastery of the new method now enabled him to solve similar problems in a more straightforward and more assured manner. Thus in the first piece the note-row is first stated in three initial chords, of four notes each, which are immediately answered by three chords (transposed inverted cancrizans), after which it unfolds in horizontal direction (transposed inverted cancrizans in treble and retrograde in bass)—an excellent example, within the shortest possible space, of the harmonic and melodic use of the twelve-note series:

Ex. 159

The last works Schoenberg wrote before his emigration to America in 1933 were *Begleitungsmusik zu einer Lichtspielszene* (Music to a Film Scene), Op. 34 (1930), which is an accompaniment to an imaginary film scene describing a mounting tension from imminent danger to fear and the final catastrophe; Six Unaccompanied Pieces, Op. 35, for men's chorus (1930), which are in a simpler contrapuntal style than his Opp. 27 and 28, and show a noticeable relaxation of the twelve-note rules, the last piece, 'Verbundenheit', even employing tonal triads; and the opera *Moses und Aron* (1932) whose completion occupied the composer during the last years of his life.

The first American composition was the Suite for Strings in G (1934), a mainly educational work written for the repertory of American school orchestras. This accounts for its being wholly tonal, though its contrapuntal writing would seem rather complex for a school work. Schoenberg's intermittent return to the tonal idiom in this and a few later compositions was at the time wrongly interpreted as a concession to American taste. Yet, apart from the fact that this assumption is amply disproved by other 'American' works in strict serial technique, Schoenberg gave it as his opinion that there was 'still a lot of good music to be written in C major' and in an article, 'On revient toujours',[1] he confessed that the wish to return to his earlier style remained constantly with him and that was 'how and why I sometimes write tonal music'.

The series of important works written during his last period began with the Violin Concerto, Op. 36 (1936), which was his first work in concerto form and obliged him to consider the, for him, novel problem of opposing a single instrument against a full orchestra. 'Opposing' here is perhaps not the right term, since soloist and orchestra are close collaborators, both being equal partners in the elaboration and development of the thematic material. It is, however, a measure of Schoenberg's skill that the work is both a symphonic concerto, in which even the most negligible figure is derived from the original row, and a virtuoso piece of the most exacting brilliance, the difficulties of the solo part being indeed so tremendous that the composer declared in jest that it needed a player 'with a sixth finger'—enormous intervallic jumps, triple and quadruple stops, double-stop harmonics, left-hand pizzicato and exploitation of extreme registers. Yet, even more than in the violin concertos of Beethoven and Brahms, the virtuoso element serves to throw the musical ideas into sharpest relief. An important feature of the general style is the prevalence of chromatic formations in the solo part, heralded in the first statement of the principal theme where the violin plays the semitones of the basic row melodically while the orchestra presents the rest of the series in chords:

[1] Reprinted in *Style and Idea* (New York, 1950), p. 211.

Ex. 160

The work, corresponding more or less to the classical concerto form, consists of a sonata Allegro, a ternary slow movement and march-like finale in rondo form, with a clear-cut and easily recognizable structure in every one of the movements. The extraordinary formal mastery of the work is matched by a rich flow of melodic invention of an intensely romantic kind, which reaches in the first two movements a rare degree of passionate intensity.

Compared with the Third String Quartet, the Fourth (written concurrently with the Violin Concerto) marks a great advance towards truly classical principles: the shape of themes is more clear-cut and sinewy, the rhythmic patterns have become more regular, and the texture shows an increased equilibrium between homophonic and contrapuntal writing:

Fx. 161

which stands in marked contrast to some works of Schoenberg's earlier style, where the impression of a polyphonic surfeit, of contrapuntal complexity for its own sake, cannot be resisted. In the Fourth Quartet there does not seem a note too many, everything falls into place; and, if the Third Quartet frequently revealed a subservience of the imagination to the twelve-note method, the later work shows absolute freedom in the way the composer bends his technical means entirely to expressive purposes. In the period following the Fourth String Quartet Schoenberg wrote a number of works, some frankly tonal, while in others the underlying note-row is so invented as to imply quasi-tonal formations. To the first group belong the *Kol Nidre*, Op. 39, for speaker, mixed chorus, and orchestra (1938), written for a Jewish organization and intended for performance on the eve of the Day of Atonement. The work is in G minor and makes use of part of the traditional *Kol Nidre* melody, which seems to be of Spanish-Moorish origin. The Chamber Symphony, no. 2, Op. 38, which was begun in 1906, at the time of the composition of the Chamber Symphony, no. 1, Op. 9, preserves its original tonal language—it is in E flat major—but the use of mirror forms, especially in the second movement, is to be traced back to the influence of the later twelve-note method. Similar in style are the Variations on a Recitative for organ, Op. 40, (1941) and Theme and Variations for Wind Orchestra, Op. 43 (1943), the first of which is written in a greatly extended D minor and the second in G minor, though intense chromaticism tends in each case to weaken the gravitational pull of the tonic.

In the second group, written in the twelve-note method, a vague and intermittent tonal feeling is perceptible—the *Ode for Napoleon*, Op. 41, for speaker, string quartet, and piano, and the Piano Concerto, op. 42 (both 1942). The *Ode* is a setting of Byron's poem written after Napoleon's abdication at Fontainebleau on 13 April 1814. It is a poem against tyranny, a passionate accusation not only of the French Emperor but of any kind of political dictatorship, containing also a wealth of historical allusions mingled with passages of mordant irony. Byron's anticipation of the advent of modern dictators lends his verses a burning actuality and it was this that prompted Schoenberg to set them to music. The work is marked by an extraordinarily violent and explosive quality, largely engendered by the prevalence of broken rhythmic patterns and by a percussive piano part which is set against short and sharply defined melodic lines on the four strings. The speaking part, in contrast to that of *Pierrot lunaire* of thirty years before, is notated on a single line giving only the rhythm at which it is to be declaimed. Despite the fact that the work falls into a number of contrasting sections, some of which are in a meditative vein, the dramatic breadth and atmosphere are well sustained. The note-row on which the work is based permits tonal chords and cadences, and the close is in a clear E flat major. Similar in character is the note-row of the Piano Concerto, containing oblique references to tonal chords and tonalities as, for instance, in the finale where the F sharp major at the beginning is opposed by the C major at the end. As in the Violin Concerto, Schoenberg skilfully solves the problem of integrating soloist and orchestra and for all the virtuoso treatment—arpeggios, wide leaps, octaves, and full chords—the piano shares the elaboration of the thematic material with the orchestra. To the Piano Concerto the composer applied the cyclic one-movement form of the Chamber Symphony, no. 1, the work consisting of four short and linked sections—an Andante which oscillates between a dream-like Viennese *Ländler* and a *siciliano*; a vigorous and, often, stormy Allegro molto; an Adagio representing the emotional climax of the work, whose ghost-like, sinister-sounding effects, after an initial section for orchestra alone, grow increasingly agitated and menacing; and a Giocoso in rondo form which completely belies the mood of the preceding section by its gay, unbuttoned character. Schoenberg, in a note found in the sketches to the Concerto, revealed something of its emotional content writing that 'life was so easy (*Andante*)—suddenly hatred broke out (*Allegro molto*)—a grave situation was created (*Adagio*)—but life goes on (*Rondo*)'.

The String Trio, Op 45 (1946), was written after an almost fatal illness and it reflects the various states of mind the composer experienced during this illness, seeming to spring from an acute awareness of the no-man's-land dividing life from death; it belongs to his most intense and most imaginative compositions opening up a world of vision entirely *sui generis*. Anxiety, agony and existential sadness, prompted by the utter solitude of man *in extremis*, mingle with a retrospect into a happy past. The work falls into three main parts and two linking episodes, of which the first and last parts convey a dark, oppressive and eschatological mood while the middle part is in a serene vein. The tone colour of what is essentially a monochrome medium shows a surprisingly wide range achieved by the use of extreme registers and by an exploitation of special effects, such as harmonics, tremolando, pizzicato, *sul ponticello*, and bowed and struck *col legno*; in addition, there are sudden contrasts of extreme dynamics.

A Survivor from Warsaw, Op. 46, for speaker, men's chorus, and orchestra (1947), the text of which is Schoenberg's own, is based on an account of a young Jew who had escaped from the atrocious battle in the Warsaw Ghetto in 1944. The composer, who had previously given eloquent expression to his Judaism in *Die Jakobsleiter, Moses und Aron* and the *Kol Nidre*, here interprets the heroic fight of the Polish Jews against their exterminators. The music has an extraordinarily disturbing effect, mounting in tension until the climax is reached, in the last pages, in the unison chorus singing the ancient Hebrew prayer, *Shema Ysrael*, the only section of the work which is sung and which achieves the effect of an emotional catharsis of remarkable power. The speaker, whose part is notated, as in the *Ode for Napoleon*, on a single line occupies four-fifths of the work. The style of the work is athematic in the sense that, except for an initial four-note motive recurring several times and an early anticipation of the theme of the Jewish prayer (horn, bars 18–21), the music unfolds in a succession of fresh thematic material of a lapidary character. The fact, however, that these various ideas derive from the basic row and its variants, is the measure of the extent to which Schoenberg developed his principle of perpetual variation.

Schoenberg's long preoccupation and increasing interest in the spirit and the ideals of Judaism and, beyond that, in religious and philosophical thought in general, began during the First World War, when he conceived the unfinished oratorio, *Die Jakobsleiter* (1915–17). This was followed in 1927 by a prose-play, *Der Biblische Weg*, the action of which centres on a young Jew who wants to found a new theocratic Israel in Africa. This play is to be taken as a preliminary study for the three-act opera, *Moses und Aron*, in that two chief characters of the latter work show traits which the hero of the play combines in his person. The first ideas for what was to be Schoenberg's last work occurred to him as early as 1923, but it was not until seven years later that he began the composition, completing the first two acts (1930–2). Although throughout the following period it was his firm intention to finish the last act the opera remained incomplete, with a sketch of only eight bars' length for the last act.

The libretto, which was Schoenberg's own and is complete, is largely based on the Book of Exodus—the calling of Moses, the revelation on Mount Sinai, the erection of the Golden Calf, and Moses's destruction of the Tablets, while between the first and second acts fall the intervening events of the massacre of the Egyptian armies, the exodus of the Israelites, and their wandering in the desert. Schoenberg interpreted these events in a manner which transcends their biblical significance and reaches far into the sphere of pure spirituality. His fundamental theme is the conflict between the characters of Moses and Aaron, a conflict already hinted at in the Old Testament: pure thought versus image, idea versus its verbal expression, the Kantian thing-in-itself versus its appearance, the abstract versus the concrete, silence versus communication, the spiritual versus the material, the numinous and unimaginable versus the visible and imaginable, reason versus instinct and emotion. In the centre of the drama stand Moses (modelled in appearance on Michelangelo's statue), who is the mouthpiece of the spirit and the law of the one God, and Aaron, the glib exponent and perverter of Moses's God-inspired message, who in his endeavour to bring this message down to the understanding of the people resorts to miracles, magic and demagogy. When Aaron asks: 'People, chosen by the one God, can you have what you cannot imagine?', Moses replies: 'No image can give you an image of the unimaginable'—an interchange which early in the opera already defines the diametrically opposed views of the two characters. The second act ends with the apparent victory of Aaron who promises the Israelites to lead them into a land of milk and honey while Moses has lost confidence in his power to carry out God's will, though he continues in his unshaken belief in God as the eternal, infinite, and omnipresent noumenon free of all phenomenal attributes. In the last act Moses challenges Aaron and accuses him of distorting the true spirit of God. When at Moses's command he is set free, Aaron falls dead—pure thought has won over the image. The ultimate message of the opera is that real life can only be the life of the spirit, and that real freedom can only be achieved in seeking a mystical union with the Supreme Being.

Text, action and music form an indissoluble unity achieved by the projection of an all-determining and all-embracing idea, and in this respect *Moses und Aron* stands entirely apart from all other modern operas. Its character oscillates between scenic oratorio, with static solo and choral ensembles, and grand opera of a tense, dramatic kind, reaching its apogee in the scene of the dance round the Golden Calf of Act II—a barbaric orgy by turns ritual, sacrificial, sexual, and suicidal. The people of Israel are given a most active role to play in the drama, recalling the *turba* of the eighteenth-century Passion, and are shown as torn between piety and hatred, lethargy and fanaticism, devotion and fickleness. From the mass there emerges a group of a few representative figures—the Priest (bass), who is shrewdly conservative and clings to the old deities, and, opposed to him, three fanatic believers in Moses's one God—a girl (soprano) and two young men (tenor and baritone). The Supreme Being is symbolized, first, by six solo voices which open the opera with four hovering tensionless chords on the syllable 'O' that stand for the notion of God's eternity and infinity. When the six voices begin to intone the text, an orchestral theme occurs representing the notion of God as an articulate Will and Thought. These are the two central musical ideas of the opera which undergo the most ingenious transformation in the course of the work, the melodic and rhythmic metamorphoses of the second theme in the dance round the Golden Calf being particularly noteworthy. In addition, there is a third, vocal, theme of primary importance, which occurs in the early part of Act I and stands for God's promise to his chosen people:

Ex. 162

(This people is chosen to be the people of the one God.)

(Ex. 162 (i) opens with the first and last three notes of the original note-row (Ex. 163) telescoped into chords; (ii) uses the notes 4 to 9 of the row, and (iii) begins with the first six notes of the retrograde, followed by the first six notes of the original). It is significant that the role of Moses should be spoken (in strict musical rhythm) which is to be taken as symbolic, speech serving as the vehicle for pure thought. Aaron, however, is a lyrical tenor whose part is often marked by quasi-oriental melismata, and the fact that his is a singing character has an equally symbolic significance, for song is the expression of the emotional, the instinctive and the sensuous—cardinal traits in Aaron's personality. The entire opera is based on a single note-row:

Ex. 163

An interesting feature of the general use of the row is the fact that the further Aaron and the Israelites move away from Moses's idea of one God, the more tenuous becomes the row in relation to the themes and motives. The formal structure of the opera alternates between freely treated sections of recitative and arioso and more or less 'closed' forms: the opening scene, for instance, is a cantata and the dance round the Golden Calf a symphony for solo voices, chorus, and orchestra, consisting of five movements. The texture is predominantly contrapuntal, though polyphony is not made an end in itself but serves the dramatic action. Imitations, stretti and canon abound: the choral Hymn of Act I utilizes a *cantus firmus*; and the Interlude before Act II is a complex double fugue, with the parts sung, whispered, and rhythmically spoken. The orchestral forces employed are very large, with triple woodwind (four clarinets), piano, celesta, two mandolines, and a wide selection of percussion instruments whose most notable use occurs in the orgy of Act II.

Moses und Aron must be accounted as Schoenberg's greatest achievement, for the width and breadth of its musical vision are monumental, the stark grandeur of its conception is comparable with that of the Old Testament itself, and it possesses a spiritual profundity whose full import has not yet been compassed.[1]

ALBAN BERG AND ANTON WEBERN

Except for the general expressionist character of their music and the adoption of the twelve-note method, Schoenberg's two most eminent pupils have little in common. Anton Webern was an 'intensive', hermetic composer who aimed at the utmost concentration and compression of form and at texture of an atomistic nature. Berg, on the other hand, was an 'extensive', expansive musician applying himself, like Schoenberg, to larger forms and achieving, alone among the three composers, a texture in which the traditional equilibrium between homophony and polyphonic writing is on the whole preserved. Webern's stylistic development led to the most attenuated lyricism, with the emotive impulse subtilized and sublimated almost out of existence, while Berg's lyrical vein is ardent, nervous, sensuous, and feminine. Berg looks backwards to the romantic past and, in spite of his whole hearted adherence to the twelve-note method, he maintained a link with tonal music by using note-rows with tonal implications and by availing himself, more or less overtly, of the traditional means of sequence, repetition and formal correspondence.

[1] For a comprehensive discussion see Karl H. Wörner, *Gottesdienst und Magie* (Heidelberg, 1959; English edition, London, 1963).

The period of Berg's creative career with which this chapter is concerned opened with his first opera *Wozzeck* (1922). For a full appreciation of the reasons that prompted Berg to choose this subject (as also that of *Lulu*) it is necessary to recall that he possessed a very marked social conscience. His compassionate humanity made him most sensible of the injustices in the political and social systems of Austria under the Habsburg monarchy, and filled him with profound sympathy for the underprivileged. It was this trait in his moral character that was in the first place responsible for selecting the play *Woyzeck* by George Büchner (1813–37) as material for his opera. The play, based on a real incident, is a violent attack on German society and German political authority before 1848. The fate of the psychopathic soldier Wozzeck, who murders his mistress and finally commits suicide, illustrates Büchner's theory that the demoralization and dehumanization of the poor derives from the cruel injustices of their social environment. The action of the play unfolds in a series of twenty-seven self-contained, fragmentary, and loosely connected scenes, not unlike a modern 'screen story'. Out of these Berg constructed a three-act libretto consisting of fifteen scenes, five scenes to each act, and for reasons of dramatic economy and condensation omitted some of the original scenes and telescoped others into a single one. The result is a tense, close-knit, and extremely well balanced drama, with exposition (Act I), development (Act II) and catastrophe (Act III). Each scene forms not only a dramatic unity but also a musical unity, Berg employing 'closed' musical forms to achieve inner cohesion. Thus the music of the first act, designed to establish Wozzeck's relationship to the surrounding characters (the grotesque Captain, the crazy Doctor who carries out scientific experiments on him, Wozzeck's mistress Marie and so on) consists of five character pieces, Suite, Rhapsody, Military March and Lullaby, Passacaglia, and Rondo. The musical structure of the second act is a five-movement symphony, while the third act is built in the form of six 'inventions'—inventions on a theme, on a note, on a rhythm, on a six-note chord, a key and on a *perpetuo mobile* movement. *Wozzeck* is, for all its novel stylistic and technical features, essentially in the line of the Wagnerian-Straussian music drama, exploring and elucidating in masterly fashion the psychology of the various characters, enhancing the nightmare unreality of the action with consummate ingenuity and adding occasional naturalistic touches in the description of external phenomena, such as the croaking of the frogs in the pond and the ripples of water in the scene of Wozzeck's drowning. The general technical style of the music is that of 'free atonality', characteristic of Schoenberg's works of the period between 1908 and 1912, but it is punctuated by tonal, polytonal and whole-tone scale features, and for the *volkstümlich* portions such as Andres's hunting song and Marie's lullaby, Berg resorts to a symmetrical arrangement of melodic phrases and to harmonies of superimposed thirds and fourths which stand in marked contrast to the irregularly built periods and dissonant (diminished and augmented) intervals of the major part of the music. In the last orchestral Interlude (invention on a key), before scene 5, Act III, the composer steps out of his role as psychological interpreter and reflects the universal significance of Wozzeck's miserable life and death, in music which is in an unambiguous D minor. (This piece derives partly from a discarded symphony of 1912 which accounts for its strong affinity with Mahler's late style.) On the other hand, serial technique is foreshadowed in the passacaglia of scene 4, Act I, where a twelve-note theme constitutes the basis of twenty-one variations, Berg using the form of a passacaglia to symbolize the Doctor's fixed ideas, as indeed the choice of all musical forms in this opera was determined by the specific character of its individual scenes. *Wozzeck* employs for the first time Schoenberg's device of the *Sprechstimme*.

Berg's second and last opera *Lulu* (1935) owes its origin to the same compassion and sympathy for the social outcast as inspired *Wozzeck*; but the action is chiefly concerned with the war between the sexes and, besides, shows a considerable ambivalence in the psychological treatment of the chief character. Berg adapted the libretto from the two plays, *Erdgeist* and *Die Büchse der Pandora*, by Frank Wedekind (1864–1918), which combine erotic satanism with mordant social satire. Lulu, the heroine of both plays, is the personification of the untrammelled sexual instinct; every type of man is attracted to her, every man takes from her what she has to offer but in so doing they meet their own destruction. While Lulu destroys, she is herself destroyed, gradually sinking into the gutter, becoming a low prostitute and finally the victim of a sexual murder. Though Wedekind takes a cynical view of woman's sexual role, it is bourgeois society that he makes ultimately responsible for its emergence in demonic form.

There is, however, a strong discrepancy between the Lulu of the text, a cold, inhuman *femme fatale*, and the Lulu characterized in Berg's music through which she is made to appear as a creature of flesh and blood capable of great suffering. This has been considered a serious dramatic flaw of the opera[1] which is certainly true in terms of the libretto and Wedekind's plays. Yet it is precisely by his musical treatment that Berg turns Lulu into an *operatic* heroine and engages the spectator's sympathy for her.

In conflating the two plays into a three-act libretto Berg achieved the

[1] Cf. Donald Mitchell, 'The Character of Lulu,' *Music Review*, xv (1954), p. 268.

same compression and unification of the dramatic action as in *Wozzeck*. The attention is most strongly focused on Lulu and on the decisive stages of her rise on the social ladder and her gradual downfall to a common prostitute, but she hardly undergoes an inner, psychological development in the accepted sense. In *Wozzeck* Berg counteracted the loose, episodic sequence of its fifteen scenes by the imposition of self-contained instrumental forms; in *Lulu*, on the other hand, a closer dramatic nexus between its seven scenes is reflected in the more 'open' on-running character of the music, in which the vocal element predominates. The title-role is for coloratura soprano, and the opera contains a number of vocal forms such as aria and arioso, canzonetta, cavatina, duet, sextet, and hymn; there are also long stretches of sung recitative (almost completely absent from *Wozzeck*) and *Sprechstimme*. Dr. Schoen and his son Alwa, however, are associated with a sonata movement and a rondo respectively, their different psychology being suggested by the different formal pattern chosen for each. In some instances Berg also resorts to contrapuntal devices—a canon between Lulu and the painter and chorale variations in the scene with the prince (both in Act I). As in *Wozzeck*, yet to a larger extent, use is made of 'reminiscences' and leitmotives, including particular harmonies, orchestral combinations, and sonorities which add to the portrayal of characters and the changing atmosphere of the drama—chord clusters on the piano for the athlete, pentatonic progressions for the Countess Geschwitz, a nonet for woodwind for Schigolch, jazz for the theatre ambience, and a solo violin playing one of Wedekind's own lute songs for Casti Piani, which becomes the theme of the variations leading to the final scene of the opera. Moreover, as in *Wozzeck*, some of the music is based on a rhythmic ostinato, as in the *monoritmica* of the duet between Dr. Schoen and the painter (scene 2, Act I), which opens with the pattern:

Ex. 164

This rhythm dominates the murder of Lulu at the hands of Jack the Ripper in the last scene of the opera.

The scoring is for a large orchestra including a jazz band off-stage, complete with saxophone, sousaphone, and banjo.

By the time he wrote *Lulu* Berg had completely assimilated the dodecaphonic method, yet his handling of it was always highly individual. The work is based on a principal note-row, but by means of most

25

ingenious permutations he derives four other series from it. The chief series is:

Ex. 165

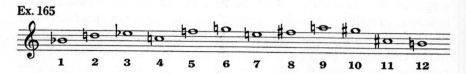

By continuous repetition of this series and by selecting from it the seventh note (not counting the first note) he arrived at the following note-row which provides the theme of Alwa's rondo:

Ex. 166

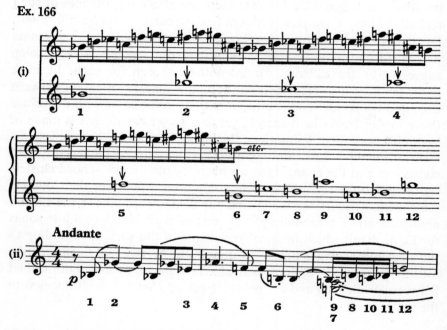

Continuous notation of the original series in which the distance between the selected notes increases and decreases at the ratio of, respectively, one, two, and three notes, etc. (again not counting the first note), yields this note-row from which emerges the energetic theme of Dr. Schoen's sonata movement:

Ex. 167

Berg left the orchestration of the final act unfinished but he had all but completed the music in short score. According to George Perle,[1] who had access to the manuscript, there are no more than twenty-two bars unfinished in the second scene of Act III, which is both musically and dramatically complete, including a full orchestration of the three fifths of scene 2 and about the same amount in scene 1. Perle found that the sections not complete in the orchestration contain no new material but are entirely based on material used in the previous two acts. Berg's intention was that the clients of Lulu in the final scene of the opera should be played by the same performers who enact her victims in Acts I and II — dramatic symbolism which is reinforced by the fact that the music of these corresponding roles is identical, except for notational differences. Moreover, in the *Lulu Symphony*, written to arouse interest in the opera and consisting of five numbers—Rondo, Ostinato, Lied of Lulu, Variations and Adagio—Berg had incorporated in its last two movements extracts from the Interlude and scene 2 of Act III. Perle argues with much justification that, despite Schoenberg's refusal in 1936 to complete the last act (for reasons entirely unconnected with the task in hand), the instrumentation of what was left in short score should not prove beyond the ability of a musician intimately conversant with Berg's late style and his technical methods.

Berg's Chamber Concerto for piano, violin, and thirteen wind instruments (1925) was written in celebration of Schoenberg's fiftieth anniversary and is the last of Berg's pre-dodecaphonic works. But the way in

[1] 'A Note on Act III of Lulu', *Perspectives of New Music* ii (1964), no. 2, p. 8. See also H. F. Redlich, *Alban Berg* (Vienna, 1957), p. 216.

which part of the melodic material is derived from an initial motto is very close to true twelve-note technique. The three different motives of which the motto is formed represent the musical letters in the names 'Arnold Schönberg', 'Anton Webern' and 'Alban Berg' and are the first indication that the number 'three' and multiples of it will determine a variety of formal, rhythmical and instrumental features of the work, in conformity with Berg's predilection for numerical correspondences. Thus the Chamber Concerto consists of three linked movements, each of which uses a different instrumental design: in the opening Theme and Five Variations, the piano is the solo instrument, in the Adagio, the violin, and in the Rondo ritmico, both instruments are combined with the accompanying wind ensemble. The writing for the two solo instruments displays a most brilliant exploitation of their expressive and technical possibilities, the virtuoso element reaching the highest pitch in the cadenza introduction for piano and violin to the last movement; while the interplay between soloists and orchestra is immensely varied and is ultimately governed by the concertante principle. Another noteworthy feature of the work is that the first two movements are brought together and amalgamated in the finale in a sonata rondo. Though the Concerto is an abstract composition, Berg's basic incentive was a programmatic one of an autobiographical character, namely to allow himself to be inspired by 'friendship, love and a world of human and spiritual references'.[1]

Berg's first essay in serial technique was his second setting of Theodor Storm's poem, *Schliesse mir die Augen beide* (1925), which he published together with his first setting of 1907, to indicate the distance he had travelled from a purely tonal style to twelve-note music. In the following *Lyric Suite* (1926) he applied the dodecaphonic method to several of its six movements, using in the first movement the same row as in his second Storm song, which was a so-called 'all-interval' series invented in 1924 by Berg's pupil, F. H. Klein. The second and fourth movements are in the free atonal manner of *Wozzeck* and the Chamber Concerto. In contrast to the Chamber Concerto, the *Lyric Suite* is loosely constructed and avoids all symphonic elaboration. Its rise in dramatic intensity, seen in the tempo indications and dynamic markings of the six successive movements, was responsible for its being called a 'latent opera'. With his love for subtle thematic relationships and correspondences between movements Berg employs a melodic fragment or motive from one movement in another. Thus, the second subject of the opening Allegretto (bars 23–25) returns in rhythmic and tempo variation in the first rondo episode of the following Andante amoroso (bars 16–23):

[1] Dedicatory letter to Schoenberg (9 February 1925).

Ex. 168

Similarly, the exposition of the fourth movement (Adagio appassionato) is anticipated in the principal theme of the Trio estatico of the preceding movement:

Ex. 169

The ground plan of the suite is analogous to an open fan: starting with the 'neutral' first movement (Allegretto gioviale), on one side are the third and fifth movements which grow increasingly faster (Allegro misterioso, Presto delirando), and on the other side are placed the second, fourth, and sixth movements which become increasingly slower (Andante amoroso, Adagio appassionato, Largo desolato), a procedure that serves to heighten the effect of contrast between the successive movements. Lyrical and dramatic elements thus alternate, enhancing each other and reaching their respective climaxes in the Adagio appassionato and the Presto delirando. A possible clue to the programmatic character of the work are the quotations, in the fourth movement, of a vocal phrase from the *Lyrical Symphony* (1923) of Alexander von Zemlinsky (to whom it is dedicated), and of the *Tristan* motive in the finale, to say nothing of the role played by Berg's symbolic figure '23' in the bar numbers of the work.

Berg's last completed composition was the Violin Concerto (1935), commissioned by the American violinist, Louis Krasner. At the start he was uncertain as to its general character and form until the death in April 1935 of the eighteen-year-old Manon Gropius, Alma Maria

Mahler's daughter by her second marriage, when he decided to write it as a kind of Requiem for the young girl, dedicating it to the 'Memory of an Angel'. In the event the concerto became Berg's own Requiem, since he died in December 1935, aged fifty. On the emotional level it stands as an eloquent testimony to the same compassion and humanity that inspired *Wozzeck* and *Lulu*. The formal organization displays a wealth of subtle correspondences between the four movements, and the virtuosic element is fully developed, reaching its acme in the third movement's accompanied cadenza for the solo violin. The tremendous technical difficulties of the cadenza are wholly subservient to the expressive ideas and are most ingeniously integrated with the demands of a symphonic concerto. The work may be taken as a symphonic poem, in the romantic tradition, whose 'programme' is the character of Manon, her tragic death and ultimate transfiguration, her specific symbol being the solo violin which accounts for the tender lyrical feeling that informs the major portion of the solo part.

The Concerto is based on a note-row so designed as to permit the employment of the violin's open strings (notes 1, 3, 5, 7). Furthermore, this row contains strong tonal implications, gratifying Berg's frequently declared wish to use serial technique without the listener being aware of it. The last four notes of the row form a whole-tone progression identical with the opening of the Bach chorale, Ex. 172(i), introduced in the finale. Although this identity was not intentional, it yet constitutes a poetic detail of the utmost emotional significance, implying that the idea of ultimate deliverance is present in the work from its very beginning:

Ex. 170

The work is in two parts each comprising two linked movements of which the first two conjure up the image of the girl's character—gentle and dreamy in the Andante, full of youthful vivacity and high spirits in the Allegretto; the latter movement is a scherzo with two trios in the second of which Berg introduces a Carinthian *Ländler* whose melody is perfectly integrated with the serial music. The second part consists of an Allegro and Adagio, the former being of a highly dramatic nature but interspersed with reminiscences from the genial Allegretto, and, as in *Wozzeck, Lulu,* and the *Lyric Suite,* Berg here resorts to a recurrent (dotted) rhythmic pattern, suggestive of Manon's inexorable fate:

Ex. 171

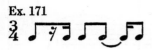

The mounting tension of the Allegro culminates in the catastrophe and the way in which afterwards the composer negotiates the link to the ensuing Adagio is a perfect example of his most subtle art of gradual transition: the first nine notes of the tone-row are telescoped into an orchestral chord while its three remaining notes are thrown up as a melodic figure played by the violin and the orchestra in octaves; this pattern is repeated five times with ever-lessening force creating the effect of a gradual collapse: on each repetition the orchestral chord is reduced by one note while at the same time the violin starts a whole-tone motive growing from one note to four, which reveals itself as an anticipation of the opening phrase of the chorale, 'Es ist genug', from Bach's sixtieth church cantata, *O Ewigkeit, du Donnerwort*. This chorale, already boldly harmonized by Bach in A major, Berg transposes a semitone up since his finale is in the freely handled tonality of B flat:

Ex. 172

(It is enough! Lord, if it please Thee.)

With the entry of the chorale Berg moves away from the torn, fragmentary texture of the preceding movement to tonally more anchored writing—another symbol—and thus achieves a reconciliation between the twelve-note method and traditional music. At the opening statement the chorale melody is accompanied in the middle part by a partial canon (Ex. 172(ii)), and, in the bass, by the note-row (transposed to F sharp) whose last note E is sounded by the chorale. The whole passage is an example of Berg's close textural thinking. In the orchestral segments of the chorale Berg adheres strictly to Bach's original harmonization. There follow two variations, both of which use an abbreviated version of the chorale; the second variation is punctuated by pointed references to the Carinthian *Ländler*. The coda, ending like Mahler's 'Abschied' in *Das Lied von der Erde* with the chord of the added sixth, employs the chorale melody shortened still further, and concludes with three repeats of the sad final 'Es ist genug!'.

Anton Webern's art is the complete antithesis of Berg's, a *multum in parvo* achieved by the utmost concentration of the musical thought and, springing from it, of projection and technical means. Webern, in fact, shows a striking affinity with certain contemporary painters, notably with Paul Klee, in the atomistic nature of his style and the severity of his vision, and he represents the most radical aspect of Schoenberg's art. With him the disintegration of melody, harmony, rhythm, and tone colour and the abolition of the difference between the horizontal and the vertical are carried as far as was then thought possible. If Webern's name is nowadays frequently juxtaposed with that of Debussy, it is because Debussy may be said to have started this process of the dissociation of the constituent elements of music.

Already Webern's early, pre-dodecaphonic works show features characteristic of his mature style—an extremely sparse texture, a pointillistic technique, the employment of silence as a principle of musical construction, a marked predilection for canonic writing (the most rigorous of the contrapuntal disciplines), and a prevalence of low dynamics which at one time earned Webern the description 'the composer of the *pianissimo espressivo*'. If, in addition, these early compositions were characterized by the utmost brevity of form and laconic utterance, this was largely due to the fact that they were in the 'free atonal' style, with its lack of any means of large-scale structure. With the adoption of Schoenberg's twelve-note method, which provided this means, Webern was enabled to tackle more extensive forms, such as sonata and variation; but the tendency to extreme compression persisted, the thematic material remained aphoristic and the fabric of his music tenuous in the extreme. In fact, Webern's essential manner scarcely changed after adopting dodecaphonic technique, which was to him a new tool for achieving structural organization and coherence but affected the character of his music very little.

Webern first used serial technique in three vocal compositions— *Drei Geistliche Volkslieder*, Op. 17, for voice, clarinet, bass clarinet, and violin (1924), *Drei Lieder*, Op. 18, for voice, E flat clarinet, and guitar (1925), and *Zwei Lieder*, Op. 19, for mixed chorus and five solo instruments (1926). If the employment of the serial method is here rather simple and even tentative, the texture on the other hand displays great contrapuntal complexity, voice and instruments forming an extremely close-knit ensemble. What is entirely novel, however, is the vocal treatment, Webern translating the phonetic tension of the words into musical, intervallic, tension; in other words, the mere verbal sound is transformed into an element of musical *structure*, a device which was to be raised to a principle in certain works of Boulez, Stockhausen, and Nono. See for instance these two examples, the first from *Drei Lieder*, Op. 18, no. 1, the second from *Zwei Lieder*, Op. 19, no. 1:

Ex. 173

(i) **Sehr ruhig**

Grünt der Ros - ma-rin,___ grünt der Myr-ten-strauss und der

Na - gerl-stock blüht im Haus

(The rosemary flourishes, the myrtle flourishes, and the carnations flower in the house.)

(ii) **Lebhaft, leicht und frei**

S.

So

A. So früh – zei-ti-ge Nar-zis - sen blü – hen

T. So___ früh-zei -

B. So früh – zei-ti-ge Nar -

früh – – zei-ti-ge Nar-zis - sen blü – hen

rei – hen-weis im Gar - ten.

- ti-ge Nar – zis - sen blü-hen rei – hen –

- zis-sen blü-hen rei-hen-weis im Gar - ten.

(So the early narcissi bloom in rows in the garden.)

The String Trio, op. 20 (1927), was Webern's first instrumental work in serial technique and marks a departure from his previous free formal writing in that it applies strict classical forms—rondo in the first movement and sonata in the second of its two movements; the latter even contains a double-bar and a repeat of the exposition, though the recapitulation is extremely well camouflaged. In the Trio it is no longer possible to discern with any clarity the individual movement of the three parts; the ear perceives, instead, a fluidum in which the musical ideas run freely from one voice to the other, grouping and regrouping, merging and disintegrating, an effect which is enhanced by the wide crossings of the parts, by the alternation of arco and pizzicato and by the introduction of numerous rests apparently interrupting the flow of the melodic line but actually used as part of its rhythmic structure and as important as the tangible, audible sound itself. The Trio marks a point of departure in Webern's style. In the Symphony, Op. 21, for nine solo instruments (clarinet, bass clarinet, two horns, harp, two violins, viola, and cello) (1928) the composer is seen to advance further in the direction of what may be defined as the use of structure *per se*, as a Kantian thing-in-itself, no longer serving conscious emotional expression but generating 'feeling' as an incidental by-product; expression thus becomes a function of construction. Moreover, minute atom-like motives in a seemingly kaleidoscopic arrangement take the place of extended thematic configurations. This method, novel in both technical and aesthetic respects, demonstrated the distance which increasingly separated Webern from Schoenberg and Berg for both of whom the *espressivo* remained a cardinal principle. Thus Webern unwittingly paved the way for the 'geometrical' construction and electronic music of the next generation of composers.

The note-row on which the Symphony is based shows a special feature: like the series used by Berg for the opening movement of his *Lyric Suite*, its second half represents the transposed *cancrizans* of the first half so that the original row is identical with its retrograde:

Ex. 174

Such structuring of the row by means of contrapuntal devices (see also Exs. 177 and 179) was highly characteristic of Webern's serial thinking which was in marked contrast to Berg's whose rows are more 'normal', less close-knit and who was also intent on evoking quasi-tonal associations through their intervallic disposition. There is, moreover, a pronounced difference between the two composers in the way they exploit their series. While the 'expansive' Berg sought to enlarge the thematic possibilities of a row by deriving from it new rows, as in several movements of the *Lyric Suite* and in *Lulu*, the 'thrifty' Webern kept strictly to the same row and even reduced its yield as a thematic reservoir by constructing some of his series in segments which represent inversions and/or retrogrades and/or transpositions of an initial motive of six, four, or three notes. On the other hand, this contrapuntal compression results in storing up kinetic energy in the row, an energy which is then discharged in the composition. In Webern's hand the series takes on a dynamic quality. It is, incidentally, probable that his marked preoccupation with the 'automatic' devices of counterpoint, notably canon, was nurtured by his intimate knowledge of Renaissance music and his editorial work on Heinrich Isaac. Indeed, from Op. 21 onwards (if not already from Op. 15) the technical models of vocal polyphony of the fifteenth and sixteenth centuries begin to emerge in Webern's output with increasing clarity leading to the masterly four-part chorale of his Second Cantata, Op. 31.[1]

In constructing for the Symphony a series (Ex. 174) which has no independent retrograde, Webern deprived himself of half of its thematic

[1] See Walter Kolneder, *Anton Webern. Einführung in Werk und Stil* (Rodenkirchen, 1961; English edition, 1968), p. 160; Eng. ed., p. 177.

possibilities; it was precisely for this reason—'the somewhat mathematical form of this series'—that Berg, in the *Lyric Suite*, altered the original row for the third, fifth, and sixth movements. But Webern's deliberate reduction of the thematic potential of his series is compensated for by the ingenuity of his contrapuntal treatment and the particular structure of the series is reflected in the frequency with which crab canons occur throughout the work. Its scoring provides an instructive example of a *Klangfarbenmelodie*, i.e. a melodic line in which individual notes or groups of notes are distributed over a variety of different instruments—a device originating in the third of Schoenberg's *Five Orchestral Pieces*, Op. 16 and perfected by Webern. Here is the opening of the first movement:

Ex. 175

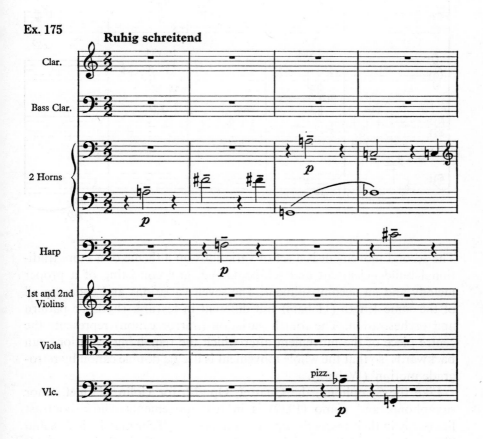

The second movement is a set of variations on a theme of a more traditional build—clear-cut and self-contained, and consisting of a proper
melody and an accompaniment. The seven variations and coda are all
of the same length (11 bars) but different in texture, rhythmic pattern
and orchestration. The fourth variation (mirror canon) represents the
centre piece of the movement after which the remaining variations run
backwards 'so that the whole movement is itself a double canon by retrograde motion' (Webern).

Like the Symphony, the Quartet, Op. 22, for violin, clarinet, tenor
saxophone, and piano (1930) is in two movements whose contrast
lies partly in their respective speeds and metres—'Sehr mässig' in 3/8 and
'Sehr schwungvoll' in (mainly) 1/2 time—and partly in their texture. It
is the only work of Webern's to show, in its particular combination and
the syncopated rhythm of the first movement, an influence of jazz. This

contrasts with Berg who employed jazz elements more extensively in the
concert aria *Der Wein* (1929) and in parts of *Lulu*. There is scarcely any
suggestion in it of a preferential treatment of one or the other instrument
—on the contrary, they are all handled alike and their individual timbre
is merely exploited to throw a given part into relief. The second movement,
more loosely woven than the first, provides a particularly good example
of Webern's predilection for microscopic motives of one, two and three
notes.

The *Drei Gesänge*, Op. 23 (1934), and *Drei Lieder*, Op. 25 (1935), for
voice and piano are settings of Webern's favourite contemporary Austrian
poet, Hildegard Jone, and show that the vocal medium made the composer to some extent relax the extreme application of his pointillist
method in favour of a more sustained, more markedly lyrical writing,
though the wide leaps and occasional rests in the voice part point to the
characteristic fingerprints of his instrumental style:

Ex. 176

es fühlt ihn an dem dunk-len Wur - zel - reich,   das an die To-ten rührt.

([The heart] feels [the spring] in the realm of dark roots which touches the dead.)

The two song cycles may be said to represent preliminary studies for the
Cantatas Opp. 29 and 31.

The Concerto, Op. 24 (1934), for flute, oboe, clarinet, horn, trumpet,
trombone, violin, viola, and piano, written in celebration of Schoenberg's sixtieth birthday, was originally to have been a solo concerto
for piano and eight instruments. A trace of this initial scheme is to be
seen in the continuity of the piano part which is the cement holding
the other parts together. The series on which the work is based, shows a
still closer inner relationship than that of Op. 21. It is built of a three-note
motive, its retrograde inversion, its retrograde and its inversion which is
like a blueprint for the structure of the Concerto as a whole:

Ex. 177

A comparison with the theme of Schoenberg's Variations for Orchestra, Op. 31 (Ex. 157(ii)), in which each of the four serial forms is stated in full (4 x 12 notes) shows the extent to which Webern carried the concentration of his serial thought. Writing about this row to Hildegarde Jone,[1] he compared it with the Latin tag:

SATOR
AREPO
TENET
OPERA
ROTAS

in which the third word is a palindrome and all the five words, read backwards and up and down, form the sentence 'Sower Arepo controls the work' and its inversion 'The work controls sower Arepo'. Just as Ex. 177 constitutes a micro-variation on the initial three-note motive, so does the whole Concerto represent a macro-variation in three movements of that motive. It is the most complete realization of Schoenberg's concept of total unity. All musical happenings spring from a single germ-cell producing an organism which Webern was fond of likening to Goethe's *Urpflanze* or primeval plant—'the root is . . . no different from the stalk, the stalk no different from the leaf, the leaf no different from the flower: variations of the same idea'.[2] The work is written in *concertante* style which is the corollary of the use of nine solo instruments. The music is thin and clear, extremely supple and sensitive. It was, significantly, from the Concerto that the concept of total serialization, i.e. the serial predetermination of all musical parameters, arose in the Germany of the early 1950s.

The Piano Variations, Op. 27 (1936), is Webern's only work for piano solo. A paramount feature of it lies in the fact that the composer, in contrast to the variation movement of his Symphony, here—not unlike Stravinsky in the variations of his Concerto for Two Pianos—dispenses with a theme so called and that the variations are not demarcated, but merge into one another. Thus the first movement opens with what is already a variation, namely a statement in canon of the basic row (right hand) and its retrograde (left hand):

---

[1] 11 March 1931. See Webern, *Briefe an Hildegard Jone und Josef Humplik*, ed. Josef Polnauer (Vienna, 1959; Eng. ed., Bryn Mawr, 1967), p. 17.

[2] *idem*, *Wege zur neuen Musik*, ed. Willi Reich (Vienna, 1960; Eng. ed., Bryn Mawr, 1963), p. 56.

Ex. 178

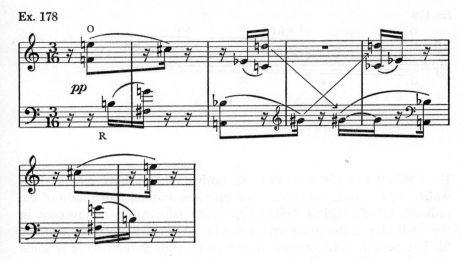

The second movement is similarly built and both movements recall, in their pianistic lay-out, a Brahmsian intermezzo. In the third movement of this 'Sonatina' (as Leibowitz calls it) Webern abandons contrapuntal texture in favour of a markedly homophonic writing and comes nearest to composing a 'theme and variations' in that he opens with the retrograde—the 'theme'—after which are deployed as 'variations' the four serial forms in various alternations and transpositions. Like the second movement of the Symphony, Op. 27 does not constitute *thematic* variations (in the sense practised by Beethoven and Brahms) but *contrapuntal* variations in which the series and its derivatives are unrolled in their totality either in combination (first two movements) or in succession (third movement). This treatment of the row as the sole generator of musical sense has been criticized as 'fetishism of the series'.[1] But this leaves out of account such aspects as figuration, dynamics, register, and accentuation which contribute to the musical sense—though in an admittedly lesser degree than structure—and which are subjected to 'real' variation in Op. 27.

The String Quartet, Op. 29 (1938), shows Webern's serial invention at its most concentrated. The basic row here consists of three four-note motives the first of which is formed of the musical letters in the name 'Bach', the second is its inversion or transposed retrograde and the third its transposition. In addition, the second half of the series represents the retrograde inversion of the first half:

---

[1] Theodor W. Adorno, *Philosophie der neuen Musik* (Tübingen, 1949), p. 74.

26

Ex. 179

Ex. 179 is the *ne plus ultra* in close motivic relationships, relationships which in *idea* are an identity, and it provides another illustration of the resemblance of a typical Webern row to the palindrome and inversion in the word play of the composer's Latin tag. As in virtually every work of his last period, strict canonic treatment prevails though there is some relaxation of it in the third movement. Webern's last instrumental composition was the Variations for orchestra, Op. 30 (1935), though its particular combination—flute, oboe, clarinet, bass clarinet, horn, trumpet, trombone, bass tuba, drum, celesta, harp, and strings—it, with the exception of the strings, used in a soloistic way and aspires to she nature of chamber music; it excels in the most delicate hues and ranges over a remarkably wide variety of tone colours. In Op. 30 the composer returns to the more traditional form of theme and variations such as he had used in the second movement of the Symphony. The theme is first alluded to in the introduction or 'Overture' and is stated in full in the first of the six variations which are clearly set off from one another by double-bars. The work shows an ingenious fusion of variation with sonata form.

Between the *Drei Lieder*, Op. 25, and the Piano Variations, Op. 27, Webern wrote *Das Augenlicht*, Op. 26, for mixed chorus and orchestra (1935), and he continued with his interest in the choral medium in the Cantata no. 1, Op. 29, for soprano, mixed chorus, and orchestra (1940), and the Cantata no. 2, Op. 31, for soprano and bass solo, mixed chorus, and orchestra (1943), the latter being his last and largest work which he compared to a *Missa brevis*. The texts of all three compositions are by Hildegard Jone and are mystical in character. As in the song cycles, Opp. 23 and 25, the vocal medium prompted him to apply his fragmentary style of writing with markedly less consistency and rigidity, treating the voices in a more sustained manner and aiming at a warmer, more lyrical mode of expression. Similarly, he returned again to a more or less clear distinction between horizontal and vertical thinking, as is shown in these examples from *Das Augenlicht*:

Ex. 180

(i)

(With as many stars as lighten the night.)

(ii)

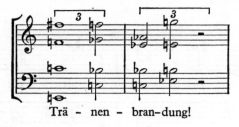

Trä - nen - bran–dung!

(O sea of vision, with the surf of tears!)

While Op. 26 is in one continuous movement, the Cantata no. 1 consists of three the second of which is for soprano solo. Its basic series is constructed like that of the String Quartet, with the same closeness of inner motivic relationships. The first entry of the chorus in the opening movement unfolds the four serial forms in a chordal texture, as indeed the whole of this setting is of a homophonic character. To counterbalance this, Webern conceived the final movement as a polyphonic piece, a four-part double fugue in which subject and countersubject are related to each other 'like antecedent and consequent in a period'. There is a wonderful flow and fluidity in the vocal counterpoint which avoids the creation of any recognizable centre of gravity:

Ex. 181

Sie - gel des Spek-trums ge - schmol - zen.

zum Sie - gel des Spek-trums ge - schmol - zen.

zum Sie - gel des Spek-trums ge - schmol - zen.

- der zum Sie - gel des Spek-trums ge-schmol - zen.

(and also the fainter image is melted as seal of the spectrum.)

In this fugue, as also in the finale of Op. 31, the voice parts are—an almost unique occurrence in Webern—doubled on the wind instruments. Op. 31 is in six markedly contrasted movements, part of this contrast lying in the choice of different vocal combinations for the individual movements. The music suggests that Webern was entering upon a phase of new simplicity. This is seen in the first place in the basic series which is a straightforward one, without any contrapuntal devices in its structure. Furthermore, the second, fourth, and sixth movements show a markedly lesser degree of textural density and the interplay between voices and instruments is almost completely free of complexities. Indeed, in the last movement there is no interplay at all, Webern doubling the four choral parts on the wind. The vocal score gives the impression that the chorus is unaccompanied, with the instruments cued in for use in rehearsal only. With its long note-values, though the tempo is very fluid, and the 'mensural' changes of the metre (2/2, 3/2 and 4/2), this movement recalls music by Heinrich Isaac whose *Choralis Constantinus* had been the subject of Webern's doctoral thesis in 1906. To all intents and purposes the finale of this Cantata *is* a chorale in the form of a four-part canon whose three verses are to be sung to the same 'tune'. Who could have foreseen that Webern would ultimately arrive at a *strophic* setting of a text?

What is the historical significance of the serial Webern? It is in the first place to be found in the almost total replacement of the romantic idea of music as a vehicle for emotional expression (Schoenberg and Berg) by the idea of music as pure sound construction, seen in his preoccupation with the contrapuntal structuring of a row and with the constructive quality of a single note and single interval which are subjected to perpetual variations in intensity, dynamics, accentuation and tone colour. With Webern the dissociation of melody, harmony, rhythm, and timbre is carried to its utmost limits, the corollary of which was the extreme fragmentation of texture. Moreover, Schoenberg's concept of the unity of the musical space finds in its most complete realization in Webern's abolition of the distinction between horizontal and vertical thinking, for his contrapuntal writing can also be interpreted as the linear projection of harmonies built from the series. Lastly, Webern reduced the means by which he exteriorized his inner vision to their essential minimum and thus achieved the highest possible degree of technical economy. In short, he drew the most radical, most uncompromising conclusions from Schoenberg's twelve-note method of composition and in so doing opened up a new vista for the succeeding generation of musicians who saw it in the serial predetermination of the totality of musical components, including pitch sequence, rhythm, duration, intensity, and method of playing. The real father-figure of the New Music of the post-Second-War period is not Schoenberg but Webern.

V

MUSIC OF THE EUROPEAN
MAINSTREAM: 1940–1960

By Peter Evans

In 1933 Anton Webern described the preceding quarter of a century's musical developments as 'an advance greater than has ever taken place before in the history of music'.[1] He was reviewing the achievement of twelve-note serial practice as the opening up of territory sought ever since music had been written, and he looked forward with confidence to the further exploration of this new world of musical order. So intrepid a reading of history demanded a visionary reading of the future, since historical significances are commonly assessed by what in fact achieves generally recognized validity; and the signs of Webern's times provided few obvious clues to a less prejudiced observer. Over three decades later we need less courage to point to significances in that period (and nowhere more certainly than in Webern's work) for these emerge in investigating our own, but of this itself little more than a record can yet be attempted. A chapter which deals with what is still present cannot indulge so freely the historian's privilege of viewing in perspective the store of knowledge: its concern must simply be with what has occupied more than parochial attention.

A simple chronological subdivision of the period 1940–60 would underline all the radical innovations in musical technique which distinguish its second decade; but this would tend unduly to obscure the continued activity of a generation already formed in earlier methods. A broad division may therefore be made between composers who, already mature before the war, lived and worked throughout this period or who achieved belated prominence during it (thus the last works of pioneers like Schoenberg, Webern, and Bartók have been discussed in a previous chapter, while Skalkottas and Valen appear here), and those of the generation which completed its apprenticeship after the war.

Of the century's earlier pioneers, Stravinsky and Hindemith demand further consideration, the former summing up in his own development

[1] *Der Weg zur neuen Musik*, ed. Willi Reich (Vienna, 1960), p. 17.

the momentous swing in the orientation of European music which may yet justify Webern's confidence. While note must also be taken of later works (for example, of Hindemith) which do not reflect a comparable change in a composer's practice, one phenomenon may be found to outweigh all others in a general survey of the middle generation—the emergence of serial method as no mere shibboleth, but as an attitude to musical material that might stimulate atrophied thought processes without taking toll of individuality. Political boycotting in Germany, and blankly uncomprehending or even virulently hostile notice elsewhere, had succeeded in bringing both the music and the ideas of Schoenberg and his pupils into almost general disrepute. Even when their music began to find more admirers, especially among composers, able to form judgements from the scores when performances were still rare, a variety of new critical positions was taken up: the works must succeed in spite of the underlying theories, or the theories could have no relevance to composers not reared in Schoenberg's Viennese environment. Yet the end of the war brought a new wave of interest in serialism that affected in varying degree composers of many countries and already versed in other styles. In Germany and Austria hostility to twelve-note music was identified with Nazi sympathies and this political circumstance gave the movement a powerful new impulse, seen most clearly in the policy of German radio stations.

These other styles, many of them related by some common factor of neo-classicism, were briefly sampled by a generation that had never known the allure they had once presented. Impatient of traditions that themselves involved historical counterfeiting in varying degrees, this new generation sought no more guidance from the past than would lead it towards an independent future The new serialism was founded on the one hand in Schoenberg's principle of regulation, as applied by Webern in his break with conventional conceptions of musical space and motion; and on the other in Messiaen's introduction to the European art of an exotic conception of musical time.

In 1940 the possibility of such a revival of serialism seemed remote; indeed it was hard to conceive of any artistic movement that could unite the talent of a continent in a common purpose. Few of the pre-eminent creative figures were able to remain in Europe, and with their emigration the focus of attention moved to America. It must be left to another chapter to chart the influences brought to bear on American music by the influx of so many of Europe's dominating composers; of reciprocal influences there are few signs. (Bartók's simplification of idiom had begun before he left Europe, though the diatonic limpidity of the Third Piano Concerto's slow movement may owe something to what

Stravinsky has called the 'Appalachian' style, and another Eastern European, Martinů, reflects this more directly in some of his symphonies.) Whether composers died in America, like Schoenberg and Bartók; chose to settle there, like Stravinsky and, much earlier, Varèse; or subsequently returned to Europe like Hindemith, their work contributes essentially to a unique European heritage.

IGOR STRAVINSKY AND THE RAPPROCHEMENT

It is clear enough that Stravinsky's changed environment hardly affected his idiosyncratic stylistic progress; indeed we may be tempted to think that his penetrating assessment of the European *avant-garde* and his characteristic opportunism with regard to its findings were helped by the perspective of distance. America did however affect his choice of media, as in his settings of English and his use of the jazz band (*Ebony Concerto*, 1945). And it is to the American reverence for the full orchestral symphony as the centre-piece of musical activity that we owe Stravinsky's two essays in this form.[1] Together with the Two-Piano Sonata (1943–4) and the Concerto in D for string orchestra (1946) they are stages in a last review of traditional form and texture that culminated in *The Rake's Progress*.

The tag 'neo-classical' is unavoidably prominent in any documentation of Stravinsky's career, yet beyond suggesting his dependence on initial stimulus from other music, it brings us little nearer an understanding of a crucial aspect of his activity. His symphonies demand not only the background of specific tradition, but a general historical awareness as extensive as his own. In both first movements the combination of simple repeated-quaver accompaniments and a persuasive motivic technique strikes a new balance between static and dynamic elements, and the use of classical progression divorced from classical timing produces an entirely personal articulation. Nominally recognizing the progressive schemes of sonata practice, the Symphony in C (1940), with brilliant irony, recaptures the rooted quality that characterizes so much Stravinsky. Its second group turns to the dominant, but adds a further section in the subdominant; the moral of this contradiction is rightly drawn by a move back to the tonic that renders the development merely ornamental. Stravinsky observes the traditional transposition of second group material on its (reversed) restatement, yet this in fact reinforces even more strongly the tonic.

> Exposition —B1 on dominant of V; B2 in IV (to I)
> Restatement—B2 in I (to V); B1 on dominant of I

[1] See Stravinsky's comments on the American commissioned symphony in Stravinsky and Craft, *Memories and Commentaries* (London, 1960), pp. 92–93.

This simultaneous acknowledgement and denial of classical precedent is stressed by hints of tonal instability in the *first* subject. By constant use of the non-committal third E–G in ambiguous harmony (avoidance of the root and use of the seventh B), Stravinsky is able to suggest E minor as an alternative meaning to the professed C major, even in the final bars of the movement, and it is on this delicate point that the apparently garrulous subject is able to hover for so long without tedium.

Ex. 182

The Symphony in Three Movements (1945) abandons this feline subtlety for harmony locked so tightly in contradiction as to provoke violent rhythmic convulsion; here the tonal plan of classical form no longer has even ironic relevance, yet the functions of development and truncated restatement are made far more vital. The material is powerful and varied, but only in the opening of the Andante is there that vein of affectionate reminiscence which can be traced throughout *The Rake's Progress* (1948–51). Whereas the symphony seeks to pursue the consequences of its pandiatonic language against a background of classical procedure, the opera places a series of classical statements in the foreground and deftly transfers them into the newer idiom. Thus, it might seem a more frivolous undertaking or, in the light of Stravinsky's subsequent work, a mere valedictory *divertissement*. Even though such a work would perhaps be a fitting monument to a public which has avidly cultivated a narrow tract of music's past to the detriment of the present, the number of specific models it brings to mind (with *Don Giovanni* prominent in Auden and Kallmann's moral tailpiece, and *Così* in the musical textures) would appear calculated impudence if Stravinsky carried us no further than the point of recognition. But his 'rare form of kleptomania'[1] is not a sentimental evocation doing duty for a personal expressive code. As a composer he does not discover the crux of what is to be expressed through any predetermined ideas, but rather discovers parallels of feeling in the course of working what may be an outmoded musical convention. The stylistic deviations prompted by these parallels are, in fact, the quintessential Stravinsky, so that it is irrelevant that the background of expressive convention may change from Bellini's to Mozart's; and the artificiality of the process is particularly appropriate to the 'framing' which has always characterized *opera buffa*.

Stravinsky's word-setting provides a simpler duality. Its apparently false accents are merely visual, for the vocal lines themselves move naturally and often show a fidelity to the inflexions of speech remarkable in one who came so late to the English language. Set against a fixed metrical accompaniment, they constantly diverge and converge in an accent-scheme whose freedom effaces what might have been stilted in the stylistic pastiche. The re-timing of conventional progressions further loosens the movement, but rarely leads to any disturbance of tonal unity within each set piece.[2]

---

[1] Stravinsky and Craft, op. cit., p. 110.

[2] See Robert Craft, 'Reflections on *The Rake's Progress*', *The Score*, ix (September, 1954), p. 24, for a study of the set-piece forms.

Ex. 183

In a fool — — ish dream, in a gloom — — y

La - by - rinth___ I_____ hunt - ed sha - dows,___ dis-

In Ex. 183 the vocal line finds its own accent-scheme from the words. The initial ambiguity of B flat and G minor persists in similar minor keys that rest on first inversions so as often to suggest majors. Having exploited the strangely exalted pathos of this device, Stravinsky finally reverts to the B flat pedal for a genuine major that has gained a transfigured clarity.

In his work on this opera, Stravinsky was assisted by a young American, Robert Craft,[1] widely versed in contemporary music, whose enthusiasms may have shortened the composer's route to serial procedure, charted with characteristic precision in the works that followed. Only a wisdom after the event notes signs of such a departure, inconceivable at the time, in some music of the forties: in the spare canon-by-inversion of the Two-Piano Sonata, or in the octave transpositions of the ten-note row (including repetitions) in the first Interlude of *Orpheus* (1947). The significance of the Mass (1948), one of Stravinsky's most accomplished works, is easier to sense than to define. In setting for liturgical use the text which, above all others, should resist the limiting effect of idiomatic cliché, he dispenses with his customary stimulus of familiar idiom. Despite broad parallels with plainsong and medieval polyphony, and incongruous echoes of his earlier work (*Benedictus*, cf. *Oedipus*), this score creates the impression of a fresh approach to simple elements of sound, a contemplation of chords and conjunct lines purged of both the furious rhythmic unrest of the *Rite* period and the automatic propulsion of pseudo-classical metre. From this attitude to Webern's contemplation of the interval and of silence may still be a long step, but it is not into an utterly foreign land.

Yet of the fundamental propositions of serialism there is no sign in

---

[1] See Robert Craft, 'A Personal Preface', *The Score*, xx (June, 1957), p. 7.

the Mass, and little of contrapuntal manipulation. The Cantata (1952) activates equally simple sounds by a ritual dance metre in the 'Lyke-Wake Dirge' verses; but the first Ricercar introduces strictly inverted canon, and the second interlocks in one line the four serial forms of a sinuous eleven-note phrase (tonal, and with many repetitions), then works out numerous possibilities of their canonic relationship.[1] Though he still uses free parts, Stravinsky is clearly able to order the total sound of an intricate polyphony by his choice of transposition and rhythmic shape. But instead of the serialist's dissolution of the row into the stream of the music, he deliberately stresses its melodic constriction and draws from this an ecstasy that reflects the text. In returning to instrumental textures with the Septet (1953), Stravinsky does not resist the lure of some well tried formulas in the sonata first movement; only the persistence of the opening motive and the complexity of the fugal development reveal his new concern for a basic unity of material. The other two movements share one sixteen-note series, still tonal though now exploiting a wide range of octave transpositions. As ground in the passacaglia it often supports an upper texture woven entirely of the same thread. The binary fugal gigue, inverted in the second half, repeats both expositions in double fugue: the simultaneous subjects deliver the identical series in different note-values. That such mastery of serial resource could be won two years after *The Rake's Progress* is remarkable enough; but that the Septet should also retain Stravinsky's unique sonority gave evidence that his rapprochement with serialism was no irresponsible gamble with fashion, but had a validity rich in consequences for music other than his own.

A variety of techniques, notably those of Bartók and Hindemith, have employed the twelve-note repertory as an enriched means of demonstrating relationships to centres of attraction. But the traditional relationships depended on scales of uneven steps, and their retention, in however elaborate a form, was inconsistent with a *fundamental* material of undifferentiated semitonal steps (and in neither Bartók nor Hindemith is this really implicit). While Schoenberg's recognition of the anomaly encouraged his adoption of the serial relations, Stravinsky chose to retain the old diatonic relations, but frequently to explore them in more than one orbit at a time. The critical hypothesis which treats the two men as poles in the music of their time[2] is supported by the results of these procedures. Whereas Schoenberg's endless revolution of the chromatic total produced a multiplicity of pseudo-leading-notes and

[1] See Colin Mason, 'Serial Procedures in the Ricercar II of Stravinsky's Cantata', *Tempo*, 61–2 (1962), p. 6.

[2] See Adorno, *Philosophie der neuen Musik* (Tübingen, 1948), and Francis Burt, 'An Antithesis', *The Score*, xviii and xix (1956–7).

therefore a sense of constant forward movement, Stravinsky's superimposed tonal pulls were often so mutually contradictory as to lead to
the suppression of classical flow and to construction from disjunct
and rhythmically autonomous segments. Despite relaxations from the
most extreme positions—Schoenberg's occasional use of petrified
rhythm[1] as well as his tonal tendencies; Stravinsky's use of 'neo-
classical' metrical accompaniment patterns—the search for common
ground was not actively encouraged while both men were alive.

In the pre-war years, the political climate of Germany and the
cultural climate of Europe in general rejected Schoenberg's school, while
an elegant imitation of the more superficial features of Stravinsky's
style was fashionable. When the stresses of war-time life led to a
widespread demand for release in artistic experience, audiences of
limited musical background found satisfaction in the classical orchestral
repertoire or such modern music as could be most easily related to it.
In these years, serial music was unknown to the public and confidently
written off by the critics. But, as Dallapiccola has pointed out, 'other
systems, having once fallen into disuse, have never reappeared, whereas
this one *did* reappear, and during the war years at that, in isolation and
in all countries independently'.[2] And a post-war generation of composers
concluded almost unanimously that the renewal they sought would set
out from serial principle, without necessarily retaining Schoenberg's
own fundamentally traditional rhetoric. Stravinsky's observation of this
phenomenon must have led to a profound analysis of the further
potentialities of his creative methods, and only the most cynical can fail
to see a decision of great moment and still greater courage in his
adoption of serial method after Schoenberg's death. In fact Stravinsky
brought at least as much to serialism as he borrowed. His curiously
oblique, though by no means careless recognition of tonal meanings, in
dodecaphony as in his earlier music, sounds an entirely different note
from Berg's yearning for tonal fulfilment. But even if the anti-tonal
implications of some of his works had been fully realized,[3] his typical
disjunct articulation and hypersensitive disposition of translucent
sonorities would have preserved the vividly personal character of his
music. The union of one of the most original creative minds and of the
most constructive thought in the music of this century led to some of
Stravinsky's most remarkable achievements; it also demonstrated a
catholic basis for the technique of composition, and this was to

[1] As Hans Keller has pointed out in the String Trio: see *The Score*, xx (June, 1957), p. 20.
[2] Luigi Dallapiccola, 'On the Twelve-note Road', *Music Survey*, iv (1951), p. 331.
[3] Stravinsky and Craft, *Memories and Commentaries*, p. 107, and see Ex. 187 from
Movements.

be welcomed in circumstances where bigoted partisanship had seemed the only alternative to despair.

Stravinsky's own progress to serialism was refreshingly free of such bigotry.[1] Far from accepting without examination the ultimate implications of constructive principles essayed in the Septet, he next explored the valuable tension set up between these principles and the promptings of a text. A simple example is provided in the first of the Shakespeare Songs (1953) where 'Musick to heare' is symbolized by revolutions of a C major scale fragment, absorbed through octave transpositions, instrumentation, and rhythmic irregularity into a texture elsewhere of the strictest serial observance. The row may be regarded as of twelve notes but is a network of inner relationships (see Ex. 184(i)), and the use of the four-note nucleus *y* as the basic compositional element is an obvious pointer to Stravinsky's study of Webern during these transitional years.

Ex. 184

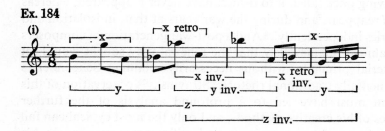

[1] Milton Babbitt, 'Remarks on the recent Stravinsky', *Perspectives of New Music* ii (2) (1964), p. 35, covers the period from the Cantata to *Movements*.

subito p

In his next work, *In Memoriam Dylan Thomas* (1954), the technical restriction against which a powerful expressive urge is pitted is a single series of five notes, retained throughout every strand of the song and of its surrounding dirge-canons (for quartets of trombones and strings). Though the concentration of such a *tour de force* is partially eased by Stravinsky's ritornello practice, the emotional concentration (the 'fierce tears' of Thomas's poem) is intensified; just as in earlier works, the crux of the feeling is discovered in the working-out of the musical material.

Webern wrote ambitiously of a large-scale work, to last half an hour even in its reduced form,[1] yet his loving research into such small musical cells never produced, even with the consummate mastery of his last period, a work exceeding half that time. So it is not surprising that Stravinsky abandoned the introspective methods of these miniatures in undertaking two larger compositions, the *Canticum Sacrum* (1955) and *Agon* (Contest) (1954–7). Not only did he enlarge the scale of his serial working by adopting at last the full twelve-note repertory, but in the very moment of recognizing resources associated with atonality, he chose also to reinvigorate his old pandiatonic style. The chronology of *Agon*[2] partly accounts for the juxtaposition, but in the *Canticum* the stylistic compatibility is deliberately and forcefully demonstrated:[3] the row manipulation of the middle movements yields clear tonal meanings, while the outer movements, at times even mono-modal, are united by one of the devices of serialism, strict retrogression. This crucial document in Stravinsky's development characteristically asserts present significance against a penetrating sense of the past. Conceived in honour

[1] In letters to Willi Reich concerning the Second Cantata, Op. 31; quoted in *Der Weg zur neuen Musik* (Vienna, 1960), pp. 69 and 72.

[2] Roman Vlad, *Strawinsky* (Turin, 1958; Eng. ed., London, 1960), p. 199; Eric Walter White, *Stravinsky, the Composer and his Works* (London, 1966), p. 450.

[3] Robert Craft, 'A Concert for Saint Mark', *The Score*, xviii (1956), p. 35; and Roberto Gerhard, 'Twelve-note technique in Stravinsky', *The Score*, xx (1957), p. 38.

of Venice's patron, Saint Mark, it draws on instrumental timbres that recall the Gabrielis, on *ricercare* and *cantus firmus* technique and on plainsong affinities hidden in its two rows. Conversely, the serial technique marks a notable step forward by harmonic compressions and linear exchanges, while a new polyrhythmic independence and a control of wide vocal intervals underline the debt to Webern.

Perhaps only in setting a sacred text can a spiritual unity be achieved that suspends disbelief in an ageless music. Certainly the piquant archaisms of *Agon* are intended to be savoured as such. Even more pointedly than the French overture which opened *Apollon*, these abstract dance movements re-create the stylizations of seventeenth-century *ballet de cour* without recourse to direct stylistic appropriation. Here the transition from the diatonic to the serial, achieved in slower stages yet in fact progressing further than in the *Canticum*, makes a fascinating summary of Stravinsky's serial artifice and its consequences for his concept of texture. The listener's impression is unified by the extreme originality of instrumental colour; sounds as arresting as the Prelude's flutes with double-bass harmonics over harp and timpani arpeggios, or the canonic opposition of acid mandoline and cloying harp in the Gaillarde, testify to an undimmed aural imagination, as empirical an arbiter in Stravinsky's serial as in his earlier music.

It is no involuntary surrender to the mechanics of a system, therefore, that gives to Stravinsky's first work on a single twelve-note row, *Threni* (Lamentations) (1957–58), its dark labyrinthine sound. A composer may choose to stress the obsessive character of strict row derivation,[1] and the smouldering gloom of Jeremiah's Lamentations is uncannily lit up in this way. Even the difficulty of the vocal writing, weaving tortuous lines without instrumental support, contributes a sense of strain which is an important part of Stravinsky's conception. (If an ability to pitch such lines precisely becomes general—and there are clear signs that this will happen—something will disappear from this work comparable perhaps to the tension lost in the change from the old natural horn to the modern instrument.) The Hebrew initial letters, retained from the original verse scheme in the Vulgate text, provide an obvious means of musical articulation but also an opportunity for a more detached, ornamental exercise of serial art. In the first movement, and 'Querimonia' section of the second, Stravinsky is content to let these beautiful sounds stand as entities (see Ex. 185(i)) or serially linked repetitions (Ex. 185 (ii)): but in 'Sensus spei', the central and most expansive section of the whole work, the eight Hebrew letters, containing twelve syllables, are equated

---

[1] Analytical studies by Hansjörg Pauli, *Tempo*, xlix (1958), p. 16, and by John S. Weissmann, *The Musical Quarterly*, xlv (1959), p. 104.

with the twelve notes, and these are sustained in turn as instrumental single or double pedals throughout the succeeding verses. The series is thus made a super-ordering such as we shall note in the music of the post-war generation, though one which is no secret formula but

Ex. 185

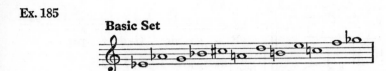

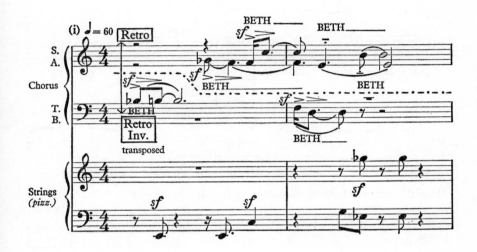

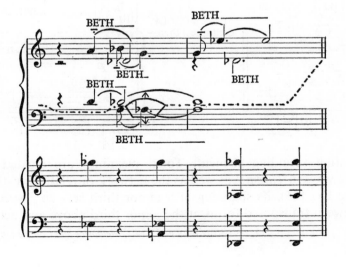

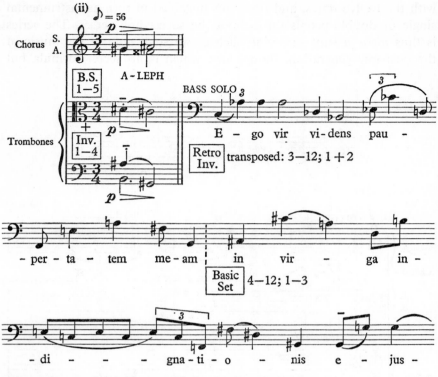

(I am the man that hath seen affliction by the rod of his wrath.)

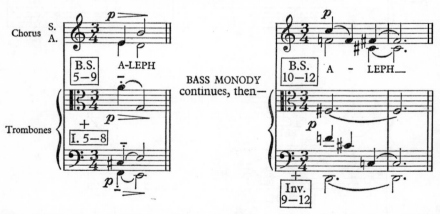

the dominating sounding element. Tonal meanings are created in innumerable ways in *Threni*:[1] as well as the network of relations within the row (see Ex. 185), its spanning of a minor third sets up a special relation between transposed forms at the minor third above and below

[1] Vlad, op. cit., Eng. ed., p. 215; also Stravinsky and Craft, *Memories and Commentaries*, p. 107.

and at the tritone. 'Querimonia' explores the rearrangement of row segments (e.g. 5–12+4–1; 3–1+12–4) and 'Solacium' reveals the simple intervals and scalic effect of two-note groupings preparing the way for genuine permutation technique (e.g. 12–10–8–6–4–2–1–3–5–7–9–11). The orchestral texture is sparse but incisive, and its conversion to Stravinskyan sonority of the *pointilliste* manner (Ex. 186) clearly foreshadows the next major work.

Even the cryptic and ambiguous title, *Movements* for piano and orchestra (1958–9), suggests some affinity with works like Stockhausen's *Gruppen* and *Zeitmasse*—though the title had already been used for the orthodox twelve-note textures of Fortner (cf. p. 413), Gilbert Amy's work is a more likely precedent for it—and Stravinsky's interest in the *avant-garde* is documented in the conversation volumes.[1] Its serial

Ex. 186

[1] Stravinsky and Craft, *Conversations*, pp. 125–33, and *Memories*, pp. 118–26.

(Remember, O Lord, what is come upon us.)

usages are intricate, often permuting the row, two hexachords of mirrored constitution. But its most significant advances towards territory pioneered by a far younger generation are in complexity and diversity of rhythmic shape (counterpointing freely the 'irrational' quintuple and septuple groupings; see Ex. 187) and in the avoidance of crystallized thematic material, though not of clear quasi-restatement correspondences. Chord formation, at the opposite extreme to wide-ranging monody in a constantly shifting textural balance remains peculiarly Stravinskyan, as does the orchestral sonority, despite a still more fragmented technique than in the previous works; and the scheme of dynamics has nothing to do with statistical distribution.

PAUL HINDEMITH AND THE GERMAN MIDDLE GENERATION

Stravinsky's cosmopolitan nature found America, like his other earlier refuges, a background to creative activity that could be accepted, even if it was with a kindly scepticism. It is typical of Hindemith that, while in America (1940–53) he associated himself enthusiastically with its musical

Ex. 187

activities and pedagogy, notably as a professor at Yale, he was eventually drawn back to a European environment. Some direct offshoots of his American years were the theoretical works[1] (developing skills on a lower level than in the *Unterweisung*), his high-minded *credo*,[2] and the English settings, especially of the Whitman Requiem,[3] a moving tribute to the dead of whatever nationality. The generally mild harmony of this work betokens no change of style, since Hindemith, after enlisting the support of natural law[4] for the simplification of idiom achieved in *Mathis*, seems to have had little difficulty in accepting his own arguments as eternal principles. If finer distinctions can be drawn, it might be held that works written for America, and especially for its symphony-concert audiences, make a more deliberate bid for popularity. How valuably this offset the ponderous textures of much late Hindemith

[1] *Elementary Training* (New York, 1946); *Traditional Harmony* I and II (New York, 1943 and 1948). For Hindemith's earlier music see Chapter IV, pp. 327–38.

[2] *A Composer's World* (1949–50 Charles Eliot Norton Lectures; New York, 1952). An important paragraph added to the German edition (Zürich, 1959) is translated in *Journal of Music Theory* (April, 1961), pp. 110–12. For some discussion of Hindemith's philosophical arguments, see Stuart Hampshire, *The Score*, vii (1952), pp. 58–62.

[3] *When lilacs last in the door-yard bloomed, a Requiem 'for those we love'* (1946).

[4] *Unterweisung im Tonsatz* (Mainz, 1937); translated as *The Craft of Musical Composition* (1942); its claims to natural law are investigated by Norman Cazden in 'Hindemith and Nature', *Music Review*, xv (1954), p. 288, Victor Landau, 'Hindemith the System Builder', *Music Review*, xxii (1961), p. 136, Richard Bobbitt, 'Hindemith's Twelve-Tone Scale', *Music Review*, xxvi (1965), p. 104 and A. Daniels, 'Hindemith's Contribution to Music Theory', *Journal of Music Theory*, ix (1965), p. 52.

is seen in the sparkle of the *Metamorphoses on themes of Weber* (1943) and the lucidity of the *Sinfonia Serena* (1946).

These symphonic works do not invite direct comparison with his orchestral music of the twenties, written in a concertante manner for adventurous groupings. Where comparison is inevitable, as between the early quartets and Nos. 5 and 6 (1943 and 1945), the later works disappoint by an unduly explicit tonal harmony, which constricts the old contrapuntal textures and encourages square-phrased forms. Favoured movement types—bulky march, lyrical pastorale, and so on—are as readily to hand as were the affective symbols of the Baroque composer.

The interludes of *Ludus Tonalis* (1942) provide a convenient summary of these, executed at a particularly high level of invention. Designed as a didactic parallel to *Das wohltemperierte Clavier*,[1] this is governed by an all-embracing tonal organization which rules the succession of the twelve keys[2] in a set of fugues according to their tonal distances from an initial point, charted by Hindemith's 'Series I'. But it is too uneasy a compromise between an archaic constructive principle and a personal hypothesis ever to approach either the topicality or the universality of its model, whatever the quality of its craftsmanship. Hindemith's mastery of contrapuntal device, rooted in the past, was perhaps intended as an object-lesson to the present: his mirror technique (the palindromic fugue in F, the totally inverted fugue in D flat, and the reversed and inverted relation of prelude and postlude) even embraces in the **B** flat fugue the four serial orders of the subject:

Ex. 188   **(Moderato scherzando)**

Piano

<hr />

[1] Heinrich Strobel, *Paul Hindemith* (Mainz, third edition, 1948), p. 127.

[2] See *supra*, p. 336. The fugue in D is recorded in *The History of Music in Sound*, x.

(S) = subject   (R) = subject in retrograde motion
(I) = subject inverted   (RI) = subject in retrograde inversion
(S.aug.) = subject augmented

Far from losing definitive form in the fluid, inextricable mesh characteristic of serial styles, they affirm tonality in a metrically patterned,
stratified texture. Movements of less subtlety, like the deft 5/8 fugue in
G or the beautifully spaced canon in B, are more persuasive testimony
to Hindemith's retention of his old imaginative powers.

A curious innovation of this period, and an antidote to the monotony
which may ensue when instrumental patterns are given their head, is the
freely rhapsodic setting of words in non-vocal contexts. Thus, in the
Two-Piano Sonata (1942) a recitative-like line declaims in piano tone
the medieval poem 'Wynter wakeneth al my care'. Other examples occur
in the 1949 Horn Concerto (to words by the composer) and in the ballet
score *Hérodiade*, a 'récitation orchestrale' after Mallarmé, 1944. In
another work used as a ballet, *The Four Temperaments* (1940), Hindemith's inventiveness takes a different form: the work consists of four
vast variations for piano and strings on a tripartite theme, preserved

with the fidelity of a *cantus firmus* throughout radical changes of tempo and rhythmic shape.[1]

The opera *Die Harmonie der Welt* (The Harmony of the World) (1956) dominates by sheer size Hindemith's output after his return to Europe. Though the orchestral movements (also playable as a symphony, as with *Mathis*) introduce some original and complex sonorities in representing the whirling of the spheres, the whole work, on the life of the astronomer Kepler, rarely recaptures the urgency with which Hindemith had once depicted Grünewald's artistic and moral crisis. Lyrical passages of great beauty and some powerful choral scenes are momentarily arresting, but nobility of purpose is not in itself sufficient to maintain an audience's expectancy through the longueurs of philosophical argument. This opera provides no evidence of radically new departures after some twenty years' reliance on the style expounded in *Mathis*; and Hindemith more strikingly affirmed his faith in that style by refashioning two operas that had symbolized earlier stages in his development, *Cardillac* (1926–1952) and *Neues vom Tage* (1929–53).

Modern opinion unanimously condemns the presumption of editors who rewrite the works in their charge, but the action of the composer who applies the lessons of maturity to the impetuosity of his own youth is almost equally debatable. Because it concerns what is perhaps Hindemith's most inspired work, the revision of the song cycle *Das Marienleben* (1923–48) has become a test case, too involved to be argued here.[2] Two short quotations (Ex. 189) from 'Rast auf der Flucht nach

Ex. 189

[1] William Hymanson, 'Hindemith's Variations', *Music Review*, xiii (1952), p. 20. The finale of the Octet (1957–8) provides a later example of this idiosyncratic variation technique.
[2] See Hindemith's introductory remarks to the new version (in English, 1953), and Rudolf Stephan, 'Hindemith's Marienleben (1922–48)', *Music Review*, xv (1954), p. 275.

(and now, on their grey mule, they endangered whole cities.)

Ägypten' show one context in which the composer's distrust of instinct has led to regulation according to principles developed later. Many changes have far-reaching effect on the structure, and several undeniably enhance the vocal flow, but only believers in absolute criteria of artistic effectiveness will applaud the transformation without hesitation; and performers have not relegated the old versions of the cycle, or of *Cardillac*, to the limbo which should logically be their fate.

Critical practice now reserves the term *Kapellmeistermusik* as a reproach, yet it represents a concept that has often justified itself. Only the regional structure of Germany's music has made possible her vast creative activity, an assured background of general competence from which the figure of pronounced originality or genius can emerge. Inevitably, few composers achieve this prominence, but new music needs the background also, of essentially derivative, second rank figures who, given sufficient stimulus, dilute or synthesize unfamiliar idioms. It was the misfortune of the German generation that came to maturity in the National Socialist period[1] that this stimulus was denied by the banning of twelve-note music and of Hindemith's works. No doubt the latter were more immediately attractive, with their mechanized counterpoint and ultimate subservience of dissonance to tonal gravitation, and Zillig has pointed out that it was an unacknowledged caricature of Hindemith's manner, pruned of its dissonance and therefore utterly vacuous in its contrapuntal bustle, which became the official Nazi style in those barren wastes of *Spielmusik* by composers better forgotten.[2]

For more adventurous minds the frustrations of aesthetic theories based on a dictator's whims[3] led to a crisis which could only be resolved in exile or in self-imposed silence. Křenek chose the first course, Hartmann the second, a courageous gesture of protest from a composer just reaching the height of his powers. His teacher, Anton Webern, had already withdrawn into an obscurity that was to outlast his life. The one progressive influence not officially proscribed, that of Stravinsky, was not encouraged by performances. And so with the end of the war and the disappearance of aesthetic dictatorship, the composers of a stunted generation reached out eagerly for all the sustenance that had been denied them. The later music of Hindemith, Stravinsky, and the Viennese School suddenly became a part of their artistic environment. By now there was a younger generation seeking a model, and its discovery of Webern is a phenomenon to be discussed later. For many of the pre-war generation however, total assimilation was harder, and the revelation served to reinvigorate a gift for cautious emulation or synthesis.

Carl Orff (b. 1895)[4] stands apart from these generalizations, for his

---

[1] A necessarily artificial but workable division is made between those composers born before 1910, who appear here, and the younger generation, discussed later.

[2] Winfried Zillig, *Variationen über neue Musik* (Munich, 1959), pp. 136 and 255.

[3] Zillig, op. cit., p. 134, on Hitler's judgement of Hindemith's Op. 38 Concerto. For an obituary devaluation of Hindemith's work, including an entirely conjectural argument that his stylistic modifications were intended to secure Nazi approval, see H. F. Redlich, 'Paul Hindemith—a re-assessment', *Music Review*, xxv (1964), p. 241.

[4] K. H. Wörner, 'Egk and Orff', *Music Review*, xiv (1953), p. 186, and Andreas Liess, *Carl Orff* (Zürich, 1955; Eng. ed., London, 1966).

individual style had finished with outside influences (mainly of the Stravinsky of *Les Noces*) by the mid-thirties. After the war his most notable advance was in the scope of his dramatic undertakings: the two operas on Hölderlin's translation of Sophocles, *Antigone* (1949) and *Oedipus* (1955), apply to larger spans the numbing reiterative technique of his immensely popular scenic cantatas. These hypnotic incantations of ancient languages or relentless probings of the primal dramatic situations codified in classical mythology have a fascination for the German that the outsider may find disturbing. Karl-Heinz Füssl claims that 'as personified wish-fulfilment of the Germans, Orff stands in Germany above all criticism'.[1] Certainly, his prodigious sense of musical theatre, which can dispense with all intricacy of purely musical development, convinces audiences not particularly inclined towards contemporary idioms that they have satisfied their responsibilities in this matter. Orff's place in the larger musical world is won by his controversial but stimulating *Schulwerk* (an educational method, revised 1950-4) and his early use of the large array of percussion instruments favoured by the new serialist composers.

Werner Egk (b. 1901), like Orff a Bavarian and by temperament a composer for the stage, has a more orthodox technique with a veneer of self-consciously French sophistication. This is most evident in scoring of an elegance unusual in Germany, but he does not consistently reveal the harmonic sensibility which should accompany it. A typical orchestral work, the *Variations on a Caribbean Theme* (1960), ranges from Gallic flute arabesques to the local colour of bongos, congas, and tom-toms, but both remain excrescences in a vulgarized Hindemithian texture whose moments of aspiration are nearer Hollywood. Such uncertainty of level is far less apparent in his operas, and his ability to find a simple but engaging formula for each dramatic situation brought widespread success to *Der Revisor* (after Gogol's *Government Inspector*). Though he has never achieved quite the degree of Orff's popular success, the genial and picturesque qualities of his early *Zaubergeige* commended him to a similar public on its 1954 revival.

As well as writing many of his own libretti, Egk supplied one for Blacher's *Abstrakte Oper* (1953). Whereas Messiaen's nonsense text for his *Cinq Rechants* seems contrived for purely musical suggestibility, and the phonetic investigations of the *avant-garde* (Stockhausen, Berio, Kagel) are directed towards a bridge between speech and music, Egk uses a free juxtaposition of syllables to give an edge to basic emotional situations, dramatically resented. pNot only the chic quality of this

---

[1] Karl-Heinz Füssl, 'Music in Austria and Germany today' in *Twentieth-Century Music* ed. Howard Hartog (London, 1960), p. 130.

experiment but its roots in an unacknowledged sentimentality seem typical of the work of Boris Blacher (b. 1903).[1] Even his use of swing formulas has a wan charm that seems an affectation beside the virile licence of jazz. In fact, Blacher has no need for these formulas, or for his echoes of Stravinsky, as spurs to a keen rhythmic imagination. Nor does he constantly rely on the mechanized arrangement of bar lengths which is his most celebrated invention. His claim that 'this variable metre is less a rhythmical problem than a formal one'[2] is justified only when the longer bars can be apprehended as entities. Too often, however, subsidiary accents and even simple syncopations destroy the effect of progression through a higher unit of time. Comparisons of this metrical ordering with that of pitch serialism bear little inspection: Blacher's method cannot set up the dense network of palpable conse-quence and coincidence implied by serial principle. Yet it can be an effective liberating agent in conventional textures (see Ex. 190 from *Orchester-Ornament*, 1953) and has been profitably borrowed by com-posers too prone to Germanic stolidity, like Hartmann and the early Henze. Blacher's preferred textures are lean, ranging between Orff's prodigal economy and Webern's excessive refinement, but often occupy-ing a middle territory that allows scope to his fluent command of academic device (see e.g. the canonic movements in the *Paganini*

[1] Cf. articles by G. F. Kosuszek, *The Score*, i (1949), J. Rufer, *Schweizerische Musik-zeitung*, lxxxviii (1948), and G. von Einem, *Schweizerische Musikzeitung*, xc (1950).
[2] Boris Blacher in a contribution to Josef Rufer, *Die Komposition mit zwölf Tönen* (Berlin, 1952; Eng. ed., 1954), p. 178 of English edition.

Variations, 1947, or the choral writing of the 1959 *Requiem*). A simple serialism is often found next to free dissonances, usually mild; these occasionally approach the internal contradiction of Stravinskyan harmony without casting off the obligations of progression. A typically deft synthesis is that of the final section in the *Orchesterfantasie* (1956), a movement which on the immediate level is characterized by Stravinsky's nervous rhythm and third reiterations, by a climax of melodic sevenths and ninths and by a canon four-in-one. On a higher time scale it is organized by the *tutti* interjection of twelve-note serial forms from the opening section, delivered in single notes at intervals reduced progressively from twenty-three bars to continuous crotchets and still further diminution. These orchestral works found a readier hearing thanks to their scoring, which is brilliantly apt though essentially traditional; in the theatre, over-anxiety to simulate a wealth of abstruse meaning (see e.g. *Rosamunde Floris*, 1960) jars with a music that is best when least pretentious.

Though the vast palindromic Amen of Blacher's *Requiem* is executed in transparent textures, it suggests a peculiarly German pride of craftsmanship (contrast e.g. the retrograde techniques of Stravinsky's *Canticum* or Nono's *Incontri*). Not surprisingly, the more usual outlet for this is a weightier contrapuntal idiom springing from a love of the Baroque and from Hindemith, whether or not it recognizes the harmonic mandate of the *Unterweisung*. Few of the innumerable composers who command such a style have more than local interest; but that it can become compelling by consummate mastery of device is shown by the best works of the Austrian, Johann Nepomuk David (b. 1895). Ernst Pepping (b. 1901) has produced admirable church music but failed to make a distinctive mark with his more ambitious work.

Wolfgang Fortner (b. 1907), who began from just such a position, has achieved international recognition. His earlier music added to the routine Hindemithian industry a strong feeling for clean sonorities deriving from Stravinsky. After the 1947 Symphony, a testimony to that period's hope and fears which played an important role in Germany's musical recovery, his assimilation of twelve-note methods (a process perhaps aided by his pupil, Henze) led to still wider prominence. Although his approach to texture and structure remains rooted in the past, he provides another instance (with Stravinsky and Dallapiccola as the most striking) of the new imaginative vistas opened to an already fluent composer who discovers in serial thought a natural medium. In the *Mouvements* for piano and orchestra (1953)[1] exemplary workmanship, with much neat dovetailing of rows, is lavished on an entirely

---

[1] Cf. comment by Francis Burt, 'An Antithesis', *The Score*, xviii (1956), p. 16.

Ex. 191

traditional sequential extension of material. The norm of dissonance is low (as the series suggests—cf. Ex. 191(i)) and textures fluctuate between neo-classical and neo-romantic, but with a preponderance of the patterned figuration that is Hindemith's legacy to a whole German generation (see Ex. 191 (ii)); the serial boogie on the other hand is a conceit that would appeal to Blacher.

Seven years later, in the *Aulodie* for oboe and orchestra (1960), Fortner's habit of transposing a segment of the row as a pseudo-classical developing motive[1] has led to the use of a single motive of three notes; the juxtaposition of its four serial orders can produce a twelve-note row. It is not only this refinement that suggests acquaintance with post-Schoenbergian developments. The rhythmic interest has increased, chord building and scoring are more varied; and the rhetorical scheme, in which pastoral solo strains and belligerent assaults are convincingly related, is new, although inordinately prolonged. The expressive release which Fortner's stylistic exploration afforded is strikingly confirmed in his vocal music; the almost embarrassing fervour of *The Creation* (1954) is stimulated as well as controlled by its technical constraints, and the Lorca opera, *Die Bluthochzeit* (The Blood Wedding) (1953) exhibits a range that no merely parochial talent could command.

As well as his important work as a teacher in Heidelberg and Freiburg,

---

[1] Cf. Fortner on his serial technique in Josef Rufer, op. cit., p. 182.

Fortner organized series of concerts in those cities under the title *Musica Viva*. In this he followed the lead given in Munich by Karl Amadeus Hartmann (1905–63). Within six months of the end of the war, Hartmann, whose withdrawal from the German musical scene has been noted, launched a campaign to re-educate composers, performers, and audiences by programmes ranging from the precursors of the new music, through the virtually unknown masterpieces of the pre-war generation to the experimental work of the emerging generation. Catholic but intelligent programme arrangement and adequately re-hearsed performances were accorded the highest importance. The results of Hartmann's labours can scarcely be overestimated: not only did the Munich audiences grow from a mere thirty to some fifteen hundred, but Munich Radio adopted the series and transmitted it to a far wider public. Its imitation in other German centres (and further afield, including Liverpool and Glasgow) brought modern music to people mistrustful of the esoteric atmosphere of Darmstadt and Donaueschingen, where the newest music has been methodically per-formed and discussed by adepts.

Hartmann's own works reflect these broad sympathies, and an alert ear immediately traces debts to Stravinsky, Bartók, Berg, and indeed, almost every important figure of the century. Yet these never deface the impression of a strongly personal musical ideal, pursued so constantly as to suggest monotony to the not wholly sympathetic listener. This ideal seems to spring from a new interpretation of Bruckner's symphonic concept that has focused on the profound adagios and bucolic scherzos of that master. Whereas the intense, rarefied mood of the former is subjected to Hartmann's impulsive but disruptive fantasy, the animal vigour of the latter is dissipated in mechanized concertante figurations. This paradox is seen most clearly in the two symphonies which under-line by their scoring a preoccupation with one of these types—the ardent, almost hysterically impassioned Symphony No. 4 (1947) for strings, framed by adagios, and the prosaically chattering *Symphonie Concertante* (No. 5, 1950) for wind, cellos, and basses, dominated by neo-Baroque allegros. The symphony completed between these two (though labelled No. 3, 1949) is more satisfactory than either, not only because of its full orchestral resources, with much bright-toned percus-sion, but also because Hartmann's use of a single continuous span compels him to cultivate some middle ground between his extreme moods and encourages him to abandon these when their initial urge is exhausted. Framed by the funereal opening and its final recall, an emotional pattern which the nineteenth century's abuse has made unfashionable is given new life by a centre-piece that demonstrates aggressive optimism in terms of cumulative fugue and ground bass. Fugal technique seems a natural solution here, but it has become a mere decorative procedure in the Sixth and Seventh Symphonies of 1952 and 1959. Hartmann's inclination to cling to mechanisms that have no essential relation to the music's growth is even more clearly seen in his fondness for mirrored writing, not pulled forward by canon but ranged immobile around a central point. In the Viola Concerto (1955), the brass chorale (a common borrowing from Bruckner) is punctuated by solo interludes (cf. Berg's Violin Concerto); despite a chromatic introversion that recalls Bartók, the strict mirror technique:

Ex. 192

has a stiffness quite foreign to that composer's symmetrical feats.

The spirited revival of German music by the generation of Blacher, Fortner, and Hartmann was one token of a determined bid for national self-respect. Blacher's music in particular, with its urbanity, efficiency, and hints of defensive irony, is a perfect counterpart to the faintly anxious good taste of the modern German hotel or office block. In sharp contrast, Austria's recovery of national autonomy was musically celebrated by an affectionate embracing of her past, or of those more recent composers (like Franz Schmidt) whose memories of it were least clouded by this century's preoccupations. Neither the Nazi ban nor their subsequent transformation of the European musical scene secured for Schoenberg's methods the championship of an Austrian public which had surrendered to its characteristic (and commercially profitable) nostalgia. The generation that should have carried on from the three great pioneers is represented only by two of their pupils, Apostel and Jelinek, and by the emigrant Křenek.

Though Hanns Jelinek (1901–69) worked indefatigably for a *Gebrauchsmusik* based on twelve-note principles, notably in the nine volumes of *Zwölftonwerk*, Op. 15,[1] he failed to find a convincing solution to the problems of his age in merely making dodecaphonic textures sound as nearly as possible traditional. Audiences that are soothed by what is familiar in such music are no nearer acceptance of any further consequences of twelve-note methods. Of course an understanding public is still less likely to be recruited if such consequences are pursued so far, and so rapidly, as to reach a private world. The remarkably varied career of Ernst Křenek (b. 1900) may be seen as a virtuosic feat of liaison. Gifted with an imagination that set him naturally among the explorers, he has sometimes been compelled by a sense of responsibility to interpret his findings in terms which the less ambitious listener can hope to understand. He remained faithful to dodecaphony after settling in America in 1938, but drew from its few basic principles a wide selection of compositional procedures[2] with as wide a range of stylistic consequences. His choral *Lamentations* (1942) reinstate a scalic norm by deriving all their material from two basic hexachordal 'modes' and the attendant modes obtained by setting out from degrees other than the first; developments of this principle in instrumental works include systematized rotations of note-order within smaller segments. In the years of these experiments, Křenek sometimes sought wider communication through a simpler technique. But the post-war emergence of young composers determined to conduct such experiments on a far broader basis found Křenek ready to learn as well as teach. As his own work had always remained traditional in its progressive development of the recognizable motive, he was reluctant to see this abandoned in favour of apparent chaos, suspicious of serial mechanisms bordering on total pre-determination, and frankly critical of electronic phenomena 'of a considerably lower intellectual level of musical consciousness than the aspirations which were associated with the music of the past'.[3] Characteristically, he tested these first reactions by the most practical method, venturing not only into schemes of multiple serialization in such works as *Kette, Kreis und Spiegel* (Chain, Circle, and Mirror)

---

[1] See also his textbook, *Anleitung zur Zwölftonkomposition* (Vienna, 1952), and its review by Křenek, *Musical Quarterly*, xl (1954), p. 250.

[2] See Křenek's writings on these in *Music Review*, iv (1943), p. 81; *Musical Quarterly*, xxxix (1953), p. 513; *Musical Quarterly*, xlvi (1960), p. 210, and in Josef Rufer, op. cit., p. 188.

[3] Ernst Křenek, 'A glance over the shoulders of the young', *Die Reihe*, i (Vienna, 1955; Eng. ed., 1958), p. 14.

(1958) but joining company with men of the next generation in exploring the mingling of electronic sound with voices in the oratorio *Spiritus Intelligentiae Sanctus* (1956).

After Křenek's intellectual curiosity has been acknowledged, it must be said that his creative achievement is disappointingly uneven, and bears no constant relation to the degree of technical innovation. If early works like *Jonny* or *Leben des Orest* showed that he dispenses with all technical stimulus at his peril, the opera *Pallas Athene weint* (1955) has shown that he also needs stimulus of another kind to reach his most impressive level. Here a burning concern for liberty is given didactic yet forceful expression through musical symbols that lose no immediacy for being derived from a personal interpretation of twelve-note practice.

THE MIDDLE GENERATION ELSEWHERE

During the years of Nazi artistic proscription, Switzerland was able to assume responsibility for the first performance of works as important as *Mathis, Lulu*, and Webern's Orchestral Variations. Her own composers remained free to profit by any example they chose, and were by national temperament inclined to choose widely. Honegger's stylistic amalgam was fused long before this period, but his development as a symphonist was touched off by an urge to comment on its dark events (in the powerful Second Symphony, for strings and trumpet, 1941); three more essays followed. A development still more remarkable was that of Frank Martin, born in 1890, but little known before the war. Stravinsky's journey from pandiatonicism to dodecaphony began as research into serial method, not necessarily demanding twelve-note material. Martin, on the other hand, was satisfied by old textural ideals, realized with considerable ingenuity and refinement, but he increasingly liberated his melodic line by use of twelve-note successions.[1] Below this surface his music often remains entirely diatonic, and the bass line regains the guiding role lost in both Schoenberg and Stravinsky. As a result, his harmonic textures, however fluid in their accommodation of chromatic line, never seethe with the inner tensions that are the source of Schoenbergian *Angst*.[2] All is so patently under control that excitement is not easily generated, though ungrudging admiration is often aroused. The popularity of the *Petite Symphonie Concertante* (1945)[3] is earned by the felicitous deployment of its varied string colours, and its counterpart

---

[1] Roman Vlad, 'Frank Martin' in his *Modernità e tradizione nella musica contemporanea* (Turin, 1955), p. 236.

[2] Martin's opposition both to Schoenberg's aesthetic and to subjugation to rule is ex pounded in articles in *Polyphonie*, iv (1948) and *Schweizerische Musikzeitung*, lxxxii (1942).

[3] Cf. Jacques de Menasce, 'Frank Martin and his *Petite Symphonie Concertante*', *Musical Quarterly*, xxxiv (1948), p. 271.

in wind tone, the 1949 Concerto, is perhaps even more adroit. But in works which demand our deeper engagement, the opera on *The Tempest* (1955) and the series of oratorios[1] dominated by *Golgotha* (1948) and *Le Mystère de la Nativité* (1959), not all Martin's concern for sonority can hide the limitation of his idiom. The first impact of serialism has proved a rich source of creative tension in many men's work, but the composer who seeks to maintain so delicate a poise is in danger of unwittingly reducing it to a pose.

On the other hand, a composer whose receptivity to new ideas is at once eager and cautious may profit for years from a gradually increasing commitment to serial procedure on his own terms, and the career of Luigi Dallapiccola (b. 1904) affords an interesting study in such assimilation.[2] Stravinsky's magisterial appropriation was achieved after serial music had become widely available, but Fascist Italy in 1940 was a less propitious environment. 'Just at the time when everyone had ceased to mention atonality or twelve-note music, I began to be passionately interested in such problems,' Dallapiccola has written.[3] In fact, Schoenberg's influence dated from a performance of *Pierrot lunaire* in 1924, which made him resolve to study composition.[4] During the following years he mastered a wholly Italian style, re-interpreting the neo-classical concepts of Busoni and Casella through a feeling for polyphonic texture that reached back to pre-classical times, yet excluding neither the Verdian cantabile nor the expressive use of instrumental colouring. Having forged a link with Italy's past, he sought one with the European present that should preserve the native qualities of his music. As he writes, 'the field which most attracted me to the twelve-note system was that of melody.'[5]

Already his melodic lines had tended to juxtapose diatonic, even modal, shapes in the wider context of the chromatic repertory; unlike Martin, Dallapiccola explored the implications of such lines in contrapuntal engagement, especially through canonic procedure. By the time of the opera *Volo di notte* (Night Flight) (1939) he had arrived at working principles that foreshadow serialism without aping the Viennese pioneers. Deprived by political prejudices from direct study of their scores, he sought inspiration in the literary procedures of Joyce and Proust.[6] But the lack of technical guidance was no obstacle to the over-

---

[1] For Martin's views on sacred music, see *Schweizerische Musikzeitung*, lxxxvi (1946).
[2] Cf. Roman Vlad, *Dallapiccola* (Milan, 1957); also articles by Vlad in *Horizon*, xx (1949). (reprinted in *Modernità . . .*) and *The Score*, xv (1956), p. 39.
[3] Luigi Dallapiccola, 'On the Twelve-Note Road', *Music Survey*, iv (i) (1951), p. 321.
[4] Cf. Vlad, *Modernità . . .*, p. 197.
[5] Dallapiccola, in Josef Rufer, op. cit., p. 180.
[6] Dallapiccola, 'On the Twelve-Note Road', loc. cit., p. 323.

whelming expressive urge of the *Canti di prigionia* (Prison Songs) (1938–1941), for the composer's own experience of political tyranny had already nourished that fanatical devotion to the cause of human liberty which is at the root of his major works.[1] A natural affinity with modal chant enabled him to make of *Dies irae* an awesome motto, but serial thought and an imaginative ear for icy sonorities (two pianos, two harps, and many percussion instruments) combined to produce the strange menace of the second movement.

Dallapiccola has stressed that mere quantitative equality of notes cannot prevent the predominance of some, due either to their placing in time, or to 'extremely subtle relationships which exist between certain notes', *polarities* which are fundamental characteristics of each row.[2] In the works which followed the *Canti di prigionia* he explored the properties of many rows,[3] never making a technical advance without assuring himself that he was still in control of the total sonority and of its immediate expressive potentiality. The seductive textures of the *Liriche greche* (Greek Lyrics) (1942–5) conceal experiments in the integration of material which made possible the fluency of *Il Prigioniero* (The Prisoner) (1944–8).[4] In an age when any compositional method but the most recent is fervently denounced, few works have been more salutary reminders than this opera that the one essential vehicle for a vital creative impulse remains a technique which, though already mastered, is still for the composer an imaginative adventure. Dallapiccola's variety of rows and motives, his evocative use of traditional chord structure, his mingled echoes of Verdi, Debussy, and Berg, all offend against *a priori* conceptions of serialism; but his right to profit as he chooses from serial discipline is vindicated by the powerful impact the work has continued to make.

The technical premises of this impassioned protest against physical and mental torture[5] could not, however, be systematized into a guarantee of further success. In Dallapiccola's 'sacra rappresentazione', *Job* (1950), the constant burden of tribulation presenting itself in many guises may have prompted his first large-scale structure from a single row.[6] Far from inducing monotony, this inspired almost too richly varied an imagery, and the spoken narrative tends to disperse the musical cumulation. After brilliantly demonstrating contrapuntal device

---

[1] Cf. R. Smith Brindle, 'Italian Contemporary Music' in Howard Hartog (ed.), *European Music of the Twentieth Century* (London, 1957), p. 176.   [2] Dallapiccola, loc. cit., pp. 325–6.
[3] Details of Dallapiccola's twelve-note work from 1942 to 1957 are given in Hans Nathan, 'The Twelve-Tone Compositions of Luigi Dallapiccola', *Musical Quarterly*, xliv (1958), p. 289.   [4] Cf. Dallapiccola, 'Notes sur mon opéra', *Polyphonie* no. 1 (1948).
[5] Cf. Vlad on the significance of *Il Prigioniero* in *The Score*, xv, (1956), p. 43.
[6] Including a form achieved by permutation; see Nathan, loc. cit., p. 291, n.3.

Ex. 193

(O brother, were our faith firm, miracles would be wrought in us.)

in the diatonic contexts of the violin Divertimento on Themes from Tartini (1951), Dallapiccola applied the same skill to a row in the 'Contrapuncti' of the *Quaderno musicale di Annalibera* (Musical album for Annalibera) (1952); like the studies in mood and texture which complete this set of piano pieces,[1] they show a new preoccupation with rhythmic variety that was to distinguish his masterpiece, the *Canti di liberazione* (Songs of Liberation) for chorus and orchestra (1955). Indeed the same series underlies both works and its choral presentation in the first *canto* is taken directly from 'Fregi' in the *Quaderno* (see Ex. 193 to bar 6—an 'all-interval series') a reminder of the vocal nature of all Dallapiccola's line. From the bass entry in bar 5 the imitations of a serial fragment with progressive diminution (but constant proportion) of note values, introduce a device used in every movement. The scale of rhythm values in use, any one of which may be treated as a basic unit, reveals a growing interest in Messiaen and the *avant-garde*. Though the frequent width of melodic interval points to Webern, Ex. 193 shows

how diatonic are the implications of the segments (although the direct octaves of *Il Prigioniero* have disappeared), and Dallapiccola's thematic use of the row elsewhere recognizes the contrasted expression of near-conjunct line.

If the scoring of this work (for full orchestra) comes near to the Bergian espressivo, much of his music shows Dallapiccola to be master of a slighter medium more typical of the period—solo voice and chamber ensemble. Works like the *Goethe-Lieder* (1953)[2] and the *Cinque canti* on Greek poems (1956), have refined instrumental textures that contribute subtle points of symbolism without ever challenging the expressive supremacy of the voice. The visual symbolism (cf. the madrigalists' 'eye-music') of note patterns that form in the score a cross in *Cinque canti* or a Christmas tree in the *Concerto per la notte di natale* (Concerto for Christmas Eve) (1957) conveys nothing to the listener, but is an illuminating commentary on the almost spiritual involvement of this composer in all he writes. These works reveal the completed assimilation of Webern's influence in their freedom of wide interval and in textures assembled from reflecting segments. But Berg remains the inspiration for the contrasting harmonic blocks of the Concerto, and the use of the

[1] Orchestrated as the *Variazioni* (1954).

[2] The German inflexions (Wagner and Schoenberg) which affect the lines of the *Goethe-Lieder* are shown in Nathan, loc. cit., pp. 294–5 and 299. Nos. 2, 3, 5, and 6 are recorded in *The History of Music in Sound*, x.

voice in two movements of this instrumental form confirms that even in his most advanced style Dallapiccola works with vocal shapes.[1]

Other composers of Dallapiccola's generation observed his serial progress with interest: Seiber noted a development that 'far from restricting his ideas or cramping his style ... seems to have liberated his colourful imagination.'[2] In Italy, the revelation of native lyricism enhanced by the twelve-note method proved an incentive to experiments that even touched figures as revered as Malipiero and Ghedini. The most thoughtful and individual compromise characterized the later work of Goffredo Petrassi (b. 1904).[3] Less dependent than Dallapiccola on the stimulus of a text, he had achieved a neo-Baroque manner which softened the rigidity of Hindemith's instrumental counterpoint but was founded in a similar extension of diatonic (and in his case modal) principle. Gatti's discovery of 'the demon of modernistic intellectualization'[4] in works like the orchestral concertos is unduly severe on Petrassi's cool but not aggressive rejection of a romantic pose he would have found uncomfortable.[5] Just as Stravinsky proved repeatedly that this attitude need not lead to a desiccated objectivity, so Petrassi with his male voice *Coro di morti* (Chorus of the Dead) (1940–1) drew a dramatic power from his treatment of Leopardi's dark verses that is the more compelling for its universal intimations. The hard sonorities (brass, three pianos, percussion, and double-basses) appear less Stravinskyan in a context that includes choral writing of an archaic (and Italian) flow and instrumental contours betraying an interest in twelve-note models.[6] Despite a number of stage works, two ballets and the operas *Il Cordovano* (1948) and *Morte dell'aria* (1950), the *Coro* was not surpassed until he worked on a subject of comparable grandeur in the cantata *Noche oscura* (Dark night of the soul) (1951). Vlad aptly cites some words of its poet, St. John of the Cross, 'mysteries are revealed through strange shapes and images',[7] to explain Petrassi's need to break loose from all diatonic ties in setting the erotic symbolism of the poem. He achieved this by allowing the serial orders of a chromatic motive to roam through musical space so as to cover, though not to regularize, the resources of dodecaphony. Serial practices reappear in the Third Orchestral Concerto (*Récréation Concertante*, 1952), and in the Fifth

---

[1] Cf. John C. G. Waterhouse, 'The Italian Avant-Garde and National Tradition', *Tempo*, 68 (1964), p. 14.

[2] Matyas Seiber, 'Composing with Twelve Notes', *Music Survey*, iv (iii) (1952), p. 486.

[3] Cf. John S. Weissmann, 'Goffredo Petrassi', *The Score*, iii (1950), p. 49, and his book of the same title (Milan, 1957); also Roman Vlad in *Modernità e tradizione nella musica contemporanea* (Turin, 1955), p. 217.

[4] Guido M. Gatti, article on Petrassi in *Grove*, 5th ed., vi, p. 689.

[5] Cf. Vlad, op. cit., p. 222.   [6] Cf. Weissmann, *The Score*, iii (1950), p. 59.

[7] Cf. Vlad, 'La *Noche Oscura*' in *Modernità . . .*, p. 234.

Concerto (1955)[1] the free permutation of a six-note row in one movement and its complement in the other produces homogeneous but
contrasted material. By the time of the 1957 String Quartet and the
Serenata (1958) Petrassi had extended his interests to the work of the
younger generation; the latter work, for flute, viola, double-bass,
harpsichord, and percussion, still betrays his old neo-classical sympathies yet manages to absorb them into a style ranging easily from simple
cantabile line to the mannered percussion writing of the *avant-garde*.

In countries more remote from the decisive happenings of modern
music, the composers best equipped to rise above a crippling pro-
vincialism were those with first-hand experience of the central lines of
development. Two pupils of Schoenberg who are comparable in this
respect are the Spaniard Roberto Gerhard (1896–1969) and the Greek
Nikos Skalkottas (1904–49), both of whom revert occasionally to a
simpler, nationalist manner. Skalkottas suffered from a self-imposed
isolation, in which he pursued his own ideas without reference to continuing developments of the Central European technique he had
acquired.[2] Yet he also lacked the stimulus or corrective of hearing his
own works in performance. Opportunities to hear the symphonic and
other extended works are still rare, which is particularly unfortunate
since the short pieces available in print, talented applications of an
individual serialism[3] to square-cut forms, relapse at times into harmonic
and textural formulas (often more reminiscent of Hindemith of the
twenties than of Schoenberg) too jaded to convey a vital expressive
urge, as in this example from the Fourth Suite for Piano:

Ex. 194   **Tempo di Polka moderato**

---

[1] Cf. Kenneth Gaburo in 'Current Chronicle', *Musical Quarterly*, xlii (1956), p. 530.
[2] Cf. John G. Papaioannou, 'Nikos Skalkottas' in Hartog, op. cit., p. 320.
[3] Ibid., p. 325.

It is difficult not to believe that more rapport with European music in Skalkottas' later years would have preserved his most personal characteristics—lithe energy, clear yet not attenuated sonorities, and a quizzical or even sardonic tone—and checked his tendency to let textural proliferation take control at moments of flagging impulse.

After the Spanish Civil War, Gerhard[1] left his own country for another territory of the musical periphery, England. His wide musical sympathies and penetrating intelligence found him a place there both as a masterly composer of incidental music and as a commentator on contemporary developments;[2] these he studied deeply and converted to his own ends. As a result, whatever Spanish inflexions or subtlety of English word-setting may contribute to its individual tone, his work reveals a European legacy that demands some mention in the present survey. This has so far been a record of composers who struck a basically diatonic stylistic balance before the war, but were in many cases impelled to modify this by some aspect of Schoenberg's thought. Dallapiccola has quoted from Gisèle Brelet's comments on atonality: 'trop tôt venu, il lui fallait attendre que surgisse chez les musiciens la conscience des problèmes auxquels il prétendait apporter une réponse.'[3] It is interesting to note that this time-lag was felt necessary even by Gerhard, a composer steeped in the Schoenbergian aesthetic and fluent in its practical consequences. In contrast to many composers, his late adoption of fully serial technique followed music written against a background of intimate knowledge of its workings; thus not only is his serial music entirely without the *gaucheries* of first experiments but it can coalesce easily with a freer style.[4] The Violin Concerto (1942–5) is a beautiful example of this,[5] his comic opera *The Duenna* (1945–7) turns again to a pointed diatonicism,[6] and in later

---

[1] Cf. *The Score*, xvii (1956), a sixtieth birthday tribute to Gerhard, with articles on his work and a catalogue.

[2] Cf. Gerhard's articles in *The Score*, vi, ix, xvi, xvii, xx, and xxiii.

[3] Gisèle Brelet, *Chances de la musique atonale* (Alexandria, 1947) quoted by Dallapiccola in 'On the Twelve-Note Road', loc. cit., p. 320.

[4] Cf. David Drew, 'The Musical Character', *The Score*, xvii (1956), p. 39.

[5] On its scoring cf. Norman del Mar, 'Gerhard as an orchestral composer', ibid., p. 17.

[6] Cf. John Gardner, 'The Duenna', ibid., pp. 20–6.

instrumental works he has used an increasingly ordered serialism. To the permutational 'inversions' of complementary hexachords which regulate tonality (in Gerhard's broad sense)[1] in the 1953 Symphony is added in the Quartet (1955) a series of time-proportions derived from the pitch set by a simple process of measuring semitonal distances.[2] With the 1959 Symphony he cast off the dependence on motivic contour which he considered tautological in serial working, and in *Collages* (1960) he tackled the problem of fusing electronic and instrumental sound. Gerhard's belief in an intelligently considered 'system of arbitrarily set-up co-ordinates'[3] as a vital spur to the creative imagination was amply justified by his own works.

Other peripheral figures have been content with narrower horizons. In Scandinavia the most notable emergence during these two decades was of the Norwegian Fartein Valen (1887–1952), though most of his music had been written earlier. Valen's link with a central tradition was through his teacher Reger, but the contrapuntal style he developed stepped out of the shadow of Bach. Despite coming under Schoenberg's influence to the extent of using twelve-note melodic rows, he did not allow them consistently to permeate the texture; and the motivic discussion which unites the parts sounds aimless once a dominating melodic strand is abandoned. Valen's enterprise deserves notice as an early venture towards territory that has still attracted few Scandinavians. More typical was the fluent but eclectic conservatism of the Dane, Vagn Holmboe (b. 1909), as indefatigable a composer of chamber concertos as was the Hindemith of the twenties, but of far less brilliance. In Sweden, Hilding Rosenberg (b. 1892)[4] wrote a series of oratorios and transmitted a catholic taste to some gifted pupils; Gösta Nystroem (1890–1966)[5], without modifying his style, produced his most distinguished work in the *Sinfonia del mare* (Sea Symphony) (1948).

The younger Scandinavian generation includes several composers who will call for discussion later. In Central and Eastern Europe too, and here even more surprisingly, the influence of the most radical advances in serial style helped to nurture some impressive talent. Of the older men, little can be reported which reflects a significant

---

[1] Cf. Gerhard, 'Tonality in Twelve-note Music', *The Score*, vi (1952), p. 23. For relevant discussion of hexachord combinational properties cf. George Rochberg, 'Harmonic Tendencies of the Hexachord', *Journal of Music Theory*, iii (1959), p. 208; for a comparable technique cf. Ernst Křenek's contribution to Rufer, op. cit., pp. 188–91.

[2] Vlad writes on both works in *The Score*, xvii (1956), p. 27; cf. also Gerhard, 'Developments in Twelve-Tone Technique', ibid., p. 61. Contrast the more elaborate derivations of time proportions from pitch series by Stockhausen.

[3] Gerhard, 'The Contemporary Musical Situation', *The Score*, xvi (1956).

[4] Cf. Moses Pergament, 'Hilding Rosenberg" *Music & Letters*, xxviii (1947), p. 249.

[5] Cf. Pergament, 'Gösta Nystroem" *Music & Letters*, xxvii (1946), p. 66.

change of reputation, and the impact of twelve-note music found no repercussions comparable to the transformation of a Dallapiccola or a Fortner. Bohuslav Martinů (1890–1959),[1] a Czech living in America, made a determined and largely successful bid for command of distinctive extended structure in his six symphonies; but his language remained nationalist, tinged by a belated impressionism or neo-classical patterning.

OLIVIER MESSIAEN

So far, this account of the middle generation's development during and after the war has been unified by one central though far from universal phenomenon—the revitalizing of style by serial thought. This may seem to invalidate the contention[2] that the philosophical speculation which brought serialism into being, and the cerebration required in its operation, were inseparable from a peculiarly Germanic musical ethos. Yet one country seems to lend some credibility to the contention: France produced no composer of distinction in direct succession to Schoenberg's ideas and technique, and vociferously rejected the importation of these into her music. In the new serialism as expounded by Boulez, not only did the letter of the old technique become a minor and inconstant observance, but values deriving from a specifically French tradition were consciously asserted.

The assimilation of principles originating outside France into a style of exclusively native tone is a familiar feature in her musical history. But the ability to maintain a character has no virtue in itself, and of the oldest French generation at work in this period, it may be said that its musical character, if unmistakable, was also weak. The only French member of Cocteau's ill-assorted 'Six' to reveal any capacity for renewal was Poulenc,[3] whose two operas, *Les Mamelles de Tirésias* (Tiresias's Breasts) (1944) and *Dialogues des Carmélites* (1956), remarkably sustain satirical and lyrical moods familiar from his songs. If the piety which rather heavily oppresses *Carmélites* stems from nineteenth-century operatic models, Poulenc's natural affinity with Gounod[4] ensures that it never becomes a pose. Such music about saintliness is acceptable in the theatre but it has little to do with religious music. In Olivier Messiaen (b. 1908) France has the only important contemporary composer whose religious belief is central to his art.

[1] Cf. Miloš Šafránek, *Bohuslav Martinů* (Prague, 1961; Eng. ed., London, 1964), Peter Evans, 'Martinů the Symphonist', *Tempo*, lv (1960), p. 19. John Clapham, 'Martinů's Instrumental Style', *Music Review*, xxiv (1963), p. 158, and Harry Halbreich, *Bohuslav Martinů: Werkvergeichnis, Dokumentation, Biographie* (Zürich, 1968).
[2] Cf. p. 388.   [3] Cf. Henri Hell, *Francis Poulenc* (Paris, 1958; London, 1959).
[4] Cf. David Drew, 'Modern French Music' in Hartog, op. cit., p. 264.

His association with Jolivet, Baudrier, and Lesur in 1936 under the title 'La Jeune France' was merely a further declaration against the smart, heartless music of the day such as he had already made in his early works. Certainly he sought no stimulus in the alliance; for this he found spiritually in a symbolical interpretation of Catholic dogma and technically in his studies of rhythm (especially Hindu), of plainsong, and of bird-song. In 1940 his freedom from the preoccupations of his contemporaries was clear, but his significance for a younger generation was still unsuspected. Now that this is generally acknowledged, it too often provides an excuse for ignoring his own erratic but considerable creative achievement.[1]

Mode, the prescription of limits within which the music may move freely, is fundamental to Messiaen's thought and a concept distinct from that of *series*, which determines the order of movement. By spanning the octave with regular patterns of pitch intervals (see Ex. 195) modes are obtained 'of limited transposition' (since the patterns repeat) which offer a variety of gravitational possibilities in place of the single point to which asymmetrical structure inevitably relates the old scales:

Ex. 195

Examples of 'Modes of limited transposition'

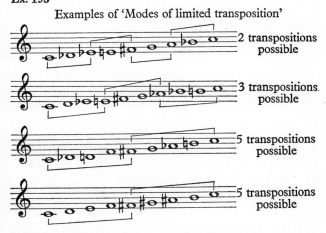

Within one of these modes tonality may remain elusive; and when two modes are at work, the texture may become fully chromatic and tonal feeling be dependent on melodic emphases. But since the selection within a given mode is left to the composer, he is equally at liberty to dwell on those notes which form conventional successions and simultaneities. Messiaen's style in fact embraces both extremes, but he has sometimes

[1] The outstanding description and critical estimate of Messiaen's work is by David Drew: 'Messiaen—a provisional study', *The Score*, x, xiii, xiv (1954–5).

irritated his disciples by his fondness for the second,[1] much as Hinde-mith favoured a comparatively small proportion of the possibilities latent in his own theory of progression. No such theory is implied by modality; Messiaen is dependent on his ear for the regulation of harmony. But like Stravinsky and Debussy, who also jettisoned the progressive mechanism, he is intent on the aural phenomenon *per se* and, like them, both scrupulous and imaginative in its construction.

If pitch-modality seems at once too defined and too imprecise to be regularly adopted by other composers (though it can be relevant to the structure of twelve-note rows), Messiaen's rhythmic principles demand consideration as leading to the most radical innovations in this branch of Western musical thought since the seventeenth-century triumph of the dance as background measurement. Treating rhythm as an absolute phenomenon separable from other considerations, he demands acute perception of the length of each note as an entity, reckoned as a multiple of a very small basic unit (present or imagined) rather than as a fraction of a palpable higher unit of time.[2] Thus, the Hindu rhythm at Ex. 196(i), one of many such patterns in the percussion writing of *Oiseaux*

Ex. 196

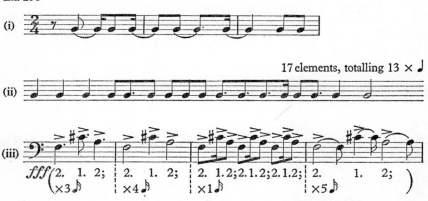

exotiques (1956), is not felt as a complex syncopation in the 2/4 measure (used for notational convenience) but as the proportions 3.2.3.5.5.2.2. In his own rhythms Messiaen avoids the emergence of a background metre, often by adroit use of small added values: see e.g. the first dotted note in Ex. 196(ii). To amplify such rhythms into structure—repetition

---

[1] Boulez's objection both to Messiaen's F sharp major penchant and to the self-deception of disguising it as modality is voiced in Antoine Goléa, *Rencontres avec Pierre Boulez* (Paris, 1958), p. 160.

[2] Cf. Preface to *Quatuor pour la Fin du Temps* (1941) and, for the most detailed exposition of Messiaen's theories, *Technique de mon langage musical* (Paris, 1944).

in toto is the simplest method: Ex. 196(ii) is the rhythmic ostinato of the Quartet's first movement. As in Machaut's isorhythmic technique, repetitions may preserve the proportions in different units; Messiaen's augmentations and diminutions are not restricted to classical two-multiples—see Ex. 196(iii) from the Quartet's sixth movement.[1] Rhythmic canon is a subtler repetition that produces cross-rhythm, and Messiaen attaches particular significance to 'rhythmes non rétrogradables' which reverse from a central value.

Rhythmic ostinato exemplifies Messiaen's view of his material as something formed in essence before the process of composition begins; ideas may be repeated literally, decorated profusely, or placed together in varying relations of time and space. Borrowing again from medieval technique, he may choose a melodic-harmonic *color* and a rhythmic *talea* of a different number of constituents (e.g. Ex. 196(ii) of seventeen rhythmic elements is set against a harmonic ostinato of twenty-nine chords)[2] and let their interaction produce constant change from what is immutable. Drew points out a still more rigid automatism in the piano piece *L'Échange* (from *Vingt Regards*): by quoting two bars and a brief key to procedure he is able to account for the following twenty-two bars.[3] Twelve-note serialism is no longer commonly held to be a Procrustean constraint on the composer's freedom of choice, but in the mechanisms of Messiaen's most painfully contrived movements may be seen the first surrender to the hazards of inadequately considered pre-determination: Webern discovers musical potentialities while Messiaen rotates statistical possibilities. The efforts of his pupils to synthesize the practices of these two explorers attracted even Messiaen himself into a position more radical than he felt willing to maintain; and it would be unjust to represent him solely by the works of those years, or to suggest that crude formulas dictate the course of his entire output. During the troubled times of the forties, his certainty of direction had no parallel among his own generation.

Though the instrumental colouring (determined by resources available in a prison-camp, 1941) makes the eight-movement *Quatuor pour la Fin du Temps* wearisome as a whole, it shows Messiaen's style fluctuating between essentially conventional harmonic forms (see the two gentle 'Louanges' in E major); and the wholly original super-imposition of blackbird and nightingale flourishes on a framework of interacting ostinati ('Liturgie de cristal'). But he may combine such

[1] Cf. Dallapiccola's practice in the *Canti di liberazione*, Ex. 193 on p. 422.

[2] Messiaen's addiction to prime numbers is more systematically revealed in e.g. *Neumes rhythmiques* (1950), the third element of which is a symmetrical rhythmic pattern expanding on repetition from a total of 41 semiquavers to 43, 47, and 53.

[3] David Drew, *The Score*, xiv (1955), pp. 46–47.

Ex. 197

extremes: in the finale of *Visions de l'Amen* (1943),[1] a rhythmic complex
(cf. Ex. 196(ii) used again in this later work) in canon at narrowing time
intervals rotates three-note groups with chromatic organum thickenings,
creating a maze of sound (Ex. 197, piano I) which enhances a chorale[2] as

[1] Cf. also Drew's discussion of *Amen des Étoiles*, ibid., pp. 41–44.
[2] The fundamentally unchanged character of Messiaen's procedures in his later style may
be seen by comparing with this the addition in *Ile de Feu 2* of the free initial theme to the
last pair of the serial permutations discussed on p. 440.

square and monotonous in itself as the feeblest effusions of the French organ school (Ex. 197, piano II). The circular key scheme (A–C sharp–F natural–A: a break with classical precedent rather than principle) of the chorale verses is literally repeated in the third of the *Petites Liturgies de la Présence Divine* (1944). This exceptionally direct work did much to establish the composer's reputation. A setting for unison female choir of his own text, it achieves dramatic compulsion from effects as simple as the clangorous reiteration without harmony of a springing pentatonic line. The scoring is for celesta, vibraphone, ondes martenot, piano, percussion, and strings, and demands a prescribed spatial arrangement of the forces. These anticipations of Boulez extend even to the use of the vibraphone to sustain vocal notes.[1]

In the first *Liturgie* the piano's bird-song introduces atonal chromatic bravura into a work which is unequivocally in A. Chromaticism of this kind, latent in Messiaen's modal theory, penetrates still further the texture of *Vingt Regards sur l'Enfant Jésus* (1944) and of the *Turangalîla-Symphonie* (1946–8).[2] This work looks ahead in such details as the association of a twelve-note succession with a scale of diminishing rhythmic values;[3] but its true importance is that of a vast compendium of Messiaen's musical language at an unusually well sustained level of invention. Though rhythmic counterpoints are superimposed in unprecedented profusion, and orchestral colourings are kaleidoscopically varied, neither thematicism nor tonality is abandoned.[4] Five years later, Messiaen returned to orchestral composition with a piano concerto, *Le Réveil des Oiseaux*, that emphasized his need to escape from the ascetic restrictive schemes of some intervening works. In *Oiseaux exotiques* (1956), a fantasy for piano, wind, and percussion, the composer continued to indulge, to the virtual exclusion of other material, his interest in Hindu and Greek rhythms (twenty patterns) and his gift for imaginative evocations of bird-song (forty-seven species). This enthusiasm has persisted in his later work, and has once again isolated the composer from the main forward movement of European music. As a result he is no longer burdened by a crippling sense of responsibility and can revert to a characteristic textural luxuriance. *Oiseaux exotiques* is in fact no pot-pourri but, for Messiaen, a remarkably strong arch-shaped movement in which the most flamboyant bird calls act as ritornelli. The texture is accumulated from the counterpoint of numerous

---

[1] Cf. Boulez, *Improvisation sur Mallarmé no. 1.*

[2] Cf. Drew, *The Score*, xiv, pp. 50–56 and Leonard Burkat, *Musical Quarterly*, xxxvi, (1950), p. 259.

[3] Cf. Drew, *The Score*, x, p. 48.

[4] See p. 45, n. 1. The F sharp movement to which Boulez objected was incorporated in *Turangalîla.*

calls, each having a fixed repertory of pitches, not necessarily adjacent, subject to rhythmic manipulation:

Ex. 198

This type of modal limitation had been systematized, together with other rationalizations of Messiaen's practice, in the piano study *Mode de valeurs et d'intensités* (1949), a work which must be discussed within the context of another generation.

THE NEW SERIALISM

In the generation that was learning its craft as the war ended there is disagreement as to the historical relationship of their musical achievements. Luigi Nono has affirmed his willingness to be judged against the background of a continuing historical process, but Stockhausen's apologist Dieter Schnebel[1] has argued that the new music implies the disappearance of such a tradition. Certainly the historical inevitability of these specific developments, though persuasively expounded by their apologists, is very debatable. It is clear that their intellectual premises came naturally to a sceptical generation which demanded explanations for creative procedure that should satisfy the mind as well as the sensibilities. To suggest that the particular equipment which has been assembled was partly due to a fortuitous interaction of circumstances is merely to recognize one of many such recoveries after crucial moments in music's history. Musical meanings are conveyed in a man-made language, and there are no *a priori* grounds for assuming that the language now evolving, by a perplexingly devious but ultimately empirical process, cannot communicate the aesthetic experience, even if its apparent remoteness from natural analogies may delay or prevent any popular acceptance.

Most composers of this generation served at least a brief apprenticeship in orthodox twelve-note techniques. The published expositions of the works of the Viennese School by the Polish-French theorist and composer René Leibowitz[2] were among their first guides in a field which many of their elders were just beginning to explore, though Martin and Dallapiccola would have been able to initiate their sometime pupils Stockhausen and Berio into personal interpretations of dodecaphony. At a time when French musicians were still overcome by Leibowitz's revelations (in performances as well as commentaries), and when there seemed high hopes of a French school of twelve-note composers,[3] Boulez enlisted as his pupil, already equipped with skills derived from Messiaen's teaching. But the most momentous revelation of serial composition came with Leibowitz's work at the Darmstadt Summer School in 1948 and 1949.

The Kranichstein Institute, founded at Darmstadt in 1946 due to the visionary zeal of one man, Wolfgang Steinecke, was intended first as a centre where young German composers could study together and hear the whole tract of contemporary music which had been denied them by Nazi proscription.[4] Their first mentor, Fortner, was still unversed in serial practice, but could demonstrate lessons he had learnt from Stravinsky and Hindemith; and in the following year Hindemith himself directed the course. So far this was only to reveal the true origin,

---

[1] See Luigi Nono, 'The Historical Reality of Music Today' (a Darmstadt lecture of 1959) in *The Score*, xxvii (1960); Dieter Schnebel, 'Karlheinz Stockhausen', *Die Reihe*, iv, p. 121.

[2] René Leibowitz, *Schönberg et son école* (Paris, 1946); *Introduction à la musique de douze sons* (Paris, 1949).

[3] Cf. Leibowitz on the work of his pupil, André Casanova, in *Music Survey*, II (iii) (1950).

[4] Cf. Antoine Goléa, *Rencontres avec Pierre Boulez* (Paris, 1958), pp. 67–80.

immeasurably more powerful than its miserable progeny, of the diluted pseudo-Hindemith of the familiar *Spielmusik* style. But Leibowitz's courses, together with the admission of foreign students from 1949, began the transformation of Darmstadt's scope: the aural experience of an almost unsuspected body of rich creative achievement and the discovery of reassuring technical bases on which they could build united the most talented (and many others) of a whole European generation. Their pursuit of that style which should satisfy a need for the intellectual underpinning of the creative impulse led them, as successive courses and private study made their models more familiar, to find this most unambiguously in Webern's music. Thus Darmstadt became the driving force behind the first consciously international movement in the music of our century.

At so close a range in time it is not possible to determine this century's most decisive moment of change.[1] The new serialism was near enough to Schoenberg to stress all that it had rejected of his methods and rhetoric,[2] but it is from Schoenberg that we must trace perpetual variation, the systematic unfolding of musical properties (with him limited to the pitch content) and as a corollary the association of sound and number. Beyond this he chose to rely on inherited formal constituents (expressive motive, phrase, and paragraph) for proportions in time, and on the ability of the row to construct proportions which should recall the traditional spanning of musical space; many composers of the middle generation devised individual means by which to sustain the same compromise. The attraction which the young generation found in Webern's music was its new expressive forms, rooted in the clarity and correspondence of intervallic and durational proportions themselves,[3] a demonstrably orderly arrangement of sonorous phenomena yielding an undemonstrable but compelling beauty. It has often been pointed out[4] that Webern's adoption of twelve-note rows created far less of a gulf in his work than had always existed between this and Schoenberg's; but it did enable him to achieve the perfect equilibrium of his later works by imposing on one idea, the construction of correspondences measured by interval, the constraint of another, serial propriety. By reducing the dominating status of the Schoenbergian *thematic* concept of the row, Webern was able to break free from the vast chain of consequences, essentially unrelated to the row as an autonomous proposition,

[1] See e.g. Th. W. Adorno, 'Modern Music is growing old', *The Score*, xviii (1956), p. 18, and the reply by H.-K. Metzger in *Die Reihe*, iv, Eng. ed. p. 63; also the essay by W.-E. von Lewinski in the same vol. p. 1, and Zillig, op. cit., p. 199.

[2] Cf. Pierre Boulez, 'Schoenberg is dead', *The Score,* vi (1952), p. 18.

[3] Cf. the analytical essays in 'Anton Webern', *Die Reihe,* ii.

[4] E.g. by Pousseur in *Die Reihe,* ii, p. 51.

and to order connexions—and ultimately structures—according to its inner potentialities. Since these prove to be virtually limitless, his characteristic row already demonstrates symmetry within its segments, so that the work makes audible 'horizontal, vertical and "diagonal" relationships'[1] stemming from a three- or four-note cell. These are the objects of the listener's attention. Although coincidence produces 'harmony' and succession 'melody', these qualities are not allowed to take on determining functions which, by re-introducing a degree of predictable movement, would divert his attention from the innate quality (which includes the duration) of the sounding moment.

Though serialism of all twelve pitches is one of the restrictions which brace Webern's style, it does not serve to guarantee the maximum separation of identical (or octave-related) notes. Indeed the close proximity of a note common to superimposed or adjacent serial forms may be pointed,[2] yet our hearing is so directed to the quality of the intervals, their forming and dissolving connexions, often across a wide total span, that such a relation is in no danger of establishing a conventional polarity. And as Webern's basic pitch-material could be reduced to the small cell, later composers have not felt bound to work with the complete pitch series.[3] Serial principle orders succession but does not of itself specify the number or nature of elements—a function, as was noted earlier, of mode. The new serialism sprang from a detailed consideration of both concepts, first brought face to face by composers who had learnt from dodecaphony and from Messiaen's methods (Boulez and Stockhausen, and—through Messiaen's teaching at Darmstadt—a far wider circle, including Nono). Messiaen's treatment of rhythmic proportions had demanded a large number of durations relatable by number, so that a rhythmic mode (a repository of different values) was already part of his equipment. Indeed he had already applied to this the principle of series in the use of rhythmic ostinato (cf. row repetition) and repetitions in various diminution and augmentation ratios (cf. row transposition), and in the importance he attached to retrograde rhythm. By contrast, in the late works of Webern could be found extremely subtle rhythmic relations,[4] including precisely timed silence as a vital contrapuntal element;[5] but despite an aural detachment from classical metre[6] and internal symmetries that prevented classical

---

[1] H.-K. Metzger, *Die Reihe*, i (Eng. ed.), p. 43.

[2] Cf. Christian Wolff, *Die Reihe*, ii, p. 62.

[3] The developments which led to the abandonment of Schoenberg's principle are discussed by György Ligeti, 'Wandlungen der musikalischen Form', *Die Reihe*, vii, p. 5.

[4] E.g. the *rhythm of connexions* discussed by Pousseur, loc. cit., p. 59.

[5] Cf. Pierre Boulez, *Die Reihe*, ii, p. 40.

[6] Webern himself, however, appears to have heard his music tensed against such a background. Cf. Peter Stadlen, 'Serialism Reconsidered', *The Score*, xxii (1958), p. 15.

flow, few signs of a treatment of duration so objectified as to be accommodated into serial logic.

The objective scrutiny of both pitch and time as musical properties that could be systematically ordered was turned, by a natural extension of the new attitude, on to other properties. Tone colour, once bound to the sense of the melodic phrase, had been fragmented in the changing chord of Schoenberg's Op. 16 pieces, and Webern's orchestration naturally pointed his construction from intervallic cells. Serialization instead of free variation of colour was a simple enough step, and as a substitute in media of limited colour (e.g. the piano) a serialization of methods of attack was thought plausible, thus rationalizing the tendency of modern music to make increasingly fine distinctions in this field. Webern's wide range of dynamic values, regarded as properties of the individual notes, suggested yet another serial ordering.

In visualizing the perpetual variation, according to a predetermined code, of each factor contributing to the distinctive quality of the musical note, the new school sought to atone for the extreme predominance accorded to pitch in Western tradition; their music should reflect the proportions of the series in a constant interplay of all the elements. For a just appreciation of the fluctuating activity within such 'global forms', the listener, brought up on precise recognition of pitch and comprehension of rhythm by the mnemonic of metre, must acquire entirely new powers of discrimination. Apart from the acquisition of similar powers, the composer's first concern must be with a means of determining the mutual relationship of his serial codes. Messiaen, already practised in simultaneously unfolding schemes of pitch and time, postulated a rudimentary solution in his piano study, *Mode de valeurs et d'intensités*, significantly inscribed 'Darmstadt, 1949'—see Ex. 199(i). True to his early principles, this uses mode, not series, but now

Ex. 199

(i)   Mode, Division I (top register)

Durational values 1 to 12 (× ♪);
in Divisions II and III the units
are ♪ and ♪ respectively.

(ii)

Piano

prescribes limits in all four fields of pitch, duration, attack, and dynamics. His pitch mode fixes the register of all twelve notes across a wide range (see Ex. 199(ii); two similar divisions correspond to the other staves and virtually cover the piano's compass) and to each of these is attached,[1] once for all, a specific attack drawn from a set of twelve, a dynamic level drawn from seven, and a duration drawn from a 'chromatic' range of one to twelve values—♪, ♪ and ♪ being the units of the three planes.

The rigid constraints of this piece (which incidentally give an almost motivic character, or at least a polarizing effect, to certain exposed pitch recurrences) do not contribute to its progress, whereas Messiaen's old interacting ostinati solved this problem at least. In another study of this set, *Ile de Feu 2*, he again sets up a fixed association of pitch and duration (though now entirely 'scalic': B ♪ B flat ♪ A ♪. &c. to C ♩, see Ex. 200(i)) but reduces the earlier, utterly impracticable differences

[1] A similar conjunction, but with a smaller range of constituents, had been attempted in *Cantéyodjayâ* (1948), p. 8.

Ex. 200

(i)

Pitch-duration mode
(12 ♪ 11 ♪   10 ♪ etc. . .)

1   2   3   4   5   6   7   8   9   10 11 12

(ii) Permutation row

7   6   8   5   9   4   10   3   11   2   12   1

Further permutations

(7	6	8	5	9	4	10	3	11	2	12	1)	see (iii)
10	4	3	9	11	5	2	8	12	6	1	7	
2	5	8	11	12	9	6	3	1	4	7	10	
6	9	3	12	1	11	4	8	7	5	10	2	
4	11	8	1	7	12	5	3	10	9	2	6	etc.
5	12	3	7	10	1	9	8	2	11	6	4	

(iii) 1st pair of permutations

Piano

in attack to four types and the dynamics to five. Messiaen reconciles here the difference between the constantly changing contour of modality and the established successions of linear serialism by the principle of permutation of all twelve notes, thus establishing at the same time a progressive mechanism. His row is the familiar pattern of semitones radiating alternately from a central note, see Ex. 200(ii),[1] and the permutation used applies the identical process (i.e. 7.6.8.5.9.4.10.3.11.2. 12.1); a few lines of the table are shown at Ex. 200(ii), from which the reader can reconstruct the course of those sections of the work based on this scheme by analogy with the first, Ex. 200(iii), noting that successive permutations are coupled in treble and bass.

Messiaen's work has been used to demonstrate simply an approach to organization of material which was also being developed by his pupils at this time. Their aim of subjecting all the elements which contribute to a musical texture (the term *parameters* was adopted) to serial procedure was extended into a structural determinant by permutation of the series according to the dictates of a super-series. These general principles were given a new interpretation in almost every work; for when so much follows from pre-compositional decisions (even if relaxations be permitted in their acceptance) they become an important field for the exercise of the composer's creative individuality. That this field may prove irksomely narrow is to be deduced not so much from the superficial impression of similarity listeners have found in multiple-serial structures—since the listening technique which these demand is both formidable and unfamiliar—as from many composers' subsequent abandonment of this extreme position. It will be profitable at this point to consider more specifically the work of some prominent representatives of the new music.

PIERRE BOULEZ

Musical history would not have immediately led us to suppose that France would provide the two most celebrated documents in the early search for strict control of every musical element—Messiaen's *Mode de valeurs et d'intensités* and Boulez's *Structures*. The pseudo-polyphony of the French Baroque, Berlioz's freedom from the tyranny of conventional progression and phrasing, and Debussy's reliance on a superb harmonic and formal instinct in abandoning orthodox tonality, suggest a native antipathy towards rigidity of procedure. Yet if the demonstrable *organization* of German music is often absent, the

---

[1] This pattern recurs in the *Livre d'Orgue* (1953). It is also a schematic serial basis much favoured by Luigi Nono; cf. p. 476.

characteristically French fantasy is governed by a meticulous feeling for *order*. Messiaen's fitful genius is somewhat exceptional in often needing the help of the controlling mechanisms noted earlier; but it is significant that, even in the *Quatre études de rhythme* (which include *Mode* and *Ile de Feu 2*), these appear in conjunction with freely rhapsodic ideas. If Pierre Boulez (b. 1925) was driven by intellectual curiosity to discover, in incomparably more precise detail, the consequences of a will to establish order in each dimension of his music, the powerful quality of his imagination has offset these statistical preoccupations.[1]

The more rigidly inhibited a piece is, the more satisfyingly accountable it becomes to the analyst, until he may even arrive at the position of being able to point out 'errors' (as distinct from infelicities or misjudgements) in the composing process. When analysis has once achieved such a status, it becomes difficult to recall its essentially subsidiary relevance to the listening experience, and a work's notoriety may come to depend more on the analyst's labours than on the listener's. This is not to decry Boulez's renowned essays in total serialization, but to stress that their place in his creative achievement has proved to be less than their importance for his development. Some of the works which preceded them, though disowned at times by Boulez, give a clearer picture of the composer's individuality, and it is a picture which more recent works have brought into still sharper focus.

After the *Psalmodies* for piano (1945), written before he knew anything of serialism, Boulez mastered orthodox row-manipulation under Leibowitz swiftly enough to explore beyond it in his next works. The 1946 Flute Sonatina uses more elaborate permutations of fully dodecaphonic thematic material than were recognized in Schoenberg's practice; but the passages of development adapt Webern's structure from much smaller cells, of a few intervals, producing an athematic texture in which attention can be concentrated on the minutiae of the sounding fabric—notably the subtle balance between rational and irrational elements in its rhythmic cells.[2] Two years later, the Second Piano Sonata established a composing process in which the plotting of rhythmic relations seems to be given precedence, and the attendant pitches develop intervallic cells without reference to any ideal twelve-note basic shape:

---

[1] Among Boulez's many writings, *Penser la musique aujourd'hui* (Paris, 1964; English translation, *Boulez on Music Today*, London, 1971), gives the most impressive account of the interplay between intellect and imagination that characterizes his work.
[2] Boulez's analysis in *Polyphonie* (1948), cited in Goléa, op cit., p. 51.

Ex. 201

Extreme dynamic changes help to convey the explosive fury characteristic of early Boulez (and a hidden menace powerfully sensed in some
later, more suave, contexts), but they still progress here according to
'expressive' rather than objectified or purely statistical dictates. Indeed
the demonstrative rhetoric (and, one might add, the length) of this work
is so far removed from Webern's highly-charged reticence that the
resulting sound gives no idea of the debt in interval treatment.[1] Aggressive timbre and splintered textures dominate the instrumental sonority,
but the contrasting quiet passages are of an exacting complexity. In the
Livre pour Quatuor, which includes ideas reworked from the Sonata,[2]
Boulez found a more congenial medium for a true counterpoint of
dynamic values and for the exercise of an easier lyricism.

These works provided impressive evidence of a compelling new
voice capable of more than one inflexion, but they gave no clear clues
to any symbolic life to be re-lived by the listener. The composer who is
intent on inculcating a new technique of acute listening may be ill-
advised to provide too soon any form of parallel to the aural phenomenon. But we may suspect one who constantly refuses to recognize
the part played by analogy in drawing musical experience from
patterned sound. (Those who find the material of *Die Kunst der Fuge*
truly 'neutral' must also find it a very dull work.) Just as Webern's
songs provide a key to his rarefaction of old expressive symbols, so
Boulez's vocal music interprets the associations he feels in newer musical
structures, and, as we saw in Stravinsky's work, this desire to wed
expressive power to an intricately regulated technique can lead to a
powerful fusion. *Le Marteau sans maître* (The Hammer without a
Master) has proved a most influential work in spreading the new music,
but Boulez had already revealed a vivid response to René Char's verse
in the early cantatas, *Le Visage nuptial* (1946–51) and *Le Soleil des eaux*
(1948/50/58). He regards the singing of a poem as a convention seriously
weakened by stylized imitation of speech rhythms and intervals; and he

[1] Drew, 'Modern French Music' in Hartog, op. cit., pp. 292–3.
[2] The *Livre* has subsequently been re-worked in a version for string orchestra.

aims instead at communicating the expressive message through the musical revaluation, rather than through the making intelligible, of texts better 'understood' simply by reading.[1] His wide range of vocal effect, even regarded purely musically, is notably free from affectation. In the first movement of *Le Soleil des eaux* the soprano monody has a suppleness which, with orchestral scoring of a beguiling clarity (even when densely contrapuntal), shows Boulez master of a peculiarly French lyricism; and the impetuous choral writing of the second movement reaches a natural climax by bursting orthodox musical bounds with elemental shouts. As the final bars recede into a limpid chamber-music texture, the whole work describes a curve of intensity that is familiar yet original.

In the instrumental works which followed, Boulez was to control such curves, here emerging from the interpretation of a poetic experience, by a statistical plan designed to embrace every other feature susceptible to analysis. The cantatas already show considerable systematization of rhythm, interval succession (including quarter-tone relations in *Le Visage nuptial*), and contrapuntal density, but in elaborating the system to the exclusion of emotional parallelism Boulez seemed to embark on an entirely new sea. The evocative titles, which related Boulez to the line of Messiaen and Debussy, were replaced by the cryptic data of *Polyphonie X* for eighteen instruments (1951) and *Structures* for two pianos (from 1952). The crossing movements which explain the former title are not merely of ascending and descending pitch patterns, but of rhythmic patterns (Messiaen's use of a rhythmic 'chromatic' scale together with its cancrizans in *Cantéyodjayâ* affords a very simple precedent) and of the governing serial processes; Ligeti's analysis of *Structure Ia* demonstrates a continuing preoccupation in Boulez's diagonal selections from his permutation tables.[2] Messiaen's *Mode* study had allowed some freedom of movement, once its fourfold but parallel restrictions were set out; but Boulez unflinchingly follows truly serial paths in each parameter. The fortuitous coincidences in *Polyphonie X* of pitch, duration, instrumental timbre, and dynamic level[3] inevitably result at times in demands which cannot be accurately realized or which repel the ear; and it seems clear that the craftsman of the sensitive translucent scoring in *Le Soleil des eaux* has abdicated momentarily in favour of the impassioned yet dispassionate researcher.

[1] Boulez on words and music in *Cahier de la Compagnie Madeleine Renaud-Jean-Louis Barrault* (May, 1958); cited by Goléa, op. cit., p. 111–13.

[2] György Ligeti, 'Pierre Boulez—Decision and Automatism in *Structure Ia*', *Die Reihe*, iv (Eng. ed., 1960), p. 36.

[3] Boulez on the inevitably approximate nature of dynamic markings: *Die Reihe*, i, p. 26; see also his *Penser la musique aujourd'hui*, pp. 68–69.

30

Boulez has described as 'totalitarian' this first essay in total serialization.[1] His *Structures* rest on as imposing a network of primary decisions, but better considered; and the most vexed problem, that of timbre, is replaced by varieties of attack in the single tone colour of two pianos. He still writes polyphony but, as Ligeti points out, 'for all its polyphonic stratification of series [the music] is formed from discrete elements of pitch and duration: because of the piano's characteristic attack, the acoustic events are concentrated into points that are well defined as to frequency and time.'[2] If we were to rate it no higher, the work would remain an invaluable contribution to the new aural training required by structures in which each note represents, not a fixed association as in Messiaen's piece, but a unique interaction of independently progressing serial mechanisms. Both his initial pitch series (but not register—a vital field for the composer's free adjustment) and duration series are borrowed from the Messiaen model (cf. Ex. 199), and in the first movement, the exposition of their simple permutations naturally produces sections of identical length ($1 \, \flat + 2 + 3 \ldots 12 = 78 \, \flat$s). Each begins with the simultaneous impact of the first note in every strand in use, the texture varying between one and six strands; and the sectional character is further stressed in that one value in the series of dynamics and attacks holds good for each strand throughout a pitch/duration combination. (Boulez writes of dynamics as 'a kind of superstructure with a demonstrable function rather than a real factor of structural organization'.)

Ex. 202

[1] Goléa, op. cit., p. 139.   [2] Ligeti, loc. cit., p. 42.

Ex. 202 shows a complete section of three strands and the first bar of a four-strand section. The correspondences across the division show how carefully planned is the super-ordering. The three pitch series here are clearly a transposition of the retrograde inversion (piano I), and two transpositions of the retrograde (piano II); the duration series are an 'inversion' and two 'basic sets'. But this terminology has no meaning apart from the permutation tables, and Boulez set these up by numbering transpositions of the pitch series, but uses them as a numerical basis for the other elements too.

The other two movements of the first book (a second book has appeared, and the composer's didactic plan comprises twelve movements) break away from the jolts—predictable and eventually monotonous, however varied the intervening patterns—caused by synchronized permutations of one simple duration series. Far more forceful oppositions can be engendered when duration series move out of alignment by using different units, when their larger values are subdivided,[1] and when the degree of activity is further raised both by a less leisurely operation of the dynamic series and, paradoxically, by the organization of durations of silence. In the formidably difficult second piece, Boulez's command of contrasted piano textures, and of their balance across a wide span, betrays a shaping impulse that can now impose itself on rigorously ordered material. This is no limp 'open form' thrown up fortuitously by the machinations of a system: its composer could turn with assurance in the following work to a dialectic founded in less demonstrable premises.

Characteristically he reverted to the problem set aside in *Structures*—the ordering of timbre, now according to an ideal of delicacy that was not among the preassumptions of *Polyphonie X*. But he also reverted, in *Le Marteau sans maître* (1953–7), to his earlier search for a new correspondence between words and music. The varied methods of vocal delivery in *Wozzeck* (for example), from speech to cantabile line, all served to underline an expressive meaning literally or implicitly preserved in the text. Boulez's scale[2] moves between a rare extreme of verbal supremacy (parlando and nominal intelligibility) and musical supremacy (vocalized sound merging with the instruments) transferring 'meaning' to a plane on which words are an intrusion. In fact the Surrealist texts of Char's poems are strangely illuminated in this process. The alto voice is identified so closely with the alto flute and viola that there is no radical differentiation when it withdraws entirely (see Ex. 203), and the instrumental 'commentaries' on the poems stand in essentially the same relation to them as do the word settings. Yet however fundamental these transitions, he has not subjected them to the strict rota ordering used by some of his contemporaries nor favoured, as they do, a deliberate sterilization of words by phonetic dissection.[3]

The popular allure of *Le Marteau* owes much to an unusual

---

[1] Subdivision is an antidote to the tendency of large values to attract more attention than is serially their due. See Ligeti, 'Wandlungen der musikalischen Form', *Die Reihe*, vii, p. 12.

[2] Stockhausen, 'Musik und Sprache', *Die Reihe*, vi, p. 36.

[3] Cf. pp. 480 and 491.

Ex. 203

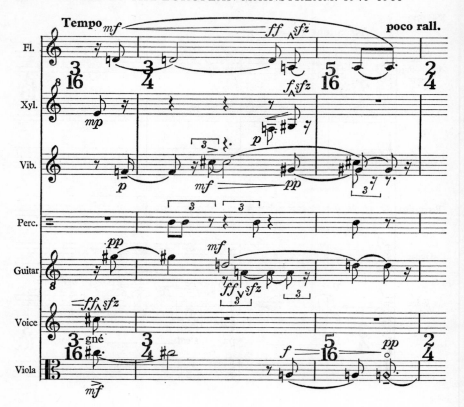

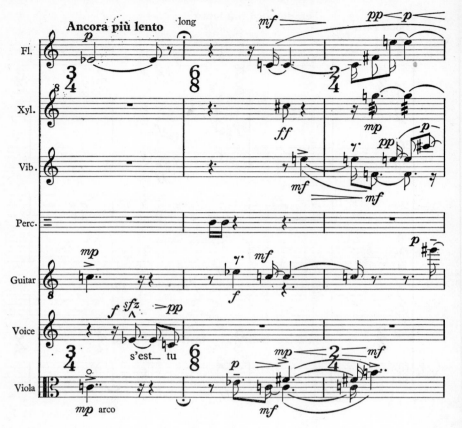

instrumentation that excludes all acerbity in a flickering interplay of high sounds. Music which never assaults the ears may be an effective narcotic; and the oriental quality of sound together with the undue length of some movements can easily deaden the listener's awareness of anything more specific than a peculiar fragrance. Boulez has pronounced his music immune against analysis,[1] but he cannot mean it to be heard in so flaccid a manner: if audiences that find this work appealing are to learn to listen discriminatingly to new music in general, they will have at least to sense the subtlety of the craftsmanship in *Le Marteau sans maître*. The variation of timbre, far from a crude *pointillisme*, includes newly imagined effects of merging and emerging colour and of 'hocketing'.[2] Rhythmic activity, which seems desperate at a first hearing,[3] is varied flexibly between an exact timing of proportioned cells (see the three commentaries on *Bourreaux de solitude* with their background of precise percussive reiteration) and a superimposition of irrational values which produces a controlled rubato. The systematic variation of octave register within the line[4] conceals yet does not entirely dissipate their tight nuclear groupings, but the prevailing impression is of an improvisatory fantasy that no longer needs Webern's crystalline correspondences.

As the works of innumerable lesser serialists show, the accumulation of restrictions must inevitably produce an increasingly arbitrary effect.[5] To have created the feeling of freedom within the ordered world of *Le Marteau* was a worthier achievement, and Boulez's characteristic reaction was to seek in his next works a controlled relation between such freedom and a fundamental strictness of technique. The second *Improvisation sur Mallarmé* is the purest example of this kind, but the Third Piano Sonata offers another freedom, an opportunity for the player to select his own permutation from serial possibilities of movement, constitution and succession planned by the composer. This element of choice, and therefore of controlled chance, had an honourable French precedent (which Boulez was quick to exploit) in Mallarmé's *Livre*,[6] but its application to music was demonstrated most radically

---

[1] Goléa, op. cit., p. 39, but see his own *Penser la musique aujourd'hui* (Paris, 1964), for a detailed account of some technical methods.

[2] Robert Craft, 'Boulez and Stockhausen', *The Score,* xxiv (1958), p. 55.

[3] Colin Mason discusses some rhythmic problems of *Le Marteau* in *Music & Letters*, xxxix (1958), pp. 198–9.

[4] That it is still possible to view the texture as linear polyphony has been made the starting point of a criticism of this work as stylized and (by implication) reactionary. See André Hodeir, *Since Debussy* (London, 1961), p. 153.

[5] Ligeti, 'Wandlungen . . .', *Die Reihe*, vii, p. 6.

[6] Hans Rudolf Zeller, 'Mallarmé und das serielle Denken', *Die Reihe*, vi, p. 5; André Boucourechliev, 'Pli selon pli', *La nouvelle revue française*, cx (1961), p. 916; Boulez, ' "Sonate, que me veux-tu?" ', *Perspectives in New Music*, i, 2 (1963), p. 32.

by the German, Karlheinz Stockhausen (b. 1928); at this point, where Boulez's leadership of the new school was first challenged, it is necessary to summarize Stockhausen's earlier work.

KARLHEINZ STOCKHAUSEN

Boulez and Stockhausen share skills derived from Messiaen's rhythmic teaching, a fervent admiration for Webern's music[1] rather than for the Viennese serial principle, and a naturally exuberant iconoclasm; and they at first retained enough in common for each to act as a valuable stimulus to the other's inventiveness. But this rivalry, industriously promoted by their disciples, never concealed fundamental divergences in sonorous ideals. These emerge clearly even in works of comparable technical complexity, so that the new music, like that of the past, is powerfully coloured by the personality of the composer.

Stockhausen's pertinacity in a long and varied training is in illuminating contrast to Boulez's brilliant but impatient apprenticeship. After acquiring conservatory disciplines under Frank Martin and Hermann Schroeder at Cologne, Stockhausen moved to Paris to study with Messiaen and Milhaud. At a time when many composers were sampling the desultory charms of *musique concrète* he abandoned them for a more systematic investigation of electro-acoustics, phonetics, and information-theory under Meyer-Eppler at Bonn. These studies contributed to the command of electronic resources displayed in his work at the Cologne Studio,[2] but the passion for analysis and synthesis which they imply has equally marked his instrumental writing. Acoustic research has proved as strong a stimulus to the imagination for Stockhausen as literary sensibilities have been for Boulez. To this more common stimulus the German might appear wholly unresponsive, yet the affecting sounds into which the biblical words of *Gesang der Jünglinge* (Song of the Youths) are transmuted spring as much from a contemplation of the text as from the wish to demonstrate a hypothesis.

The hyphen in Stockhausen's title *Kontra-punkte* (1953) underlines one technical assumption of this first published work (the earlier *Kreuzspiel* (Cross Play) has subsequently been issued in a revised version). But strict *pointillisme* is not the only relation in which he sets the tone colours of ten instruments, reduced progressively to solo piano. Already there are examples of an opposite extreme—superimpositions of rapid passages which fuse into aurally inextricable entities of a given pitch width. Interval correspondences rarely reproduce Webern's sim-

---

[1] Cf. the tributes to Webern by Boulez and Stockhausen in *Die Reihe*, ii, (Eng.) pp. 40 and 37.
[2] Cf. pp. 489–92.

plicity but are no less persistent: innumerable patterns are derived by octave transposition from the addition of a perfect and an augmented fourth (see the last two bars of Ex. 204(i), and in Ex. 204(ii) the assembly of the chromatic total from these intervals). Permuted dodecaphonic successions are used, but a less expected link with Schoenberg is provided by occasional weighty 'chromatic'[1] harmonic texture, especially in the piano, as at Ex. 204(i). Accurate realization of the many irrational rhythmic groups is made more hazardous by their dispersal among the instruments, yet they remain calculable against an essentially rigid 3/8 beat.

With the *Klavierstücke I–IV* (1954),[2] experimental pages revealing little of Boulez's natural pianistic élan, Stockhausen abandoned the restrictions of the humanly practicable in his notation of simultaneous

Ex. 204

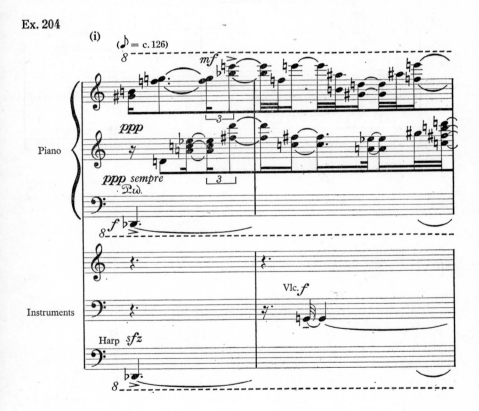

[1] i.e. retaining the tension of chromatic texture such as Schoenberg's Op. 11, no. 3, written when tonality was so recently exorcized; contrast the weightless sound characteristic of Webern.

[2] The third piece is analysed by Dieter Schnebel in 'Karlheinz Stockhausen', *Die Reihe*, iv, (Eng.) pp. 126–31.

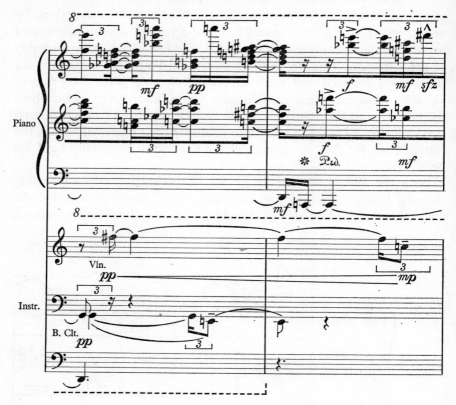

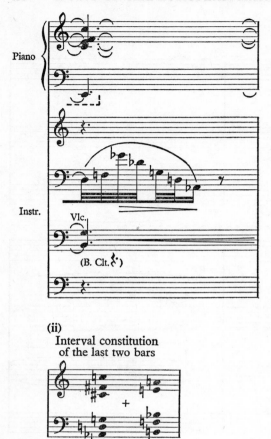

(ii)

Interval constitution
of the last two bars

dynamics—see Ex. 205(i)—and duration-proportions. His demands
(e.g. the doubly irrational groups in Ex. 205(ii)) are so detailed that it is
disconcerting to learn that the player, after familiarizing himself with
their complex relation to a metronomic tempo (as fast as possible), may
reinterpret them as less taxing proportions in varying tempi. Patient
study of such notational problems might conceivably lead to a control,
tauter than that of an impromptu rubato, of the discontinuous tempi
essential to the structure. But Boulez has written in an implied reference to these pieces, 'it is better to substitute an alteration of tempo',[1]
and the distinction he then makes between concepts of time appropriate

---

[1] Boulez, 'At the ends of fruitful land', *Die Reihe*, i, (Eng.), pp. 23–24; see also comments
by Nicholas Ruwet and Henri Pousseur in *Die Reihe*, vi, pp. 67–68 and 77–78.

Ex. 205

to electronic and instrumental music respectively is fundamental to an understanding of Stockhausen's development:

In the first case, an unchanging *tempo* within which durations may be subjected to almost unlimited degrees of variation; in the second a *tempo* which is itself subject to the greatest degree of variation but within which there are limits to the degree to which values may be varied.[1]

This wide-ranging essay by Boulez abounds in such speculations, often brilliantly apposite but not always reflected in his own music. Stockhausen prefers to work out the implications of his ideas in both composing and theorizing. His next instrumental works, *Zeitmasse* (Measures of time) (1955–6) and *Gruppen* (Groups) (1955–7), apply the concept of fluctuating tempo to a small chamber group and to large orchestral forces, while his essay on musical time[2] has become a required text in that study. The five wind players of *Zeitmasse*, although their parts present unprecedented difficulties, are not required constantly to interrelate them on the basis of an identical beat. At times each moves at an

---

[1] Boulez, loc. cit., p. 25.
[2] Stockhausen, 'How time passes . . .', *Die Reihe*, iii, (Eng.) p. 10.

even but individual tempo, or several parts engage in an independent accelerando or ritardando with or without even tempi elsewhere; or one part may rely entirely on cues provided by another. Stockhausen's theory of *time-fields*,[1] degrees of permissible deviation from mathematical precision in the realization of complex rhythmic notation or in ensemble performance at tempi without common multiples, rationalizes the tendency of post-war composers to break free of the old constraint imposed on horizontal movements in time by rigid vertical 'harmonic' alignment. In Webern interval-patterns vary freely between the successive and the simultaneous, but it is only when intervals as objects for individual perception have been abandoned in favour of complexes of a given note-content (see e.g. bar 2 in Ex. 207(iii)) that the composer may claim that discrepancies in the progress-through-time of the total sound-constituents no longer impairs intelligibility. In fact, Stockhausen ensures that his simultaneous tempi do not lose the proximity he intends and can resume precise alignment; he has calculated the superimpositions with the musical craftsman's awareness of instrumental possibilities. *Action-durations*,[2] such as the time which a competent executant will take to play a given passage 'as fast as possible' or the time dictated by the requirement 'as slowly as possible, in one breath', provide at once a feeling of freedom to the player and a measure of some tolerance rather than of utter unpredictability.

Clearly, such freedom could not be extended far beyond the confines of a small chamber group, and *Zeitmasse* has become legendary for its rehearsal demands. In writing for bigger forces, Stockhausen concentrated on freedom of movement between, rather than within, the tempi of three orchestras, each with its conductor, and enhanced this for the listener by separating them in space.[3] *Gruppen* demonstrates the composer's view, prompted by his electro-acoustic researches, of time relations as a reflection in the 'macro-structure' of those existing in the 'micro-structure' (i.e. as vibration frequencies). As a pitch doubles its value in our conventional temperament after twelve increases by the twelfth root of two, he experiments with a comparable 'chromatic' scale of tempi[4]—contrast Messiaen's additive scale of durations; see pp. 439–40 and 446, and Ex. 206(i) and (ii).

This scale can be arranged serially, and with three orchestras each may have rests in which to prepare the next tempo (see Ex. 206(iii)). Having equated tempi with *chromatic* fundamental pitches, Stockhausen then equates constituent rhythmic values with the superimposition of

---

[1] Stockhausen, loc. cit., p. 30.   [2] Stockhausen, loc. cit., pp. 34–35.
[3] Stockhausen, 'Musik im Raum', *Die Reihe*, vi, pp. 61–62.
[4] Stockhausen, 'How time passes . . .', *Die Reihe*, iii, (Eng.) p. 21.

Ex. 206

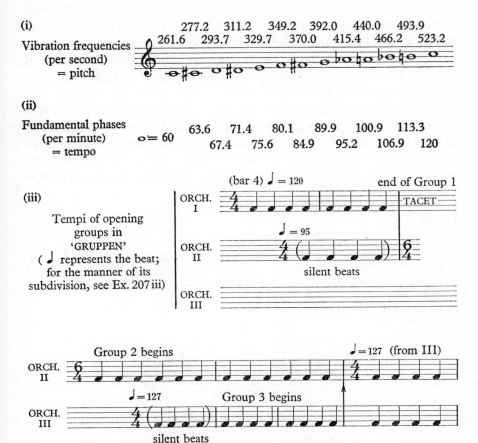

(i)

Vibration frequencies
(per second)
= pitch

      277.2 311.2   349.2 392.0   440.0   493.9
261.6 293.7 329.7   370.0 415.4 466.2 523.2

(ii)

Fundamental phases
(per minute)
= tempo

$\circ$ = 60

  63.6   71.4   80.1   89.9 100.9 113.3
   67.4   75.6   84.9   95.2 106.9 120

(iii)

Tempi of opening
groups in
'GRUPPEN'
(♩ represents the beat;
for the manner of its
subdivision, see Ex. 207 iii)

harmonic partials that produces tone-colour, overlaying his fundamental tempo phases—e.g. the semibreves in Ex. 206(ii)—with a variety
of 'formants', fractions which coincide to reinforce the beginning of
each fundamental phase[1] (see Ex. 207(ii)). Thus the use of irrational
values foreshadowed by Webern and favoured by Stockhausen's
generation, is interpreted as a magnification of the natural phenomenon
of timbre: 'rhythm of the sound' is paralleled as 'rhythm of the bar'.
This brings us no nearer aural perception of the analogy, since a wealth
of formants[2] suggests no transformation into a higher unity, though it
does merge like a wealth of partials into an inextricable sound. Yet

[1] Ibid., pp. 16–18.
[2] Ibid., pp. 26–28, gives an explanation of the 'formant spectra' which regulate the
selection of formants sounded.

31

Stockhausen's theory does enable him to plot the fluctuations in rhythmic density so typical of his work, and many transitions in *Gruppen* exploit the territory between apprehension of rhythmic activity as tempi and as eventful but opaque, and therefore immobile, sound.

A similar distinction is made between co-existent instrumental textures that merge and those with a high degree of 'permeability'.[1] But Stockhausen's spatial lay-out also permits arresting motions of a uniform timbre; a quasi-fugal exposition of nine brass entries is distributed in space and its climax-chords dynamically manipulated so as to swirl round the orchestras. By a clear scheme of timbre predominances and transitions almost two hundred small 'groups' of material are welded into far longer sequences. Together with organization of tempo

Ex. 207

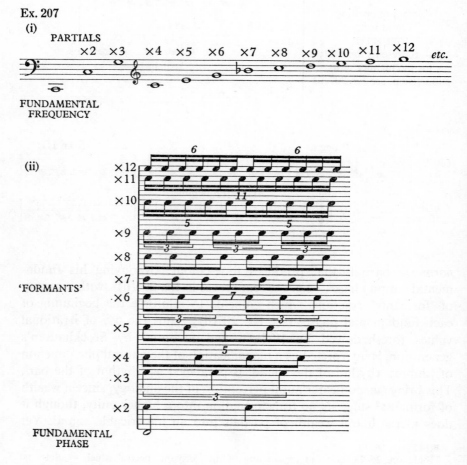

---

[1] Ligeti, 'Wandlungen der musikalischen Form', *Die Reihe*, vii, pp. 8 and 14.

Chromatic segment
('band width')

Fundamental phase: ♩
Formants: 2. 3. 4. 5. 6. 7. 8. 9. 10.

and timbre a third serialism, of 'band-widths', functions no less directly. Activity within the groups is often no more than a constant flickering of many formants between pitches selected by a super-row, but these present the utmost diversity between a tight cluster of semitones (see e.g. the first bar in Ex. 207(iii) and its activation in the next bar) and a punctiliously spaced wide distribution of twelve pitches (occasionally more—octaves pass unnoticed at moments of densest activity)[1]. As many of these distinctive sound patterns remain immediately recognizable despite reorganization of scoring and rhythms, they provide another source of the work's remarkably integrated effect. The formidable theoretical concepts of *Gruppen* are reflected in diversity of detail contributing to a form of powerful simplicity. The espressivo of its string writing and the furious vigour of its jazz-influenced climax provide the closest ties with familiar rhetoric in all Stockhausen, while its frank emphasis on the spectacular element natural to orchestral performance may yet help to establish this score as a valuable bridge between the composer and an uninitiated public.

Stockhausen's spatial distribution of orchestral sound logically resolved the contradiction posed by the delicate elaboration of post-war serialism and the gargantuan apparatus of the nineteenth-century orchestra: when composition is stratified the listener can concentrate on local detail or broader relationships. His example was followed by many of his contemporaries, including Boulez (in *Doubles*, performed in 1958 but subsequently rewritten), Nono, and Pousseur, and has also had important consequences for a natural fusion of electronic and instrumental sound. In *Carré* (1960), Stockhausen essayed spatial writing for four choral-orchestral ensembles. This comprehensive score has many impressive (and some humorous) moments, but seems to lack the dramatic cogency of both *Gruppen* and *Gesang der Jünglinge*. Meanwhile Stockhausen's pioneering had attracted at least as much emulation in another field.

Klavierstück XI (1956) has gained a notoriety incommensurate with its absolute worth as a prototype of indeterminacy and the musical 'mobile'. (The term was used by analogy with the artistic forms of Calder and others, in which spatial relations are variable.) Chance modified only the synchronization of the strata in *Zeitmasse* and *Gruppen*, but in writing for a single performer Stockhausen allowed it to regulate the succession and quality of events. Nineteen pieces of piano-texture face the player, who chooses their order at random but follows instructions in each one as to the manner (i.e. tempo, dynamics and mode of attack) in which he shall play his next choice. This provision does ensure con-

---

[1] Ligeti, loc. cit., p. 8.

PLATE VI

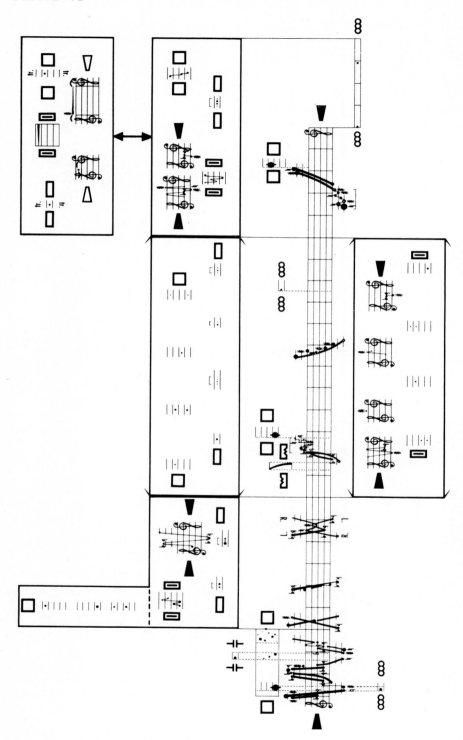

STOCKHAUSEN'S *ZYKLUS*, 1959 (*see p. 465*)

A page from the score

trasts of material, but means that pitch and rhythm relations have been composed with no fixed idea of the kind of music they represent. From this attitude to one which abandons all concern for the precise notes played may appear a small step, and it had already been taken by the American, John Cage, and in the 'graphic notation' used for works like Sylvano Bussotti's *Piano Pieces for David Tudor*.[1] Having recognized the vanity of earlier dreams of absolute control through multiple serialism, some composers decided to relinquish what has traditionally been regarded as their prime function, the construction of exact sound relationships. However his disciples may have profiteered from this cheapening of their craft, Stockhausen still retained too much of traditional German skills to exercise his aural imagination merely in peripheral matters and to decline responsibility for the sounding substance. His *Zyklus* (1959),[2] for an enormous battery of percussion instruments controlled by one player, explores a field of sound in which pitch continuity is naturally exceptional. Here operations of chance and idiosyncratic notation both contribute to a *tour de force* that admits yet directs the improvisatory vehemence associated with these instruments in their most developed environments—tribal music and jazz. In the *Refrain* for piano, celesta, and vibraphone (1959), the effect of spontaneity does not exclude a keen regulation of sonorities, and this short attractive piece suggested that Stockhausen's use of his talents was not to be dictated simply by the principle of novelty at any price.

Boulez first introduced some freedom of performing procedure in works that appeared later than Stockhausen's. Whether he was at least as early in conceiving the principle[3] is less significant than his distinctive view of it. In allowing an incredibly large number of possible orders of events in *Klavierstück XI*, Stockhausen shed the artist's responsibility to create what he believes to be effective order. Even if we regard cumulative rhetoric as dependent on tonality and substitute discontinuous 'open' forms, the very existence of music as an art presupposes that some sequences of sound are more satisfying than others; and it is a perversion of the serial ideal to insist that we should discover these only by dint of working through many less engaging permutations.

Boulez was repelled by the artistic indifference implied by the infinitely variable mobile and 'indeterminate' notations, and in his Third Piano Sonata he can be seen weighing the effect of permitted

---

[1] Stockhausen lectured on 'Music and Graphic Arts' at Darmstadt in 1959; see report by K. H. Wörner, *Musical Quarterly*, xlvi (1960), p. 271. Cf. also 'Notation-Interpretation' by Cornelius Cardew in *Tempo*, 58 (1961), p. 21. Cardew was responsible for the 'realization' of Stockhausen's *Carré*: see his article in *Musical Times*, cii (1961), pp. 619 and 698.

[2] See pl. VI.

[3] See Goléa, op. cit., pp. 228–9.

modifications on structures whose broad design remains within his control.[1] The five 'formants' may be placed in various orders, but the massive 'Constellation' or its alternative retrograde version, 'Constellation-Miroir', must remain the centrepiece. Within the movements the interpreter must choose from alternative routes according to principles so carefully drawn up that no haphazard presentation of the total material is countenanced. In the simplest piece, 'Antiphonie', each of the two sections may be played in either the original version or in a variation printed on the opposite page, a degree of liberty scarcely exceeding that of many a Baroque structure. 'Trope' is published in a spiral-backed form that allows a variety of starting points in the cycle of its four sections; as one of them ('Commentaire') appears twice but is to be performed on only one of these occasions, a wider range of possible orders emerges. In addition, two of the sections are composed of obligatory and optional fragments in constant alternation; thus, it is unlikely that the enterprising player will ever reproduce the same pattern, yet the *sequence* is always one that Boulez has planned. Similarly the alternation of *blocs* (dense harmonic textures) and *points* in 'Constellation' leaves the player free to choose innumerable different itineraries from this 'map of an unknown city',[2] but the composer ensures that he does not double in his tracks. The remaining formants, 'Strophe' and 'Séquence', have not yet achieved their final shape and, given this concept of the sonata as 'a moving, expanding universe',[3] it is to be expected that every modification to one movement will tend to change the composer's attitude to those he had thought to have perfected.

The influence of Mallarmé's *Livre* on the flexible shape of this sonata has been noted. At least four more works by Boulez already performed remained for long, or still exist as, 'work in progress', due to his view of form as intelligent compilation and to his enthusiasm for revision. The most ambitious of these, *Pli selon pli* for soprano and orchestra, is a tribute to Mallarmé built around three *Improvisations* on his verses. The impression of the whole work is of the composer's most mature achievement, in which his splenetic violence and lyrical sonority contribute not so much to bizarre contrasts as to a comprehensive pattern. Boulez has acknowledged his debt to a study of Debussy and Ravel's Mallarmé settings,[4] and the influence of the former is not far to

[1] Ibid., pp. 229–30; Boulez's views on chance are expounded in 'Alea', *La Nouvelle Revue Française* (November 1957) and *Perspectives of New Music*, iii, 1 (1964), p. 42. On the Third Sonata in its first form see Ligeti, 'Zur III. Klavier-sonate von Boulez', *Die Reihe*, v, pp. 38–40; on a later stage, see Boulez, ' "Sonate, que me veux-tu?" ', *Perspectives of New Music*, i, 2 (1963), p. 32.

[2] Boulez, loc. cit.   [3] Ibid.   [4] Goléa, op. cit., p. 251.

seek in the evocative, hovering harmonies. The initial poise of the vocal line gives way to ecstatic convolutions of multiple grace-notes (producing an inevitably free tempo); and though the orchestra in the final 'Tombeau' reaches a climax of dense improvisatory activity, it is with the impassioned return of the voice that the work's great circle is completed. Among the provisions for interpretative liberty built into it are alternative circuits of procedure selected by the conductor, and durational schemes controlled by the singer's breath (cf. *Zeitmasse*): in Ex. 208, from the second *Improvisation*, all the instrumental groups are played freely between the singer's moves.

Ex. 208

The general transition of the *avant-garde* from a fanatical ordering of every detail in time to such fluidity has sometimes seemed a *volte face* explained only by capriciousness or despair; but for Boulez this withdrawal of attention from the precise construction of each moment has never involved the purely fortuitous, and has encouraged a breadth of structure so far without parallel among his contemporaries.

THE *AVANT-GARDE* IN ITALY AND ELSEWHERE

Despite differences of musical temperament that confirm national traditions, Boulez and Stockhausen showed obvious parallels, even reciprocity, in their early technical development. A third composer whose name was often linked with theirs, Luigi Nono (b. 1924), presents a further, and very distinctive, national inflexion, but also a single-minded direction of technique towards the immediate expressive purpose, often of a dramatic urgency. Both Nono and another Venetian, Bruno Maderna (1920–73), owe much to the teaching of Hermann Scherchen, a conductor and profound student of modern music who championed Webern and foresaw his importance for the new generation. Maderna acquired professional skill as conductor and composer while Nono was still reading law, and could therefore guide his early development. Their attendance at the Darmstadt courses in 1950 founded contacts between the European advanced movement and the composers of Northern Italy which flourished in the succeeding decade and produced some of its most distinguished music. These cultural ties, altogether closer than may be traced in Petrassi's neo-classicism or Dallapiccola's dodecaphonic allegiance, imply no renunciation of national predilections. Nono's *Intolleranza 1960* was the first opera of the *avant-garde*, but its passionate involvement in the endless protest against oppression recalls not only Dallapiccola but the revolutionary Verdi. And Dallapiccola's concern for lucid sonority and lyrical flow are reflected, despite constructional devices far more schematic than his, in the works of his sometime pupil, Luciano Berio (b. 1925).

In basing his Canonic Variations (1950) on a twelve-note row by Schoenberg, Nono paid tribute to Viennese expressionism and to dodecaphonic principle, both of which he was to transmute in forging his mature style. The chamber medium of *Polifonica-Monodia-Ritmica* (1951)[1] prompted an uncharacteristic sharpness of line, but the *Epitaph for Federico Garcia Lorca* (1951) included Nono's first attempts to pit constructive ingenuity against the expressive compulsion generated by a text, to 'live in a state of tension between rational and emotional creative thought'.[2] The *Due Espressioni* (1953) are important studies in the conversion of Schoenberg's *Klangfarbenmelodie* to the ambivalent textures, immobile yet quivering throughout with restless activity, that have become Nono's distinguishing sound. Such textures, of constantly fluctuating colour, dynamics, spacing and density of events, invite the description *pointilliste* since instruments and even voices frequently contribute no more than isolated notes. Here too an ambivalence is apparent, for the sense of cohesion is stronger than that of isolation. Much of Nono's art lies in his scrupulous dispersal across many registers of notes that are firmly tied together in serial durational

---

[1] Udo Unger, 'Luigi Nono', *Die Reihe*, iv, (Eng. ed.) p. 5.
[2] Ibid., p. 10.

successions (several strata operate at once, based on different sub-divisions of a fundamental beat) and by the constant, indeed automatic, revolution across the events in time of a pitch-series: see Exx. 209(i) and 210(iii). By 1955, many composers had abandoned the fixed twelve-note succession as a working principle, but Nono's *Incontri* (Encounters) for twenty-four instruments consists of forty-one reiterations of a row and the repetition of the entire structure in reverse. Yet the very auto-matism of the procedure reveals how far it is from the privileged thema-tic status of the Schoenbergian series: here the succession merely ensures an even supply of homogeneous material, while the listener's attention is occupied by endlessly new engagements between the same notes due to activity in the other parameters and to register changes (see Ex. 209(ii)). Repeated-note flourishes in conflicting durational strata generate a conventionally 'rhythmic' excitement and make a climactic epigram of the central bar, in which the first and last notes of the row compete before they exchange roles; but, as with *Le Marteau*, an impression of uniformly attractive or intriguing sound may in fact dull response to the changing 'encounters' produced by this method.

In *Il canto sospeso* (The interrupted song) (1956), variation of or-chestral and vocal resources in nine short movements ensures a continued freshness of sound. Due to the consistency of colour within a choral texture even *pointilliste* distributions tend to cohere as melodic strata, while the solo voices still more forcefully reinstate melodic criteria; it is perhaps not only for ease of singing that Nono forms near-tonal groupings (overshadowed but not concealed by their contexts) in setting texts of such simple but harrowing pathos as these last letters of Resistance workers condemned to death; see Ex. 210(i). To use such potent literary raw material is to risk disrupting the poise, the distillation of the experience, without which music becomes inchoate; the more powerful the impact of such lines on the composer, the greater his need to discipline his means of communicating it. Nono has denied Stock-hausen's claim that his technique of sharing dissected words among the voices (see Ex. 210(ii)) deliberately masks their intelligibility,[1] but the

Ex. 209
(i)

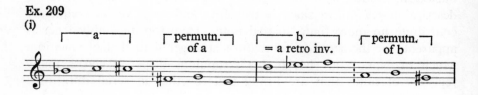

---

[1] Stockhausen, 'Musik und Sprache', *Die Reihe*, vi, p. 42, and see footnote on p. 44.

(all instruments notated at sounding pitch)

listener finds that it often disperses their immediacy while elevating their meaning, a traditional and unique function of music. Stockhausen's discovery of a serialization of vowel sounds in *Il canto sospeso* may reveal more of his own cast of thought than of Nono's; but the latter's practice of flooding the whole musical fabric with the colour of specific vowels (see Ex. 210(iii)(c)) identifies him with a general preoccupation of his contemporaries with the sounds of language.

The technique is essentially that of *Incontri*; though the straight row (Ex. 210(ii)(c); cf. Messiaen's row at Ex. 200(i)) is not preserved for every movement, Ex. 206(iii) shows a typical unfolding of it across four durational strata (units ♪^{5}, ♪, ♪^{3} and ♩—see Ex. 210(iii)(a)) according to a proportional series produced by successive additions—1.2.3.5.8.13;[1] dynamics are also serialized, by a dual ordering.[2] Indeed, of the works of this period which have impressed audiences as putting artifice to the service of expressive ardour, *Il canto sospeso* is superficially nearest to the unsubtle rigidity of totally predetermined texture. Though the composer's choice of register has been noted as the key to the beauty of the sound, it is his choice of different determining mechanisms which is elevated here to a decision involving all his artistry. For the dramatic contrasts spring directly from this. The overwhelming menace of the wedge of choral sound widening from a vast unison at the words 'Le porte s'aprono. Eccoli i nostri assassini' (The gates open. There are our murderers), or the powerful compassion of the crescendo-diminuendo arch in the orchestral interlude surrounded by shimmering close spectra of string harmonics, realize designs that are in themselves triumphs of the creative spirit.

Whether Nono surpassed this achievement in essaying a still more ambitious and overtly dramatic scheme in *Intolleranza* (1960) is debatable. The elaborate symbolism of Angelo Maria Ripellino's libretto has not encouraged as unified a vision, and the note of protest sometimes rings shrill; but Nono remained the composer most likely to re-create a peculiarly Italian tradition in terms of the new art. Other works after *Il Canto* show greater intricacy in applying basically unchanged methods. The *Cori di Didone* (1958) to lines by Giuseppe Ungaretti exploit fanwise chromatic movement and syllabic dissection still further, yet the level of musical intensity directly reflects the words. Nono has declared himself against indeterminacy,[3] but the possibility of an entirely accurate performance of this work seems dubious. And in the

[1] See analyses by Stockhausen, loc. cit.; R. Smith Brindle in *Musical Quarterly*, xlvii (1961), p. 247, and Unger, loc. cit., p. 10, all are in fact oversimplified accounts of Nono's procedures.

[2] Stockhausen, loc. cit., pp. 48–49.

[3] Nono, 'The Historical Reality of Music Today', *The Score*, xxvii (1960), p. 41.

Ex. 210

(i)

(ii)

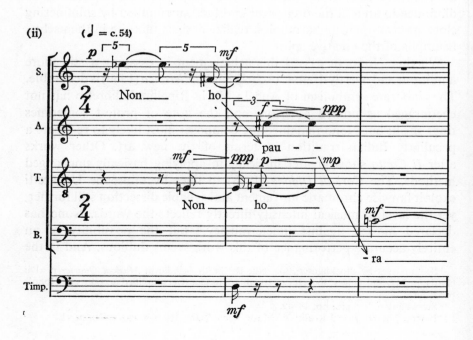

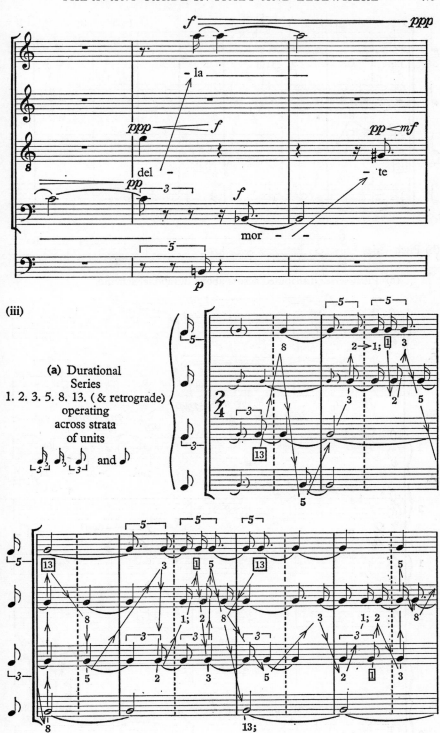

(iii)

(a) Durational
Series
1. 2. 3. 5. 8. 13. (& retrograde)
operating
across strata
of units

(b) Pitch series

(c) Pitch series distributed across above durational scheme

orchestral stereophony of his *Composizione 2* (*Diario polacca 1958*) (Polish Diary 1958) he demands of a vast apparatus (such as Stockhausen devised for the flexible relation of tempi), a precision of timing across the four orchestral groups which is vital to his purpose yet extravagantly taxing. The opening bars, at Ex. 211 (brass only), show comparatively simple entry-delays that move the focal point of the sound.

Nono's recognition began in Germany, and for some years his work was scarcely known in his own country. In contrast, Luciano Berio played a decisive part in stimulating Italian interest in new music, as founder of the Milan electronic studio in 1955, of the concert series 'Incontri Musicali' in 1956, and as editor of the journal of that title. In his early works he excelled in sensitive orchestral colouring and in handling variation-forms easily apprehended as such. This might

32

Ex. 211

Pitch series (cf. Ex. 210 iii, b)

suggest a merely decorative talent, but the arrangement of material in *Omaggio a Joyce*[1] is cumulative, and the five variations of the early orchestral piece *Nones* (from material for an oratorio on Auden's poem) are formed into a larger structure. Berio deliberately reinstates here

[1] Cf. p. 492.

pitch polarities (their serial superstructure permitting spacious articulation) and the octave—as a unique phenomenon that can be neither surreptitiously overlooked nor systematically excluded. By building on a symmetrical row (see Ex. 212) that includes two Ds, he is able, dramatically yet logically, to expose the open octave as the opposite extreme

Ex. 212

to the density of the total chromatic spectrum.[1] The middle territory includes many familiar chordal formations, and the work has more of the Schoenbergian espressivo than is implied by its technical premises of multiple serialism; the sudden dissolution of climax-texture to quiet string harmony is a gesture much used in later works. In *Quaderni I* (1960), it is almost a cliché, and the widening or narrowing chromatic spectrum is a very direct means of controlling emotional tension; the orchestral invention may have been stimulated by experience with electronic processes yet it remains idiomatic and unfailingly attractive. Although the five sections may be played in various successions, their inner forms retain Berio's characteristic simplicity. The String Quartet (1956) seeks to compensate for an essentially monochromatic medium by systematic use of vibrato, pizzicato, *sordino*, and *col legno* effects, influenced in this by Maderna's quartet of the previous year.[2] Here too variation-principle is at work,[3] on material of great nervous intensity. But Berio avoids overtaxing the listener by diluting the stream of events at times, and his practice of dividing long durations into repeated notes even provides a link with the rhythmic world of Stravinsky and Bartók (see Ex. 213).

Berio's *Allelujah II* (1956–8) profits from the example of *Gruppen* in its spatial and temporal conception of five instrumental bodies, but the scoring and the chain of transformations forged from the initial material maintain personal traits. *Circles* (1960), for soprano, harp, and two percussion players, supplements Stockhausen's views on the progression between tone and noise, intelligibility and basic speech elements.[4] The

[1] R. Smith Brindle, *Musical Quarterly*, xliv (1958), pp. 95–101; Piero Santi, 'Luciano Berio', *Die Reihe*, iv (Eng. ed.) pp. 99–100.

[2] On Maderna's quartet, see Giacomo Manzoni, 'Bruno Maderna', *Die Reihe*, iv (Eng. ed.) pp. 115–18.

[3] Santi, loc. cit., p. 100.   [4] Cf. pp. 470–3 and 491.

Ex. 213

[V.O. = vibrato ordinario]

disintegration of language is begun here by the poet, E. E. Cummings, but taken by the composer to the point at which individual consonants are recognized as additional percussion instruments. Similarly the musical content is also gradually reduced to 'noise', and the entire process is then reversed for the second half of the piece. The percussion writing derives from *Zyklus*, each player controlling fifteen types of instrument; and its improvisatory practices include the free 'expression' of words omitted in the singer's restatement (see Ex. 214(ii)), while the singer is twice required to walk to a new position. Although this work was denounced as a farrago of modernism,[1] in fact it demonstrates a notable gift for evocative imagery that has nothing to do with theoretical speculation (see Ex. 214(i)) and an arched form naturally adapted to its descent into elemental sound and recovery of musical meaning.

Ex. 214

[1] See the review by R. F. Goldman, *Musical Quarterly*, xlvii (1961), p. 239.

(ii)

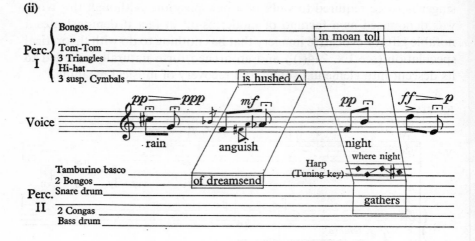

As two of the most forceful creative personalities of the new music, Boulez and Stockhausen strongly influenced the development of numerous lesser men. Any well-publicized artistic movement will attract untalented imitators, to some of whom the *avant-garde* implies only the pursuit of the *dernier cri*. The restrictions of total serialism and the freedoms of indeterminacy are equally easy to reproduce, and innumerable personal foibles can be devised by any composer merely intent on writing an impressive score. When the average score is of formidable complexity, the number of those capable of mentally formulating its sound must be very small; and so the historically un-precedented position arises in which works reach performance because no one has felt able to pronounce with certainty that they were unworthy of it. Fortunately the deception cannot be sustained indefinitely, and the barrage of technical information thrown up around many new works—another curiosity of this period—is unlikely to conceal from the experienced listener evidence of patent ineptitude in the manipula-tion of sound relationships, rather than of their symbols on paper.

The charlatanism of music that simply apes the fashionable must not discredit the efforts of composers whose genuinely exploring cast of mind attracts them naturally to the new paths. Not all of these composers depended slavishly on the enterprise of the two pioneers. The Belgian, Henri Pousseur (b. 1929), an associate of Stockhausen in the earliest electronic investigations, has also shown the German's influence in his instrumental works. But his individual treatment of texture has developed from a detailed study of Webern,[1] and from

[1] Henri Pousseur, 'Webern's Organic Chromaticism', *Die Reihe*, ii, (Eng. ed.) pp. 51–60; also his comparative study of Schoenberg and Webern, *Incontri Musicali*, i (Milan, 1956).

speculation of evident integrity.[1] His important analysis of Webern's 'organic chromaticism'—chains of connexion through the semitone and its octave-transpositions that dispel the polarizing tendencies of other intervals (even including the octave)—has led directly to the predominance in his idiosyncratic harmonic system of the major seventh and minor ninth. Twelve-note serialism is not relevant to his schemes, but the Quintet (1955) in memory of Webern adapts the interval succession of the row in that composer's Op. 22 Quartet. Each interval is regarded as a chromatic scale segment, all its semitonal constituents appearing, but as octave-transpositions; as their order of appearance within a given time-span is free, the relations of the various strata can be regulated so as to control the by-product of other intervals.[2] In later works, Pousseur has diversified his consistent but monotonous harmonic material by acknowledging non-chromatic intervals as primary factors, but systematically neutralizing their polar tendencies through added chromatic relations. Ex. 215 from his *Impromptu* shows a simple example founded in whole-tone intervals:

Ex. 215

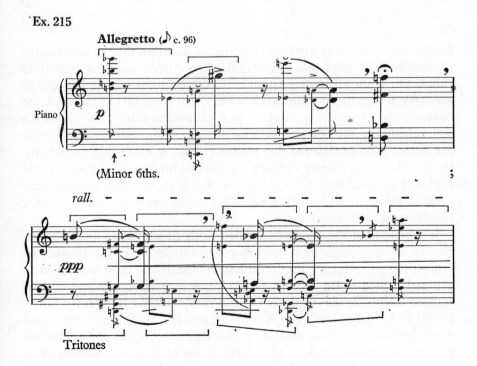

[1] Pousseur, 'Outline of a Method', *Die Reihe*, iii, (Eng. ed.) pp. 44–88.
[2] See the critical analysis of the Quintet's procedures in G. M. Koenig, 'Henri Pousseur', *Die Reihe*, iv, (Eng. ed.) pp. 16–28.

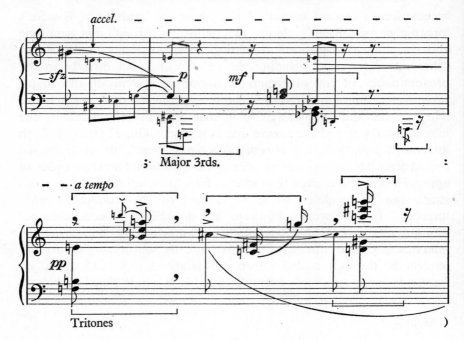

It also shows an early attempt to perfect a notation for the 'qualitative relationship' of durations, freed not merely from complex irrational values but from all numerical rigidity. Grace-notes within the square brackets are included within the main note- (or rest-) value, and the conventions of commas, dashes, and plus-signs allow the player to concentrate on immediate subtleties of proportion such as the listener can detect. The *Mobile* for two pianos (1958), in extending this liberty to two players, naturally exploits the flexible relation of the strata first explored by Stockhausen[1] and possibilities of their varied arrangement such as Pousseur had already provided in his electronic piece *Scambi* (Exchanges) (1957).

It was among the circle associated with Stockhausen in Cologne, mostly of musicians from peripheral countries, that the pursuit of innovation sometimes outstripped any demonstrable urge towards new expressive media. Bo Nilsson (b. 1937), a Swedish composer of precocious talents, in his vocal works *Mädchentotenlieder* (Dirges for Girls) (1958) and *Ein irrender Sohn* (A straying son) (1958) fluently synthesized vocal resources and instrumental colourings reminiscent of *Le Marteau* with the temporal freedom and stereophony of *Gruppen*, adding some distinctive treatment of octaves (as tone colour) and of near-conventional line. The nervous sensitivity of these works is signally lacking in

[1] Pousseur, 'Musik, Form und Praxis', *Die Reihe*, vi, pp. 82–83.

the grotesque *Zwanzig Gruppen* (Twenty groups) for piccclo, oboe, and clarinet. By applying simultaneously the action-durations of Stockhausen's *Zeitmasse* and the 'mobile' principle, Nilsson contrives to accumulate up to one hour's sound from the superimpositions of diverse unequal lines selected in random order from sets of twenty per player. Since no further control is imposed, and indeed entirely unforeseen juxtapositions must be the only subjects of the listener's attention, it is difficult not to believe that an indistinguishable effect could be produced from any suitably complex material; a few random groups (Ex. 216) will reveal the contrast between their meticulous performing directions and the anarchy of their relations.[1]

Ex. 216

[1] Cf. Hans Rudolf Zeller, 'Mallarmé und das serielle Denken', *Die Reihe*, vi, p. 29, n. 11. On Nilsson's divorce from practicalities in devising an electronic score, see G. M. Koenig, 'Bo Nilsson', *Die Reihe*, iv, (Eng. ed.) pp. 85–88.

The Argentinian, Mauricio Kagel (b. 1931), has sought constantly to
enlarge the sonorous possibilities of familiar media, introducing quarter-
tone harmony as well as familiar indeterminacies in his String Sextet
(1953–7) and creating some beautiful new piano sounds through the
percussion player in *Transicion II* (John Cage's influence is more than
modish here), but his *Anagrama* (1957–8) extends its play on the
assonances of a speaking choir to an inordinate length without aspiring
to the musicality of Berio's *Omaggio*.

Behind such projects, however admirably executed, lurks the temptation to 'épater le bourgeois'. Confidence in the essential vitality of the
new movement is sustained by many musicians from all over Europe
who accept some of its idioms as a natural vehicle for undemonstrative
craftsmanship of a very high order. The adoption of advanced serial
techniques by composers of the Eastern bloc, and the contemporary

music festivals there (Warsaw, from 1956), might be interpreted as nostalgia for old artistic alliances or as spirited repudiation of Soviet aesthetic ideology, but the development of men like Haubenstock-Ramati (b. 1919) and Witold Lutosławski (b. 1913) suggests a less factitious sympathy with new methods. Roman Haubenstock-Ramati, in his *Symphonies de timbres* (1957), finds a convincing role for development and (reversed) restatement of material, a fluid rhythmic variety that stops short of insuperable difficulties, and a distinguished range of orchestral colourings; evidence of such mastery compelled respectful investigation of later, more enigmatic, scores like the *Mobile for Shakespeare* (1960). Haubenstock left Poland in 1950, but Włodzimierz Kotoński (b. 1925) took the lessons of Darmstadt back to Warsaw and worked at the electronic studio there. His *Kammermusik* (1958) and *Musique en relief* (1959) show a gifted miniaturist with a remarkable ear for ingratiating textures; so gentle an introduction to modern techniques may well win them an audience. Krzysztof Penderecki (b. 1933) set out from a similar position, and in his subsequent career he has shown a remarkable ability to adapt new techniques to ends which quite unsophisticated listeners find compelling: the opaque textures (for fifty-two string parts) of his *Tren—Ofiarum Hiroszimy* (Threnody for the victims of Hiroshima) (1961) marked an important stage in this development. Lutosławski's *Muzyka żałobna* (Funeral music) for Bartók (1958) similarly marked the beginning of a new style in a development which has shown initiative and imagination in the use of new techniques.

MUSIC ON TAPE

The rough distinction made earlier[1] between a French ordering by instinct and a German organization by system is reinforced by the different approaches in these countries towards a music that eliminates the interpreter. *Musique concrète* is above all an art of tasteful arrangement of existing sound shapes, while electronic music, faced with an infinite wealth of sound potentialities, must shape according to rigidly restrictive principles if it is to avoid a chaotic prodigality. Their direct construction of the means of production is perhaps no more significant ultimately than their recognition of finer distinctions in aural phenomena formerly classed indiscriminately as 'noise', distinctions which may contribute to the balance and contrast that form musical experience. In this respect, electronic music, founded in acoustic synthesis, offers incomparably more precise criteria for a new tabulation of sound since it can order its inner structure.

[1] Cf. pp. 441–2.

The patchwork construction of forms from an arbitrary assembly of 'concrete' pieces of sound (by manipulation of magnetized recording tape) offers an obvious parallel to *collage* methods in the visual arts. Both demand of the creator more aesthetic judgement than conventional craftsmanship, and both may confuse our sensibility to the whole by an appeal to sentimental associations with still recognizable constituent objects. The works which have achieved the widest note since Pierre Schaeffer's experiments[1] began in Paris in 1948 are frankly directed towards programmatic or impressionistic ends. In the *Symphonie pour un homme seul*, by Schaeffer and Pierre Henry, a technique which has proved admirable for prompting a wealth of suggestions during a few moments of incidental sound is used to produce an evocative pattern far more ramified than that of *L'Après-midi d'un faune* with means often cruder than those of *Pacific 231*. Ballet, which has so often reduced the status of music intended to be self-sufficient, has come to the rescue of this type of concrete music by providing a visual continuity around which the sound can conjure up its momentary fantasies.

Several French composers, intent on a music that should justify its continuity by an inherent logic, experimented with the equipment assembled by Schaeffer. Though his stock of sounds was too *ad hoc* to offer possibilities for a permutational treatment of their constitution—rather than of their juxtaposition, already practicable in serialized instrumental timbre—the techniques of tape montage[2] did offer a guaranteed precision in the execution of complex rhythmic superimpositions such as seems likely to remain for ever beyond instrumentalists' skill. Boulez constructed two *Études* (1951–2) setting out respectively from a single sound and six types of sound, but he was satisfied by his results only in the field of durations.[3] Messiaen's essay *Timbres-durées* (1952) merely worked out at greater length some formulas of his contemporary instrumental music. By now most composers whose ideas call for direct contact with the sounding material are more attracted by the wider and measurable resources of electronic sound-generation. Yet the unusually penetrating quality of Stockhausen's *Gesang der Jünglinge* and Berio's *Omaggio a Joyce* springs from an analytical treatment of the most evocative of all 'concrete' sources—the sound of the human voice.

When such existent sources are abandoned and musical composition

[1] Schaeffer, *A la recherche d'une musique concrète* (Paris, 1952); see also Lowell Cross, 'Electronic Music 1948–53', *Perspectives of New Music*, vii (1968), p. 32.

[2] On *musique concrète* see Schaeffer, op. cit., and Goléa, op. cit., pp. 150–3; on electronic music, various articles in *Die Reihe*, i; see also the bibliography in Aurelio de la Vega, 'Regarding Electronic Music', *Tempo*, 75 (1966), and in *Journal of Music Theory*, vii (1963).

[3] Boulez has stressed that his concern was for organized duration, not for a mere juggling with the physically impracticable: *Die Reihe*, i, (Eng. ed.), p. 24.

begins from the electro-acoustic fundamentals (the pure sinusoidal tone and, at the other extreme, the 'white noise' in which all pitches are present), the composer can only abandon a rhetoric based on principles of physical tension and relaxation that no longer have any relevance to a patently 'effortless' aural phenomenon. All sounds—of whatever pitch, duration, volume, density, or timbre—are then without associations of graded human achievement and are *a priori* equally feasible. This limitless repertoire did not become available until a few years after composers writing for conventional resources had begun to attempt a music that should order these parameters simultaneously (Webern and Messiaen) or make distinctions as fine in the sphere of noise as in that of note (Varèse). In fact timbre, never the most satisfactory element in the total serialization process, has ceased to be a parameter in the old sense and is recognized as the organization at another level (the micro-structure) of relations of time (i.e. vibration-frequencies)[1] and intensity, the familiar tone colours being no more than particular examples (with their partials in 'harmonic' proportions) from a continuously variable and thus serially permutable range.

An appropriate attitude to its control on two levels therefore existed before the new medium, but its surrender to such control emphasized how much instrumental performance had been fertilized by individual unpredictability and idiosyncrasy. The investigation of this latter field has been noted;[2] but at the same time as 'live' music was being made to depend increasingly on the unique, unrepeatable quality of the individual performance, music for mechanical means of production, instead of being the petrifaction of one such performance, was seen to be most aptly conceived as a precise correlation of measured sounds. The onus remained with the composer-operator to demonstrate in the process anything more widely compelling than the appeal of the underlying pattern of calculations. Yet he was confronted at each stage of his work by the aural implications of his theories,[3] and so empiricism inevitably became an important modifying factor.

The challenge was taken up with enthusiasm, if not with consistent success. Within a few years of the establishment in 1951 of the first studio, at Cologne under the direction of Herbert Eimert (1897–1972),[4] attempts to synthesize familiar sounds[5] were rejected as distractions

---

[1] Cf. p. 460 for some consequences of this attitude in Stockhausen's instrumental music.
[2] Cf. pp. 464–8.
[3] See G. M. Koenig, 'Bo Nilsson', *Die Reihe,* iv, (Eng. ed.) pp. 85–88, on the folly of planning an electronic composition without access to its realization in sound.
[4] Herbert Eimert, loc. cit., p. 5; Stockhausen, 'Elektronische und instrumentale Musik', *Die Reihe*, v, p. 50.
[5] E.g. Eimert's *Glockenspiel* (1953–4), based on an analysis of bell sounds.

from the task of relating an external musical order to the internal acoustical order: 'everything is designed not to escape from the nature of electronic sound but to go further into it'.[1] Stockhausen's *Studie I* (1953)[2] was restricted to sinusoidal tones, but their superimpositions were determined by a serial plan relevant to the structure of the whole piece,[3] not by a deliberate creation of harmonic series fusing into single timbres nor by any restriction to the tempered twelve-note scale. As well as some rather characterless chords, i.e. combinations without fusion, it uses the less familiar and aurally intriguing phenomena known as tone-mixtures, combinations in which the constituent pure tones merge to some extent, yet not so as to produce the impression of a single note. Eimert's *Etüde über Tongemische* (Study in tone-mixtures) (1954)[4] deploys five mixtures, each of nine partials and each transposed to nine different registers, with results far more congenial to the medium than the relapses into instrumental styles of his *Fünf Stücke* (1954–5).

Though the new territory of tone-mixtures was the most immediately attractive, investigations were made on both sides of it. Paul Gredinger in *Formanten* reached back towards the nature of instrumental sound in seeking to regulate the harmonic ordering of partials so as to produce a gradually changing timbre.[5] Stockhausen, in *Studie II* (1954),[6] the first electronic work to be published as a diagram,[7] varied the widths of mixtures and the closeness of their superimpositions, often approaching the dense band of adjacent frequencies of 'coloured noise' (i.e. a filtered segment of white noise, referable only to a pitch area); the durational plan of this short piece is heard as a rhythmic life, diverse yet coherent. Here the recognition of individual pitches is no longer of prime importance and the music is characterized by just that 'atonality' which Schoenberg scorned as an impossibility. In the *Klangfiguren* by Gottfried Michael Koenig,[8] the material is restricted to 'noise', so diversely graded as to suggest a musical potential higher than that of a conventional percussive apparatus.

In Stockhausen's *Gesang der Jünglinge* (1955–6),[9] electronic sounds take on a disturbing 'otherness' when set in relief by the humanity of a boy's voice, racked at times out of intelligibility, but never out of

[1] Eimert, loc. cit., p. 10.   [2] Recorded on DGG LP 16133.
[3] Stockhausen's analysis in *Technische Hausmitteilungen des NWDR* 6 (1954) is summarized by Burt in 'An Antithesis', *The Score*, xix (1957), p. 64.
[4] DGG LP 16132.
[5] Pousseur, 'Formal Elements in a New Compositional Material', *Die Reihe*, i, (Eng. ed.) p. 32, and Gredinger, 'Serial Technique', ibid., p. 40.
[6] DGG LP 16133.
[7] Vienna, 1956.
[8] G. M. Koenig, 'Studio technique', *Die Reihe*, i, (Eng. ed.) pp. 52–54; 'Studium in. Studio', *Die Reihe*, v, p. 74; *Klangfiguren* is recorded on DGG LP 16134.
[9] DGG LP 16133.

recognition, by the dissection of its speech elements. Effects such as the distant murmur of multitudinous identical voices have a dramatic impact far more direct than Stockhausen's comments on the work would suggest; his concern is to incorporate vocal sounds as natural stages (complemented electronically) in the continuum that links tone to noise, vowel to consonant.[1] His vivid imagination for broad effects is further revealed in the spatial direction and movement of the sound by multi-channel distribution.[2] This has subsequently become a crucial aspect of electronic composition and has helped to combat the faintly ridiculous sensation with which an audience concentrates on sounds emanating from a single 'pseudo-instrument'.[3] Stockhausen's fanatical devotion to this art is sustained by a vision of public music rooms (spherical ideally) giving continuous performances of spatial music.[4] However reminiscent this may seem of some deplorable cinematic techniques, complex stereophony is an altogether natural development of machine-music and may help it to achieve a persuasive idiom owing nothing to instrumental practice.

Another achievement which lies ahead is that of a basis for the criticism of electronic music. Such 'scores' as exist are instructions to the technician but a dubious boon to the musical, rather than acoustic, analyst;[5] often the composer who has constructed his own work keeps no record of his procedures and has no further interest in them. In this unprecedented historical situation the critic must rely largely on an instinctive perception of formal balance. His recognition of certain broad classes of sound may become as automatic as that of fixed instrumental timbres, but there will always remain a degree of uncertainty in the means which will compel him to consider more searchingly the end. The pointed avoidance of emotional overtones in such titles as *Continuo* or *Perspectives* should discourage him from seeking *raisons d'être* outside the sounds themselves. This quandary may ultimately be beneficial, but meanwhile electronic works have found more receptive ears when presented less enigmatically. *Artikulation*, for example, by György Ligeti (b. 1923) is acknowledged to be humorous in intent.[6] Its sounds, individually suggestive of screams and whistles, pistol-shots and bath-water, were long ago drained of risible potential, but are juxtaposed and

---

[1] Stockhausen, 'Musik und Sprache', *Die Reihe*, vi, p. 52; 'Actualia', *Die Reihe*, i, (Eng. ed.) p. 45.

[2] Stockhausen, 'Musik im Raum', *Die Reihe*, v, p. 60.

[3] Boulez, 'At the ends of fruitful land . . .', *Die Reihe*, i, (Eng. ed.) p. 28.

[4] Stockhausen, *Die Reihe*, v, p. 60.

[5] See however B. Fennelly, 'A Descriptive Language for the Analysis of Electronic Music', *Perspectives of New Music*, vi (1967), p. 79.

[6] Stockhausen, 'Elektronische und instrumentale Musik', *Die Reihe*, v, p. 53; see also Ligeti, 'Wandlungen der musikalischen Form', *Die Reihe*, vii, p. 14.

counterpointed here with so much wit and musical craftsmanship that the piece is exhilarating rather than farcical.

The facilities of the Cologne Studio could not provide for all the composers with ideas that called for realization in the new medium. Under the direction of Maderna and Berio, a studio was opened at Milan in 1955, and Pousseur worked there until facilities were available at Brussels in 1958, while a Dutch studio was used by Henk Badings. Eastern European interest in Western musical developments was confirmed in the institution of a studio at Warsaw and, still further afield, America and Japan joined the pioneering movement. Many of the early works produced at these centres are no more than studies, but two pieces made at Milan call for notice. Pousseur's *Scambi* (1957) attempts to compensate for absence of the interpreter by introducing the element of choice so industriously cultivated in instrumental music like his own *Mobile* for two pianos. The individual strata of *Scambi* are composed by a characteristic application of precise filtering-techniques to the random phenomena of white noise, and the operator may select from a variety of possible schemes his own sequence and superimposition.[1] Berio's *Omaggio a Joyce* (1958) depends more heavily than does Stockhausen's *Gesang* on the *concrète* medium of a human voice, here reading a passage from *Ulysses*. Having analysed these sounds, Berio proceeds to manipulate them into an edifice of disturbing beauty in which 'musical' values—of colour as well as pitch—become far more important than verbal intelligibility. The lyricism of this work and its satisfying emotional curve are Italian qualities which remain recognizable in more orthodox pieces like Berio's *Momenti* and Maderna's *Notturno*. Both composers have also experimented with the confrontation of electronic and instrumental sound.

A pointer towards such synthesis was provided by Edgar Varèse (1883–1965). After the intrepid acceptance in his early works of 'noises' as essential extensions of music's basic material—sound (this in itself being a concept for which few were ready in the early thirties)[2]—Varèse had withdrawn from composition, but not from vigilant enquiry into the nature of noise. More than any eccentric of this century's music he saw his ideas pass into common currency, for the perfection of tape-recording techniques and of electronically generated sound gave them an unsuspected validity. Though his early works have been discovered with enthusiasm, the example of *Déserts* (1954) has been more widely followed in its combination of instrumental sounds (piano, wind, and

[1] Marc Wilkinson, 'Two Months in the Studio di Fonologia', *The Score*, xxii (1958), p. 45.

[2] Wilkinson, 'An Introduction to the music of Edgar Varese', *The Score*, xxi (1957), p. 5; Milton Babbitt, 'Edgard Varèse: a few observations of his music,' *Perspectives of New Music*, iv (1966), p. 14.

percussion) and a recorded tape (of noise sources); its crude vitality proved his musical nerves to be as strong as ever, and his later *Poème électronique* (1958), dispensing with instruments, is a *tour de force* constructed for the multi-channel reproducers of Corbusier's pavilion at the Brussels World Fair. Meanwhile the integration of player and machine proceeded through forms as various as Maderna's *Musica su due dimensioni* (1958) in which a solo flute plays against electronic background, and Pousseur's *Rimes pour différentes sources sonores* (1959) which engages three orchestral groups and two loudspeaker channels. In this field too, Stockhausen attempted an exhaustive exploration: his *Kontakte* (1959–60) aims once again at a sound continuum (electronic sources providing transitional stages between instrumental) but he brings a new ingenuity to spatial disposition and rotation of sound produced from a circular formation of four loudspeakers with the two players (piano and percussion) at its hub.[1] Though these were among the earliest essays in synthesis, they already suggested that audiences welcome the guidance of palpable patterns of human achievement. This does not invalidate electronic media, and may indeed hasten their development and recognition as artistic expression through the ordering of sound—in short, as music.

CONSERVATISM AND COMPROMISE

Although many writers consistently deplored the manifold innovations which obsessed some of the most notable creative talent in European music during the sixth decade of this century, it was no longer possible to envisage the emergence of a serious style which would show no trace of the new strategic ordering of musical time, pitch, intensity, and colour. There were composers, not belonging to the *avant-garde*, who found that their slower progress had none the less brought them to a point where they were able to contribute to some valid synthesis. Such men, sometimes intelligently interested in their contemporaries' explorations, found themselves a territory among the diverse technical advances made but not fused during the first half of the century. Conservatism proved the refuge of scarcely more of the untalented than were to be found in esoteric circles, and was by no means automatically a dismal academicism. The common sense that views tradition as a measure of, not a defence against, the present can often adapt or interpret new idioms in forms acceptable to a wider public.

Whatever the varieties of individual method to be found among the

---

[1] The theoretical basis of *Kontakte* is discussed by Stockhausen in 'The Concept of Unity in Electronic Music,' *Perspectives of New Music*, i, 1 (1962), p. 39.

33

new serialists, they could draw confidence from their essential unity of purpose; and they present a 'movement' that will continue to engage historians' attention. Outside their confines no such solidarity exists, and the species of craft practised permit no neat classification. Switzerland, always unsympathetic to extremist doctrines, provides a typical cross-section in the work of three composers of the generations after Frank Martin. The operas of Heinrich Sutermeister (b. 1910) have a devoted public, for their musical language firmly excludes any trace of recent developments. Comparison of this innocuous diatonicism with Britten's[1] flatters a pedestrian talent with none of Britten's gift for the unpredictable reassessment of the apparently obvious. Sutermeister's exact contemporary, Rolf Liebermann, has yoked twelve-note method to an elegance that its originator never sought, notably by the use of triadic rows;[2] these provoke none of Berg's unrest but a stream of figurative chatter owing something to Hindemith. The Concerto for Jazz Band and Orchestra fails to find much common ground between elements so disparate as jazz and dodecaphonic music, but a keen sense of musical theatre makes his operas apt, if rarely penetrating. The work of Klaus Huber (b. 1924) represents the moderation of a later generation. Taught by Blacher and familiar with all the resources developed in the first half of the century, he has sought a personal synthesis, one that will convey a mood rarely explored during those years, of religious mysticism; his chamber cantata *Auf die ruhige Nachtzeit* (At the quiet night-time) (1958) captures this in a serene contemplation of musical symmetries.

Synthesis does not always achieve this poise, and may do no more than appropriate technical gains without a distinctive expressive note. Karl-Birger Blomdahl (1916–1968) had an impressive command of techniques that included serialism, and in his *chef d'œuvre*, the opera *Aniara* (1957–9), he also drew on tape montage. This work bravely attempts to provide a comprehensive document for an age in which obsessions of impending catastrophe are diverted by visions of planetary exploration. But the score has little of the keen fantasy demanded by its subject: its dodecaphonic basis merely produces a monotonously uniform harmonic level in stubbornly traditional textures and rhythms (see Ex. 217), and so, instead of an imaginatively prophetic music, it presents studies in the conventionally horrific, lascivious, or ecstatic, which rarely suspend disbelief. Blomdahl was a pupil of Hilding Rosenberg, as were two other Swedish composers who have shown the same determination to escape from a paling nationalism through Central European tech-

[1] Winfried Zillig, *Variationen über neue Musik* (Munich, 1959), p. 221.
[2] See Liebermann's contribution to Rufer, *Composition with Twelve Notes* (London, 1954), pp. 191–3.

Ex. 217

(I long for the land that is not)

niques. Sven Erik Bäck (b. 1919) and Ingvar Lidholm (b. 1921) have now moved towards multi-dimensional ordering; despite the difficulties of his compromise position, Blomdahl's work suggests the strongest talent. In Denmark, an unpretentious synthesis of serialism with strong inflexions of Stravinskyan choral style is practised in the church music of Bernhard Lewkovitch (b. 1927).

To detail the innumerable personal solutions worked out by European composers who have stopped short of complete association with the advanced movement would be both tedious and confusing. Men like Roman Vlad (b. 1919) in Italy,[1] Marius Constant (b. 1925) in France or

---

[1] Ronald Stevenson, 'An Introduction to the Music of Roman Vlad', *Music Review* xxii (1961), p. 124.

Tadeusz Baird (b. 1928) in Poland, are evidently conversant with the recent developments but cautious in profiting from them. The music of such composers plays a vital part in the endless process of acclimatizing audiences to sounds they would once have found incoherent, and its craftsmanship may well surpass that of some who assist in the more spectacular extension of the frontiers. Yet only an unusually compelling creative power can give it a dominating position in the contemporary scene: in the music of Hans Werner Henze (b. 1926), compromise achieves its most persuasive justification.

Germany's role as chief patron of the new serialism soon extended beyond the Darmstadt schools and the Donaueschinger Musiktage (revived in 1950) to the commissioning of many scores by the various radio stations. Their policy was enlightened and their nominations catholic; good performances were ensured and audience figures were not a determining factor. Thus the composer whose position was secured might freely indulge an exploring spirit, seeking no stimulus outside that of like-minded colleagues. These hermetic conditions inevitably favoured extravagant innovation for its own sake, but the liberal dissemination of experimental music perhaps re-orientated some German composers originally inclined towards more moderate idioms. Bernd Alois Zimmermann (1918–1970) for example, whose Symphony (1953) is an admirable mosaic of expressionist textures, in subsequently pruning this opulence added to Webernian interval proportions a strict regulation of other dimensions.[1] Giselher Klebe (b. 1925)[2] was a pupil of Boris Blacher, and the early two-piano sonata suggests no aspirations beyond the mixture of Stravinskyan rhythmic acuity, chromaticized diatonicism and swing formulas to be found in the work of his talented fellow-pupil, Heimo Erbse (b. 1924).[3] But Klebe's need to control a piquant fantasy by intellectual disciplines led him through orthodox twelve-note techniques handled with virtuosic ease— as in the String Quartet (1950) or the *Römische Elegien* (1952)—to an individual treatment of serial durations.[4] Neither this nor his experience of electronic composition[5] has led him to abandon a refined thematicism or the wealth of traditional 'expressive' analogy; yet his fastidious concern for craftsmanship has deprived his works, including the opera *Die Räuben* (The Robbers), of the wider currency accorded those of the more flamboyant Henze. Transition in the opposite direction, though excep-

[1] Reinhold Schubert, 'Bernd Alois Zimmermann', *Die Reihe,* iv, (Eng. ed.) pp. 103–13.
[2] W.-E. von Lewinski, 'Giselher Klebe', *Die Reihe,* iv, (Eng. ed.), pp. 89–97, and A. D. McCredie, 'Giselher Klebe', *Music Review,* xxvi (1965), p. 220.
[3] Francis Burt, 'An Antithesis', *The Score,* xix (1957), p. 71.
[4] Lewinski, loc. cit., pp. 92–94, on the *Elegia Appassionata* Trio (1955).
[5] Giselher Klebe, 'First Practical Work', *Die Reihe,* i, (Eng. ed.) p. 17.

tional, may seem a surer guarantee of popular success. Gottfried von Einem (b. 1918), an Austrian pupil of Blacher, has shown increasing attachment to a diatonicism seasoned with glib references to popular idioms; his *Dantons Tod* (Death of Danton) (1947) was a landmark in the post-war recovery of German opera, but a signal decline from the Büchner opera it in some respects aped.

When the Nazi downfall permitted the vigorous resurgence of German music, educators like Blacher and Fortner must have visualized a return to musical literacy less violent than that which has reshaped the language. Yet if they could not foresee a Stockhausen, they might well have foreseen a Henze, for in many ways he was to remain faithful to the ideals of those years. This is not to say merely that he became the supreme exponent of a synthesis composed of all the major influences of the first half-century, but that he pointedly dissociated himself from his contemporaries' belief in intellectual canons as an arbiter of sound-construction. The composer who in 1947 was seeking 'widely-ranging tender cantilenas'[1] was still intent on 'tender beautiful noises'[2] twelve years later, and this sonorous vision was far more fundamental to his art than any one of the techniques he sampled in realizing it. Indeed, he turned to twelve-note serialism largely because, under the spell of Berg, he saw in it a way to a rich lyricism, not a substitute for tonal coherence (cf. Schoenberg) nor one factor in predetermining structure (cf. the early 'post-Webern' experiments). As he soon abandoned its consistent use, his typical methods have sometimes seemed to be as dependent as were Stravinsky's on the empirical juxtaposition of apt sounds. But his training under Fortner and Leibowitz has ensured that spontaneously invented ideas suggest appropriate, and often subtle, means for their structural extension: 'structural rules emerge from ideas laid down at the beginning of a work; their development and variation are subject to no arrangement imposed from without'.[3]

His earliest works show the assimilation of Hindemith and Stravinsky which was then the routine German apprenticeship, and these influences persist in works which adhere painstakingly to the serial letter. The Piano Variations (1948) strive to reproduce the manner of Schoenberg's first serial period (see Ex. 218(i)), yet hesitate to indulge his fearless pungency of dissonance; the tonal implications of the row, Ex. 218(ii), naturally produced harmony nearer Berg, but Hindemith and Stravinsky

---

[1] Henze on his Violin Concerto, quoted by Reinhold Schubert in 'Bernd Alois Zimmermann', *Die Reihe*, iv, (Eng. ed.) p. 105.

[2] Henze's guidance to his librettists, quoted by W. H. Auden and Chester Kallman in 'Genesis of a Libretto', *Glyndebourne Festival Programme Book* (1961), p. 37.

[3] Henze, lecture at the Braunschweiger Festliche Tage Neuer Kammermusik 1959, quoted by Diether de la Motte, *Hans Werner Henze—Der Prinz von Homburg* (Mainz, 1960), p. 60.

sometimes affect texture and rhythm. In the Second Symphony (1949), though the row bristles with cadential possibilities (see Ex. 218(ii)) and is progressively transposed, the harmony is already beginning to explore the Stravinskyan immobility bred of inner contradictions (Ex.218(iii)(a)). German influences still predominate however: the movement structure is indebted to Hartmann, the scherzo's twelve-note ground, Ex. 218(iii)(b), uses Blacher's variable metres, wittily reversed in the *da capo* after a palindromic trio, and the finale emulates Hindemith's motoric

Ex. 218

(ii)

Basic set of Piano Variations

Triadic or quasi-triadic groups
Leading notes
Tonal groups

Basic set of Second Symphony

(iii) **Lento**

(a) Orch.

(b)

counterpoint even to the *Mathis*-like climax in a chorale. One more serial essay, the String Quartet (1952), is noteworthy for the technical feat of preserving (free) twelve-note horizontal successions while distributing the series vertically,[1] but such skill only serves to emphasize the faint aura of academicism which surrounds Henze's early instrumental music.

Academicism implies the mastery of a technique without a proportionate urge to expression through it. Though much *avant-garde* music is academic, that of a composer like Stockhausen reflects a preoccupation with the material's possibilities so ardent as to constitute his most characteristic expression. For Henze, the nature of what is to be expressed is the stimulus to composition, and this assumes more tangible form in a verbal equivalent: the sonorous formulas cited provide less pointedly the guidance commonly found in a literary text or a scenario, and it was inevitable that he would discover his *métier* in word-setting and the musical theatre. Experience in writing ballet music (*Jack Pudding* reveals the flirtation with jazz which few German composers can resist), vocal chamber music like the delicate *Apollo et Hyacinthus* (1949, his most distinguished serial work of this period), and operatic essays after Cervantes and Kafka, was summed up in the opera *Boulevard Solitude* (1951), a reworking of Prévost's *Manon Lescaut*. Having found the key to his most personal utterance in these fields, he was reluctant to abandon it in writing for instruments, and the *Ode to the West Wind* (1953) for cello and orchestra follows Hindemith's example[2] in using Shelley's poem as a continuous verbal undercurrent to the music.

The extent of literary indebtedness is exceptional here, but a series of instrumental works confirmed Henze's dependence on poetic moods (*Quattro Poemi*, 1955; *Drei Dithyramben*, 1958). An attitude so redolent of the previous century demands the qualities it prized: 'harmony' as a basic concept (not a product of exceptional textural conditions), contributing with orchestral colour to sounds considered in themselves 'expressive', though often used as background to one dominating melodic line. Henze's employment of complex chords that, because of their constitution from several contradictory triads, have piquancy rather than acidity, provides an unexpected extension of orthodox harmonic theory—see Ex. 219 from *Drei Dithyramben*. This luxuriance stems from Berg yet avoids turgidity thanks to an ear for orchestral clarity as scrupulous and inventive as Stravinsky's. Henze's melody

---

[1] See Henze's note on this in Rufer, op. cit., p. 185; also Rudolph Stephan, 'Hans Werner Henze', *Die Reihe,* iv, (Eng. ed.) pp. 32–34.

[2] Cf. p. 406.

Ex. 219

is less consistently striking, but his admiration of Italy led him to
emulate the Verdian cantabile, often most effective when least aspiring,
as in the engaging *Five Neapolitan Songs* (1956). Yet these revaluations
of traditional means did not deter him from profiting by the innovations of his contemporaries. Comparison of the ground from the
second Dithyramb (Ex. 220) with an earlier ground (see Ex. 218(iii)(b))
reveals how much of the new concept of line and rhythm he has
accepted. The 1959 Piano Sonata suggests a need to demonstrate his
freedom of movement in *pointilliste* textures, even to witticism at their
expense in the final fugue, while the pantomime *The Emperor's
Nightingale* (1960) exploits the bravura flute writing and exotically
bright chamber sonorities beloved of the *avant-garde* as symbols
particularly appropriate to the legend.[1]

Such a range of style need not be disconcerting in an opera composer
who recognizes the principle of set numbers and the value of parody
techniques. After the prodigality of *König Hirsch* (King Stag) (1956)
Henze curbed a fantasy sometimes too facile in meeting the challenge of

[1] Colin Mason, 'Hans Werner Henze', *The Listener* (17 November 1960), p. 913.

Ex. 220

a drama so powerful, and apparently so unsusceptible to musical en-
hancement, as *Der Prinz von Homburg* (1960). His association of
intervals with characters is no guarantee of musical cogency, but developments of material such as the battle scene, a typical application of
serial principle to free thematicism, later pared down to a twelve-note
row, reveal how effectively his craft reinforces his dramatic instinct.[1]
Henze's admiration for Britten, a composer whose sublime simplicity
and fleetness he does not naturally share but most nearly captured in
Kammermusik 1958 (dedicated to Britten), may have prompted his
chamber opera *Elegy for young lovers* (1961). In its characterizing
instrumental colourings and its use of idioms ranging from jazz to 'post-
Webernian' vocal *fioritura*, this summed up Henze's peculiar gifts, and
emphasized the role that synthesis would continue to play in realizing so
personal a vision of sound.

[1] Diether de la Motte, op. cit., pp. 32–38.

VI

MUSIC IN BRITAIN 1916–1960

By ARTHUR HUTCHINGS

INTRODUCTION

DURING the years immediately after 1918 music in Great Britain passed through a tunnel rarely cheered by gleams of the light into which it was eventually to emerge. Until nearly 1930 discerning critics had the uneasy impression that Delius and Elgar towered head and shoulders above their successors. One of the most intelligent representatives of the younger generation, Constant Lambert, in his *Music Ho! A Study of Music in Decline*,[1] showed the effect of war coinciding with the climax of a nationalist movement among artists who had little or no commerce with the *avant-garde* of other countries, for the war had prolonged that delay of technical stimuli from abroad which has always flattered insular conservatism. The last German romantic who had been hailed as ultra-modern, Richard Strauss, was still deeply venerated, but there was no comparable cult of French music except among pianists and singers, some of whom belatedly recognized Fauré's subtlety and veiled power. Debussy and Ravel were not explored, but were represented by frequent performances of two or three pieces which provided a Latin sauce to the basic German fare. Sibelius's symphonies enjoyed a popularity in Great Britain that had no parallel in Germany but the Strauss cult affected not only the importing of other central European music but also indigenous composition.

Native new music offered no technical advance upon Strauss's and did not approach the professional invention or design of even his poorest works. The so-called 'nationalists' at least offered a different flavour; but it was several years before they offered more than songs and short vocal or instrumental lyrics, mostly pastoral in character.

In 1919 Holst and Vaughan Williams re-entered the lists. Holst's suite *The Planets*, which had been played only privately in 1918, was given at a public concert in 1920. Though it was immediately acclaimed it could not easily be reconciled with the composer of *Sāvitri* (1908) and some short choral works which Holst had published before the war.

[1] London, 1934.

Vaughan Williams, whose name and appearance were almost symbolically insular, had secured a reputation for consistent advance by *Toward the Unknown Region* (1907), *A Sea Symphony* (1910), the song cycle *On Wenlock Edge* (1909) and the *Fantasia on a Theme by Tallis* (1910); but his *London* and *Pastoral* symphonies, first heard in 1920 and 1922 respectively, were more striking leaps forward. They were symptomatic of the persistent British obsession with the symphony.

While the ambitious young French or Italian composer hoped to write a successful opera or ballet, his British counterpart lost time in straining to produce grandiose symphonies. Before considering those who are held to have succeeded we should consider one who preceded them.

BAX AND HIS ROMANTIC CONTEMPORARIES

In *The Garden of Fand* (1916), *Tintagel* (1917), and *November Woods* (1917) Arnold Bax (1883–1953) had demonstrated his rare command of the orchestral palette. His imaginative use of other materials is shown in certain chamber works, especially his exquisite Nonet and some piano sonatas, and *Mater ora Filium* (1921), a virtuosic motet for double choir. The seven symphonies which he composed between 1923 and 1939 were well received, especially the Third (1929), which was less bitter and turbulent than its predecessors; for Bax, shy even among the friends who marvelled at the facility with which he translated complex orchestral score into keyboard terms, seemed to release in these symphonies dark moods and passions, their violence offset by dreamy lyricism that suggested exhaustion after protest. Both passages quoted here illustrate the last point, though they were not chosen to do so. Ex. 221, from the Second Symphony (1925), shows how Bax could write appealing melodies that fall just short of memorability and distinction:

Ex. 221

Ex. 222, from the Third Symphony, how adroitly he improvised what
was needed at any point in a long work—in this case the coda to a big
movement:

Ex. 222

Bax disproves the belief that *Tristan* or *Elektra* pushed chromatic
harmony to a point beyond which classical tonality finishes, or that
continental composers left little more to be drawn from a large romantic
orchestra. His weakest music is less banal than Strauss's but his

strongest, rivalling Strauss in imagination, does not equal him in coherence and distinction. Bax loved Celtic literature, the Irish landscape and seascape, and though his symphonies are not overtly programmatic their movements begin as if they were intended as tone poems evoking Celtic legends, or as music for films set in a Celtic atmosphere.

Bax and Cyril Scott (1879–1970) have been the two most inadequately assessed among those of Strauss's and Debussy's British contemporaries who are not labelled 'nationalist'. To the surprise of his compatriots Scott was thought by many continental musicians to be 'the leading representative of modernism in England', perhaps because his composing chiefly for the pianoforte made him easily accessible. Moreover his appeal is made almost entirely by impressionist harmony, usually more complex than that of Debussy or Ravel, and sounding 'perfumed' or 'exotic' to an aesthetic served by Vaughan Williams.

Few others who aspired to symphonic poems, romantic symphonies, music dramas, or works that would have been acceptable before the war in France or Germany are remembered today. The ambitious attempts by Joseph Holbrooke (1878–1961) and Rutland Boughton (1878–1960) at Celtic emulations of Wagner's dramas are virtually forgotten. A few of the many songs and part-songs of Granville Bantock (1868–1946) are still heard, but not his tone poems nor his choral works, and he is honoured chiefly because he used an official appointment for the encouragement of young musicians. The only exceptions are two composers who did not publish anything too ambitious for their talents. Frank Bridge (1879–1941) might be known to very few concert goers if it were not for Britten's acknowledgement of his indebtedness to a fine teacher and mentor, yet so notable a 'musician's musician' as Bridge deserves mention. He was a fine enough violinist and viola player to deputize in the Joachim Quartet, and his name was often the first suggested to direct a concert or opera at short notice. Though an admirable advance can be traced through the major works he composed before and after the war, his music has no strong public personality, but is cherished among players of chamber music who recognize his remarkable feeling for the character of their instruments.

John Ireland (1879–1962) also advanced his technique without fertilization from Teutonic or Latin sources (except Debussy, who influenced his keyboard style). Ireland's are among the most satisfying of the many settings of verses from A. E. Housman's *A Shropshire Lad*; and although he is best known by a few conservative works—the choral and orchestral *These things shall be*, which is not far removed from the cantatas of Parry and Stanford, or the picturesque *A London Overture—*

his true artistic worth is better measured by the songs from poems by Thomas Hardy (1925), the much later piano pieces, *Sarnia*, and fine chamber works, such as the Fantasy Sonata for clarinet and piano. Obviously Ireland took least risk with the largest forces: the basically traditional harmony of his Piano Concerto, for instance, is merely disguised by added notes and other decoration. This caution and his small, finely wrought output testify to shrewdness, not insincerity.

RALPH VAUGHAN WILLIAMS

Most of the next generation are widely regarded as satellites of Ralph Vaughan Williams (1872–1958) whose discovery of a distinctively English idiom is said to have provided a catalyst for talents which might otherwise have remained ineffective, if not inarticulate, attempting to do what Strauss and Debussy had done better.

Vaughan Williams was older than any of the musicians mentioned hitherto, each of whom might have described himself, as Bax did, as 'a hopeless romantic'. He was therefore more of a pioneer. We shall see that he was partly led by a distaste for what he thought weak in late-romantic music. The medical or psychological truth in the diagnosis 'a late developer' is not easily judged when the subject is an artist whose strong will and financial independence enable him to learn or do only what seems to suit his purpose. Vaughan Williams was no more docile than Beethoven; but it is foolish to pretend that an Englishman who in 1909 secured the orchestral effects, the adroit modulations and witty technical points of Vaughan Williams's incidental music to *The Wasps* was less than clever—although this was an epithet which he disliked by temperament and upbringing. The apparent weaknesses of the music—coarse scoring, missing climax, vague transition etc.—may be no more due to inadvertence or incompetence than Beethoven's unorthodox counterpoint and unorthodox treatment of instruments.

A clue to the solution of this problem is offered by his choice of words for six operas, about fifty choral works, and some hundred solo, unison and part songs. This friend and admirer of romantics shows distaste for several favourite romantic emotions. He shuns words of a kind sought by composers from Schubert to Mahler and by Britten and others today. The self-pity and despair which cover a large field of the best English verse from Shakespeare to Eliot are passed by; grief and anger are represented, notably in *Riders to the Sea* (1937), but only from the mouths of the strong or the brave. Erotic material is for mockery or satire, and in *Flos Campi* (1925) even the Song of Solomon is sublimated to chastity, its luxury a strong man's vision. There is more human feeling than private devotion in his treatment of religious words, though these are surprisingly frequent in the output of a confessed agnostic. In fact his choice and interpretation of words plainly reflect the liberal humanitarianism of his family and of Parry, together with the ethic of his school mentors. Although openly hostile to imperialism and insolent privilege, he paradoxically cherished pride as a virtue rather than the first of the Seven Deadly Sins, seeing man as 'a being darkly wise and rudely great', not by the grace and mercy of God but by his own effort and courage—a conception directly opposed to orthodox Christian doctrine. He found the best of humanity either in the strong and naïve 'naturals' of folk-song, unspoiled by urban meanness and sophistication, or in idealistic optimists like Whitman who exulted above sophistication. Endurance—whether in Job, in Scott of the Antarctic, in the bereaved heroine of *Riders to the Sea*, or in the political prisoner—always inspired him, and he supported those who showed it even when he could not support their cause.

His music neither complains nor protests, but reflects the endurance of men braver than the 'stout of heart', for they are past hope or fear and know only the duty to stand, not to understand. One might suppose this seeming negation of feeling to be beyond music if it were not that such a piece as the fourth movement (epilogue) of the Sixth Symphony (1948), pianissimo and *senza cresc.* throughout, finds what music can convey and words cannot.

Vaughan Williams's limitations and strength came first from his upbringing, which was fortunate enough to prevent his associating the words 'noble' and 'manly' with philistines. Romantic and impressionist, he reacted against what he thought unmanly and weak in romantic and impressionist music. This fact, not an archaeological interest, led him to old music. The trunk and oldest branches of a tree are the strongest and so are the earliest growths of an ascendant musical style. The most powerful of effects is the unison; the most stark of harmonies are the bare fifth and fourth; the modal melodic cadence which rises by a tone seems stronger than one which rises by a semitone from a leading note. Triads are strong chords; among the 'weak' and over-used are dominant sevenths, ninths, elevenths, and chromatics other than those of chromatic triads; but 'accidentals' cease to be chromatic when they become the degrees of empirical or exotic modes and scales. Now as in the sixteenth century the strength of counterpoint lies less in rhythmic contrast than in the thrust of discord. Hence the 'marching basses', alike in orchestral movements and in hymns or unison songs by Holst and Vaughan Williams, a bass note often chosen for no other reason than its recalcitrance with the upper harmony. Investigation of the development of Vaughan Williams's technique shows him instinctively seeking a higher degree of dissonance, though not chiefly violent dissonance. He cannot be reproached for begetting or reaching high tension so early in a movement that he cannot secure climax without adventitious vulgarity.

Although it has been truly observed that the ear cannot always tell whether Vaughan Williams's melodies are entirely his or whether they are from folk-song, he would surely have found a technique for 'manly' expression if he had known no old music at all. Vaughan Williams took what he recognized as his own in old music. That throughout his life he gave far more than he took may be observed from two examples chosen almost at random from his music.

The first is the beginning of the *Pastoral Symphony* (1922) omitting the first three bars:

Ex. 223

In it will be recognized the influence of impressionism and folk melody, although only short phrases of melody can (unprofitably) be described as in this or that mode, which may well be contradicted by the harmony. The second quotation takes us forward thirteen years to the fourth and most aggressively dissonant of his symphonies, but it is chosen from the quietest movement:

Ex. 224

Here only the rhythmic contours in the violin melody show any connexion with folk music. The passage is not difficult to grasp yet it is neither diatonic, atonal, nor polymodal. It comes beautifully to rest on G, yet G is not its tonic; it does not need more counterpoint to be fully effective but it badly needs its context.

Here, as often when his effect is most clearly achieved, the composer has patiently exercised his complex intelligence. The first movement of the Fifth Symphony (1943), as original in its own way as the strident Fourth, will provide a further example:

Ex. 225

Vaughan Williams's reputation abroad was established with the 1909 song-cycle *On Wenlock Edge* for tenor, piano, and string quartet, several features of which do not recur in his many later songs; his repute in Great Britain was notably increased by two works first given in the following year at provincial festivals. The choral and orchestral effects in *A Sea Symphony* (1910) sometimes attain a splendour (distaste may call it grandiosity) that did not recur even in occasional and exultant pieces like the *Benedicite* (1931). In *A London Symphony*, we encounter instead another quality which became all-pervading in Vaughan Williams and may be called remoteness. It touches the symphony only in a few places, notably the slow movement, 'O vast rondure swimming in space', but we find it in the other admired work of 1910, *Fantasia for Double Orchestra on a Theme of Tallis*.

Vaughan Williams has made his own not only Tallis's long and lovely melody but its descant. The *Fantasia* and much subsequent music seemed severe because it stirred the spirit more than the blood. 'Remote' had been used in judgement of romantic artists whose subjects included 'old, unhappy, far-off things', the remote figures of legend, the remote lands of heart's desire, objects of longing and aspiration, hills and landscapes that were romantic precisely because they were remote, and horizons that were unattainable. Vaughan Williams's remoteness is post-romantic and often extra-romantic, for in his music even rage, pain, and desire become removed, no longer subjective. His aesthetic as much as his ethical beliefs required restraint of the immediate cry; man should endure these emotions, contemplate them and recognize with awe their universal power. Little wonder, then, that he was attracted by the story of Job.

Job: A Masque for Dancing (1931)[1] resembles *Petrushka*, in that its conception embraces two planes which must perforce be separate; and just as the same figures in the most corporeal of the arts must here be seen on both planes, so the same music makes a direct physical impact yet encompasses a drama too vast to be contemplated until it is made sufficiently remote. The physical appeal of this music is not just an effect of its combination with stage scenes and personages, for it sounds as fine when taken out of the stage pit to the concert hall. Here its climax of terror—Job's first vision of heaven with Satan enthroned—is enhanced by a sudden crash of the full organ, a grim 'deadweight' use of this instrument without parallel except in the third movement of *Sinfonia antartica* (1953) where it adds the expression of diabolical hostility to that of the vastness and remoteness of the polar regions. The music of *Job* is far from disembodied and does not exclude the pulsation of dancing, but the rhythms of pavane, galliard, sarabande, and minuet impart a statuesque dignity rarely attempted in the theatre after Gluck's tragedies.

Vaughan Williams supplied for *Job* a more admirable score than any since *Flos Campi*, a suite for viola solo, small orchestra and wordless chorus. Unconventional alliances of instruments, unbalanced or bizarre textures, and opacity are here calculated effects. The inexact unison between muted brass and reed instruments conveys Satan's baleful exultation, the oily saxophone tone the false commiserations of Job's comforters; and the thickening of harmonies by divided cellos gives what would otherwise be too courtly and human a 'Galliard of the Sons of the Morning' the kind of impression produced by the angels on a Byzantine mosaic or Romanesque tympanum.

There is a wealth of melismatic rhapsody in *Job* outside the 'Dance of Youth and Beauty', which recalls *The Lark Ascending* (1914). The composer's rhythmic sense and wit were bent away from classic-romantic contours, and posterity may yet praise him for his pioneer work in showing that rhythm is not metre. If one of his movements seems to lose grip, the fault is rarely attributable to loss of rhythmic interest. He possessed the symphonist's ability to compose coherent and large movements rich in ideas, to develop with fine rhetoric a single thought, and to expand themes by other means than classical metabolism.

It would be easy to distinguish grades of workmanship if whole movements could be regarded as failures—the somewhat facile cavatina in the Eighth Symphony (1956), for instance, or the movement originally

---

[1] See pl. VII.

PLATE VII

VAUGHAN WILLIAMS'S *JOB*, 1931 (*see p. 512*)

A painting by Gwen Raverat of a design for the original stage production at the Cambridge Theatre, London

associated, in a film, with seals and penguins in *Sinfonia antartica*. But often the best of Vaughan Williams's music is inextricably entangled in floundering growth. The finale of the Fourth Symphony, for example, very clearly sets out upon the classical sonata plan, with first and second groups of strong personality. Then, where we expect a sonata-coda, comes the astounding fugal epilogue upon the chief motto-idea of the whole symphony, savagely devouring the sonata themes as counter-subjects.

GUSTAV HOLST

Gustav Holst (1874–1935), Vaughan Williams's contemporary and friend, was born at Cheltenham and sprang from a milieu of professional musicians very different from Vaughan Williams's. He was 'a musician's musician' because he was fascinated by the technique of the art, indeed by any musical sounds or music from any race. Though his technical explorations were made at the prompting of creative desire they are often held to have hindered its realization. He produced no series of symphonies, nor indeed any large-scale undertakings which can easily be examined as a series. It is significant that Stravinsky fascinated Holst, who may well have had genius enough (if he had been born into another tradition and granted health and freedom) to compose equivalents of *The Fire Bird* or even *The Rite of Spring*, though he rarely achieved the effortless coherence found even in smaller Stravinsky works like *Apollon Musagète*. Could the composer of *Ode to Death* (1919), and *The Hymn of Jesus* (1920) have achieved equivalents of *A Symphony of Psalms*, *Oedipus Rex*, and *Threni*? The question is less vain than most of its kind, because we cannot claim outright for Holst those symphonic qualifications that were conceded to Vaughan Williams. However great our admiration of Holst's achievement, in circumstances that would have frustrated most men, it seems clear that he commanded his musical materials better than their germinating processes, and could have found a convincing synthesis in more than two or three works if he had lived to be less interested in fertilizers than in the ground to which they were applied—often too liberally for immediate absorption. Vaughan Williams evolved large-scale contexts for 'tune' (as distinct from prose-like line) which was derived from folk-song, though often neither bucolic nor deliberately insular. Holst, having found in folk-music and modes, or in empirical and eastern scales and rhythms, an escape from Anglo-German melody, continued with explorations that produced wholly individual flavours. Yet when he wanted a 'tune' he continued to the end of his life to introduce the contour of folk-song or dance into refractory and recalcitrant textures.

It seems fair to illustrate some of these points from *The Hymn of Jesus*. Near the opening the music passes from 'Pange lingua' to 'Vexilla regis' with an easy mastery remarkable from a British composer in 1917; the effect at the first performance in 1920 was as electrifying as that of the subsequent full chorus:

Ex. 226

After a verse from each hymn in unaccompanied unison the orchestra makes its next transition:

Ex. 227

A short passage of routine imitation leads to the first of many six-four chords, then more imitative work on the first half of the motive, the harmonies becoming just sufficiently biplanar to avoid commonplace. A few bars before the much-quoted biplanar 'To you who gaze, a lamp am I':

Ex. 228
[Orchestral and lower voice parts omitted]

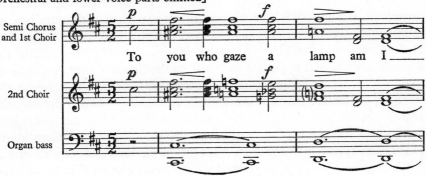

we find harmony, in itself not despicable, that belongs to Stanford's Anglican church music.

Analogies with *Pelléas et Mélisande* and *Oedipus Rex* suggest that Holst's unification would have been less easy if the text (from the apocryphal *Acts of St. John*) had been too slavishly followed from image to image, or if the emotional content had been full-blooded instead of allusive. Holst himself, for all his avoidance of publicity, was no more the recluse, no more austere than many a man whose work nobody has thought frigid; yet people once called him cold, severe, or 'mystical'. If a mystic is one who expresses experiences that are incommunicable except by a language of symbolism it is difficult to see why Holst is more mystical than a host of others. His art is ill-suited to the sort of subjects that appealed to Verdi, but he is more often mysterious than mystical; and the more forbidding or abstract his theme the stronger his brush. 'Saturn, the Bringer of Old Age' and 'Neptune, the Mystic' are the best of *The Planets*, and *Egdon Heath* is his finest orchestral work. This reflection poses what is surely the ultimate problem about Holst, and it concerns the man rather than his technical experiments.

The Hymn of Jesus was greeted with an enthusiasm that bewildered the composer. He was unwise enough to concoct his own libretto and indulge in elaborate parody of German and Italian opera for *The Perfect Fool* (1923); but in the same year the brilliantly scored ballet music from this opera, together with *The Planets* and *A Fugal Concerto* raised the composer to a peak of popularity. Then, during the twelve years left to Holst, his new works were treated either with curious respect or frank dislike. His daughter[1] records such press comments as: 'the chilly vacillations of its harmonies, where cerebration tamed and bridled inspiration'—referring to the Choral Symphony, for which even Vaughan Williams felt only 'a cold admiration'. By 1931 Holst 'was always feeling exhausted' and 'dreaded that his ideas were drying up'.[2]

Nevertheless the orchestral piece *Egdon Heath* (1927), the *Lyric Movement* for viola and orchestra (1933) and *Scherzo* for orchestra (1935) already show such 'third period' features as a simpler harmony and a new integration of purpose and style. Undoubtedly what we must call vision, for lack of another term, seems to have become intense and steady in Holst's last major works. Though *Egdon Heath* evokes Hardy's description (in *The Return of the Native*) of an upland tract of Dorset that is 'mysterious in its swarthy monotony', the music itself does not sprawl or flounder. By the clock this is a short piece that merely suggests man's reaction to the vast, inhospitable landscape. It does not relent to entertain the musician with points of technical interest as most of Holst's works certainly do. Imogen Holst says: 'There is no hint of exile in the loneliness of *Egdon Heath*: it is a home-coming.'[3] Clear vision betokens the genuine mysticism that is less concerned to suggest mystery than to pierce it and reveal the truth which it obscures.

Does the steady vision alone support belief in a 'third period'? Holst defies chronological classification. Few of his published works fit into a 'first period' that reflects as much of the nineteenth century as Beethoven's did of the eighteenth; and if penetration into regions (not necessarily of the mystic) where nobody can guide him puts a man's music into a 'third period' then most of Holst's major works belong to it. Other classifications than the chronological are also unsatisfactory. To speak of his 'Sanskrit period' is misleading unless we mean only that between 1907 and 1912. Holst taught himself to read Sanskrit and composed the *Hymns from the Rig Veda* and the one-act opera *Sāvitri* (from the *Mahabharata*) to his own translations. Their musical features —the spare texture, the recourse to quintuple and septuple time signatures, the reticent declamation—are not just of one period. His leaning towards the arabesque of eastern melodic lines does not belong only to

---

[1] Imogen Holst, *Gustav Holst* (London, 1938), pp. 115–6.   [2] Ibid., p. 149.
[3] Idem, *The Music of Gustav Holst* (London, 1951), p. 101.

one stage in his output or only to works like *Beni Mora* and *Two Eastern Pictures*. He needed it as he had needed folk-song, because its scales and rhythms took him away from convention. (There is no actual *râga* music in Holst's work as there is in *Padmâvati* for he was not, like Roussel, a connoisseur of oriental music.)

William McNaught wrote in 1939:[1]

. . . Holst occupied himself with intricate textural problems that seemed to the outer world to be of little importance. A typical instance was a three-part vocal canon with a different key-signature to each part . . . Either openly or implicitly he was given to the solving of out-of-the-way problems of his craft that kept him to the borders of the true road of music. His tremendous creative power was partly frittered away by this preoccupation with artifice, and it was only because the diminished impetus of that power was so great that he made his impression.

Some years later Wilfrid Mellers[2] wrote at length about the debt of subsequent musicians to Holst's treatment of the English language.

Holst did not see in the folk-song cult any wistful reversion to a simpler form of existence . . . he was interested in [folk-song] because words and tune had grown up together. . . . His own melodic idiom has affinities with that of English folk-song . . . [ ] more 'primitive' but completely unsentimental, it arouses expectations which it does not fulfil . . . Holst does sublimate speech into a phrase of some considerable extent, but not to the pitch of song.

The lyricism compatible with polyphony in Weelkes, Dowland, Purcell and many more of Holst's heroes seems to have been shunned. Within Holst's part-song settings from Robert Bridges are found some of his rare foreshadowings of the polyphonic ease assumed by his pupil Rubbra.

This austerity would be understandable in a minor composer for whom words meant more than line and harmony, rhythm and texture, but Holst was primarily interested in 'pure' music, music that did not duplicate what words could say, but began where words failed. We are left asking 'Why?' after reading Mellers's perceptive comments:[3]

The link with folk-song still prevails—for instance in the pentatonic feeling . . . but both the rhythmic plasticity and the tonality have acquired a sub-dued wavering instability which gives to the line its coldly desolate effect . . . His unique position, his oddity as a cultural phenomenon, consists precisely in his allowing the prose phrase integral expression without trying to emotionalize it or to compensate *for* it with a sensuous harmonic vocabulary.

And our 'Why?' is implied by the severest of all his critics, the composer

[1] *Modern Music and Musicians* (London, 1946), p. 47.
[2] Wilfrid Mellers, *Studies in Contemporary Music* (London, 1948) p. 145.
[3] Ibid., p. 147.

himself. Imogen Holst tells us that, listening to Schubert's C major Quintet in 1930:[1]

he realized what he had lost, not only in his music but in his life. He could cling to his austerity. He could fill his days with kindliness and good humour. He could write music that was neither commonplace, unmeaning, nor tame. And he could grope after ideas that were colossal and mysterious. But he had missed the warmth of the Schubert Quintet. At the moment, it seemed as if this warmth might be the only thing worth having.

Holst's peculiar psychosis of austerity was purely artistic. It did not belong only to the last years when he sat 'huddled over the fire . . . as if the spirit itself were numb'. *Sāvitri* dates from 1908, before the worst onset of neuritis or the effects of concussion after a fall, but its lack of sensuous appeal has earned it a reputation as 'an opera for spiritual and intellectual aristocrats'.

PETER WARLOCK AND HIS CONTEMPORARIES

The three or four men who produced distinctive work during the decadence of the nationalist movement also refreshed themselves directly from folk-music and the works of Tallis, Byrd, Weelkes, Wilbye, Dowland, Gibbons and Purcell. The limited achievement of E. J. Moeran (1894–1950) was exclusively lyrical, partly because he studied the violin as a schoolboy and partly because he had absorbed the Norfolk folk-songs which he collected. The best of his original songs approach the quality of Warlock's and his arrangements of Norfolk songs are neither timid nor clumsy. In his works more ambitious than songs none rises above the commonplace unless the original lyric gift is to the fore. His Symphony in G minor (1937) fails to fulfil the promise of an eloquently melodic opening; subsequent ideas lose character in turgid passages that seem to derive their menacing moods from Sibelius. On the other hand Moeran's Violin Concerto of 1942 has few *longueurs* because instead of an imposing façade it offers simple geniality. Moeran's attempts to emulate other men's complex harmony or structure betray the student, not the master; when he was wholly himself, as in two pieces of 1931 for small orchestra, he could realize forms of quiet beauty that maintain their appeal. The second of these two pieces uses the Norfolk song 'Lonely Waters' which he had already issued for voice; the other, 'Whythorne's Shadow', pays tribute to a beautiful song from Thomas Whythorne's collection of 1571.[2]

Twelve of Whythorne's songs had been published in 1927 by Philip

[1] *The Music of Gustav Holst*, p. 142.
[2] See Vol. IV, pp. 84 and 200.

Heseltine (1894–1930) whose own music was issued under the name Peter Warlock. While still a boy he was moved deeply by the music of Delius, with whom he became personally acquainted through a relation who lived near Delius at Grez-sur-Loing. Later he became an enthusiastic disciple of Bernard Van Dieren (1884–1936) who migrated from Holland in 1909 and became 'an enigmatic and portentous figure in the background'[1] of London music between the wars. Under his own name Heseltine published books on Delius, Gesualdo,[2] and *The English Ayre*. Under his pseudonym he brought out editions of Dowland's *Lachrimae*, Locke's and Purcell's fantasies and other consort music, and numerous songs and ayres of the sixteenth and seventeenth century. In his own compositions archaism and preciosity could sometimes be indulged with overt panache and wit, as in the *Capriol Suite* for string orchestra (1927) which uses dance tunes from Thoinot Arbeau's *Orchésographie* of 1589, or in the piquant accompaniments to songs of sly gallantry and tavern roistering. He could set a nursery or nonsense verse (as in the albums of 1923 called *Peterisms* and *Lilligay* with the consummate mastery that he expended on verses from Shakespeare.

These veins of his muse are associated with his gnomic pseudonym, but from the first songs which he published during the First War to the last set of 1929–30 there came from time to time the expression of pity, melancholy, or passionate devotion unparalleled in the setting of English poetry since Purcell. His tragic expression owes its effect to economy, and his taste for exactitude and orderliness is manifest even in the frenzied nausea of 'Take, O take those lips away'. This short song perfectly catches a climactic moment in Shakespeare, yet does so largely by a superb use of rich Delian harmonies that sound over-ripe and bitter and suggest a passion that has been poisoned. Among the finest of his sombre songs are two in his last four, settings of Bruce Blunt's poems 'The Frostbound Wood' and 'The Fox'. This set also includes the exquisitely tranquil 'Bethlehem Down'. Perhaps his supreme achievement lay in works for solo voice with a small group of instruments. A setting of Yeats's 'The Curlew' for tenor voice, flute, cor anglais, and string quartet, which foreshadows Britten's skill in dealing with a chamber group and solo voice, is surely one of the most beautiful evocations of desolate melancholy produced outside opera by any musician since Schubert.

Poverty, malnutrition and tuberculosis, following the effects of wounds, gas and shell-shock, deprived first of his reason and then of his life Ivor Gurney (1890–1937), a lyric poet of talent and a composer

---

[1] McNaught, ibid., p. 53.
[2] *Carlo Gesualdo, Prince of Venosa: Musician and Murderer* (London, 1926).

who excelled in the setting of English words. His musical remains are insufficient in bulk and maturity to justify speculation as to whether he would have reached Warlock's command of other accomplishments than a wonderfully sensitive vocal line. Gurney's malady overtook him before he had mastered the integration of vocal melody with harmony and other points of technique, despite striking passages in which chords or modulations perfectly fit verbal imagery. Few of the poems he wrote while serving in France were set to music. An exception, 'Severn Meadows', made his finest song which, with some of his Housman settings, e.g. 'Loveliest of trees', 'Desire in Spring', 'Lights Out', and 'An Epitaph', justify an echo of Grillparzer's tribute to Schubert: 'a rich treasure, but still fairer hopes'.

Gurney's friend Herbert Howells (b. 1892) was, like him, a Gloucester chorister who earned a scholarship at the Royal College of Music. His affection for the cathedral atmosphere has elicited a large number of anthems, motets, and canticles, some dedicated to particular foundations, as well as more ambitious works for voices and orchestra, such as *Hymnus Paradisi* (1950) and *Missa Sabrinensis* (1953). His music for the concert-hall is less familiar than his rhapsodic organ pieces and his two suites for clavichord. The fastidiousness of his textures, with their restless polyphony, makes exacting demands, but both instrumental and vocal effects are calculated with the imagination of a craftsman in filigree.

ARTHUR BLISS

Among composers who had already shown promise before the end of the First War was Arthur Bliss (b. 1891), one of the generation of Stanford pupils which included Howells and Gurney. He has been given insufficient credit for initiating before 1920 the reaction associated with the twenties in works musically superior to many which achieved a *succès de scandale*. Bliss lacks a personal idiom. He has therefore been most successful in works where strong personality is less important than deft technique, the securing of telling effects and a high order of general intelligence—in the films *The Shape of Things to Come* (1935), *The Conquest of the Air* (1937), and *Men of Two Worlds* (1945), in the incidental music to several plays, and in the ballets *Checkmate* (1937), *Miracle in the Gorbals* (1944), and *Adam Zero* (1946).

His career as a composer has been unusual because, instead of moving farther and farther away from his teachers, he seemed by the end of the twenties to turn towards their ideals. It was in these works that he revealed his full calibre and not just his enviable facility and humour. Among them are *Pastoral: Lie Strewn the White Flocks* (1928) and the admirably controlled yet rhapsodic Clarinet Quintet of 1931. The Quintet is manifestly English, whereas the *Pastoral* draws most appropriately upon the technique and flavours of the nationalists in settings for solo and chorus, with flute, strings, and percussion, of poems by Jonson, Fletcher, Theocritus, and others. Bliss lets the singer bear the main responsibility for details of interpretation and uses the instruments with reticence, as in his background music for films. That is probably why his choral symphony *Morning Heroes* (1930) moves without discrepancy from a portion of the Iliad (Hector's farewell to Andromache) to poems by Whitman, Li-Po, Wilfred Owen, and Robert Nichols. The work requires an orator with chorus and orchestra.

The best of Bliss's earlier works, *Rout* for soprano and ten instruments, using nonsense syllables purely for their sound (without the associative subtlety of Edith Sitwell's verses that were issued chiefly as studies in rhythm) and his *Conversations* for three string and three wind instruments, both date from 1919 and represent more than reaction against the amplitude of the romantic orchestra. The chamber groups and the employment of the voice as another instrument were means to musical wit in the strict sense of the word; every point, humorous or serious, is rooted in the forms and processes of music. There is wit not only in 'The Committee Meeting' and 'In the tube at Oxford Circus' (*Conversations*)[1] but also in the *Colour Symphony* (1922) which is serious, even romantic, for the four movements evoke the symbolic associations of purple, red, blue and green respectively: and Bliss's wit does not forsake him in more sinewy and classicist textures like the later *Music for Strings* (1935) and his two quintets (1931 and 1937). A piano concerto written for the New York World Fair (1939) is a clever attempt to revive the grand manner and opulent scale of the late nineteenth century.

Lord Berners (1883–1950) succeeded to his barony in 1918 but, as Gerald Tyrwhitt, had already published such musical facetiae as *Trois petites marches funèbres* (for a statesman, a canary, and a rich aunt) (1914), and the parodistic *Lieder Album* (1913) and *Valses bourgeoises* (1917). Later he achieved originality in ballets which include general parody of nineteenth-century music and manner, notably *The Wedding Bouquet* (1936) with his own French provincial sets and costumes and a chorus to a text devised by Gertrude Stein for its phonetic effect. *The Triumph of Neptune* (1926) was produced by Dyagilev with nautical scenes devised by Sacheverell Sitwell from a Victorian toy theatre, and *Luna Park* (1930) was included in one of Cochran's revues.

----

[1] Both recorded in *The History of Music in Sound*, x.

ALAN BUSH

Alan Bush (b. 1900), an important influence upon adolescent talent and judgement during the twenties and thirties, received his chief professional training in Berlin, and his leadership before the war is attributable less to his composition than to his strong personality and didactic power. He has been compared with Hindemith, sometimes ineptly, for though he respects (as fulfilling an obligation to society) what he calls 'educated music' which may not be treasured by posterity, he has formulated no harmonic-structural system to serve the composer who needs premises. Consequently pupils do not need to unlearn Bush's teaching in order to follow examples as diverse as those given by Stravinsky, Webern, Blacher, or Martin.

Bush's music is polyphonic, and his first notable success was achieved with one string quartet (1924) which won a Carnegie award, and another (*Dialectic*, 1929) is still considered his masterpiece. If he sometimes achieves only *Kapellmeistermusik*, of a solidity which suggests the church musician rather than the 'people's composer', it is sometimes his commission that has prevented his using strings or voices in a first-class demonstration of thematic argument; sometimes, as in the choral finale of his Piano Concerto (1937) he cannot rise above an ephemeral or naïve text. The best of Bush's instrumental works, such as the C major Symphony (1940), *Lyric Interlude* for violin and piano (1944), and Violin Concerto (1948), commended themselves to their first admirers on more valid grounds than a technique not quite like that of Rawsthorne, Rubbra or any other Englishman. Why, since he admired Schoenberg and actually used twelve-note themes in two movements of his C major Symphony, did Bush decline to join the radical serialists? Plainly for reasons which are bound up with his acceptance of Soviet composers' manifestos concerning proletarian understanding of ambitious music. Possibly Bush's style would have become less complex quite apart from his political conscience; but whatever the explanation, this simplification furthered the composition of Bush's operas, whose heavily slanted librettos have won them success in East Germany— *Wat Tyler* (1951) and *Men of Blackmoor* (1955). Musically these works are chiefly distinguished by their strong choral writing, foreshadowed by *The Winter Journey* of 1946, a cantata in which Bush treats the Christmas theme non-religiously.

CONSTANT LAMBERT AND WILLIAM WALTON

The first publications of three composers of the next generation— Constant Lambert (1905–51), William Walton (b. 1902), and Lennox

Berkeley (b. 1903)—associated them with the reaction against patriotism, romanticism, and high moral seriousness. Yet these young composers of the 1920s were more considerable than any of 'Les Six' except Honegger. However questionable the opinions in Lambert's *Music Ho!*, their bitterness is passionately serious; and so, beneath sophisticated mannerisms, is Walton's poignantly pessimistic lyricism, notably in the slow movement of his *Sinfonia concertante* for orchestra with piano (1927) and the outer movements of his Viola Concerto (1929).

In 1926 Lambert, still a student at the Royal College of Music, was the first Englishman whom Dyagilev asked to compose a ballet. *Romeo and Juliet* is set in a dancing school and has a 'rehearsal' plot culminating in an elopement by aeroplane. Young Lambert's eighteenth-century dances, with spicings and occasional jazzings, proved him an adroit rather than an original composer, for the work called for parody and pastiche. It immediately secured the commission for *Pomona*, also with choreography by Nizhinska, but without farcical elements. To judge only from the concert suite, *Pomona* (produced in Buenos Aires early in 1927) presented its pastoral myth in a manner as nearly 'straight' as does, say, *Apollon Musagète*; certainly it gave scope for mannered yet vital melody, presented less with contrapuntal device than with attractive contrapuntal features. Despite the large orchestra required, this athletic harmony and instrumentation commended *Music for Orchestra* (1927) to its first audience; its urbanity seemed clean, yet neither sterile nor made palatable with pseudo-sentiment from the jazz world. Some thematic material from *Music for Orchestra* (Ex. 229), shown with a short specimen of word setting from *Summer's Last Will and Testament* (1935) (Ex. 230), will suggest the quality of Lambert's mind:

Ex. 229

Ex. 230

He was a polymath who occasionally wrote incidental or film music, transcribed old music, made arrangements for ballets, and was so fully employed as a conductor and writer that his only other considerable orchestral work was *Aubade héroïque*, finished in 1942 but suggested by an early morning of 1940 when the Vic-Wells Ballet Company was escaping from Holland before the German invaders.

Before appearing as composer and conductor Lambert had been the speaker in his friend Walton's *Façade* (1923), an entertainment devised as a *Gesamtkunstwerk*, in which Edith Sitwell's verses, described as 'studies in rhythm, sound, and association of ideas', were spoken through a megaphone in a screen which prevented any distraction caused by the appearance of the speaker or of the instrumental ensemble which played Walton's pieces. The score, virtuosic both in its original form and in the full orchestral dress of its concert suite, and Walton's brilliant *Sinfonia Concertante* (1927), which included brittle rhythms of the kind associated with Milhaud's confections and some of jazz provenance, were largely responsible for the coupling of Walton's name with Lambert's. These early works have been disparaged as 'highbrow jazz', a defensive growth against the pathetic quasi-moral Philistinism of schools or the drab and even more tyrannical Philistinism of democracy. 'The perverse highbrowness which indulges in the low, having gone beyond the primitive earnestness of the romantics',[1] expressed during the twenties the thwarted desires of so large a section of urban society that in Germany and Russia government officials and indoctrinated artists fulminated against it. Its frivolity, as much as the querulousness of later generations, repels balanced minds. But Walton and Lambert were convinced of the need to doff the prophetic mantle, to learn from light music and jazz, just as the nationalists had learned from primitive and folk-music; and Walton and Lambert wrote very little inferior music before they passed to a less inhibited revelation of romantic earnestness.

It is mistaken to suppose that *Façade* is inferior Walton or to recognize the ephemeral superficies of the *Sinfonia Concertante* and not the poignant beauty to be found chiefly, but not only, in its slow movement; to suppose that Lambert published his Piano Sonata (1929) and his Concerto for Piano and Nine Instruments (1931) only to be fashionable, or to regard Walton's acid harmonies as 'wrong note' effects like those in the more vulgar pieces of Prokofyev and 'Les Six'. Though Walton proved more romantic and rhetorical, Lambert as a composer was either intellectually more serious, as in *Horoscope* (1937) with its elaborate musical palindrome, or emotionally more serious, as in the *Dirge from*

---

[1] Chapter on Walton by Colin Mason in *British Music of Our Time*, ed. Alfred Bacharach (London, 1946).

Cymbeline (1940) and *Summer's Last Will and Testament* (1935) with its
'King Pest' rondo and the culminating 'Sarabande':

> Queens have died young and fair;
> Dust hath closed Helen's eye:
> I am sick—I must die.
> Lord have mercy on us!

Lambert scored one extraordinarily popular success in 1927, with
a setting of Sacheverell Sitwell's *The Rio Grande* for chorus and
orchestra, ineptly described as symphonic jazz; not even the brilliant
solo piano part or the 'damask' blues chords in the quiet middle
section ('The noisy streets are empty and hushed is the air') keep to jazz
idiom which, according to the composer, 'is a more plastic basis than
folk song or pre-jazz popular song. Jazz, like much exotic music,
depends more upon rhythmic and melodic inflection than upon a
square-cut scheme.' Lambert was aware of the limitations of standard
jazz syncopations and jazz harmony, not altogether unlike the deficiencies in all but the best music of the nineteenth-century German
romantic school, as Wagner himself was aware. Beethoven's scherzos
were a serious composer's development from minuets 'as rhythmically
effete as commercial jazz' and Walton's *Portsmouth Point* (1925) included jazz rhythms but produced 'an atmosphere as far removed from
Harlem' as Beethoven's was from the eighteenth-century dancing room.
'The jazz composer is now stagnating, bound to a narrow circle of
rhythmic and harmonic devices and neglecting the possibilities of form.
It is for the highbrow composer to take the next step.' Lambert shrewdly
noticed the ineffectiveness of many attempts to bring jazz into the
concert room; and he particularly disliked composers like Gershwin
who used 'only the non-barbaric, non-vital elements . . . Jazz is not
raw material but half-finished material in which European sophistication
has been imposed over coloured crudity. There is always danger that
the highbrow composer may . . . leave only the sophisticated trappings
. . . as in the *Rhapsody in Blue*.'[1]
     Perhaps the clearest statement of his belief lies in the words: 'I see
no reason . . . why a composer should not be able to rid himself as much
from the night-club element in jazz as Haydn did from the ballroom
element in the minuet, and produce the modern equivalent of those
dance suites of Bach which we treat with as much seriousness as the
sonatas of Beethoven.'
     The development of Walton's own temperament revealed a strain
of brooding and melancholy at odds with the sharp wit and smart

---

[1] *Music Ho!*, p. 228.

exterior features of his style. This is seen notably in his deservedly popular dramatic oratorio, *Belshazzar's Feast* (1929), upon a text skilfully arranged by Osbert Sitwell from the biblical narrative. Walton, like Rubbra, Rawsthorne, and other British musicians born between 1900 and 1905, found in traditional quarries a seam scarcely large enough for one man's needs throughout a normal working life. He was put to unusual labour whenever he avoided the obvious recourse to older seams with which he made shift in commissioned and ceremonial music, and his completion of major work has always been slow; but British musicians of Walton's generation were more talented than most of their immediate predecessors, and it is mistaken to attribute their restricted range entirely to limitations of musical gifts. Without abnormal competence they had little chance of a hearing. If they could not appear original by adopting foreign styles they could do so only by idiosyncracy of style. This Walton commanded without affectation and cultivated in his best work by genuine compulsion. He begins the slow movement of his First Symphony (1935) with a melody as poignant as Ex. 231:

Ex. 231

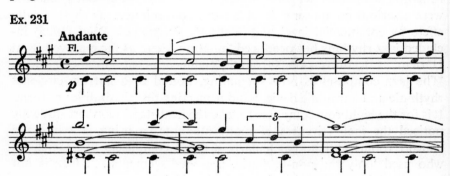

and, despite echoes of its contours, throws it away until it is used as an epilogue. He presented impassioned music like:

Ex. 232

and vehement music like Exx. 233 and 234 (also from the First Symphony):

Ex. 233

Ex. 234

with detachment, sometimes implied amusement, remains urbane even in the haunting close of the Viola Concerto (1929), embedding the jaunty first theme of the finale within the soft valedictory texture, offsets *con malinconia* with *con malizia*, reconciles Stravinskyan subleties of accentual rhythm with long-phrased melody never commanded by Stravinsky, finds a place in symphonic structure for fastidiously sensuous orchestral effects, even to finely judged dynamics for Chinese block, castanets, and minor percussion, and was not afraid of the taunt that he reflected the taste of a sophisticated intelligentsia. There is no insincerity in Walton's style, which is true to the man, known for taciturn good humour and the sardonic wit that informs his scherzos.

Walton's occasional additions to his musical vocabulary, for example in his Cello Concerto (1959) or the passacaglia-finale of his Second Symphony (1961), reveal no significant refreshment of his powers, and he has not always succeeded in attempts to make his style serve a wider range of expression than it did before the war. In his opera *Troilus and Cressida* (1954), for example, the choruses and the witty music for Pandarus showed the familiar Walton to his first operatic audience. But his music for the protagonists rarely rises to lyricism as poignant as in his best purely instrumental music, and hardly ever to ecstasy. He often seems rather to be translating into his own idiom the responses by which successful opera composers before him met the situations requiring different moods and aspects of the grand passion. Aware both of increased skill and also of an artistic impasse, Walton has from time to time offered a work that resembles a second, perhaps more accomplished, fulfilment of an earlier task. Thus the overture *Scapino* (1941) is better constructed than *Portsmouth Point* yet does not fully match its youthful verve; the great beauty and skill of the Violin Concerto (1939) would be admired without reserve if this work (by other points than two quiet and lyrical outer movements enclosing an astringently witty one) did not invite comparison with the Viola Concerto, which is not only among the most attractive specimens of its genre but also Walton's most consummate achievement. A similar comment is invited by the Second Symphony (1960).

EDMUND RUBBRA

At almost every point of personal temperament and musical style Rubbra is Walton's antithesis. Despite his wide reading, historical knowledge, and interest in the graphic arts, Rubbra cannot be described as urbane. His music almost excludes epigram, impressionistic digressions or sudden brilliance; most of its ideas have high lyrical potential and may be suffused with lyrical sentiment from the beginning (as at the opening of the Fourth Symphony) but they usually need ample time to become impassioned. The rhetoric moves steadily to its climaxes, where emotion glows to full incandescence as in filaments at some distance from their source of power. Rubbra's achievement has been to combine the classical principle of expanding variation with a continuously polyphonic texture—polyphonic not just in the Wagnerian sense, but in a sense that has made people regard some of his movements as gigantic motets. Indeed, the claim to have linked renaissance with modern musical organisms, falsely made for composers whose texture was at least half impressionistic (Vaughan Williams's Mass, for instance, has more of Debussy than Byrd in it) can be sensibly made for Rubbra and only for him. Rubbra does not seek incidental colour for its own sake. Most of his ideas are song-like and grow by polyphonic texture wherein the long phrases reach inexorably forward into big paragraphs—not of balanced sequences and patterns of figuration, but of asymmetrical sentences.

His First Symphony (1938) is fashioned from the materials Rubbra has continued to use—the diatonic scales, with a predilection for the melodic minor and a sparing use of chromatics except the sixth and seventh degrees of the ascending minor scale. Contrary motion of the parts, including that between the two directions of this scale, gave a measure of discord unremarkable at the time, but the Symphony sounded hard-driven because the ideas were hard-driven. They are so in many of Rubbra's subsequent movements, across which may be written the technical description *tema ricercata*, but less and less forcing was needed as the ideas themselves became more fertile.

Already in the First Symphony Rubbra had established several characteristic forms of *tema ricercata*, some of them by no means motet-like or fugue-like. Only the two most strongly contrasted can be described here. The movement corresponding with the minuet or scherzo of a classical symphony is called 'Périgourdine'. A dance-like length of tune recurs without episode and with only such variation-development as Purcell uses to vary the key in a long 'ground'. Passing harmonies, textures, and counter-themes seem to clutch at the swift gliding tune, increasing the effect of unhesitating motion. The second movement of Rubbra's Fifth Symphony (1948):

Ex. 235

Theme by augmentation

shows comparable treatment of a most attractive tune—apparently more naïve than the 'Périgourdine' yet in fact extremely subtle, and full of spores which are transplanted for accompanying material but not allowed to interfere with the main thread, in which the complete tune recurs through all twelve major keys. This pruning back, with the suppression of threatened climaxes in deference to the pattern of repetitions, produces an effect of intense energy. The corresponding first movements show a very different form springing from a song-like idea, which gathers counterpoint but does not germinate only by counterpoint and is not planned with countersubjects. In the initial stages of this type of organism the main stem of melody will normally make sense and suggest the play of smaller and larger climax even if shorn of accompanying material. Some of these movements with a strong 'main stem' have elicited the description 'monistic' from writers who are well aware that its propriety, like that of 'monothematic', has usually been questioned when applied to movements of symphonic dimensions. When Rubbra reached more genial expression than his First Symphony, he was not untrue to himself in allowing contrasts that deceptively suggest as much relaxation as there is in most classical symphonies. Thus the staid melody which opens his Third Symphony (1939) is at first paced rather than countered, gathers tension by generating polyphony, reaches a distinct cadence (Ex. 236) and passes to what seems to be an entirely new, contrasting idea of plain chords which resembles the beginning of a classical 'second group'; its punctuation by a four-note figure from the previous polyphony is no stronger a means of integration than the corresponding feature in the lyrical second subject of Beethoven's Fifth Symphony. Yet when this homophonic passage reaches its finish in the key from which it began, we recognize it as a long extension of the cadence. The polyphony continues where it left off, gathering up the opening theme of the movement along with the punctuating figure of the episode as if to compensate for the relaxation.

Ex. 236

If works on a symphonic scale did not take great time and labour, we might wonder that Holst's disciple has written little vocal music. What he has written achieves distinction (notably in the choral *Dark Night of the Soul*, 1935 and *The Morning Watch*, 1941) and, when liturgical, reconciles scrupulous propriety with imaginative power. Moreover, it sometimes serves, like some of his few chamber works, to disprove the supposition that he is never inclined towards the impressionist's love of colourful or alluring effect. As a fine pianist, who as a boy loved the late romantics, Rubbra has a connoisseur's appraisal of harmony that makes an immediate impact, yet it cannot be denied that his best chamber music reflects his symphonic breadth. His Cello Sonata (1946) is among the noblest of its kind, his String Quartet, no. 2 (1952), within its proper limits, secures emotional intensity within imposing forms, and a piece for recorder and piano for Carl Dolmetsch, *Meditazioni sopra Cœurs désolés*, contains within a mere five pages an epitome of his art; yet his symphonies are his masterpieces.

Rubbra's symphonies, of which there are so far eight, stand unique in British music. In them are combined inheritances that had been thought irreconcilable—polyphony similar in principle to that in which the greatest British composers of the past excelled, the dimensions of romantic symphonies and their scale of climax and tension.

LENNOX BERKELEY

Although Berkeley (b. 1903) exemplifies the Parisian and Stravinskyan influences of the 1920s, he belongs to no group, French or English, and was little known until the 1920s were over. After a normal university career, not devoted to music, in 1925 Berkeley went to Paris and worked as a pupil of Nadia Boulanger in order to become effectively articulate. Many have testified to those parts of Nadia Boulanger's courses that are designed to broaden knowledge and taste; but in Berkeley (and in his contemporaries under her discipline—Copland and Harris for instance) it is possible to observe the effect of a complementary concentration upon certain composers from Monteverdi to Stravinsky and upon composition for prescribed groups and small groups of instruments. The first long work which Berkeley sent to England, the oratorio *Jonah* (1929), was scarcely coherent, somewhat congested and bloodless; despite inventive and sensitively scored passages it rarely inspired fine singing by soloists or chorus. Yet among the mature Berkeley's chief merits are his assured clarity of thought and texture and his outstandingly attractive vocal writing. Perhaps the most notable example of the latter is Lady Nelson's soliloquy at the end of Act II in *Nelson* (1953), but Berkeley's St. Teresa songs for contralto and string orchestra (1947) touch an extraordinarily high level of inspiration as well as craftsmanship.

To recognize his cautious but assured growth into a distinct personality one should compare his String Trio of 1944 with his Horn Trio of 1954, or his two Symphonies of 1940 and 1958. None of these four works is imposing or solemn; yet the advance in unpretentious musical architecture during the eighteen years which separates them is as clear as Mozart's more speedy advance from the serenade-like Salzburg symphonies and concertos to the Viennese works, with their motivic and contrapuntal integration.

Unlike the preclassical masters, Berkeley was not forced to earn by purveying music of serenade gravity; but having abandoned the promptings that led to his oratorio, he published between 1935 and 1950 a series of works which made people regard him as primarily 'a divertimento composer'. He was content to keep his movements short and largely unrhetorical, to hold interest by buoyant rhythm, neat harmony, and attractive fragments of melody rather than by the musical equivalent of 'great thoughts'. His Serenade for Strings (1939), Divertimento (1945), Concerto for Two Pianos (1943), Nocturne and

Sinfonietta, or his Piano Sonata (1941) and Six Preludes, suggested that Berkeley was capable of composition on a grander scale. Berkeley would still rather charm than bore, but with the charm there was now a concentration occasionally amounting to earnestness. An exception is *Nelson* (1953) which nowhere depends upon 'good theatre' to hide weak musical seams. In any other European country *Nelson*, as well as *Ruth* (1956) and the amusing chamber opera *The Dinner Engagement* (1954), would be valued. Admittedly *Nelson* is dramatically unequal and episodic; so also are most of the established favourites of the lyric stage.

ALAN RAWSTHORNE

Alan Rawsthorne (1905–71) courted neither public nor minority favour. He issued a score of admirable works, almost all instrumental and with simple musical titles—quartet, sonata, concerto etc. An exception is *The Creel* (1940), a fascinating suite of short pieces for piano duet, each corresponding with one of Isaak Walton's 'characters' of freshwater fish (see Ex. 237(i)). Rawsthorne's nationality is sometimes said to betray itself in turns of melody, especially in lyrical passages. Yet there are long stretches of this music, from the Symphonic Sketches to the splendid Violin Sonata (1959), which could deceive Swiss, Dutch, German, or Scandinavian listeners who did not know Rawsthorne (an important condition, for he has a personal style) into believing that they were hearing works by their compatriots. The First Violin Concerto, one of the works which occupied him during his war service in the army (though not played until 1948), was dedicated to Walton; yet here again the similarities to Walton are often less striking than affinities with such composers as Hindemith and Frank Martin.

Rawsthorne's music sometimes resembles Hindemith's (in passing, not in broad structure) simply because he shares some of his aesthetic ideals. He offers athletic design and neat figuration; hence the frequent observation that his phrasing, patterning and decorative counterpoint recall the baroque masters. But it is the score-reading eye rather than the ear which links it with baroque technique. Undoubtedly his 'conception of variation is not the melodic one of Haydn and Mozart but rather that of Bach in the Goldberg Variations'.[1] Probably the most personal element in his idiom is his very fluid harmony; and if he had been required to theorize, he would probably have said with Hindemith that he avoided atonal techniques because he needed a hierarchy of tensions and relaxations among the degrees and intervals of the tempered chromatic scale. His use of a twelve-note series has no more

---

[1] Mellers, op. cit., p. 176.

significance than Walton's or Britten's; in the Quintet for wind instruments and piano (1962), it merely emphasizes the unchanged elements in his style.

Though Rawsthorne shapes complete movements as assuredly and precisely as he does paragraphs and sentences, at least some of his persistent characteristics can be observed in short excerpts which, taken from very diverse sources, also show how intelligently self-imposed limits have not restricted his range of imagination and expression as they might have done. Scanning the following excerpts, we see the variety of patterning and decorating but do not hear it as neo-baroque pastiche:

'The Sprat', No. 2 of *The Cree*

Ex. 237

Baroque patterning is a superstructure over a thoroughbass; in Rawsthorne's texture functions are reversed, for it is the figuration or the
contrapuntal superstructure that holds together the mercurial harmonies—the slippings from augmented triads, the constant major-minor
alternations, and the elusive tonality.

If Berkeley had not composed religious songs and a romantic opera,
his temperamental as well as his technical affinity with Rawsthorne
might have been more often noticed. The French atmosphere of his
work should not blind us to several parallels with Rawsthorne's
methods; and Rawsthorne's music is far from being a bloodless
exhibition of design and form. There has been no need for Rawsthorne
to compose a *Nobilissima Visione*, or even his admirable *Street Corner
Overture* (1944), merely to prove the redness of his blood.

GERALD FINZI

The songs of Gerald Finzi (1901–56) treat English verse as sensitively
as Wolf's did German. Three cycles of songs from Thomas Hardy and
one from Shakespeare, issued between 1933 and 1949 (especially the
Hardy cycle of 1936 entitled *Earth and Air and Rain*) earn Finzi a
greater distinction than he has secured by music more frequently heard
in public, such as his cantata *Dies Natalis* (1939), a setting of five
Traherne poems for voices and strings, or his Concerto for Clarinet and
Strings (1949). A light polyphony resembling some of Rubbra's less
intense orchestral textures gives a quasi-symphonic effect to Finzi's
accompaniments.

MICHAEL TIPPETT

After 1945 only extreme pessimists could fear a dearth of new and original native music, for the 1940s confirmed the impression that Michael Tippett (b. 1905) would stimulate controversy with every new work; and Benjamin Britten (b. 1913), some of whose instrumental works of the late 1930s (especially the concertos) had produced uncertainty whether the spate of his ideas would run deep or shallow, now produced three fine operas in three successive years—*Peter Grimes* in 1945, *The Rape of Lucretia* in 1946, *Albert Herring* in 1947.

Despite the disparity of their ages, Tippett and Britten have temperamental affinities. They read more widely than most musicians and are interested in other arts than music. They differ greatly as composers yet are both attracted by subjects (in songs, operas, or cantatas) dominated less by direct expression of the primitive passions than by the pity, fear, disgust, or amusement with which we contemplate their survival or perversion among supposedly civilized men. They would be assured of lasting distinction if they had been no more than the first modern English composers whose operas aroused international interest, or the first whose declamation has challenged the artistry of singers and invited a new examination of dramatic word-setting from Purcell to Mussorgsky.

Tippett's deep interest in the polyphonists and in Purcell was not merely instilled but grew from inner compulsion. Tippett once confessed himself unable to select the greatest composers of this century, but he was willing to name the most important ones for himself and other British musicians: Stravinsky, Hindemith, Bartók, and Berg. He admired Purcell's emulation of the Italians and esteemed English composers of the twentieth century for what they did not share. Bartók, he declared, was well served by the asymmetry and fertilizing 'barbarity' of the folk-music he collected, whereas English composers had been ensnared by their lyrical folk-music.

Tippett's works are few in number and make no bid for the modicum of popularity elicited by work that can be allotted to stylistic niches. There are few points of style common to Tippett's quartets, cantatas, and operas; few indeed can be traced from one quartet to another. Some extracts from his Second Quartet may serve to show the originality of his instrumental polyphony, indebted to English consort music but not finding its integration, as that music did, in the kind of rhythmic and melodic symmetry associated with the high baroque and classical styles:

Ex. 238

(i) 2nd. movt. Andante

(ii) 3rd movt. Presto

The claim that bar lines are purely for the reader's convenience can be justly made for a good deal of Tippett's musical thought; but he did not reach a consistent and integrated instrumental style. His music can be irritatingly insubstantial even when it seems polyphonic and, to the eye, suggests rhythmic subtlety. The figuration of his accompaniments (to vocal or instrumental lines) seems often to intrude unconvincingly with ornamental figuration, not to support or challenge; and even his popular Concerto for Double String Orchestra (1939) owes much to an illusion of solidity produced by its medium.

His important vocal works are few and all are set to carefully chosen words at the bidding of complex ideas, the symbols without which he seems unable to express simple enough truths. The complexity of his symbolism, and the fact that it begins before the further symbolism of music has been imposed, would have distinguished Tippett from Britten even if their music itself had not been so different—Tippett's involved, elusive, sometimes inchoate, and Britten's disarmingly direct and paradoxically both sophisticated and naïve. To be fully articulate Tippett needs words and the human voice; and even when he strains the voice and sets syllables to melisma without obvious reason, he communicates the anxiety of a high intelligence. Whether spare or elaborate, his music is produced by intense mental labour; so is Britten's, but Britten rarely betrays labour.

Two exceptional and daring essays in seemingly incongruous juxta-position have been made by Tippett and Britten, the first in *A Child of our Time* (1941) by employing Negro spirituals as Bach did chorales, the second in his *War Requiem* (1962) by interposing the operatic declamation of Wilfred Owen's poems within liturgical treatment of the Latin choruses from the *Missa pro defunctis*. Each caused a sensation at first, yet Tippett's cantata is as innocent of vulgarity as Britten's masterpiece. In the past, opera has been more effective when we have been caught up in the feelings of protagonists than when we have been presented with psychological symbolism and moral reflection, but Tippett's cantata should be judged as a work *sui generis*. The difficulty of doing this is increased by Tippett's tripartite plan. Each section begins with a chorus and ends with a spiritual, suggesting parallels with Bach's Passions. As in Bach, both choral and solo sections are used for narration as well as for reflection. The intermingling of story and commentary, the quantity and brevity of 'numbers', and Tippett's elusively complex rhythms enhance the effect of the spirituals which are presented without translation to the texture and harmony of other items.

The Midsummer Marriage (1952) brought into the theatre much of the Tippett of *A Child of our Time*. He wrote his own libretto, giving himself little scope for 'characterization' and much for symbolic representation; his music is allied with moral problems which are beyond the bounds of musical expression. Yet for its understanding the listener-spectator needs no more than the barest outline of the composer's explanations. Tippett observes that the classic comic plot presented hindrances to a marriage, and that they were largely social; the chief modern hindrances to a good marriage or to any successful relationship are ignorance and illusions, especially about ourselves. Therefore in the course of his plot the characters discover their true selves, and he himself has declared that 'the moral of *The Midsummer Marriage* is enlightenment' when in a final tableau we see the young lovers transfigured in light, like Hindu deities. A sensitive young man and a hard young woman ('whose illusions are spiritual'), a tycoon and his vulgar innamorata ('whose illusions are social'), a mechanic, a clairvoyante, ancient Greeks, priests and priestesses, ritual dancers, splendidly and diversely caparisoned choruses, a spiral staircase that stops in mid-air like something out of Cocteau, a cavern with gates, the play of light from dawn to nightfall, the different seasons of nature—here is ample mechanism for opera and for a phantasmagoria of symbolism which seems to be the necessary catalyst for a Tippett opera; for, as *A Child of our Time* shows, Tippett's music does not necessarily become second-rate when his text becomes philosophic.

Music is powerful not only because it intensifies what words and spoken drama can convey, but also because it expresses reactions of our subconscious and shades of emotion which words can neither describe nor even name. Tippett and Britten are modern composers because they have sped music on this process of discovery; that their success varies, or that their styles may be considered conservative, matters little beside the fact that their sensibilities have kept pace with the ideas of twentieth-century thinkers, poets and dramatists. Their libretti may be symbolical or historical, but produce modern, even 'problem' operas which disturb comfortably settled minds.

BENJAMIN BRITTEN

If Britten had died before setting libretti which tax both mind and musical sensibility, he would still be acclaimed as one of the most imaginative of composers, distinguished by the degree to which his imagination is aural. Few composers so marvellously command the acoustic and instrumental materials of music that they always secure, by notation and a few spoken directions at rehearsal, the effects they imagined before a note was written. This faculty in Britten almost disarms criticism. Faced with a level of professional competence reached by no other British composer since the seventeenth century, one may dislike this or that effect and try to defend an objection of mere taste; but it is normally dangerous to suggest improvements in the means by which the effect is secured. The point may be illustrated from the Sunday morning scene in *Peter Grimes*, during which Ellen's pleadings and Grimes's expostulations are heard against evocations of the sea and of the service proceeding in the nearby church. An initial suspension of disbelief which accepts scenery and music that is only religiously picturesque seems less vulgar than a series of adjustments to convention at each change from the liturgical to the operatic. *Peter Grimes* wonderfully captures the style of the English village service from our grandfathers' time to ours; but the parson's intonings, the congregational responsory and the incurably intrusive electronic organ reached those outside church in spasms. Britten could hardly have flecked his score with stray sounds of worship as Debussy did *Fêtes* with distant sounds of the fairground; yet had he not overstrained his mind's ear by trying to assimilate sections of church-parody into his tense dramatic dialogue? No. There is no incongruity between the stylized and the onomatopoeic —between Britten and Victorian church chant.

Almost as disarming is Britten's professional seriousness, for it has often contradicted first impressions. The most conscientious artist may occasionally pass what seem the idle thoughts of a busy fellow, and when he is extraordinarily gifted as well as conscientious, the listener may easily believe that he has been content with 'facile brilliance' or 'shallow cleverness'. In addition to his share of salutary adverse criticism Britten has also received adverse criticism that was contradicted after subsequent closer acquaintance with the music. The instrumental *Sinfonia da requiem* of 1940 (Ex. 239(i) and (ii)) illustrates the kind of expression to which few people had become accustomed in 1940, when Britten was twenty-seven:

Ex. 239
(i)

(iii) **Andante**

Britten perplexed his early critics because he could be related neither to a recognized contemporary school nor to a tradition. None of Britten's English predecessors, whether nationalists or disciples of continental leaders, entirely abandoned criteria of harmony and texture formed by 'the classics'. His major works seemed insubstantial in the same sense as Turner's later pictures—all air and light. When he decided, as in *The Young Person's Guide to the Orchestra* (1946), to make his peroration with a fugue he sloughed parts or ran them into unison to avoid opacity. Similarly chaconnes, canons, and pedals are allowed no more complexity than is required for a desired total effect.

Britten's fugues and his Second String Quartet (1945)—the movements of which are of more traditional design that most of Britten's— suggest that certain designs discover his limitations. He does not resemble the English teachers for whom he has expressed admiration and affection—Frank Bridge, John Ireland, and Arthur Benjamin (1893–1960). It has already been pointed out that these were among the least nationalist of their generation and the least attached to any school. Unlike Hindemith and Nadia Boulanger, they do not seem to have inclined towards the manner of any modern composer or school. If we did not know their names not even the title of the most virtuosic of Britten's early instrumental works, the string Variations on a Theme of Frank Bridge (1937), would lead one to mention their influence, although Arthur Benjamin's *The Devil Take Her* (1932), a sparkling and splendidly composed one-act opera, is one of the few pre-Britten English works that might pass for Britten's, if we could postulate for him an operatic 'first period'. Benjamin wrote five works for the stage: unfortunately the best music is found in the incomplete *Tartuffe*, which contains spoken parts and is an English adaptation of Molière's *Le Misanthrope*.

Britten is at his best when a plot, text, or vocal line provides the thread that helps to make explicit the purport of his texture as a whole and also bears the chief concentration of integrating technique. It is possible that the revaluation of *Sinfonia da requiem* has been largely the consequence of familiarity with his treatment of the voice and his response to dramatic and pictorial situations; the thematic material is subtly linked from movement to movement and there are also derivations from harmonic formulae; moreover the three movements bear titles and could have occurred in an opera or cantata. The examples from the third and final movement, 'Requiem aeternam', provide a slight anchorage for the listener. The instrumentation of Ex. 239(i) is possibly from Stravinsky and Ex. 239(ii) is Mahlerian; in both excerpts the rhythms are conservative and the harmonies basically so. The flutes clash, and several bass notes are discords, yet the sound is gently luminous.

Britten's harmony is as personal as his structure, and so linked with structure that we must qualify the label 'impressionist'. Britten is an impressionist in so far as his chords are not conceived within a framework of symmetrical harmonic rhythm. Singly, in pairs, or in short groups they may be sustained, repeated, or varied as long as he needs their initial effect. He rarely uses the lush chords of post-romantic impressionists but is fond of triads with added notes, augmented triads, and indeed just plain triads divorced from traditional contexts. His juxtapositions look simple but are not prefabricated 'progressions'. The lullaby from *The Rape of Lucretia* quoted in Ex. 239(iii) seems an exception in Britten of four-part harmony with a regular tread, yet it is both impressionistic and original in a way which only the dramatic circumstances and the proper instruments fully reveal. Britten's chords, unlike Bartók's or Stravinsky's, are rarely built up from fourths; he favours the piling of thirds—triad, seventh, and ninth.

We cannot class Britten with impressionists who continued the refinement of erotic romanticism, nor with those whose evanescent harmonies and colours are mixed with mere wisps and scrappets of melody, for the strongest of all his materials of expression is his vocal line. It has been imitated but remains unique. Britten's 'line' (vocal or not) gives the complete texture a tighter integration than was necessary for former impressionists.

In *Peter Grimes* several passages of arioso seem to flaunt the ideal of 'heightened speech'. Lawyer Swallow's declamations, of which Ex. 240 is a specimen, were quoted as examples of perversity:

Ex. 240

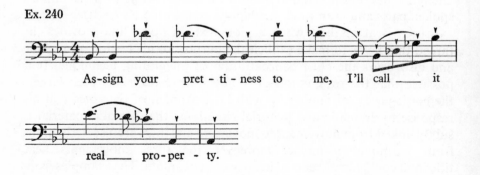

In his twenties Britten was manifestly attracted by Purcell's inspired flamboyance, yet he never emulated Purcell to the extent of sounding neo-baroque. Undoubtedly, however, seventeenth-century words in *The Holy Sonnets of John Donne* (1946) have prompted his most Purcellian settings. The point could be best shown from No. 7, 'At the round earth's imagined corners', but one forbears to excise a quotation from a song that is unified by a ground-bass technique, and therefore Ex. 241 is taken from No. 9, 'Death, be not proud'. The extract is the transformation of a quiet theme introduced at the words 'From sleepe and rest, which but thy pictures bee':

Ex. 241

Such direct and fiery Purcellisms now represent a comparatively early stage in a composer who could hardly have reached the subtle integration of his later settings and yet retained vivid illustrative power if his flamboyance had not been strong enough for pruning. He is now rarely opulent and never ostentatious, but his refinement is not emaciated, timid or affected; it comes from an invention so fertile that it might have lost much of its power if it had run riot.

The stages by which Britten came to mastery in dealing with English words invite psychological as well as musical inquiry. According to Peter Pears[1] his thorough study of Purcell was not undertaken until the general directions of his style were fixed and his originality recognized. The 1936 settings of satirically sententious and sometimes obscure verses by Auden in *Our Hunting Fathers* were by no means a waste of his abilities; still less questionable was his determination not to set familiar English verses from Elizabethan and Jacobean lyrics, or from later sources, until he had met the challenge of French in *Les Illuminations* (Rimbaud) and Italian in *Seven Sonnets of Michelangelo* (both 1940).

---

[1] *Benjamin Britten: a Commentary on his works*, ed. Donald Mitchell and Hans Keller (London, 1952), p. 64.

Pears's comments on the factors which ordained Britten's course need not be echoed here, but we should draw one clear conclusion— that, as Byrd declared in a misquoted and misunderstood passage, the 'hidden power' which elicits music at the reading of the right words comes not from the words themselves but (Byrd's phrase) from the 'thoughts underlying the words', and therefore Britten's self-imposed course was neither perverse nor affected. Before returning to his native language he wished to kill any temptation to accept without question a reciter's values.

Britten's return to English poets was signalized in 1943 by the publication of one of his most attractive works, the Serenade for tenor solo, horn obbligato, and string orchestra. The subject of evening and nightfall links its six texts, chosen from different periods so that an anonymous fifteenth-century dirge is flanked by familiar verses from Blake and Tennyson, Jonson and Keats; but Britten's wish to unify the cycle precludes any attempt to relate musical styles to literary periods. Particularly fine, both in itself and in its effect as a 'frame' is the paragraph for solo horn that forms the prologue and is repeated distantly ('off stage') for epilogue. It is to be played on the natural harmonics: the feeling for the instrument, the punctuation of the paragraph and the extraordinary power of its phrases to suggest both the main theme of the cycle and a concentration of associations and memories testify to a rare quality of musicianship.

The Serenade is among the most deservedly popular of Britten's non-operatic works, but the key documents to his mature, unostentatious integration in arioso are the three *Canticles*. For subtlety of organization Britten has never surpassed *Canticle 3* (1955) a setting of Edith Sitwell's 'Still falls the rain'. The verses are interspersed with variations for horn and piano, and only a long quotation could show the variation technique as well as the relation between vocal and instrumental movements.

There is hardly a better manual of Britten's later vocal style than a set of songs which, unlike the *Canticles* or *Nocturne*, are almost domestic music, though singer and pianist must be worthy of a modern Schubertiad. *Winter Words* (1954) is an album of eight lyrics from Thomas Hardy. The first, 'At close of day', accommodates a wealth of illustration in variations of an initial idea, yet at the finish leaves us aware that the dips of the line throughout depict the background of the poem, the swaying of 'tall trees'. The motor pattern of the second song, about a poor lad's railway journey from home on a bleak night, is a traditional integrator; but the Purcellian melisma in the voice part produces a total effect by no means traditional. The deliberately

Purcellian arioso in No. 5, 'The Choirmaster's Burial', is self-explanatory. The last song, 'Before Life and After', is useful for short quotation. Its trudging triads offer in themselves little scope for varied expression but make a superb background for highly expressive vocal inflexion. In Ex. 242 we note how they are halted, Schubert-wise, at key points in the poem, the third time with an unemphatic false relation which gives 'no sense was stung' a vividness which eludes the words alone:

Ex. 242

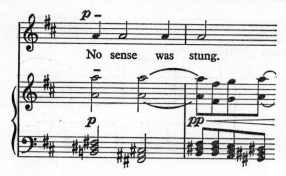

No sense was stung.

Britten withdrew his first opera, *Paul Bunyan,* and no part of it has been heard in public. *Peter Grimes* (1945), comparable in resources and musical ingredients with Verdi's *Otello* rather than any German music-drama, remains his most popular work, having been translated into many languages and acclaimed in many countries. *The Rape of Lucretia* (1946) requires a string and a wind quintet with two percussion players, and a cast of three men and three women to whom are added one man and one woman who stand on either side of the proscenium as commenting chorus. It is customary to call this work and the ensuing *Albert Herring* (1947) chamber operas, though *Lucretia* touches levels of pathos reached in Britten's full-scale operas and *Herring* is one of the better comic operas of our century. It is possible to deplore the new forms of puritanism, manifest in gratuitous moralizing and in an emphasis upon squalid *verismo* for *The Beggar's Opera* and in the implication that we are wickedly heartless to acquiesce in Gay's idea of 'A Newgate Pastoral'; yet one may still marvel at Britten's ability to meet Tyrone Guthrie's dialogue and to extend or vary the original music without once suggesting academic exercise. *The Beggar's Opera* (1949) is rightly described as 'opera in three acts' and wrongly as 'a new realization of John Gay's Ballad Opera 1728'.

The Turn of the Screw (1954) also engages 'single' instruments. This work, to which 'chamber' should never be applied as a diminutive, is the finest as well as the most ingenious of Britten's operas. The less complex and very directly appealing *Billy Budd* (1952)[1] which, marking Britten's return to Verdian broadness, full cast, and orchestra, may be considered the successor to *Grimes.* Its naval setting and consequent all-male cast seems not to have affected its success. For the coronation *festa teatrale* at Covent Garden in 1953 Britten provided *Gloriana,* an episodic piece upon the relations between Elizabeth I and her favourites; the two ballet sections and the incongruous spoken scene at the end are

[1] See pl. VIII.

PLATE VIII

BRITTEN'S *BILLY BUDD*, 1952 (*see p. 554*)

A scene from the original production at the Royal Opera House, Covent Garden

not the only features of this work which prove it to be no exception to the rule that first-class operas cannot be secured from the most giftep composer if he is restricted in choice of subject or given a time-limit.

Another work in a class by itself is *A Midsummer Night's Dream* (1960). Abbreviating Shakespeare so that cutting or botching is nowhere evident, Britten and Pears prepared a libretto which offers even more scope than the tragic operas for Britten's characteristic techniques. More than a dozen personages are thematically distinguished, their musical characterization high-lighted by strong contrasts—Titania and the transformed Bottom, the drugged and therefore fawning or scorning lovers—and the already wealthy motivic apparatus is further enriched by the palpable characterization of such concepts as The Wood, or Sleep. Oberon's is a countertenor part and Puck's a speaking part for a boy-acrobat; the dances and the onomatopoeic and scenic effects are not the only wonderful features of a score without modern rival for the variety of suggestive magic that is drawn from the quieter registers of a large orchestra. Particularly original is the use of the lighter percussion instruments.

In every one of Britten's operas the music carries the drama, is itself the drama. *The Rape of Lucretia*, based on a play adversely criticized for its preciosity, is furnished with an English text in the pseudo-poetry practised by teachers and students of prosody. Yet objection is irrelevant. If such a sentence as 'Home is what man leaves to seek' were merely 'set' to the kind of music designed to let words speak for themselves, we should suppose it to be a literal and obscure translation. As it comes through an exquisite instrumental texture from the female chorus (during the folding of linen) nobody strains to catch its meaning: it is simply part of a musical picture of domestic womanhood. The text of *Lucretia* is no more a musical handicap than that of *Grimes* which, based on George Crabbe, contains phrases not easily 'caught' as so many words, e.g. 'But when the crowner sits upon it, who can dare to fix the guilt?' It is as a musician that Britten is a consummate dramatist, and he would have been so even if he had not composed his operas.

From the unpretentious, divertimento-like Cello Sonata to *A Midsummer Night's Dream* Britten's sheer composition has no parallel in any British music by younger composers. And, with all its variety, it is remarkably—and unconsciously—consistent. Britten expressed amazement when shown the similarity between the chords used in Ex 243(i), for the setting of Keats's 'Sonnet to Sleep' in the Serenade, and those employed nearly twenty years later to evoke a similar atmosphere in *A Midsummer Night's Dream* (Ex. 243(ii)). In neither case did the fact that four chords utilized all twelve semitones signify any indebtedness to Schoenberg or his technical successors. Britten's *conscious* aim was to produce equal unexpectedness between the four chords and provide a large enough basis for variations.

Ex. 243

ELISABETH LUTYENS

Despite the structural use of twelve-note rows in *The Turn of the Screw* (1954) and the *Cantata Academica* (1960), celebrating the 500th anniversary of Basle University, these are not twelve-note compositions; the music is, as always with Britten, essentially diatonic.

The first 'twelve-note' British musician was Britten's senior. To Elisabeth Lutyens (b. 1906) must go the credit of first employing in England the full Schoenbergian 'method of composing with twelve notes'. As a viola player Lutyens had been attracted by Purcell's fantasias, and it was her attempt to 'organize "atonal" conceptions in accordance with an indigenous tradition' in a five-part string fantasia which 'gave birth unconsciously to a twelve-note theme'.[1] She turned permanently to serial technique in the Concerto for Nine Instruments of 1940, but she had shown full understanding of Webern in the String Trio of the previous year. Until her Sixth String Quartet of 1952, however, she seemed curiously limited in rhythmic invention, although she was said to be an admirer of Bartók. Her music is most impressive when it includes voices, e.g. her setting of Rimbaud's *O saisons, O châteaux*

[1] *Grove's Dictionary* (fifth edition) (London, 1954), v, p. 448.

for soprano, mandoline, harp, guitar, and strings (1946), *The Pit* (1947) for tenor and bass soloists, with women's chorus and orchestra, her Op. 27 Motet (1954) to words selected from Wittgenstein, and her chamber opera *Infidelio* of the same year. Her contemporary, Benjamin Frankel (1906–73), and two rather younger women-composers of her generation, Elizabeth Maconchy (b. 1907), and Phyllis Tate (b. 1911), are more conservative.

IMMIGRANT COMPOSERS

Three continental musicians of wide experience and forward-looking temperament settled in Britain during the 1930s. Egon Wellesz (b. 1885), though esteemed chiefly for his studies of Byzantine chant and of early baroque music, has composed eight symphonies and nine string quartets, much better known in Central Europe than in the land of his adoption, as well as operas and liturgical works. A close friend of Bruno Walter and Schoenberg he did not follow Schoenberg's path but was constantly influenced by his historical studies—eastern, medieval, baroque, romantic, and modern. His music is recognizably Viennese and includes many points of experimental interest, a fact which explains his wide influence on adventurous young musicians, exercised not by expecting them to imitate him but by shrewd understanding of European and English traditions and by unfailing optimism and sympathy.

Ex. 244 is from his Eighth String Quartet (1963). The extended Mahlerian character of this passage is clear in the wide intervals of the melodic line in the first violin part and the reining-in before the irregular metre of the climax.

Ex. 244

Roberto Gerhard (1896–1970) must have been the least docile and the least Teutonic among Schoenberg's pupils.[1] Although his father was Swiss and his mother French, he was brought up as a Catalan near Barcelona. He came to England at the end of the Spanish Civil War and lived in Cambridge.

In 1945 Gerhard adapted Sheridan's *The Duenna* for an opera in which the juxtaposition of techniques is no more incongruous than Sheridan's mixture of verses and conversational prose, or his relaxations and accelerations of dramatic action. Gathering tensions among the characters sometimes produce a Bergian polyphony, and the transitions between arias and dialogue-music often engage serial technique. On the other hand the charming verses are set to attractive rhythms in a style that is often less complex than that of the strophic items in Stravinsky's *The Rake's Progress*. Much in the declamatory and conversational vocal line shows both subtlety of characterization and an awareness of English speech inflexions that at times actually recalls Britten's.

An even more powerfully individual artist emerged in the instrumental works which Gerhard composed after 1950, when he became an established twelve-note composer, though without losing the love of sensuous harmony with which his earliest work showed him to be abnormally endowed. Gerhard has provided a clue to the harmonic and orchestral allure which he achieves in works like the serial Violin Concerto of 1945, Piano Concerto (1951), Symphony (1955), Harpsichord Concerto and String Quartet (both 1956). He arranges and permutes divisions of the twelve notes of a series (e.g. tetrachords or hexachords) as one does when spacing or inverting chords of three, four, five, or six notes in tonal harmony. In some ways he was more like Schoenberg than Webern was, and could claim just as validly to have developed from a point at which Schoenberg left off.

The third notable immigrant, Mátyás Seiber (1905–60), was a less original and audacious composer than Gerhard, but more representative of central European advances in composition as observed by a superb teacher who assiduously practised composition in all styles.

Seiber, who settled in England in 1935, was among Kodály's pupils and was much influenced by Bartók both before and after his appointment at Frankfurt-am-Main in 1928 as director of the newly opened jazz department of the Hoch Conservatoire. Such essays in orthodox Schoenbergian dodecaphony as the Second String Quartet (1935) and the chamber cantata *Three Fragments* (1957) (the texts taken from Joyce's *A Portrait of the Artist as a Young Man*) attracted less attention than the Third String Quartet (*Quartetto lirico*, 1951) and the cantata

[1] On Gerhard, see also p. 426.

Ulysses (1949) in which Seiber set passages from Joyce's book for tenor, chorus, and orchestra. Here we find, without obvious debt to Berg or anyone else, Seiber's easy absorption of dodecaphonic methods along with others. *Ulysses* disproved the charge that serial music is impractical or ineffective for choral groups, and Seiber's work in general answered critics who supposed that dodecaphonic serialism cannot sustain lyrical rapture or that it cannot be integrated with techniques avoided by its Viennese pioneers.

Ex. 245 is from *Ulysses*. Characteristic of Seiber are both his consideration for the singers, whose individual lines are easy to pitch, and his combination of canonic writing with *bouche fermée* to create an atmospheric effect which is nevertheless truly, even traditionally musical in the strictest sense.

Ex. 245

HUMPHREY SEARLE

The writings of Humphrey Searle (b. 1915), who studied with Webern, include *Twentieth Century Harmony* and translations of Schoenberg's *Structural Functions of Harmony* and Rufer's *Composition with Twelve Notes*. As a composer Searle glanced towards Stravinsky in *Gold Coast Customs* for speakers, male chorus and orchestra (1949), but achieved more distinction by his interest in Liszt. Searle hardly did more than defy fashion with his first Lisztian piano concerto in 1944 but he proved in the next few years that a Webern pupil need not abjure the reflective beauty of his native song. His Intermezzo for Eleven Instruments, his setting for soprano, flute, oboe, and string quartet of W. R. Rodgers's *Put away the flutes*, and his best work, the somewhat Bergian Poem for Twenty-two Strings (1950) as well as the Variations and Finale for Ten Instruments (1958) are stronger works than the more grandiose Piano Sonata (1951) with romantic bravura and a Lisztian thematic technique, and five symphonies (1953, 1958, 1960, 1962, and 1964). *The River-Run* of 1951 affords more pleasure from the orchestral texture than from the speaker of James Joyce's words with Dublin intonations.

THE YOUNGER GENERATION

The new composers who emerged after the Second World War include Peter Racine Fricker (b. 1920), Malcolm Arnold (b. 1921), Robert Simpson (b. 1921), Iain Hamilton (b. 1922), Anthony Milner (b. 1925), and Thea Musgrave (b. 1928). Fricker has given time and labour to a relatively small output of high quality. Conscious of developments abroad he owes allegiance to no single school or method, and even his admitted indebtedness to Bartók is far from obvious. He took lessons with Mátyás Seiber, and his 1949 Quartet is clearly influenced by Bartók's Third. Before Fricker could have been at all considerably influenced by Bartók he had produced harsh but emotional effects by his textures; and if he did not command Bartók's rhythmic fertility, Fricker has proved himself to be a master of rhythm in the broader sense in movement after movement although (or maybe because) his rhythmic *articula* are built into contrapuntal designs derived from those used in classical teaching. What gives such distinction to the result is the frequent composition of an athletic texture in which vigour, though generated by ubiquitous counterpoint, appears to be concentrated in an expansive, finely phrased, but urgent melody as in this excerpt from the first movement of his Second Symphony:

Ex. 246

Admirable thematic organization makes Fricker's Second Symphony (1951) as a whole more rewarding than the First (1949), despite the First Symphony's finale where inspired integration transcends its complex detail. Perhaps the most assuring aspect of Fricker's composition is its consistency and reliability. The symphonies and the Viola Concerto of 1952 happen to be impressive because they use the full orchestra, but the same standard of composition is found in the String Quartet of 1949, the Violin Sonata of the following year, and some works for small orchestra composed at about the same time—a Violin Concerto and the particularly attractive Prelude, Elegy, and Finale for strings, from which part of the middle movement may be quoted on account of its lyrical appeal:

Ex. 247

Fricker does not seem to have introduced any serial features into his compositions until 1955 with *Litany* for Double String Orchestra and *Sonnets for Piano*. Even when his texture is unusually lean Fricker does not write music like Webern's, but has brought twelve-tone melodies, figurations, and chords into an already assured style. In his Twelve Studies for Piano (1960) the contrasts are not between styles learnt from this or that source—Hindemith, Stravinsky, Bartók, Webern—but of keyboard technique in varying moods invented by an integrated imagination.

Fricker successfully cast his First String Quartet (1949) in one movement; his Violin Sonata (1950) and Second Quartet (1952) finish with third movements that are also the slowest; all three movements of his Second Symphony he regards as rondos. His command of extended form served him well in 1958, when he undertook his only commission for an imposing choral work, choosing for his text Cynewulf's *Christ* interwoven with Hallelujahs and extracts from the Mass, and entitling the whole work *The Vision of Judgement*. It moves from a stern penitential atmosphere to sustained apocalyptic glory, and is grateful to chorus, soloists and the many instrumentalists required. The normal tautness of his musical textures is relaxed in the immediately attractive Octet of 1958.

Iain Hamilton showed honest romantic rapture in his Op. 1 Variations for Strings, but a Symphony heard first in 1951 could not avoid comparison with Fricker's of that year. It took wing powerfully in fine melody and reached no satisfactory culmination in its finale. Fricker's, on the other hand, showed its first movement to be the shortest, remaining menacing and restrained even during passages of sultry lyricism; expansive magniloquence crowned the work in its finale. Hamilton's Violin Concerto of the following year was well designed and intensely emotional in its appeal, but he then turned from this romantic mode of expression, with its high violin melodies poised above alluring discords. Since then he has experimented with chamber works, song-settings, piano pieces, Scottish dances, a concerto for jazz trumpet, and, more recently, serial works, following his study of Webern, Stockhausen, and other Europeans. It is only in these later works, which lie outside the scope of this chapter, that Hamilton achieves a fully assured style.

Neither Anthony Milner (b. 1925) nor Malcolm Williamson (b. 1931) has followed Fricker in concentrating upon concert-hall instrumental composition. They have had little difficulty in finding words, liturgical and secular, to excite their musical imagination towards an expression as full-blooded as sincerity and modern sophisticated taste will allow. Milner is the less romantic of the two and the more conservative technically.

Milner's efficient chamber and orchestral pieces show that he is dependent upon words or religious concepts to stimulate his invention. In addition to an unaccompanied Mass and setting of vespers-psalms, Milner's best works include his *Improperia* for double chorus, strings, and organ (1949) which, from its recourse to instruments, cannot be intended for church use in the Good Friday liturgy, *The City of Desolation* (1955), a cantata with soloists and orchestra, *The Water and the Fire* (1962), a Three Choirs Festival oratorio on texts chosen by him incorporating material from the Easter Liturgy, *Our Lady's Hours* (1957), a song cycle for soprano and piano, and Variations for Orchestra (1959) upon a fifteenth-century theme.

Williamson was born in Australia and heard little twentieth-century music until his first visit to Europe in 1950. His deprivation did him little harm, for he suffered no pressure from vogue and could form his own judgements on Delius, Shostakovich, and the scores of 'musicals'. He was ready to receive and examine any music in which he recognized vitality. By 1953, when he settled here permanently, he had taken lessons with Elisabeth Lutyens and been persuaded to use serial techniques. His conversion to Roman Catholicism awakened his interest in Dunstable and other medieval musicians (he uses isorhythm in the organ variations on the Coventry Carol, *Vision of Christ-Phoenix*) as well as in the music and theories of Messiaen. His one-time employment as a night-club pianist and his admiration of tunes in Richard Rodgers's musicals led to his own writing of more advanced musicals, including *No Bed for Bacon*.

Williamson's exuberance finds full rein in his concertos, as it did in the opera *Our Man in Havana* (1963). (One of his best works before this was the unaccompanied *Symphony for Voices* of 1962.) *Our Man in Havana* was an audacious and unequal undertaking, but its best parts are not confined to the most serious or the most serial.

To choose names from among the still younger composers becomes increasingly invidious. Of those who had begun to make their mark before 1960, which is the chronological limit of this chapter, and have gone on to prove their worth, one must mention Alexander Goehr (b. 1932), Hugh Wood (b. 1932), Peter Maxwell Davies (b. 1934), Harrison Birtwistle (b. 1934), and Nicholas Maw (b. 1935). Goehr, Davies, and Birtwistle have become known as 'the Manchester school' since they were fellow-students there; Wood studied with Milner, Hamilton, and Seiber, Maw with Berkeley and Nadia Boulanger.

VII

AMERICAN MUSIC: 1918–1960

(i) Music In The United States

By RICHARD FRANKO GOLDMAN

THE BACKGROUND

WESTERN musical art is essentially international, but its expressions and institutions vary locally. We can often distinguish English, French, German, Italian, or Russian music by idiosyncracies of style, and can trace these elements of style to national or regional backgrounds of folk-music deriving from a remote past and from traditions of composition handed down from one generation to another by a succession of acknowledged masters. Elaborated or sophisticated art, and the institutions for its presentation and dissemination, depend on a sense of continuity and on a consciousness of a more or less homogeneous culture. It is evident that these conditions for the development of an indigenous art did not prevail in America for many generations, and that an American music of consequence could not have evolved earlier than the twentieth century.

American music inevitably reflected, as did American culture as a whole, the diversity of its European origins. Musicians born or settled in America were content to make the best effort within their powers to continue, or perhaps to discover, the traditions of a highly developed musical language. Musicians arriving from Europe in each generation brought with them their ideas, traditions, and technical skills. There were, unfortunately, no composers of dominating personality or important attainment among them. American-born composers, until the beginning of the twentieth century, necessarily went back to Europe, and principally to Germany, to learn their craft. With few exceptions, they became very minor German composers; and although almost since the settling of the continent there had been a sense of the need for discovering an artistic America, this discovery could not be effected by exhortation. If certain American materials were already present, the conditions for their recognition were not. And while Americanism as such remained a preoccupation, there was at the same time an intense desire to perpetuate, without the historical and social conditions that had made them possible, many of the institutions and practices of European artistic life. One feels that many of these efforts were primarily competitive in impulse, and to some extent based on an idea of what was proper rather than what was necessary.

In considering any aspect of American culture, a fundamental condition of American society must always be kept in mind: that the country was settled by immigrants from every European background, and that eventually the consciousness of an African background also became an element of primary importance. Thus a part of the problem of the American artist has always centred on his search for a real and usable past, and one that could be assimilated in a sense as a common past for all Americans. The first social and cultural traditions were of course English, and English became the language to be learned by Germans, Mediterraneans, East Europeans, and all others. But the English past, including English folk-song or English hymnody as passed on through New England musicians, represented a tradition alien to increasing numbers of Americans of non-English background. The theoretical 'melting-pot' produced its tensions and conflicts, and it would be a rash historian who would claim that these have ever been completely resolved in American society.

Thus, while nineteenth-century American composers of serious inclination and ambition were endeavouring to establish an American art of conventional English and German pattern, they failed to notice a lively and diversified popular art which was developing all about them. The work of these composers was a provincial echo of the most facile styles of Europe. From time to time, gestures were made in the direction of the native picturesque, beginning with Hans Gram's *Death Song of an Indian Chief* (1791), said to be the first orchestral score published in the United States, and on through a variety of naïve and condescending evocations of the noble Indian and the happy, carefree Negro. Exception must be made for the more interesting efforts of William Henry Fry (1813–64), the first musical Americanist of consequence, and of Louis Moreau Gottschalk (1829–69), a virtuoso pianist of New Orleans, who took a genuine and cultivated interest in the Creole music of the Caribbean as heard in Louisiana, and attempted to recapture its flavour in many of his once-popular piano pieces. But in general, a genteel and conservative manner, typical of provincial urban society, set the tone of American concert life, and the representative composers, from John Knowles Paine (1839–1906) to Edward MacDowell (1862–1908) and Horatio Parker (1863–1919) echoed the styles of Raff or Grieg. The so-called Boston school, beginning with Paine, did however establish a standard of professional competence and craft, and provided a basis for the schooling of later musicians. Paine became the first Professor of Music at Harvard University in 1875; Parker later held a similar post at Yale, and MacDowell at Columbia. They helped to establish the important precedent of the teaching of composition and other branches of musical art in American universities, a development of the greatest significance for American music in the twentieth century.

Popular music in nineteenth-century America was not (nor is it yet) a unified folk-music, if indeed it was a folk music at all within the usual European definition. Perhaps that is why it was not recognized as such even by those composers who most vehemently lamented the absence of a folk tradition in America. American popular music was the music of a diversity of people remote from the traditions of the concert hall or of German symphonic music. It embraced hymns, revival songs, temperance tunes, Negro work songs and spirituals, imitation ('black-face') Negro music of the minstrel shows, brass band quicksteps, the composed songs of Stephen Collins Foster (1826–64) and others, and, in a number of areas, survivals of British, Spanish, French, or German secular folk tunes. Eventually ragtime and jazz, a fusion of many elements, emerged in and around New Orleans. But all of these vigorous manifestations of idiosyncratic music were considered, until the twentieth century, as beneath the proper concern of cultivated musicians, with the sole exception of the surviving strains of British folk-song. These latter were regarded by some few composers as the only proper and respectable sources for an American idiom; all else remained either vulgar or alien. A new American consciousness, evolving in the twentieth century, was required for the recognition and absorption of popular diversity—cultural, racial, and even sectional—as the most genuine possibility for an indigenous expression.

American music owes a great debt to Antonín Dvořák. Dvořák was among the first composers of universally acknowledged stature to visit the United States (1893–5), and the first to advise the American composer to look about him at home, with particular attention to the music of the Negro. Although Dvořák's own knowledge of Negro music was superficial, he at least took this music seriously and gave others the artistic courage to do so. He contributed greatly towards the creation of the new environment for the American musician that began to take shape in the early years of the twentieth century. The fact that he was a Czech was not without importance. Gilbert Chase[1] correctly points out that MacDowell's contemptuous dismissal of Dvořák's advice was probably motivated by the fact that Dvořák was not a German composer. But other composers were stimulated by Dvořák's

[1] *America's Music* (New York, 1955), p. 392.

example and advice. Arthur Farwell (1872–1951) is best remembered for his serious study of Indian music, undertaken as a direct result of Dvořák's influence. But in 1903 Farwell also declared that music other than German—French and Russian especially—needed hearing in the United States. Farwell, an important figure in American musical history (although his compositions have not survived in the repertoire), felt strongly the need for an American manner of expression which, in his view, would embrace ragtime, as well as the music of the Negro and Indian, and which also would demand 'new and daring expressions'. In 1902 Farwell founded the Wa-Wan Press for the publication of new American music, with the expressed purpose of launching 'a progressive movement for American music, including a definite acceptance of Dvořák's challenge to go after our folk music'. The Wa-Wan Press is important in American music as the first concrete and organized effort to offer an opportunity of publication to composers representing a new orientation and spirit.

Among the composers published by the Wa-Wan Press was Henry F. B. Gilbert (1868–1928). Although Gilbert was MacDowell's first American pupil, his musical aesthetic was diametrically opposed to that of his teacher. Gilbert, like Farwell, saw the importance of the native background. He travelled widely throughout the United States, earning his living in a variety of ways, and absorbed a great deal of what he heard. Like Gottschalk, he was attracted by the Creole music of New Orleans, and based his symphonic poem *The Dance in Place Congo* (performed as a ballet-pantomime in 1918 at the Metropolitan Opera House) on tunes published in 1886 by the New Orleans writer George W. Cable. Gilbert's *Comedy Overture on Negro Themes* (1911) is still played occasionally. In other compositions, Gilbert turned his attention to ragtime, to the music of Latin America, and to the hitherto neglected tunes made popular in the blackface minstrel shows of the 1850s and 1860s. Gilbert was perhaps the first to recognize that these tunes had become a kind of American folk-music.

Farwell and Gilbert, and other composers of their generation, represented what would eventually become one of the main streams of American musical development. They were aware of the great variety of unexplored and unexploited material available, and their work, though not in itself of permanent musical value, prepared the ground for later composers by calling attention to that material and to its possibilities. Their contribution towards the establishing of an American musical consciousness can be seen at a distance as more important than that of MacDowell, who was recognized without question in his time (and for some time thereafter) as the 'greatest' American composer. MacDowell achieved something of an international reputation, the first American composer to do so; and this accomplishment was important in that it gave Americans of his time a sense that a native composer of acknowledged stature had finally appeared. MacDowell's music has been overpraised and under-estimated; at its best it has charm and individuality, but the style he represented was that of a period reaching its end, and its connexion with the major movements of musical art was that of a late arrival.

American music may be said to have been, until the end of the First World War, in the process of discovering itself. The war of 1914–18 marked a turning point in the cultural as well as the political history of the United States. America's emergence as a world power brought with it a heightened national consciousness and a sense of history that could be translated into a new and vigorous expression. Earlier consciousness, as for example in Whitman, had been largely prophetic. The Transcendentalists had spoken for the individual. But the new sense of awareness was both collective and retrospective; a new identity, formed of European elements but in spirit non-European, took shape for the first time. It was not accident that the variety of memories and traditions existing during the periods of immigration and settlement should at this time have begun, at many levels of American culture, to fuse into memories and traditions with some meaning for all. The material of American culture required synthesis, and in so far as American culture can be said to have a character, it is synthetic in the literal meaning of the term. In art, as in politics, the emergence of Americans of other than English or German origin, dates effectively from 1918, and it is again not by accident that in order to be American, American art had first to acquiesce in internationalism. The prominence of American composers of, for example, Italian descent (Walter Piston, Paul Creston, Peter Mennin, Norman Dello Joio, Gian Carlo Menotti) and of Jewish descent (George Gershwin, Ernest Bloch, Aaron Copland, William Schuman, Marc Blitzstein, Hugo Weisgall, Leonard Bernstein, Leon Kirchner) is a purely twentieth-century phenomenon.

From this standpoint, a more immediate interest and awareness of contemporary European currents was also of importance. The end of an age throughout the world, reflected in art as conscious revolt, gave American artists a sense of being able to overcome the lateness of their start and to begin a new movement on an almost equal footing. The universal awareness of new aesthetic orientations and ideals had a liberating influence, both technically and psychologically, on artists throughout the world, with whom, for the first time, Americans were able to feel a sense of community and of contemporaneity. The

38

American musician felt a welcome sense of release at being able to throw off, at the same time as everyone else, the weight of competition with Beethoven, Brahms, and Wagner, or even with Raff and Grieg. A surge of freedom, reflected in 'advanced' music, was necessary not only as an assertion of independence, but even as a condition for making conservative music once again interesting.

The influence of European events was felt not only as a result of travel and communication, but also through the arrival in the United States as permanent residents of musicians of the quality of Edgard Varèse (1916) and Ernest Bloch (1916). Whether Varèse and Bloch are to be considered American composers and musicians is open to question, but one cannot question their importance and influence in the American musical scene. A younger 'immigrant' whose importance was temporary, but who attracted much attention for a brief period, and who did much to make the public conscious of a radical new stream of musical thought, was the Russian-born Leo Ornstein (b. 1895). In the years before 1920, a small current of French music and influence was reflected in the compositions of Charles Martin Loeffler (1861–1935), born in Alsace, but long resident in Boston, and of Charles Tomlinson Griffes (1884–1920). Griffes was a composer of marked gifts, and several of his works entitle him to continued respect and attention. Among these are *The Pleasure Dome of Kubla Khan*, written as a piano piece in 1912, and performed in an orchestral version in 1919. *The White Peacock* was similarly composed for piano in 1915, and orchestrated in 1919. The *Poem for Flute and Orchestra* (1918) and the Sonata for Piano (1918–19) are also representative. Griffes may be described as an eclectic composer, but he was alive to the interesting currents of his time, and much of his music can still be heard with pleasure. He was aware of the contributions of Debussy, Busoni, and Stravinsky, and he was interested in Arabian, Japanese, and Amerindian music. It is worth noting that among those who encouraged him most strongly was Farwell.

CHARLES IVES

Before turning to the main currents of American musical activity in the 1920s, it is necessary to consider the extraordinary phenomenon of Charles Ives, one of the truly great 'originals' in the history of music. Ives was born in Danbury, Connecticut, on 20 October 1874, and died in New York on 19 May 1954. His life thus spans the entire period in which American music may be said to have established itself. The extraordinary circumstance of Ives's life and work is that none of his music was heard or known, even in professional circles, until the 1920s, and that important public performances of his major works did not take place until 1939 and after. With the exception of the *Concord Sonata*, which Ives had privately printed in 1919, and a collection of 114 Songs, similarly printed in 1922, none of Ives's music was available in published form until 1929, by which time he had ceased composing.

The position of Ives in American music, indeed in the history of contemporary music, is unique. One need not agree fully with his biographers, Sidney and Henry Cowell, that he was one of 'the four great creative figures of the first half of the twentieth century'—the others being Schoenberg, Stravinsky, and Bartók—but it is impossible to question his originality, his power or his authenticity. He anticipated many of the 'discoveries' of his contemporaries and juniors, using techniques not widely accepted until a generation later, including harmony based on fourths, polytonality, tone-clusters and poly-rhythms of extreme complexity. Passages in his work have a freedom and boldness of imagination that is not only astonishing for its time (all of Ives's work was done between 1891 and 1921—the most important was completed by 1916) but that still seemed inventive and advanced to musicians at the mid-point of the century. Most important, however, he was the first to realize completely what it might mean to be an American composer, and his career and work illuminate in the most telling manner what it is to discover a musical world.

The world of Charles Ives was a world in which Beethoven and Bach met Stephen Foster, New England hymn-singing, ragtime, circus quick-steps, country fiddling, and every variety of spontaneous music-making that characterizes the activity of a rural environment. This world was shaped by an imagination conditioned in childhood to believe substance more important than style and to shun dependence on musical customs and habits. But it was an imagination coupled with intellect, with deep roots in the New England past, and strengthened by a complete acceptance of the New England environment as expressed in its most ideal terms by Emerson and Thoreau. Ives had the independence that can come only from tradition and discipline, the solid base over which the most diverse elements can be assimilated and made into a new unity.

Ives received a conventional training from his father, a bandmaster and music teacher who was himself ceaselessly interested in experiment and fascinated by the nature of sound itself to the extent of improvising devices for the performance of quarter tones. Beside giving his son a conventional training, he invented exercises designed 'to stretch our ears and strengthen our musical minds'. Later, young Ives studied under Horatio Parker at Yale, doing 'correct' exercises for the classroom, but writing for his own satisfaction music that shocked everyone but himself. His *Variations on 'America'* for organ, composed in 1891, employed bitonality, and other pieces composed before 1900 utilized other techniques and materials that could only have seemed incomprehensible to his contemporaries. Here is an extract:

Ex. 248

Characteristically, these early pieces include works based on or para-phrasing hymn-tunes, circus marches, or other types of popular music, set in textures ranging from extreme simplicity to extreme dissonance and rhythmic complexity.

Ives evolved his techniques and chose his materials not according to any formulated theory of musical composition, but rather in an attempt to solve what to him were important questions about the nature of art and expressiveness. To write 'correct' music (which he was quite able to do) was of no interest to him. Ives sought to express a variety of things (this was his view of 'substance' as opposed to 'style') that to him were vital and meaningful: the particular quality of life as perceived and enjoyed by a given man in a given time and place, here, in New England, and beyond that the transcendental reality of man and the universe in terms that had come most immediately from Emerson. Ives was not afraid of large thoughts; his own philosophy was forceful and articulate, and for him an art divorced from life, whether eternal life or daily life, was utterly without point.

Whatever the merits of Ives's philosophy, the student of American music can learn much by reading his *Essays before a Sonata*,[1] privately printed in 1920 as an adjunct to the *Concord Sonata* for piano. It becomes clear that Ives is the first composer in America who did not look to European music for models, but to Bach and Beethoven as if he felt that he understood what they meant.

It is not surprising that Ives could find no audience. No public was ready for this music, and Ives decided soon after leaving the university that he would have to make his living as a business man. Characteristi-cally, he did not feel that this involved any conflict. In a statement made for the Southern poet and novelist Henry Bellamann, Ives wrote:[2] 'The fabric of existence weaves itself whole. You cannot set an art off in the corner and hope for it to have vitality, reality and substance. There can be nothing "exclusive" about a substantial art. It comes directly out of

[1] Reprinted in *Three Classics in the Aesthetic of Music* (New York, 1962).
[2] 'Charles Ives: the Man and his Music', *Musical Quarterly*, xix (1933), p. 45.

Ex. 249

the heart of experience of life and thinking about life and living life. My work in music helped my business and my work in business helped my music.'

Occasionally Ives was able to hear portions of some of his works in readings by friends or occasionally members of local theatre orchestras, hired at his own expense. For a time he made efforts to have his work performed, but the total lack of understanding, and in many cases the derision, with which he met, eventually discouraged him. A reading of parts of his First Symphony by Walter Damrosch in about 1910 produced only annoyance on all sides. Ives resigned himself to the fact that his way would have to be made slowly. In 1919 he decided to publish himself some of the works he had written, hoping that if enough copies were distributed (*gratis*, of course) a few, through the operation of the law of averages, would find sympathetic readers. This proved true, and the first sympathetic notices of Ives's music were written by Bellamann. Some time afterwards, the enthusiastic interest of a number of musicians, including Nicolas Slonimsky and Henry Cowell, and eventually many others, was aroused, and by about 1930 (though not earlier) the name of Ives began to be current in *avant-garde* circles. The first major performance of a major work of Ives was that of *Three Places in New England*, performed by an orchestra directed by Slonimsky in 1930 in Boston. Examination of Ex. 249 will give the reader some idea of the harsh dissonances, polyrhythms, and performance difficulties involved in this work. It was not, however, until the performance of the entire *Concord Sonata* by John Kirkpatrick in New York in 1939 that Ives achieved anything approaching 'recognition' by even a small part of the musical public. This example from *The Anti-Abolitionist Riots* will give the reader an idea of Ives's style of writing for the piano, as well as of his improvisatory style without bar-lines:

Ex. 250

Adagio Maestoso

Ives wrote much, including four symphonies, a variety of music for various small and large instrumental combinations, some chamber music, choral works, music for piano, and songs. The songs are extraordinary in their variety, and often in their originality, and they constitute in themselves a chapter in American music. No other American composer has approached Ives's richness or power in this field. The *Concord Sonata*, actually entitled 'Second Piano Sonata "Concord, Mass., 1840–60" ', is almost universally recognized as the most powerful and impressive work of its kind in American music. Its technical problems are great; Ives was notoriously indifferent to practicability and at times wrote music that he himself admitted might be impossible to perform (see Ex. 250). This constituted, in his view, no reason for not writing it, if the expression in itself was justified by what he felt necessary to say. It was not until 1964, for instance, that Leopold Stokowski was finally able to present a complete performance of the Fourth Symphony.

The *Concord Sonata* is in four large movements, each an evocation of Concord's past. The first is entitled 'Emerson'; the second, 'Hawthorne'; the third, 'The Alcotts'; and the final movement, 'Thoreau'. Ives himself wrote programmes for each of the movements, and described the work as 'an attempt to present one person's impression of the spirit of transcendentalism . . .' He uses the terms 'impression' and 'impressionistic' several times; yet the music is not what is generally associated with impressionism. It is intensely strong, with a structure obeying its own organic laws; there is nothing else quite like it in the literature of the piano. Powerful dissonances alternate with quiet quotations of hymns, delicate passage work with brash allusions to circus parades. It is an impression of all that Ives knew of New England both in thought and in sound, an impression of a New England universe. The scope is not exaggerated; among the many sketched and unfinished works of Ives is a *Universe* or *Universal Symphony*, 'not intended to be completed by the composer himself or by any other man, because it represents aspects of life about which there is always more to be said'.

That Ives was ahead of his time in many ways hardly needs emphasis. When first written his harmonies could not have failed to seem barbarous, his melodies and sonorities crude or vulgar, his rhythms unplayable, and his musical orthography merely eccentric. By the time his music became known, however, most of his 'innovations' had become familiar in the works of other composers, and his use of popular materials had become a part of American musical language. But Ives's importance does not reside in his discoveries or anticipations; it resides in the facts that his music communicated life and vigour, that he was neither a miniaturist nor a docile follower, and that what he had to express spoke persuasively to a few musicians in the 1920s and 1930s and to a large public thereafter. It is perhaps incidental, but by no means unimportant, that Ives's music was clearly the first music of large intent and dimension that could not have been written by any but an American. He believed strongly in himself as a man living in an environment which he conceived in a way no one before him had done. That is why his place is large in American musical history, and why he has come to be an image of great importance for so many American musicians. It is the substance that in the end justifies Ives, as he himself would have wished. There are crudities in the style. Some of these might have been resolved had he had the opportunity of hearing more of his music, though this cannot be certain. Aaron Copland suggested[1] that Ives 'lacked neither the talent nor the ability nor the métier nor the integrity of the true artist, but what he most shamefully and tragically lacked was an audience'. And further, '. . . the drama of Ives . . . is that of every American composer of serious pretensions. The problem of the audience—not a passive audience but an active one—an audience that *demands* and *rejects* music, that acts as a stimulus and a brake, has never been solved.'

Obviously, Ives's influence, both technical and spiritual, could not have been felt until his music had become known, and in the 1920s it was known to very few. But many of the strands of American music in that decade were converging towards the kind of synthesis that Ives had in a sense achieved, and one can see how justly the discovery of his music coincided with the emergence of a new generation of American composers. The native materials of ragtime, jazz, and popular hymnody were put to use by a number of composers who were at the same time learning the devices and techniques of 'modern' music from Stravinsky, Milhaud, Hindemith, Ravel, Bartók, Prokofyev, and the other new masters in Europe, as well as from experimenters at home. It remained only for the impact of Schoenberg and his school to be absorbed, some years later, for American music to become completely international.

THE DECADE 1920–30: GERSHWIN AND COPLAND

The 1920s were eventful years, not only because of the arrival on the scene of a number of strikingly gifted composers, but also because for the first time concerted efforts were made to give their works a hearing. The International Composers' Guild was founded in 1921 by Edgard Varèse (1885–1965) and Carlos Salzedo (1885–1961) for that purpose,

---

[1] *Our New Music* (New York, 1941), pp. 160–1.

as was The League of Composers two years later. The New Music Society of San Francisco was founded by Henry Cowell in 1927, and, beginning in 1928, Aaron Copland and Roger Sessions joined forces to produce the stimulating Copland-Sessions concerts. These were among the most important groups, but there were others; and contemporary music, with special emphasis on contemporary American music, began to engender an atmosphere of enthusiasm and excitement. These groups not only performed, but did active propaganda, and although they could not bring new music to the attention of the great public, the stir they created eventually spread. A few sympathetic critics, notably Paul Rosenfeld, appeared on the musical scene, and many of the composers themselves turned their hands to writing. The magazine *Modern Music*, established by The League of Composers in 1925, was, until its discontinuation in 1947, an influential force in American musical life.

The atmosphere of the early twenties is suggested by some lines of Paul Rosenfeld, written in 1922. 'It is . . . no longer true . . . that there is no vitality in the native musical production. What has been characteristic of the painting and the writing of the land has now become characteristic of the music. The country can produce really gifted youth. Society has become sufficiently settled to permit the talent to assert itself; there is even . . . enough of a real community to permit the musical gesture, the gesture of the interpenetrated group, to be made.'[1]

It may be said that the characteristic of American music during the decade was its diversity of style and its unity of spirit. The spirit was one of new confidence and assertiveness; composers (and some performers) felt united in a common cause, that of new music and the modern temper. For the first time, too, American musicians felt that they were part of the main current, and not timorous artisans on the periphery. The atmosphere was lively and the activity enormously accelerated. This was the decade in which the names, and the music, of Aaron Copland, Roger Sessions, Roy Harris, Virgil Thomson, Henry Cowell, Walter Piston, Randall Thompson, Howard Hanson, George Antheil, Carl Ruggles and Wallingford Riegger were becoming known, and in which George Gershwin composed his *Rhapsody in Blue*. It was of course also the decade in which the musical style known as jazz was for the first time taken seriously, as something vital and new and unquestionably American.

The jazz-influenced idiom was but one of the manifestations of American music in the twenties. John Alden Carpenter (1876–1951) of Chicago had employed a type of ragtime jazz in his Concertino for Piano and Orchestra (1915), in his 'jazz pantomime' *Krazy Kat*

[1] Paul Rosenfeld, *Musical Chronicle, 1917–1923* (New York, 1923).

(1921), and in *Skyscrapers* (1926). Carpenter's music enjoyed a vogue for a time, for it was basically conservative enough to appeal even to the conductors of major orchestras and their audiences. A more seriously assimilated jazz appeared in several works by Louis Gruenberg (1884–1964), one of the composers active in the early days of the International Composers Guild and The League of Composers. Gruenberg's *The Daniel Jazz* (1923) and *The Creation* (1924), both for voice and a combination of eight instruments, had some solidity and originality as stylizations of Afro-American material. (It is interesting to note that *The Daniel Jazz* and Milhaud's *La Création du Monde* were written in the same year.) But it remained for two composers of quite different orientation to establish definitely the consciousness of jazz as an artistic reality in American music.

George Gershwin (1898–1937) achieved early fame as a writer of popular tunes and musical comedies. But he studied music seriously with Rubin Goldmark, then the most esteemed teacher of composition in New York, and felt that material derived from jazz and the idiom of American popular songs could be used in works on a larger scale, even symphonically. The *Rhapsody in Blue*, designed as a demonstration of 'symphonic jazz', was commissioned by the band leader Paul Whiteman, and was first performed on 12 February 1924, in New York. Its success was instantaneous, and the date is a memorable one in American music. Probably no work written in America is as well known, nor is there any other work that has appealed to such an extent to audiences on every level. It may be termed one of the genuine American 'classics'. This is not to make a musical judgement, for the *Rhapsody in Blue* is a hybrid work, which in fact is not jazz, but which combines a real feeling for American popular style with a romantically eclectic harmonic and orchestral style. Ex. 251, showing one of the *Rhapsody*'s principal themes, clearly illustrates these features:

Ex. 251

Nevertheless, the *Rhapsody in Blue* was a genuinely original conception, realized with great success; and although the idea of 'symphonic jazz' could not survive its inherent contradictions, the *Rhapsody* influenced American music both positively and negatively. It demonstrated both what could be accomplished on a large scale by a talented composer using a popular idiom, and at the same time the serious limitations of using a conventional 'symphonic' style as a vehicle for this type of musical speech. The *Rhapsody* compelled the attention of both serious and popular musicians, however, and the effects of its success cannot be under-estimated. Gershwin continued active in both musical comedy and serious composition for the remainder of his life. His works in the latter category include a Concerto in F for Piano (1925), Three Preludes for Piano (1926), the orchestral *An American in Paris* (1928), a Second Rhapsody (1932), the *Cuban Overture* (1934), and his masterpiece, the opera *Porgy and Bess* (1935).

Gershwin's natural language was made up of ragtime, the blues and jazz, to which in *Porgy and Bess* he added melodic contours resembling spirituals. Out of these elements he made something unmistakably his own. *Porgy and Bess* has not only never been equalled in its genre, it has not even been approached. Gershwin called it a 'folk opera', and whether or not it is opera at all, in the conventional definition, would hardly seem to matter. Its tunes are part of the American vocabulary, and it has outlasted every other American work for the musical stage. Gershwin had the instinct of a natural dramatist, and while *Porgy and Bess* may be defective in terms of formal operatic convention, or even material, it is moving and compelling. Its success, not only at home, but throughout Europe, indicates that it makes its point as authentic American music that could have come from no other place in the world.

On 11 January 1925, not quite one year after the first performance of the *Rhapsody in Blue*, the first major work of another young American composer was performed in New York. This was the Concerto for Organ and Orchestra by Aaron Copland. Copland, born in Brooklyn in 1900, was, like Gershwin, a pupil of Goldmark's, but he had gone to France where he had become a student of Nadia Boulanger. His striking talent was recognized not only by her, but also by the American composer Marion Bauer, who had called his name to the attention of The League of Composers. Copland came on the scene with considerable force; his first works demonstrated unusual power and originality, and there was little question from the start that a major voice in American music had arrived. The Organ Concerto had many derivative elements, notably from Stravinsky, and was not wholly successful (Copland later rewrote it as his First Symphony, without organ). But Copland's next work, commissioned by Sergey Kussevitsky, stands, like the *Rhapsody in Blue*, though on a different plane, as a milestone in American music. This was *Music for the Theater*, a suite in five movements for small orchestra. Here a 'jazz' style, combined with sophisticated twentieth-century techniques of composition, including polytonality, resulted in a work of exuberant vitality which for the first time indicated how effectively 'Americanized' the international idiom could become. Although Milhaud had already written his 'jazz' ballet, *La Création du Monde*, a comparison of the two works makes clear how much more direct and meaningful was Copland's relation to jazz material.

Jazz is the essential American contribution to the world's music, but it has given rise to disputes that come near to being as subtle as those of the medieval scholastics. It was not, historically, until the 1940s that the discussion of jazz assumed the dimensions of a new musicology, with learned and pseudo-learned contentiousness devoted to defining what is, or was, jazz, and what is not. From the purist point of view, jazz must be improvisatory, among other things. Although this is true, it also remains true that it can be the informing element in music that is not literally jazz, but that is either an evocation of jazz in art music, or else the reflection, in formal terms, of some of its characteristics. In the 1920s, no such fine lines were drawn, and the distinction between what is today properly called jazz and the music that derives from it was neither sharp nor consistent. The historian of American music must note that 'true' jazz had actually to be *revived* in the 1940s and 1950s, and again in the 1970s.

With these reservations, Copland's early style must still be described as a 'jazz' style. All the works of this period, and notably the Piano

Concerto of 1926, are based on characteristically American rhythms which Copland himself understood as jazz. He used them consciously until he felt that he had exhausted their expressive possibilities. He noted also at the time that the use of a jazz style was 'an easy way to be American in musical terms';[1] but later in his career he found other, and equally persuasive, ways of writing recognizably American music.

After 1930 Copland's music alternated between what has been called his 'austere' style, best represented in the Piano Variations (1930), the *Short Symphony* (1933), and *Statements for Orchestra* (1934), and a style based on folk-music elements, designed to appeal more immediately to a large public. An important inner evolution seems to have taken place in the years immediately preceding 1930, and the Piano Variations and *Statements for Orchestra* remain fundamental for any evaluation of Copland's mature achievement. These works, which are tight-knit, strongly dissonant, vigorous, and hard in sonority, may properly be called severe in style. The Piano Variations has remained, thirty years after its composition, a landmark in American composition; all of the works of this period, taken together, revealed to musicians the emergence of an original personality in full command, intellectually and emotionally, of a striking and forceful idiom.

Copland himself felt that these works might be too advanced for any but the most sophisticated audiences, and in the mid-'thirties began to make a conscious effort toward achieving what he termed 'an imposed simplicity'. To accomplish this simplification, and to please a wide audience without losing the marks of a personal style is a difficult task, yet Copland's success in this respect must be considered remarkable. Among the first works in this more accessible vein were the orchestral *El Salón México*, and a small opera, *The Second Hurricane*, written for performance by high-school students, both completed in 1936. *El Salón México* is based on authentic Mexican folk and popular tunes, handled with great brilliance and vigour, with characteristically colourful orchestration and shifting rhythms. The use of folk-tunes, or of material related to folk-music, was carried a step further in scores composed for the dance productions *Billy the Kid* (1938), *Rodeo* (1942), and *Appalachian Spring* (1944), all of which were recast in concert form. *Appalachian Spring* remains the work by which Copland is probably best known to the general public, and through which he most effectively realized his hope of communicating with an audience not exclusively composed of devotees of *avant-garde* music. The diatonic and folk-like Copland manner may be studied in the excerpt from *Appalachian Spring* (Ex. 252) where a simple Shaker tune ('The gift to be simple') is treated

---

[1] *Our New Music*, p. 227.

39

Ex. 252

canonically in a texture of great transparency. Many of his works in this vein have not only remained in the standard American concert repertoire, but have also received frequent performances by school orchestras and bands, a sure proof that they have deeply penetrated the American musical consciousness. Copland's scores for films are generally also in his simpler style, and have aided in making his idiom familiar. These scores are extraordinarily sensitive, and several must rank with the best music of this genre that has yet been produced. Copland's film scores include *Of Mice and Men* (1939), based on the Steinbeck novel; *Our Town* (1940), based on the Thornton Wilder play; and *The Heiress* (1948), after the novel by Henry James. Related in many ways to his film scores as well as to his dance scores is the opera *The Tender Land* (1954), one of the few major works of Copland that has not enjoyed either popular or critical success. It may be said that Copland's music, while full of strength and motor energy, is on the whole more lyrical than dramatic in quality. The vocal writing in *The Tender Land* is sensitive, as it is in his settings of *Twelve Poems of Emily Dickinson* (1950), yet it is perhaps too elegant and refined to succeed on the large scale of the operatic stage.

That Copland's work has been frequently imitated, or has served as a stylistic point of departure, seems evidence enough that the music exhibits a very personal and easily distinguishable style. This is true of both the 'austere' and the 'accessible' styles, which are in fact not as different as they may often appear to be on the surface. One may find elements of both manners in the Piano Sonata of 1951 or the Sonata for Violin and Piano of 1943,[1] and certainly in the Third Symphony of 1946. Copland always writes with clarity and brevity, with an honest lyricism and lack of grandiloquence, and an elegance of line and phrase. The sound is generally open and lean, with a remarkable sense of timbre and spacing. These qualities remain constant in his work throughout his career and through what appears to be his adoption of different manners.

In later works, such as the Piano Quartet (1950), the Piano Fantasy (1957) and the Nonet (1960), Copland adapted serial techniques, and although his previous work is essentially diatonic, while freely dissonant, the similarity in fundamental musical orientation to his earlier Piano Variations is striking. Copland's music is often open in texture, occasionally bitonal, and marked by the frequent occurrence of simple triads. The language is severely disciplined and the craftsmanship impeccable. The first page of the Piano Fantasy, with its wide spacing and isolated sonorities, is representative of Copland's more 'severe' style:

[1] The slow movement of which is recorded in *The History of Music in Sound*, x.

Ex. 253

Slow ♩ ; (♩ = circa 76)★ *in a very bold and declamatory manner*

*Metronome markings throughout are to be understood as approximations only.

During the second quarter of the century, no composer in America exercised greater influence on his contemporaries, both through his music (and his leadership in exploiting varieties of material), and through his activities as teacher and lecturer, organizer, and propagandist for his colleagues. Copland was one of the first to make important contributions to music for those twentieth-century media, the radio and the motion picture. His contribution towards the musical re-orientation of the American musical scene cannot be overestimated.

Apart from the débuts of Copland and Gershwin in the 1920s, there was an immense and spontaneous variety of musical activity along many lines. In retrospect, it must seem that this decade was in many ways the most expansive and optimistic of recent times. Financial support for 'modern' art was forthcoming from enlightened patrons, and the artist, as well as the small but growing audience, seemed to be looking (despite the often-cited disillusionment of the post-war period) confidently at the present and future. After the First World War, Western civilization in general began to look at its past in a new light— to reinterpret or paraphrase what it did not actively reject. Leadership in style and manner still came from the great European figures: Stravinsky, Picasso, Joyce; later, in music, Schoenberg and Webern; and the American artist felt closer to these than he ever could have felt to Wagner or Brahms or Debussy.

The decade was one, moreover, in which the new art—whether music or painting or literature—was not taken for granted. By mid-century, novelty as such was assumed as a matter of course to be a *sine qua non* in art; the composer was expected to produce a new technique or a new theory each week. But in 1925, the new could still be surprising and often pleasant, and attitudes could be tried out to see if they were possible to maintain. Experiment was fresh rather than desperate. Critical and public hostility towards new art may have been helpful, although not apparently so at the time to the artists concerned; it solidified their ranks in a way that has not been known since that period, when musical currents had not become as schismatic and mutually exclusive as they were to become later.

All composers of any standing were 'modern'. Some inclined more than others towards experiment for its own sake, or towards the exploration of 'new musical resources', as Henry Cowell phrased it. But even some of the most conservative composers felt that they were part of an important tide. Thus, for example, Howard Hanson (b. 1896) wrote symphonies and other large-scale works in a romantic style perhaps continuing the manner of MacDowell with echoes of Sibelius; yet Hanson as Director of the new Eastman School of Music organized in 1925 a series of American Composers' Orchestral Concerts which were extremely important in helping to make new American music known, and in giving composers a chance (for the most part denied them by the established symphony orchestras) of hearing their larger work. Hanson's opera *Merry Mount* (1934) was one of the few works by Americans presented by the Metropolitan Opera Association; others heard in the 1920s and 1930s were two by the even more conservative Deems Taylor (1885–1966), *The King's Henchman* (1927) and *Peter Ibbetson* (1931). The most interesting American opera produced by the Metropolitan was Gruenberg's *The Emperor Jones* (1933), a 'jazz' opera based on the play by Eugene O'Neill.

RADICALS OF THE 1920s

The *avant-garde* groups could hardly afford to present large orchestral works, much less operas, and their presentations had to be limited to chamber music and music in smaller forms. But much of this was memorable. The stir created by performances of the French-born Varèse's *Octandre* and *Hyperprism* (1924) still seems vivid. Cowell's pounding of tone-clusters on the piano (often with the aid of a board) seemed outrageous, and gave Cowell a notoriety that unfortunately obscured his achievements in other experimental aspects of composition, and for a long time made people forget the mastery of dissonant counterpoint shown in such works as his Sinfonietta of 1925. Virgil Thomson appeared on the American scene, as a young man returned from Paris, with *Capital, Capitals*, a setting of words by Gertrude Stein for four men's voices and piano, performed at one of the Copland-Sessions concerts of 1928, and with other works in which the inspiration of Satie and 'Les Six' made its most effective American appearance. The greatest public sensation of the time was made by the *Ballet mécanique* of George Antheil (1900–59), a former pupil of Ernest Bloch's who had spent the years 1922–5 in Europe, where he had aroused interest by his compositions utilizing jazz elements. The *Ballet mécanique*, scored for ten pianos and an assortment of noise-producers not usually employed in orchestration, proved, when revived many years later in New York, a rather dated expression of 'futurism'. Nevertheless it was a scandal in its time and so made its contribution towards a public awareness of the changing climate.

Carl Ruggles (1876–1971) is a minor composer of some interest who was associated with the 'radicals' of the 1920s. With Varèse, Riegger, Cowell, and others, he was active in the Pan American Association of Composers. One can hardly place Ruggles in the mainstream of musical development in America, and it is questionable that his tiny output of work has exerted much influence. His half-dozen or so completed compositions have, however, had ardent admirers. The four major works of Ruggles were all written between 1921 and 1933; they include *Angels* (1921), originally for six trumpets, later re-written for four violins and three cellos, or four trumpets and three trombones; *Men and Mountains* (1924) for chamber orchestra; *Portals* (1926) for string ensemble or string orchestra; and *The Sun Treader* (1933) for large orchestra. All these works are characterized by extreme dissonance and concentration. The technique is linear and very free, though calculated with extreme care. The music is non-tonal, and gives an impression of great intensity. Ruggles was an original voice, though a small one. For many years his music was rarely heard, though often discussed, and it was only in the 1950s that it became generally known and admired.

Works such as these caused the greatest amount of excitement, opposition, and noise. Many of them have been forgotten; the works of Varèse (1883–1965), on the other hand, were understood by very few when they were first heard, and the importance and vitality of his work came to be appreciated only very much later. In every important respect, Varèse anticipated the *musique concrète* of the 1950s, and showed a musicality and verve that make many of the newer 'abstract' composers seem inhibited by their own theories. Varèse was influenced by the famous Italian 'Futurist' manifesto of 1913, and his training in mathematics and engineering makes him seem a destined precursor of the mathematically serialized music, and the electronic experiments, of a later generation. His works of the 1920s lead directly to his *Poème Electronique* of 1958, composed directly on electronic tape for the World's Fair of Brussels; they can be seen in retrospect as early examples of what Varèse termed 'organized sound'. *Ionization*, composed in 1931, is scored entirely for percussion: thirteen players, using thirty-seven instruments, including two sirens, with chimes, celesta and piano heard briefly towards the end of the work. It differs basically from the *Poème Electronique* only in the means of sound production. *Hyperprism* (Ex. 254), composed in 1924, also uses an extraordinary assortment of percussion, and a small orchestra composed entirely of wind instruments. All these works are original and striking; although stark, after many years they no longer impress as being brutal. The music of Varèse seems to reflect the positive achievement of a mechanical and technological civilization, not its doubts, nor does it give that impression of retreating which is characteristic of so much twentieth-century art. Like Ives, Varèse was at least a generation ahead of his audience.

HENRY COWELL

The early work and activity of Henry Cowell (1897–1965) placed him in the foreground of attention as a radical and controversial figure in the 1920s. During his very active career as composer, performer, author, and lecturer, Cowell was associated with almost every development in American music. In the 1920s he was a radical among radicals, producing works in a bitingly dissonant counterpoint and exploring new possibilities in rhythmic organization. At the same time he startled audiences with his novel piano pieces in which he used what he termed 'tone-clusters' (massed chords of any size built on major and minor seconds) and also struck, plucked or brushed the strings directly, used

Ex. 254

harmonics, and employed the instrument in other unconventional ways. *Tiger* (Ex. 255) illustrates Cowell's piano technique admirably, and the bars of 5 against 4 show another of the composer's musical preoccupations:

Ex. 255

In 1927, Cowell founded the New Music Society in San Francisco, for the promotion of *avant-garde* music, and edited the *New Music Quarterly*, which published works of Ives and other American and European composers at a time when no other outlet was available to them. Cowell devoted a great deal of his inexhaustible energy to the cause of contemporary music itself, and did much to make American music aware of its own strength.

Cowell had an extraordinary childhood, and was largely self-taught until he attracted the attention of Charles Seeger (b. 1886), a remarkable composer and musicologist who taught at the University of California. Cowell later went to Germany where he studied comparative musicology under Hornbostel and attended Schoenberg's lectures. Webern performed Cowell's *Sinfonietta* in his concerts in Vienna, one of the first American works of the period to be heard in Europe. Cowell in turn helped introduce music of Schoenberg and Webern, as well as Bartók, to *avant-garde* audiences in America. His interest in oriental music, stimulated by his study with Hornbostel, led him to further explorations, and to an attempt at the reconciliation of music of the East and West which became a life-long pre-occupation. Cowell was essentially an eclectic composer, taking material where and how he found it, and using it without inhibition in compositions of all types. His work demonstrates his extraordinary interest in all musical phenomena, of any time and place, and the amount of music he left is as huge as it is varied.

As early as 1914, Cowell had hit on the idea of the serialization of rhythm, and had experimented with aleatory music, and with novel instruments, including an electronic sound-producer invented by Lev Theremin (b. 1896). With Joseph Schillinger he had experimented with a 'Rhythmicon' as an aid in construction with cross-rhythms of great complexity. In later years, Cowell explored American popular hymnology, folk music of all types, and 'exotic' material of widely varying kinds. There is, over the years, no single Cowell style, and this has puzzled and annoyed critics and historians who feel a compulsion to classify. Copland once said of Cowell that he was more of an inventor than a composer, but this is a judgement that time may not bear out. Cowell composed with natural enthusiasm and facility and much of his work is both original and well-realized. His later works, including most of his nineteen symphonies, are on the whole more conservative than the earlier ones, yet the entire body of work has a kind of consistency that a highly personal view of phenomena can bring to a variety of materials and idioms. Cowell's experiments, and his musical interests and aims, have had considerable influence both direct and indirect on many of his contemporaries and juniors, notably John Cage and Lou Harrison.

VIRGIL THOMSON AND OTHERS

Virgil Thomson (b. 1896) went from Harvard to Paris, where he studied with Nadia Boulanger and where he remained almost un-interruptedly until 1940. Thomson found the attitudes and aesthetic of Satie and 'Les Six' sympathetic, and became the outstanding American exponent of their spirit. But Thomson was an artistic personality of great originality and sophistication in his own right, and the deceptive simplicity of his usually diatonic and triadic idiom was as representative of a new spirit in music as the complex constructions of many of his contemporaries. Thomson abandoned the neo-classic style of his *Sonata da Chiesa* (1926), in which he introduced a tongue-in-cheek tango, and among his early works of distinct individuality his *Symphony on a Hymn Tune* (1928) stands as one of the first after Ives to utilize this type of American material. The work that established Thomson's reputation was the opera *Four Saints in Three Acts*, composed to a libretto of Gertrude Stein (1928). Its production in America in 1934 was a memorable event. Thomson's second opera with Miss Stein, *The Mother of Us All* (1947), remains, with the earlier work, a classic of the American theatre. Both works are inimitably original; the music is witty, imaginative, subtle, and daring in its innocence (which is only apparent). It makes delicate allusions to a variety of sources, from modal melodies to folk hymns and ballads and the mock-heroic style, but in a way that no one has done before or since. The delicious pseudo-simplicity characteristic of Thomson's music is illustrated in this quotation from his *Four Saints in Three Acts*:

Ex. 256

These same qualities are apparent in much of Thomson's work in other media, and are especially notable in his scores for the motion pictures *The Plow That Broke the Plains* (1936), *The River* (1937) and *Louisiana Story* (1948). Thomson has occasionally written in a more dissonant chromatic style, and has even explored aspects of twelve-note technique; but the essential quality of his writing remains a subtle simplicity that can take materials ranging from the commonplace to the recondite and transform them into a sophisticated personal idiom. Thomson's handling of prosody, as demonstrated in his operas, his miscellaneous vocal music and his Mass (1959), is masterly. From 1940 to 1954 Thomson served as music critic of the New York *Herald-Tribune*, his work marking a high point in American musical journalism.

Thomson is one of the true 'originals' in American music, or, for that matter, in international music of the twentieth century. He does not appear to be interested in striking out on new paths, or in the complications of technique that characterize most contemporary music. Yet it is obvious that his path is a new one, and that he is well aware of every technical procedure that is current. The music he writes is the product of a serious and refined intelligence brought to bear on an immediate problem or need for making music. He is not afraid of being banal, or of not being 'significant'. One of the mechanisms that makes his music effective is his manner of making alarming juxtapositions; one could say that he makes Paris and Kansas City realize what they have in common, by the fact of his having reconciled them. This is beyond mere wit and cleverness. Thomson is one of the few contemporary artists in any field with a true sense of high comedy. Lesser artists use parody, satire, farce, or irony; but the appearance of comedy is indeed rare.

While jazz and the more interesting varieties of novel or experimental music were attracting by far the greatest amount of attention, a number of American composers were quietly and solidly writing music that made its way more slowly. Walter Piston (b. 1894), Quincy Porter (1897–1966), Randall Thompson (b. 1899), Bernard Rogers (1893–1968), Wallingford Riegger (1885–1961), Douglas Moore (1893–1969), Leo Sowerby (1895–1968), Roger Sessions (b. 1896), and Otto Luening (b. 1900), were names not on everyone's tongues before 1930. No one of them burst on the scene with the impact of Copland or Gershwin, or aroused the kind of violence that met Varèse or Antheil or Cowell. Nor were they acclaimed as extravagantly as Roy Harris was to be only a few years later. The music of these composers represents a wide variation in style and temper, from the moderately academic conservatism of Sowerby, Thompson, and Porter to the more ruggedly dissonant and

40

involved style of Sessions and the more or less atonal style of Riegger. Of the composers born before 1901, these were the ones whose work remained of greatest interest at mid-century. There were of course many others whose work attracted attention, and the names of Arthur Shepherd (1880–1958), John J. Becker (1886–1961) and Frederick Jacobi (1891–1953) deserve mention.

Thompson, Moore, Rogers, Antheil, Porter, and Sessions all were at one time pupils of Ernest Bloch (1880–1959), whose importance in American music requires no further emphasis. Bloch himself wrote some of his most important works in the United States, including the Suite for Viola and Piano (1919), the Piano Quintet (1924), the 'epic rhapsody' *America* (1925), the fine neo-classic Concerto Grosso (1925), said to have been written as a model for his pupils, the *Sacred Service* (1933), perhaps his most significant work, and the Violin Concerto (1937). With Bloch one is faced squarely with the problem of defining just who is an American composer, for although Bloch spent more than half his life in the United States, it is difficult to think of this remarkable man as anything but a musician belonging to a world in which nationality is meaningless. Bloch can perhaps best be classed with Dvořák, Schoenberg, Milhaud, Hindemith, Křenek, Stravinsky, Bartók, Toch, and Wolpe, as visitors from another world who lived in America for shorter or longer periods (many of them becoming American citizens), and who had great influence as teachers and composers on several generations of American musicians.

Bloch's influence is not easy to discern in most of the composers who studied under him, but there is an almost unanimous testimony as to its importance. Bloch should be ranked with Boulanger (whose students included Copland, Thomson, Piston, Harris, Carter, and a long list of younger composers) as one of the two musicians who did most to shape American music in the first half of the twentieth century. And many of their pupils, notably Sessions, Porter, Rogers, Piston, Moore, Copland, Thomson, became in turn important teachers of a succeeding generation.

Douglas Moore, after his studies with both Bloch and Boulanger, joined the faculty of Columbia University in 1926, where he eventually succeeded to the Professorship endowed in memory of Edward MacDowell. His music is conservative and showed from the start a rejection of both contemporary French and German styles. Moore developed a simple personal idiom, the originality of which was not perceived at once; it was based on a deep understanding of American vernacular music and an ability to translate this into an uncomplicated musical language that was both sentimental and sophisticated. Moore firmly believed in musical Americanism, in much the same sense as Ives, but he wrote without Ives's complexities. Moore's was a traditional Americanism, not a cosmopolitan one. His first orchestral work to attract attention was *The Pageant of P. T. Barnum* (1924). This was followed by *Moby Dick* (1928), *Overture on an American Tune* (1931) and other works clearly reflecting a commitment to American themes. With *The Devil and Daniel Webster* (1938), a one-act opera based on a story of Stephen Vincent Benét, Moore showed that vocal writing and the musical theatre were his natural media. This unpretentious but original work enjoyed great success and has held the stage as a minor classic in American music. Moore's greatest accomplishment, and the work that finally brought general recognition of his unique talent, was the opera *The Ballad of Baby Doe* (1956), based on a true story of the American West, with libretto by John LaTouche. With this work, late in life, Moore achieved an American opera with greater success than any of his contemporaries or juniors had hitherto succeeded in producing.

INTERNATIONAL STYLES—WALLINGFORD RIEGGER, ROGER SESSIONS, WALTER PISTON

Piston, Sessions, and Riegger are, each in his way, composers in international styles. Each has gained in reputation since first attracting notice in the 1920s. By the middle of the century no critic or historian could have done other than place them as among the most interesting and significant American composers of their time. Riegger, the oldest of the three, was the last to gain recognition. His career was curiously chequered. He began as a thorough conservative, a student of Goetschius in New York and later of Bruch and of the American Edgar Stillman Kelley (1857-1944) in Germany. After winning several prizes for his early works, Riegger decided to rest and to reconsider for a period of three years. At the end of this time, he produced his *Study in Sonority* (1927) for ten violins, a work of extremely dissonant tension, using two mixed and extremely acid harmonic complexes as arbitrary tonic and dominant, and, as the title suggests, exploring string timbres in an unusual way. In his *Dichotomy* (1932) for chamber orchestra Riegger utilized two 'note-rows', and the music remains consistently within the rather general definition of 'atonality'. This was at a time when Riegger was entirely unfamiliar with the work or theories of Schoenberg. Riegger's style progressed from the orthodox to the radical as he grew older, although in general he adhered to classic forms, which he handled with the assurance of an expert craftsman. Yet Riegger remained for many years a rather neglected composer, and despite a volume of interesting work (much of it composed for dance companies)

Ex. 257

he was relatively unknown to the American public until his Third Symphony (1948). His use of twelve-note techniques is demonstrated in this work, and also in his First String Quartet (1938). Riegger employed row construction in a personal and free manner, and combined it with traditional structure. He was not a purist, but a composer who took materials as he needed them, and employed them with assurance. His Second String Quartet (1948) and his *Music for Brass Choir* (1949) show other aspects of his highly personal and sharply dissonant style, his strong rhythmic drive, and brilliant sense of instrumental sonority. *Music for Brass Choir* (Ex. 257) has been described as 'the apotheosis of the tone cluster'. The effect of these massed sounds on the brass instruments, and the imaginative handling of line and mass throughout this work are indeed original and impressive.

The career and reputation of Riegger illuminate one aspect of American musical life by underlining the importance of prizes, festivals, and energetic seeking of public notice. Riegger had been known to musicians for many years as a composer of considerable importance, and had, in fact, been an active associate of Ives, Varèse, Ruggles, and Cowell in the Pan American Association of Composers during the 1920s. But public recognition came to him only after his Third Symphony, written when he was 62 years of age, had received an award from New York's music critics. Fortunately, the impression made by this work (which was, incidentally, the first major commission Riegger had ever received) resulted in performances of Riegger's other music and brought him further commissions for new works. For the last decade of his life, Riegger enjoyed some of the recognition and influence he clearly deserved, and was at last able to hear his music performed by major orchestras and other performing groups. His works after 1948 included his Fourth Symphony (1957), much chamber and choral music, and two fine sets of variations, for Piano and Orchestra (1953) and for Violin and Orchestra (1959). Like Schoenberg, Riegger occasionally returned to tonal writing throughout his career, as in the *Canon and Fugue for Strings* (1941) and the *Suite for Younger Orchestras* (1954).

Basically, Riegger's music, despite its wealth of invention and the depth of its technical vocabulary, is uncomplicated. Riegger strove for clarity and logic, and felt that the enlargement of the tonal vocabulary in the twentieth century was not a licence to greater freedom for the composer, but on the contrary imposed on him an ever greater need for control and discipline. Riegger's influence on younger composers became more evident during the later years of his career, as the original nature of his contribution became more generally appreciated.

Roger Sessions, like Riegger, is a composer of marked individuality who has also been influenced by twelve-note methods without becoming a doctrinaire adherent of the school. Again like Riegger, his musical thought gravitated towards serial techniques at a middle stage of his career as a composer, although in the case of Sessions this evolution was gradual. Sessions's early works, of which the most representative is the suite extracted from his music for Andreyev's play *The Black Maskers* (1923), show an inclination towards the richness and complexity of Central European styles, and reflect the influences of Bloch, Mahler, and Strauss. The complexity and richness of texture remain through most of Sessions's later work, which from the beginning has had a strong appeal to musicians but has never commanded a wide public following. The tonal works of Sessions's early period, including the First Symphony (1927) and First Piano Sonata (1930), show a solidity of technique and sense of musical logic that are very striking, and in their straining at the bounds of tonality foreshadow later developments in Sessions's music. The key work and turning point in Sessions's composition is the Second Symphony (1946), in which the impulsion towards a completely chromaticized style reaches the threshold of atonality. It is after this work that Sessions began to adopt twelve-note serial techniques, using them never in the sense of a system, but, again like Riegger, deriving thematic material and relationships freely and flexibly. Sessions's music is much more inward and intense than Riegger's, and is essentially more involved and elusive. At the same time, it often has a brooding and disquieting lyricism, perhaps at its most evocative in the Second String Quartet (1951). Sessions's chamber music is always impressive and satisfying. The Quintet for Strings (1958) shows his style at its least opaque and most accessible, and also illustrates his very personal use of twelve-note themes.

In addition to the Third and Fourth Symphonies (1957 and 1958), Sessions's major production includes a Violin Concerto (1935), a Piano Concerto (1956), a Mass (1958), and a setting of an *Idyll of Theocritus* for soprano and orchestra (1954). Sessions is not a prolific or casual composer. An intellectual and spiritual affinity to Schoenberg is evident in all of his work, although in none of it is there any rigid application of Schoenberg's theory or practice; the affinity is entirely one of attitude and mentality. The essentially inward temperament perhaps is the reason that Sessions seems less happy and successful in works for the stage, such as the one-act opera, *The Trial of Lucullus* (1947), after Brecht.

Sessions was at mid-century a figure of the greatest importance on the American musical scene, not only as a composer highly respected

Ex. 258

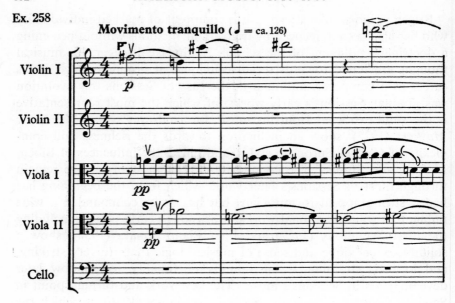

by all, but also as a teacher and as a direct and indirect influence on an entire generation of younger composers. Many of his students, including Ross Lee Finney, Hugo Weisgall, Leon Kirchner, Milton Babbitt, and indeed a host of others, have achieved prominence not only as composers, but also, in turn, as teachers.

Piston, too, has had great influence as a teacher. While Sessions taught at California and at Princeton, Piston was at Harvard from 1926 to 1961. Both Piston and Sessions have written books on harmony that have been widely used in American schools and conservatories. But while Sessions's music reminds one in texture and aesthetic of Central Europe, Piston's music is that of a neo-classicist. His early works, such as his First String Quartet (1933), impressed his contemporaries by their elegance, control, and craftsmanship. This impression was confirmed by the composer's later work, all of which exhibited a polish and mastery of medium that was as refreshing as it was rare. Piston's symphonies (his Seventh was completed in 1961) constitute the central portion of his work, although he has written in all conventional forms of chamber music as well.

Unlike Sessions or Riegger, Piston has had a fairly wide public success. His music is accessible and fluent, in an idiom that is recognizably of the twentieth century, but it is not 'advanced' or radical or apparently complicated by theoretical problems or considerations. It is essentially related to early and middle Stravinsky, with occasional overtones of Hindemithian counterpoint. Basically it is conservative and even academic, and, in an entirely non-pejorative sense, it may be said that Piston represents the legitimate continuation of the 'Boston School' of Paine, Chadwick, and Parker.

ROY HARRIS

If Piston's music is characterized by its sureness and craftsmanship, the opposite must be said of the music of Roy Harris (b. 1898). Harris's arrival on the American musical scene can only be described as explosive; as with so many explosions, however, the aftermath is less exciting to describe. Harris was for some time a major force in American music, and suffered the unfortunate fate of becoming almost a legend at a time when American music was searching for something resembling a hero sprung directly from the soil. Harris did emerge from the West, appropriately enough from a log cabin; he did not decide to be a composer until he was twenty-four, when he studied briefly with Farwell, who launched him with considerable effectiveness. An Andante for Orchestra was performed by Howard Hanson in 1926, and gained Harris the immediate interest of his colleagues. He then went to Paris, on Copland's advice, to study with Boulanger; and his Sextet for Clarinet, Piano, and Strings (1927) and his first Piano Sonata (1928) are among the best works of this period. Indeed they must still be counted among the best Harris has written. His First Symphony (1933) aroused the enthusiasm of Kussevitsky, the Russian-born conductor of the Boston Symphony who almost alone among the conductors of major orchestras encouraged and performed the larger works of American composers a this time. Harris's Third Symphony (1939) (see Ex. 259) seems in retrospect to mark the high point of his achievement. Hailed immediately as an American masterpiece, it exerted a powerful influence on musical thought for many years, and must be counted among the half-dozen most important American works of the century. Its interest and appeal are difficult to analyse, yet its intensity and novelty made themselves felt immediately among musicians and laymen alike. The Symphony appeared to be an expression of all that was vast, aspiring and nostalgic in American life; it was all things to all people, yet it appealed as being peculiarly and unmistakably American in each of its aspects. The material ranges from the home-spun (the hymn-tune, as in Ives, Copland and Thomson) to the epic-heroic: chorale-like brass passages and fanfares. Harris's style, as exhibited in this Third Symphony, found immediate imitators, and its technical and emotional mannerisms have had many echoes in American music.

Harris's music usually has a long line, more often modal or diatonic than chromatic. He is fond of canon and fugue (or of canonic and fugal devices); his phrase-structure and rhythm are often irregular and shifting. He is fond of triads in non-functional relationship, as sonorities in their own right, but often uses a polyharmonic texture, producing an overlay of dissonance in an essentially simple tonal context. Cyclical structure occurs in many of his larger works. Harris reasons and writes about his music, but it remains the music of an instinctive rather than of an intellectually disciplined composer, and a lack of a self-critical faculty is often evident. In later works Harris proclaimed his mission as an American composer through a more obvious and naïve use of folk and patriotic materials and motives.

As early as 1941, Aaron Copland (like Cowell and Thomson a most perceptive critic of new music) pointed out the qualities and deficiencies of Harris's music in a summation that has not since been surpassed for acuteness and balance. Copland, after noting the sweep and breadth, the power and emotional depth, of Harris's best pages, and noting too the indefinably 'American' quality of his tunes and rhythms, pointed out that Harris often seemed not to know what to make of his materials. Formal deficiencies in the music, Copland pointed out, are so obvious

Ex. 259

as to make it evident that Harris's 'insecure critical faculty' handicapped him seriously. Many of his pieces lack a sense of direction, and also fail to correspond to the copious 'spiritual' explanations that Harris so often provided. Yet, in the end, Copland concluded that 'Whatever one may think, it is useless to wish Harris otherwise than he is. One may show how much better his work might have been . . . But there is no gainsaying that, such as it is, with all its faults and qualities, it is enormously important to us in the immediate scene. Plenty of Americans have learned how to compose properly, and it has done us little good. Here is a man who, perhaps, may not be said to compose properly but who will do us lots of good. We can let posterity concern itself with the eternal aspect of Harris's music, if any. The important thing is that it has something for us here and now.'[1]

Harris's influence on the music of the late 1930s and 1940s has not been, on the whole, justly estimated. Its positive qualities are best seen in the work of his pupil, William Schuman (b. 1910), and in aspects of the work of such composers as Vincent Persichetti (b. 1915) and Peter Mennin (b. 1923). But its weaknesses, too, have been reflected in a great deal of pseudo-Americana and nationalistic bombast, and in a tendency towards the formation of a right-wing school of composition based on nostalgia. With the emergence of Harris as a major influence on American music, one is aware that the mood of a period has changed, and that 'modernism' is no longer a primary concern. A music for the people became the preoccupation of many composers; Harris himself felt strongly the need to communicate on a wide scale, and his Fourth Symphony (1941), based on folk-songs, and his Sixth (1944), based on Lincoln's Gettysburg Address, were evidence not only of what Harris believed, but also of what the results might be in terms of musical content and style. It was at about this time that Copland first produced his folk-style ballet scores, in a much more transparent and easily assimilable manner than his early works, and that Cowell abandoned radical experiment for an innocently folklorish manner. The urge towards creating a people's music was felt also in the work of a consciously 'proletarian' school, of which the most important productions were the stage works of Marc Blitzstein (1905–64). Among these, *The Cradle Will Rock* (1936) made a great impression by its directness and force, and helped to create a public for a native opera not based on the conventions of the Italian or German grand style.

Many factors, both musical and social, contributed to the establishment of new tendencies in American music during the 1930s. The financial crisis of 1929 and the depression that followed brought a

[1] *Our New Music*, p. 175.

number of changes to American life and thinking, and these affected the American artist directly and indirectly. The relief programmes of public works instituted during the Roosevelt administration included projects designed to provide both opportunity and sustenance to writers, painters and composers. The Works Progress Administration (WPA), under which musicians were given employment, instituted concerts, 'forums' and a variety of projects including the collection of folk-songs. The WPA orchestras provided more opportunities than had previously been available for the performance of new American works, and were in general a vitally stimulating influence. Was it a coincidence that the number of composers seemed to increase vastly? Certainly the WPA provided an encouragement that has since come to be expected by American artists, and which has, in fact, been perpetuated through the extraordinary abundance since World War II of grants, fellowships, awards, and commissions, which appear to fall to the talented and the untalented in about equal proportions. During the period of the depression, American composers acquired a new sense of their position and function in society, and became increasingly aware of the possibility of effective collective action not only towards economic improvement, but also towards the establishment of an awareness of composers as a body politic.

THE 1930s—THE IMPACT OF EUROPEAN IMMIGRANTS

A further major influence on the development of music in America was the arrival as permanent residents in the United States of some of the most eminent composers of Europe. Arnold Schoenberg came to the United States in 1933, and after a brief residence in Boston moved to California, where he remained until his death in 1951. Ernst Toch arrived in 1934, Kurt Weill in 1935, Hindemith in 1937, Křenek and Wolpe in 1938, Stravinsky, Milhaud, and Vittorio Rieti in 1940, Martinů and Bartók in 1941. All of these composers, except Stravinsky and Weill, made their presences felt in the most direct manner, by teaching; but it is evident that the immediate impact of their personalities and the performances of their music were also of great importance. Nearly all of these distinguished emigrés became members of the music faculties of American colleges and universities: Schoenberg at the University of Southern California, Křenek at Vassar and Hamline (St. Paul, Minnesota), Hindemith at Yale, Milhaud at Mills, Toch also at the University of Southern California, Martinů at Princeton, Bartók at Columbia. The importance and prestige of the teaching of composition at American universities, begun by Paine and Parker, was greatly emphasized by the presence of these acknowledged masters. Even

Stravinsky, who never wished to be officially a teacher of composition, gave the series of lectures at Harvard University later published as *Poétique musicale*, a document of major interest in twentieth-century aesthetic.

Of the very great number of composers active in the United States in the 1930s, a few began to emerge as well-defined musical personalities towards the end of the decade. They represent, for the most part, a generation trained in America and directly profiting by the work, both musical and propagandistic, of their immediate elders. Among the composers achieving prominence around 1940, and maintaining their positions during the following twenty years, were Samuel Barber (b. 1910), Ross Lee Finney (b. 1906), Paul Creston (b. 1906), William Schuman, Norman Dello Joio (b. 1913), Morton Gould (b. 1913), David Diamond (b. 1915), Vincent Persichetti and Gian Carlo Menotti (b. Italy, 1911). Others, equally prominent in the years following World War II, had not yet attracted comparable attention.

The music of these men reflects the customary American diversity of style, temperament, and training, but on the whole it is consistently conservative and eclectic. It reflects an acceptance and mastery of the less adventurous techniques of twentieth-century European masters, but with the exception of Finney's later music (after 1950) demonstrates no influence of the Schoenbergian disciplines and little desire to enlarge musical boundaries. On the other hand, it contains ample evidence of the already strong influences of Copland and Harris, added to those of the neo-classic Stravinsky, of Hindemith, and to a much smaller extent, of Prokofiev. The musical idioms range from the rather sober elegance of Barber, through the boisterous vehemence of Schuman, to the popular-music style of Gould and the theatricality of Menotti.

Barber provides an excellent illustration of the internationally-oriented traditionalist in American music. His music was readily accepted by conservative audiences, and he was the first American composer to be performed by Arturo Toscanini (*Essay for Orchestra*, 1937, and Adagio for Strings, 1936). Barber's music has often been described as 'neo-romantic', a vague word used to suggest the fact that the music flows smoothly, is not excessively dissonant, is traditional in form, and gives the impression of both warmth and refinement. Barber has, however, written in the 'neo-classic' style (*Capricorn Concerto*, 1944) and there are elements of greater dissonance and freer concepts of tonality in his *Second Essay for Orchestra* (1942), the *Medea* Suite (1947), and the Piano Sonata (1949). Barber's work after 1950 shows a tendency to become more complex, but without losing its mastery of line, form, and mood. His opera *Vanessa* (1958), with libretto by

Menotti, and his *Antony and Cleopatra* (1966), are among the few by American composers to have been produced by the Metropolitan Opera in New York.

Menotti himself has proved to be much more a composer (and author) for the theatre than most of his American-born contemporaries, and his success in an idiom remarkably his own has helped to interest the American public in new works for the operatic stage. He first attracted widespread attention with his one-act *opera buffa, Amelia Goes to the Ball* (1937), produced at the Metropolitan in 1938. Menotti came to the United States in 1928 and was trained, like Barber, at the Curtis Institute in Philadelphia. Although fundamentally Italianate as a composer, Menotti is identified with the American musical scene, and has been without question an important factor in the development of an American musical theatre. *The Medium* (1946) and *The Consul* (1950), both serious, if rather melodramatic, works, enjoyed unprecedented success in the commercial theatre, and have been performed frequently throughout the United States and Europe. The chamber opera *Amahl and the Night Visitors* (1951) was commissioned by the National Broadcasting Company (a private enterprise) especially for television, and has been presented annually on Christmas Eve. The unqualified success of Menotti's work with even the very broadest public has been valuable to other American musicians, creating an awareness of opera as a still effective art form and as a potential medium for communicating with audiences larger than those available for symphonic music. The appeal of Menotti's work, continued with *The Saint of Bleecker Street* (1954), lies in his unerring dramatic flair and directness. The musical material is conventional, but treated imaginatively, and the vocal line is always handled with mastery.

William Schuman and Norman dello Joio were among the best known and most widely performed American composers during the 1940s and 1950s. Dello Joio's music poses no problems; it is expertly made and quite conservative in style. Dello Joio's principal teacher was Hindemith, and his music reflects the influence of that master. If dello Joio's music is less angular and has more obvious warmth than his master's, that is perhaps a reflection of an Italian heritage. Dello Joio has frequently used modal melodic material, including Gregorian chant, in a mildly dissonant texture. His use of contrapuntal techniques is skilful. Dello Joio is an accomplished pianist and organist and is one of the few American composers (Persichetti is another) who has written interesting music for the keyboard. Among dello Joio's orchestral works, his *Variations, Chaconne and Finale* (1948) has been often performed by American orchestras.

41

The chief distinguishing character of Schuman's music is the quality of its motor energy. It derives both in spirit and in technique from Harris, but goes beyond Harris in achievement. Like Harris, Schuman is often concerned with being an American composer; he is, however, essentially an urban American, and his music seems a reflection of the drive, the buoyancy and the tension of American life. The orchestral piece that first brought him notice was an *American Festival Overture* (1939), a brilliantly orchestrated work of great liveliness. His Third Symphony (1941) established him securely among American composers of his generation, and his work has continued to be performed more and more widely. Schuman's work in the 1940s and 1950s includes seven symphonies, two concertos, various other orchestral pieces, four string quartets, and the music for several dance productions, notably *Undertow* (1945), *Night Journey* (1947) and *Judith* (1949). Schuman has writtens ongs, piano music, and choral works as well, and one opera, *The Mighty Casey* (1953), based on a celebrated mock-epic of baseball. With many other American composers (Cowell, Luening and Finney among them) Schuman rediscovered the work of one of America's authentic 'primitives', the New England composer William Billings (1746–1800), whose name is associated with sturdy hymns, patriotic anthems and what he himself termed 'fuguing tunes'. Schuman based his *New England Tryptych* (1956) on music by Billings, and this example of musical Americana has been one of his most popular works. Schuman's music is basically tonal, although at times extremely dissonant. He is fond of major-minor triads and is not afraid of harsh conflicts. Like Harris, he often employs a long melodic line and makes frequent use of canonic and fugal techniques. The flow of Schuman's music is often punctuated by brittle rhythmic passages. It is the drive and restlessness of the rhythms, and the brilliance of the orchestration, that first attract attention to Schuman's music. A passage from his Sixth Symphony (Ex. 260) shows the long string line opposed to the noisy rhythmic punctuation of the entire brass section.

THE SITUATION IN 1950—THE DECADE 1950–60

At the mid-point of the century the American musical scene was one of tremendous activity. Among the 'established' composers, the most important appeared to be Copland, Barber, Piston, Schuman, Dello Joio, Thomson, Sessions and Riegger; and Ives's reputation was rising. But new developments were under way, and other young and middle-aged composers were coming to the fore. Almost all the composers named above, with the exceptions of Ives and Sessions and possibly of

Ex. 260

Riegger, were well received in polite musical circles and regarded as conservative by a younger generation. Most of the newer composers were interested neither in simplicity nor in Americanism. The influence of Schoenberg and Webern was beginning for the first time to be strongly felt and reflected by American composers, and Stravinsky's conversion to serialism prompted a further movement towards the international *avant-garde* style. Prominent among the composers working in serial techniques were Milton Babbitt (b. 1916), Ben Weber (b. 1916), George Perle (b. 1915), and George Rochberg (b. 1918). Many others followed, and the influence of the post-Webernists continued to become more marked. Copland and Thomson themselves experimented with note-row construction, and a number of more or less neo-classical composers, such as Arthur Berger (b. 1912), followed the new Stravinsky line of the 1950s. At the same time, new composers also emerged on the right wing and in a middle group. Some of the most interesting figures, among them Elliott Carter (b. 1908), Hugo Weisgall (b. Bohemia, 1912) and Leon Kirchner (b. 1919) could be described as left of centre without being committed to serialism or to any other easily identifiable school. The original and controversial work of John Cage (b. 1912) also attracted attention during the fifties, and the equally original work of Harry Partch (b. 1901) began to interest the musically curious, without, however, reaching a large public or exerting much influence on musical thought or practice.

The range of interest and of musical style continued to widen during the decade 1950–60, so that composers of one extreme tendency seemed hardly to exist in the same world as those at the other extreme. This was merely a reflection in America of the international situation in music; but the important difference for American music lay in the fact that it had finally reached a point of development at which it was abreast of European currents, instead of being anywhere from ten to fifty years behind them. Increased facility of communication was of course a primary factor, but it was the achievement of several generations of American composers that provided the technical and artistic basis for this new relation to the musical art of the world. In the 1950s, the work of new European composers such as Boulez and Stockhausen made an immediate impact in America, and for the first time a few American composers, notably Carter, Cage, and Babbitt, produced music other than jazz that was of some influence on musicians of Europe. American music had finally become part of the international scene rather than a provincial echo.

It is obviously impossible, in a brief essay, to mention all of the many dozens of composers whose works commanded some attention during the decade 1950–1960, nor is it possible to pretend to any degree of historical perspective in evaluating an enormous volume and variety of production that is still so recent. But among the many composers occupying the broad middle ground of musical style at mid-century, one should cite some of those who attracted attention and achieved some prominence. In such a list one would find the names of Peter Mennin and Vincent Persichetti (already mentioned), as well as those of Lukas Foss (b. Germany, 1922), Leonard Bernstein (b. 1918), Robert Palmer (b. 1915), Ingolf Dahl (b. Germany, 1912–1970), Irving Fine (1914–1962), Alexei Haieff (b. Russia, 1914), Elie Siegmeister (b. 1909), Robert Ward (b. 1917), William Bergsma (b. 1921), Andrew Imbrie (b. 1921), and Alan Hovhaness (b. 1911). To cite these names and to omit others is not to make either a critical or an historical judgement. Nor should it be assumed that these composers constitute a group in any sense; they represent a variety of personalities and musical orientations, and have in common only the fact that all were active and respected in their time and place, and that their music was performed and known. At so short a remove in time, one cannot know if a Charles Ives remains undiscovered, or if an Edward MacDowell enjoys a fame beyond his deserts.

Of these composers, brief accounts must suffice. Mennin's style, best seen in his symphonies, is broad and singing, rhythmically alive, and shows an impressive command of large contrapuntal forms. Ward, like Mennin a student of Hanson and Bernard Rogers, has written in an easy and recognizably American style in his overture, *Jubilation* (1946), and has progressed to an effective dramatic music in his very successful opera *The Crucible* (1960). Palmer and Dahl write for the most part in a vein of Hindemithian neo-classicism, while Fine and Haieff represent a neo-classicism deriving from Stravinsky. Bergsma's music is generally classical and conservative, but has great sensitivity and elegance. Imbrie, a pupil of Sessions, has some of his teacher's intensity and drive, and his music represents the Sessions influence at its best. Persichetti's style is one in which influences of Copland, Harris and Schuman seem to be fused. Foss continued to evolve an expression of his own after arriving in the United States at the age of fifteen. Influenced strongly by Hindemith, later by Stravinsky and eventually by Copland, Foss later turned to serialism in his *Time Cycle* (1960) for soprano and orchestra, and to experiment with improvisatory techniques. Hovhaness, of Armenian descent, has attempted in his prolific output of composition to reconcile music of the East and West, and has succeeded in producing work of quite distinct profile. Bernstein, like Foss a gifted pianist and conductor, is a Protean composer, whose serious symphonic works derive from Stravinsky and Copland (with occasional overtones of German nineteenth-century composers), but whose most convincing accomplishments so far are in the popular musical theatre, as *West Side Story* (1957).

The techniques and mannerisms of electronic music, aleatory and improvisational music, totally serialized music and other manifestations of contemporary musical thought or exploration commanded attention in the United States as they did in Europe. Among the first to experiment with music composed on electronic tape were Otto Luening and his colleague at Columbia University, Vladimir Ussachevsky (b. Manchuria, 1911). A first concert of their compositions for tape recorder was given in New York in 1952. A grant from the Rockefeller Foundation in 1959 established a laboratory for electronic music at Columbia, where further experiment is carried on under the direction of Luening and Ussachevsky, with Milton Babbitt and Roger Sessions of Princeton. Sessions himself has not composed electronic music; Babbitt, on the other hand, has been among the most active in this field, and his work, both in theory and in application, has been extremely influential. Coincidental with the rise of electronic music, as a phenomenon of major interest, was the reappearance, after a silence of many years, of Varèse. Varèse had in many ways anticipated the aesthetic of electronic music, and the evolution of its techniques, by a singular poetic justice, re-emphasized the daring and originality of the music he had written in the 1920s. *Deserts* (1954), his first new work in almost twenty years, was composed for conventional instruments (including much percussion) with interludes of 'organized sound' recorded on tape. With this remarkable piece, Varèse once again proved himself to be a composer of imagination, power, and vitality.

Among the independent explorers of new musical styles, none was more prominent during the fifties than John Cage. Cage first attracted attention with his music for 'prepared' piano in the 1940s, taking up a line of development first indicated by Cowell. Cage has been influenced also by Varèse, by oriental music, by Anton von Webern, and by a variety of philosophical or speculative ideas. He was perhaps the first to use chance as a basic element in musical construction; and his work antedates by some years the aleatory music fashionable in Europe late in the fifties. His *Imaginary Landscape*, for twelve radios, was performed in 1951 at what proved to be the final concert of the New Music Society. This work, the principle of which is that it can never repeat itself, depends entirely on the chance of what will be on the air at the time of performance. 'Form' is indicated, but the essence of 'content' is absolute randomness. The spirit of Cage's work is reminiscent of Parisian Dada;

if its absolute value is difficult to estimate, its influence on many of Cage's contemporaries cannot be denied.

Among other composers of an experimental and non-conformist tendency, Lou Harrison (b. 1917), a pupil of Cowell, and Henry Brant (b. Canada, 1913) deserve mention. Harrison, in addition to some highly sensitive, though eclectic, works for conventional instruments and voices, has composed a number of works for percussion orchestra, including such unorthodox sound-producers as brake-drums, iron pipes, and packing boxes, and these are often of a surprising gentleness and astonishing effectiveness. Brant, whose teachers included Antheil, Copland, and Riegger, among others, but who was also very strongly influenced by Ives and Cowell, was a juvenile prodigy whose early works showed a bewildering exuberance and cleverness. He has worked as a professional arranger for radio and other commercial media, and after repudiating many of his early compositions, has turned his attention to experiments in multi-planed music, using separated and independent groups of players. The groups are often of unusual constitution. Typical of Brant's work is his *Grand Universal Circus* (1956), a theatre-piece in three 'acts' which embodies Brant's ideas of stereophonic distribution and polyphonic tempi. Of Brant's music, Henry Cowell commented that 'it constitutes audaciousness in the grand manner . . . and [is] deserving of a place in Ives' idea of a *Universal Symphony*, to which all composers with doughty ears and strong-sounding music are invited by Ives to contribute. . . .'

Considerably less controversial, and with no elements either of Dada or of 'scientific' objectivity or abstraction, is the music of Carter, Kirchner and Weisgall, who achieved recognition in the fifties as composers of impressive stature. Kirchner studied with both Schoenberg and Sessions, and his music has a complexity and intensity reminiscent of these composers. But Kirchner's music also shows affinities with the music of Berg and Bartók. Kirchner first attracted attention with a rhapsodic Duo for Violin and Piano (1947) and followed this with a Piano Sonata (1948) and a String Quartet (1949):

Ex. 261

His Concerto for Piano (1953) is representative of his mature work in large forms. There is great force, even violence, in Kirchner's music, which at all times remains highly personal and indifferent to theoretical positions. Kirchner succeeded Piston as professor of composition at Harvard, after many years at Mills College in California.

Hugo Weisgall also studied with Sessions, and writes in a highly dissonant atonal style that recalls the expressionist manner of Central Europe. Weisgall's *forte* is vocal music, and his setting of English is extraordinarily effective. His principal work is in the field of opera; he is almost the only American composer of the fifties to write opera in a dissonant, powerfully dramatic style. Ex. 262 from his *Athaliah* illustrates also the restless semiquaver notation characteristic of Weisgall's music. *The Tenor* (1950) and *The Stronger* (1952), based on Wedekind and Strindberg respectively, made Weisgall known as among the most interesting new American composers for the serious musical theatre. *Six Characters in Search of an Author* (1956), after the Pirandello play, and *Purgatory* (1958), after Yeats, established the composer firmly as one of the most forceful on the American scene.

Elliott Carter was among the most respected composers in America at the end of the decade. Carter studied with Piston and Boulanger, and his early compositions were of a neo-classical trend, with echoes of Stravinsky and Copland. Not until 1948 did Carter find an expression that was entirely his own, and one that he has developed with increasing originality and authority with each succeeding work. In the Sonata for Cello and Piano of 1948, he joined the ranks of the 'experimental' composers, but his distinction in this category is that such experiment

Ex. 262

end of Part One

as the work represented was subordinate to a remarkable musical realization. In this work Carter for the first time utilized his invented principle of 'metrical modulation', a technique for controlling and changing the absolute speeds of musical time units. This alone would demand attention, but the Sonata also exhibited an expressive power of the highest degree and a command of spacing and sonority already fore-shadowed in the Piano Sonata of 1946. Carter's work during the follow-ing years, the *Eight Etudes and a Fantasy* for woodwind quartet (1950), the String Quartet (1951), the Variations for Orchestra (1955) and the Second String Quartet (1960), all impressed as being of major impor-tance. Carter's works may be described as intellectual machines in which an unusually forceful musical impulse supplies the momentum. His ideas in the fields of form and organization, his successful creation of a music evolving on several simultaneous planes, had already exercised wide influence by 1960. In some respects Carter solved some of the problems in polyrhythm and multi-planed music that Ives had posed many years before. Ex. 263, from the 1951 String Quartet, is typical of his music in this respect:

Ex. 263

Carter's music is always rigidly disciplined, but it is without formula. Its texture is generally dense and its colour dark. The calculation of sonorities and balances is extremely delicate, and each new work has seemed to indicate further progress into still unexplored areas of musical thought.

It is impossible to foresee how the music of the 1950s will appear in even the very near future. Judgement becomes increasingly difficult not only because of the great diversity of styles and techniques—and the consequent possibility that the mid-century on the whole represents a point of transition and synthesis—but also because of the enormous numbers of composers at work, and the unprecedented rapidity with which musical fashions continue to evolve, and in many cases to disappear. All these phenomena are characteristic of the twentieth century everywhere, and in every field, but they seem to take on peculiarly exaggerated forms in America. One is safe only in assuming that American music at the beginning of the second half of the century possessed both the environment and the tradition to keep abreast of the remainder of the world.

(ii) Music in Latin America
By GERARD BÉHAGUE

NATIONALISM

DURING the first half of the twentieth century Latin-American art music was largely dominated by the nationalist trend, with notable exceptions. Composers sought in the various folk-music traditions of their countries the substance of their works. The large majority of the considerable music production for all media at this time reveals varying degrees of national concern, from the direct use of folk and popular sources to a more subjective assimilation of folk material. Through their nationalistic works Latin-American composers were able to win unprecedented international recognition, and only in the late 1950s and the 1960s did musical nationalism suffer an obvious decline.

The major exponents of Latin-American art music during the period under consideration include Heitor Villa-Lobos, Carlos Chávez, Domingo Santa Cruz, and Alberto Ginastera, respectively from Brazil, Mexico, Chile, and Argentina. They and their contemporaries, however, were not exclusively nationalist. Frequently they have attempted to incorporate twentieth-century European styles and techniques into certain national idioms. In many cases they have also followed such trends as impressionism, neo-classicism or serialism, in which no trace of nationality can be detected.

In Brazil, Heitor Villa-Lobos (1887–1959) dominated the local scene throughout his career. Extremely prolific and imaginative, he wrote about a thousand works (including various arrangements of many pieces) in all possible genres and media. By 1913 he had written some fifty-five compositions, among which the *Suite dos cântigos sertanejos* (Folk-song suite) (1910) indicates his first elaboration of thematic material derived from folk sources. Further involvement with typical national subjects is evidenced in his tone poems and ballets of the late 1910s, such as *Uirapurú* and *Amazonas*, introducing concurrently characteristic harmonic and rhythmic elements of popular music as well as children's song-tunes in his piano pieces, such as *A prole do bêbê* (Baby's family) *no. 1* (1918) and *Lenda do caboclo* (Tale of a peasant) (1920). During the 1920s Villa-Lobos travelled to Paris where he succeeded in establishing himself as a composer and conductor. This period had a particular significance for him because he then completed the series of the *Chôros*, considered together with the *Bachianas brasileiras* his best contribution to modern music. Inspired by the native background of the *chôros* (popular strolling ensembles of serenaders in Rio de Janeiro at the turn of the century), he wrote sixteen compositions bearing this title. Not in chronological order, they are intended for the most varied media, from solo guitar (*Chôros no. 1*) to full orchestra with mixed chorus (*Chôros no. 10*). The only common stylistic traits result from a highly subjective recreation of various popular and primitive musical traditions. *Chôros no. 10* quoting the popular song 'Rasga o coração' reveals the assimilation of advanced techniques: predominance of rhythm and percussion instruments, polytonality, and atonality with tone-clusters. The 1920s were also the years of his piano masterpieces including the *Cirandas* (Rounds) (1926), sixteen pieces of high virtuosity based on children's songs, and *Rudepoema* (Rude poem) (1921–26), dedicated to Arthur Rubinstein. The *Bachianas brasileiras*, the last seven symphonies, and the last thirteen quartets dominated Villa-Lobos's production during the last twenty-seven years of his life. According to the composer himself the *Bachianas* were inspired by the atmosphere of J. S. Bach's work, considered by him as a universal source of music. Consisting of nine pieces they are written as dance suites preceded generally by a prelude and ending with a fugue-like or toccata-like movement. The use of baroque composition processes is in fact small, although fugue as a formal principle could be construed as a 'neo-baroque' device, demanding a clarity of horizontal movement and the presence of systematic imitation. Ostinato figures and long pedal notes also indicate neo-classic devices. This series was meant as a free adaptation of such 'baroque' devices applied to Brazilian folk music.

Among Villa-Lobos's Brazilian contemporaries, Oscar Lorenzo Fernândez, Luciano Gallet, and Francisco Mignone represent the folk-music orientation of their time. The best known composers of the next generation include Camargo Guarnieri, Luiz Cosme, Radamés Gnatalli, and José Siqueira.

The 1910 revolution had an extraordinary impact on Mexico's artistic life. As a result of patriotic fervour musicians adhered to musical nationalism whose sources of expression were sought in either Indian or mestizo cultures. Manuel M. Ponce (1882–1948), considered the pioneer of nationalism in Mexico, drew on all types of mestizo folk music incorporated into a neo-Romantic style. The post-revolutionary period saw the emergence of the so-called Aztec Renaissance and the consequent *indianista* movement in the arts. Carlos Chávez (b. 1899), the most influential Mexican composer of the twentieth century has been particularly successful in evoking subjectively the remote past, character, and cultural setting of the pre-conquest Indian. His works of clear Indian inspiration comprise the ballet *Los cuatro soles* (The Four

Ages), *Sinfonía India*, *Xochipilli-Macuilxóchitl* ('An Imagined Aztec Music'), a Piano Concerto, and the well known Toccata for percussion, rearranged as a ballet and titled *Tóxcatl*. In his most abstract compositions such as his *Sinfonía de Antígona*, *La hija de Cólquide* (The daughter of Colchis), his Violin Concerto, and numerous piano pieces, Chávez's highly personal style and Mexican sense appear so intimately connected that his music has been characterized as 'profoundly non-European'. As a conductor he has also had a brilliant career. He founded the Orquesta Sinfónica de México in 1928 and directed it for over eighteen years. Chávez's contemporary, Silvestre Revueltas (1899–1940), became internationally known especially through his works *Ocho por Radio* and *Sensemayá*.

Outstanding Cuban composers associated with nationalism were Amadeo Roldán (1900–39) and Alejandro García Caturla (1906–40) who found in Afro-Cuban music the most suitable source of national expression. José Ardévol (b. 1911) assumed a position of leadership in Cuba as a composer and teacher from the 1930s to the middle 1950s, founding in Havana the *Grupo Renovación Musical* (1943) which promoted contemporary music and rejected nationalism.

Musical nationalism in Chile is represented mainly by Pedro Humberto Allende (1885–1959), who utilized native elements within an impressionist style, Carlos Lavín (1883–1961), and Próspero Bisquertt (1881–1959). The best known Chilean composers, however, are Domingo Santa Cruz (b. 1899) and Juan Orrego-Salas (b. 1919), both of neo-classic rather than nationalist tendencies. Santa Cruz has laid the foundation of professional musical life in his country through the promotion of music education and the creation of music and concert societies. His large production as a composer includes mostly abstract works for symphony orchestra, chamber and choral works. Orrego-Salas's output comprises a large number of chamber works, such as his *Sonata a quattro*, Op. 55 (1964), three symphonies, ballets, choral pieces, and an opera.

Nationalistic tendencies emerged in Argentina in the works of Alberto Williams (1862–1952), the most prolific and influential composer of his generation, and of Arturo Berutti (1862–1938), who treated national themes in his operas (*Pampa, Yupanki*). Alberto Ginastera (b. 1916), one of the leading creative personalities in contemporary Latin-American music, has evolved from a nationalistic orientation in the 1930s and 1940s (in such works as *Impresiones de la Puna*, the ballets *Panambi* and *Estancia*, the series of *Pampeanas*) to a neo-classical current in the 1950s (a Piano Sonata, *Variaciones concertantes*, and others). In the 1960s he turned to an effective manipulation of atonal and serial

42

techniques, mixed with a meticulous preoccupation with timbres (*Cantata para América Mágica*, a Piano Concerto, a Violin Concerto, the operas *Don Rodrigo*, *Bomarzo*, and *Beatrix Cenci*). In some works, such as *Estudios sinfónicos*, Op. 35 (1967), he combined serial and microtonal textures with fixed and aleatory structures.

MODERNISM AND THE *AVANT-GARDE*

In opposition to the prevailing nationalist current, a number of Latin-American composers active in the 1940s and 1950s practised an abstract style through neo-classic, dodecaphonic, and post-Webernian serialist idioms. In Argentina Juan Carlos Paz (b. 1897), one of the founders of the *Grupo Renovación* and the *Agrupación Nueva Música*, favoured the expressionistic aesthetic and became already in 1930 a strong supporter and follower of twelve-note techniques. In Chile Carlos Isamitt (b. 1887), though interested in Indian materials did not neglect serial techniques; and Gustavo Becerra (b. 1925) cultivated expressionist atonality and serialism before engaging himself actively in experimental music.

In Brazil Schoenberg's theories were first introduced by the German-born composer Hans-Joachim Koellreutter (b. 1915) and followed in the 1940s by such composers as Claudio Santoro (b. 1919) and César Guerra-Peixe (b. 1914). Among the younger generation Edino Krieger (b. 1928) has found some interesting compromises within a modernistic neo-classic style, as shown by his first string quartet of 1956. The Argentineans Roberto García Morillo (b. 1911) and Roberto Caamaño (b. 1925) represent the same tendency. The Colombian Luis Antonio Escobar (b. 1925) has alternated his style from a neo-classic trend to a post-Webern serialism. In Peru an internationalist current appears with composers such as Enrique Iturriaga (b. 1918), Celso Garrido Lecca (b. 1926), Enrique Pinilla (b. 1927), and others, while in Uruguay the most advanced techniques of composition have been used by León Biriotti (b. 1929) and Sergio Cervetti (b. 1940).

Avant-garde tendencies have emerged especially in Argentina, Chile, Brazil, Uruguay, Peru, and Mexico. In spite of the limited means of the Latin-American scene for experiments in new music, numerous young composers (several of them active in Europe or the U.S.A.) have advocated and used electronic musical resources, aleatory techniques, and indeterminacy, thus breaking definitely with musical nationalism.

VIII

MUSIC IN THE SOVIET UNION

By GERALD ABRAHAM

THE POLITICAL BACKGROUND

FEW events in political history have produced such fundamental cultural consequences as the October 1917 Revolution in Russia. But the consequences followed only by very slow degrees, except in so far as individual composers were concerned. Stravinsky was abroad and decided to stay there; Rakhmaninov went into self-imposed exile in December and was followed the next year by Prokofyev (though not before he had conducted the first performance of his Classical Symphony in April 1918). These departures, like the deaths during 1914–18 of Lyadov, Skryabin, Taneyev and Cui, impoverished Russian musical life and seemed to draw a line under the end of an epoch; but a great deal in the new Russia was for some time very much like the old so far as music was concerned. Glazunov (1865–1936) remained at the head of the Petrograd Conservatoire, Mikhail Ippolitov-Ivanov (1859–1935) became president of the Society of Writers and Composers in 1922 and remained director of the Moscow Conservatoire until 1924, when he returned to Tiflis to organize musical life in the Georgian Republic; Reinhold Glier (1875–1956) was director of the Kiev Conservatoire until his transfer to Moscow in 1920. All three were Rimsky-Korsakov pupils. A fourth, Nikolay Myaskovsky (1881–1950) was still in the Army and not demobilized until 1921. Rimsky-Korsakov's son-in-law, Maximilian Steinberg (1883–1946) was the principal composition professor at Petrograd and became Director of the (by this time Leningrad) Conservatoire in 1934. From the very first the cultural policy of the new régime was directed by Lunacharsky, who was no enemy of 'bourgeois culture', and when the Commissariat of Education formed a music section in July 1918 its first head was Arthur Lourié (1892–1966), a disciple of Debussy, Skryabin, and Schoenberg. The pre-Revolutionary academics and the pre-Revolutionary *avant-garde* might have been supposed to have no enemies but each other. Even the earliest experiment in 'proletarian culture', the movement known as *Proletkult* (1918–23), largely directed to the training of workers and peasants in writing and the practice of the arts in naïve 'leftist' directions, was tempered by the common sense of some of its leaders; these included Aleksandr Kastalsky (1856–1926), an authority on choral music and folk-song, whose choral folk-song arrangements were deservedly popular during the nineteen-twenties. So long as the Civil War and Polish War lasted, that is, until 1921, composers were more concerned with the production of music of this kind, and 'mass-songs' for or about the Red Army or the workers, than with symphony or opera. The mass-songs of this period not only served as models for the later ones of Aleksandr Aleksandrov (1883–1946) (who in 1940 was to compose the 'Hymn of the Soviet Union') and other composers, but often left their broad, undistinguished, diatonic stamp on Soviet symphony and opera when these appeared.

The end of the fighting brought a period of relative relaxation, stock-taking, and policy-formulating. Lenin had said that

Art belongs to the people. It must penetrate with its deepest roots into the very thick of the broad working masses. It must be understandable by these masses and loved by them. It must unite the feeling, thought and will of these masses, inspire them. It must awaken in them artists and develop them.[1]

These are admirable sentiments, which many eminent Russians, from Chernïshevsky and Mussorgsky to Stasov and Tolstoy, would have endorsed; but, like so many utterances of politicians, they are capable of various interpretations. In one sense it was easy to see what should be done—and, so far as music was concerned, it was done with a thoroughness that put the rest of the world to cultural shame. Musical education in the widest sense was put within the reach of all and professional musical education raised to the highest imaginable level. 'The masses' were brought into opera-house and concert-hall, and not only choirs and orchestras of popular instruments but symphony orchestras and string quartets were sent to factories and barracks. But the questions 'What music is to be understood and loved by the masses? What should be the nature of the music of our Brave New World?' remained unanswered. Lenin himself knew there were no quick answers, and in 1921 he gave a public warning that 'cultural problems cannot be decided as quickly as political and military problems',[2] but there were two bodies who were confident they knew the answers: the [later: Rossiyskaya] Assotsiatsiya proletarskikh muzïkantov (Association of Proletarian Musicians: known as APM or RAPM) founded in 1923, and the Assotsiatsiya sovremennoy muzïki (Association for Contemporary Music: ASM) founded in 1924, the year when Western

[1] O literature i iskusstve (Moscow, 1957), p. 583.
[2] Sochineniya, xxxiii (Moscow, 1950), p. 55.

musicians began to visit the Soviet Union and full cultural contacts with the outside world were made. APM was the successor to, and in some respects the negation of, *Proletkult*. *Proletkult* had believed in bringing the workman and the peasant to art, including contemporary art; RAPM not only detested contemporary music but denounced the classics as 'bourgeois' and had little use even for national folk-art; to them 'Soviet music' was music immediately comprehensible to the simple workman or peasant. ASM stood for the 'contemporary' in the international sense and became closely associated with the International Society for Contemporary Music. It held that 'music is not ideology' and defended the autonomy of the creative musician. Naturally each body suffered internal dissensions and secessions—ASM, for instance, had a more conservative wing in which Myaskovsky, Yury Shaporin (1887–1966), and Vissarion Shebalin (1902–63) were prominent—and some of the older composers (Glazunov, Glier, Ippolitov-Ivanov) and their followers kept aloof from both, preserving 'active neutrality'. But broadly speaking these two bodies polarized the main opposing tendencies throughout the nineteen-twenties and early nineteen-thirties. Thanks to the greater influence of ASM, particularly in Leningrad, Soviet Russia was able during 1925–8, the period of maximum artistic freedom, to hear such operas as Schreker's *Der ferne Klang*, Prokofyev's *Love for Three Oranges,* Křenek's *Der Sprung über den Schatten, Wozzeck, Le roi David, Mavra* and *Oedipus Rex, Jonny spielt auf* and the *Dreigroschenoper.* 'Persimfans', the conductorless Moscow orchestra which flourished for ten years or so from 1922, played not only the classics but Bartók, Skryabin, Stravinsky, Honegger, Ravel, Falla, and Prokofyev.

The 'modernist' wing of ASM included Skryabin's old champion, the critic Leonid Sabaneyev, and Lev Knipper (b. 1898), Nikolay Roslavets (1881–1944), Alexander Mosolov (b. 1900), Leonid Polovinkin (1894–1949), and Gavriil Popov (b. 1904) among the composers. The real founder of ASM, Boris Asafyev ('Igor Glebov') (1884–1949), the doyen of Soviet musical criticism, played an ambiguous rôle: conservative and uninspired as a composer, he was at first the critical champion of advanced Western modernism but as early as 1924[1] he began to sound warnings about the dangers of subjective composition and holding aloof from the masses, and by the mid-nineteen-thirties he had become one of the severest critics of everything ASM had stood for. RAPM was at first insignificant both numerically and in the nature of its membership; its only distinguished original member, Kastalsky, died

---

[1] 'Krizis lichnovo tvorchestva', *Sovremennaya muzïka* (1924) no. 4, p. 98, and 'Kompozitorï, pospeshite', ibid., no. 6, p. 146.

in 1926. It was only in 1929, when it was reinforced by the *Prokoll*,[1] a group of young graduates from the Moscow Conservatoire—including Alexander Davidenko (1899–1934), Boris Shekhter (1900–61), Viktor Bely (b. 1904), Dmitry Kabalevsky (b. 1904), and Marian Koval (1907–1971)—that it began to carry much professional weight,[2] though its ideals naturally appealed to a much bigger public than those of ASM. The battle was already going badly for the 'contemporaries'; their organ *Sovremennaya muzïka*, founded in 1924, ceased publication in 1929, and in 1931—weakened by the secession of Myaskovsky and Shebalin—ASM finally collapsed. But the triumph of RAPM was short-lived; it was intolerant, dictatorial, and many of its members were technically incompetent. Under the 'proletarian' régime, standards at the Moscow Conservatoire fell so low that composition-students needed to offer only two or three mass-songs as their leaving exercise.[3]

Parallel struggles had been going on in literature and the other arts and on 23 April 1932 the Central Committee of the All-Union Communist Party stepped in. In 1925, while expressing pious hopes for the future 'hegemony' of proletarian writers, it had resolved that 'the Party cannot connect itself in any way with any tendency in the domain of literary form. . . . A style corresponding to the epoch will be created but it will be created by other methods; the solution of the problem is not yet in sight. . . . The Party must declare for the free rivalry of different groups and tendencies. . . . The Party cannot allow a monopoly by any group whatever, even to that which is proletarian in ideology: this would lead in the first place to the ruin of proletarian literature'.[4] Now it took Soviet culture firmly in hand and put an end to both crude proletarian art and sophisticated contemporary 'formalism' (art for art's sake). Before long Soviet artists and writers were given a phrase of Gorky's as their slogan: 'Socialist realism'. Soviet art must be understandable and loved by the masses, but it must be worthy of its ancestry in classic Russian and world art; and by its strength and optimism it must help to build socialism. The artistic debate was henceforth not between creeds but about the correct interpretation of the only true creed. RAPM was dissolved and the Union of Soviet Composers was established in order to safeguard 'socialist realism' in Soviet music.

[1] Portmanteau form of 'Proizvodstvenny kollektiv studentov-kompozitorov Moskovskoy konservatorii' (Production group of the student-composers of the Moscow Conservatoire), founded in 1926: see Sergey Ryauzov, 'Vospominaniya o "Prokolle" ', *Sovetskaya muzïka*, (1949), no. 7, p. 54.

[2] The RAPM programme at this moment of triumph is translated by Nicolas Slonimsky, *Music since 1900* (3rd edition, New York, 1949), p. 655.

[3] See the collective work, *Istoriya russkoy sovetskoy muzïki*, i (Moscow, 1956), p. 58.

[4] Resolution of 18 March 1925.

THE BEGINNINGS OF SOVIET OPERA AND BALLET

During its first decade Soviet opera[1] had practically only one theme, revolution, and its dramaturgy was hardly more sophisticated than that of the 'Western' film. One of the aberrations of the early nineteen-twenties was the performance of operatic classics with new, 'revolutionary' libretti; thus *Tosca* was produced at Leningrad in 1924 as *Borba za Kommunu* (The Fight for the Commune). Similarly *Les Huguenots*, which under Nicholas I had had to be disguised as *I Guelfi e i Ghibellini*, now appeared as *Dekabristï* (The Decembrists). The centenary in 1925 of the Decembrist rising, however, also suggested two new operas, Vasily Zolotarev's *Dekabristï* which was produced in that year and Shaporin's *Pauline Goebel*, of which only a few scenes were produced at the time. (It had to wait till 1938 before even the first version was nearly completed under the title *Dekabristï*.)[2] 1925 was the true birth-year of Soviet opera, for it saw not only the 'Decembrist' works but Andrey Pashchenko's *Orliny bunt* (The Eagles' Revolt), Peter Triodin's *Stepan Razin*, and *Za Krasny Petrograd* (For Red Petrograd) by Arseny Gladkovsky and E. V. Prussak. These were not actually the first new operas after the Revolution; but Triodin's *Knyaz Serebryany*, based on A. K. Tolstoy's historical novel (1923), and Yurasovsky's *Trilby* (1924)[3] neither belonged to the new age nor possessed the breath of life. Pashchenko's opera on the Pugachev rising, Triodin's second opera, and the Gladkovsky-Prussak picture of the defenders of Petrograd against the White army under Yudenich also failed to survive, but the last has at least historic interest as the earliest opera on a Soviet theme. The score was mainly the work of Gladkovsky (1894–1945), a competent conventional composer, while his collaborator Prussak contributed some grotesque, satirical music for the Whites; their fighting heroine, Dasha, is characterized by music suggesting revolutionary workers' songs and her comrades by quotations from the Internationale and 'Yablochko' (The little apple), the enemy by 'Vzveytes, sokolï, orlami' (Soar, hawks, like eagles), a song popular in the White armies. However, after thirteen performances, the opera succumbed to protests from both modernists and *Proletkult*. Gladkovsky's later version of it, *Front i tïl* (Front and Rear) (1930) 'does not contain one single Soviet man who is given individual characterization'.[4] Pashchenko (b. 1885) was more

---

[1] On early Soviet operas see the chapter by I. Rïzhkin and S. Levit in *Istoriya russkoy sovetskoy muzïki*, i, p. 155, and M. Iordansky, P. Kozlov, and V. Taranushchenko, 'K probleme sovetskoy opere', *Sovetskaya muzïka* (1933), no. 1, p. 19.

[2] See p. 688.

[3] In this chapter the dates of operas are those of the first production; for all other works the dates are those of composition.

[4] Rïzhkin, op. cit., p. 187.

successful with his Pugachev opera,[1] not so much with the individual
characters as with the broad folk-songish crowd-scenes; it was performed all over Russia and held the stage for ten years or so. His Civil
War opera, *Cherny yar* (The Black Crag) (1931) was a failure.
Zolotarev's *Dekabristï* also survived at least into the mid-nineteen-
thirties. A minor pupil of Rimsky-Korsakov, Zolotarev (1873–1934) had
a real, if unoriginal vein of lyrical-elegiac melody which enabled him to
make the Decembrist poet Rïleyev, the real hero of the opera, a live and
sympathetic character. Inability to create character in musical terms
was the general failing of the Soviet opera-composers of this period.
Even when given strong literary characters, such as Ivan Shishov
(1888–1947) found for his *Tupeyny khudozhnik* (The Toupee Artist)
(1929) in Leskov's terrible story of the love of a serf-hairdresser for a
serf-actress, they are apt to be musically lost against their social background, though Shishov comes near to success in a quintet for the
fugitive lovers Lyuba and Arkady, the wretched priest and his wife who
have betrayed their hiding-place, and the enraged Count:

Ex. 264

[1] See Asafyev's article in *Zhizn iskusstva*, 1925, no. 46, reprinted in his *Izbrannïe trudï*, v
(Moscow, 1957), p. 113.

Go - - re gor - ko - e.
Oy!   mya - tezh - ni - ki!
pro - - - - u - chu ya ikh
Akh! tï do - lyush - ka
Akh!

(*Lyuba:* Oh, the lot of the
un-free, bitter woe.
Priest and Wife: Disobedi-
ent! Rebels!
Count: I'll teach them.
Arkady: Bitter woe. Oh, the
lot of the un-free.)

Yet another work in a similar old-fashioned nationalist idiom and with
a little life, at least in the heroine, was *Prorïv* (The Break-Through, i.e.
of Mamontov's cavalry, raiding far in the rear of the Red Army in 1919)
(1930) by Sergey Pototsky (b. 1883). *Tupeyny khudozhnik* at least
brought a refreshing change from the themes of revolt and civil war.
Aleksandr Krein (1883–1951) and Sergey Vasilenko (1872–1956) sought
variety by transposing the themes into other lands—in Krein's opera
Zagmuk (1929), into a far distant age as well: the revolt of Babylonian
slaves against their Assyrian oppressors. In *Sïn solntsa* (Son of the Sun,
also 1929) Vasilenko turned to the China of the Boxer Rising, with a
tragic love-affair between a Boxer hero and Aurora Walter, daughter of
the American General Hamilton; ten years later he produced a parallel
piece, *Buran*, about the struggle of the Uzbeks with the 'Tsarist
colonizers'.

The settings of Krein's and Vasilenko's operas also allowed alter-
natives to Russian musical idioms; Vasilenko's Boxers were predominantly pentatonic. Throughout the nineteen-twenties the basic
language of Soviet opera was not unnaturally that of the quarter-
century before the Revolution, which in turn had been on the whole a
period of conservatism and epigonism. The only new elements were the
militant mass-songs, the 'leftist' pop-art modernism of *Proletkult*, and
'contemporary Western' modernism; and these new elements were
generally associated with Bolsheviks and their supporters. Opera-
production tended to be 'modernistic', sometimes incongruously at
variance with the music, particularly in Leningrad. The least conventional works, no doubt inspired conceptually if not musically by
Stravinsky's *Histoire d'un soldat*, were Klimenty Korchmarev's *Ivan-
soldat* (1927) and Pashchenko's *Tsar Maximilian* (1929), satirical essays

in musical folk-theatre, with clowning and popular song. The impact in 1930 of Dmitry Shostakovich's *Nos* (The Nose) (after Gogol's story) and Knipper's *Severny veter* (North Wind), the one grotesquely comic and with no political content, the other tragic—based on the never forgotten or forgiven shooting of the Baku commissars—but both genuinely contemporary in musical idiom, must have been severe. Their jagged, nearly atonal melodic lines, motor-rhythms and dissonant harmony come from the world of Hindemith and Prokofyev, Křenek and Stravinsky's *Mavra*; even the diatonic banalities of *The Nose* are more likely to have their roots in Křenek than in *Proletkult*. Ex. 265 shows the hotchpotch of styles in which the only common factor is anti-romanticism: (i) parody coloratura *à la Mavra* and Hindemithian counterpoint; (ii) from the *galop* interlude preceding the solemn sounds of the scene in the Kazan Cathedral where the Nose sings (i).

Ex. 265 (i)

(What do you mean? Explain.)

(ii)

Molto allegro ($\stackrel{.}{\sqcap} = 106$)

It must, however, be remembered that caricature by means of parody and the grotesque was by no means always inspired from the West; it was constantly employed—for instance, in *Za Krasny Petrograd* as we have seen—against the past and present enemies of the Revolution by composers who were anything but modernists.

Soviet ballet[1] can claim a longer history than Soviet opera, for Asafyev, who had composed four ballets in pre-Revolutionary days, wrote a *Carmagnole* during the first winter of the new régime and produced it with piano—played by himself—in a Petrograd workers' club on the first anniversary of the October Revolution. After that, Asafyev contented himself for a long time with the compilation of ballet-scores from the music of better composers (Grieg, Tchaïkovsky) and returned to original composition only in 1932 with *Plamya Parizha* (The Flames of Paris), after which came *Bakhchisaraysky fontan* (The Fountain of Bakhchisaray, after Pushkin) (1934)[2] and a series of works which all failed to achieve lasting success. Vasilenko and Korchmarev also tried their hands at ballet. Vasilenko's second effort, *Iosif prekrasny* (based on the Old Testament story of Joseph), was the first new ballet to

---

[1] On the early Soviet ballets, see M. Rittikh in *Istoriya*, i, p. 202.

[2] Asafyev's own accounts of these works are reprinted in *Izbrannïe trudï*, v (Moscow, 1957), pp. 138 and 141.

be staged at the Bolshoy in Moscow after the Revolution (March 1925); and Korchmarev's *Krepostnaya balerina* (The Serf Ballerina) (1927), another glorification of the Pugachev rising, won success through its beautiful, folk-songish score. But by far the most successful Soviet ballet of this period was Glier's *Krasny mak* (The Red Poppy) (1927; revised version, 1949), set in contemporary China, with wicked imperialists and reactionaries and splendid Soviet sailors; part of its success was no doubt due to the ballerina Ekaterina Geltser, who danced the Chinese heroine; but Glier's score included numbers such as the 'Dance of the Soviet Sailors' (variations on the popular song 'Yablochko') which became popular on their own account.

EARLY SOVIET ORCHESTRAL MUSIC [1]

The earliest, and for thirty years the senior, Soviet composer of symphonies was Myaskovsky.[2] He may not cut a very impressive figure when seen in world-perspective but, compared with most of the composers whose operas and ballets have just been enumerated, he was outstanding: a master of his craft, fertile in invention, mildly original in thought, a genuine supporter of the Revolution, though far from being a revolutionary in music. His pre-war compositions had been subjective, rather pessimistic in tone, and couched in a late-romantic idiom influenced by middle-period Skryabin. Of the two symphonies, Nos. 4 and 5, which he wrote at Revel in the first half of 1918, No. 5 in D—bright and idyllic, with humour and suggestions of folk-music—suggests a new departure and has been seen as 'the beginning of Soviet symphonism'; but the idea of 'a quiet symphony (E, G, D?) in four movements; *Andante* mysterious, with chief theme of lullaby character' had come to him in April 1914.[3] The Sixth Symphony, completed in 1923, was a different matter. There are still subjective elements; the two middle movements were written under the direct impression of the deaths of two persons very dear to the composer; the middle section of the second suggests a mysticism akin to Holst's:

---

[1] See particularly 'Glebov', 'Russkaya simfonicheskaya muzïka za 10 let', *Muzïka i revolyutsiya* (1927), no. 11; Viktor Belyaev, '10 let russkoy simfonicheskoy muzïki', *Sovremennaya muzïka* (1927), no. 24.

[2] The chief source of information about Myaskovsky is *N. Y. Myaskovsky: stati, pisma, vospominaniya*, edited by S. Shlifshteyn, two vols. (Moscow, 1959 and 1960). There is a good short survey of his work by Kabalevsky in *Sovetskaya muzïka* (1951), no. 4, p. 18, reprinted in M. A. Grinberg (ed.), *Sovetskaya simfonicheskaya muzïka* (Moscow, 1955), p. 36. On the first twelve symphonies see particularly Tamara Livanova in *Istoriya*, i. p. 233; on the later symphonies see ibid. ii, p. 384, iii, p. 359, and iv (2), p. 235. Studies in periodicals are very numerous.

[3] Shlifshteyn, op. cit. ii, p. 394.

Ex. 266

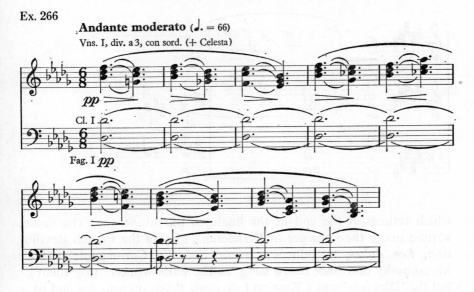

and the main theme of the third:

Ex. 267

which returns at the end of the finale, is Skryabinesque. The finale, written under the influence of Verhaeren's play of the French Revolution, *Les Aubes*, introduces 'Ça ira' and 'La Carmagnole' (which Myaskovsky had once heard sung 'as the Paris workers sing them'),[1] but the 'Dies irae' and a Russian folk-song, taken up near the end by a chorus, which sings of the soul being parted from the body and going before the judgement of God, seem to triumph over the revolutionary songs. On the other hand, the Symphony is undeniably 'monumental' in scale and conception; it contains a great deal of lyrical diatonic music; the end can be construed as an apotheosis of those who gave their lives for the Revolution. Modelled on Berlioz rather than Mahler, whose music Myaskovsky knew but considered 'rather banal',[2] it is the recognized forerunner of the various 'monumental' Soviet symphonies that have come since. Livanova compares it with Blok's poem 'The Twelve' 'not only in the analogous treatment of the theme, but for its place in the history of Soviet art';[3] both are documents of a period when a portion of the *intelligentsiya* were still preoccupied with a 'sacrificial' conception of the Revolution.

Myaskovsky's later symphonies were not all so acceptable. No. 8 (1925), based largely on appropriate folk-songs, reflects—like the contemporary operas of Pashchenko and Triodin—the current interest in historical peasant-risings, in this case Stepan Razin's. But the one-movement No. 10 (1927), inspired by the crazy hero of Pushkin's 'Bronze Horseman', was regarded as a deviation in the direction of 'false modernism', and No. 11 (1932) was (as he admitted) 'subjective'.

---

[1] Shlifshteyn, op. cit. i, p. 198, and ii, p. 15. The author of the thematic analysis of the Sixth Symphony in the ASM organ, *Sovremennaya muzïka* (1924), no. 3, p. 86, failed to recognize either tune. See also M. Tarakanov, 'Shestaya simfoniya N. Y. Myaskovskovo', *Sovetskaya muzïka* (1956), no. 7, p. 11.

[2] Shlifshteyn, op. cit. i, p. 211.　　　[3] Livanova, op. cit., p. 245.

He made amends in the lyrical No. 12 (1932), conceived as a 'Collective Farm' Symphony and dedicated 'To the Fifteenth Anniversary of the October Revolution'.

Throughout the nineteen-twenties Soviet orchestral music maintained a more 'modernistic' line than opera. The 'proletarians' were not interested in the symphony and the symphonists felt no strong compulsion to indulge in musical ideology. Beside Myaskovsky among the more conservative members of ASM stood his talented pupil Shebalin, who produced two very Myaskovskian symphonies (1925 and 1929)—Myaskovskian in their leaping, energetic *allegro* themes, their plastic, long-drawn lyrical ones, their chromatic harmony, and their slightly incongruous folk-elements—and a much older man, Aleksandr Gedike (1877–1957), organist and Bach scholar, whose Third Symphony (1922) and Concerto for organ and strings (1926) are solid, academic works. But there were orchestral essays in more modern idiom, such as Knipper's *Skazki gipsovovo Buddï* (Tales of the Plaster Buddha) (1924) and D minor Symphony (1929), Mikhail Gnesin's *Simfonichesky monument: 1905–1917* (with chorus singing a poem by Esenin) (1925), Krein's First Symphony (1925) and *Traurnaya oda* (Funeral Ode—for Lenin) (1926), Polovinkin's *Teleskopï I, II,* and *III*[1] (1926–8), and Shebalin's earlier symphonies (1926 and 1928). Modernistic in a more vulgar sense, betraying the influence of *Proletkult*—which gladly accepted 'modernistic constructivism', the 'neo-classicism' of the West, as an alternative to 'individualistic subjectivism' (bourgeois romanticism)—was Mosolov's ballet suite *Stal* (Steel) (1926), perhaps an attempt to emulate Prokofyev's *Pas d'acier*; the first movement of this suite the noisy, realistic 'Zavod' (Foundry), achieved a notoriety, even outside the Soviet Union, far beyond its deserts.

However, the outstanding orchestral work of the nineteen-twenties, the only one to win world recognition and establish a permanent place in the repertory, was the First Symphony (1925) of Steinberg's young pupil Shostakovich (b. 1906).[2] The F minor Symphony was his 'diploma work' on leaving the Petrograd Conservatoire and some of the material is nearly identical with that of still earlier works, such as the Piano Trio, Op. 8 (1923). It is eclectic in the sense that the music of any young composer is eclectic: one easily detects the shades of this or that older Russian composer or of Prokofyev. But, whereas in the later *Nose* the

---

[1] 'For me a telescope is a symbol for gazing into the distance or at great manifestations—often the same thing', the composer explained: 'K moemu avtorskomu kontsertu', *Sovremennaya muzïka* (1928), no. 30, p. 140.

[2] On Shostakovich's symphonies, see particularly Genrikh Orlov, *Simfonïï Shostakovicha* (Leningrad, 1961) which has an excellent bibliography, and (on the first six only) M. D. Sabinina, *Simfonizm Shostakovicha: put k zrelosti* (Moscow, 1965).

influences are heterogeneous, in the Symphony they are homogeneous and have been so far absorbed that a clear and new musical personality is revealed. The symphony is 'pure'—or, as a Soviet critic would say, 'formalistic'—music, marked as Asafyev pointed out[1] by 'the rare quality of laconicism' and the ability to 'seize upon the characteristic quality of a thought and reveal it plastically'; it was only years later that Soviet critics began to discover its 'heroic-tragic' nature and the 'festively monumental style' of its conclusion.

Shostakovich's next two symphonies were by no means 'pure' music. The Second ('October') Symphony (1927)—the first and only edition (Moscow, 1927) is entitled 'To October: symphonic dedication', with no claim that it is a 'symphony'—and the Third ('First of May') (1929) are both single-movement works, each with a final chorus. Each is marked by a good deal of brass declamation against bustling, washed-in backgrounds; each has a curious little quasi-*concertino* episode for solo instruments unaccompanied (in the Second, violin, clarinet, and bassoon; in the Third, piccolo, oboe, clarinet, and bassoon). But there are also considerable differences. The Second opens Largo, with a remarkable built-up sound of muted strings, *ppp*, against which a solo trumpet begins to declaim an angular theme. The main Allegro, indicated only by a new metronome mark ($\bf{J} = 152$), begins in the manner of the First Symphony, but the *concertino* episode develops in pure counterpoint:

Ex. 268

[1] 'Glebov', 'Russkaya simfonicheskaya muzïka'.

which soon reaches eleven independent parts. A great climax is reached and then a transition effected for the entrance of the chorus, which sings a typical *Proletkult* slogan-poem by Bezïmensky. The final words,

> There is the banner, the name of the living generations:
> October,
> The Commune
> and Lenin

are shouted, not sung. The music of this section, of which Ex. 269 (from near the end)—'October! Herald of the wished-for sun'—gives a fair idea:

Ex. 269

is purely diatonic, in the strongest contrast to what has gone before.
Whatever the composer may have intended, the effect is that of an ASM
orchestral piece with RAPM finale, and the work was at first actually
accepted—with reservations—by both parties. The Third Symphony is
a more successful attempt to integrate Shostakovich's earlier style with
a proletarian one. The idiom is essentially, if somewhat eccentrically,
diatonic throughout. Some features, such as the opening clarinet call,
suggest the impact of Mahler, whose symphonies had been performed
several times in Leningrad during 1925–7: the already known Fifth
once (1925), the Fourth once (1927), and the Second three times (1926).
The purely instrumental part of Shostakovich's Third is merely a string
of episodes, which forecast—they were not (as some Soviet critics
have claimed) influenced by—his successful activity as a composer of
film- and theatre-music. But they are not, at any rate in intention,
formalistic; one can guess their meaning. The unaccompanied duet for
two clarinets, following the solo call, obviously evokes the breath of
spring:

Ex. 270

A trumpet calls, inevitably, and keeps on calling; human excitement
grows. A march for brass and side-drum suggests the gathering for a
meeting; the twittering quasi-*concertino* that interrupts it perhaps
represents young Pioneers, but it leads not to anything like Ex. 268 but
to a quiet episode slightly reminiscent of the second subject of the First
Symphony. The climax of the instrumental part seems intended to
suggest the excitement of a vast May Day meeting, the entire orchestra
in octaves against an *fff* roll on side-drum and kettle-drum (high G)
declaiming rhetorical, quasi-recitative phrases punctuated by the *fff*
cannon-shots of a bass-drum:

Ex. 271

The chorus then sings Kirsanov's May Day poem in block harmonies or unison.

The Third Symphony was unlucky in that its first performance was delayed till November 1931, only five months before the proclamation of the ideal of 'socialist realism'. On 15 February 1932 Shostakovich announced in *Sovetskoe iskusstvo* that he had begun 'a great symphonic poem with orchestra, chorus and solo vocal numbers. Its theme is "From Karl Marx to our own days"'. The words had been written by a *Proletkult* poet, Nikolay Aseyev, and the first of the five parts was already composed; the work was intended to last an entire evening. But *Proletkult* was not socialist realism. How much, if any, of the music survives in other compositions, we can only conjecture.

EARLY SOVIET MUSIC IN OTHER FIELDS

Chamber music, piano music and solo song were cultivated only by the conservative academics and the modernist formalists. These kinds of music were for the few, the already cultured; they tended to express individual ideas and subjective emotion, and the proletarians were actively hostile to them. Recitals were given mainly under the aegis of ASM, but the predominant idiom was that of fastidious late-romantic lyricism.

One of the earliest post-Revolutionary string quartets must have been the veteran Glazunov's Sixth (1921). (His Seventh and last, was written in 1930 after his emigration.) Like Glier's Third (1928), it is a return to a medium abandoned a quarter of a century earlier. And quite a number of 'Soviet' chamber-compositions were really refurbishings of works written or at least sketched before the Revolution: Aleksandrov's Quartet, Op. 7, Lyapunov's Piano Sextet, the third and fourth of the quartets Myaskovsky brought out as Op. 33. (And Op. 33, nos. 1 and 2, composed about 1930, are inferior inhabitants of the same world.) Myaskovskian, too, are the Op. 2 quartet (1923) and the String Trio, Op. 4 (1924) of Shebalin, and Kabalevsky's First Quartet (1928): works of promise rather than achievement. Only in Shebalin is there a whiff of Prokofyev's brand of anti-romanticism, with tougher modernism represented by the quartets, trios, and violin sonatas of Roslavets and by Popov's Sextet.

The piano music of the period is similar in spirit but technically more accomplished. The sonatas of Myaskovsky, Anatoly Aleksandrov (b. 1888), and Samuil Feinberg (1890–1962) belong to the aesthetic worlds of Skryabin, Medtner, or Rakhmaninov. It is music for the recital-platform; later they had to learn to write in a more intimate style and for humbler performers. Nothing could be in sharper contrast with this refined if rather etiolated art than the early piano works of Shostakovich, the *Fantastic Dances*, First Sonata and *Aforizmï* (1922–7), which emulate by turns Prokofyev, Stravinsky, and Hindemith.[1] The two wings of ASM piano music may be illustrated by (i) the opening of Feinberg's Prelude, op. 8, No. 1, (ii) the opening of the slow movement of Shostakovich's First Sonata:

---

[1] For a 'socialist-realist' judgement on these works and their immediate successors, see Mikhail Druskin, 'O fortepiannom tvorchestve D. Shostakovicha', *Sovetskaya muzïka* (1935), no. 11, p. 52.

Ex. 272

(i)

sempre marcato e cantando

(ii)

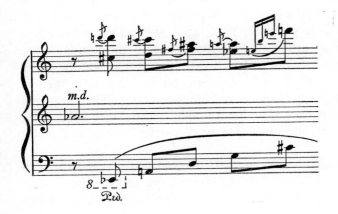

Both were written in 1926; both were objectionable to the proletarians. Equally objectionable was another piano-piece of the same year: the 'coarsely naturalistic' railway noises of *Relsï* (The Rails), by the *Prolet-kult* composer Vladimir Deshevov (1889–1955). Polovinkin, always more original in his titles (for instance, his *Elektrifikat* for piano) than in his music, having composed four sonatas during 1924–6, marked the 'crisis in the Soviet piano sonata' by naming No. 5 (1928) *Poslednyaya sonata* (Last Sonata).

All these piano composers, with one exception, composed also for voice and piano. (The exception was Shostakovich, whose solo songs of the nineteen-twenties—settings of two Krïlov fables (1921–2), which already show his gift for satire, and of Japanese poems (1928)—have orchestral accompaniment.) To them we must add one too-little known composer, Vasily Nechaev (1895–1956), a true song-writer who is at his best in his Blok and Esenin settings of 1926–8. Their choice of poets was symptomatic; instead of the young Soviet poets, they generally preferred translations from the Japanese or of Sappho, the Russian classics and (above all) the Symbolists and 'Perfectionists'—Balmont, Blok, Gippius, Akhmatova. The music is essentially a continuation of the polished Russian art-song of the pre-Revolution period. There is no social or political awareness; even composers, such as Myaskovsky, who had shown it in their orchestral works, naturally felt free here to retreat into a private world of personal dreams and emotions. Only the egregious Mosolov set to music a collection of *Gazetnïe obyavleniya* (Newspaper advertisements) (1926). An art like theirs could hardly be expected to flourish under the triumphant proletarianism of 1929–31 or even in the freer air of early 'socialist realism'.

SOCIALIST REALISM IN OPERA

Given the Marxian postulates, reinforced by the nineteenth-century Russian view of the function of art, the Party had to lay down a new and firm literary-artistic policy in 1932; and, granted those premises, the policy was not so arbitrary as it may seem to the non-Russian. ASM had been hopelessly out of touch with 'the people'; on the other hand RAPM had not only lowered standards but had been so intolerant that, by comparison, early 'socialist realism' was liberal. The Party was at this point legislating for a situation, though, as usual with benevolent paternalism, it made no allowances for the eccentricities of exceptionally gifted children.

The composers and other creative artists even had a year or two to work out in the new Union of Soviet Composers and parallel bodies their own interpretation of 'socialist realism'. This was naturally more difficult in music than in literature, though least difficult in opera. As always at these policy changes there was trouble with works in progress. At the beginning of the nineteen-thirties two composers had been working independently on operas dealing with the serf-rising against Shuysky led by Ivan Bolotnikov in 1606: Nechaev and Valery Zhelobinsky (1913–46). Nechaev had shown very mild leanings to 'modernism' and his *Ivan Bolotnikov*, though accepted for production in 1932 by Stanislavsky, never reached the stage even in its second version of 1936–7. Zhelobinsky's *Kamarinsky muzhik*[1] was produced in 1933. His model was clearly *Boris*—there is even a Polish scene, with mazurka, and a Polish seductress; the hero was meant to be simply a symbol of the oppressed people; the idiom is predominantly vocal, folk-songish melody or melodic recitative. But, apart from the fact that Zhelobinsky was no Mussorgsky, his characters are lay-figures and he was criticized both for his failure to show Bolotnikov's connexion with the people and for his 'grotesque', 'ironical' treatment of the boyars. The comic quartet for the bass princes in scene 4, accompanied only by the orchestral basses, certainly recalls Puccini's Ping, Pang, and Pong:

Ex. 273

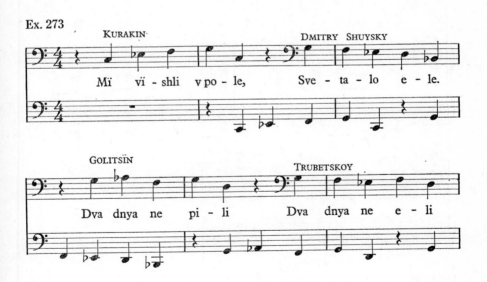

[1] See M. Glukh, '*Kamarinsky muzhik*—opera V. Zhelobinskovo', *Sovetskaya muzïka* (1934), no. 8, p. 3, and S. Levit in *Istoriya russkoy sovetskoy muzïki*, i (Moscow, 1959), pp. 176 ff.

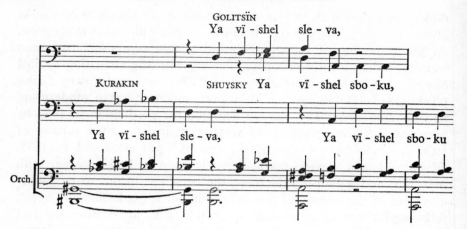

(We went out in the fields. It was scarcely daylight. For two days we didn't drink. For two days we didn't eat. I went left. I went sideways.)

The chorus of serfs in the last scene is typical of Zhelobinsky's folk-songish melodic style and flaccid harmony—and also of a great deal of other Soviet opera:

Ex. 274

(The tomtit languishes in prison; it neither eats nor drinks nor sings.)

PLATE IX

SHOSTAKOVICH'S *THE LADY MACBETH OF THE MTSENSK DISTRICT*, 1934 (*see p. 663*)

A scene from the original production in Moscow

Indeed *Kamarinsky muzhik* is in subject and musical style typical of a whole genre of Soviet operas, from Pashchenko's *Orliny bunt* onward, while his *Imeninï* (The Name-day) (1935), based on a nineteenth-century story of a serf-musician's tragedy, is an obvious attempt to emulate Shishov's *Tupeyny khudozhnik*.

These second-rate works are completely overshadowed by an opera which, whatever its faults and however adventitious its fame, is the only Soviet opera to make its way all over the world: Shostakovich's *Lady Macbeth Mtsenskovo uezda* (The Lady Macbeth of the Mtsensk District) or, to give its alternative title, *Katerina Izmaylova*.[1] Although not produced until 22 January 1934, it had been composed during 1930–2 and is marked, like the Third Symphony, by a mixture of incompatible styles. Side by side with beautiful or powerful invention, as in the passacaglia entr'acte in Act II, and Act IV as a whole—its tragic key-note sounded by the old convict's song at the beginning:

Ex. 275

(Mile after mile the long file trudges, burned by wearying heat.)

[1] See pl. IX.

there is a great deal of parodic and burlesque music, associated not only with the old Izmaylov (where it is defensible and even admirable) but with the anti-hero Sergey and the policemen of Act III. And Leskov's sombre realistic story is falsified not only by this conversion into a satire on the nineteenth-century provincial merchant-class but by the attempt to make the triple murderess Katerina a sympathetic figure. The dramatic incongruity is as marked as the musical. Yet there are master-strokes, such as the subtle recall of Katerina's song of melancholy boredom (a nice parody of the sentimental Russian 'romance' of the eighteen-forties) in the third scene of the First Act (i) when she thinks of the 'deep black lake in the forest' near the end of the last (ii):

Ex. 276

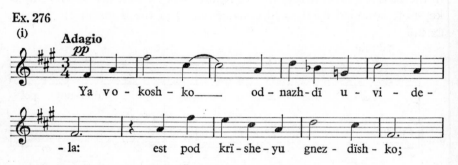

(Once from the window I saw a little nest under the eaves;)

(quite round, very deep, and its water black—like my conscience, black.)

and it is not difficult to see why, amid the operatic mediocrity of the time, it was hailed as 'a most significant landmark on the road of the creative development of Soviet musical art', a genre *sui generis*— 'tragic satire'.[1] Nevertheless when the Party in 1936 decided that composers were interpreting the directive of 1932 altogether too loosely, it was specifically at *The Lady Macbeth* and Shostakovich's recent collective-farm ballet *Svetly ruchey* (Clear Stream) that the official thunderbolts were directed. On 28 January 1936 *Pravda* printed its now historic article 'Sumbur vmesto muzïki' (Confusion instead of music)[2] asserting that 'from the first minute the listener to *The Lady Macbeth* is dumbfounded by a deliberately discordant, confused stream of sounds'; the music was 'modernist formalism' of the worst kind. The defining of 'socialist realism' was too serious a matter to be left to musicians; it was taken over by a government Committee for Artistic Affairs. The notorious modernist-formalist Mosolov, who made a public protest in a Moscow restaurant on 31 January, was unanimously expelled from the Union of Soviet Composers for drunken brawling, withdrew to Buryat-Mongolia, and reappeared as a composer of simple, conservative music only in 1939.

The opera publicly approved by Stalin and Molotov as a model Soviet opera, eleven days before the *Pravda* condemnation of *The Lady Macbeth*, was *Tikhy Don* (The Quiet Don) by Ivan Dzerzhinsky (b. 1909).[3] Based on Sholokhov's novel of Don Cossack life during the 1914 War and the Revolution, *Tikhy Don* was first produced in 1935 as a result, ironically, of the help and encouragement of Shostakovich to whom it is dedicated. Unlike earlier Soviet operas on similar subjects, it is concerned with genuine characters who are typical of the masses without being mere types; unhappily the simple lyrical score never brings them to musical life. A few bars from the episode of the soldier half-crazy from shellshock in Act III (Ex. 277) will not at all unfairly illustrate the naïve technique and dramatic impotence of the entire opera.

Apart from its wealth of rather undistinguished melody in a diluted folk-song idiom, the merits of *Tikhy Don* are mostly negative; there is no trace of any influence more modern than early Debussy; even

---

[1] A. Ostretsov, '*Lady Macbeth Mtsenskovo uezda*: opera Dmitriya Shostakovicha', *Sovetskaya muzïka* (1933), no. 6, p. 9. For a much later Russian study of the opera, see Iosif Rïzhkin in *Istoriya russkoy sovetskoy muzïki*, ii (Moscow, 1959), pp. 196 ff.

[2] Reprinted in *Sovetskaya muzïka* (1936), no. 2, p. 4, the second article, 'Baletnaya falsh', ibid. p. 6; translated excerpts from both in Gerald Abraham, *Eight Soviet Composers* (London, 1943), pp. 25–26; longer excerpt from the first, Slonimsky, op. cit., p. 402.

[3] On *Tikhy Don* and Dzerzhinsky's views on Soviet opera, see Abraham, op. cit., pp. 81 ff., A. Budyakovsky, '*Tikhy Don*' I. Dzerzhinskovo', *Sovetskaya muzïka* (1935), no. p. 11, 38, and Rïzhkin, op. cit., ii, pp. 215 ff.

Ex. 277

(Oh, have pity, I want to live, don't destroy me, give me a hand, food, stretch out your feet and I'll wash them with bitter tears.)

the reactionary Listnitskys, father and son, are not caricatured in grotesque music. Dzerzhinsky also composed an opera on the sequel to Sholokhov's novel, *Podnyataya tselina* (Virgin soil upturned) (1937)[1] but neither this nor Dzerzhinsky's later operas achieved success comparable with that of *Tikhy Don*.

The way pointed by *Tikhy Don* was followed by Oles Chishko

[1] See Budyakovsky, 'Ivan Dzerzhinsky i evo opera *Podnyataya tselina*', *Sovetskaya muzïka* (1937), no. 10–11, p. 44, and Rïzhkin, op. cit., ii, pp. 227 ff.

(b. 1895) in *Bronenosets Potemkin* (The Battleship *Potyomkin*) (1937),[1] Zhelobinsky in *Mat* (The Mother, after Gorky) (1938),[2] Leon Khodzha-Eynatov (1904–54) in *Myatezh* (The Revolt, on a story by the 'proletarian' Dmitry Furmanov) (1939) and *Semya* (The Family, based—like Chishko's opera—on a film) (1940), and Tikhon Khrennikov (b. 1913) in *V buryu* (In the Storm, based on Nikolay Virta's notable novel *Odinochestvo*) (1939).[3] Aesthetically similar to these, but refreshingly set in sixteenth-century Burgundy, is Kabalevsky's *Master iz Klamsi* (The Master of Clamecy, based on Romain Rolland's *Colas Breugnon*—by which name the opera has become generally known) (1938),[4] a lyrical, if not very original, score with at least one rounded, musically living character, Colas himself. But a greater musician than any of these had been waiting for seven or eight years in the wings; in 1940 he stepped on to the Soviet stage with a ballet and an opera.

Prokofyev had always been the idol of ASM. In 1927, when he paid his first visit to Russia after the Revolution, he was greeted as composer and soloist with wild enthusiasm; and late in 1932, when the RAPM reaction seemed to have been crushed, he decided to return permanently and settle in Moscow. But at first he wrote relatively little:[5] mostly incidental music or film-music—notably for *Poruchik Kizhe* (Lieutenant Kizhe) (1933) and *Aleksandr Nevsky* (1938)—and, although he had finished the ballet *Romeo and Juliet* in 1936, only concert suites from it were performed. Now in January 1940 *Romeo and Juliet* was at last produced and on 23 June his first Soviet opera *Semen Kotko*. It aroused an immediate storm and was contrasted with Khrennikov's *V buryu* very much as *The Lady Macbeth* had been with *Tikhy Don*.

V buryu has a great deal in common with *Tikhy Don*: the folk-song idiom, relieved here and there by watered-down Tchaïkovsky (in scene 4), and the general weakness of characterization. But it is a better *Tikhy Don*, less helpless technically and with little tonal twists that relieve the melodic insipidity, as in Aksinya's song in scene 2:

[1] See Rïzhkin, op. cit., ii, pp. 237 ff. and A. Steinberg, 'Opera o "Bronenostse Potemkine" ', *Sovetskaya muzïka* (1937), no. 10–11, p. 55.

[2] See M. A. Grinberg, 'Opera *Mat* V. Zhelobinskovo,' *Sovetskaya muzïka* (1939), no. 5, p. 9, and Levit, op. cit., ii, pp. 241 ff.

[3] See Ivan Martïnov, '*Bratya*—opera T. Khrennikova' (*Bratya*—Brothers—was the original title), *Sovetskaya muzïka* (1937), no. 10–11, p. 64, and '*V buryu*—T. Khrennikova', ibid. (1939), no. 11, p. 55, and Rïzhkin, op. cit., ii, pp. 249 ff. On Virta's novel, see Gleb Struve, *25 Years of Soviet Russian Literature* (2nd ed., London, 1944), p. 281.

[4] See Abraham, op. cit., pp. 73 ff., L. Danilevich, '*Master iz Klamsi*', *Sovetskaya muzïka* (1937), no. 12, p. 35, and Levit, op. cit., pp. 289 ff.

[5] See infra, pp. 672. As early as 1934 he courageously drew attention to the danger of Soviet music becoming 'provincial'.

Ex. 278

(The falcons flew away to different lands, left and forgot the native nest.)

The action is laid in and around a Tambov village in 1921, with most of
the peasants at first uncertain whether to side with the Bolsheviks or
with Antonov's counter-revolutionaries. The drama of decision is
decided in the minds of the heroine Natasha (a passive character like
so many heroines in Russian opera), her lover (whose brother is already
a convinced Bolshevik) and her father, and has an emotional parallel in
the love-affair; but Khrennikov has no power to convey deep emotion.
An artificial high-light introduced in the version produced in 1939—it
does not occur in the unperformed original version of 1937—is the visit
which Natasha's father and Listat, the Bolshevik brother, pay to Lenin
in Moscow (scene 5); this was Lenin's first appearance on the opera-
stage, but he was not allowed to sing; when he speaks the music stops.

   Semen Kotko is a different matter. As early as 1933 Prokofyev had
expressed the wish to write an opera on a Soviet theme, 'heroic and
constructive',[1] and he at last found this theme in a story by Valentin
Kataev. Like *V buryu*, it is a peasant drama of the Civil War, played out

---

[1] Prokofyev, 'Zametki', *Sovetskaya musïka* (1933), no. 3, p. 99.

in 1918 when the Communists in the Ukraine still had to contend with
German troops as well as the counter-revolutionaries. The characters
are not unlike those of Khrennikov's opera, but Prokofyev was far more
gifted and much better equipped. Instead of relying almost exclusively
on a song-based idiom, he commanded one compounded of melodic
and declamatory elements which enabled him to convey shades of
feeling and draw character with a subtlety, power and flexibility quite
beyond the range of his younger colleagues. Consider Remenyuk's
farewell to the bodies of his murdered comrades:

Ex. 279

Drug moy,   Va - sya Tsa - rev, —   Va - si - ly Tsa-rev, ve —

- se - ly mat - ros   s Cher-no- mor-sko-vo flo - ta.

(My friend, Vasya Tsarev, merry sailor from the Black Sea Fleet—)

or compare the heart-rending lament of Tsarev's sweetheart, Lyubka,
out of her mind at his death, with Dzerzhinsky's half-mad soldier
(Ex. 277):

Ex. 280

LYUBKA   Kuk - la   bez dvi -

KHIVRYA   Ve - li - ko mu-che-ni-tsa pre-po-dob - na - ya

44

(*Lyubka:* Doll without movement. . . *Khivrya:* May the holy martyr Khivrya pardon and intercede!)

(The older woman, Khivrya, meanwhile comments in her own accents.) There is plenty of strong, long-breathed diatonic melody, especially in connexion with the hero Semyon Kotko; it is employed romantically in the manner of Rimsky-Korsakov to set the mood of the summer night and the three pairs of lovers at the beginning of Act III;[1] here much of it is related to Ukrainian folk-song, such as the 'Rano ranenko' (Early in the morning) melody heard as the second subject of the overture, the wedding chorus in Act II, and sung by Semyon and his sweetheart, Sofya, at the end of the opera. There is humour, as when Semyon instructs the young partisans in manning a field-gun in Act IV, and in the love affair of his young sister. The Germans are not caricatured but characterized, as they had already been in *Aleksandr Nevsky*, by viciously dissonant harmony. All these qualities were widely recognized at the time but they failed to save the opera: it quickly disappeared from the repertory and was revived—in concert form—only in 1958.[2]

SOCIALIST REALISM IN THE CONCERT HALL

The achievement of true socialist realism proved still more difficult in symphonic music. Even Myaskovsky, who produced no fewer than nine symphonies, Nos. 13 to 21, as well as a Violin Concerto, during the period 1933–40, found it difficult to maintain the right note. Nos. 14, 16, and 21 were considered the most satisfactory

---

[1] Quoted by Nestyev, *Prokofyev* (Moscow, 1957): English edition (London, 1960), p. 316.
[2] The prolonged controversy about *Kotko* filled the Soviet musical press for some time and is discussed in all the literature on Prokofyev. On this, and the work generally, see particularly M. Sabinina, *'Semen Kotko' i problemi opernoy dramaturgii Prokofyeva* (Moscow, 1963).

but in his autobiography[1] he confessed to various backslidings into subjectivism. But his 'monumental' Sixth was matched in 1932 by a work of irreproachable orthodoxy by Shaporin.[2] As always with Shaporin, the musical language is conservative yet he contrives to say fresh things in it. The Symphony employs chorus, brass band, and piano in addition to a large orchestra and is planned in four movements: (1) introducing themes suggesting Russia's remote heroic past, in the manner of Borodin, and recalling the heroic days of the more recent past ('Yablochko'); (2) a dance-scherzo; (3) a dark-coloured lullaby for female chorus, which leads into (4) 'Campaign', a broad, powerful movement that does indeed suggest 'the movement of colossal human masses'.[3] Six years later, in a much finer 'symphony-cantata' Shaporin crystallized similar ideas and emotions around a cycle of poems by Blok: *Na pole Kulikovom* (On the field of Kulikovo).[4] Here, as in the symphonic cantata which at about the same time Prokofyev developed from his *Aleksandr Nevsky* film music[5] and in the 'oratorio' *Emelyan Pugachev* by Marian Koval (1907–71), heroes from Russia's past were glorified, in two cases princely and patriotic, not revolutionary, heroes who distinguished themselves against foreign invaders. The increasing threat of Nazi Germany led to official encouragement of patriotic art. *Kulikovo* and *Aleksandr Nevsky* are outstanding in a genre hitherto rare in Russia: large-scale secular choral composition. In both works, as in Koval's, the choral scoring is very dull by Western standards; the choirs sing almost entirely in solid harmony or unison, without contrapuntal interest; the half-dozen bars of imitative writing in the 'Lullaby' of *Kulikovo* are quite exceptional but the massive effects in the fourth and last movements of *Nevsky*, and the first and third movements and Epilogue of *Kulikovo* are splendid. There is a certain parallel between the works as wholes; in each the fifth movement is a battle-scene and is followed by a beautiful soprano solo, in one case a lament over the Russian dead, in the other the reassuring lullaby of a Russian mother.

Symphonies and other orchestral works glorifying the Red Army or more peaceful activities of the Soviet Union had already appeared: Knipper's Symphonies, Nos. 3 ('Far Eastern') (1932), 4 ('Poem of the

---

[1] 'Avtobiograficheskie zametki o tvorcheskom puti', *Sovetskaya muzïka* (1936), no. 6, p. 3; reprinted in M. A. Grinberg (ed.), *Sovetskaya simfonicheskaya muzïka* (Moscow, 1955), p. 20.

[2] See Abraham, op. cit., pp. 90 ff. On Shaporin generally, see Levit, *Yury Aleksandrovich Shaporin* (Moscow, 1964).

[3] A. Ostretsov, 'Sovetskoe simfonicheskoe tvorchestvo', *Sovetskaya muzïka* (1935), no. 4, p. 19.

[4] See S. Skrebkov and V. Protopopov in *Istoriya*, ii, pp. 169 ff., and Abraham, op. cit., pp. 94 ff.

[5] Skrebkov and Protopopov, ibid., pp. 163 ff., and Abraham, ibid., pp. 38 ff.

Fighting Komsomols') (1934), 6 (dedicated to the Red Cavalry but 'dry, abstract and formalistic') (1936) and 7 ('Military') (1938),[1] Polovinkin's Fourth Symphony ('Red Army') (1933), Steinberg's Fourth ('Turksib') (1933), Shebalin's Fourth ('Perekop') (1935), Vasilenko's *Red Army Rhapsody* (1938). Another group of works manifested the interest of Russian composers in the native music of the non-Slavonic republics of the U.S.S.R.,[2] which they were officially encouraged to visit—both to study folk-lore and to stimulate the development of native art. As early as 1927 Glier's Azerbaydzhanian opera *Shakh-Senem* had been produced at Baku,[3] and about 1931–3 Knipper composed a series of orchestral works on Tadzhik themes,[4] notably the suite *Vanch*, Shekhter a *Turkmenia* suite, and the veteran Ippolitov-Ivanov various Uzbek and Turkmenian 'pictures' and 'fragments' for orchestra. And before long a native Armenian, Aram Khachaturyan (b. 1903), was to appear with a Trio for piano, violin and clarinet (1932), a First Symphony (1934), a First Piano Concerto (1936), a Violin Concerto (1940),[5] essentially Russian but coloured by the folk-music of Armenia and Uzbekistan.

'Pure' orchestral music became rare after 1932. Kabalevsky's First Symphony (1932) was inspired by Gusev's poem 'The Year 1917', though his attractive Second—in three movements with a scherzo-finale (1934)—and Khrennikov's First (1936) are abstract works and so, despite their conservative idiom, aroused little enthusiasm. As for Popov's First Symphony, not performed till 1935, it had been conceived as early as 1927—in the high noon of *sovremennost* ('contemporariness') —and was now condemned out of hand. Prokofyev, after devastating adverse criticism of his *Simfonicheskaya pesn* (Symphonic Song) (1933), his first composition after his return to his homeland, wrote a Second Violin Concerto, in G minor (1935), but refrained at this period from venturing on a symphony. Shostakovich was bolder but ran into trouble. After a deliberately vulgar Piano Concerto (1933), in which a solo trumpet plays a scarcely less important part than the piano, he had made an almost wholly serious essay in pure instrumental music, a Cello Sonata (1934), and followed this in 1936 with a Fourth Sym-

[1] On these symphonies by Knipper, see Abraham, op. cit., pp. 55–60.
[2] See infra, pp. 699–700.
[3] On *Shakh-Senem* see Ostretsov, '*Shakh-Senem*', *Sovetskaya muzïka* (1938), no. 2, p. 45, and Rïzhkin, *Istoriya*, i, pp. 165 ff.
[4] See Viktor Belyaev, 'Tadzhikskie narodnïe temï v syuite *Vanch* L. Knippera', *Sovetskaya muzïka* (1937), no. 4, p. 49.
[5] On these works, see Abraham, op. cit., pp. 45 ff., Georgy Khubov, *Sovetskaya muzïka* (1939), no. 9–10, p. 18, Martïnov, ibid. (1938), no. 5, p. 26, and Tumanina, *Istoriya*, ii, pp. 450 ff.

phony.[1] Like so much of Shostakovich's music, it is a mixture of styles—to which, as will be apparent from the openings of the second movement and slow introduction to the third (the finale):

Ex. 281

that of Mahler was now added. The concertino element of the Second and Third Symphonies reappears in the first movement but there is little of their revolutionary rhetoric. As with Mahler himself, an unmistakably personal utterance emerges from the heterogeneous musical fabric. And the work ends with a faint question mark: against the very long-held C minor triad of the strings and celesta, the solo trumpet takes 18 bars to resolve its F sharp on G. The Fourth Symphony was on

[1] See L. Danilevich, *Nash sovremennik: Tvorchestvo Shostakovicha* (Moscow, 1965), pp. 127 ff.

the eve of performance when the storm over *The Lady Macbeth* broke. Shostakovich decided that it did not exemplify socialist realism in the symphony and withdrew it; it was first heard in December 1962. Its successor (1938) was described by Shostakovich himself as 'a Soviet artist's practical creative reply to just criticism'.[1]

The theme of my symphony is the stabilization of a personality. In the centre of this composition—conceived lyrically from beginning to end—I saw a man with all his experiences. The finale resolves the tragically tense impulses of the earlier movements into optimism and joy of living.

Lyricism and the optimistic D major of the finale cancelled out the subjective elements of the earlier movements. But the socialist realism of the Sixth Symphony (1939) was more doubtful:[2] the slow first movement was found too elegiac, the remaining two movements too noisy, empty, and formalistic.

From this period also date two notable chamber-works by Shostakovich, the Piano Quintet (1940) and the first (1938) of his series of string quartets. Chamber music and solo piano music had flourished briefly in the early days of socialist realism, though the piano music— for instance, Shostakovich's Twenty-four Preludes (1932–3), Khachaturyan's Toccata (1932), and Kabalevsky's Sonatinas, op. 13 (1930)— tended to be technically less demanding, as if written for domestic use rather than the concert-platform. In the field of solo song composers conscious of the dangers of subjective expression turned to arrangements of folk-song but no longer limited themselves exclusively to Russia or the sister-republics: in 1933 both Anatoly Aleksandrov and Feinberg published sets of 'songs of the Western peoples' (including a number of Hebridean, Lowland Scottish, and English examples). Koval, on the other hand, searched the Russian classics for socially significant poems and published sets of Pushkin and Nekrasov songs: his *Pushkiniana* (1934)[3] is a cycle of ten rather declamatory songs, interspersed with readings from Pushkin's diaries and note-books. Koval was a former 'proletarian' composer and one of his most lyrical Pushkin songs may be instructively compared with one from the same period by a former 'contemporary', Mosolov:

---

[1] On the Fifth Symphony see particularly Khubov, 'Pyataya simfoniya D. Shostakovicha', *Sovetskaya muzika* (1938), no. 3, p. 14, and Orlov, op. cit., pp. 62 ff.

[2] Orlov as usual quotes and summarizes the contemporary criticisms, op. cit., pp. 102 ff.

[3] See Shlifsteyn, '*Pushkiniana* M. Kovalya', *Sovetskaya muzika* (1937), no. 2, p. 42.

Ex. 282

(i)

(Useless gift, chance gift; life, why art thou given me?)

(ii)

(Into your little room, my tender friend, I come for the last time.)

The Pushkin centenary was also marked by the appearance of a number of finely wrought settings of his more lyrical verse by Shaporin, Aleksandrov and Feynberg. In particular Shaporin's five Pushkin songs, op. 10 (1935), with his *Dalekaya yunost* (Far-off Youth) (1935–40) and his *Elegii*, op. 18 (1945), despite the conservatism of their idiom, entitle him by their poetic sensitivity and beautiful craftsmanship to a place beside all but the greatest of Russian song-composers.

PROKOFYEV'S 'WAR AND PEACE'

The outbreak of the 'Great War for the Fatherland' evoked a great upsurge of patriotic feeling which found the most varied outlets of musical expression: in great symphonic works, opera, and even ballet. (Khachaturyan, for instance, drastically recast his first ballet, *Schastye* (Happiness) (1939), with a fresh, bellicose scenario as *Gayane* (1942).) Opera-composers drew inspiration first from national heroes of the past —Vasilenko in *Suvorov*, Koval in *Emelyan Pugachev* (to whom he had already dedicated an oratorio), Boris Mokrousov (b. 1909) in *Chapaev* (all three produced in 1942)—later from heroic events in the German war itself: Dzerzhinsky's *Krov naroda* (The Blood of the People) (1942) and *Nadezhda Svetlova* (1943), Kabalevsky's *Pod Moskvoy* (Near Moscow: also known as *V ogne*, In the Fire) (1943), Koval's *Sevastopoltsï* (The Defenders of Sevastopol) (1946). Now and again, a composer would be content to turn to a literary classic, as Viktor Trambitsky did to Ostrovsky's *Groza* (The Storm) (1942) and Anatoly Aleksandrov to Lermontov in *Bela* (produced 1946, but completed several years earlier), but such operas were exceptional. Some of the war operas proved hardly more than ephemeral; all were overshadowed by

Prokofyev's *Voyna i mir* (War and Peace) (original version, 1943; produced 1946).[1]

Tolstoy's novel seems an impossible opera-subject; its vast field of vision, the multitude of fully conceived characters, above all that sense of time passing and a whole generation of youth achieving maturity—all this is beyond theatre, and music could add nothing to it. What Prokofyev did was to extract on the one hand the principal characters, and the personal tragedy of Andrey's love for Natasha and her seduction by Kuragin, on the other the great set-pieces of 1812: the Battle of Borodino, the council of war at Fili (one of the new scenes of the second version), the burning of Moscow, and the French retreat. Indeed the opera divides naturally into two parts. The first seven scenes are all personal drama; at the end of the seventh, when Pierre has put Kuragin to shame and flight, Denisov enters with the news that 'Napoleon has advanced his troops to our border'. After that, only in the wonderful twelfth scene where Natasha comes to the dying Prince Andrey (and Prokofyev gives a choral embodiment to 'the soft, whispering voice' of his heart—Andrey did not know whether it was delusion or reality—'incessantly and rhythmically repeating "i-piti-piti-piti" '):

Ex. 283

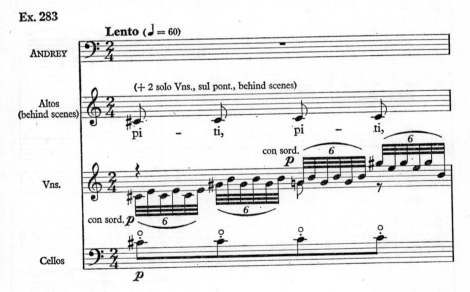

---

[1] The original version consisted of 11 scenes; only eight scenes were produced in 1946. Prokofyev later made cuts but also substantial additions, including two completely new scenes; 11 scenes of this version were crowded into one night in 1955, the complete 13-scene form was produced only in 1957. On *War and Peace*, see particularly A. Khokhlovkina, '*Voyna i mir* Sergeya Prokofyeva', *Sovetskaya muzïka* (1946), no. 8–9, p. 15, Nestyev, op. cit. (English ed.), pp. 445 ff,. and Rïzhkin, *Istoriya*, iii, pp. 211 ff.

(Why is it white by the door?)

do we return to the personal drama. We see Pierre at the redoubt at Borodino, arrested in captured Moscow, talking to the peasant Karataev, rescued (not by Cossacks as in the book but by *partizani*), but we do not apprehend what is going on in his heart and mind. The hero is now the Russian people and Kutuzov, the embodiment of its immanent will. Like other great Russian operas—*Boris* itself—*War and Peace* is a masterpiece not because of its wholeness but because of the greatness of its parts.

The music is worthy of the subject. In this score, better than in any other, Prokofyev showed how a great creative artist, denied total freedom of musical speech, may yet achieve unmistakably individual utterance. Even his earlier works, written in the West, had shown a vein of strong diatonic melody; he found this an ever valuable resource after his return to Russia; and in *War and Peace*, as in *Romeo and Juliet*, he achieves a cool classic beauty that is rare in Russian music. It is heard straight away in the very first scene, as Andrey sits by the open window at Otradnoe in the May moonlight, when the flute plays the melody—borrowed from incidental music to a stage version of *Eugene Onegin* (1936)—that is to be associated throughout with Natasha:

Ex. 284

(Bright spring sky, is not this perhaps an illusion?)

At times the diatonic idiom is handled artlessly, as in Kutuzov's noble but too Borodin-like monologue on the abandonment of 'white-stoned mother Moscow' after the council of war. Much more typical are the harmonic twists and rhythmic energy that stamp Andrey's assurance to Pierre before Borodino: 'But I tell you: be that as it may, we shall win this battle'. Even the big war scenes, spectacular as in Meyerbeer or Wagner, remind one more of Mussorgsky than of 'grand' opera—in many more details than the reading of the proclamation and the appearance of the madmen in captured Moscow. Nothing even in Mussorgsky is more moving than the scene of Andrey's dying.

The first version of *War and Peace* was produced on 12 June 1946; less than five months later (3 November) came another Prokofyev opera, one that had been on the point of production five years before, when war broke out: *Obruchenie v monastïre* (Betrothal in a Priory: after Sheridan's *Duenna*).[1] In spite of his declared intention, Prokofyev allowed the comic side, with its brilliantly subtle declamation and characterization, to outweigh the lyrical music of the two pairs of lovers; the boozing friars in scene 8 might have come from *The Three Oranges*. But the lyrical vein is as unmistakably Prokofyev's here as in *War and Peace*; good examples are the quartet at the end of scene 5 and Clara's aria in

[1] For Prokofyev's own account of the inception of the work, see S. I. Shlifshteyn, *S. S. Prokofyev: materialï, dokumentï, vospominaniya* (Moscow, 1956), p. 112; English version, Moscow, n.d., p. 122). On the opera generally, see Nestyev, op. cit., pp. 389 ff., and Rïzhkin, *Istoriya*, iv (1) (Moscow, 1963), pp. 408 ff.

scene 7, and when Louisa is plotting with the Duenna in scene 2 Prokofyev contrives to write a purely diatonic love-theme in D flat ('Yes, I love so much that more I cannot love') which yet avoids the almost inevitable lusciousness associated with the key. Here again the melody is cool and classic.

INSTRUMENTAL MUSIC, 1941–7

Orchestral music no less than opera reflected the patriotic mood of the war-period, sometimes directly, often by emphasis on the national music of the non-Russian peoples of the Soviet Union. (The wholesale evacuation of composers first to Nalchik in the northern Caucacus, then to Tbilisi (Tiflis), naturally heightened their interest in the national musics.) Thus Myaskovsky's Twenty-second Symphony (1941) was styled 'Symphony-ballad of the Great War for the Fatherland', the first of its three connected movements depicting 'peaceful life into which breaks a menace', while the other two were conceived as 'Apprehending the horrors of war' and 'And the enemy faltered' (a reference to Taneyev's song, Op. 26, no. 8), while his Twenty-third (also 1941) was, like Prokofyev's Second String Quartet, based on Kabardinian themes. Indeed one or two are common to both works and the contrasts in treatment are striking:

Ex. 285

Prokofyev's other compositions of the war and immediate post-war period included the ballet *Zolushka* (Cinderella) (produced 1945), the Fifth and Sixth Symphonies (1944 and 1947), and his last three piano sonatas. The symphonies and sonatas all belong more or less to the musical world of *War and Peace*. This is particularly true of the 'heroic' Fifth Symphony, the opening of which might well be part of the characterization of Andrey, while the second movement might have served for the caricaturing of Napoleon and the D flat 'Russian' theme in the finale for the glorification of Kutuzov. Equally, the middle movement of the Eighth Sonata (also 1944) would not be out of place in the ball-scene. Neither the Fifth nor the Sixth Symphony has a programme, but both were written under the impression of the war, present or in retrospect.

The same is certainly true of the Seventh and Eighth Symphonies of Shostakovich (1941 and 1943), while his Ninth (1945) presumably reflects the high spirits of victory. Only the first movement of the Seventh, the so-called *Leningrad*, is actually programmatic, the development section being replaced by a long-drawn orchestral crescendo in the manner of Ravel's *Bolero*—the major part of the movement—suggesting the inexorable advance of the invading armies, while the recapitulation brings back the material of the 'peaceful' exposition partly in the minor and in mournful distortion; the beginning of the recapitulation is marked by *fff* octave declamation by practically the entire orchestra in the oratorical manner of the Third Symphony. But although the composer had originally intended to give titles to all four movements—'War', 'Remembrance', 'The Wide Spaces of our Land', 'Victory'[1]—he suppressed them and later gave no more detailed clues than that the second movement, with its echoes of Mahler's *Ländler*[2] in the 'humorous' middle section, is 'an intermezzo, very lyrical, gentle—no sort of programme, fewer "concrete facts" than in the first movement', and the third, 'a pathetic *adagio* with a dramatic middle section'. In the finale his intention was to compose 'an Ode sounding from all the ends of the earth and triumphantly growing', a statement which has a more Mahlerian ring than the music itself. Whatever the extra-musical ideas underlying the Eighth Symphony, there can be no doubt of its relationship to the Seventh, even though the relationship seems to be antithetical. There are even thematic relationships; the very first entry of the first violins broodingly takes up the opening of the 'invasion' theme of the Seventh; the third movement is again concerned with cruel, in-

---

[1] Shostakovich, 'O podlinoy i mnimoy programmnosti', *Sovetskaya muzïka* (1951), no. 5, p. 76.

[2] Orlov, op. cit., p. 168, sees a relationship between the first part of the movement and an episode in the finale of *Das Lied von der Erde*.

human automata. But there is now no triumphant conclusion. The Eighth Symphony is a tragic monument, one of Shostakovich's most powerful and individual scores, but so pessimistic and couched in such pungent harmonic terms that in 1948 it was, with Prokofyev's Sixth, denounced as 'formalistic' and both works disappeared from the repertory for nearly ten years.

By comparison with these symphonic giants, Shostakovich's Ninth, thrown off in a few weeks in August 1945, is a lightweight: short, scored for a smaller orchestra, humorous but not without serious passages (for instance, the obviously programmatic introduction to the finale). It is a counterpart to Prokofiev's *Classical* and, like that work, may be expected to outlive the Second Symphonies of Khachaturyan, Khrennikov and Popov (all 1943) or Muradeli's, 'dedicated to the victory of the Soviet people over Fascism' (1945).

Another significant stage in Shostakovich's career was now marked by increasing preoccupation with chamber music. Before the war, he had—after some juvenilia—produced only a decidedly eclectic Cello Sonata (1934), a rather naïve String Quartet, said to be based on memories of childhood and youth (1938), and a fine, if suite-like Piano Quintet (1940, but published only in 1956). The year 1944 brought a Piano Trio and a Second Quartet, which is also rather naïve and suite-like, consisting of overture, recitative and romance, valse,[1] and theme with variations. But with the Third Quartet (1946) Shostakovich first showed his mastery of the medium and embarked on that series of compositions which established him not only as the finest Soviet quartet-composer but as also the most prolific.[2] (The ever-fertile Myaskovsky produced six more quartets, nos. 7–12, during the period 1941–7.) Two other Soviet string quartets of this period stand out: Kabalevsky's Second (1945) and Shebalin's Fifth (1942). Kabalevsky's Quartet, like his Second Piano Sonata (written in the same year), is dramatic and thematically related to his operas *V ogne* and *Semya Tarasa* (Taras's family). Shebalin's, the *Slavonic*, is based on Russian and Ukrainian folk-themes in its first and fifth movements, Polish, Slovak and Serbian tunes in the middle ones. (The Serbian theme of the fourth movement is that on which Tchaïkovsky based his *Slavonic March*.) Shebalin further exploited the Russian folk-song vein with fine craftsmanship in his Seventh Quartet (1948) and the variation-finale of his Piano Trio (1949). Beside these established masters, a newcomer appeared in this field: Shostakovich's pupil Yury Sviridov (b. 1915).

---

[1] Recorded in *The History of Music in Sound*, x.
[2] See L. Raaben, *Sovetskaya kamerno-instrumentalnaya muzïka* (Moscow, 1963) and Colin Mason, 'Form in Shostakovich's Quartets', *Musical Times*, ciii (1962), p. 531.

Sviridov's two quartets, his Piano Quintet, and his Piano Trio all date from 1945–6, although the Trio and Quintet were thoroughly revised ten years later; as one might expect, they show the influence of his teacher's Trio and Third Quartet—in more ways than their suite-like structure—but also individual traits, indeed more of the latter than in some of Sviridov's later, more highly praised works.

VOCAL MUSIC, 1941–7

The solo song was cultivated during these years more than might have been anticipated. Naturally heroic, declamatory elements are prominent, as in Anatoly Aleksandrov's cycle *Tri kubka* (Three goblets) (1942) and Nechaev's *O doblestyakh, o podvigakh, o slave* (Of heroism, great deeds, and fame) (1943). The nineteenth-century form of the narrative ballad was also revived in art-song as well as mass-song; for instance, the heroism of the airman Gastello was celebrated by both Viktor Bely ('Ballada o kapitane Gastello') and Khachaturyan ('Kapitan Gastello'). The wartime alliance also evoked not only a great many arrangements of English and Scottish folk-songs but also numerous original settings of English and Scottish verse. Shostakovich led the way with his six bass songs, op. 62 (1942), to translations of Shakespeare, Walter Raleigh, and Burns, originally with piano, later with orchestral accompaniment; his attempt at Sonnet 66 must be one of the worst Shakespeare settings in existence, but he was more successful with Burns. Indeed Burns (in Marshak's generally good translations) became a favourite with other composers, including Khrennikov. But the Russian classic lyric poets—Pushkin, Fet, Tyutchev—were not neglected, and Shebalin composed a Heine cycle.

Yet the most remarkable solo vocal composition of the war years was wordless: the Concerto for voice (coloratura soprano) and orchestra (1943) by the veteran Glier. It is in two movements, a lyrical Andante and a brilliant final valse or *jota*. The idiom is that of half a century earlier but it is a true concerto, highly effective, and it has easily maintained a place in the Russian concert repertoire.

Of the larger works for chorus and orchestra, the patriotic cantatas and so-called oratorios, Kabalevsky's *Rodina velikaya* (The great motherland) (1942), Myaskovsky's *Kirov s nami* (Kirov is with us) (1943) and Shaporin's *Skazanie o bitve za Russkuyu zemlyu* (Story of the fight for the Russian land) (1944)[1] are perhaps the best. They are rhythmically square-cut, diatonic, with a preponderance of block common chords: official art carried out with the technical competence

[1] On these and other similar works, see Tumanina in *Istoriya*, iii, pp. 137 ff.

and occasional flashes of real invention one expects of these composers, but even Shaporin's *Skazanie* is far inferior to *The Field of Kulikovo*.

POLITICAL BACKGROUND AFTER 1947

While the works just mentioned, and many others, conformed absolutely to the strictest demands of socialist realism, there were some which did not. During the war the Soviet Government and the Central Committee of the Communist Party had not been paying close attention to literary and artistic orthodoxy and, with control thus relaxed, writers and artists had insensibly begun to take liberties; the old evils of 'formalism' and 'subjectivism' were creeping back. As early as August 1946 the Central Committee had begun to worry about literature and journalism, about the theatrical repertory, and about films; and writers were sharply reminded that 'there are not and cannot be other interests than the interests of the people, of the state. . . . Hence all preaching of that which has no idea-content, of the apolitical, of "art for art's sake", is foreign to Soviet literature, harmful to the interests of the Soviet people and state, and must have no place in our journals'. Writers of the rank of Akhmatova and Zoshchenko were coarsely abused in public speeches by the Committee's spokesman, Andrey Zhdanov, and the Union of Composers did not fail to notice the danger-signals.[1] But more than a year passed before the Committee turned its attention to music. Just as in 1936, the immediate occasion was a specific opera: this time *Velikaya druzhba* (The great friendship) by the Georgian-born Vano Muradeli (1908–70), produced in Moscow on 7 November 1947, to mark the thirtieth anniversary of the Revolution. The highest members of the Government and Party were present and reacted precisely as they had done to *The Lady Macbeth*. Little more than a month later (25 December) the performance of Prokofyev's Sixth Symphony in Moscow made matters much worse. (It had been acclaimed in Leningrad in October.) In January Zhdanov sternly addressed a three-day conference of musicians in Moscow, from which Myaskovsky absented himself[2] and on 10 February the Central Committee published its ordinance 'On the opera *The Great Friendship* by V. Muradeli',[3] which not only denounced Muradeli's work in terms practically identical with those applied (with much less injustice) to *The*

[1] See the unsigned article, 'Problemï sovetskovo muzïkalnovo tvorchestva', *Sovetskaya muzïka* (1946), no. 8–9, p. 3, and the account of the week-long plenary meeting of the organizing committee of the Union of Soviet Composers, ibid., no. 10, p. 3.

[2] For a copious, though not quite complete, report of the conference, see Alexander Werth, *Musical Uproar in Moscow* (London, 1949), pp. 47 ff.

[3] Full translation of the resolution, Zhdanov's speech, and various statements by composers in Slonimsky, op. cit., pp. 684 ff.; long excerpts, with commentary, in Werth, op. cit., pp. 28 ff.

45

Lady Macbeth and *Clear Stream* twelve years before but also attacked as 'anti-national formalists' the far more important composers Shostakovich, Prokofyev, Khachaturyan, Shebalin, Popov, and Myaskovsky. From the composers' side, the official view was endorsed most enthusiastically by Khrennikov; some—notably Shebalin—defended themselves with spirit or remained silent; the majority, including Muradeli and Shostakovich, abased themselves and confessed their errors.

The so-called 'Zhdanov period' lasted in its full rigour until the death of Stalin—on the same day as Prokofyev—in March 1953. A slow 'thaw' then set in, officially acknowledged in 1956, though it was not until 18 May 1958 that the Central Committee published another resolution 'correcting errors of evaluation' in the ordinance of 1948, for which 'J. V. Stalin's subjective approach to works of art' was blamed. Nevertheless this was no charter of liberty; those who had misread it in that sense were put right by Khrushchev in March 1963.

OPERA: 1948–60

Muradeli's *The Great Friendship* is a weak opera[1] and the accusations of lack of memorable melody or true local colour were justified, but the charges of 'chaos' and 'continuous discord' against so innocuous a score were ludicrous. It contains no harmony more pungent than such passages as this:

Ex. 286

THE
COMMISSAR

pa - kha-rya, kto nad so-khoy sklo-nyon

---

[1] See Rïzhkin, *Istoriya*, iv (1), pp. 327 ff.

(the ploughman who bends over the plough, and the shepherd who works day and night, the miner who all day follows his dark road underground,)

and a very great deal that is less. Perhaps the music was really considered less objectionable than the libretto, which purported to show the reconciling by a Political Commissar of (allegedly non-existent) enmity between the Russians and Lesgians in the Northern Caucasus but concentrated instead on a romantic-melodramatic plot which would serve equally well for a 'Western' film. It is historically important only for the deathly hush that followed its condemnation. Prokofyev completed his

Povest o nastoyashchem cheloveke (The story of a real man) but it had only one private concert performance in December 1948; it was not produced till 1960, seven years after his death. Even the *Semya Tarasa* of the more conservative and 'correct' Kabalevsky, which had been tried out in Moscow in November 1947, was drastically rewritten and produced in its revised form in 1950.[1] (Both these operas are on war-subjects; Kabalevsky's depicting the patriotism of a worker's family in a part of the Ukraine overrun by the Germans, Prokofyev's the heroic will-power of an airman who overcomes the loss of his feet.) In the operatic silence were heard only such small, quiet voices as that of the Odessa-born Antonio Spadavecchia (b. 1907), a former composition-pupil of Shebalin and Prokofyev, with his *Khozyayka gostinitsï* (The Hostess at the Inn) (based on Goldoni's *Locandiera*) (1949), and the official one of Khrennikov with his uninspired comedy *Frol Skobeyev* (1950).

By far the most notable opera of the nineteen-fifties was Shaporin's *Dekabristï* (The Decembrists), produced on 23 June 1953 after more than a quarter of a century of gestation. The original conception had been the personal drama of the young nobleman Annenkov, who has brought back from the West liberal ideas and a French shopgirl, Pauline, whom he is determined to marry—despite his mother's violent opposition. He is drawn into the Decembrist conspiracy and sentenced to exile; at a masked ball Pauline was to plead in vain with the Tsar for her husband's pardon and resolve to accompany him to Siberia. The political events provided no more than a background except in two scenes, the equivalents of the definitive fourth and sixth: the meeting on the eve of the rising (a scene in which Annenkov's part was insignificant) and the great spectacular scene in the Senate Square when the rising collapsed. In this form the opera was nearly completed in 1938, with only the Senate Square scene and the ball scene unwritten.[2] In the final version Annenkov was supplanted by Shchepin-Rostovsky and Pauline by Elena Orlova, the daughter of an impoverished neighbouring land-owner. The personal drama remained the same, though the lovers lost some beautiful music, but it was now pushed into the background of the historical events. (Spadavecchia's *Khozhdenie po mukam* (1954), based on A. N. Tolstoy's well-known novel of the Revolution, translated under the title *Darkness and Dawn*, underwent a precisely similar change.) The hero of the final version is no longer Annenkov/Shchepin but the Decembrists collectively and, while it would be quite untrue to

[1] Ibid., pp. 283 ff.
[2] See the account, with lengthy musical examples, by A. Lepin, '*Dekabristï*—opera Y. Shaporina', *Sovetskaya muzïka* (1938), no. 7, p. 20.

say that the Decembrist leaders are not differentiated, they are certainly
more important as a group than as individuals. Instead of a lyrical-
dramatic opera, *The Decembrists* thus became a series of historic
tableaux in the tradition of *Prince Igor*. (One would say 'of *Boris
Godunov*', if only there were one central character, hero or villain,
studied in depth, but neither Rïleyev nor Pestel, nor Nicholas I, is so
studied.) Elena and Shchepin become hardly more important than
Musorgsky's Marina and Pretender-as-lover. Yet, granted this
dramatic weakness and the conservative nature of Shaporin's musical
idiom, the score contains far too many memorable things to be dismissed as mere epigonism: the beautiful folk-song chorus that opens the
first and last scenes, the arioso in which Shchepin tells his mother of
his love (Russian romantic lyricism at its best), Bestuzhev's song of the
winter road that ends scene 2, the polyphony of folk-songs sung by
four choral groups in the fair-scene:

Ex. 287

(*Girls:* Fly, my horse, so the wind doesn't catch you! *Stesha:* Hoi, little road, my distant way ... *Chorus I:* Hey, beer is good! Wine's better! *Chorus II:* Yes, they mentioned in the pot-house!)

the broad, massive handling of the spectacular scene in the Senate Square, the waltz (worthy of Tchaïkovsky) to which the Emperor pursues Elena at the ball. No other Soviet opera comes so near to challenging *War and Peace* on its own ground.

The diatonic melody and harmony which came naturally to Shaporin were cultivated deliberately, in conformity with the Party directive, but with much less technical skill, by the younger men: Dzerzhinsky in *Daleko ot Moskvï* (Far from Moscow) (1954) and *Groza* (Ostrovsky's Storm) (1956), Kabalevsky in *Nikita Vershinin* (1955), Kirill Molchanov (b. 1922) in *Kamennïy tsvetok* (The Stone Flower) (1954, and therefore after the composition but before the production of Prokofyev's ballet on the same subject), *Zarya* (The Dawn) (1956), and *Ulitsa del Korno* (Del Corno Street) (1959), and Khrennikov in *Mat* (The Mother, after Gorky) (1956), Even the best Soviet composers failed in the struggle for unnatural simplicity. Shostakovich's 'musical comedy' with spoken dialogue, *Moskva, Cheremushki* (1958), is banal beyond belief, and Prokofyev's *Story of a Real Man,* when it was produced at last post-humously in 1960, only showed that his avowed striving for 'clear

melodies and the simplest harmonic language possible'[1] could sometimes be fatal in his case, too. Only here and there for a few bars, as in
no. 14 when old Mikhaylo tells how the maimed Aleksey has dragged
himself along:

Ex. 288

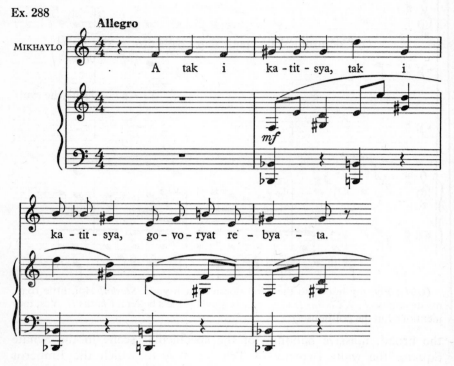

(And so it goes, so it goes, as children say.)

is there any hint of the old Prokofyev. Indeed there is more of 'the old
Prokofyev' in Shebalin's often witty *Ukroshchenie stroptivoy* (The
Taming of the Shrew) (1957).

INSTRUMENTAL MUSIC: 1948–60

The Party resolution of 1948 had similar effects in the field of instrumental music; works that might have incurred the charge of formalism
were laid aside and composers cultivated simple diatonic melody and
harmony. Major instrumental composition, so liable to formalistic
lapses, was indeed largely superseded for a time by the writing of
cantatas and 'oratorios' with ideologically irreproachable texts.

[1] Quoted by Nestyev, op. cit., p. 403.

Shostakovich temporarily suppressed his Violin Concerto (composed in 1948 as Op. 77) and his Fourth Quartet (1949), and composed a banal 'oratorio', *Pesn o lesakh* (Song of the Forests) (1949) and *Twenty-Four Preludes and Fugues* for piano (1950-1) in emulation of Bach.[1] Another field much cultivated during this period of enforced innocence was that of music for children—not so much for children to perform as for children to listen to: Kabalevsky's concertos for violin, cello and piano, Opp. 48-50 (1948-9), Prokofyev's *Zimniy koster* (Winter Bonfire) for readers, chorus of boys, and orchestra (1949), and Shostakovich's Concertino for two pianos (1953). Even Prokofyev's Seventh Symphony (1952), a lyrical and rather weak work, was originally conceived as a 'symphony for children' and Shostakovich's Second Piano Concerto (1957) were products of the same impulse. Not unnaturally, the stronger creative talents show to less advantage within such limitations than composers whose more modest powers needed less restraint. Kabalevsky's Violin Concerto is a charming little work with an *andantino* melody in the middle movement worthy of Tchaïkovsky himself:

Ex. 289

whereas the corresponding theme in Shostakovich's Second Concerto sounds like Baroque pastiche:

Ex. 290'

[1] See S. Skrebkov, 'Prelyudii i fugi D. Shostakovicha' *Sovetskaya muzïka* (1953), no. 9, p. 18, and V. Protopopov, *Istoriya*, iv (2), (Moscow, 1963), pp. 190 ff.

The second subject of Kabalevsky's finale has an appropriate affinity with the song of Nastya and the Komsomols in Act I of *Semya Tarasa*:

Ex. 291

(We part with friends, perhaps for ever. Farewell, friends, it's time to leave!)

Stalin was no sooner dead than Shostakovich embarked on a Tenth Symphony, written during the summer of 1953 and performed in December. Judged by purely musical criteria, it is arguably the finest of all his symphonies, stamped from beginning to end with his creative personality and free both from the cheaper forms of grotesque humour which intrude so often in his best scores and from concessions to official conservatism. Such a work was bound to attract the charge of 'formalism', and few new symphonies can have been debated so fiercely and immediately by the composer's colleagues as this.[1] The Symphony manifestly has no quasi-literary programme but it is equally certainly not abstract music; it is not so much 'formalistic' as 'subjective' and 'pessimistic', which, from the Marxist point of view, is just as bad. That

[1] See Orlov, op. cit., pp. 249 ff., for particulars and references.

much of the Symphony is in some sense tragic is hardly deniable; the problems that agitated Shostakovich's colleagues were whether the tragedy was personal or national (still the aftermath of the war) and whether the tragedy might be regarded as 'overcome' in the end.[1] In the perspective of ten years, the authors of the official *History of Russian Soviet Music*[2] were able to sum up in 1963:

The tragic element in Shostakovich, particularly in his later works, is optimistic in tendency. He seeks a way to overcome a tragic beginning. His humanistic ideals as a Soviet artist, loving life and freedom, fighting for peace and happiness, cannot fail to lead him to life-affirmation. It is possible to argue about this or that degree of artistic conviction and about the forms in which the tragic is overcome in Shostakovich's works—arguments which still continue in musical criticism—but there can be no doubt of the general effort to overcome tragedy.

'Optimistic tragedy' is a phrase commonly met with in Soviet criticism; both Shaporin's *Decembrists* and Kabalevsky's *Taras's Family* are 'optimistic tragedies'. But Shostakovich was taking no chances with his next two symphonies, No. 11 (1957) and No. 12 (1961), which are both programmatic—with programmes beyond political reproach—and, particularly No. 12, written in a musical idiom comprehensible to mass-audiences. Each is dedicated to a revolution. The four movements of No. 11 (entitled *The Year 1905*) are headed 'The Palace Square' (i.e. in Petersburg), '9 January', 'Eternal Memory', and 'Tocsin', and Shostakovich has based most of the score on revolutionary tunes of the period,[3] not simply quoting and varying them, but sometimes even fusing them into fresh entities. Thus the melodic line of the horns just before fig. 107 in the third movement is derived partly from the song 'Baykal', partly from 'Boldly, comrades, keep in step'. The funeral-march third movement is based mainly on the song, 'Vï zhertvoyu pali' (You fell as a sacrifice), which was solemnly sung by Lenin and his companions in exile when they heard the news of 'Bloody Sunday',[4] and the title of the finale almost certainly refers to his article 'Revolution in Russia' in the *émigré* journal *Vpered* on 11 January 1905. No. 12 is a companionpiece, *The Year 1917*, with movements entitled 'Revolutionary Petrograd', 'Razliv' (where Lenin lay low before the October Revolution), 'The *Aurora*' (the cruiser which dealt the decisive blow to the Provisional Government), and 'The Dawn of Humanity'. The

---

[1] See, for instance, Andrey Volkonsky, 'Optimisticheskaya tragediya', *Sovetskaya muzïka* (1954), no. 4, p. 25.

[2] *Istoriya*, iv (2), p. 145.

[3] See Orlov, op. cit., pp. 286 ff., and L. Lebedinsky, 'Revolyutsionnïy folklor v Odinnadtsatoy simfonii D. Shostakovicha', *Sovetskaya muzïka* (1958), no. 1, p. 42.

[4] N. K. Krupskaya, *Vospominaniya o Lenine* (Moscow), 1957, p. 89 (quoted by Orlov, op. cit., p. 303).

Thirteenth Symphony (1962), on poems by Evtushenko, is less a symphony than a cantata for baritone, male chorus and orchestra, while the Fourteenth (1969), settings of Lorca, Guillaume Apollinaire, Küchelbecker and Rilke for soprano, bass and orchestra, is no more— but no less—a symphony than Mahler's *Lied von der Erde*.

But the best of Shostakovich at this time was put, not into the symphonies (with the exception of the Tenth) but into the Cello Concerto (1959)—inspired, like Prokofyev's *Sinfonia concertante* for cello and orchestra (1952, but a reworking of material from the Cello Concerto of 1938), by the playing of Mstislav Rostropovich—and the string quartets from No. 4 onward. The Fourth Quartet itself was written soon after the outstanding song-cycle *From Hebrew Folk Poetry* (1948) and both are related, either thematically or emotionally, to the Piano Trio of 1944, the finale of which is said to have been inspired by the discovery of the Jewish death-camp at Majdanek. Rabinovich says[1] that both the Fourth and Fifth Quartets were 'composed in the same atmosphere of thoughts and emotions in which the future Tenth Symphony took form' and 'perhaps, either directly or indirectly, prepared the way for it'. They are even related thematically, and stamped as essentially 'personal' works, by the appearance in all three, in various permutations and transpositions, of the notes D-E♭-C-B♮ representing the composer's initials 'D.Sch.' (Sch being the German transliteration of the single Russian letter which begins his surname) a motive that was to appear again in the concertos for violin and cello, and in other works. One can trace no similar connexion between the later quartets and symphonies. The Eleventh and Twelfth Symphonies are public utterances; the quartets are intensely personal and subtle in workmanship. This is particularly true of No. 8 (1960), with its numerous references to the 'D. Sch.' theme, prominent from the very beginning, and quotations from the composer's earlier works[2]—the opening of the First Symphony near the very beginning, and the second subject of the finale of the Piano Trio in the second movement (p. 9 of the miniature score)—as well as the revolutionary song 'Zamuchen tyazheloy nevoley' ('Worn out by heavy slavery') and a passage from *The Lady Macbeth* in the middle of the fourth movement.

The other older composers continued to produce in their familiar veins. Kabalevsky's Fourth Symphony (1956), Shebalin's Seventh, Eighth and Ninth Quartets (1948, 1961 and 1963) and Fifth Symphony (1962), Knipper's Symphonies 10–14 (1946–54), Aleksandrov's Piano Sonatas 9–11 (1946–55) are all well-written works, with fine passages

[1] D. Rabinovich, *Dmitry Shostakovich* (London, 1959), p. 129.
[2] Keldïsh, 'An Autobiographical Quartet', *Musical Times*, cii (1961), p. 226.

(e.g. the Andante of Shebalin's Seventh Quartet), which nevertheless add nothing essential to the composers' images. Khachaturyan's
colourful ballet *Spartak* (Spartacus) (1954; produced 1956) is no
more than a counterpart of *Gayane*. Nor can it be said that the
generation born just before or not long after the Revolution brought
forth anything startlingly new. There have been some very successful works: Rodion Shchedrin's ballet *Konek-Gorbunok* (The little
humpbacked horse) (1955), the 'oratorios', *Pamyati Sergeya Esenina*
(In memory of Esenin) (1955) and *Pateticheskaya oratoriya* (Pathetic
Oratorio) (1959) by Sviridov, and *Dvenadtsat* (Blok's 'The Twelve')
(1957) by Vadim Salmanov (b. 1912). But neither in these nor in
the orchestral works of Andrey Eshpay (b. 1925) and Boris Chaykovsky
(b. 1925)—to name the best composers of their generation—is there
much, if anything, that could not have been written half-a-century,
even a century, earlier. Consider, for instance, the theme of the
storm-wind which not only opens Salmanov's *The Twelve* but plays an
important part throughout:

Ex. 292

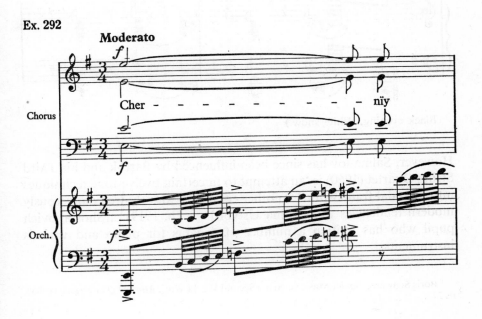

(Black evening, White snow.)

However, Salmanov has since been influenced by Bartók and his Third
String Quartet (1960) is 'an attempt to fit certain twelve-tone techniques
into a modal framework.[1] Another composer who showed dangerously
modern tendencies was Galina Ustvolskaya (b. 1919), a Shostakovich
pupil who has written a number of sonatas for piano and various
instruments.

---

[1] Boris Schwarz, 'Soviet Music since the Second World War', *Musical Quarterly*, li (1965),
p. 277.

THE *AVANT GARDE*

A genuine *avant-garde*, employing twelve-note and aleatory techniques, emerged when the composers born during the 1930s came to maturity thirty years later. They even managed to get a respectful hearing for some of their work. When Andrey Volkonsky (b. 1933) first performed in public his twelve-note piano suite *Musica Stricta* (1957) it was dismissed as 'fashionable experiment and nothing more'[1] but his later work won toleration though not official approval. Born in Geneva of *émigré* parents, Volkonsky had studied as a child with Nadia Boulanger; but he made his home in Russia and completed his studies in Moscow under Shaporin. He first attracted attention with a setting of Paul Eluard's *Poèmes pour la paix* for mezzo-soprano, chorus, organ, and orchestra (1952) and a Piano Quintet (1955). By 1962 he was writing a *Game in Three* for violin, flute, and harpsichord, suggested by Stockhausen's *Kreuzspiel*. Aleatory works by other composers followed: for instance, the *Dialogï* for wind quintet (1964) by Sergey Slonimsky (b. 1932), which employ both aleatory and serial techniques, and the *Crescendo e diminuendo* for twelve strings and kettledrum (1965) of Edison Denisov (b. 1929). A more important work of Denisov's is *Soleil des Incas*, a cantata for soprano and eleven solo instruments on a text by Gabriela Mistral (1964). Other leading composers of this *avant-garde*, whose works are publicly performed and seriously discussed, are Boris Tishchenko, a pupil of Ustvolskaya, Salmonov, and Shostakovich, Valentin Silvestrov (b. 1937), and two Estonians, Arvo Päärt (b. 1935) and Kuldar Sink (b. 1942). Sink has experimented with both electronic music and *musique concrète*.

MUSIC IN THE NON-RUSSIAN REPUBLICS

The interest taken by Russian musicians such as Glier and Ippolitov-Ivanov (in the nineteen-twenties) and Myaskovsky and Prokofyev (during the War) in the music of the Caucasian peoples of the Soviet Union has already been mentioned. Such interest was not in itself new, of course; but it was of a different nature from the interest of nineteenth-century tourists like Balakirev and Taneyev.[2] The Soviet Government from the very early days attached great importance to the stimulation of the native arts in the Asiatic republics of the Union, and Russian musicians and musicologists were sent to study their folk-musics[3] and

[1] Václav Kučera, *Nové proudy v sovetské hudbé* (Prague, 1967), p. 19.

[2] Taneyev's study of Kabardinian folk-music, 'O muzïke gorskikh Tatar', is printed in V. Protopopov (ed.), *Pamyati S.I. Taneeva: 1856–1946* (Moscow, 1947), p. 195, with Belyaev's commentary, ibid., p. 212.

[3] The results have been published in such monographs as Viktor Uspensky and Viktor Belyaev, *Turkmenskaya muzïka* (Moscow, 1928), and Belyaev, *Ocherki po istorii muzïki narodov SSSR*, i and ii (Moscow, 1962 and 1963).

foster the development of more ambitious musical forms on the basis of folk-art. Such works as Glier's operas *Shakh-Senem* (Baku, 1927), *Leyli i Medzhnun* (Tashkent, 1940) and *Gyulsara* (Tashkent, 1949)—the last two in collaboration with the Uzbek composer, Talib Sadïkov (b. 1907)—and Knipper's orchestral suites *Vanch* (on Tadzhik themes) (1937), *Turkmenskie eskizï* (Turkmenian sketches) (1940), and *Kurumkan* (on Buryat-Mongolian themes) (1948), are essentially different from nineteenth-century Russian essays in orientalism; they are attempts to provide models for authentic Caucasian or Central Asian art-music. Conversely Caucasian composers—the Armenian Khachaturyan is the outstanding example—have settled in Russia and, without sacrificing their native accents, made notable contributions to Russian music. Others, such as the Georgian, Andrey Balanchivadze (b. 1906), himself the son of a composer (Meliton Balanchivadze, 1862–1937), the Azerbaidzhanian Kara Karaev (b. 1918), a pupil of Shostakovich, the Armenian Eduard Mirzoyan (b. 1921) and the Georgian Sulkhan Tsintsadze (b. 1925), have preferred to stay in their native lands. The piano concertos of Balanchivadze and the string quartets of Tsintsadze have won popularity all over the U.S.S.R.

Even the Ukraine has produced composers who have followed Mïkola Lïsenko (1842–1912) in refusing to allow themselves to be swallowed by Great Russian culture—notably Boris Lyatoshinsky (b. 1895), Mikhail Verikovsky (b. 1896), and Gleb Taranov (b. 1905). But Ukrainian musical nationalism is perhaps a dying cause.

BIBLIOGRAPHY

The bibliography for Chapters III and V is by John Arnn, and for Chapter VI by Lewis Foreman

GENERAL

ABRAHAM, GERALD: *A Hundred Years of Music* (London, 3rd ed., 1964).

ADORNO, T. W.: *Philosophie der Neuen Musik* (Tübingen, 1949).

AUSTIN, W. W.: *Music in the Twentieth Century* (New York, 1966).

BAUER, MARIAN: *Twentieth-Century Music* (New York, 1933).

CALVOCORESSI, M. D.: *Musicians' Gallery* (London, 1933).

CARNER, MOSCO: *A Study of Twentieth-Century Harmony* (London, 1942).

COOPER, MARTIN: *French Music* (*From the death of Berlioz to the death of Fauré*) (London, 1951).

CORTOT, ALFRED: *La Musique française de piano* (Paris, three vols., 1930, 1932 and 1944).

DUNWELL, WILFRID: *The Evolution of Twentieth-Century Harmony* (London, 1960).

DYSON, GEORGE: *The New Music* (London, 1924).

HARTOG, EDWARD (ed.): *European Music in the Twentieth Century* (2nd ed., London, 1961).

LISSA, ZÓFIA: 'Geschichtliche Vorform der Zwölftontechnik', *Acta Musicologica*, vii (1935).

MELLERS, WILFRID: *Caliban Reborn: Renewal in Twentieth-Century Music* (London, 1968).

——*Studies in Contemporary Music* (London, 1947).

MERSMANN, HANS: *Die moderne Musik seit der Romantik* (Potsdam, 1931).

——*Musik der Gegenwart* (Berlin, 1923).

MITCHELL, DONALD: *The Language of Modern Music* (London, 1963).

MYERS, ROLLO: *Modern French Music* (Oxford, 1971).

——Twentieth-Century Music (2nd ed., London, 1968).

ROHOZINSKI, L. (ed.): *Cinquante ans de musique française* (Paris, 1925).

SCHOENBERG, ARNOLD: *Style and Idea* (New York, 1950).

SLONIMSKY, NICOLAS: *Music since 1900* (New York, 4th ed., 1972).

SOUVTCHINSKY, PIERRE: *Musique russe* (Paris, 1953).

STEIN, ERWIN: *Orpheus in New Guises* (London, 1953).

STEPHAN, RUDOLF: *Neue Musik* (Göttingen, 1958).

STUCKENSCHMIDT, H. H.: *Twentieth-Century Music* (London, 1969).

Twentieth-Century Composers. In 5 vols.:

——Vol. 1 American Composers since 1910. By Virgil Thompson.

——Vol. 2 Germany and Central Europe. By H. H. Stuckenschmidt (1970).

WEBERN, ANTON: *Wege zur neuen Musik* (Vienna, 1960).

WELLESZ, EGON: *Die neue Instrumentation* (Berlin, two vols., 1928 and 1929).

WÖRNER, KARL H.: *Musik der Gegenwart* (Mainz, 1949).

——*Neue Musik in der Entscheidung* (Mainz, 1954).

CHAPTERS I AND II

THE APOGEE AND DECLINE OF ROMANTICISM and THE REACTION AGAINST ROMANTICISM: 1890–1914

(i) *General*

BUSONI, FERRUCCIO: *Von der Einheit der Musik* (Berlin, 1922; English translation, London, 1957).

LANDORMY, PAUL: *La Musique française de Franck à Debussy* (Paris, 1943).

LENORMAND, RENÉ: *Étude sur l'harmonie moderne* (Paris, 1913; English translation, London, 1915).

ROLLAND, ROMAIN: *Musiciens d'aujourd'hui* (Paris, 1908).

(ii) *Individual Composers* (books and articles dealing with their non-operatic works of the period 1890–1914)

Bartók

'Bartók' numbers of *Musikblätter des Anbruch* (1921) and *Tempo* (1949–50).

MASON, COLIN: 'Bartók's Rhapsodies', *Music and Letters*, xxx (1949).

——'Bartók's Early Violin Concerto', *Tempo*, 49 (1958).

——'Bartók's Scherzo for Piano and Orchestra', *Tempo*, 65 (1963).

NÜLL, EDWIN VON DER: *Béla Bartók: Ein Beitrag zur Morphologie der neuen Musik* (Halle, 1930).

STEVENS, HALSEY: *The Life and Music of Béla Bartók* (New York, 2nd ed., 1964).

——'Some "Unknown" Works of Bartók', *Musical Quarterly*, lii (1966).

UJFALUSSY, JÓZSEF: *Bartók* (Budapest, 1965; English translation, Budapest, 1971).

Berg

CHADWICK, NICHOLAS: 'Berg's Unpublished Songs in the Österreichische Nationalbibliothek', *Music and Letters*, lii (1971).

LEIBOWITZ, RENÉ: 'Alban Berg's Five Orchestral Songs, Op. 4', *Musical Quarterly*, xxxiv (1948).

REDLICH, HANS F.: *Alban Berg: Versuch einer Würdigung* (Vienna, 1957; English condensation, London, 1957).

REICH, WILLI: *Alban Berg* (Vienna, 1937).

——*Alban Berg: Leben und Werk* (Zürich, 1963; English translation, London, 1965).

STUCKENSCHMIDT, H. H.: 'Debussy or Berg? The Mystery of a Chord Progression', *Musical Quarterly*, li (1965).

Busoni

'Busoni' numbers of *Musikblätter des Anbruch* (1921) and *Rassegna musicale* (1940).

DEBUSMANN, EMIL: *Ferruccio Busoni* (Wiesbaden, 1949).

DENT, EDWARD J.: *Ferruccio Busoni: a Biography* (Oxford, 1933).

LEICHTENTRITT, HUGO: 'Ferruccio Busoni', *Music Review*, vi (1945).

SITSKY, LARRY: 'The Six Sonatinas for Piano of Ferruccio Busoni', *Studies in Music* (Perth, Western Australia), ii (1968).

STUCKENSCHMIDT, H. H.: *Ferruccio Busoni, Zeittafel eines Europäers* (Zürich, 1967; English translation, London, 1970).

VLAD, ROMAN: 'Busoni's Destiny', *Score*, 7 (1952).

Chausson

BARRICELLI, PIERRE, and WEINSTEIN, LEO: *Ernest Chausson: the Composer's Life and Works* (Norman, Oklahoma, 1955).

'Chausson' number of *Revue musicale* (1925).

Debussy

D'ALMENDRA, JULIA: *Les Modes grégoriens dans l'oeuvre de Claude Debussy* (Paris, 1948).

BRAILOU, CONSTANTIN: 'Pentatony in Debussy's Music', *Studia Memoriae Bélae Bartók Sacra* (3rd ed., London, 1959).

DAWES, FRANK: *Debussy: Piano Music* (London, 1969).

'Debussy' numbers of *Revue musicale* (1920, 1926, 1964).

FISCHER, KURT VON: 'Bemerkungen zu den zwei Ausgaben von Debussys *Ariettes oubliées*', *Symbolae Historiae Musicae* (Federhofer Festschrift), (Mainz, 1971).

GERVAIS, FRANÇOISE: *Debussy et l'évolution de la musique au XXe siècle* (Paris, 1965).

GRUBER, GERNOT: 'Zur Funktion der "primären Klangformen" in der Musik Debussys', *Symbolae Historiae Musicae* (Mainz, 1971).

JAKOBIK, ALBERT: *Die assoziative Harmonik in den Klavier-Werken Claude Debussys* (Würzburg, 1940).

JANKÉLÉVITCH, VLADIMIR: *Debussy et le mystère* (Neuchâtel, 1949).

KOECHLIN, CHARLES: *Debussy* (Paris, 1927).

KOLSCH, HANS F.: *Der Impressionismus bei Debussy* (Düsseldorf, 1937).

LIESS, ANDREAS: *Claude Debussy: das Werk im Zeitbild* (Strasbourg, 1936).

——*Claude Debussy und das deutsche Musikschaffen* (Würzburg, 1939).

——'L'harmonie dans les oeuvres de Claude Debussy', *Revue musicale* (1931).

LOCKSPEISER, EDWARD: *Debussy* (revised edition, London, 1951).

——*Debussy: his Life and Mind* (two volumes, London, 1962 and 1965).

MELLERS, WILFRID: 'The Later Work of Claude Debussy', in *Studies in Contemporary Music* (London, 1947).

NICHOLS, ROGER: 'Debussy's Two Settings of "Clair de lune"', *Music and Letters*, xl (1967).

PHILLIPS, C. HENRY: 'The Symbolists and Debussy', *Music and Letters*, xiii (1932).

SCHAEFFNER, ANDRÉ: 'Debussy et ses rapports avec la musique russe', in *Musique russe*, i (ed. P. Souvtchinsky) (Paris, 1953).

SCHMITZ, ROBERT: *The Piano Works of Claude Debussy* (New York, 1950).

STORB, ILSE: *Untersuchungen zur Auflösung der funktionaler Harmonik in den Klavierwerken von Claude Debussy* (Cologne, 1967).

STUCKENSCHMIDT, H. H.: 'Debussy or Berg? The Mystery of a Chord Progression', *Musical Quarterly*, li (1965).

VALLAS, LÉON: *Claude Debussy et son temps* (Paris, 1932; English translation, London, 1933).

——*Les Idées de Claude Debussy, musicien français* (Paris, 1927; English translation, 1929).

Delius

ABRAHAM, GERALD: 'Delius and his Literary Sources', in *Slavonic and Romantic Music* (London, 1968).

BEECHAM, THOMAS: *Frederick Delius* (London, 1959).

COOKE, DERYCK: 'Delius and Form: a Vindication', *Musical Times*, ciii (1962).

'Delius' number of *Tempo* (1952).

HESELTINE, PHILIP: *Frederick Delius* (revised ed., London, 1952).

HOLLAND, A. K.: *The Songs of Delius* (London, 1951).

HUTCHINGS, ARTHUR: *Delius* (London, 1948).

PALMER, CHRISTOPHER: 'Delius and Poetic Realism', *Music and Letters,* li (1970).

——'Delius, Vaughan Williams and Debussy', *Music and Letters*, l (1969).

PAYNE, ANTHONY: 'Delius's Stylistic Development', *Tempo*, 60 (1961).

Dukas

'Dukas' number of *Revue musicale* (1936).

FAVRE, GEORGES: *Paul Dukas: sa vie – son oeuvre* (Paris, 1948).

Elgar

DANN, MARY, G.: 'Elgar's Use of the Sequence', *Music and Letters*, xix (1938).
'Elgar' number of *Music and Letters* (1935).
KENNEDY, MICHAEL: *Elgar: Orchestral Music* (London, 1970).
MCVEAGH, DIANA M.: *Edward Elgar: his Life and Music* (London, 1955).
MAINE, BASIL: *Elgar: his Life and Work* (London, 1933).

Falla

MAYER-SERRA, OTTO: 'Falla's Musical Nationalism', *Musical Quarterly*, xxix (1943).
PAHISSA, JAIME: *Vida y obra de Manuel de Falla* (Buenos Aires, 1947; English translation, 1954).
TREND, J. B.: *Manuel de Falla and Spanish Music* (London, 1930).
——'Manuel de Falla in "Arabia"', *Music and Letters*, iii (1922).

Fauré

'Fauré' numbers of *Revue musicale* (1922) and *Monthly Musical Record* (1945).
FAVRE, MAX: *Gabriel Faurés Kammermusik* (Zürich), 1948.
JANKÉLÉVITCH, VLADIMIR: *Gabriel Fauré: ses mélodies – son esthétique* (revised and enlarged edition, Paris, 1951).
KOECHLIN, CHARLES: *Gabriel Fauré* (Paris, 1927; English translation, London, 1945).
MELLERS, WILFRID: 'The Later Work of Gabriel Fauré' in *Studies in Contemporary Music* (London, 1947).
SUCKLING, NORMAN: *Fauré* (London, 1946).

Granados

COLLET, HENRI: *Albeniz et Granados* (Paris, 1926).
'Granados' number of *Revista musical catalana* (1916).
LIVERMORE, ANN: 'Granados and the Nineteenth Century in Spain', *Music Review*, vii (1946).

Grieg

ABRAHAM, GERALD (ed.): *Grieg: a Symposium* (London, 1948).
FISCHER, KURT VON: *Griegs Harmonik und die nordländische Folklore* (Berne, 1938).
HORTON, JOHN: 'Grieg's "Slaatter" for Pianoforte', *Music and Letters*, xxvi (1945).
SCHJELDERUP-EBBE, DAG: *A Study of Grieg's Harmony* (Oslo, 1953).

Holst

HOLST, IMOGEN: *The Music of Gustav Holst* (London, 1951).

d'Indy

'd'Indy' numbers of *Revue musicale* (1932, 1937).
SAINT-SAËNS, CAMILLE: *Les Idées de M. Vincent d'Indy* (Paris, 1919).
SÉRIEYX, AUGUSTE: *Vincent d'Indy* (Paris, 1914).
VALLAS, LÉON: *Vincent d'Indy* (Paris, two vols. 1946 and 1950).

Koechlin

CALVOCORESSI, M. D.: 'Charles Koechlin's Instrumental Works', *Music and Letters*, v (1924).
MELLERS, WILFRID: 'Charles Koechlin' in *Studies in Contemporary Music* (London, 1947).

Magnard

CARRAUD, GASTON: *La Vie, l'oeuvre et la mort d'Albéric Magnard* (Paris, 1921).

Mahler

ADLER, GUIDO: *Gustav Mahler* (Vienna, 1916).
BARFORD, PHILIP: *Mahler: Symphonies and Songs* (London, 1970).

BEKKER, PAUL: *Gustav Mahlers Sinfonien* (Berlin and Stuttgart, 1921).
LOCKSPEISER, EDWARD: 'Mahler in France', *Monthly Musical Record*, xc (1960).
MAHLER, ALMA M.: *Gustav Mahler: Erinnerungen und Briefe* (Amsterdam, 1940; enlarged and revised English translation, London, 1968).
MAHLER, GUSTAV: *Briefe, 1879–1911* (Berlin, Vienna and Leipzig, 1924).
'Mahler' numbers of *Die Musik* (1911) and *Musikblätter des Anbruch* (1920, 1930).
MITCHELL, DONALD: *Gustav Mahler: The Early Years* (London, 1958).
NEWLIN, DIKA: *Bruckner—Mahler—Schoenberg* (New York, 1947).
PAMER, FRITZ EGON: 'Gustav Mahlers Lieder', *Studien zur Musikwissenschaft*, xvi (1929) and xvii (1930).
RATZ, ERWIN: 'Zum Formproblem bei Gustav Mahler: Eine Analyse des ersten Satzes der IX. Symphonie', *Musikforschung*, viii (1955).
——'Zum Formproblem bei Gustav Mahler: Eine Analyse des Finales der VI. Symphonie', *Musikforschung*, ix (1956).
REDLICH, HANS F.: *Bruckner and Mahler* (London, 1955).
SCHAEFERS, ANTON: *Gustav Mahlers Instrumentation* (Düsseldorf, 1935).
STEFAN, PAUL: *Gustav Mahler* (enlarged and revised edition, Munich, 1920).
TISCHLER, HANS: 'Mahler's "Das Lied von der Erde"', *Music Review*, x (1949).
——'Mahler's Impact on the Crisis of Tonality', *Music Review*, xii (1951).
WELLESZ, EGON: 'The Symphonies of Gustav Mahler', *Music Review*, i (1940).

Nielsen
NIELSEN, CARL: *Levende Musik* (Copenhagen, 1925).
SIMPSON, ROBERT: *Carl Nielsen, Symphonist* (London, 1952).

Rakhmaninov
CULSHAW, JOHN: *Sergei Rachmaninov* (London, 1949).
'Rakhmaninov' number of *Tempo* (1951).
TSITOVICH, T. E. (ed.): *S. V. Rakhmaninov: sbornik statey i materialov* (Moscow and Leningrad, 1947).
VASINA-GROSSMAN, V. A.: 'Romansï Rakhmaninova', in *Russkiy klassicheskiy romans XIX veka* (Moscow, 1956).
ZHITOMIRSKY, D.: 'Fortepiannoe tvorchestvo Rakhmaninova', *Sovetskaya muzïka: sbornik statey*, 4 (1945).

Ravel
AKERET, KURT: *Studien zum Klavierwerk von Maurice Ravel* (Zürich, 1941).
BRUYR, JOSÉ: *Maurice Ravel, ou le lyrisme et les sortilèges* (Paris, 1950).
CALVOCORESSI, M. D.: 'When Ravel composed to order', *Music and Letters*, xxii (1941).
JANKÉLÉVITCH, VLADIMIR: *Ravel* (2nd ed., Paris, 1956).
JOURDAN-MORHANGE, HÉLÈNE: *Ravel et nous* (Geneva, 1945).
ORENSTEIN, ARBIE: 'Maurice Ravel's Creative Process', *Musical Quarterly*, liii (1967).
'Ravel' numbers of *Revue musicale* (1925, 1938).
ROLAND-MANUEL: *A la gloire de Ravel* (Paris, 1938; English translation, London, 1947).

Reger
BAGIER, GUIDO: *Max Reger* (Stuttgart and Berlin, 1923).
COENEN, PAUL: *Max Regers Variationsschaffen* (Berlin, 1935).
DENECKE, H. L.: 'Max Regers Sonatenform in ihrer Entwicklung', *Festschrift Fritz Stein* (Brunswick, 1939).
GATSCHER, E.: *Die Fugentechnik Max Regers in ihrer Entwicklung* (Stuttgart, 1925).
HUESGEN, R.: *Der junge Reger und seine Orgelwerke* (Schrammberg, 1935).
MOSER, HANS JOACHIM: 'Max Regers Orchesterwerke', *Festschrift Max Reger* (Leipzig, 1953).

RAHNER, HUGO E.: 'Max Regers Choralfantasien für die Orgel', *Heidelberger Studien zur Musikwissenschaft* (Kassel, 1936).

'Reger' number of *Die Musik* (1921).

STEIN, FRITZ: *Max Reger* (Potsdam, 1939).

——*Thematisches Verzeichnis der im Druck erschienenen Werke von Max Reger* (enlarged edition, Leipzig, 1953).

THERSTAPPEN, H. J.: 'Über die Grundlagen der Form bei Max Reger', *Festschrift Fritz Stein* (Brunswick, 1939).

WEHMEYER, GRETE: 'Max Reger als Liederkomponist', *Kölner Beiträge zur Musikforschung* (Regensburg, 1955).

WURZ, R. (ed.): *Max Reger: eine Sammlung von Studien aus dem Kreise seiner persönlichen Schüler* (Munich, four *Hefte*, 1920–3).

Roslavets

GOJOWY, DETLEF: 'Nikolaj Andreevic Roslavec, ein früher Zwölftonkomponist', *Musikforschung*, xxii (1969).

ROSLAVETS, NIKOLAY: 'Nik. A. Roslavets o sebe i svoem tvorchestve', *Sovremennaya muzïka*, no. 5 (1924).

Roussel

BERNARD, ROBERT: *Albert Roussel* (Paris, 1948).

DEANE, BASIL: *Albert Roussel* (London, 1961).

HOÉRÉE, A. R.: *Albert Roussel* (Paris, 1938).

LOCKSPEISER, EDWARD: 'Roussel and Ravel', *Music and Letters*, xix (1938).

MELLERS, WILFRID: 'Albert Roussel and *La Musique française*', in *Studies in Contemporary Music* (London, 1947).

PINCHERLE, MARC: *Albert Roussel* (Geneva, 1957).

'Roussel' numbers of *Revue musicale* (1929, 1937).

Satie

AUSTIN, WILLIAM: 'Satie before and after Cocteau', *Musical Quarterly*, xlviii (1962).

DANCKERT, WERNER: 'Der Klassizismus Erik Saties und seine geistesgeschichtliche Stellung', *Zeitschrift für Musikwissenschaft*, xii (1929–30).

MELLERS, WILFRID: 'Erik Satie and the "Problem" of Contemporary Music', in *Studies in Contemporary Music* (London, 1947).

MYERS, ROLLO H.: *Erik Satie* (London, 1948).

TEMPLIER, PIERRE-DANIEL: *Erik Satie* (Paris, 1932; English translation, London, 1969).

Schmitt

HUCHER, YVES: *Florent Schmitt, l'homme et l'artiste, son époque et son oeuvre* (Paris, 1953).

Schoenberg

ARMITAGE, MERLE (ed.): *Arnold Schoenberg* (New York, 1939).

BERG, ALBAN: *Gurrelieder (Führer)*, (Vienna, 1913).

——*Kammersinfonie, Op. 9 (Thematische Analyse)*, (Vienna, n.d.).

——*Pelleas und Melisande, Op. 5 (Kurze thematische Analyse)* (Vienna, n.d.).

——'Warum ist Schönbergs Musik so schwer verständlich?', reprinted in Willi Reich, *Alban Berg* (Vienna, 1937).

BOULEZ, PIERRE: 'L'Oeuvre pour piano de Schönberg', in *Relevés d'apprenti* (Paris, 1966; English translation, 1968).

BRINKMANN, REINHOLD: *Arnold Schönberg: Drei Klavierstücke Op. 11 (Studien zur frühen Atonalität bei Schönberg)* (Wiesbaden, 1969).

EHRENFORTH, K. H.: *Ausdruck und Form (Schönbergs Durchbruch zur Atonalität in den George-Liedern, Op. 15)* (Bonn, 1963).

FRIEDBERG, RUTH: 'The Solo Keyboard Works of Arnold Schönberg', *Music Review*, xxiii (1962).

FRIEDHEIM, PHILIP: *Tonality and Structure in the Early Works of Schoenberg* (Diss. New York Univ., 1963).

HOPKINS, G. W.: 'Schoenberg and the "Logic" of Atonality', *Tempo*, 94 (1970).

JALOWETZ, HEINRICH: 'On the Spontaneity of Schoenberg's Music', *Musical Quarterly*, xxx (1944).

NEWLIN, DIKA: *Bruckner—Mahler—Schoenberg* (New York, 1947).

PAYNE, ANTHONY: *Schoenberg* (London, 1968).

RUFER, JOSEF: *Das Werk Arnold Schönbergs* (Kassel, 1959; English translation, London, 1962).

SCHOENBERG, ARNOLD: *Harmonielehre* (Vienna, 1911).

——*Style and Idea* (New York, 1951).

——'Schoenberg' Festschriften (Munich, 1912 and Vienna, 1925 and 1934); 'Schoenberg' numbers of *Musikblätter des Anbruch* (1924), *Pult und Taktstock* (1927), etc.

WELLESZ, EGON: *Arnold Schönberg* (Vienna, 1921; English translation, London, 1925; new edition, 1972).

WILLE, RUDOLF: 'Reihentechnik in Schönbergs opus 19, 2', *Musikforschung*, xix (1966).

Sibelius

ABRAHAM, GERALD (ed.): *Sibelius: a Symposium* (London, 1947).

GRAY, CECIL: *Sibelius: the Symphonies* (London, 1935).

HILL, WILLIAM G.: 'Some Aspects of Form in the Symphonies of Sibelius', *Music Review*, x (1949).

LAYTON, ROBERT: *Sibelius* (London, 1965).

PARMET, SIMON: *Sibelius Symfonier* (Helsinki, 1955; English translation, London, 1959).

ROIHA, EINO: *Die Symphonien von Jean Sibelius: eine formanalytische Studie* (Jyväskylä, 1941).

TANZBERGER, ERNST: *Die symphonischen Dichtungen von Jean Sibelius* (Würzburg, 1943).

TAWASTSTJERNA, ERIK: *The Compositions of Sibelius* (Helsinki, 1957–).

Skyrabin

BERKOV, V.: 'Nekotorïe voprosï garmonii Skryabina', *Sovetskaya muzïka*, xxiii (1959).

COOPER, MARTIN: 'Scriabin's Mystical Beliefs', *Music and Letters*, xvi (1935).

DICKENMANN, PAUL: *Die Entwicklung der Harmonik bei A. Skrjabin* (Berne, 1935).

GLEICH, C. C. J. VON: *Die sinfonischen Werke von Alexander Skrjabin* (Bilthoven, 1963).

KELDISH, YURY: 'Ideynïe protivorechiya v tvorchestve A. N. Skryabina', *Sovetskaya muzïka*, xvi (1950).

LISSA, ZOFIA: 'O harmonice A. N. Skrjabin', *Kwartalnik muzyczny*, viii (1930).

SABANEYEV, LEONID: *A. N. Skryabin* (Moscow, 1922).

——*Vospominaniya o Skryabina* (Moscow, 1925).

Skryabïn, N. A., 1915–1940: Sbornik k 25-letiyu so dnya smerti (Moscow, 1940).

'Skryabin' number of *Muzïkalny sovremennik* (1916).

WESTPHAL, KURT: 'Die Harmonik Scrjabins', *Musikblätter des Anbruch*, xi (1929).

Strauss

DEL MAR, NORMAN: *Richard Strauss: a Critical Commentary on his Life and Work* (three volumes, London, 1963, 1969 and 1972).

GYSI, FRITZ: *Richard Strauss* (Potsdam, 1934).

MUELLER VON ASOW, E. H.: *Richard Strauss: Thematisches Verzeichnis* (two volumes, published Vienna, 1955 and 1959).

LORENZ, ALFRED: 'Neue Formerkenntnisse angewandt auf Richard Straussens "Don Juan"', *Archiv für Musikforschung*, i (1936).

SCHUH, WILLI (ed.): *Richard Strauss Jahrbuch* (Bonn, 1954–00).

SPECHT, RICHARD: *Richard Strauss und sein Werk* (Vienna, 1921).

STEINITZER, MAX: *Richard Strauss* (Berlin, revised and enlarged edition, 1922).

TENSCHERT, ROLAND: 'Die Kadenzbehandlung bei Richard Strauss', *Zeitschrift für Musikwissenschaft*, viii (1925–6).

——'Versuch einer Typologie der Richard Strausschen Melodik', *Zeitschrift für Musikwissenschaft*, xvi (1934).

WACHTEN, EDMUND: 'Der einheitliche Grundzug der Strausschen Formgestaltung', *Zeitschrift für Musikwissenschaft*, xvi (1934).

Stravinsky

BOYS, HENRY: 'Stravinsky: A Propos his Aesthetic', *Score*, 2 (1950).

——'Stravinsky: The Musical Materials', *Score*, 4 (1951).

DREW, DAVID: 'Stravinsky's Revisions', *Score*, 20 (1957).

EVANS, EDWIN: *Stravinsky: 'The Fire-Bird' and 'Petrushka'*, (London, 1933).

'GLEBOV, IGOR' (Boris Asafyev): Kniga o Stravinskom (Leningrad, 1929).

HOPKINS, G. W.: 'Stravinsky's Chords', *Tempo*, 76 and 77 (1966).

SCHAEFFNER, ANDRÉ: *Stravinsky* (Paris, 1931).

SCHUH, WILLI: 'Zur Harmonik Igor Strawinskys', *Schweizerische Musikzeitung*, xcii (1952).

SMALLEY, ROGER: 'The Sketchbook of *The Rite of Spring*', *Tempo*, 91 (1969).

STRAVINSKY, IGOR: *Poétique musicale* (Cambridge, Mass., 1942; English translation, Cambridge, Mass., 1947; revised edition, Paris, 1952).

'Stravinsky' numbers of *Revue musicale* (1923 and 1939), *Musical Quarterly* (1962) and *Tempo* (1948, 1967 and 1971).

TANSMAN, ALEXANDRE: *Igor Stravinsky* (Paris, 1948; English translation, New York, 1949).

VLAD, ROMAN: *Stravinsky* (Milan, 1958; English translation, 2nd edition, London, 1967).

WHITE, ERIC WALTER: *Stravinsky: The Composer and his Works* (London, 1966).

Szymanowski

CHOMINSKY, JOZEF: 'Szymanowski i Skryabin', in *Russko-polskie muzïkalnïe svyazi* (ed. Igor Belza), (Moscow, 1963).

LOBACZEWSKA, STEFANIA: *Karol Szymanowski: Życie i twórczosc* (Cracow, 1950).

STUCKENSCHMIDT, H. H.: 'Karol Szymanowski', *Music and Letters*, xix (1938).

Vaughan Williams

DICKINSON, A. E. F.: *An Introduction to the Music of R. Vaughan Williams* (London, 1928).

FOSS, HUBERT: *Ralph Vaughan Williams* (London, 1950).

HOWES, FRANK: *The Music of Ralph Vaughan Williams* (London, 1954).

KENNEDY, MICHAEL: *The Works of Ralph Vaughan Williams* (London, 1964).

KIMMEL, WILLIAM: 'Vaughan Williams's Choice of Words', *Music and Letters*, xxi (1938).

——'Vaughan Williams's Melodic Style', *Musical Quarterly*, xxvii (1941).

PAYNE, ELSIE: 'Vaughan Williams and Folksong', *Music Review*, xv (1954).

VAUGHAN WILLIAMS, RALPH: *National Music* (London, 1934).

Webern

CONE, EDWARD T.: 'Webern's Apprenticeship', *Musical Quarterly*, liii (1967).

KOLNEDER, WALTER: *Anton Webern: Einführung in Werk und Stil* (Rodenkirchen, 1961; English translation, London, 1968).

CHAPTER III

STAGE WORKS: 1890–1918

(i) *General*

GILMAN, LAWRENCE: *Aspects of Modern Opera* (London, 1924).

GROUT, DONALD JAY: *A Short History of Opera* (New York, 1947; 2nd ed., 1965).

ISTEL, EDGAR: *Die moderne Oper vom Tode Wagners bis zum Weltkrieg* (Leipzig, 1915; 2nd ed., 1923).

——'German Opera since Richard Wagner', *Musical Quarterly*, i (1915).

KLEIN, JOHN W.: 'Verdi's Italian Contemporaries and Successors', *Music and Letters*, xv (1934).

LOUIS, RUDOLF: *Die deutsche Musik der Gegenwart* (Munich, 1909; 3rd ed., 1912).

PROD'HOMME, JACQUES GABRIEL: 'The Recent Fiftieth Anniversary of the "New Opera"', *Musical Quarterly*, xii (1926).

SCHULLER, KENNETH GUSTAVE: *'Verismo' Opera and the Verists* (Diss. Washington Univ., 1960).

(ii) *Individual Composers*

d'Albert

RAUPP, WILHELM: *Eugen d'Albert. Ein Künstler und Menschenschicksal* (Leipzig, 1930).

SCHMITZ, EUGEN: 'Eugen d'Albert als Opernkomponist', *Hochland*, vi (1909).

TORCHI, LUIGI: *'Ghismonda*, opera in tre atti di Eugenio d'Albert', *Rivista musicale italiana*, iii (1896).

Bartók

LENDVAI, ERNÖ: 'A kékszakállu herceg vára' (*Duke Bluebeard's Castle*), *Magyar Zene*, i (1961).

VERESS, SANDOR: 'Bluebeard's Castle', *Tempo*, xiii (1949); xiv (1949–50); repr. in *Béla Bartók: A Memorial Review* (New York, 1950).

Bloch

COHEN, ALEX: 'Ernest Bloch's *Macbeth*', *Music and Letters*, xix (1938).

GATTI, GUIDO MARIA: 'Two *Macbeths*: Verdi-Bloch', *Musical Quarterly*, xii (1926).

HALL, RAYMOND: 'The *Macbeth* of Bloch', *Modern Music*, xv (1938).

HASTINGS, JOHN: 'Ernst Bloch and Modern Music', *Music Review*, x (1949).

NEWLIN, DIKA: 'The Later Works of Ernest Bloch', *Musical Quarterly*, xxxiii (1947).

TIBALDI-CHIESA, M.: *Ernest Bloch* (Turin, 1933).

Busoni

DENT, EDWARD J.: 'Busoni's *Doctor Faust*', *Music and Letters*, vii (1926).

GATTI, GUIDO MARIA: 'The Stage Works of Ferruccio Busoni', *Musical Quarterly*, xx (1934).

GOSLICH, SIEGFRIED: 'Das Wandbild: Othmar Schoeck und Ferruccio Busoni', *Musica*, xi (1957).

GUERRINI, GUIDO: *Ferruccio Busoni: la vita, la figura, l'opera* (Florence, 1944).

STUCKENSCHMIDT, HANS HEINZ: 'Rede über Busonis *Doktor Faust*', *Schweizerische Musikzeitung*, xcvi (1956).

Charpentier
DELMAS, MARC: *Gustave Charpentier et le lyrisme français* (Paris, 1931).
HIMONET, ANDRÉ: *Louise de Gustave Charpentier: Étude historique et critique, analyse musicale* (Paris, 1922).
HOOVER, KATHLEEN O'DONNELL: 'Gustave Charpentier', *Musical Quarterly*, xxv (1939).

Debussy
ACKERE, JULES VAN: *Pelléas et Mélisande, ou le recontre miraculeuse d'une poésie et d'une musique* (Brussels, 1952).
APPLEDORN, MARY JEANNE VAN: *A Stylistic Study of Claude Debussy's Opera 'Pelléas et Mélisande'* (Diss. Univ. of Rochester, 1966).
CHAILLEY, JACQUES: 'Le Symbolisme des thèmes dans *Pelléas et Mélisande*', *L'information musicale*, lxiv (1942).
DAVISON, ARCHIBALD T.: *The Harmonic Contribution of Claude Debussy* (Diss. Harvard Univ., 1908).
EMMANUEL, MAURICE: *'Pelléas et Mélisande': étude historique et critique, analyse musicale* (Paris, 1925).
GOLÉA, ANTOINE: *'Pelléas et Mélisande': Analyse poétique et musicale* (Paris, 1952).
LOCKSPEISER, EDWARD: *Debussy* (London, 1936; 3rd ed., 1951).
——*Debussy: His Life and Mind* (2 vols., London, 1962–5).
——'Mussorgsky and Debussy', *Musical Quarterly*, xxiii (1937).
PIZZETTI, ILDEBRANDO: *'Pelléas et Mélisande* ... Debussy', *Rivista musicale italiana*, xv (1908).

Delius
HUTCHINGS, ARTHUR: *Delius* (London, 1948).
——'Delius's Operas', *Tempo*, xxvi (1952–3).
KLEIN, JOHN W.: 'Delius as a Musical Dramatist', *Music Review*, xxii (1961).

Dukas
BUSNE, HENRY DE: *'Ariane et Barbe-bleue* de M. Paul Dukas', *Mercure musicale*, iii (1907).
PIZZETTI, ILDEBRANDO: *'Ariane et Barbebleue* ... de Paul Dukas', *Rivista musicale italiana*, xv (1908).

d'Indy
KUFFERATH, MAURICE: *'Fervaal* ... di V. d'Indy', *Rivista musicale italiana*, iv (1897).
ROLLAND, ROMAIN: *'L'Étranger* de Vincent d'Indy', *Rivista musicale italiana*, xi (1904).
VALLAS, LÉON: *Vincent d'Indy* (2 vols., Paris, 1946–50).

Mascagni
POMPEI, EDOARDO: *Pietro Mascagni* (Rome, 1912).
TORCHI, LUIGI: *'Guglielmo Ratclif* ... di Pietro Mascagni', *Rivista musicale italiana*, ii (1895).
——'Iris ... di Pietro Mascagni', *Rivista musicale italiana*, vi (1899).

Massenet
BRUNEAU, ALFRED: *Massenet* (Paris, 1935).
MASSENET, JULES-EMILE-FRÉDÉRIC: *Mes souvenirs* (Paris, 1912).
POUGIN, ARTHUR: 'Massenet', *Rivista musicale italiana*, xix (1912).

Pfitzner
BERRSCHE, ALEXANDER: *Kurze Einführung in Hans Pfitzners Musikdrama 'Der arme Heinrich'* (Leipzig, 1910).
HALUSA, KARL: *Pfitzners musikdramatisches⁻Schaffen* (Diss. Vienna, 1929).

MANN, THOMAS: *Pfitzners 'Palestrina'* (Berlin, 1919).
PFITZNER, HANS ERICH: *Gesammelte Schriften* (3 vols., Augsburg, 1926).
RUTZ, HANS: *Hans Pfitzner: Musik zwischen den Zeiten* (Vienna, 1949).

Puccini
BILLECI, A.: *'La Bohème' di Giacomo Puccini: Studio critico* (Palermo, 1931).
BONACCORSI, ALFREDO: *Giacomo Puccini e i suoi antenati musicali* (Milan, 1950).
CARNER, MOSCO: 'The Exotic Element in Puccini', *Musical Quarterly*, xxii (1936).
——*Puccini: A Critical Biography* (London, 1958).
——'Puccini's Early Operas', *Music and Letters*, xix (1938).
GATTI, GUIDO MARIA: 'The Works of Giacomo Puccini', *Musical Quarterly*, xiv (1928).
MARIANI, RENATO: 'L'ultimo Puccini', *Rassegna musicale,* ix (1936).
PARKER, DOUGLAS C.: 'A view of Giacomo Puccini', *Musical Quarterly*, iii (1917).
RICCI, LUIGI: *Puccini interprete di se stesso* (Milan, 1954).
SARTORI, CLAUDIO (ed.): *Giacomo Puccini* (Milan, 1959).
TORCHI, LUIGI: '*Tosca*, di G. Puccini', *Rivista musicale italiana*, vii (1900).

Schillings
LEPEL, FELIX VON: *Max von Schillings und seine Oper 'Mona Lisa': Ein Ruhmesblatt für die stadtische Oper in Berlin-Charlottenburg* (Berlin-Charlottenburg, 1954).

Richard Strauss
DEL MAR, NORMAN: *Richard Strauss* (3 vols., London, 1962, 1969, 1972).
ERHARDT, OTTO: *Richard Strauss, Leben, Wirken, Schaffen* (Freiburg/Breisgau, 1953).
FÄHNRICH, HERMANN: 'Richard Strauss über das Verhältnis von Dichtung und Musik (Wort und Ton) in seinem Opernschaffen', *Musikforschung*, xiv (1961).
GREGOR, JOSEF: *Richard Strauss, der Meister der Oper* (Munich, 1939).
JEFFERSON, ALAN: *The Operas of Richard Strauss in Britain, 1910–1963* (London, 1963).
KRALIK, HEINRICH: *Richard Strauss, Weltbürger der Musik* (Vienna, 1963).
KRÜGER, KARL-JOACHIM: *Hugo von Hofmannsthal und Richard Strauss* (Berlin, 1935)
MANN, WILLIAM: *Richard Strauss. A Critical Study of his Operas* (London, 1964).
ROTH, ERNST (ed.): *Richard Strauss Bühnenwerke* (London, 1954).
SCHMITZ, EUGEN: *Richard Strauss als Musikdramatiker* (Munich, 1907).
SCHUH, WILLI: *Hugo von Hofmannsthal und Richard Strauss, Legende und Wirklichkeit* (Munich, 1964).
——*Über Opern von Richard Strauss* (Zurich, 1947).
STRAUSS, RICHARD and HANS VON BÜLOW: *Correspondence* (English translation, London, 1955).
——and HUGO VON HOFMANNSTHAL: *Briefwechsel* (Zürich, 3rd ed., 1964).
——English translation as *A Working Friendship* (New York, 1961).
——and ROMAIN ROLLAND: *Correspondence,* ed. R. Meyers (Berkeley, Calif., 1968).
——and FRANZ WÜLLNER: *Briefwechsel,* ed. D. Kämper (Cologne, 1963).
TENSCHERT, ROLAND: 'Versuch einer Typologie der Richard Strausschen Melodik', *Zeitschrift für Musikwissenschaft,* xvi (1934–5).
——*Dreimal sieben Variationen über das Thema Richard Strauss* (Vienna, 1944).
TRENNER, FRANZ: *Richard Strauss: Dokumente seines Lebens und Schaffens* (Munich, 1954).

Wolf
BOLLERT, WERNER: 'Hugo Wolfs *Corregidor*', *Musica*, xiv (1960).
HELLMER, ELMUND (ed.): *'Der Corregidor' von Hugo Wolf* (Berlin, 1900).
HERNRIED, ROBERT: 'Hugo Wolf's "Four Operas"', *Musical Quarterly,* xxxi (1945).

REICH, WILLI: 'Dokument eines Gesprächs (Zur Wiener Erstauffführung von Wolfs *Corregidor*)', *Musica,* xiv (1960).

WALKER, FRANK: *Hugo Wolf* (London, 1951; 2nd ed., New York, 1968).

Wolf-Ferrari

GRISSON, ALEXANDER CAROLA: *Ermanno Wolf-Ferrari* (Zürich, 2nd ed., 1958).

PFANNKUCH, WILHELM: *Das Opernschaffen Ermanno Wolf-Ferraris* (Diss. Kiel Univ., 1953).

RINGO, JAMES: 'Ermanno Wolf-Ferrari: An Appreciation of his Work', *Rivista musicale italiana,* xlix (1949).

TORCHI, LUIGI: 'La vita nuova di E. Wolf-Ferrari', *Rivista musicale italiana,* x (1903).

WOLF-FERRARI, ERMANNO: 'Meine Beziehung zur komischen Oper', *Zeitschrift für Musik,* cviii (1941).

ZENTNER, WILHELM: 'Zum Opernschaffen Ermanno Wolf-Ferraris', *Zeitschrift für Musik,* cviii (1941).

CHAPTER IV

MUSIC IN THE MAINLAND OF EUROPE: 1918–1939

(i) *General*

AUSTIN, WILLIAM W.: *Harmonic Rhythm in Twentieth-Century Music* (Diss. Harvard Univ., 1951).

BABBITT, RICHARD B.: *The Harmonic Idioms in the Works of Les Six* (Diss. Boston Univ., 1963).

COLLAER, PAUL: *La musique moderne, 1905–1955* (Paris, 1955; English translation, as *A History of Modern Music,* Cleveland, 1961).

COOPER, GROSVENOR W.: *An introduction to the Analysis of Certain Contemporary Harmonic Practices* (Diss. Harvard Univ., 1939).

DAVIES, LAURENCE: *Paths to Modern Music* (London, 1971).

DERI, OTTO: *Exploring Twentieth Century Music* (New York, 1968).

DUMESNIL, RENÉ: *La Musique en France entre les deux guerres 1919–1939* (Geneva, 1946).

FRANCES, ROBERT: *La perception de la musique* (Paris, 1958).

HILL, EDWARD BURLINGAME: *Modern French Music* (Boston, 1924).

HÄUSLER, JOSEF: *Musik in 20 Jahrhundert von Schönberg zu Penderecki* (Bremen, 1969).

HODIER, ANDRÉ: *Since Debussy: A View of Contemporary Music* (English translation, New York, 1961).

KŘENEK, ERNST: *Music Here and Now* (1937; English translation, New York, 1939).

——'The New Music and Today's Theatre', *Modern Music,* xiv (1937).

——'Opera between the Wars', *Modern Music,* xx (1943).

KOMOROWSKI, HANS-PETER: *Die 'Invention' in der Musik des 20. Jahrhunderts,* (*Kölner Beiträge zur Musikforschung,* lxii) (Regensburg, 1971).

KROHER, EKKEHART: *Impressionismus in der Musik* (Leipzig, 1957).

LANG, PAUL HENRY and NATHAN BRODER (eds.): *Contemporary Music in Europe* (New York, 1965).

MACHLIS, JOSEPH: *Introduction to Contemporary Music* (New York, 1961).

MELLERS, WILFRID: *Studies in Contemporary Music* (London, 1948).

MERSMANN, HANS: *Musik der Gegenwart* (Berlin, 1923).

MEYER, LEONARD B.: *Music, the Arts, and Ideas: Patterns and Predictions in Twentieth-Century Culture* (Chicago, 1967).

MYERS, ROLLO H. (ed.): *Twentieth-Century Music* (London, 1960).

PERLE, GEORGE: *Serial Composition and Atonality: An Introduction to the Music of Schoenberg, Berg, and Webern* (Berkeley, Calif., 1962).

PEYSER, JOAN: *The New Music* (New York, 1971).
RETI, RUDOLPH: *The Thematic Process in Music* (New York, 1951).
——*Tonality, Atonality, Pantonality: A Study of some Trends in 20th Century Music* (New York, 1958).
SALAZAR, ADOLFO: *La música moderna: Las corrientes directrices en el arte musical contemporáneo* (Buenos Aires, 1944; English translation as *Music in Our Time: Trends in Music Since the Romantic Era*, New York, 1946).
SALZMAN, ERIC: *Twentieth-Century Music: An Introduction* (Englewood Cliffs, N.J., 1967).
SCHWARTZ, ELLIOTT and BARNEY CHILDS (eds.): *Contemporary Composers on Contemporary Music* (New York, 1967).
SMITHER, HOWARD E.: *Theories of Rhythm in the Nineteenth and Twentieth Centuries, with a Contribution to the Theory of Rhythm for the Study of Twentieth-Century Music* (Diss. Cornell Univ., 1960).
STUCKENSCHMIDT, HANS HEINZ: *Neue Musik;* Vol. II: *Zwischen den beiden Kriegen* (Berlin, 1951).
——'Opera in Germany Today', *Modern Music*, xiii (1935).
——*Twentieth-Century Music* (English translation, New York, 1969).
VETTER, HANS JOACHIM: *Die Musik unseres Jahrhunderts* (Mainz, 1968).
VLAD, ROMAN: *Storia della dodecafonia* (Milan, 1958).
WEISSMANN, ADOLPH: 'Germany's Latest Music Dramas', *Modern Music*, iv (1927).
WESTPHAL, KURT: *Die moderne Musik* (Leipzig, 1928).
YATES, PETER: *Twentieth Century Music* (New York, 1967).

(ii) *Individual Composers*

Bartók
ABRAHAM, GERALD: 'The Bartók of the Quartets', *Music and Letters*, xxvi (1945).
BABBITT, MILTON: 'The String Quartets of Bartók', *Musical Quarterly*, xxxv (1949).
BATOR, VICTOR: *The Béla Bartók Archives: History and Catalogue* (New York, 1963).
Béla Bartók: A Memorial Review (New York, 1950).
CITRON, PIERRE: *Bartók* (Paris, 1963).
DILLE, DENIJS (ed.): *Documenta Bartókiana* (Budapest, 1964–   ).
GOMBOSI, OTTO: 'Béla Bartók, 1881–1945', *Musical Quarterly*, xxxii (1946).
KODÁLY, ZOLTÁN: 'Béla Bartók', *Revue musicale*, ii (1921).
MOREUX, SERGE: *Béla Bartók* (Paris, 1955).
STEVENS, HALSEY: *The Life and Music of Béla Bartók* (New York, 1953).
VINTON, JOHN: 'Bartók on his own Music', *Journal of the American Musicological Society*, xix (1966).
WEISSMANN, JOHN S.: 'Béla Bartók: An Estimate', *Music Review*, vii (1946).

Berg
ARCHIBALD, ROBERT B.: *Harmony in the Early Works of Alban Berg* (Diss. Harvard Univ., 1965).
BERG, ALBAN: 'A Word about Wozzeck', *Modern Music*, v (1927).
——*Écrits*, ed. and tr. Henri Pousseur (Monaco, 1957).
FORNEBERG, ERICH: '*Wozzeck' von Alban Berg* (Berlin-Lichterfelde, 1963).
KLEIN, JOHN W.: '*Wozzeck*—A Summing Up', *Music and Letters,* xliv (1963).
PERLE, GEORGE: '*Lulu:* The Formal Design', *Journal of the American Musicological Society*, xvii (1964).
——'The Music of *Lulu:* A New Analysis', *Journal of the American Musicological Society*, xii (1959); corrections: *Journal of the American Musicological Society*, xiv (1961).

PLOEBSCH, GERD: *Alban Bergs 'Wozzeck'* (Strasbourg, 1968).
REDLICH, HANS FERDINAND: *Alban Berg: Versuch einer Würdigung* (Vienna, 1957; English condensation, *The Man and his Music,* New York, 1957).
REICH, WILLI: *Alban Berg* (Vienna, 1937; 2nd ed. Zurich, 1963; English translation, *The Life and Works of Alban Berg,* London, 1965).
——'Alban Berg's *Lulu*', *Musical Quarterly,* xxii (1936).
——'Alban Berg's Oper *Lulu*', *Melos,* xix (1952).
——'*Lulu*—the Text and Music', *Modern Music,* xii (1935).
——'A Guide to *Wozzeck*', *Musical Quarterly,* xxxviii (1952).
STEIN, ERWIN: 'Berg and Schoenberg', *Tempo,* xliv (1957).

Casella
D'AMICO, FEDELE and GUIDO M. GATTI: *Alfredo Casella: con saggi ... appendice biobibliografica* (Milan, 1958).
CASELLA, ALFREDO: 'Matière et timbre', *Revue musicale,* ii (1921).
——*I segreti della Giara* (Florence, 1941).
CASELLA, ALFREDO and VIRGILIO MORTARI: *La tecnica dell'orchestra contemporanea* (Milan, 1950).
CORTESE, LOUIS: *Alfredo Casella* (Genoa, 1935).

Dallapiccola
D'AMICO, FEDELE: 'Luigi Dallapiccola', *Melos,* xx (1953).
VLAD, ROMAN: *Luigi Dallapiccola* (English translation, Milan, 1957).

Falla
ARIZARA, RODOLFO: *Manuel de Falla* (Buenos Aires, 1961).
CAMPODONICO, LUIS: *Falla* (French translation, Paris, 1959).
JAENISCH, JULIO: *Manuel de Falla und die spanische Musik* (Zürich, 1952).
MAYER-SERRA, OTTO: 'Falla's Musical Nationalism', *Musical Quarterly,* xxix (1943).
MILA, MASSIMO (ed.): *Manuel de Falla* (Milan, 1962).
PAHISSA, JAIME: *Vida y obra de Manuel de Falla* (Buenos Aires, 1947; English translation, *Manuel de Falla: His Life and Works,* London, 1954).
WÖRNER, KARL H. 'Manuel de Falla', *Musica,* i (1947).

Hindemith
BLITZSTEIN, MARC: '*Hin und Zurück* in Philadephia', *Modern Music,* v (1928).
BOATWRIGHT, HOWARD: 'Paul Hindemith as a Teacher', *Musical Quarterly,* i (1964).
GUTMAN, HANS: 'Tabloid Hindemith', *Modern Music,* vii (1930).
HENSEL, HERMAN R.: *On Paul Hindemith's Harmonic Fluctuation Theory* (Diss. Univ. of Illinois, 1964).
HINDEMITH, PAUL: *A Composer's World: Horizons and Limitations* (New York, 1961).
——*The Craft of Musical Composition* (New York, 1945).
REICH, WILLI: 'Paul Hindemith', *Musical Quarterly,* xvii (1931).
ROSNER, HELMUT: *Paul Hindemith: Katalog seiner Werke. Diskographie, Bibliographie, Einführung in das Schaffen* (Frankfurt/Main, 1970).
SCHILLING, H. L.: *Die Oper 'Cardillac' von P. Hindemith* (Diss. Freiburg/Breisgau, 1957).
STONE, KURT: *Paul Hindemith: Catalogue of Published Works and Recordings* (New York, 1954).
STROBEL, HEINRICH: *Paul Hindemith* (Mainz, 1928; 3rd ed., 1948).
WILLMS, FRANZ: *Führer zur Oper 'Cardillac' von Paul Hindemith* (Mainz, 1926).
——'Paul Hindemith: Ein Versuch', *Von neuer Musik,* i (1925).

Honegger
BRUYR, JOSÉ: *Honegger et son oeuvre* (Paris, 1947).
DELANNOY, MARCEL: *Arthur Honegger* (Paris, 1953).
GEORGE, ANDRÉ: *Arthur Honegger* (Paris, 1926).
GÉRARD, CLAUDE: *Arthur Honegger* (Brussels, 1945).)
HOÉRÉE, ARTHUR: *(Honegger) La vie, l'oeuvre, l'homme* (Paris, 1942).
HONEGGER, ARTHUR: *Incantation aux fossiles* (Lausanne, 1948).
——*Je suis compositeur* (Paris, 1951; German translation, Zürich, 1952).
PRUNIERES, HENRY: 'Honegger's *Judith*', *Modern Music*, iii (1926).
TAPPOLET, WILLY: *Arthur Honegger* (Boudry-Neuchâtel, 1957).

Janáček
BROD, MAX: *Leoš Janáček: Leben und Werk* (Vienna, 1956).
GERLACH, REINHARD: 'Leoš Janáček und die Erste und Zweite Wiener Schule', *Musikforschung*, xxiv (1970).
HOLLANDER, HANS: 'Leoš Janáček and his Operas', *Musical Quarterly*, xv (1929).
——*Leoš Janáček: His Life and Work* (English translation, London, 1963).
——'Leoš Janáček in seinen Opern', *Neue Zeitschrift für Musik*, cxix (1958).
RACEK, JAN: 'Der Dramatiker Janáček', *Deutsches Jahrbuch der Musikwissenschaft*, v (1961).
——'Leoš Janáčeks und Béla Bartóks Bedeutung in der Weltmusik', *Studia Musicologica*, v (1963).
ŠTĚDROŇ, BOHUMIR: *The Work of Leoš Janáček* (Prague, 1959).
VOGEL, JAROSLAV: *Leoš Janáček: Leben und Werk* (Prague, 1958; English translation, London, 1963).

Kodály
EÖSZE, LÁSZLÖ: *Kodály Zoltán* (Budapest, 1956; English translation, *Zoltán Kodály, his Life and Work*, London, 1962).
MASON, COLIN: 'Kodály and Chamber Music', *Studia Musicologica*, iii (1962).
STEVENS, HALSEY: 'The Choral Music of Zoltán Kodály,' *Musical Quarterly*, liv (1968).

Martin
ANSERMET, ERNEST: 'Der Weg Frank Martins', *Österreichische Musikzeitschrift*, xi (1956).
KLEIN, RUDOLF: *Frank Martin: sein Leben und Werk* (Vienna, 1960).
KOELLIKER, ANDRÉ: *Frank Martin* (Lausanne, 1963).
TUPPER, JANET E.: *Stylistic Analysis of Selected Works by Frank Martin* (Diss. Indiana Univ., 1964).

Martinů
CLAPHAM, JOHN: 'Martinů's Instrumental Style', *Music Review*, xxiv (1963).
HALBREICH, HARRY: *Bohuslav Martinů: Werkverzeichnis: Dokumentation: Biographie* (Zürich, 1968).
MIHULE, JAROSLAV: *Symfonie Bohuslava Martinů* (Prague, 1959).
ŠAFRÁNEK, MILOŠ: 'Bohuslav Martinu', *Musical Quarterly*, xxix (1943).
——*Bohuslav Martinů: zivot a dilo* (Prague, 1961; English translation, London, 1964).

Messiaen
GOLEÁ, ANTOINE: *Rencontres avec Olivier Messiaen* (Paris, 1961).
MESSIAEN, OLIVIER: *La Technique de mon langage musicale* (Paris, 1944; English translation, Chicago, 1957).
SAMUEL, CLAUDE: *Entretiens avec Olivier Messiaen* (Paris, 1967).

Milhaud

BECK, GEORGES: *Darius Milhaud. Étude suivi du catalogue chronologique complet de son ouvrage* (Paris, 1949; *Supplément* (Paris, 1956).
COLLAER, PAUL: *Darius Milhaud* (Antwerp, 1947).
LOPATNIKOFF, NIKOLAI: 'Christophe Colomb', *Modern Music*, vii (1930).
MASON, COLIN: 'The Chamber Music of Milhaud', *Musical Quarterly*, xliii (1957).
MILHAUD, DARIUS: 'La mélodie', *Melos*, iii (1922).
——'Polytonalité et atonalité, *Revue musicale*, iv (1923).
——*Notes sans musique* (Paris, 1949; 2nd ed., 1963; English translation, London, 1952).
——*Entretiens avec Claude Rostand* (Paris, 1952).

Petrassi

WEISSMANN, JOHN: *Goffredo Petrassi* (Milan, 1957).
——'Goffredo Petrassi and his Music', *Music Review*, xxii (1961).

Pizzetti

GATTI, GUIDO MARIA: *Ildebrando Pizzetti* (Turin, 1934; 2nd ed., Milan, 1955; English translation, London, 1951).
GAVAZZENI, GIANANDREA: *Altri studi pizzettiani* (Bergamo, 1956).
——*Tre studi di Pizzetti* (Como, 1937).

Poulenc

DUREY, LOUIS: 'Francis Poulenc', *The Chesterian*, xxv (1922).
HELL, HENRI: *Francis Poulenc, musicien français* (Paris, 1958; English translation, London, 1959).
ROY, JEAN: *Francis Poulenc: l'homme et son oeuvre* (Paris, 1964).
SCHAEFFNER, ANDRÉ: 'Francis Poulenc, musicien français', *Contrepoints*, i (1946).

Prokofyev

BROWN, MALCOLM J.: *The Symphonies of Sergei Prokofiev* (Diss. Florida State Univ., 1967).
NESTYEV, IZRAEL V.: *Prokofyev* (Moscow, 1957; English translation, Stanford, 1960).
——and G. EDELMAN (eds.): *Sergey Prokofyev 1953–1963: stati i materialï* (Moscow, 1962).
SHLIFSHTEYN, S. I.: *S. S. Prokofyev: materialï, dokumentï, vospominaniya* (Moscow, 2nd ed. 1961; English translation, Moscow, 1960).
——*S. S. Prokofyev: notografichesky spravochik* (Moscow, 1962).

Ravel

FARGUE, LÉON-PAUL: *Maurice Ravel* (Paris, 1949).
JOURDAN-MORHANGE, HÉLÈNE: *Ravel et nous: l'homme, l'ami, le musicien* (Geneva, 1945).
MACHABEY, ARMAND: *Maurice Ravel* (Paris, 1947).
ROLAND-MANUEL, ALEXIS: *Maurice Ravel* (Paris, 1938; English translation, London, 1947).
——*Maurice Ravel et son oeuvre dramatique* (Paris, 1928).
SEROFF, VICTOR: *Maurice Ravel* (New York, 1953).

Respighi

MILA, MASSIMO: 'Probleme di gusto ed arte in Ottorino Respighi', *Rassegan musicale,* vi (1933).
RESPIGHI, ELSA: *Ottorino Respighi: dati biografici ordinati* (Milan, 1954; English translation, London, 1962).
RINALDI, MARIO: 'Ottorino Respighi', *Musica d'oggi*, iv (1961).

Satie

APOLLINAIRE, GUILLAUME: *Selected Writings* (English translation, New York, 1948).
AUSTIN, WILLIAM W.: 'Satie before and after Cocteau', *Musical Quarterly*, xlviii (1962).
COCTEAU, JEAN: *Fragments d'un conférence sur Erik Satie* (1920; repr. Liège 1957 and *Music Review*, v (1944)).
ÉCORCHEVILLE, JULES: 'Erik Satie', *Bulletin de la Société internationale de musique*, vii (1911).
MYERS, ROLLO H.: *Erik Satie* (London, 1948).
TEMPLIER, PIERRE-DANIEL: *Erik Satie* (Paris, 1932).

Schoenberg

ADORNO, THEODOR WIESENGRUND: 'Arnold Schönberg', *Die grossen Deutschen*, iv (1957).
BORETZ, BENJAMIN and EDWARD T. CONE (eds.): *Perspectives on Schoenberg and Stravinsky* (Princeton, N.J., 1968).
BROEKEMA, ANDREW J.: *A Stylistic Analysis and Comparison of the Solo Vocal Works of Arnold Schoenberg, Alban Berg, and Anton Webern* (Diss. Univ. of Texas, 1962).
BUCHANAN, HERBERT B.: 'A key to Schoenberg's *Erwartung* (Op. 17)', *Journal of the American Musicological Society*, xx (1967).
CLIFTON, THOMAS J.: *Types of Ambiguity in the Tonal Compositions of Arnold Schoenberg* (Diss. Stanford Univ., 1966).
EPSTEIN, DAVID M. *Schoenberg's 'Grundgestalt' and Total Serialism: Their Relevance to Homophonic Analysis* (Diss. Princeton Univ., 1968).
FRIEDHEIM, PHILIP: 'Rhythmic Structure in Schoenberg's Atonal Compositions', *Journal of the American Musicological Society*, xix (1966).
HILL, RICHARD S.: 'Schoenberg's Tone-Rows and the Tonal System of the Future', *Musical Quarterly*, xxii (1936).
LEIBOWITZ, RENÉ: *Introduction à la musique de douze sons* (Paris, 1949).
——*Qu'est-ce que la musique de douze sons?* (Liège, 1948).
——*Schoenberg et son école: l'étape contemporaine du langage musical* (Paris, 1947: English translation, New York, 1949).
LESTER, JOEL: *A Theory of Atonal Prolongations as used in an Analysis of the Serenade, Op. 24 by Arnold Schoenberg* (Diss. Princeton Univ., 1970).
NAMENWIRTH, SIMON M.: *Twenty Years of Schoenberg Criticisms: Changes in the evaluation of once unfamiliar music* (Diss. Univ. of Minnesota, 1965).
ODEGARD, PETER S.: *The Variation Sets of Arnold Schoenberg* (Diss. Univ. of California, Berkeley, 1964).
PISK, PAUL A.: 'Schoenberg's Twelve-Tone Opera', *Modern Music*, vii (1930).
RUFER, JOSEF: *Komposition mit zwölf Töne* (Berlin, 1952; English translation, London, 1954).
——*Das Werk Arnold Schönbergs* (Kassel, 1959; English translation, New York, 1963).
SCHOENBERG, ARNOLD: *Style and Idea* (New York, 1950).
——*Structural Functions of Harmony*, ed. H. Searle (New York, 1954).
STEFAN, PAUL: 'Schoenberg's Operas', *Modern Music*, ii (1925) and vii (1929–30).
STUCKENSCHMIDT, HANS HEINZ: *Arnold Schönberg* (Zürich, 1951; 2nd ed. 1957; English translation, New York, 1960).
SUDERBURG, ROBERT C.: *Tonal Cohesion in Schoenberg's Twelve-Tone Music* (Diss. Univ. of Pennsylvania, 1966).
WÖRNER, KARL H.: *Gotteswort und Magie. Die Oper 'Moses und Aaron' von Arnold Schönberg* (Heidelberg, 1959; English translation, *Schoenberg's 'Moses and Aaron'*, New York, 1964).
——'Arnold Schoenberg and the Theatre', *Musical Quarterly* xlviii (1962).

Stravinsky

BLITZSTEIN, MARC: 'The Phenomenon of Stravinsky', *Musical Quarterly*, xxi (1935).
BORETZ, BENJAMIN and EDWARD T. CONE (eds.): *Perspectives on Schoenberg and Stravinsky* (Princeton, N.J., 1968).
CRAFT, ROBERT: *Stravinsky: Chronicle of a Friendship 1948–1971* (New York, 1972).
FLEISCHER, HERBERT: *Stravinsky* (Berlin, 1931).
FREDERICKSON, LAWRENCE: *Stravinsky's Instrumentation: A Study of his Orchestral Techniques* (Diss. Univ. of Illinois, 1960).
HANDSCHIN, JACQUES: *Igor Strawinsky: Versuch einer Einführung* (Zurich, 1933).
KIRCHMEYER, HELMUT: *Igor Stravinsky: Zeitgeschichte im Personlichkeitsbild: Grundlagen und Voraussetzungen zur modernen Konstructionstechnik* (Regensburg, 1958).
LANG, PAUL HENRY (ed.): *Stravinsky: A New Appraisal of His Work* (New York, 1963).
NABOKOV, NICHOLAS: *Igor Strawinsky* (Berlin, 1964).
RAMUZ, CHARLES FERDINAND: *Souvenirs sur Igor Strawinsky* (Paris, 1929; 2nd ed., Lausanne, 1952).
SCHAEFFNER, ANDRÉ: *Strawinsky* (Paris, 1931).
STRAVINSKY, IGOR: *Autobiography* (New York, 1962).
——*Poétiques musicales* (Cambridge, Mass., 1942; English translation, *Poetics of Music*, New York, 1956).
VLAD, ROMAN: *Strawinsky* (Turin, 1958; English translation, London, 1960),
WADE, CARROLL D.: 'A selected Bibliography of Igor Stravinsky', *Musical Quarterly*, xlviii (1962); repr. in Paul Henry Lang, ed., *Stravinsky: A New Appraisal of his Work* (New York, 1963).
WHITE, ERIC WALTER: *Stravinsky: The Composer and His Works* (London, 1966).

Szymanowski

GAVEZZENI, GIANANDREA: 'Karol Szymanowski e il *Re Ruggiero*', *Rassegna musicale*, x (1937).
JACHIMECKI, ZDZISŁAW: *Karol Szymanowski* (Cracow, 1927).

Varèse

CHOW WEN-CHUNG: 'Varèse: A Sketch of the Man and his Music', *Musical Quarterly*, lii (1966).
COWELL, HENRY: 'The Music of Edgard Varèse', *Modern Music*, v (1928).
VARÈSE, LOUISE: *Varèse: A Looking-Glass Diary*. Vol. I: 1883–1928 (New York, 1972).
VIVIER, ODILE: 'Innovation instrumentale d'Edgar Varèse', *Revue musicale*, ccxxvi (1955).

Webern

ANTHONY, DONALD B.: *Microrhythm in the Published Works of Anton Webern* (Diss. Stanford Univ., 1968).
Anton Webern, special issue of *Die Reihe*, ii (German ed., 1955; English ed., 1958).
BROWN, ROBERT B.: *The Early Atonal Music of Anton Webern: Sound Material and Structure* (Diss. Brandeis Univ., 1965).
KARKOSCHKA, ERHARD: *Studien zur Entwicklung der Kompositiontechnik im Frühwerk Anton Weberns* (Diss. Tübingen, 1959).
KOLNEDER, WALTER: *Anton Webern: Einführung in Werk und Stil* (Rodenkirchen, 1961; English translation, London, 1968).
MCKENZIE, WALLACE CHESSLEY: *The Music of Anton Webern* (Diss. North Texas State College, 1960).
PERLE, GEORGE: 'Webern's Twelve-Tone Sketches', *Musical Quarterly*, lvii (1971).
REICH, WILLI (ed.): *Anton Webern: Weg und Gestalt. Selbstzeugnisse und Worte der Freunde* (Zurich, 1961).

WEBERN, ANTON: *Der Weg zur neuen Musik*, ed. by Willi Reich (Vienna, 1960; English translation, *The Path to the New Music*, Bryn Mawr, Pa., 1963).
Webern Archive of the Moldenhauer Collection at the University of Washington (Seattle, 1963). (Now located at Northwestern University, Evanston, Ill.)

Weill
BLITZSTEIN, MARC: 'On *Mahagonny*', *The Score* (1958).
DREW, DAVID: 'Topicality and the Universal: The Strange Case of Weill's *Die Bürgschaft*', *Music and Letters*, xxxix (1958).
——'Weill's School Opera *Der Jasager*', *Musical Times*, cvi (1965).
GUTMAN, HANS: '*Mahagonny* and Other Novelties', *Modern Music*, vii (1930).
KOTSCHENREUTHER, HELLMUT: *Kurt Weill* (Berlin, 1962).
STEFAN-GRUENFELDT, PAUL: 'Antinomie der neuen Oper: Kurt Weill und Strawinsky', *Musikblätter des Anbruch*, x (1928).
TOLKSDORF, CÄCILIE: *John Gay's 'Beggar's Opera' und Bert Brechts 'Dreigroschenoper'* (Diss. Bonn Univ., 1934).

CHAPTER V

MUSIC OF THE EUROPEAN MAINSTREAM 1940–1960

(i) *General*
ADORNO, T. W.: *Philosophie der neuen Musik* (Tübingen, 1948).
——'Modern Music is growing old', *The Score*, xviii (1956).
BASART, ANN PHILLIPS: *Serial Music: a Classified Bibliography on 12-tone and Electronic Music* (Berkeley, 1961).
CROSS, ANTHONY: 'The Significance of Aleatoricism in twentieth-century Music', *Music Review*, xxix (1968).
EVANS, PETER: 'Compromises with Serialism', *Proceedings of the Royal Musical Association*, lxxxviii (1962).
FORTE, ALLEN: *Contemporary Tone Structures* (New York, 1955).
GERHARD, ROBERTO: 'Developments in twelve-note technique', *The Score*, xvii (1956).
——'Tonality in twelve-note music', *The Score*, vi (1952).
KŘENEK, ERNST: 'New developments of the twelve tone technique', *Music Review*, iv (1943).
——'Extents and limits of serial techniques', *Musical Quarterly*, xlvi (1960).
LANG, PAUL HENRY and BRODER, NATHAN (eds.): *Contemporary Music in Europe* (New York, 1965).
RUFER, JOSEF: *Composition with Twelve Notes related only to one another* (London, 1954).
RUWET, NICOLAS: 'Contradictions within the serial language', *Die Reihe*, vi (1964).
VLAD, ROMAN: *Modernità e tradizione nella musica contemporanea* (Turin, 1955).
ZILLIG, WINFRIED: *Variationen über neue Musik* (Munich, 1959; reissued as *Die neue Musik: Linien und Porträts*, 1963).

(ii) *Individual Composers*

Boulez
BOULEZ, PIERRE: 'Propositions', *Polyphonie*, ii (1948).
——'At the ends of fruitful land', *Die Reihe*, i (1955).
——'Sonate, que me veux-tu?', *Perspectives of New Music*, i (1963).
——'Alea', *Perspectives of New Music*, iii (1964).
——*Penser la musique aujourd'hui* (Paris, 1964; English translation, *Boulez on Music Today*, London, 1971).
GOLEA, ANTOINE: *Rencontres avec Pierre Boulez* (Paris, 1958).

Dallapiccola

DALLAPICCOLA, LUIGI: 'On the twelve-note road', *Music Survey*, iv (1951).
NATHAN, HANS: 'The twelve-tone compositions of Luigi Dallapiccola', *Musical Quarterly*, xliv (1958).
——'Luigi Dallapiccola' (conversations), *Music Review*, xxvii (1966).
VLAD, ROMAN: *Luigi Dallapiccola* (Milan, 1957).

Egk

WÖRNER, K. H.: 'Egk and Orff', *Music Review*, xiv (1953).

Gerhard

DREW, DAVID: 'Roberto Gerhard—the musical character', *The Score*, xvii (1956).

Henze

HENZE, HANS WERNER: *Essays* (Mainz, 1964).

Hindemith

BRINER, ANDREAS: *Paul Hindemith* (Zürich, 1971).
HINDEMITH, PAUL: *The Craft of Musical Composition* (London, 1942).
——*A Composer's World* (New York, 1952).
KEMP, IAN: *Hindemith* (London, 1970).
LANDAU, VICTOR: 'Paul Hindemith: a Case Study in Theory and Practice', *Music Review*, xxi (1960).
——'Hindemith the System Builder: a Critique', *Music Review*, xxii (1961).
REDLICH, H. F.: 'Paul Hindemith: a Reassessment', *Music Review*, xxv (1964).
STEPHAN, RUDOLPH: 'Hindemith's *Marienleben* (1922–48): an assessment of its two versions', *Music Review*, xv (1954).
STROBEL, HEINRICH: *Paul Hindemith* (3rd edition, Mainz, 1948).
THOMPSON, WILLIAM: 'Hindemith's Contribution to Music Theory', *Journal of Music Theory*, ix (1965).

Ligeti

LIGETI, GYÖRGY: 'Metamorphoses of Musical Form', *Die Reihe*, vii (1965).

Messiaen

DREW, DAVID: 'Messiaen—a provisional study', *The Score*, x, xii and xiv (1954–5).
GOLÉA, ANTOINE: *Rencontres avec Olivier Messiaen* (Paris, 1961).
MESSIAEN, OLIVIER: *Technique de mon langage musicale* (Paris, 1944).

Orff

WÖRNER, K. H.: 'Egk and Orff', *Music Review*, xiv (1953).

Petrassi

WEISSMANN, JOHN: *Goffredo Petrassi* (Milan, 1957).

Pousseur

POUSSEUR, HENRI: 'Music, Form and Practice', *Die Reihe*, vi (1964).
——'Outline of a Method', *Die Reihe*, iii (1959).

Schaeffer

SCHAEFFER, PIERRE: *À la recherche d'une musique concrète* (Paris, 1952).

Schoenberg

See Bibliography to Chapter IV.

Skalkottas

PAPAIOANNOU, YIANNIS: 'Nikos Skalkottas', in Hartog (ed.), *European Music in the Twentieth Century* (2nd ed., London, 1961).

Stockhausen
HARVEY, JONATHAN: 'Stockhausen: Theory and Music', *Music Review*, xxix (1968).
MARCUS, GENEVIEVE: 'Stockhausen's Zeitmasse', *Music Review*, xxix (1968).
STOCKHAUSEN, KARLHEINZ: 'How time passes . . .', *Die Reihe*, iii (1959).
——'Electronic and Instrumental Music', *Die Reihe*, v (1961).
——'Music in Space', *Die Reihe*, v (1961).
——'Music and Speech', *Die Reihe*, vi (1964).
——'The Concept of Unity in Electronic Music', *Perspectives of New Music*, i (1962).
WÖRNER, K. H.: *Karlheinz Stockhausen, Werk und Wollen* (Rodenkirchen, 1963).

Stravinsky
BABBITT, MILTON: 'Remarks on the recent Stravinsky', *Perspectives of New Music*, ii (1964).
CONE, E. T.: 'The Uses of Convention: Stravinsky and his Models', *Musical Quarterly*, xlviii (1962).
——'Stravinsky: the Progress of a Method', *Perspectives of New Music*, i (1962).
GERHARD, ROBERTO: 'Twelve-note technique in Stravinsky', *The Score*, xx (1957).
PAULI, HANSJORG: 'On Stravinsky's *Threni*', *Tempo*, xix (1958).
STEIN, ERWIN: 'Stravinsky's Septet—an Analysis', *Tempo*, xxxi (1954).
STRAVINSKY, IGOR and CRAFT, ROBERT: *Conversations with Igor Stravinsky* (London, 1959).
——*Memories and Commentaries* (London, 1960).
——*Expositions and Developments* (London, 1961).
——*Dialogues and a Diary* (London, 1963).
See also Bibliography to Chapter IV.

Varèse
BABBITT, MILTON: 'Edgard Varèse: a few observations of his music', *Perspectives of New Music*, iv (1966).
CHOW WEN-CHUNG: 'Varèse: a sketch of the man and his music', *Musical Quarterly*, lii (1966).
WHITTALL, ARNOLD: 'Varèse: and organic athematicism', *Music Review*, xxviii, (1967).
WILKINSON, MARC: 'An Introduction to the Music of Edgard Varèse', *The Score*, xix (1957).

Webern
See Bibliography to Chapter IV.

CHAPTER VI

MUSIC IN BRITAIN: 1918–1960

(i) *General*
BACHARACH, A. L. (ed.): *British Music of Our Time* (Harmondsworth, 2nd ed., 1951).
BLOM, ERIC: *Music in England* (Harmondsworth, rev. ed., 1947).
BOOSEY & HAWKES (publishers): 'England-Heft' (Bonn, n.d., *c.* 1953), *Musik der Zeit*, Heft iv.
BORNOFF, JACK: 'Musikleben in England', *Melos* (March 1950).
BOULT, SIR ADRIAN: *My Own Trumpet* (London, 1973).
BRADBURY, ERNEST: 'Modern British Composers', in *Choral Music*, ed. Arthur Jacobs (Harmondsworth, 1963).
BRITTEN, BENJAMIN: 'England and the Folk-Art Problem', *Modern Music* (1940).
CASSINI, LEONARD: 'Neue Englische Musik', *Musik und Gesellschaft*, ix (1956).
FOREMAN, R. L. E.: *The British Musical Renaissance: a Guide to Research*, (thesis, London, 1972).

Foss, Herbert and Goodwin, Noel: *London Symphony* (London, 1954).

Frank, Alan: *Modern British Composers* (London, 1953).

Harris, Rex: 'The Influence of Jazz on English Composers', *Penguin Music Magazine* (1947).

Howes, Frank: *The English Musical Renaissance* (London, 1966).

Lee, Edward: *Music of the People: a study of popular music in Great Britain* (London, 1970).

Lockspeiser, Edward: 'Trends in Modern English Music', *Musical Quarterly*, xxviii (1942).

Manning, Rosemary: *From Holst to Britten* (London, 1949).

Mellers, Wilfrid: 'Recent Trends in British Music', *Musical Quarterly*, xxxviii (1952).

Milner, Anthony: 'English Contemporary Music', in *European Music in the Twentieth Century*, ed. Hartog, (London, 1957).

Palmer, Christopher: 'The Post Impressionists in England', *Impressionism in Music* (London, 1973).

Porter, Andrew: 'Some New British Composers', in *Contemporary Music in Europe: a comprehensive survey*, eds. Lang and Broder, (New York, 1965).

Raynor, Henry: 'Influence and Achievement: some thoughts on Twentieth-Century English Song', *Chesterian*, xxx (1956).

Routh, Francis: *Contemporary British Music: Britain's Musical Tradition since the War* (London, 1972).

Searle, Humphrey: 'Growing Pains in England', *Modern Music* (1939).

Searle, Humphrey and Layton, Robert: *Britain, Scandinavia and the Netherlands* (Twentieth Century Composers, vol. v) (London, 1972).

The Times: *Musical Britain in 1951* (London, 1951).

Thompson, Kenneth: *A Dictionary of Twentieth-Century Composers (1911–1971)* (London, 1973).

Wood, Hugh: 'English Contemporary Music', in, *European Music in the Twentieth Century*, ed. Hartog (Harmondsworth, paper-back edition, 1961).

(ii) *Individual Composers*

Alwyn

Hold, Trevor: 'The Music of William Alwyn', *Composer* (1972).

Arnold

Mitchell, Donald: 'Malcolm Arnold', *Musical Times*, xcvi (1955).

Bantock

Anderton, H. Orsmond: *Granville Bantock* (London, 1915).

Bantock, Myrrha: *Granville Bantock: a personal portrait* (London, 1972).

Bax

Foreman, R. L. E.: 'Bibliography of Writings on Arnold Bax', *Current Musicology*, No. 10 (1970).

Hull, Robin, M.: *A Handbook on Arnold Bax's Symphonies* (London, 1933).

Scott Sutherland, Colin: *Arnold Bax* (London, 1973).

Benjamin

Boustead, Alan: 'Arthur Benjamin and Opera', *Opera* (1964).

Keller, Hans: 'Arthur Benjamin and the problem of popularity: a critical appreciation', *Tempo*, xi (1950).

Bennett, Richard Rodney

Maw, Nicholas: 'Richard Rodney Bennett', *Musical Times*, ciii (1962).

Berkeley
DICKINSON, PETER: 'The Music of Lennox Berkeley', *Musical Times*, ci (1963).
——'Lennox Berkeley', *Music and Musicians*, xiii (1965).
——'Berkeley's Music Today', *Musical Times*, cix (1968).
HULL, ROBIN: 'The Style of Lennox Berkeley', *Chesterian*, xxiv (1950).
REDLICH, HANS F.: 'Lennox Berkeley', *Music Survey* (1951).

Bliss
BLISS, SIR ARTHUR: *As I Remember* (London, 1970).
HASKELL, ARNOLD L.: *Miracle in the Gorbals: a study* (Edinburgh, 1946).
SCHOLES, PERCY A.: *A Few Notes upon the Work of Arthur Bliss and Especially upon his Colour Symphony* (London, 1922).
THOMPSON, KENNETH L.: *The Works of Arthur Bliss* (London (rev. ed.) n.d. (1971)). Originally published in *Musical Times*.

Boughton
HURD, MICHAEL: *Immortal Hour: the life and period of Rutland Boughton* (London, 1962).

Brian
FOREMAN, LEWIS: 'Havergal Brian: a new view', *Composer* (1971–2).
MACDONALD, MALCOLM: *Havergal Brian: perspective on the music* (London, 1972).
NETTEL, REGINALD: *The Life and Music of Havergal Brian* (London, 1937). A revised and enlarged version of *Ordeal by Music* (London, 1945).

Bridge
PAYNE, ANTHONY: 'The Music of Frank Bridge', *Tempo*, xxxiv (1973).
PIRIE, PETER J.: *Frank Bridge* (London, 1971).

Britten
BROWN, DAVID: 'Britten's Three Canticles', *Music Review*, xxi (1960).
KENDALL, ALAN: *Benjamin Britten* (London, 1973).
MITCHELL, DONALD and KELLER, HANS (eds.): *Benjamin Britten: a commentary on his works from a group of specialists* (London, 1952).
WHITE, ERIC WALTER: *Benjamin Britten—his life and operas* (London, 1970). Revised and expanded version of *Benjamin Britten—a sketch of his life and works* (London, 1948; 2nd ed., 1954).

Bush, Alan
STEVENSON, RONALD: 'Alan Bush—committed composer', *Music Review*, xxv (1964).
Tribute to Alan Bush on his fiftieth birthday—a symposium. (London, 1950).

Cooke
CLAPHAM, JOHN: 'Arnold Cooke: the achievement of 20 years', *Music Survey* (1951).

Elgar
See Bibliography to Chapters I and II.

Finzi
FERGUSON, HOWARD: 'Gerald Finzi (1901–1956)', *Music and Letters*, xxxviii (1957).

Fricker
ROUTH, FRANCIS: 'Peter Racine Fricker', in *Contemporary British Music* (London, 1972).

Gerhard
'Gerhard' issue of *The Score*, xvii (1956).

Goossens
GOOSSENS, EUGENE: *Overture and Beginners* (London, 1951).

Gurney
'Gurney' number of *Music and Letters*, xix (1938).
BURTCH, M. A.: 'Ivor Gurney—a revaluation', *Musical Times*, xcvi (1955).

Hadley
PALMER, CHRISTOPHER: 'The Music of Patrick Hadley', *Musical Times*, cx (1969).

Hamilton
MILNER, ANTHONY: 'Some Observations on the Music of Ian Hamilton', *Musical Times*, xcvii (1956).

Holst
HOLST, IMOGEN: *Gustav Holst—a biography* (London, 2nd ed., 1969).
——*The Music of Gustav Holst* (London, 3rd ed., 1974).
MELLERS, W. H.: 'Holst and the English Language', in *Studies in Contemporary Music* (London, 1947).
RUBBRA, EDMUND: *Gustav Holst* (Monaco, 1947).
    'Gustav Holst as Teacher', *Monthly Musical Record*, lx (1930).
TIPPETT, MICHAEL: 'Holst, Figure of Our Time', *Listener* (13/11/1958).
TOVEY, DONALD F.: Essays in *Essays in Musical Analysis*, ii, iv and v (London, 1936–7).
WARRACK, JOHN: 'A New Look at Holst', *Musical Times*, civ (1963).

Howells
PALMER, CHRISTOPHER: 'Herbert Howells at 80—a retrospect', *Musical Times*, cxiii (1972).
SPEARING, ROBERT: *HH—Herbert Howells . . .* (London, 1972).

Ireland
DICKINSON, A. E. F.: 'The Progress of John Ireland', *Music Review*, i (1940).
HOLBROOKE, JOSEF: 'John Ireland', in *Contemporary British Composers* (London, 1931).
LONGMIRE, JOHN: *John Ireland—Portrait of a Friend* (London, 1969).

Lambert
McGRADY, RICHARD: 'The Music of Constant Lambert', *Music and Letters*, li (1970).
SHEAD, RICHARD: *Constant Lambert* (London, 1973).

Leigh
WIMBUSH, ROGER: 'Walter Leigh', *Monthly Musical Record*, lxviii (1938).

Leighton
COCKSHOOT, JOHN V.: 'The Music of Kenneth Leighton', *Musical Times*, xcviii (1957).

Lutyens
LUTYENS, ELIZABETH: *A Goldfish Bowl* (London, 1972).

Maconchy
'Living British Composers—Elizabeth Maconchy', *Hinrichsen Musical Yearbook* No. 6 (1949/50).
MACONCHY, ELIZABETH: 'A Composer Speaks', *Composer* (1971–2).

Milner
BRADBURY, ERNEST: 'The Progress of Anthony Milner', *Musical Times*, civ (1963).

Moeran
FLEISCHMANN, ALOYS: 'The Music of E. J. Moeran', *Envoy* (1951).

Musgrave
BRADSHAW, SUSAN: 'Thea Musgrave', *Musical Times*, civ (1963).

Rawsthorne
BERKELEY, LENNOX: 'Alan Rawsthorne—1', *Composer* (1971–2).
GREEN, GORDON: 'Alan Rawsthorne—2', *Composer* (1972).
HOWELLS, HERBERT: 'A Note on Alan Rawsthorne', *Music and Letters*, xxxii (1951).
MELLERS, WILFRID: 'Alan Rawsthorne and the Baroque', in *Studies in Contemporary Music* (London, 1947).

Rubbra
DAWNEY, MICHAEL: 'Edmund Rubbra and the Piano', *Music Review*, xxxi (1970).
HUTCHINGS, ARTHUR: 'Edmund Rubbra's Second Symphony', *Music and Letters*, xx (1939).
MELLERS, WILFRID: 'Rubbra and the Dominant Seventh', in *Studies in Contemporary Music* (London, 1947).
OTTAWAY, HUGH: 'Rubbra's Symphonies', *Musical Times*, cxii (1971).
PAYNE, ELSIE: 'Edmund Rubbra', *Music and Letters*, xxxvi (1955).

Scott
DEMUTH, NORMAN: 'Cyril Scott', *Musical Opinion*, lxxx (1957).
HULL, A. EAGLEFIELD: *Cyril Scott: Composer, Poet and Philosopher* (London, 1971).
SCOTT, CYRIL: *Bone of Contention* (London, 1969).

Searle
LOCKSPEISER, EDWARD: 'Humphrey Searle', *Musical Times*, cxvi (1955).
RAYMOND, MALCOLM: 'Searle—avant garde or romantic', *Musical Times*, cv (1964).

Seiber
KELLER, HANS: 'Matyas Seiber', *Musical Times*, xcvi (1955).
——'Matyas Seiber 1905–1960', *Tempo*, xxi (1960).

Simpson
JOHNSON, EDWARD (ed.): *Robert Simpson—fiftieth birthday essays* (London, 1971).

Tate
CARNER, MOSCO: 'The Music of Phyllis Tate', *Music and Letters*, xxxv (1954).

Tippett
ATKINSON, NEVILLE: 'Michael Tippett's Debt to the Past', *Music Review*, xxiii (1962).
KEMP, IAN (ed.): *A Symposium for Michael Tippett's 60th Birthday* (London, 1965).
MILNER, ANTHONY: 'The Music of Michael Tippett', *Musical Quarterly*, 1 (1964).

Van Dieren
APIVOR, DENIS: Bernard van Dieren, *Music Survey* (June 1951).

Vaughan Williams
'Vaughan Williams Centenary' number of *Opera*, (1972).
'Ralph Vaughan Williams 1872–1958', memorial number of *R.C.M. Magazine*, (1959).
DAY, JAMES: *Vaughan Williams* (London, 1961).
DICKINSON, A. E. F.: *Vaughan Williams* (London, 1963).
DOUGLAS, ROY: *Working with R.V.W.* (London, 1972).
FOREMAN, LEWIS: 'V.W.—a bibliography of dissertations', *Musical Times*, cxiii (1972).

Foss, Hubert: *Ralph Vaughan Williams—a study* (London, 1950). (Includes 'A Musical Autobiography' by Vaughan Williams.)

Kennedy, Michael: *The Works of Ralph Vaughan Williams* (London, 1964).

Ottaway, Hugh: *Vaughan Williams: Symphonies* (London, 1972).

Payne, Elsie M.: 'Vaughan Williams' Orchestral Colourings', *Monthly Musical Record* (1954).

——'Vaughan Williams and Folk-Song', *Music Review*, xv (1954).

Schwartz, Elliott S.: *The Symphonies of Ralph Vaughan Williams* (Amherst, Mass., 1964).

Vaughan Williams, Ursula: *R.V.W.: a biography of Ralph Vaughan Williams* (London, 1964).

Young, Percy M.: *Vaughan Williams* (London, 1953).

Walton

'William Walton at 75' number of *Musical Times*, cxiii (1972).

Craggs, Stewart: *Sir William Walton, O.M.: a catalogue, bibliography and discography* (Thesis, London, 1973).

Foss, Hubert: 'William Walton', *The Chesterian*, xi (1930).

——'William Walton', *Musical Quarterly*, xxvi (1940).

Howes, Frank: *The Music of William Walton* (London, 1965; 2nd ed. 1973).

Lambert, Constant: 'Some Recent Works by William Walton', *The Dominant*, i (1928).

Mitchell, Donald: 'Some Observations on William Walton', *The Chesterian*, xxvi (1952).

Tovey, Donald F.: 'Walton's Viola Concerto', in *Essays in Musical Analysis*, iii (London, 1936).

Warlock

Copley, Ian A.: 'Peter Warlock's Vocal Chamber Music', *Music and Letters*, xliv (1963).

——'The Published Instrumental Music of Peter Warlock', *Music Review*, xxv (1964).

——'Peter Warlock's Choral Music', *Music and Letters*, xlv (1964).

Gray, Cecil: *Peter Warlock—a memoir of Philip Heseltine* (London, 1934).

Van Dieren, Bernard: 'Philip Heseltine', *Musical Times*, lxxii (1931).

Wellesz

Mellers, Wilfrid: 'Egon Wellesz', in *Studies in Contemporary Music* (London, 1947).

Ridley, Anthony: 'The Later Works of Egon Wellesz', *Composer* (1966).

Schollum, Robert: *Egon Wellesz—eine Studie* (Vienna, 1964).

Symons, David: 'Egon Wellesz and Early Twentieth Century Tonality', *Studies in Music* (No. 6, 1972).

Williamson

Mason, Colin: 'The Music of Malcolm Williamson', *Musical Times*, cv (1962).

CHAPTER VII

AMERICAN MUSIC: 1918–1960

(i) The United States

(i) *General*

Barzun, Jacques: *Music in American Life* (New York, 1956).

Chase, Gilbert: *America's Music* (2nd ed., New York, 1967).

Copland, Aaron: *Our New Music* (New York, 1941).

COPLAND, AARON: *Copland on Music* (New York, 1960).
COWELL, HENRY: *New Musical Resources* (New York, 1930).
——(ed.): *American Composers on American Music* (Stanford, 1933).
GOSS, MADELEINE: *Modern Music-Makers: Contemporary American Composers* (New York, 1952).
HITCHCOCK, WILEY: *Music in the United States: a Historical Introduction* (New York, 1969).
HOWARD, JOHN TASKER: *Our American Music* (3rd ed., New York, 1946).
LAHEE, HENRY C.: *Annals of Music in America* (Boston, 1922).
LANG, PAUL HENRY (ed.): *100 Years of Music in America* (New York, 1961).
MELLERS, WILFRID: *Music in a New Found Land* (London, 1964).
REIS, CLAIRE: *Composers in America* (New York, 1947).
——*Composers, Conductors and Critics* (New York, 1955).
ROSENFELD, PAUL: *Musical Chronicle 1917–1923* (New York, 1923).
——*Discoveries of a Music Critic* (New York, 1936).
——*An Hour with American Music* (Philadelphia, 1929).
SABLOSKY, IRVING: *American Music* (Chicago, 1969).
SAMINSKY, LAZARE: *Living Music of the Americas* (New York, 1949).
THOMSON, VIRGIL: *The Musical Scene* (New York, 1945).
——*Music Right and Left* (New York, 1951).
——*The State of Music* (New York, 1939; 2nd ed., 1963).

(ii) *Individual Composers*

Babbitt

BRUNO, ANTHONY: 'Two American Twelve-tone Composers' (Milton Babbitt and Ben Weber), *Musical America*, xxxvii (1951).
KOSTELANETZ, R.: 'Two Extremes of Avant Garde Music' (A Discussion of the music of Milton Babbitt), *New York Times Magazine*, 15 Jan. 1967.

Barber

BRODER, NATHAN: *Samuel Barber* (New York, 1954).
——'The Music of Samuel Barber', *Music Quarterly*, xxxiv (1948).

Becker

RIEGGER, WALLINGFORD: 'John J. Becker', *Bulletin of the American Composers Alliance*, ix (1959).

Bergsma

SKULSKY, ABRAHAM: 'William Bergsma', *The Juilliard Review*, Spring 1956.

Bernstein

BRIGGS, JOHN: *Leonard Bernstein: the Man, His Works and His World* (Cleveland, 1961).

Brant

SANKEY, STUART: 'Henry Brant's Grand Universal Circus', *The Juilliard Review*, Fall 1956.

Cage

DUNN, ROBERT (ed.): *John Cage* (New York, 1962).
KOSTELANETZ, RICHARD: *John Cage* (New York, 1970).

Carter

GOLDMAN, RICHARD FRANKO: 'The Music of Elliott Carter', *Musical Quarterly*, xliii (1957).
SKULSKY, ABRAHAM: 'Elliott Carter', *Bulletin of the American Composers Alliance*, iii (1953).

Copland

BERGER, ARTHUR: *Aaron Copland* (New York, 1953).

COLE, HUGO: 'Aaron Copland', *Tempo*, Spring and Summer, 1966.

SMITH, JULIA: *Aaron Copland: His Work and Contribution to American Music* (New York, 1955).

Cowell

GERSCHEFSKI, EDWIN: 'Henry Cowell', *Bulletin of the American Composers Alliance*, iii (1953).

GOLDMAN, RICHARD FRANKO: 'Henry Cowell: A Memoir and an Appreciation', *Perspectives of New Music*, Spring-Summer 1966.

WEISGALL, HUGO: 'The Music of Henry Cowell', *Musical Quarterly,* xlv (1959).

Creston

COWELL, HENRY: 'Paul Creston', *Musical Quarterly*, xxxiv (1948).

Dello Joio

DOWNES, EDWARD: 'The Music of Norman Dello Joio', *Musical Quarterly*, xlviii, (1962).

Finney

COOPER, PAUL: 'The Music of Ross Lee Finney', *Musical Quarterly*, liii (1967).

Gershwin

ARMITAGE, MERLE: *George Gershwin, Man and Legend* (New York, 1958).

GOLDBERG, ISAAC: *George Gershwin, A Study in American Music* (New ed. Supplemented by Edith Garson. New York, 1958).

RUSHMORE, ROBERT: *The Life of George Gershwin* (New York, 1966).

Gilbert

DOWNES, OLIN: 'An American Composer' (Henry F. B. Gilbert), *Musical Quarterly*, iv (1918).

Griffes

BAUER, MARION: 'Charles T. Griffes as I Remember Him', *Musical Quarterly*, xxix (1943).

MAISEL, EDWARD M.: *Charles T. Griffes: The Life of an American Composer* (Cleveland, 1961).

Hanson

ALTER, MARTHA: 'Howard Hanson', *Modern Music*, xviii (1941).

TUTHIL, BURNETT C.: 'Howard Hanson', *Musical Quarterly*, xxii (1936).

Harris

FARWELL, ARTHUR: 'Roy Harris', *Musical Quarterly*, xviii (1932).

Harrison

YATES, PETER: 'Lou Harrison'. *Bulletin of the American Composers Alliance* ix (1960).

Ives

BELLAMANN, HENRY: 'Charles Ives: The Man and His Music', *Musical Quarterly*, xix (1933).

COPLAND, AARON: '(Ives's) One Hundred and Fourteen Songs', *Modern Music*, xi (1934).

COWELL, HENRY and SIDNEY: *Charles Ives and His Music* (New York, 1955).

GRUNFELD, FREDERIC: 'Charles Ives . . . Yankee Rebel', *Bulletin of the American Composers Alliance*, iv (1955).

STONE, KURT: 'Ives's Fourth Symphony: A Review', *Musical Quarterly*, lii (1966).

YATES, PETER: 'Charles Ives', *Arts and Architecture*, lxvii (1950).

Kirchner
RINGER, ALEXANDER L.: 'Leon Kirchner', *Musical Quarterly*, xliii (1957).

Loeffler
ENGEL, CARL: 'Charles Martin Loeffler', *Musical Quarterly*, xi (1925).
——'News and Reviews' (A eulogy of Charles Martin Loeffler), *Musical Quarterly*, xxi (1935).

Mennin
HENDL, WALTER: 'Peter Mennin', *The Juilliard Review*, Spring 1954.

Ornstein
BUCHANAN, C. L.: 'Ornstein and Modern Music', *Musical Quarterly*, iv (1918).

Palmer
AUSTIN, WILLIAM: 'The Music of Robert Palmer', *Musical Quarterly*, xlii (1956).

Partch
MELLERS, WILFRID: 'An American Aboriginal', *Tempo*, Spring 1963.

Persichetti
EVETT, ROBERT: 'Vincent Persichetti', *The Juilliard Review*, Spring 1955.

Piston
CARTER, ELLIOTT: 'Walter Piston', *Musical Quarterly*, xxxii (1946).
CITKOWITZ, ISRAEL: 'Walter Piston . . . Classicist', *Modern Music*, xiii (1936).

Porter
BOATWRIGHT, HOWARD: 'Quincy Porter', *Perspectives of New Music*, Spring-Summer 1967.

Riegger
BECKER, JOHN J., COWELL, HENRY and GOLDMAN, RICHARD FRANKO: 'Wallingford Riegger . . . A Tribute', *Bulletin of the American Composers Alliance*, ix (1960).
GOLDMAN, RICHARD FRANKO: 'The Music of Wallingford Riegger', *Musical Quarterly*, xxxvi (1950).

Rogers
DIAMOND, DAVID: 'Bernard Rogers', *Musical Quarterly*, xxxiii (1947).

Ruggles
SEEGER, CHARLES: 'Carl Ruggles', *Musical Quarterly*, xviii (1932).
HARRISON, LOU: *About Carl Ruggles* (New York, 1946).

Schuman
BRODER, NATHAN: 'The Music of William Schuman', *Musical Quarterly*, xxxi (1945).
SCHREIBER, FLORA RHETA and PERSICHETTI, VINCENT: *William Schuman* (New York, 1954).

Sessions
CONE, EDWARD T.: 'Conversation with Roger Sessions', *Perspectives of New Music*, Spring-Summer 1966.
IMBRIE, ANDREW: 'Roger Sessions: In Honor of his Sixty-Fifth Birthday', *Perspectives of New Music*, Fall 1962.
SCHUBART, MARK A.: 'Roger Sessions: Portrait of an American Composer', *Musical Quarterly*, xxxii (1946).

Thompson
FORBES, ELLIOT: 'The Music of Randall Thompson', *Musical Quarterly*, xxxv (1949).

Thomson

GLANVILLE-HICKS, P.: 'Virgil Thomson', *Musical Quarterly*, xxxv (1949).
HOOVER, KATHLEEN: *Virgil Thomson* (New York, 1959).
THOMSON, VIRGIL: *Virgil Thomson* (New York, 1966).

Varèse

BABBITT, MILTON: 'Edgard Varèse: A Few Observations of His Music', *Perspectives of New Music*, Spring-Summer 1966.
COWELL, HENRY: 'The Music of Edgard Varèse', *Modern Music*, Jan.-Feb. 1928.
CHOW WEN-CHUNG: 'Varèse: A Sketch of the Man and His Music', *Musical Quarterly*, lii (1966).
DALLAPICCOLA, LUIGI, CARTER, ELLIOTT, NIN, ANAIS, SZATHMARY, ARTHUR, FELDMAN, DORTON and WILKINSON, MARC: 'In Memoriam: Edgard Varèse', *Perspectives of New Music*, Spring-Summer 1966.
WALDMAN, FREDERICK: 'Edgard Varèse', *The Juilliard Review*, Fall 1954.
WILKINSON, MARC: 'An Introduction to the Music of Edgar Varèse', *The Score*, No. 19 (1957).

Ward

STAMBLER, BERNARD: 'Robert Ward', *Bulletin of the American Composers Alliance*, iv (1955).

Weber

BRUNO, ANTHONY: 'Two American Twelve-tone Composers' (Milton Babbitt and Ben Weber), *Musical America*, Feb. 1951.

Weisgall

ROCHBERG, GEORGE: 'Hugo Weisgall', *Bulletin of the American Composers Alliance*, vii (1958).

(ii) *Latin America*

(i) *General*

ALMEIDA, RENATO: *História da música brasileira* (Rio de Janeiro, 1942).
AUZA, ATILIANO: *Dinámica musical en Bolivia* (La Paz, 1967).
AZEVEDO, LUIZ HEITOR CORREA DE: *150 Anos de música no Brasil (1800–1950)* (Rio de Janeiro, 1956).
——*Música e músicos do Brasil* (Rio de Janeiro, 1950).
CALCAÑO, JOSÉ ANTONIO: *La Ciudad y su música. Crónica musical de Caracas* (Caracas, 1958).
CARPENTIER, ALEJO: *La música en Cuba* (Mexico, 1946).
CHASE, GILBERT: *A Guide to the Music of Latin America* (Washington, D.C., 1962).
ESCOBAR, ROBERTO: *Músicos sin Pasado: Composición y compositores de Chile* (Barcelona, 1971).
LIST, GEORGE & ORREGO-SALAS, JUAN (eds.): *Music in the Americas* (Bloomington, 1967).
MARIZ, VASCO: *Figuras da música brasileira contemporanea* (Brasilia, 1970).
MAYER-SERRA, OTTO: *Música y músicos de latinoamérica* (Mexico, 1947).
——*Panorama de la música mexicana* (Mexico, 1941).
PERDOMO ESCOBAR, JOSÉ I.: *Historia de la música en Colombia* (Bogotá, 1963).
RAYGADA, CARLOS: 'Guia musical del Perú', *Fénix*, xii, xiii, xiv, (1956–64).
SALAS VIU, VICENTE: *La creación musical en Chile* (Santiago, 1952).
SALGADO, SUSANA: *Breve historia de la música culta en el Uruguay* (Montevideo, 1971).
SLONIMSKY, NICOLAS: *Music of Latin America* (New York, 1945).
STEVENSON, ROBERT: *Music in Mexico* (New York, 1952).

(ii) *Individual composers*

Ardévol
ARDÉVOL, JOSÉ: 'El Grupo Renovación de La Habana', *Revista musical chilena*, xxvii (1947).
CARPENTIER, ALEJO: 'La música contemporánea de Cuba', *Revista musical chilena*, xxvii (1947).

Becerra
MERINO, LUIS: 'Los cuartetos de Gustavo Becerra', *Revista musical chilena*, xcii (1965).

Chávez
CHÁVEZ, CARLOS: *Musical Thought* (Cambridge, Mass., 1961).
GARCIA MORRILO, ROBERTO: *Carlos Chávez: vida y obra* (Mexico, 1960).
(HALFFTER, RODOLFO): *Carlos Chavez, catálogo completo de sus obras* (Mexico, 1971).

Cosme
BÉHAGUE, GERARD: 'Luiz Cosme (1908–1965): Impulso creador versus conciencia formal', *Yearbook* (Inter-American Musical Research Institute), v (1969).

Ginastera
CHASE, GILBERT: 'Alberto Ginastera: Argentine composer', *Musical Quarterly*, xliii (1957).
SUAREZ URTUBEY, POLA: *Alberto Ginastera* (Buenos Aires, 1967).

Mignone
VERHAALEN, MARION: 'Francisco Mignone: His music for piano', *Inter-American Music Bulletin*, lxxix (1970–1).

Orrego-Salas
ORREGO-SALAS, JUAN: *Pasado y presente de la música chilena* (Santiago, 1960).

Ponce
PONCE, MANUEL M.: 'Apuntes sobre música mexicana', *Boletin latino-americano de música*, iii (1937).

Paz
PAZ, JUAN CARLOS: *Introducción a la música de nuestro tiempo* (Buenos Aires, 1955).

Revueltas
MAYER-SERRA, OTTO: 'Silvestre Revueltas and Musical Nationalism in Mexico', *Musical Quarterly*, xxvii (1941).

Santa Cruz
SALAS VIU, VICENTE: 'Las obras para orquesta de Domingo Santa Cruz', *Revista musical chilena*, xlii (1951).

Villa-Lobos
MARIZ, VASCO: *Heitor Villa-Lobos* (Rio de Janeiro, 1949).
NOBREGA, ADHEMAR: *As Bachianas Brasileiras de Heitor Villa-Lobos* (Rio de Janeiro, 1971).
ORREGO-SALAS, JUAN: 'Villa-Lobos: Man, Work and Style', *Inter-American Music Bulletin*, lii (1966).
PEPPERCORN, LISA M.: *Heitor Villa-Lobos. Leben und Werk des brasilianischen Komponisten* (Zürich, 1972).

CHAPTER VIII

MUSIC IN THE SOVIET UNION

(i) *General*

ASAFYEV, B. V.: *Izbrannïe trudï*, v (Moscow, 1957).

BERGER, KARLHANNS: *Die Funktionsbestimmung der Musik in der Sowjetideologie* (Wiesbaden, 1963).

BERNANDT, G. and DOLZHANSKY, A.: *Sovetskie kompozitorï: kratkiy bibliograficheskiy spravochnik* (Moscow, 1957).

GRINBERG, M. and POLYAKOVA, N. (ed.): *Sovetskaya opera: sbornik kriticheskikh statey* (Moscow, 1953).

GRINBERG, M. A. (ed.): *Sovetskaya simfonicheskaya muzïka: sbornik statey* (Moscow, 1955).

KABALEVSKY, D. B., *et al* (ed.): *Istoriya russkoy sovetskoy muzïki* (four vols., Moscow, 1956–63).

KREBS, S. D.: *Soviet Composers and the Development of Soviet Music* (London, 1970).

KUČERA, VACLAV: *Nové proudy ve sovetské hudbé* (Prague, 1967).

OLKHOVSKY, ANDREY: *Music under the Soviets* (London, 1955).

ORLOV, G.: *Russkiy sovetskiy simfonizm* (Moscow and Leningrad, 1966).

——*Sovetskiy fortepianniy kontsert* (Leningrad, 1954).

PRIEBERG, F. K.: *Musik in der Sowjetunion* (Cologne, 1965).

SCHWARZ, BORIS: *Music and Musical Life in Soviet Russia 1917–1970* (London, 1962).

(ii) *Individual Composers*

Myaskovsky

IKONNIKOV, A.: *Myaskovsky, his Life and Work* (New York, 1946).

SHLIFSTEYN, S. (ed.): *N. Y. Myaskovsky: Stat'i, pis'ma, vospominaniya* (two vols., Moscow, 1959 and 1960).

Prokofyev

ARANOVSKY, M.: *Melodika S. Prokof'eva* (Leningrad, 1969).

BLOK, V.: *Kontsertï dlya violoncheli s orkestrom S. Prokof'eva* (Moscow, 1959).

——'Osnovnie osobennosti neimitatsionnoy polifonii Prokof'eva' in G. A. Orlov *et al* (ed.), *Problemï muzïkal'noy nauki*, i (Moscow, 1972).

BOGANOVA, T.: *Natsional'no-russkie traditsii v muzïke S. S. Prokof'eva* (Moscow, 1961).

DELSON, V.: *Fortep'yannïe kontsertï S. Prokof'eva* (Moscow, 1961).

GAKKEL, L.: *Fortep'yannoe tvorchestvo S. S. Prokof'eva* (Moscow, 1960).

KHOLOPOV, Y.: *Sovremennïe chertï garmonii Prokof'eva* (Moscow, 1967).

MNATSAKANOVA, E. A.: *Opera S. S. Prokof'eva 'Voyna i mir'* (Moscow, 1959).

——*Opera S. S. Prokof'eva 'Obruchenie v monastïre'* (Moscow, 1962).

NESTYEV, I. V.: *Prokof'ev* (Moscow, 1957; English translation, London, 1961; revised and enlarged edition, *Zhizn' Sergeya Prokof'eva*, Moscow, 1973).

——and EDELMAN, G. Y. (ed.): *Sergey Prokof'ev, 1953–1963. Stat'i i materialï* (Moscow, 1962; rev. and enlarged ed., 1965).

OLIVKOVA, V. B.: '*Romeo i Dzhuletta*' *S. Prokof'eva* (Moscow and Leningrad, 1952).

ORDZHONIKIDZE, G.: *Fortep'yannïe sonatï Prokof'eva* (Moscow, 1962).

POLYAKOVA, L. V.: '*Voyna i mir*' *S. S. Prokof'eva* (Moscow, 1960).

ROGOZHINA, N.: *Vokal'no-simfonicheskie proizvedeniya S. Prokof'eva* (Moscow and Leningrad, 1964).

SABININA, M.: '*Semen Kotko*' *i problemï opernoy dramaturgii Prokof'eva* (Moscow, 1963).

SHLIFSTEYN, S. (ed.): *S. S. Prokof'ev: materialï, dokumentï, vospominaniya* (Moscow, 1956; English translation, Moscow, n.d.).
SLONIMSKY, S.: *Simfonii Prokof'eva* (Moscow and Leningrad, 1964).
SOROKER, Y.: *Skripichnoe tvorchestvo S. Prokof'eva* (Moscow, 1965).
TARAKANOV, M.: *Stil' simfoniy Prokof'eva* (Moscow, 1967).
VOLKOV, A.: 'Ob odnom printsipe formoobrazovaniya u Prokof'eva', in Orlov (ed.), *Problemï muzikal'noy nauki*, i (Moscow, 1972).
——*Skripichnïe kontsertï Prokof'eva* (Moscow, 1961).
Chertï stilya S. Prokof'eva: Sbornik teoretciheskikh statey (Moscow, 1962).

Shaporin
LEVIT, S.: *Yuriy Aleksandrovich Shaporin: ocherk zhizni i tvorchestva* (Moscow, 1964).

Shebalin
BELZA, I. F. and PROTOPOPOV, V. V. (ed.): *Vissarion Yakovlevich Shebalin: stat'i, vospominaniya, materialï* (Moscow, 1970).

Shostakovich
BERGER, L. (ed.): *Chertï stilya Shostakovicha* (Moscow, 1962).
BOBROVSKY, V.: *Kamernïe instrumental'nïe ansambli Shostakovicha* (Moscow, 1961).
BOGDANOVA, A.: 'Sochineniya D. Shostakovicha konservatorskikh let (1919–1925)', in A. Kandinsky (ed.), *Iz Istorii russkoy i sovetskoy muzïki* (Moscow, 1971).
DANILEVICH, L. L.: *D. D. Shostakovich* (Moscow, 1958).
——*Nash sovremennik: Tvorchestvo Shostakovicha* (Moscow, 1965).
MARTINOV, I.: *D. D. Shostakovich* (Moscow and Leningrad, 1946).
ORLOV, G.: *Simfonii Shostakovicha* (Leningrad, 1961).
RABINOVICH, D.: *Dmitry Shostakovich* (English translation only, Moscow and London, 1959).
SABININA, M. D.: *Simfonizm Shostakovicha: put k zrelosti* (Moscow, 1965).

LIST OF CONTENTS OF

THE HISTORY OF MUSIC IN SOUND

VOLUME X

The History of Music in Sound is a series of volumes of gramophone records, with explanatory booklets, designed as a companion series to the *New Oxford History of Music*. Each volume covers the same ground as the corresponding volume in the *New Oxford History of Music* and is designed as far as possible to illustrate the music discussed therein. The records are issued in England by E.M.I. Records Ltd. (H.M.V.) and in the United States by R.C.A. Victor, and the booklets are published by the Oxford University Press. The editor of Volume X of *The History of Music in Sound* is Gerald Abraham.

The History of Music in Sound is available on LP records, and the side numbers are given below.

Band 4   *Zápisník zmizelého* (Diary of one who vanished), Nos. 15, 16, 17, and 18 (tenor and piano) (Janáček)
Band 5   *Stillung Mariä mit dem Auferstandenen* (from *Das Marienleben* for voice and piano, 1923) (Hindemith)
Band 6   *Fuga Octava in D* (from *Ludus Tonalis* for piano solo) (Hindemith)

12-NOTE MUSIC

Band 7   March from *Serenade*, Op. 24 (Schönberg)
Band 8   *Goethe-Lieder*, Nos. 2, 3, 5, and 6 (for mezzo-soprano and three clarinets) (Dallapiccola)

MODERN ECLECTICISM

Side IV   Band 1   *Allegro moderato* from *Trio for violin, viola, and cello*, Op. 58 (Roussel)
Band 2   *Valse* from *String Quartet, No. 2*, Op. 69 (Shostakovich)
Band 3   *Lento* from *Sonata for violin and piano* (Copland)
Band 4   *Sanctus, Benedictus,* and *Agnus Dei,* from *Missa Cantuariensis*, Op. 59 (Rubbra)
Band 5   *Poco lento* from *Quartet for clarinet, viola, and cello* (Rawsthorne)

INDEX

Compiled by G. W. Hopkins